The Neolithic of the Irish Sea

Materiality and traditions of practice

The Neolithic of the Irish Sea

Materiality and traditions of practice

Edited by
Vicki Cummings and Chris Fowler

Oxbow Books

Published by
Oxbow Books, Park End Place, Oxford OX1 1HN

ISBN 1 84217 109 7

A CIP record for this book is available from the British Library

This book is available direct from
Oxbow Books, Park End Place, Oxford, OX1 1HN
(Phone: 01865-241249; Fax: 01865-794449)

and

The David Brown Book Company
PO Box 511, Oakville, CT 06779, USA
(Phone: 860-945-9329; Fax: 860-945-9468)

or

via our website
www.oxbowbooks.com

*Front cover: Port Sonachan chambered cairn, western Scotland.
Photo: Vicki Cummings*

Printed in Great Britain at
The Alden Press
Oxford

For Alasdair and Julian

Contents

Preface

Julian Thomas

The concept of an 'Irish Sea zone' in prehistory is one that has a long history (Waddell 1991). It is curious, then, that it should now be re-emerging as part of a new phase in the development of Neolithic and early Bronze Age studies. Gordon Barclay (2001) has cogently argued that our study of these periods has been dominated by an over-emphasis on certain 'luminous centres', principally Wessex and Orkney. These areas have plentiful upstanding monuments, and as a consequence have attracted the attention of antiquarians and archaeologists for many generations. Numerous excavations have been undertaken, and museum basements have been filled with project archives and stray finds. None of this means, however, that these areas were necessarily of pre-eminent importance in the Neolithic. Other traditions of monumentality from those that characterise the 'core' areas of study, which leave a less durable trace, and other social practices entirely, may have been of equal importance to people in the past.

This history of research has had other consequences. In the early 1980s, a series of new approaches to the Neolithic and early Bronze Age began to emerge, influenced by recent developments in archaeological thought (Bradley and Gardiner 1984; Braithwaite 1984). These accounts of the period addressed themes of ideology, social power, material symbolism, stylistic variation, depositional activity, identity and ritual action, and were critical of culture-historic narratives based around 'peoples' and 'invasions'. In order to create more subtle analyses, they often required extensive sets of evidence: suites of burials, well-recorded and contextually located assemblages of ceramics, lithics and faunal remains. The tendency was to seek these in the geographical areas that had seen the most intensive field research, thereby reinforcing the hegemony of Wessex and Orkney. This was particularly the case because much of this work was undertaken by research students, who lacked the resources to carry out extensive field projects of their own. The areas surrounding the Irish sea, save for Ireland itself, have had a reputation for producing rather scarce assemblages of material culture, and were somewhat neglected by the social archaeologies the 1980s.

More recently, a series of changes in the character of research have contributed to a shift of focus. Firstly, there has been a growing interest in the experiential aspects of landscape, architecture and monuments (Cooney 2000; Tilley 1994). While excellent work had been continuing in western Scotland, Wales and the Isle of Man throughout (e.g. Gibson 1994; Smith and Lynch 1987), these preoccupations drew a new generation of researchers to work in these areas (Cummings 2002; Fowler 2001). Secondly, there was a greater willingness to make the most of the supposedly meagre artefactual resources of the Irish Sea area (Burrow 1997; Peterson 2003; Squair 1998). Thirdly, some of the very scholars who were prominent in the Wessex and Orkney-centred archaeology of the early 1980s, subsequently expanded their fieldwork interests into other zones (e.g. Bradley 2000; Bradley and Edmonds 1993). Finally, there was a growing appreciation of the extent of regional variation in the Neolithic and early Bronze Age (Sharples 1992), which lent credence to arguments like Barclay's, criticising a myopic focus on one or two regions judged to be paradigmatic of the period.

The papers in this volume address a series of regions, some of which have been judged to be 'peripheral' in previous work. But importantly, they do so within the broader framework of the Irish Sea zone. There is, of course, a danger of reifying such an entity into a 'cultural hearth' of some kind. But it is valuable to consider the interactions, similarities and contextual variations in the use of material things between communities surrounding a major body of water, thereby undercutting the illusory homogeneity of 'English prehistory', 'Welsh prehistory', 'Irish prehistory' or 'Scottish prehistory'.

References

Barclay, G. 2001. 'Metropolitan' and 'parochial'/'core' and 'periphery': a historiography of the Neolithic of Scotland. *Proceedings of the Prehistoric Society* 67, 1–18.

Bradley, R.J. 2000. *The good stones: a new investigation of the Clava Cairns*. Edinburgh: Society of Antiquaries of Scotland.

Bradley, R. and Edmonds, M. 1993. *Interpreting the axe trade*. Cambridge: Cambridge University Press.

Bradley, R.J. and Gardiner, J. (eds) 1984. *Neolithic studies*. Oxford: British Archaeological Reports British Series 133.

Braithwaite, M. 1984. Ritual and prestige in the prehistory of Wessex c.2000–1400 BC: a new dimension to the archaeological evidence. In D. Miller and C. Tilley (eds), *Ideology, power and prehistory,* 93–110. Cambridge: Cambridge University Press.

Burrow, S. 1997. *The Neolithic pottery of the Isle of Man: a study in production, decoration, and use.* Unpublished Ph.D. thesis: University of Bournemouth.

Cooney. G. 2000. *Landscapes of Neolithic Ireland.* London: Routledge.

Cummings, V. 2002. Between mountains and sea: a reconsideration of the Neolithic monuments of south-west Scotland. *Proceedings of the Prehistoric Society* 68, 125–46.

Fowler, C. 2001. Personhood and social relations in the British Neolithic, with a study from the Isle of Man. *Journal of Material Culture* 6, 137–64.

Gibson, A. 1994. Excavations at Sarn-y-bryn-caled cursus complex, Welshpool, Powys. *Proceedings of the Prehistoric Society* 60, 143–224.

Peterson, R. 2003. *Neolithic pottery from Wales: traditions of construction and use.* Oxford: British Archaeological Reports British Series 344.

Sharples, N. 1992. Aspects of regionalisation in the Scottish Neolithic. In: N. Sharples and A. Sheridan (eds), *Vessels for the ancestors,* 322–31.Edinburgh: Edinburgh University Press.

Smith, C.A. and Lynch, F.M. 1987. *Trefignath and Din Dryfol: the excavation of two megalithic tombs in Anglesey.* Cardiff: Cambrian Archaeological Association.

Squair, R. 1998. *The Neolithic of the Western Isles.* Unpublished Ph.D. Thesis: University of Glasgow.

Tilley, C.Y. 1994. *A phenomenology of landscape.* Oxford: Berg.

Waddell, J. 1991. The Irish Sea in prehistory. *Journal of Irish Archaeology* 6, 29–40.

List of Contributors

MARCUS BRITTAIN
School of Art History and Archaeology
University of Manchester
Oxford Road
Manchester M13 9PL

KENNETH BROPHY
Department of Archaeology
Gregory Building
University of Glasgow
Lilybank Gardens
Glasgow G12 8QQ

GABRIEL COONEY
Archaeology Department
John Henry Newman Building
University College Dublin
Belfield Campus
Dublin 4, Ireland

VICKI CUMMINGS
School of History and Archaeology
PO Box 909
Cardiff University
Cardiff CF10 3XU

TIMOTHY DARVILL
School of Conservation Sciences
Bournemouth University
Fern Barrow
Poole
Dorset BH12 5BB

PETER DAVEY
Centre for Manx Studies
6 Kingswood Grove
Douglas
Isle of Man

THOMAS DOWSON
School of Art History and Archaeology
University of Manchester
Oxford Road
Manchester M13 9PL

EDWARD EVANS
School of Art History and Archaeology
University of Manchester
Oxford Road
Manchester M13 9PL

HELEN EVANS
Graduate School of Archaeology and
Archaeological Science
West Court
2 Mappin Street
Sheffield S1 4DT

CHRIS FOWLER
School of Art History and Archaeology
University of Manchester
Oxford Road
Manchester M13 9PL

COLE HENLEY
School of History and Archaeology
PO Box 909
Cardiff University
Cardiff CF10 3XU

ANDREW JONES
Department of Archaeology
University of Southampton
Avenue Campus
Southampton SO17 1BF

TREVOR KIRK
School of Archaeology
Trinity College
Carmarthen SA31 3EP

DAVID MULLIN
1 Ockeridge Cottage
Chance's Pitch
Colwall
Malvern WR13 6HP

RICK PETERSON
SCARAB Research Centre
University of Wales College Newport
Caerleon Campus
PO Box 179
Newport NP18 3YG

KEITH RAY
County Archaeologist
Planning Services
Herefordshire Council
Hereford HR1 2YH

COLIN RICHARDS
School of Art History and Archaeology
University of Manchester
Oxford Road
Manchester M13 9PL

RICK SCHULTING
School of Archaeology and Palaeoecology
The Queen's University of Belfast
Northern Ireland BT7 1NN

ALISON SHERIDAN
Department of Archaeology
National Museums of Scotland
Chambers Street
Edinburgh EH1 1JF

JULIAN THOMAS
School of Art History and Archaeology
University of Manchester
Oxford Road
Manchester M13 9PL

AARON WATSON
Department of Archaeology
University of Reading
Whiteknights
PO Box 227
Reading RG6 6AB

ALASDAIR WHITTLE
School of History and Archaeology
PO Box 909
Cardiff University
Cardiff CF10 3XU

JENNY WOODCOCK
Department of Archaeology
William Hartley Building
University of Liverpool
Liverpool L69 3BX

Acknowledgements

This volume began life as a conference held in the University of Manchester in April 2002. Many people assisted with the organisation and running of the conference and we are particularly grateful to the British Academy for help with funding the event. We owe a great debt also to our respective universities (Cardiff and Manchester) who have provided a great deal of support and assistance along the way. Vicki would also like to thank the Board of Celtic Studies, and Chris would like to thank the Leverhulme Trust, for their support during this project. On the technical side of things, John Morgan assisted with the scanning process and Aled Cooke helped with hardware and software.

We would like to offer particular thanks to the contributors to this volume, who made the original conference such an enjoyable event, and this such an interesting volume. And finally we offer thanks to our respective mentors, Alasdair Whittle and Julian Thomas, who have offered immeasurable amounts of help, advice and support over the years. We dedicate this book to them with thanks.

Vicki Cummings and Chris Fowler
Cardiff and Manchester, March 2003

1   Introduction: locating *The Neolithic of the Irish Sea: materiality and traditions of practice*

Vicki Cummings and Chris Fowler

Introduction

More by way of setting the scene of these conference proceedings than providing a traditionally neutral introduction or brief review of the papers collected here, we begin by offering a series of comments on the history and future of research into material culture, culture, and trends of practice in the Neolithic around the Irish Sea.

A history of research into the Neolithic around the Irish Sea

It seems that O.G.S. Crawford was the first archaeologist to recognise the significance of the Irish Sea as an area of cultural interaction in his 1912 paper on the distribution of gold *lunulae* and flat celts across Cornwall and south-west Wales (Bowen 1970). In this paper Crawford suggested the presence of an 'isthmus' route across Cornwall and south-west Wales in the Bronze Age (Bowen 1970, 14; Crawford 1912). In 1915, H.J. Fleure published a paper on the spread of megalithic monuments along the west coast of Britain. In particular he discussed routes across the Lleyn peninsula and Pembrokeshire. His emphasis on the importance of the Irish seaways may have been inspired by his work on the Isle of Man, at the very centre of the Irish Sea. By 1932, Cyril Fox had published a map of the western sea routes of the British Isles in *The Personality of Britain*. He suggested considerable interactions across the Irish Sea area and noted the importance of sea-routes between north-east Ireland and Galloway, the Clyde and the Isle of Man, Dublin Bay and the Isle of Man, and Anglesey and north Pembrokeshire. All this research was part of a broader objective of pinpointing the spread of cultural traits and groups from Europe into Britain (e.g. Childe 1927; also see Waddell 1991). Like much work of the period, this early phase of research was concerned with routes of diffusion and cultural contact. The earliest conceptions of the Irish Sea zone as an area of interaction were therefore dominated by culture-historical approaches which assumed that the Neolithic originated in the Mediterranean (Piggott 1954; 1965; Trigger 1989).

From the 1940s onwards, discussion on the Irish Sea zone became more widespread, as the precise origins of particular culture groups were sought. In 1941 Glyn Daniel discussed what he described as the dual nature of the megalithic colonisation of north-west Europe, suggesting that there was a primary spread of monuments across Europe followed by the evolution of local monument types (Daniel 1941). These local variants then diffused across smaller areas. In this model the western sea routes played a critical role in the punctuated spread of monumentality from the Atlantic seaboard throughout the Irish Sea. An influential paper by Margaret Davies in 1945 also studied the distribution of monuments around the Irish Sea and considered the role of the tides and the sea as a crucial factor in the formation of a cultural province. The significance of the Irish Sea as an area of cultural interaction was subsequently followed by a number of leading scholars of the time including Stuart Piggott (1954) and Rúaidhrí de Valera (1960) to name but two. Diffusionist approaches were retained, but modified in attending to interaction at the more local level.

By the late 1960s scholars were increasingly concerned to illustrate regional differences and emphasise detailed chronological sequences. The publication of Powell, Corcoran, Lynch and Scott's *Megalithic Enquiries in the West of Britain* in 1969, for example, detailed the monuments of north Wales and the Clyde cairns of Scotland while Audrey Henshall's 1964 and 1972 inventories of Scottish cairns fitted them into a comprehensive comparative scheme. Important work was also conducted in Ireland with the publication of inventories of the megalithic tombs from the 1960s onwards (de Valera 1960; de Valera and Ó Nualláin 1961; 1964; 1972). This kind of research into the Irish Sea zone seems to have culminated in 1970 with the publication of *The Irish Sea Province in Archaeology and History* which contained a summary of research into the Irish Sea zone by E.G. Bowen as well as a paper by Michael Herity on the spread of monuments around the Irish Sea basin. Bowen's general summary of the study of cultural interaction covered both prehistoric and historic periods and gave a strong sense of the significance of the Irish Sea as an enduring routeway, stressing that it should not be seen as a barrier to cultural interaction. He cited evidence of widespread and repeated contacts across this area (Bowen 1970). Herity's focus was on specific monument types which are found on either side of the Irish Sea, which he argued left us with a 'pattern of Neolithic and early Bronze Age colonisation and settlement' which covered that area. Passage graves, for example, spread from the continent to the Irish Sea zone, followed by a secondary spread from Ireland into Wales (Herity 1970, 30).

After 1970 the idea that the Irish Sea was an area of significant cultural interaction slowly began to fall into the background. The Irish Sea area was still considered in several important articles, for example in a paper by Frances Lynch published in 1989 and a 1991 paper by John Waddell. Lynch (1989) reconsidered early Neolithic connections between Wales and Ireland, seeing the Irish Sea as a 'linking highway' for incoming farmers from Continental Europe. Waddell (1991) strongly advocated the Irish Sea an a focal area for interaction and exchange in prehistory, based on the distribution of a number of material forms (e.g. court cairns and porcellanite axes).

While the continued character of work across this region has largely emphasised that prehistoric contact took place, a parallel course of investigation has also demonstrated that some features of the British and Irish Neolithics were rather different and drew on distinct indigenous patterns of activity (e.g. Cooney 1997; 2001). While there are differences in the development of the Neolithic in these areas, there are also a variety of different histories to the Neolithic at a smaller scale (cf. Cooney 1997). The recent emphasis on regional studies (e.g. Brophy 1999; Burrow 1997; Cleal 1995; Cummings 2001; Fowler 1999; Holgate 1988; A. Jones 1997; Leivers 2000; Lucas 1994; MacGregor 1999; Peterson 1999; 2003; Phillips 2003; Richards 1993; Squair 1998; Thomas 1988; 1991 and cf. Barclay and Brophy forthcoming) indicates that parallel yet different processes of cultural change took place throughout the British Isles as a whole. These studies have illustrated patterns of local distinctiveness that also articulate with studies of the wider picture. One of the aims of this volume was to bring together some of these regional perspectives and compare them across the Irish Sea area. The volume therefore provides a basis for comparison which supports studies of regional diversity alongside broader long-term trends in prehistoric activity.

The last two decades has also seen a number of key projects in the Irish Sea area which throw light on both long-distance interaction and regional developmental sequences. For example, there have been projects studying axes throughout the area, including important work on the Langdale axes in Cumbria and axe sources and distributions in Ireland (e.g. Bradley and Edmonds 1993; Cooney and Mandal 1998). There has been considerable work on the movement of material culture across the Irish Sea area (Cooney 2000; Saville 1994; Sheridan

1986; Sheridan *et al.* 1992). There has also been a range of excavation, survey and archive work, including key projects in Ireland (e.g. the Discovery Programme initiative, and excavations beyond the Boyne Valley such as at Ballynahatty; Hartwell 1998), western Scotland (Bradley 1997; RCAHMS 1999; and the excavations at Nether Largie) the excavation of non-megalithic monuments in south-west Scotland (Thomas 1999; 2000) and work on the Isle of Man (e.g. Darvill 2001).

The thematic background to the conference

Therefore, although recent years have seen a proliferation of research on the Neolithic of the Irish Sea, little work has been produced which critically reassesses the culture-historical approaches which were forwarded from the 1930s to the 1960s. At the same time contemporary issues in studies of the Neolithic have been concerned with identity (e.g. Brück 2001; Fowler 2001; A. Jones 1997; Last 1997; Lucas 1996; Thomas 1996; 2000), landscape (e.g. Bender 1993; Tilley 1994), place (e.g. Bender 1998; A. Jones 1997; Pollard 1999; 2001) experience (e.g. Cummings 2002; A. Jones 1998; Thomas 1992; 1993; Watson and Keating 1999), and the interpretation of materiality (e.g. Fowler and Cummings 2003; Richards 1996; Thomas 1998). The conference itself aimed to bring together scholars from both sides of the Irish Sea in order to reconsider the nature of the Neolithic in this area, in order to address and assess previous models in the light of more recent issues and approaches. We asked colleagues in particular to address several key issues. Can different monuments and material culture be mobilised in producing similar kinds of experiences or social effects? Different material forms are traditionally seen to indicate the actions of different ethnic groups, referred to as cultural groups. Were there other ways to explain these patterns in past practice, for example, as kinds of social strategies that could be turned to many ends by diverse interest groups? Were there practices that were shared across the Irish Sea area linking different styles of monuments and material culture, or were the media intrinsic to the message? And what kinds of information can archaeologists draw on in moving interpretations of the prehistoric past beyond the limits of data gleaned from a conventional notion of an 'archaeological record' (cf. Barrett 1988; 2001, 156–7)? In sum, can new approaches to material culture, monuments and social effects let us rethink cultural interaction across the Irish Sea zone? While no single contribution should be expected to directly answer all these questions, the collection as a whole provides a thinking point for these and many other issues. The questions themselves stem from our interest in understanding what can broadly be described as the relationship between culture and practice. We would like to explain that interest by briefly exploring the role of these concepts in contemporary prehistoric archaeology.

The origins of culture

The idea of 'culture' seems to have originated in the Renaissance which promoted a new way of looking at and understanding the world (Gramsch 1996, 24). Humans, and the environment in which they lived, were increasingly separated out as distinct entities (Cosgrove 1989, 121), in the beginnings of a division between culture (people) and nature (environment). The concept of nature originated from the Latin *nascere* which means to be born, to come into being (Olwig 1993, 313). The concept of culture stemmed from the Latin *colere* which meant to inhabit, to cultivate and to honour with worship; it also implied cyclical processes and the agricultural 'scaping' of the land by people (Olwig 1993, 313). In Enlightenment thought culture would ideally reflect and perfect human nature. Gradually, the meaning shifted to the human control of and domination over nature. The two concepts became separated and then opposed (Jordanova 1989). The modern notion of culture increasingly lay over the top of nature; both secondary to it and also countermanding it, struggling to control it.

Cultures

Shanks (2001, 285) describes how the idea of *cultures* emerged from the Enlightenment conception of human culture. The pluralising of culture to cultures was intended to emphasise that peoples outside Europe were also possessed of cultural worlds, even though some did not exhibit the traits that were diagnostic of civilised culture in the eighteenth and nineteenth centuries. These other cultures shared human nature, but were culturally different. While conception of many human cultures would seem to value the diversity of all human experiences as equal but different, in practice the history of eighteenth to twentieth century European engagement with such 'other cultures', was also marked by genocide and exploitation. Through social Darwinism and related nineteenth and twentieth century discourses culture became a reflection of different natures or biologies. The idea of cultures, through the work of Kossinna (1911) and Childe (1927; 1929), among others, became heavily ingrained in the study of European prehistory in the twentieth century (Trigger 1989). While Childe (1942) came to reject such ideas, the connection between cultures, material or practical traits, and underlying pre-existing differences remained, influencing many other leading scholars (e.g. Piggott 1954). The culture-historical approach suggested that different material cultures indicated different cultural groups. In this way, material culture could simply be interpreted as the material remains of particular culture groups. Indeed, much of the history of research into the Neolithic of the Irish Sea outlined above fits this paradigm.

However, a number of studies, including that by David Clarke (1968), have demonstrated serious problems with the notion of interpreting cultures from material culture. Through his study of language groups, material culture forms, and ethnic identity among the Bantu, Clarke concluded that while each of these features of identity overlapped they were not entirely commensurable. Clarke illustrated that material culture alone cannot be used to identify an ethnic group: the boundaries of material traits and ethnic identities do not match one another. This phenomenon was assessed more completely from the 1980s onwards. Although Hodder conducted rather different studies of the use of material culture in relation to cultural grouping in the 1970s and 1980s, he came to broadly similar conclusions as Clarke's (e.g. Hodder 1977; 1978a and 1978b; 1982). His studies showed that while some consistent associations of artefacts did match ethnic identities, many others did not. Roy Larick's (1986) ethnographic studies in particular showed that one generation could adopt material styles from a neighbouring and rival community in expressing a difference of identity to their elders. Clearly, this would appear as a classic case of enculturation in the archaeological record, though no such process had occurred. Numerous studies of the use of material culture in the generation of meaning illustrated that no safe assumptions should be made about the nature of stylistic boundaries (cf. Shanks and Tilley 1987, 137–71). More recently Marek Zvelebil (1996) has discussed suggestions that a range of evidence for cultural groups should be compared in assessing past cultural groups (including linguistic, genetic, dietary, material culture). While this seems, as Zvelebil argues, the most plausible approach, plural cultural influences are often adopted and manipulated by different members of any social group. As a result,

> If we accept the archaeological culture as a multi-dimensional phenomenon, we cannot then automatically equate it with any coherent ethnic, economic, social or demographic unit. This means, for example, that an archaeological culture such as Funnel Beaker, can have diverse origins (Midgeley 1993; Solberg 1989), and the unifying features which give it apparent coherence (recognised and acknowledged archaeologically) may be a result of broad processes such as contact/exchange networks, ideological/symbolic change, [and] adoption of farming by local (diverse) hunter-gatherer groups.
> Zvelebil (1996, 155–6)

At the same time as these critiques were developing, Neolithic archaeology in the British Isles has been taking shape around a series of ethnographic observations about identity, ancestry, community and landscape (e.g. Edmonds 1999; Tilley 1994). These approaches have had the effect of firming up the relationship between place and social group, accentuating how communities belong to ancestral places. However, negotiations of belonging and identity are also social interactions, and may be contested and claimed (e.g. Bender and Winer 2001). Material culture, past places and monument-building were all key features in the repeated contestation of kinship, community and heritage. Monuments and material culture were undoubtedly key contexts and icons through which such identities were reworked, but their significance cannot be presumed to have been securely fixed in their forms.

These arguments do not mean that there were not instances in the past when one group of people, however associated, moved and colonised or attempted to colonise other regions of northern Europe. However, what this does indicate is that the perceived boundaries between forms of material culture are not good indicators of boundaries between social groups. Patterns in material culture, or patterns in social practices, will not on their own allow us to identify ethnic groups in the Neolithic. Where cultural trends can be identified they do not necessarily match social groups nor do they represent homogenous patterns of social relations (cf. S. Jones and Richards 2000). Jones' detailed analysis of ethnicity (1997) also suggests that attempting to locate such bounded units leads archaeology down a blind alley. She instead illustrates how identities are produced through deliberate participation in patterns of practice drawing on many different materials, symbols and forms. Strategies of practice are themselves of great interest to prehistorians, and tracing these practices may open up studies of identity and community that are not tied directly to presumptions about ethnic boundaries. Instead of searching for cultures, and the limits and interactions between them, we would like to turn to the *interpretation* of culture as a practical interaction with and through the material world.

Traditions of practice

Archaeological research tends to reify traditions from the patterns of Neolithic practices, particularly those relating to monuments. Through these practices Neolithic people continually reinterpreted and revalued the past around them. Our interpretations may recognise trends in prehistoric *habitus*, trends in 'doing'. While these do not equate with trends in ethnic identity or even overtly acknowledged cultural fields (S. Jones 1997, 122–3) they may denote ways of carrying out social relations, including relations with things, people, animals and places. The practices that have historically characterised the Neolithic are: practices of production, agriculture, and the manu-facture of pots, axes, or monuments. These are the practices that have therefore been placed at the heart of Neolithic cultural traditions. However, it is also clear that consumption was a vital Neolithic practice, not simply in a dietary sense, although this is clearly a matter of importance, but also in the sense of how Neolithic people consumed material culture (Thomas 1988; 1996). This also includes how Neolithic people lived among their pasts, and interpreted the material media of their lives (Barrett 2001; Bradley 2002).

Since culture-historical approaches to the Neolithic have conventionally placed the emphasis on the pro-duction of food, pots and monuments, the traditions traced are often traditions of production. Yet in studying material remains of past actions Neolithic archaeologists are arguably closer to the context of consumption. It is through such practices that the world is interpreted, that material culture is made sense of, and the effects of the material world affect those who dwell within it. Julian Thomas has frequently alluded to the process of *bricolage* in Neolithic engagements with material culture (Thomas 1988; 1991; 1999a). *Bricolage* is both the production of meaning and also the consumption of prior symbols; it illustrates how acts of consumption produce new meanings. Through this approach Thomas has outlined a material core to the Neolithic, that the Neolithic was a social engagement with a particular and flexible suite of things. This clearly moves the emphasis away from any initial context in which a template of those things might originate, and creates a fluid approach to the Neolithic, whereby the archaeologist can trace the repeated engage-ment with any phenomenon or type of object through time. These phenomena need not belong to any cultural group, but are interpreted through plural and successive social contexts, strategies, and traditions of interpretation. The use of particular kinds of material culture may therefore become embedded in cultural practices shared by many different communities. However, which practice new forms of material culture become embedded in may be quite different from one area to another. Each pheno-menon is the result of different traditions reinterpreted and brought together, and the basis of future divergent phenomena. Here we could perhaps imagine something like the carinated bowl, found widely in early Neolithic Britain, as a meaningful item interpreted and employed in numerous contexts. Other pot styles may have been connected to more localized identities and histories, or used in a more restricted range of social contexts. Critically, it may have been the contexts in which different forms of material culture were consumed that was the most significant element, so that broader connections and more localized meanings were not mutually exclusive. In a similar way we could imagine monuments working at multiple levels, making connections with broader traditions of monument construction and understandings of landscape, while evoking regional or local meanings and histories.

Cultural groups are therefore intersected by traditions of practice transmitted and consumed in different ways through a range of social contexts. While some of these contexts may be related to ethnic identities, many others could relate to gender, age, caste, personhood or any other means of framing and producing contexts of inclusion and exclusion. Some of these aspects of identity are yet to be assessed as potential features of prehistory. Similar strategies for doing things may be adopted by groups with different interests and lent towards different ends. The principles through which action is structured are transposed between different areas of identity, so that gender and ethnicity for example are produced in similar ways in a given context. Discourses on gender, ethnicity and other features of identity therefore overlap, and run in parallel, but are not entirely fixed to one another. There are different kinds of ethnic identity, not just different ethnic groups all with identical means of producing ethnicity (S. Jones 1997, 98–99). Equally, discourses on gender or kinship may be shared by some communities but at odds with others. Some prehistoric communities may have shared, for instance, means of tracing kinship that were at odds with others, or means of investing certain kinds of power in specific persons which were otherwise distributed or absent in neighbouring communities. Forms of social and material relations may therefore cut across cultural groups: in some cases these may have left traces in what we currently delimit as the archaeological record, while in other cases they may not.

This kind of practice-based approach has nourished studies that link the large-scale and long-term concern with cultural traditions to the seemingly more ephemeral issue of experience (e.g. Bradley 1998; A. Jones 2001; 2003; Thomas 1996; Tilley 1996). In particular the roles of memory, and the citation of past actions, are stressed by considering the central role of Neolithic materiality. The generation of these experiences draws on particular strategies in producing material relations, and these can be investigated both at the local experiential level, and in comparison with larger scale trends. These approaches place scrutiny on material media, and on the social contexts which activate and give value to them; to social technologies (e.g. Barrett 1994; Brück 2001b; Fowler 2001; 2003; A. Jones 2002; 2003; S. Jones and Richards 2000; Thomas 2000b; 1998; Williams 2003). They prioritise relations not just between people, but between people and things. Barrett (2001) presents society not as a structure or group of people, but as relations with others, and with things. He stresses the way that people learn about their world, and live among material conditions of the past. Cultural traditions are not so much transmitted as interpreted and reinvented in each interaction with the past. These interactions are constrained and enabled by those material conditions and the efficacy of patterns in practice in reproducing the same kind of social relations. In this view, material things are the media through which social relations are negotiated and re-negotiated. The emphasis rests on how communities consume and reinterpret the past in creating a particular present and future. Approaches to the Neolithic which have proliferated over the last fifteen years have increasingly relied on attention to the effects of particular

kinds of material context on human experience. While these approaches may be criticised as over-privileging specific experiences (cf. Brück 1998), they relocate those long-term and large-scale processes with which archaeologists are concerned in the ongoing present that people live through. Experience is studied not as specific to individual people, but as a social effect produced in negotiation with the material world. This means that cultural tradition may not be seen as an ongoing force, the 'dead hand of tradition', but as an active social engagement with the material conditions people live through. The relationship between people and material things or conditions is therefore opened up to consideration as a vital feature of past societies.

Materiality

Studies of materiality therefore take an interest in how substances, forms and conditions are re-evaluated through engagement, experience and practice. Material culture is not studied to match form to form, but to think about the relative effects produced by experiencing, constructing, using, and modifying material things. Things from the past already have value so that even natural substances have a place in the cultural understanding of the world. Coupled with theories of practice or experience, studies of materiality allow interpretation not just of changing meanings in the past, but changing social, political and cultural effects created by human participation with the material world and with one another.

A diversity of approaches

Many of the papers presented in this volume do approach the evidence from the Irish Sea area with these notions of practice and materiality in mind. But perhaps the strength of this collection of papers is that they illustrate the *diversity* of research taking place within studies of the Neolithic around the Irish Sea, and the plurality of viewpoints that currently exist. In editing this volume we have included contributions taking a wide range of theoretical approaches to the question of cultural engagement within the material world, and we hope this demonstrates how these approaches provide a stronger foundation for further study of the Neolithic in the British Isles when brought together than when kept apart. While the viewpoint presented in this introduction is clearly our own it is also at least partly a result of having organised the conference and edited these papers. We hope that reading this book will inspire both answers to the questions raised here, and further questions to be asked of Neolithic archaeology.

Acknowledgements

Many thanks to Alasdair Whittle and Julian Thomas for commenting on earlier drafts of this paper.

References

Barclay, G. and Brophy, K. (eds). forthcoming. *Regional diversity in the Neolithic of Britain and Ireland.* Oxford: Oxbow.

Barrett, J.C. 1988. Fields of discourse: reconstituting a social archaeology. *Critique of Anthropology* 7, 5–16.

Barrett, J.C. 1994. *Fragments from antiquity.* London: Routledge.

Barrett, J.C. 2001. Agency, the duality of structure, and the problem of the archaeological record. In I. Hodder (ed.), *Archaeological theory today*, 141–64. Cambridge: Polity Press.

Bender, B. (ed.) 1993. *Landscape: politics and perspectives.* Oxford: Berg.

Bender, B. 1998. *Stonehenge: making space.* Oxford: Berg.

Bender, B. and Winer, M. (eds) 2001. *Contested landscapes: movement, exile and places.* Oxford: Berg.

Bowen, E.G. 1970. Britain and the British Seas. In D. Moore (ed.), *The Irish Sea province in archaeology and history*, 13–28. Cardiff: Cambrian Archaeological Association.

Bradley, R. 1997. *Rock art and the prehistory of Atlantic Europe: signing the land.* London: Routledge.

Bradley, R. 1998. *The significance of monuments: on the shaping of human experience in Neolithic and Bronze Age Europe.* London: Routledge.

Bradley, R. 2002. *The past in prehistoric societies.* London: Routledge.

Bradley, R. and Edmonds, M. 1993. *Interpreting the axe trade.* Cambridge: Cambridge University Press.

Brophy, K. 1999. *The cursus monuments of Scotland.* Unpublished Ph.D. Thesis: University of Glasgow.

Brück, J. 1998. In the footsteps of the ancestors: a review of Christopher Tilley's *A phenomenology of landscape: places, paths and monuments. Archaeological Review from Cambridge* 15, 23–36.

Brück, J. 2001a. Monuments, power and personhood in the British Neolithic. *Journal of the Royal Anthropological Institute* 7, 649–67.

Brück, J. 2001b. Body metaphors and technologies of transformation in the English middle and late Bronze Age. In J. Brück (ed.), *Bronze Age landscapes: tradition and transformation*, 149–60. Oxford: Oxbow.

Burrow, S. 1997. *The Neolithic pottery of the Isle of Man and its relationship to that of surrounding areas: a study in production, decoration and use.* Unpublished Ph.D. Thesis: Bournemouth University.

Childe, V.G. 1927. *The dawn of European civilisation.* London: Kegan Paul.

Childe, V.G. 1929. *The Danube in prehistory.* Oxford: Clarendon Press.

Childe, V.G. 1942. *What happened in history.* Harmondsworth: Penguin.

Clarke, D. 1968. *Analytical archaeology.* London: Methuen.

Cleal, R. 1995. Pottery fabrics in the fourth to second millennia BC. In I. Kinnes and G. Varndell (eds), *Unbaked urns of rudely shape: essays on British and Irish pottery*, 185–94. Oxford: Oxbow.

Cooney, G. 1997. In P. Topping (ed.), *Neolithic landscapes*, 23–32. Oxford: Oxbow.

Cooney, G. 2000. *Landscapes of Neolithic Ireland.* London: Routledge.

Cooney, G. 2001. Bringing contemporary baggage to Neolithic landscapes. In B. Bender and M. Winer (eds), *Contested landscapes: movement, exile and places*, 165–80. Oxford: Berg.

Cooney, G. and Mandal, S. 1998. *Irish stone axe project monograph 1.* Dublin: Wordwell.

Cosgrove, D. 1989. Geography is everywhere: culture and symbolism in human landscapes. In D. Gregory and R. Walford (eds), *Horizons in human geography*, 118–35. London: MacMillan.

Crawford, O.G.S. 1912. The distribution of early Bronze Age settlements in Britain. *Geographical Journal* 40, 299–303.

Cummings, V. 2001. *Landscapes in transition? Exploring the origins of monumentality in south-west Wales and south-west Scotland.* Unpublished Ph.D. thesis: Cardiff University.

Cummings, V. 2002. Experiencing texture and touch in the British Neolithic. *Oxford Journal of Archaeology* 21, 249–61.

Daniel, G.E. 1941. The dual nature of the megalithic colonisation of prehistoric Europe. *Proceedings of the Prehistoric Society* 7, 1–49.

Darvill, T. 2001. Neolithic enclosures in the Isle of Man. In T. Darvill and J. Thomas (eds), *Neolithic enclosures in north-west Europe*, 77–111. Oxford: Oxbow.

Davies, M. 1945. Types of megalithic monuments of the Irish Sea and north Channel coastlands: a study in distributions. *Antiquaries Journal* 25, 125–44.

de Valera, R. 1960. The court cairns of Ireland. *Proceedings of the Royal Irish Academy* 60, 9–140.

de Valera, R. and Ó Nualláin, S. 1961. *Survey of the megalithic tombs of Ireland. Volume 1, County Clare.* Dublin: Stationery Office.

de Valera, R. and Ó Nualláin, S. 1964. *Survey of the megalithic tombs of Ireland. Volume 2, County Mayo.* Dublin: Stationery Office.

de Valera, R. and Ó Nualláin, S. 1972. *Survey of the megalithic tombs of Ireland. Volume 3, Counties Galway, Roscommon, Leitrim, Langford, Westmeath, Laoighis, Offaly, Kildare, Cavan.* Dublin: Stationery Office.

Edmonds, M. 1999. *Ancestral geographies of the Neolithic.* London: Routledge.

Fleure, H.J. 1915. Archaeological problems of the west coast of Britain. *Archaeologia Cambrensis* 15, 405–20.

Fowler, C. 1999. *On discourse and materiality: personhood in the Manx Neolithic.* Unpublished PhD thesis: University of Southampton.

Fowler, C. 2001. Personhood and social relations in the British Neolithic with a study from the Isle of Man. *Journal of Material Culture* 6, 137–63.

Fowler, C. 2003. Rates of (ex)change: decay and growth, memory and the transformation of the dead in early Neolithic southern Britain. In H. Williams (ed.), *Archaeologies of remembrance – death and memory in past societies*, 45–64. London: Kluwer Academic Press.

Fowler, C. and Cummings, V. 2003. Places of transformation: building monuments from water and stone in the Neolithic of the Irish Sea. *Journal of the Royal Anthropological Institute* 9, 1–20.

Fox, C. 1932. *The personality of Britain*. Cardiff: National Museum of Wales.

Gramsch, A. 1996. Landscape archaeology: of making and seeing. *Journal of European Archaeology* 4, 19–38.

Hartwell, B. 1998. The Ballynahatty complex. In A. Gibson and D.D.A. Simpson (eds), *Prehistoric ritual and religion. Essays in honour of Aubrey Burl*, 32–44. Stroud: Sutton.

Henshall, A. 1963. *The chambered tombs of Scotland, volume one*. Edinburgh: Edinburgh University Press.

Henshall, A. 1972. *The chambered tombs of Scotland, volume two*. Edinburgh: Edinburgh University Press.

Herity, M. 1970. The early prehistoric period around the Irish Sea. In D. Moore (ed.), *The Irish Sea province in archaeology and history*, 29–37. Cardiff: Cambrian Archaeological Association.

Hodder, I. 1977. The distribution of material culture items in the Baringo district, western Kenya. *Man* 12, 239–69.

Hodder, I. 1978a. Simple correlations between material culture and society: a review. In I. Hodder, (ed.) *The spatial organisation of culture*, 3–24. London: Duckworth.

Hodder, I. 1978b. The spatial structure of material 'cultures': a review of some of the evidence. In I. Hodder, (ed.) *The spatial organisation of culture*, 93–111. London: Duckworth.

Hodder, I. 1982. *Symbols in action: ethnoarchaeological studies of material culture*. Cambridge: Cambridge University Press.

Holgate, R. 1988. *Neolithic settlement of the Thames Basin*. Oxford : British Archaeological Reports, British Series 194.

Jones, A. 1997. *A biography of ceramics: food and culture in Late Neolithic Orkney*. Unpublished Ph.D .thesis: University of Glasgow.

Jones, A. 1998. Where eagles dare: landscape, animals and the Neolithic of Orkney. *Journal of Material Culture* 3, 301–24.

Jones, A. 2001. *Archaeological theory and scientific practice*. Cambridge: Cambridge University Press.

Jones, A. 2002. A biography of colour: colour, material histories and personhood in the early Bronze Age of Britain and Ireland. In A. Jones and G. MacGregor (eds) *Colouring the past*, 159–74. Oxford: Berg.

Jones, A. 2003. Technologies of remembrance: memory, materiality and identity in early Bronze Age Scotland. In H. Williams (ed.), *Archaeologies of remembrance – death and memory in past societies*, 65–88. London: Kluwer Academic Press.

Jones, S. 1997. *The archaeology of ethnicity: constructing identities in the past and present*. London: Routledge.

Jones, S. and Richards, C. 2000. Neolithic cultures in Orkney: classification and interpretation. In A. Ritchie (ed.), *Neolithic Orkney in its European context*, 101–106. Oxford: Oxbow.

Jordanova, L. 1989. *Sexual visions*. London: Harvester Wheatsheaf.

Kossinna, G. 1911. *Die Herkunft der Germanen*. Leipzig: Kabitzsch.

Larick, R. 1986. Age grading and ethnicity in the style of Loikop (Samburu) spears. *World Archaeology* 18, 269–83.

Last, J. 1998. Books of life: biography and memory in a Bronze Age barrow. *Oxford Journal of Archaeology* 17, 43–53.

Leivers, M. 1999. *The architecture and context of mortuary practice in the Neolithic period in north Wales*. Unpublished Ph.D. Thesis: University of Southampton.

Lucas, G. 1994. *Genealogies. Classification, narrative and time: an archaeological study of eastern Yorkshire 3700–1300 BC*. Unpublished PhD thesis: University of Cambridge.

Lucas, G. 1996. Of death and debt: a history of the body in Neolithic and early Bronze Age Yorkshire. *Journal of European Archaeology* 4, 99–118.

Lynch, F. 1989. Wales and Ireland in prehistory: a fluctuating relationship. *Archaeologia Cambrensis* 138, 1–19.

MacGregor, G. 1999. *The Neolithic and Bronze Ages of Aberdeenshire: a study of materiality and historical phenomenology*. Unpublished Ph.D. Thesis: University of Glasgow.

Midgley, M. 1993. *TRB culture: the first farmers of the north European plain*. Edinburgh: Edinburgh University Press.

Olwig, K. 1993. Sexual cosmology: nation and landscape at the conceptual interstices of nature and culture: or what does landscape really mean? In B. Bender (ed.), *Landscape: politics and perspectives*, 307–43. Oxford: Berg.

Peterson, R. 1999. *The construction and use of categories of Neolithic pottery from Wales*. Unpublished Ph.D. Thesis: University of Southampton.

Peterson, R. 2003. *Neolithic pottery from Wales: traditions of construction and use*. Oxford: British Archaeological Reports, British Series 244.

Phillips, T. 2002. *Landscapes of the living, landscapes of the dead: the location of chambered cairns of northern Scotland*. Oxford: British Archaeological Reports, British Series 328.

Piggott, S. 1954. *The Neolithic cultures of the British Isles*. Cambridge: Cambridge University Press.

Piggott, S. 1965. *Ancient Europe from the beginnings of agriculture to classical antiquity: a survey*. Edinburgh: Edinburgh University Press.

Pollard, J. 1999. 'These places have their moments': thoughts on settlement practices in the British Neolithic. In J. Brück and M. Goodman (eds), *Marking places in the prehistoric world*, 76-93. London: University College London Press.

Pollard, J. 2001. The aesthetics of depositional practice. *World Archaeology*, 33, 315–33.

Powell, T., Corcoran J., Lynch, F. and Scott, J. 1969. *Megalithic enquiries in the west of Britain*. Liverpool: Liverpool University Press.

RCAHMS 1999. *Kilmartin: an inventory of the monuments extracted from Argyll*. Edinburgh: Royal Commission of Ancient and Historic Monuments Scotland.

Richards, C. 1993. *An archaeological study of Neolithic Orkney: architecture, order and social classification*. Unpublished PhD thesis: University of Glasgow.

Richards, C. 1996. Henges and water: towards an elemental understanding of monumentality and landscape in late Neolithic Britain. *Journal of Material Culture* 2, 313–36.

Saville, A. 1994. Exploitation of lithic resources for stone tools in earlier prehistoric Scotland. In N. Ashton and A. David (eds), *Stories in stone*, 57–70. London: Lithic Studies Society.

Shanks, M. 2001. Culture/archaeology: the dispersion of a discipline and its objects. In I. Hodder (ed.), *Archaeological theory today*, 284–305. Cambridge: Polity Press.

Shanks, M. and Tilley, C. 1987. *Reconstructing archaeology*. London: Routledge.

Sheridan, J.A. 1986. Porcellanite artefacts: a new survey. *Ulster Journal of Archaeology* 49, 19–32.

Sheridan, J.A., Cooney, G. and Grogan, E. 1992. Stone axe studies in Ireland. *Proceedings of the Prehistoric Society* 58, 389–416.

Solberg, B. 1989. The Neolithic transition in southern Scandinavia: internal development or migration? *Oxford Journal of Archaeology* 8, 261–96.

Squair, R. 1998. *The Neolithic of the Western Isles.* Unpublished PhD thesis: University of Glasgow.

Thomas, J. 1988. Neolithic explanations revisited: the Mesolithic-Neolithic transition in Britain and south Scandinavia. *Proceedings of the Prehistoric Society* 54, 59–66.

Thomas, J. 1991. *Rethinking the Neolithic.* Cambridge: Cambridge University Press.

Thomas, J. 1992. Monuments, movement, and the context of megalithic art. In A. Sheridan and N. Sharples (eds), *Vessels for the ancestors,* 143–55. Edinburgh: Edinburgh University Press.

Thomas, J. 1993. The hermeneutics of megalithic space. In C. Tilley (ed.), *Interpretative archaeology,* 73–98. London: Berg.

Thomas, J. 1996. *Time, culture and identity.* London: Routledge.

Thomas, J. 1998. An economy of substances in earlier Neolithic Britain. In J. Robb (ed.), *Material symbols: culture and economy in prehistory,* 70–89. Carbondale: Southern Illinois University Press.

Thomas, J. 1999a. *Understanding the Neolithic.* London: Routledge.

Thomas, J. with contributions by K. Brophy, C. Fowler, M. Leivers, M. Ronayne and L. Wood. 1999b. The Holywood cursus complex, Dumfries: an interim account 1997. In A. Barclay and J. Harding (eds), *Pathways and ceremonies: the cursus monuments of Neolithic Britain and Ireland,* 107–18. Oxford: Oxbow.

Thomas, J. 2000a. The identity of place in Neolithic Britain: examples from south-west Scotland. In A. Ritchie (ed.), *Neolithic Orkney in its European context,* 79–90. Oxford: Oxbow.

Thomas, J. 2000b. Death, identity and the body in Neolithic Britain. *Journal of the Royal Anthropological Institute* 6, 603–17.

Tilley, C. 1994. *A phenomenology of landscape.* Oxford: Berg.

Tilley, C. 1996. *An ethnography of the Neolithic.* Cambridge: Cambridge University Press.

Trigger, B. 1989. *A history of archaeological thought.* Cambridge: Cambridge University Press.

Waddell, J. 1991. The Irish Sea in prehistory. *The Journal of Irish Archaeology* 6, 29–40.

Watson, A. and Keating, D. 1999. Architecture and sound: an acoustic analysis of megalithic monuments in prehistoric Britain. *Antiquity* 73, 325–36.

Williams, H. (ed.) 2003. *Archaeologies of remembrance - death and memory in past societies.* London: Kluwer Academic Press.

Zvelebil, M. 1996. Farmers; our ancestors and the identity of Europe. In P. Graves-Brown, S. Jones, and C. Gamble (eds), *Cultural identity and archaeology,* 145–66. London: Routledge.

2 Neolithic connections along and across the Irish Sea

Alison Sheridan

Introduction

While some other papers in this volume focus on the ways in which individuals experienced and made sense of their world, in examining Neolithic connections around and across the Irish Sea, this contribution looks at the spatial and chronological patterns in material culture and practices that we, from our privileged and distanced perspective, can make out. It will be argued that three kinds of linkage were responsible for creating these patterns, each operating over a different timescale and varying in spatial extent. These can be characterised in the following terms:

1. *Commonality of origins*: in other words, the earliest communities whom we identify as 'Neolithic' shared the same, continental ancestry and so brought the same basic traditions to Britain and Ireland. This is the basis for understanding the similarities in material culture and traditions of practice in the centuries around 4000 BC.
2. *Regular or sporadic contact* between communities on either side of the Irish Sea; once established, this might be described as a kind of 'kissing cousins' relationship, although of course the degree of actual kinship will have varied considerably.
3. *Relatively long distance and probably relatively exclusive connections*, towards the end of the fourth millennium BC.

In seeking to explain this choice of interpretations, it will be clear that certain rather unfashionable concepts, reminiscent of the writings of Stuart Piggott (1954), will be entertained. This writer is not seeking to create a retrograde, culture-historical view of the past, as some critics of this kind of approach tend to suggest (e.g. Kinnes 1988; 1995; Thomas 1996). Rather, it is felt that the information currently available to us invites certain interpretations that may seem relatively simple, yet which match the data significantly better than others. The reader can decide whether this is the case or not.

Commonality of origins

This first kind of connection is the one which has been most vigorously debated, particularly over the last decade: it concerns the nature of the Mesolithic-Neolithic transition. In brief, it appears that a range of novel resources, technologies, artefacts and practices appeared over most of Britain and Ireland in the centuries around 4000 BC[1]. These signalled the appearance of new life-ways: people were not wholly dependent on the use of wild or semi-domesticated resources for their subsistence; rectilinear timber houses, some of them substantial, appeared for the first time; and new funerary practices, some involving monumental structures, also appeared. The degree to which these novelties constitute a 'Neolithic package', and the speed, nature and agency of the transformation, have been extensively debated (e.g. Cooney 2000; Monk 2000; Rowley-Conwy 2003; Schulting 2000; Schulting and Richards 2002a; 2002b; Thomas 1996; 1998; 1999; Woodman *et al.* 1999). It is not intended to rehearse the various arguments in detail here; suffice it to say that, for most of Britain and all of Ireland, the evidence *against* Julian Thomas' model of a gradual transformation, with indigenous forager communities being the main agent of change, appears overwhelming – at least to this author.

What is of present interest is whether the observed patterning of these novelties constitutes one 'Neolithic' or several. In this author's opinion, the latter is the case; for reasons outlined below, these 'Neolithics' are viewed in terms of various movements of incoming farming communities from the continent. The number of people involved in each movement need not have been great, but in some cases the distances covered (principally by sea) were substantial. The main strands of these movements can be characterised thus:

1. *Atlantic*: from southern Brittany, up the Irish Sea and along the west coast of Scotland and the north coast of Ireland.
2. *'Cross-Channel-west'*: various movements from northern Brittany and Normandy to southern England.

3. *'Cross-Channel-east'*: various movements from different areas along the Channel coast between the Région of Haute-Normandie to the Netherlands.

Of these, the Atlantic and the 'Cross-Channel-east' are the ones which affected both sides of the Irish Sea, and will therefore be considered here. As for the hypothetical 'Cross-Channel-west' movements, these are arguably attested in phenomena such as the Norman/Channel-Islands-style simple passage tomb at Broadsands, Devon (Radford 1958), and the marked similarity between the trapezoidal long mound at Colombiers-sur-Seulles, Calvados (Chancerel and Kinnes 1998) and examples in southern England and elsewhere (e.g. Beckhampton Road, Wiltshire). Such movements may be responsible (in part, at least), for some of the diversity of southern English early Neolithic ceramics (see below on the problems of pinpointing areas of origin).

The Atlantic movement

This has been dealt with in detail elsewhere by this author (Sheridan 2000; 2003a; b; in press), so only the principal points will be reiterated here. The evidence for this hypothetical northwards 'diaspora' up the Irish Sea consists of small, closed polygonal megalithic chambers and small simple passage tombs which are found on or near the coast in Wales, western Scotland and Ireland. Examples of these monuments are shown in Fig. 2.1, and their distribution in Fig. 2.2 (see Sheridan 2003 b for details of their similarities and differences from area to area). As explained in that publication, these simple structures appear to lie at the beginning of the long and complex sequence of passage tomb development in Ireland and Scotland. In Wales, by contrast, this particular funerary tradition seems not to have 'taken root', the later and more elaborate passage tombs representing a subsequent adoption of practices from Ireland (see below and Lynch 2000, 73–7).

The reason for regarding these closed chambers and simple passage tombs as a southern Breton phenomenon is not simply the fact that reasonable parallels for their design and construction can be found in the Morbihan area of Brittany. At Achnacreebeag in the west of Scotland, pottery found in a simple passage tomb that was secondary to a closed chamber has been positively identified as being of late Castellic style, as used in simple passage tombs in the Morbihan between *c* 4300 and 3900 BC (Fig. 2.3; Boujot and Cassen 1992; 1997; 1998; Cassen 2000; 2001; Ritchie 1970). One of the closest parallels for the 'rainbow'-decorated bipartite bowl from Achnacreebeag (Fig. 2.3.1) is shown in Fig. 2.3.2, and represents a northern outlier of the late Castellic style, from Vierville in Normandy (Verron 2000).

Support for the date of this hypothetical movement has recently been provided by the substantial number of new, AMS, radiocarbon dates obtained for closed chambers and simple passage tombs at the cemetery of Carrowmore, County Sligo on the north-west coast of Ireland (Burenhult 2001). These indicate construction of these monuments within the 4200–3800 BC date range. (See Sheridan 2003 b for a discussion of all the radiocarbon dates relating to this cemetery.) Additional indirect support is offered by the evidence from Ballintoy, County Antrim (Mogey 1941), where a simple passage tomb was constructed on the site of a pyre associated with Carinated Bowl pottery, for which a date of *c* 4000 BC can be suggested, thereby providing a *terminus post quem* for the passage tomb.

The fact that Breton-style pottery has not (yet) been found in the few Welsh[2] and more numerous Irish examples of these monuments does not invalidate the hypothesis. At Carrowmore, re-use of tombs is likely to have taken place as the cemetery expanded; direct dating of the cremated bone found inside them should demonstrate whether this is the case or not (see Lanting and Brindley 1998 on dating cremated bone).

Apart from the structural and ceramic links with southern Brittany outlined above, the reasons for interpreting this scatter of monuments in terms of an incoming group of settlers are: a) the lack of Mesolithic precedents in any of these areas for *either* a funerary tradition involving monument construction *or* the use of pottery; b) the lack of evidence for contact between late Mesolithic communities around the Irish Sea or between this area and north-west France at this time; and c) the absence of an obvious reason why, even if there had been such contact, the Mesolithic communities around the Irish Sea should choose to adopt these novel practices. By contrast, Boujot and Cassen's interpretation of developments in the Morbihan provides us with a plausible reason why some people might have chosen to leave the area and make a new life elsewhere at this time (Boujot and Cassen 1992; 1997; 1998; Cassen 2000; 2001). The transition to a mode of subsistence dominated by the use of domesticated resources, documented in the very bones of the individuals concerned (Schulting and Richards 2001), seems to have involved social, ideological and perhaps also cosmological *bouleversements*, as expressed in the destruction of earlier monuments (stelae) and their incorporation within a new style of funerary monument, the passage tomb. The population of the Morbihan may have been fairly dense; the inhabitants had a long tradition of seafaring expertise (Cassen 1993; Kinnes 1984); therefore departure of some families westwards then northwards by sea at this time of change does not seem far-fetched.

'Cross-Channel-east' movements

As with 'Cross-Channel-west' movements, a series of separate movements may well have occurred, some of them involving just the relatively short sea journey to

Figure 2.1. *Closed chambers and simple passage tombs. Top left: Bodowyr, Anglesey (photo: V. Cummings); top right: Achnacreebeag, Argyll (closed chamber; photo: G. Ritchie, Crown copyright); bottom left: Lennaghbeg, Co. Antrim; bottom right: Carrowmore grave 7, Co. Sligo (author's own photos).*

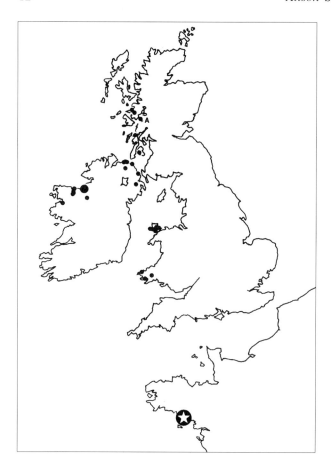

Figure 2.2. *Distribution of closed chambers and simple passage tombs in Britain and Ireland. A = Achnacreebeag; large dot: Carrowmore cemetery; star: Morbihan area of Brittany. Note: the Broadsands tomb and the Cotswold-Severn 'rotundae' are excluded. Based on Lynch 1975; 2000 and Sheridan 1986, with amendments.*

southern England. (Evidence in favour of such a view includes the results of Anne Tresset's work on patterns of animal husbandry and consumption in southern England, where she has identified close similarities with those seen in the Paris Basin and adjacent areas: Tresset 2000.)

The movement – or series of movements – of particular interest to the matter at hand is that which brought the use of Carinated Bowl pottery (and all the novelties associated with it, including non-megalithic funerary practices and rectangular timber houses) to Britain and Ireland. Discussed intelligently by Herne (1988), but nevertheless still lacking an overall, definitive distribution map or *corpus*, this type of pottery is found extensively over Britain and Ireland (with numerous recent Irish discoveries being described in Armit *et al.* 2003). The consistency of the earliest Carinated Bowl pottery is very striking, as is the skill in its manufacture (Fig. 2.4); and the radiocarbon dating evidence, notwithstanding its various problems, suggests that there was no significant

time lag between its appearance in different parts of Britain and Ireland. In other words, another 'diaspora'-type movement of its makers and users, from Continental Europe, is implied from its distribution. Once again, no convincing model of indigenous Mesolithic agency in its appearance has been presented. In Ireland, the Thomasian model is especially weak since, in addition to the unlikelihood of the indigenous foragers rapidly and simultaneously gaining expertise in pottery manufacture, there is a striking contrast in the distribution of late Mesolithic and Carinated Bowl findspots (with the former being found almost exclusively in coastal, riverine and lacustrine areas: Woodman *et al.* 1999).

A perennial problem in the debate over the 'colonisation' hypothesis has been the fact that no specific point(s) of origin for the Carinated Bowl 'package' has successfully been identified, even though there has been long-standing and widespread acknowledgement of affinities with some northern Chassey and Michelsberg pottery (e.g. Childe 1932; Kinnes 1988). Louwe Kooijmans has pointed out that the most similar pottery in the Netherlands appears to be a contemporary congener, rather than an ancestral precursor (Louwe Kooijmans 1976; 1980). Against this it must be stressed that our knowledge and understanding of the Neolithic across the Channel around 4000 BC is far from complete. As recent discoveries in Normandy (e.g. Verron 2000) and Belgium (Vanmontfort 2001) have demonstrated, models that may have been accepted a decade ago have had to be revised substantially in the light of new and different evidence. Even though the recent developer-funded fieldwork connected with road and rail construction in the Régions of Haute-Normandie, Picardie and Nord-Pas de Calais, and in Belgium, has not produced our hypothetical point(s) of departure for Carinated Bowl users, this does not mean that such areas will not be found in the future. The same may indeed be true as far as ceramic links in other cross-Channel movements are concerned. While Serge Cassen's attempt to identify connections between Castellic pottery and the early Neolithic decorated wares as seen, for instance, at Windmill Hill (Cassen 2000, 435–59) is unconvincing (not least because of a chronological disjunction); it may be, nevertheless, that Basse-Normandie will produce closer parallels in future.

Regularity of contact: 'kissing cousins' connections

There is abundant and varied evidence to suggest that the Neolithic communities around the Irish Sea communicated with each other and exchanged objects, ideas and probably also people. A few specific examples should suffice, namely: a) contacts, throughout the Neolithic, between north-east Ireland and Scotland (particularly the south-west); b) more sporadic north-south contacts along

Figure 2.3. *1 (top) Decorated bipartite bowl from Achnacreebeag (photo: NMS). 2 (bottom) Late Castellic bowl from Vierville, Normandy (drawing: Verron 2000; photo: Musée de Normandie, Caen).*

Figure 2.4. *Carinated bowl from Ballintaggart, Co. Armagh (photo: Ulster Museum).*

the Irish Sea; and c) contacts between eastern and southern Ireland and the areas across the Irish Sea (for which see also Darvill this volume, which deals specifically with Manx relationships).

Connections between north-east Ireland and Scotland

The evidence for such links is well documented, so only a summary description will be offered here. Communities on either side of the North Channel appear to have been in regular contact throughout the Neolithic – as indeed has been the case throughout prehistory and history. Within the last 150 years, for example, the inhabitants of the Antrim coast found it easier to sail to Galloway to obtain supplies than to cross the high Antrim plateau.

The indisputable movement of artefacts and partly-worked raw materials is documented in the porcellanite axeheads and roughouts found in Scotland, their sources being Tievebulliagh and Brockley, Rathlin Island in County Antrim (Cooney and Mandal 1998; Scott 1973; Sheridan *et al.* 1992); in individual artefacts and hoards of high-quality Antrim flint found in south-west Scotland (Saville 1999; Scott 1973); and in finds of Arran pitchstone in Ireland (Simpson and Meighan 1999). Porcellanite items have a particularly extensive distribution in Scotland, with possible examples having been found as far north as the Northern Isles. While much of the mainland Scottish distribution pattern might be accounted for by the transmission of axeheads across networks of contacts, the Hebridean and west coast examples might have been acquired directly from the source areas, by sailing down the coast. This is suggested by the fact that pottery of distinctive Hebridean character has been found in the sandhills at Portstewart on the north Antrim coast (Herity 1982, fig. 77.1–2; Sheridan 1985, fig. 5.56; see also below)[3].

The sharing of ideas and traditions is shown in the design of pottery and of megalithic tombs in north-east Ireland and south-west Scotland. The ceramic links have been discussed elsewhere (Sheridan 1985; 1995; 2000); of these, one of the most interesting is the use of decorated bipartite bowls that are clearly derived from the late Castellic tradition mentioned above. Their course of development in Scotland, Ulster and elsewhere in Ireland is presented in Sheridan 2000, figs. 5 and 6; these are the vessels variously described by others as 'Beacharra II carinated bowls', 'Ballyalton bowls' and 'Drimnagh style bowls' (see Sheridan 1995 for details).

The similarities and differences in megalithic tomb design between 'Clyde cairns' and Irish court tombs have been discussed exhaustively elsewhere, not always productively (e.g. Corcoran 1960; 1972; Henshall 1972; Scott 1969; 1973). Suffice it to say that, in the light of evidence for non-megalithic precursors (in the form of timber mortuary chambers, some segmented, and some with long mounds and façades: Kinnes 1992), it seems likely that

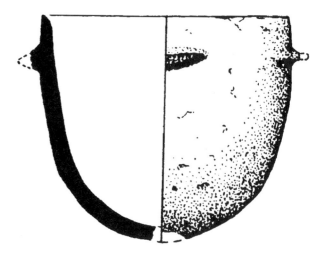

Figure 2.5. *Lugged plain bowl from Clachaig, Arran (from Henshall 1972)*

on both sides of the sea we are seeing a translation into stone of non-megalithic monuments. Part of the similarity between Clyde cairns and court tombs may therefore be due to the 'shared ancestry' as mentioned above. However, some specific points of similarity do suggest an exchange of design ideas across the North Channel: for example, some Clyde cairns feature the Irish-style jamb-and-sill arrangement for chamber segmentation (Scott 1973).

Early Neolithic north-south contacts along the Irish Sea

That a certain amount of north-south Irish Sea movement occurred is suggested principally by the presence of an unmistakably south-west English pottery form in a few assemblages in north-east Ireland and west/south-west Scotland. This is the deep, undecorated, lugged fineware bowl form (Fig. 2.5), which is one of the classic components of the 'south-western style' (Whittle 1977; also known as 'Hembury Ware': Piggott 1954, 67–71) but which was absent from the Carinated Bowl repertoire. On current reckoning, this kind of pottery was in use around 3600 BC, if not slightly earlier (Sharples 1991, 253; Whittle *et al.* 1999, especially 116–20).

In Scotland, this type of pot has been found in several Clyde cairns, including the northern (and slightly unusual) outlier at Clettraval on North Uist (Henshall 1972, 507–12). Jack Scott (1964) has classified it as part of the 'Beacharra tradition', which is a catch-all term covering early to mid-Neolithic pottery in south-west Scotland and the Hebrides (cf. Sheridan 2000 fig. 6). In Ireland, it has been found at two coastal sandhills locations in the north-east, at Dundrum, County Down, and at Portstewart, Co. Derry (Evans 1945)[4]. The fact that Hebridean decorated pottery has also been found at Portstewart (see above) might indicate that the proximate

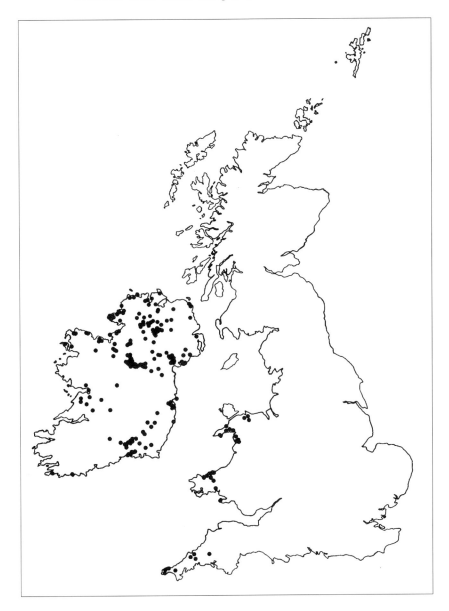

Figure 2.6. The distribution of portal tombs (based on Lynch 1969; 2000; Waddell 1998).

source of the design idea for the Portstewart pot (if not the actual vessel itself) might have been the Outer Hebrides, rather than somewhere to the south.

Other evidence for north-south Irish Sea contacts is more fragmentary and contentious. As far as pottery is concerned, one of the bowls from the megalithic chamber at Ballymacaldrack, County Antrim, resembles the baggy bowls with sub-rim perforations as seen at Windmill Hill (Evans 1938, pot B), but otherwise there is no strong connection between assemblages as a whole in north-east Ireland and southern England. There are hints of a possible northerly trickle of axeheads: Cooney and Mandal (1998, 175) have concluded that there may be a few specimens of Cornish gabbro in Ireland and there are a few definite and possible examples of Welsh axeheads in Scotland, including a fragment of a Group VII (Graig Lwyd) axehead in a pre-henge context at

Cairnpapple, West Lothian (Piggott 1950). As far as the design of megalithic monuments is concerned, there has been much speculation as to the influence of Cotswold-Severn design on court tombs (e.g. Corcoran 1972, Scott 1969; 1973); but, despite generalised similarities (e.g. in the use of drystone walling) the evidence is not wholly convincing, and the arguments were formulated without considering the contribution of non-megalithic precedents for some of the design elements, such as the use of a trapezoidal mound.

Contacts across the sea, involving eastern and southern Ireland

Various strands of evidence suggest contacts at different times during the Neolithic. One obvious early Neolithic pattern is the circum-Irish Sea distribution of portal tombs

(Fig. 2.6). Once again, there has been much discussion of the origin and significance of these tombs (e.g. Corcoran 1972; Lynch 1972; 2000). For what it is worth, it is this author's opinion that they might represent the elaborated translation into stone of a simple, non-segmented timber chamber form that may have been in widespread currency during the early Neolithic (see Sheridan in press b for a discussion of non-megalithic funerary traditions in Ireland). Their date within the first half of the fourth millennium has been established not only by the Carinated Bowl type pottery from Dyffryn Ardudwy (Lynch 2000) and some Irish sites, but also, arguably, by the suite of dates on human bone from Poulnabrone, Co. Clare (Cooney 2000, 94–7; Lynch 1990. It has been suggested, however, that the human bones may have been curated for several centuries before their deposition in this tomb). As far as the current discussion is concerned, the design similarities on either side of the Irish Sea may well indicate a degree of contact among their builders, and not just a shared ancestry of funerary tradition.

Other evidence for contact across the Irish Sea includes the now fairly substantial number (101) of axeheads of Great Langdale tuff in Ireland (Cooney *et al.* 1998), together with the scatter of Irish porcellanite axeheads in England, Wales and the Isle of Man (Sheridan *et al.* 1992, fig. 6). There are also a few axeheads of possibly Welsh origin in Ireland (Cooney and Mandal 1999, 175; note that the two County Antrim axeheads identified by Keiller (1936) as of Group XIII rock from the Preseli Hills were subsequently dismissed: Evens *et al.* 1962, 219). In terms of ceramics, there are strong similarities between some of the Irish Impressed Wares (e.g. those found at Townleyhall, County Louth and Knowth, County Meath) and Welsh Impressed Ware (Gibson 1995; Redknap 2003, 160; Sheridan 1995). Furthermore, the idea of using Grooved Ware appears to have been adopted in Ireland from across the water, even though the precise area/s of contact is still open to debate (Brindley 1999a; b; see below and Sheridan in press c for a possible Orcadian link).

Finally, the aforementioned 're-introduction' of the passage tomb tradition to Wales, this time from eastern Ireland, has been persuasively argued by Frances Lynch (2000). Not only tomb design but also the use of megalithic 'art' – not only in north Wales but also at the destroyed Merseyside passage tomb, the Calderstones (Shee Twohig 1981, 228–9, figures 261–5) – indicates the strength of the connection with Irish developed passage tombs.

Long-distance connections across, along and beyond the Irish Sea during the late fourth millennium BC

It has long been recognised that the largest passage tombs in the Boyne Valley have far-reaching resonances – in their ground plan and construction, in the designs pecked and incised into them, and in the objects found within them – which link the Boyne with Orkney to the north, Wales to the east and Brittany and Iberia to the south (e.g. Bradley and Chapman 1984; Eogan 1999). The easterly connection to Wales has already been mentioned. The Iberian connection was observed in a handful of items from the Boyne Valley and elsewhere. At Knowth, a grooved stone object found close to the entrance to the western tomb of the largest mound (no. 1) finds its only convincing parallels in tombs around Lisbon in southern Portugal (Eogan 1980). A bone or antler pin with zig-zag decoration from a smaller passage tomb at Knowth, a similar pin from Fourknocks, County Meath, and groove-decorated pendants from Carrowmore and Carrowkeel (County Sligo) and Loughcrew (County Meath), were compared with similar bone pendants from the Lisbon area and around Alicante. More hesitatingly, some peculiarly-shaped natural stone concretions found near the entrance to Knowth 1 west were compared with the stone 'baetyls' found near the entrances of some Los Millares passage tombs (Eogan 1980; although whether the *comparanda* are likely to be contemporary is a moot point). Similarly-shaped stones were associated with the largest passage tomb and with a smaller passage tomb at Newgrange; the main Newgrange tomb also produced a small carved pebble, closely paralleled in north-west Iberia (O'Kelly 1982, 192; Shee Twohig 1981, 126).

A Breton connection, again involving the Morbihan area, is apparent in the megalithic 'art' (O'Kelly 1982, 192; O'Sullivan 1997; Shee Twohig 1981, 126). More tentatively, one could also suggest certain similarities in passage tomb design, such as the fact that the western tomb at Knowth 1, enlarged from an initial simple shape by the addition of an angled passage, recalls Breton 'allées coudées' (Sheridan 1986). The similarities in the 'art' are not generalised, but are specific and concern a small number of monuments, suggesting a phase of contact within the otherwise differing trajectories of passage tomb development in the Boyne and Brittany.

The Orcadian connection is relatively strong, being reflected not only in passage tomb design and 'decoration', but also in artefacts and possibly, as we shall see below, in non-funerary practices associated with Grooved Ware. The parallelism in tomb design is shown in the cruciform (or otherwise cellular) chamber shape and long passages of Orcadian Maes Howe-type passage tombs, and also in the fact that Maes Howe, like Newgrange, was orientated on a significant astronomical phenomenon (the setting sun at midwinter solstice; cf. sunrise at

Newgrange; Davidson and Henshall 1989; Eogan 1992). The use of spiral and similar motifs, pecked into the lintel stones of several extant or destroyed passage tombs, is another feature adopted from Irish practice (Davidson and Henshall 1989; Shee Twohig 1981); the close picking marks and incised designs seen at Maes Howe have also been compared with Irish megalithic 'art' (Eogan 1992). As Kinnes (1995) and others have pointed out, the spiral design has also been found elsewhere in Britain, on portable artefacts such as carved stone balls and Grooved Ware as well as on fixed monuments and rock outcrops.

Artefactually, the deliberately burnt, broken pestle macehead from the western tomb at Knowth 1 is of a type commonly found in Orkney, where the practice of deliberately breaking such maceheads is also attested (Simpson and Ransom 1992); and the magnificent spiral-decorated Maesmawr-type macehead from the eastern tomb at Knowth 1 (Eogan and Richardson 1982) has an Orcadian link insofar as the closest parallel for this particular spiral design comes from the destroyed passage tomb at Pierowall on Westray (Simpson and Ransom 1992). Maesmawr-type maceheads are also known from elsewhere in Britain.

Ceramically, the infamous Grooved Ware sherd from Skara Brae, shown on the cover of Piggott's 1954 volume, has been claimed as having a particularly close link with Boyne Valley megalithic 'art'. While some link is indeed likely, it must be pointed out that Piggott 'doctored' the image slightly, as Kinnes has noted (1995; Clarke *pers. comm.*). There is also the issue, touched upon above, of whether the practice of using Grooved Ware could have been introduced to Ireland from (or via) Orkney, where it appears to have originated (Brindley 1999a; 1999b; Cowie and MacSween 1999; Eogan and Roche 1999; MacSween 1992). While no timber circle analogous to the Irish examples from Knowth (Eogan and Roche 1994; 1999) and Ballynahatty (Hartwell 1998) has been found in Orkney, a suspicious trail of Grooved Ware finds, some associated with tall timber or stone circles along the west coast of Scotland, in the Hebrides (Calanais, Unival) and on Arran (Machrie Moor), would appear to offer a possible chain of evidence. Unfortunately space does not permit this matter to be explored at greater length here; see Sheridan in press c for a full discussion.

Finally, a recent discovery in the field of animal genetics has produced new and startling evidence to support the idea of long-distance connections during the late fourth millennium BC. The Orkney Vole (*microtus arvalis orcadensis*, Fig. 2.7), now found only in Orkney, was discovered to have a genetic makeup indicating that it can only have arrived in Orkney from either western France or Iberia, travelling in a single step (Haynes *et al.* in press). Since it is known to be present at the sites of Skara Brae and the Links of Noltland, which are roughly contemporary with Maes Howe-type passage tombs, it is tempting to suggest that its appearance was linked with the same kind of long-distance movements that are thought

Figure 2.7. The Orkney Vole (photo: Peter Reynolds).

to be responsible for the phenomena outlined above.

Observing such phenomena is one thing; interpreting them intelligently, as Kinnes has pointed out (1995), is something else entirely. Bradley and Chapman (1984) and this author (1986) proposed a kind of 'peer polity interaction' model, in which long-distance travel and the acquisition and use of exotic items or ideas was fundamental to the maintenance and enhancement of the elites' power. Certainly the construction of the massive passage tombs in the Boyne Valley, Brittany and Iberia (and arguably also the technically-accomplished Maes Howe tomb) would seem to imply a markedly ranked society; the role of cosmology and ancestor-related practices in maintaining the elite's temporal power in this society has been discussed at length elsewhere (e.g. Bradley and Chapman 1984; Sheridan 1986). Against this, Kinnes has counselled against the 'facile' equation of pattern with inter-regional contact, and has emphasised the need for much firmer chronological and contextual information. While nobody would dispute the need for more and better data, this author feels that Kinnes is falling into the same trap as those who eschew notions of colonisation by continental farmers around 4000 BC. By ridiculing much earlier attempts to explain the widespread distribution of the spiral motif within an *ex oriente lux* model, his reluctance to cross the boundary between describing material evidence and actively interpreting it does not move the debate forward. Notwithstanding the shortcomings of the data, it is surely unlikely that the currently-accepted pattern is due solely to chance.

Conclusion

It is hoped that this brief review of the evidence for contacts across and around (and indeed beyond) the Irish Sea has revealed the wealth of information available and will stimulate further debate as to how best to interpret it. The explanations offered here are merely suggestions, and they beg many questions (such as why the relatively long east-west crossing of the Irish Sea was undertaken: was it to maintain the same kind of inter-community relations as experienced on either side of the North Channel?). There is no doubt more to be said about the extent and nature of long-distance movements/contacts, particularly those involved with the 'Grooved Ware phenomenon', which cannot adequately be covered here. And there is clearly a need for the integration of this kind of perspective with the insights gained from a phenomenological approach to the Neolithic inhabitants of the Irish Sea area.

Ian Kinnes berated much current methodology as 'a curious combination of absolutist interpretation (this is how I say it was) and abrogation (the language which I employ does not commit me)' (1995, 52). If this paper succeeds in avoiding the worst excesses of such an approach, well and good. It is offered as a challenge to others to produce a more convincing narrative and better fit with the data.

Notes

1 An earlier but isolated episode of contact, between western France and the south coast of Ireland around 4500–4300 BC, has been suggested to account for the early dated cattle bone from Ferriter's Cove: Tresset 2000.
2 A large plain baggy bowl found in Carreg Samson, while clearly not part of the Carinated Bowl repertoire, remains hard to pinpoint in terms of ceramic traditions.
3 The Hebridean connections of these two pots were not recognised by Herity. The sherds are from the Wellcome Collection in the Ulster Museum and there is a slight doubt as to whether they came from Portstewart or elsewhere on the Antrim coast; Herity refers to them as 'possibly County Antrim'.
4 Evans mistakenly gave the findspot of this pottery as Whitepark Bay; documentation in the Ulster Museum demonstrates that it was from Portstewart. Furthermore, in his illustration, Evans linked the rim of the lugged bowl with the base of a completely different, decorated pot.

Acknowledgements

The extreme patience of the editors is very greatly appreciated, and Vicki Cummings is also thanked for allowing reproduction of her image of Bodowyr. The Musée de Normandie, Caen (and particularly Sandrine Berthelot), is thanked for permission to reproduce the photograph of the Vierville bowl; the Ulster Museum, for Fig. 2.4, and Peter Reynolds, for Fig. 2.7.

References

Armit, I., Murphy, E., Simpson, D.D.A. and Nelis, E. (eds) 2003. *Neolithic settlement in Ireland and western Britain.* Oxford: Oxbow.
Boujot, C. and Cassen, S. 1992. Le développement des premières architectures funéraires monumentales en France occidentale. *Revue d'Archéologie de l'Ouest, Supplément no. 5*, 195–211.
Boujot, C. and Cassen, S. 1997. Néolithisation et monumentalité funéraire: explorations du tertre de Lannec er Gadouer à Erdeven (Morbihan, France). In A. Rodríguez Casal (ed.), *O Neolítico Atlántico e as orixes do megalitismo*, 211–32. Santiago de Compostela. UISPP.
Boujot, C. and Cassen, S. 1998. Tertres armoricains et tumulus carnacéens dans le cadre de la Néolithisation de la France occidentale. In J. Guilaine (ed.), *Sépultures d'occident et genèses des mégalithismes (9000–3500 av. notre ère)*, 107–26. Paris: Editions Errance.
Bradley, R.J. and Chapman, R. 1984. Passage graves in the European Neolithic – a theory of converging evolution. In G.Burenhult, *The archaeology of Carrowmore: environmental archaeology and the megalithic tradition at Carrowmore, Co. Sligo, Ireland*, 348–56. Stockholm: G. Burenhults Förlag.
Brindley, A. 1999a. Irish Grooved Ware. In R. Cleal and A. MacSween (eds), *Grooved Ware in Britain and Ireland*, 23–35. Oxford: Oxbow.
Brindley, A. 1999b. Sequence and dating in the Grooved Ware tradition. In R. Cleal and A. MacSween (eds), *Grooved Ware in Britain and Ireland*, 133–44. Oxford: Oxbow.
Burenhult, G. 2001. *The illustrated guide to the megalithic cemetery of Carrowmore, Co. Sligo.* Stockholm: G. Burenhults Förlag.
Cassen, S. 1993. Le Néolithique le plus ancien de la façade atlantique de la France. *Munibe 45*, 119–29.
Cassen, S. 2000. *Eléments d'architecture: exploration d'un Tertre Funéraire à Lannec er Gadouer (Erdeven, Morbihan). Constructions et reconstructions dans le Néolithique morbihannais. Propositions pour un lecture symbolique.* Chauvigny: Éditions Chauvinoises.
Cassen, S. 2001. Stelae reused in the passage graves of western France: history of research and sexualization of the carvings. In A. Ritchie (ed.), *Neolithic Orkney in its European context*, 233–46. Cambridge: McDonald Institute for Archaeological Research.
Chancerel, A. and Kinnes, I.A. 1998. Du bois dans l'architecture: le tumulus de la Commune Sèche à Colombiers-sur-Seulles (Calvados), *Révue archéologique de l'Ouest, supplément 5*, 17–29.
Childe, V.G. 1932. The continental affinities of British Neolithic pottery. *Archaeological Journal 88*, 37–66.
Cooney, G. 2000. *Landscapes of Neolithic Ireland.* London: Routledge.
Cooney, G., Byrnes, E. and Mandal, S. 1998. Case study: Group VI axes in Ireland. In G. Cooney and S. Mandal, *The Irish stone axe project. Monograph I*, 111–73. Bray: Wordwell.
Cooney, G. and Mandal, S. 1998. *The Irish stone axe project. Monograph I.* Bray: Wordwell.
Corcoran, J.X.W.P. 1960. The Carlingford culture. *Proceedings of the Prehistoric Society 26*, 98–148.
Corcoran, J.X.W.P. 1972. Multi-period construction and the origins of the chambered long cairn in western Britain and Ireland. In F. M. Lynch and C. Burgess (eds), *Prehistoric man in Wales and the west: essays in honour of Lily F. Chitty*, 31–63. Bath: Adams and Dart.
Cowie, T.G. and MacSween, A. 1999. Grooved Ware from

Scotland: a review. In R. Cleal and A. MacSween (eds), *Grooved Ware in Britain and Ireland*, 48–56. Oxford: Oxbow.

Davidson, J.L. and Henshall, A.S. 1989. *The chambered cairns of Orkney*. Edinburgh: Edinburgh University Press.

Eogan, G.1980. Objects with Iberian affinities from Knowth, Ireland. *Revista de Guimarães* 89, 3–7.

Eogan, G. 1992. Scottish and Irish passage tombs: some comparisons and contrasts. In N.M. Sharples and J.A. Sheridan (eds), *Vessels for the ancestors: essays on the Neolithic of Britain and Ireland in honour of Audrey Henshall*, 120–7. Edinburgh: Edinburgh University Press.

Eogan, G. 1999. Megalithic art and society. *Proceedings of the Prehistoric Society* 65, 415–46.

Eogan, G. and Richardson, H. 1982.Two maceheads from Knowth, Co. Meath. *Journal of the Royal Society of Antiquaries of Ireland* 112, 123–38.

Eogan, G. and Roche, H.A. 1994. A Grooved Ware wooden structure at Knowth, Boyne Valley, Ireland. *Antiquity* 68, 322–30.

Eogan, G. and Roche, H.A. 1999. Grooved Ware from Brugh na Bóinne and its wider context. In R. Cleal and A. MacSween (eds), *Grooved Ware in Britain and Ireland*, 98–111. Oxford: Oxbow.

Evans, E.E. 1938. Doey's cairn, Dunloy, Co. Antrim. *Ulster Journal of Archaeology* 1, 49–78.

Evans, E.E. 1945. Field archaeology in the Ballycastle district. *Ulster Journal of Archaeology* 8, 14–32.

Evens, E.D., Grinsell, L.V., Piggott, S. and Wallis, F.S. 1962. Fourth report of the sub-committee of the south-western group of museums and art galleries on the petrological identification of stone axes. *Proceedings of the Prehistoric Society* 28, 209–66.

Gibson, A. 1995. First impressions: a review of Peterborough Ware in Wales. In I.A. Kinnes and G. Varndell (eds), *'Unbaked urns of rudely shape': essays on British and Irish pottery for Ian Longworth*, 23–39. Oxford: Oxbow.

Hartwell, B. 1998. The Ballynahatty complex. In A. Gibson and D.D.A. Simpson (eds), *Prehistoric ritual and religion: essays in honour of Aubrey Burl*, 32–44. Stroud: Sutton.

Haynes, S., Jaarola, M., Searle, J. and Dobney, K. in press. The origin of the Orkney vole: a proxy for reconstructing human movements. In R. Housley and G. Coles (eds), *Atlantic connections and adaptations: economies, environments and subsistence in the north Atlantic realm*. Oxford: Oxbow.

Henshall, A.S. 1972. *The chambered tombs of Scotland. Volume 2*. Edinburgh: Edinburgh University Press.

Herity, M. 1982. Irish decorated Neolithic pottery. *Proceedings of the Royal Irish Academy* 82C, 247–404.

Herne, A. 1988. A time and a place for the Grimston bowl. In J. Barrett and I.A. Kinnes (eds), *The archaeology of context in the Neolithic and Bronze Age: recent trends*, 9–29. Sheffield: Department of Archaeology and Prehistory, University of Sheffield.

Keiller, A. 1936. Two axes of Presely stone from Ireland. *Antiquity* 10, 220–1.

Kinnes, I.A. 1984. Microliths and megaliths: monumental origins on the Atlantic fringe. In G. Burenhult, *The archaeology of Carrowmore: environmental archaeology and the megalithic tradition at Carrowmore, Co. Sligo, Ireland*, 367–70. Stockholm: G. Burenhults Förlag.

Kinnes, I.A. 1988. The Cattleship Potemkin: the first Neolithic in Britain. In J. Barrett and I.A. Kinnes (eds), *The archaeology of context in the Neolithic and Bronze Age: recent trends*, 2–8. Sheffield: Department of Archaeology and Prehistory, University of Sheffield.

Kinnes, I.A. 1992 *Non-megalithic long barrows and allied structures in the British Neolithic*. London: British Museum.

Kinnes, I.A. 1995. An innovation backed by great prestige: the instance of the spiral and twenty centuries of stony sleep. In I.A. Kinnes and G. Varndell (eds), *'Unbaked urns of rudely shape': essays on British and Irish pottery for Ian Longworth*, 49–53. Oxford: Oxbow.

Lanting, J. and Brindley, A. 1998. Dating cremated bone: the dawn of a new era. *Journal of Irish Archaeology* 9, 1–7.

Louwe Kooijmans, L.P. 1976 Local developments in a border land. *Oudheidkundige Mededelingen uit het Rijksmuseum van Oudheden te Leiden* 57, 227–97.

Louwe Kooijmans, L.P. 1980. The middle Neolithic assemblage of Het Vormer near Wijchen and the culture pattern around the southern North Sea, c. 3000 B.C. *Oudheidkundige Mededelingen uit het Rijksmuseum van Oudheden te Leiden* 61, 113–208.

Lynch, A. 1990. Poulnabrone portal tomb, Co. Clare. In R.E.M. Hedges, R.A. Housley, I.A. Law and C.R. Bronk, Radiocarbon dates from the Oxford AMS system: *Archaeometry* datelist 10. *Archaeometry* 32, 106.

Lynch, F.M. 1969. The megalithic tombs of North Wales. In T.G.E. Powell, J.X.W.P. Corcoran, F.M. Lynch and J.G. Scott, *Megalithic enquiries in the west of Britain*, 107–48. Liverpool: Liverpool University Press.

Lynch, F.M. 1972. Portal dolmens in the Nevern Valley, Pembrokeshire. In F. M. Lynch and C. Burgess (eds), *Prehistoric man in Wales and the west: essays in honour of Lily F. Chitty*, 67–84. Bath: Adams and Dart.

Lynch, F.M. 2000. The earlier Neolithic. In F.M. Lynch, S. Aldhouse-Green and J.L. Davies (eds), *Prehistoric Wales*, 42–78. Stroud: Sutton.

MacSween, A. 1992. Orcadian Grooved Ware. In N.M. Sharples and J.A. Sheridan (eds), *Vessels for the ancestors: essays on the Neolithic of Britain and Ireland in honour of Audrey Henshall*, 259–71. Edinburgh: Edinburgh University Press.

Mogey, J.M. 1941. The Druid stone ('Mount Druid'). *Ulster Journal of Archaeology* 4, 49–56.

Monk, M. 2000. Seeds and soils of discontent: an environmental archaeological contribution to the nature of the early Neolithic. In A. Desmond, G. Johnson, M. McCarthy, J. Sheehan and E. Shee Twohig (eds), *New agendas in Irish prehistory: papers in commemoration of Liz Anderson*, 67–87. Bray: Wordwell.

O'Kelly. M.J. 1982. *Newgrange: art, archaeology and legend*. London: Thames and Hudson.

O'Sullivan, M. 1997. Megalithic art in Ireland and Brittany. Divergence or convergence? In J. L'Helgouac'h, C.T. Le Roux and J. Lecornec (eds), *Art et symboles du mégalithisme Européen*, 81–96. Rennes: Centre National de Recherche Scientifique.

Piggott, S. 1950. The excavations at Cairnpapple Hill, West Lothian, 1947–48. *Proceedings of the Society of Antiquaries of Scotland* 87, 68–123.

Piggott, S. 1954. *Neolithic cultures of the British Isles.* Cambridge: Cambridge University Press.

Radford, C.A.R. 1958. The chambered tomb at Broadsands, Paignton. *Proceedings of the Devon Archaeological Exploration Society* 5, 47–67.

Redknap, M. 2003. Llanbedrgoch: a Viking site on Anglesey. *Current Archaeology* 184, 160–5.

Ritchie, J.N. G. 1970. Excavation of the chambered cairn at Achnacreebeag. *Proceedings of the Society of Antiquaries of Scotland* 102, 31–55.

Rowley-Conwy, P. 2003. How nomadic was the north-west European Neolithic ? In. G. Burenhult (ed.), *Stones and bones: formal disposal of the dead in Atlantic Europe during the Mesolithic-Neolithic Interface, 6000–3000 BC*, 115–43. Oxford: British Archaeological Reports (International Series 1201).

Saville, A. 1999. A cache of flint axeheads and other flint artefacts from Auchenhoan, near Campbeltown, Kintyre, Scotland. *Proceedings of the Prehistoric Society* 65, 83–123.

Schulting, R.J. 2000. New AMS dates from the Lambourn long barrow and the question of the earliest Neolithic in southern England: repacking the Neolithic package? *Oxford Journal of Archaeology* 19, 25–35.

Schulting, R.J. and Richards, M.P. 2001. Dating women and becoming farmers: new palaeodietary and AMS data from the Breton Mesolithic cemeteries of Téviec and Hoëdic. *Journal of Anthropological Archaeology* 20, 314–44.

Schulting, R.J. and Richards, M.P. 2002a. The wet, the wild and the domesticated: the Mesolithic-Neolithic transition on the west coast of Scotland. *European Journal of Archaeology* 5, 147–89.

Schulting, R.J. and Richards, M.P. 2002b. Finding the coastal Mesolithic in southwest Britain: AMS dates and stable isotope results on human remains. *Antiquity* 76, 1011–25.

Scott, J.G. 1964. The chambered cairn at Beacharra, Kintyre, Argyll. *Proceedings of the Prehistoric Society* 30, 134–58.

Scott, J.G. 1969. The Clyde cairns of Scotland. In T.G.E. Powell, J.X.W.P Corcoran, F.M. Lynch and J.G. Scott (eds), *Megalithic enquiries in the west of Britain*, 175–222. Liverpool: Liverpool University Press.

Scott, J.G. 1973. The Clyde cairns of Scotland. In G.E. Daniel and P. Kjaerum (eds), *Megalithic graves and ritual*, 117–28. Copenhagen: Gyldendal.

Sharples, N.M. 1991. *Maiden Castle: excavations and field survey 1985–6.* London: Historic Buildings and Monuments Commission for England.

Shee Twohig, E. 1981. *The megalithic art of western Europe.* Oxford: Clarendon.

Sheridan, J.A. 1985. *The role of exchange studies in 'social archaeology', with special reference to the prehistory of Ireland from the fourth to the early second millennium bc.* Unpublished Ph.D. thesis: University of Cambridge.

Sheridan, J.A. 1986. Megaliths and megalomania: an account, and interpretation, of the development of passage tombs in Ireland. *Journal of Irish Archaeology* 3 (1985/6), 17–30.

Sheridan, J.A. 1995. Irish Neolithic pottery: the story in 1995. In I.A. Kinnes and G. Varndell (eds), *'Unbaked urns of rudely shape': essays on British and Irish pottery for Ian Longworth*, 3–21. Oxford: Oxbow.

Sheridan, J. A. 2000. Achnacreebeag and its French connections: vive the 'Auld Alliance'. In J.C. Henderson (ed.), *The prehistory and early history of Atlantic Europe,* 1–15. Oxford: British Archaeological Reports, International Series 861.

Sheridan, J.A. 2003a. French connections I: spreading the *marmites* thinly. In I. Armit E. Murphy, D.D.A. Simpson and E. Nelis (eds), *Neolithic settlement in Ireland and western Britain.* Oxford: Oxbow.

Sheridan, J.A. 2003b. Ireland's earliest 'passage' tombs: a French connection ? In G. Burenhult (ed.), *Stones and bones: formal disposal of the dead in Atlantic Europe during the Mesolithic-Neolithic Interface, 6000–3000 BC,* 9–25. Oxford : British Archaeological Reports (International Series 1201).

Sheridan, J.A. in press a. Les éléments d'une origine bretonne autour de 4000 av. J.-C. en Écosse: témoignages d'alliance, d'influence, de déplacement, ou quoi d'autre?, *Bulletin de la Societé Préhistorique Française.*

Sheridan, J.A. in press b. A non-megalithic funerary tradition in early Neolithic Ireland ? In M. Meek (ed.), *The modern traveller to our past: festschrift in honour of Ann Hamlin.* Belfast.

Sheridan, J.A. in press c. Going round in circles? Understanding the Irish Grooved Ware 'complex' in its wider context. In H. Roche, E. Grogan, J. Bradley, J. Coles and B. Raferty (eds), *From megaliths to metals.* Oxford: Oxbow.

Sheridan, J.A., Cooney, C. and Grogan, E. 1992. Stone axe studies in Ireland. *Proceedings of the Prehistoric Society* 58, 389–416.

Simpson, D.D.A. and Meighan, I. 1999. Pitchstone – a new trading material in Neolithic Ireland. *Archaeology Ireland* 13, 26–30.

Simpson, D.D.A. and Ransom, R. 1992. Maceheads and the Orcadian Neolithic. In N.M. Sharples and J.A. Sheridan (eds), *Vessels for the ancestors: essays on the Neolithic of Britain and Ireland in honour of Audrey Henshall,* 221–43. Edinburgh: Edinburgh University Press.

Thomas, J. 1996. Neolithic houses in mainland Britain and Ireland – a sceptical view. In T. Darvill and J. Thomas (eds), *Neolithic houses in northwest Europe and beyond.* Oxford: Oxbow.

Thomas, J. 1998. Towards a regional geography of the Neolithic. In M.Edmonds and C. Richards (eds), *Understanding the Neolithic of north-western Europe,* 37–60. Glasgow: Cruithne Press.

Thomas, J. 1999. *Understanding the Neolithic.* London: Routledge.

Tresset, A. 2000. Early husbandry in Atlantic areas. Animal introductions, diffusions of techniques and native acculturation at the north-western fringe of Europe. In J. C. Henderson (ed.), *The prehistory and early history of Atlantic Europe,* 17–32. Oxford: British Archaeological Reports, International Series 861.

Vanmontfort, B. 2001. The group of Spiere as a new stylistic entity in the middle Neolithic Scheldt Basin. *Notae Praehistoricae* 21, 139–43.

Verron, G. 2000. *Préhistoire de la Normandie.* Rennes: Éditions Ouest-France.

Waddell, J. 1998 *The prehistoric archaeology of Ireland.* Galway: Galway University Press.

Whittle, A.W.R. 1977. *The earlier Neolithic of southern*

England and its continental background. Oxford: British Archaeological Reports, Supplementary Series 35.

Whittle, A.W.R., Pollard, J. and Grigson, C. 1999. *The harmony of symbols: the Windmill Hill causewayed enclosure, Wiltshire.* Oxford: Oxbow.

Woodman, P.C., Anderson, E. and Finlay, N. 1999. *Excavations at Ferriter's Cove, 1983–95: last foragers, first farmers in the Dingle Peninsula.* Bray: Wordwell.

3   An Irish sea change: some implications for the Mesolithic-Neolithic transition

Rick J. Schulting

Introduction

Recent discussions of the beginnings of the Neolithic have downplayed the importance of a shift in the subsistence economy. New research, however, is showing a very sharp disjunction between the Mesolithic exploitation of wild resources and, in the Irish Sea region especially, marine resources, and the Neolithic husbandry of domestic animals and the cultivation of domestic plants. Yet the implications of this have been little explored. A substantial change in the subsistence economy would have enormous consequences for the use and perception of the landscape and seascape, the routines of daily lives, the utilisation of symbols and the construction of identity. This paper briefly presents the evidence for a strong economic shift in the Irish Sea region and begins to explore some of the implications for the transition to the Neolithic. It is argued that we have an insufficient understanding of the materiality of food production systems.

The last few decades have seen a considerable backlash against the study of the Neolithic subsistence economy, and its importance as a factor in the Mesolithic-Neolithic transition (Thomas 1999). To some extent this was certainly justified, as the methodologies and views put forward in economic approaches were at times exceedingly narrow. However, it can be argued that the current orthodoxy has swung too far in the opposite direction. It is not that detailed studies of Neolithic subsistence practices are entirely lacking, but they are fewer than what one might expect given the radical revision that has taken place over the last ten years as to the nature of the Neolithic subsistence economy. This is now, with very few exceptions, seen as largely continuing a 'Mesolithic' tradition of hunting and foraging, with a few exotic domesticated additions thrown in for ritual flavour. But what is this based on? Largely the ubiquitous presence of hazelnuts on Neolithic sites (and the debate over the interpretation of this is well-known, see for example: Jones 2000; Moffett *et al.* 1989), and on the one or two sites where wild fauna can be said to outnumber domestic fauna (such as the aptly-named Coneybury Anomaly, where even the numerically dominant roe deer are overshadowed by domestic cattle in terms of meat weight).

Subsistence has become a bad word, as if people could live off the ritual wafer rather than the daily bread (see also Kinnes 1998). In many ways this is puzzling, since many accounts profess a concern with Bourdieu's (1977) concept of *habitus*, with an understanding of daily routines. Yet the focus for the most part has remained firmly on monuments, their architecture and their placement in the landscape. Monuments were undoubtedly extremely important and resonant places, but were they so central in the daily lives of Neolithic people? The amount of material deposited in and around them, and the number of bodies interred in them suggests that they were visited at best intermittently. Perhaps, like the ancestral tombs of the Merina in Madagascar, they were avoided most other times as the abodes of restless and dangerous ghosts. Certainly this would be one way of enhancing the status and power of those that, when the time did come, were able to safely orchestrate the funerary rituals and see the deceased's spirit on its way. So, if we want to understand daily routines, perhaps we would better experience Neolithic lives by taking up farming for a season or two (see for example Pryor 1996; 1998), or by visiting an abattoir.

My thesis is simply that subsistence matters. In many small-scale societies around the world, food looms large in the daily thoughts and actions of people. Of course it is not *just* about food. Obtaining, serving and consuming food, as we all know, is bound up with issues of identity, of status, of gender and sociality in general (e.g. Caplan 1994; Hugh-Jones 1978; Wiessner and Schiefenhövel 1996). But, in emphasising the various social and symbolic aspects, we have perhaps moved too far away from what might be called the materiality of food and food production systems. How do they work? What constraints and possibilities would be faced by those taking up an agro-pastoral economy? What consequences, perhaps unintended, would follow? What I propose to do here is to briefly summarise the evidence from stable isotope analysis as it relates to the diets of prehistoric coastal communities. My focus is on the Mesolithic-Neolithic transition on the east side of the Irish Sea zone, but also on different contexts – monumental and non-monumental – within the Neolithic. I will then proceed to explore some of the implications of this evidence for the nature of earlier Neolithic society, and to raise some concerns regarding our current level of understanding. My eventual goal is to integrate the subsistence economy more closely with Neolithic society.

A sea change

Stable isotope analysis on human bone collagen provides a direct means of assessing the protein make-up of an individual's diet over the medium to long term, say a period of 5–10 years (Schoeninger and Moore 1992). Thus it allows us to approach the timescale of less than the individual lifetime, a rarity in prehistoric archaeology (Schulting in prep). The technique works particularly well in differentiating marine and terrestrial-based diets, and so it is best applied to humans living near the sea. Two striking patterns have emerged over the last few years (Richards and Hedges 1999; Richards and Mellars 1998; Schulting 1998; Schulting and Richards 2000; 2002a; 2002b). One is that Mesolithic humans living near the coast typically show a high degree of utilistation of marine foods, on the order of from one-third to nearly complete reliance on marine protein (there are some intriguing exceptions that require further investigation). The other is that Neolithic humans do not (Fig. 3.1). The pattern emerging in Britain is of course not unique: an even more striking shift has long been noted for Denmark (Tauber 1981; 1986).

It does not seem to matter whether Neolithic humans lived at sites immediately next to the sea, five km inland, or 50 km inland: they made little or no appreciable use of marine foods. Ongoing research in Scotland, Wales, and south-west England continues to support this pattern. Whatever we may think of the increasing trend towards emphasising regional variation in the Neolithic (Barclay 2000; Harding 1995; Thomas 1998), one thing seems to be consistent, and that is a near-total avoidance of sea-foods, from Devon to northern Scotland. This is seen equally in humans interred in coastal caves as it is in those from coastal monuments (Gower peninsula: Red Fescue Hole and Spurge Hole caves vs. Parc le Breos chambered tomb; Oban: Carding Mill Bay and Raschoille Cave vs. Crarae chambered tomb) (Schulting and Richards 2002a; 2002b). There seems to be no difference in this regard, which should serve to dispel the idea that those buried in monuments were an 'elite' with a completely different diet from that of the remainder of the population.

While it is true that the stable isotope technique does not easily distinguish between terrestrial wild and domestic plants and animals (although there are some possibilities in this regard that have been little explored), it stretches the bounds of reason to argue that the isotopic evidence from coastal Neolithic sites indicates anything other than a high degree of reliance on domestic resources.

First, why should Neolithic people switch to wild plants and animals when, assuming indigenous adoption, their immediate predecessors had relied to such a great extent on the sea. This is not 'continuity'. Second, where is the faunal evidence for this supposed dominance of wild game? The argument that the majority of the available faunal evidence comes from 'special' sites, while again true, is getting a bit long in the tooth. To assume that the faunal evidence presents a completely biased picture, and that daily subsistence focused on wild resources, argues for such a complete separation between 'ritual' and 'domestic' economies that I find it hard to accept, both on evidential and theoretical grounds. In fact this goes completely against the grain of any attempt to more closely integrate these two aspects of social life. It is well known that in many 'pastorally inclined' societies animal meat will only be consumed on what are seen as 'special occasions' (e.g. Keswani 1994). Yet such special occasions can include not only the grander events that might normally come to mind: births, marriages and deaths; but also more everyday events ranging from someone having a toothache to a neighbour visiting (e.g. Condominas 1994; A. Richards 1948). The numerous occasions for ritual slaughter, together with natural deaths and the need to slaughter excess male animals, resulted in a steady supply of beef even among societies of the East African 'cattle complex', who were notoriously loath to slaughter their animals but instead saved them for social transactions (Barfield 1993, 26).

Cows and fish don't get along

Let us take the position for the moment that earlier Neolithic society around much of the Irish Sea was based primarily on keeping cattle, with a variable but generally minor contribution of cereals, hunted game, gathered plants, and fish. This currently seems a reasonable position (although there is a nagging doubt that cereals are being too quickly dismissed). But at the moment a more pastoral view of the British Neolithic presents something of an emerging consensus (Barclay *et al.* 1999; Caulfield 1983; Fowler 1981; Kinnes 1988; Legge 1981; Pryor 1996; 1998; Stallibrass and Huntley 1996; Thomas 1999; Tresset 2000). Now how can this be explained? It is often thought that Mesolithic communities may have been more attracted to pastoralism than to agriculture because it had more in common with their traditional focus on red deer and other large game hunting. Both provided for a relatively mobile lifestyle, emphasising a high proportion of animal protein in the diet. Meat is almost invariably the most highly desired food item in pre-industrial societies (Abrams 1987; Speth and Spielman 1983). But this image is harder to retain in coastal areas. There is little in common between fisher folk and pastoralists. Indeed the argument used to run that settled coastal Mesolithic populations would be in

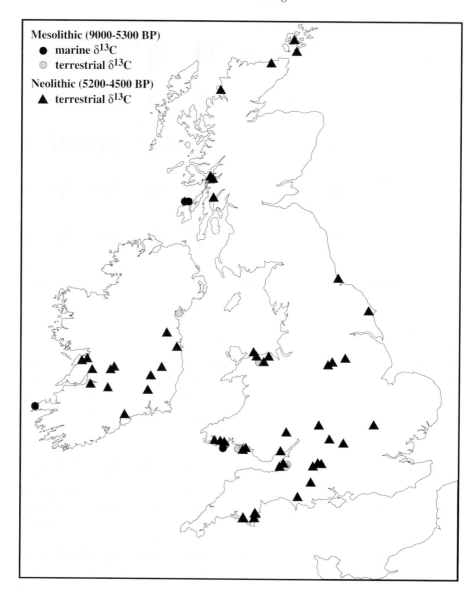

Figure 3.1. *Map of the British Isles showing locations of directly dated human remains and associated dominant dietary regime as shown by stable isotope analysis. The cut-off point for a marine vs. terrestrial signature is a $\delta^{13}C$ value of = -17‰. For the Neolithic measurements, no results are greater than -19‰, which indicates a minimal input of marine protein. Source: Schulting n.d..*

some sense 'pre-adapted' to agriculture because of their more sedentary lifestyle (Rowley-Conwy 1983).

So how and why did coastal Mesolithic groups take up farming? Or did they? Perhaps fishing communities persisted for as long as possible in their way of life, but were soon ousted by pastoralists who desired their rich coastal grazing lands. The origin of these pastoralists might be more inland locations in the British Isles, locations that might previously have been regarded as somewhat backwards when compared with coastal groups. The late dates on very much marine-oriented humans from Oronsay provide some hint of this (Richards and Sheridan 2000; Schulting and Richards 2002a). Con-

temporary humans on the mainland show no contribution of marine protein, and are best viewed within a 'Neolithic' context. Microliths associated with what *may* be a early Neolithic domestic pig at Lydstep in south Wales provide another possible glimpse of more antagonistic relations between Mesolithic and Neolithic communities (Schulting 2000).

However, let us assume that coastal Mesolithic communities did take up the new economy. Not gradually, not partially, but very quickly and completely. What kinds of explanations could be offered for this? The classic 'population-resource imbalance' model (e.g. Binford 1968) can probably be ruled out. There is no evidence for subsistence stress in the late Mesolithic (but then there is little evidence for the late Mesolithic economy full stop), and there seems to be little evidence for a dramatic environmental change of the kind that would necessitate such an economic transformation (although see Baillie 1992; Bonsall *et al.* 2002). But ruling this out does not exhaust the possible 'economic' explanations that could be offered. As intimated above, we understand far too little of the consequences of the two options in terms of what I have called the materiality of food production. An option that provided a predictable and plentiful source of fat-rich meat may have proven irresistible to Mesolithic peoples. Once begun it may have been difficult to control the process. Animals make demands, demands on time, on movement, on ideas of ownership; demands that may have been incompatible with a marine-based economy. In addition, we understand little about how the forest-grazing or coastal pasturing of cattle would affect the ability of a territory to support wild game. Gregg (1988, 124), for example, suggests that red deer can only flourish with little or no competition from livestock.

And there may be other considerations. Prejudices against the consumption of fish are strikingly common among pastoralists who keep cattle (Almagor 1978; Malainey *et al.* 2001; Schwabe 1988; Simoons 1994). Pastoralists seem to have a very powerful sense of identity; one might even call it intolerant. Maasai who loose their cattle through drought or disease and are forced to take up farming or fishing are seen as inferior by other Massai (Simoons 1994, 263), and indeed may even loose their ethnic identity (Chang 1982). There is a Turkana saying that, if a well-to-do man eats fish, his cows will no longer give milk (Beech 1911, 10–11). These cultural pro-scriptions are impressive enough, but a recent paper by Malainey *et al.* (2001) argues that something else might be going on. Taking a physiological approach, they note that the body's digestive system is homeostatically regulated and adjusts to foods regularly eaten. When the food most commonly eaten is lean red meat, switching seasonally to fat-rich fish can cause severe illness (such as dysentery). This fact was consciously recognised by a number of Plains Indian groups who practiced strong fish avoidance. There is a bit of a leap in applying such an idea to the British Neolithic (for one thing the leanness of cattle would be highly variable; as noted above, fat-rich meat would be the most desirable), but that is not really what I am suggesting. The point is that there are many aspects of both the production and consumption of food that we simply do not understand, at the gut level (so to speak), let alone the symbolic level.

Another possible corollary of a pastoral economy that has received scant attention is an increase in inter-group conflict. In societies that rely heavily on cattle, their possession tends to take on enormous connotations of wealth and high socio-political status (A. Richards 1948). This, combined with their mobility, makes them attractive targets for theft. Additional sources of conflict are over access to the best pasture, water, and control over/inheritance of the herds. Indeed, the images that the term 'pastoral' conjure up for us, of a peaceful rural idyll, are far from the reality of most known pastoral societies, in which feuding and warfare are endemic (Barfield 1993; E. Thomas 1965; Turney-High 1991). For example, in the recent past among the Rwala Bedouin, over 80% of males died from wounds received in inter-tribal warfare (Musil 1928 cited in Turney-High 1991). Evidence – albeit limited – for violent conflict has long been recognised in the British Neolithic, most dramatically at the small number of enclosures with evidence of having been attacked (Mercer 1999). But an ongoing re-analysis of extant human skeletal collections is beginning to document more examples of conflict, although its context remains poorly understood (Schulting and Wysocki 2002; Wysocki and Whittle 2000).

Social networking

Keeping domestic plants and animals, making pottery and building monuments could have been part of a relatively coherent package that gave access to a wider network of social participation. This is comparable to a phenomenon noted by those studying the emergence of complex trans-egalitarian societies in Mesoamerica, which is that there are watersheds of change crossed simultaneously by entire regions (Clark and Blake 1994). The reality of this wider network in the Neolithic British Isles is clear. One thing that plainly distinguishes the Neolithic from the Mesolithic in the Irish Sea region is the far greater evidence for wider contacts in the Neolithic (Lynch 1989). The Irish Sea seems to have formed a much stronger barrier to interaction in the Mesolithic than it did in the Neolithic (which is odd given Mesolithic peoples' reliance on the sea for subsistence). As has long been recognised, very similar monument forms are shared between western Scotland and Northern Ireland (Collins 1973; Corcoran 1973). Pitchstone is much more widely distributed in the Neolithic (Saville 1994; Simpson and Meighan 1999); stone axes from sources in Ireland are found in western Britain, and stone from Britain is found in Ireland (Sheridan and Cooney 1992). Rectangular timber structures – let us call them houses – are increasingly common at least in Ireland, and again show a strong disjunction with the Mesolithic, having more in common with a limited (but steadily increasing) number of sites in Britain (Cooney 1999; 2000). Finds of jadeite axes show that connections stretched even further afield (Bishop *et al.* 1978; Riqc-de Bouard 1993). This stands in contrast to the decidedly insular late Mesolithic of Ireland (Cooney 1988; Woodman 1985; 2000).

So, in addition to sharing certain ideas about the treatment of the dead, about how to serve food, about the value of stone and its use to create and maintain relationships, it may be that the ability to serve up cattle on important occasions, to offer them as bride-price, for death payments, and at life transition events, constituted the currency by which a comparatively large-scale social network operated. Once such a system got going, the choice of whether or not to participate in it would become less and less of an option. Those who did not would be increasingly marginalised (Douglas and Isherwood 1996). The need for alliances would be especially critical if an element of conflict appeared at this time. Loss of cattle through raiding would threaten not only a community's means of subsistence, but also its ability to participate in the social network, and even its very sense of identity (Chang 1982).

In one sense I find this 'social network' model both a plausible and powerful explanation of the transition, one which importantly better integrates the evidence for a sharp economic change. In a way this also represents an emerging consensus, as highlighted by a number of papers, as well as the discussion, at the conference on which this volume is based. But it is perhaps still too quick and too easy a conclusion. At least from my own perspective, there is too little understanding of the detailed workings of food production systems, of possible incompatibilities with other ways of living, and of the physiological consequences associated with certain combinations of food. It is just these areas that will require more thought and research.

If we are to turn our attention to the rhythms of daily lives in the Neolithic, then surely it is the daily matter of making a living that we should be focussing on, rather than the occasional ceremonies that took place at monuments. This is emphatically not to say that subsistence activities themselves are purely 'practical' and devoid of cultural and symbolic meaning. But to focus on the latter so exclusively, as now seems to often be the case, no longer furthers our understanding of the workings of Neolithic society. People's accounts of their own lives as recorded in ethnographies from around the world again and again show a deep and abiding concern with and interest in matters that we too easily dismiss as simple and uninteresting: the day-to-day activities surrounding growing cereals, keeping animals, preparing and serving food.

Meanwhile, the sea in the Neolithic was perhaps still seen as a very resonant and powerful place, but its associations would have changed dramatically from those it held in the Mesolithic. No longer was it viewed as a place where one where one toiled to provide food for one's family and community, and for larger social gatherings. The associations the sea held for Neolithic people may have had more to do its use as a communication route, and so with trade, exchange, alliance, raiding, acquiring marriage partners, and visiting. Indeed, there may have been surviving stories and myths concerning the arrival of the first domestic plants and animals from across the sea. Perhaps this is why so many monuments face the sea.

References

Abrams, H.L. 1987. The preference for animal protein and fat: a cross-cultural survey. In M. Harris and E.B. Ross (eds), *Food and evolution: toward a theory of human food habits*, 207–23. Philadelphia: Temple University Press.

Almagor, U. 1978. *Pastoral partners*. Manchester: Manchester University Press.

Baillie, M.G.L. 1992. Dendrochronology and past environmental change. *Proceedings of the British Academy* 77, 5–23.

Barclay, A. and Hey, G. 1999. Cattle, cursus monuments and the river: the development of ritual and domestic landscapes in the Upper Thames Valley. In A. Barclay and J. Harding (eds), *Pathways and ceremonies: the cursus monuments of Britain and Ireland*, 67–76. Oxford: Oxbow.

Barclay, G. J. 2000. Between Orkney and Wessex: the search for the regional Neolithics of Britain. In A. Ritchie (ed.), *Neolithic Orkney in its European context*, 275–85. Cambridge: McDonald Institute for Archaeological Research.

Barfield, T.J. 1993. *The nomadic alternative*. Englewood Cliffs, New Jersey: Prentice-Hall.

Beech, M.W.H. 1911. *The Suk, their language and folklore*. Oxford: Clarendon.

Binford, L. 1968. Post-Pleistocene adaptations. In S. Binford and L. Binford (eds), *New perspectives in archaeology*, 313–41. Chicago: Walter de Gruyter.

Bishop, A.C., Woolley, A.R., Kinnes, I.A. and Harrison, R. 1978. Jadeite axes in Europe and the British Isles: an interim study. *Archaeologia Atlantica* 2, 1–8.

Bonsall, C., Macklin, M., Anderson, D. and Payton, R. 2002. Climate change and the adoption of agriculture in northwest Europe. *European Journal of Archaeology* 5, 9–23.

Bourdieu, P. 1977. *Outline of a theory of practice*. Cambridge: Cambridge University Press.

Caplan, P. 1994. *Feasts, fasts, famine: food for thought*. Oxford: Berg Occasional Papers in Anthropology 2.

Caulfield, S. 1983. The Neolithic settlement of North Connaught. In T. Reeves-Smyth and F. Hammond (eds), *Landscape archaeology in Ireland*, 195–216. Oxford: British Archaeological Reports British Series 116.

Chamberlain, A.T. 1996. More dating evidence for human remains in British caves. *Antiquity* 70, 950–53.

Chang, C. 1982. Nomads without cattle: East African foragers in historical perspective. In E. Leacock and R. Lee (eds), *Politics and history in band societies*, 269–82. Cambridge: Cambridge University Press.

Clark, J.E. and Blake, M. 1994. The power of prestige: competitive generosity and the emergence of rank societies in lowland Mesoamerica. In E.M. Brumfiel and J.W. Fox (eds), *Factional competition and political development in the New World*, 17–30. Cambridge: Cambridge University Press.

Collins, A.E.P. 1973. A re-examination of the Clyde-Carlingford tombs. In G. Daniel and P. Kjærum (eds), *Megalithic graves and ritual*, 93–103. Copenhagen: Jutland Archaeological Society.

Condominas, G. 1994. *We have eaten the forest*. New York: Kodansha.

Cooney, G. 1988. Irish Neolithic settlement and its European context. *Journal of Irish Archaeology* 4, 7–11.

Cooney, G. 1999. A boom in Neolithic houses. *Archaeology Ireland* 47, 13–16.

Cooney, G. 2000. *Landscapes of Neolithic Ireland*. London: Routledge.

Corcoran, J.X.W.P. 1973. The chambered cairns of the Carlingford Culture: an enquiry into origins. In G. Daniel and P. Kjærum (eds), *Megalithic graves and ritual*, 105–16. Copenhagen: Jutland Archaeological Society.

Douglas, M. and Isherwood, B. 1996. *The world of goods: towards an anthropology of consumption*. London: Routledge.

Fowler, P.J. 1981. Wildscape to landscape: 'enclosure' in prehistoric Britain. In R. Mercer (ed.), *Farming practice in British prehistory*, 9–54. Edinburgh: Edinburgh University Press.

Gregg, A. 1988. *Foragers and farmers: population interaction and agricultural expansion in prehistoric Europe*. Chicago: University of Chicago Press.

Harding, J. 1995. Social histories and regional perspectives in the Neolithic of lowland England. *Proceedings of the Prehistoric Society* 61, 117–36.

Hugh-Jones, C. 1978. Food for thought: patterns of production and consumption in Pirá-Piraná society. In J.S. LaFontaine (ed.), *Sex and age as principles of social differentiation*, 41–66. London: Academic Press.

Jones, G. 2000. Evaluating the importance of cultivation and collecting in Neolithic Britain. In A.S. Fairbairn (ed.), *Plants in Neolithic Britain and beyond*, 79–84. Oxford: Oxbow.

Keswani, P.S. 1994. The social context of animal husbandry in early agricultural societies: ethnographic insights and an archaeological example from Cyprus. *Journal of Anthropological Archaeology* 13, 255–77.

Kinnes, I. 1988. The cattleship Potemkin: the first Neolithic in Britain. In J. Barrett and I. Kinnes (eds), *The archaeology of context in the Neolithic and Bronze Age: recent trends*, 2–8. Sheffield: Department of Archaeology and Prehistory, Sheffield University.

Kinnes, I. 1998. From ritual to romance: a new western. In A.M. Gibson and D.D.A. Simpson (eds), *Prehistoric ritual and religion*, 183–89. Stroud: Sutton.

Legge, A.J. 1981. Aspects of cattle husbandry. In R. Mercer (ed.), *Farming practice in British prehistory*, 169–81. Edinburgh: Edinburgh University Press.

Lynch, F. 1989. Wales and Ireland in prehistory: a fluctuating relationship. *Archaeologia Cambrensis* 138, 1–19.

Malainey, M.E., Przybylski, R. and Sherriff, B.L. 2001. One person's food: how and why fish avoidance may affect the settlement and subsistence patterns of hunter-gatherers. *American Antiquity* 66, 141–61.

Mercer, R.J. 1999. The origins of warfare in the British Isles. In J. Carman and A. Harding (eds), *Ancient warfare*, 143–56. Stroud: Sutton.

Moffett, L., Robinson, M. A. and Straker, V. 1989. Cereals, fruits and nuts: charred plant remains from Neolithic sites in England and Wales and the Neolithic economy. In A. Milles, D. Williams & N. Gardner (eds), *The beginnings of agriculture*, 243–61. Oxford: British Archaeological Reports International Series 496.

Pryor, F. 1996. Sheep, stockyards and field systems: Bronze Age livestock populations in the Fenland of Eastern England. *Antiquity* 70, 313–24.

Pryor, F. 1998. *Farmers in prehistoric Britain*. Stroud: Tempus.

Richards, A. 1932. *Hunger and work in a savage tribe. A functional study of nutrition among the Southern Bantu*. London: Routledge.

Richards, M.P. and Hedges, R.E.M. 1999. A Neolithic revolution? New evidence of diet in the British Neolithic. *Antiquity* 73, 891–97.

Richards, M. P. and Mellars, P. 1998. Stable isotopes and the seasonality of the Oronsay middens. *Antiquity* 72, 178–84.

Richards, M.P. and Sheridan, J.A. 2000. New AMS dates on human bone from Mesolithic Oronsay. *Antiquity* 74, 313–15.

Riqc-de Bouard, M. 1993. Trade in Neolithic jadeite axes from the Alps: new data. In C. Scarre and F. Healy (eds), *Trade and exchange in prehistoric Europe*, 61–7. Oxford: Oxbow.

Rowley-Conwy, P. 1983. Sedentary hunters: the Ertebølle example. In G. Bailey (ed.), *Hunter gatherer economy in prehistory*, 111–26. Cambridge: Cambridge University Press.

Saville, A. 1994. Exploitation of lithic resources for stone tools in earlier prehistoric Scotland. In N. Ashton and A. David (eds), *Stories in stone*, 57–70. London: Lithic Studies Society Occasional Paper 4, British Museum.

Schoeninger, M. and Moore, K. 1992. Stable bone isotope studies in archaeology. *Journal of World Prehistory* 6, 247–96.

Schulting, R.J. 1998. Slighting the sea: the transition to farming in northwest Europe. *Documenta Praehistorica* 25, 203–18.

Schulting, R.J. 2000. New AMS dates from the Lambourn long barrow and the question of the earliest Neolithic in southern England: repacking the Neolithic package? *Oxford Journal of Archaeology* 19, 25–35.

Schulting, R.J. In prep. The times they are a changin': [14]C chronology and the beginning of the Neolithic. Manuscript on file with author.

Schulting, R.J. and Richards, M.P. 2000. The use of stable isotopes in studies of subsistence and seasonality in the British Mesolithic. In R. Young (ed.), *Mesolithic lifeways: current research from Britain and Ireland*, 55–65. Leicester: University of Leicester Press.

Schulting, R.J. and Richards, M.P. 2002a. The wet, the wild and the domesticated: the Mesolithic-Neolithic transition on the west coast of Scotland. *European Journal of Archaeology* 5, 147–89.

Schulting, R.J. and Richards, M.P. 2002b. Finding the coastal Mesolithic in southwest Britain: AMS dates and stable isotope results on human remains from Caldey Island, Pembrokeshire, South Wales. *Antiquity*.

Schulting, R.J. and Wysocki, M. 2002. Cranial trauma in the British earlier Neolithic. *Past* 41, 4–6.

Schwabe, C.W. 1988. *Unmentionable foods*. Charlottesville: University Press of Virginia.

Sherdian, A. and Cooney, G. 1992. Stone axe studies in Ireland. *Proceedings of the Prehistoric Society* 58, 389–416.

Simoons, F.J. 1994. *Eat not this flesh: food avoidances from prehistory to the present*. Madison: University of Wisconsin Press.

Simpson, D.D.A. and Meighan, I. 1999. Pitchstone – a new trading material in Neolithic Ireland. *Archaeology Ireland* 13, 26–30.

Stallibrass, S. and Huntley, J.P. 1996. Slim evidence: a review of the faunal and botanical data from the Neolithic of northern England. In P. Frodsham (ed.), *Neolithic studies in no-man's land*, 35–42. Northern Archaeology Volume 13/14, Journal of the Northumberland Archaeological Group.

Tauber, H. 1981. 13C evidence for dietary habits of prehistoric man in Denmark. *Nature* 292, 332–33.

Tauber, H. 1986. Analysis of stable isotopes in prehistoric populations. *Mitteilungen der Berliner Gesellschaft für Anthropologie, Ethnologie und Urgeschichte* 7, 31–38

Thomas, E.M. 1965. *Warrior herdsmen*. New York: Alfred A. Knopf

Thomas, J. 1998. Towards a regional geography of the Neolithic. In M. Edmonds and C. Richards (eds), *Understanding the Neolithic of north-western Europe*, 37–60. Glasgow: Cruithne Press.

Thomas, J. 1999. *Understanding the Neolithic*. London: Routledge.

Tresset, A. 2000. Early husbandry in Atlantic areas. Animal introductions, diffusions of techniques and native acculturation at the north-western fringe of Europe. In J. C. Henderson (ed.), *The prehistory and early history of Atlantic Europe*, 17–32. Oxford: British Archaeological Reports International Series 861.

Wiessner, P. and Schiefenhövel, W. (eds) 1996. *Food and the status quest: an interdisciplinary perspective*. Providence: Berghahn.

Woodman, P.C. 1985. Prehistoric settlement and environment. In K.J. Edwards and W.P. Warren (eds), *The quaternary history of Ireland*, 251–78. London: Academic Press.

Woodman, P.C. 2000. Getting back to basics: transitions to farming in Ireland and Britain. In T.D. Price (ed.), *Europe's first farmers*, 219–59. Cambridge: Cambridge University Press.

Wysocki, M. and Whittle, A. 2000. Diversity, lifestyles and rites: new biological and archaeological evidence from British earlier Neolithic mortuary assemblages. *Antiquity* 74, 591–601.

4   Connecting the mountains and sea: the monuments of the eastern Irish Sea zone

Vicki Cummings

Introduction

Neolithic monuments are found along the coasts of the eastern Irish Sea zone and in this paper I would like to suggest that their setting in the landscape was of crucial importance to their meaning within Neolithic society. In particular I will emphasise the significance of the location of monuments in relation to mountains and the sea. At one level, the builders of these sites seem to have constructed monuments in order to create connections across the wider Irish Sea zone. I will also suggest that these monuments were intimately connected to the local topography, drawing upon features of local significance. Therefore it is possible to suggest that monuments were carefully positioned in the landscape in order to create a range of interwoven connections that worked at different levels. I will go on to suggest that these connections referred to a new sense of community that was created at the beginning of the Neolithic in the Irish Sea zone.

The monuments of the eastern Irish Sea

Stone-built monuments dating to the Neolithic period are found in discrete concentrations in south-west Wales, north-west Wales, the Isle of Man and south-west Scotland (Fig. 4.1). Typologically, the monuments of the eastern Irish Sea zone are diverse, including sites classified as Clyde monuments in south-west Scotland (Henshall 1972), court tombs on the Isle of Man (Burrow 1997; Darvill 2000) portal dolmens in south-west and north-west Wales (Lynch 1969; 1972) as well as a whole range of sites which do not fit into any of these classifications. Elsewhere along the eastern Irish Sea coast there are 'blank' areas where no stone-built monuments are found, although there is evidence which suggests that these areas were utilised by people in the Neolithic (see papers in this volume by Mullin and Peterson). In the past, connections between the monuments of these areas has been sought in the morphology of the monuments themselves. Similarities and differences in monument style and form have been used to suggest areas of interaction between these areas and with Ireland (e.g. de Valera 1960; Lynch 1989; Piggott

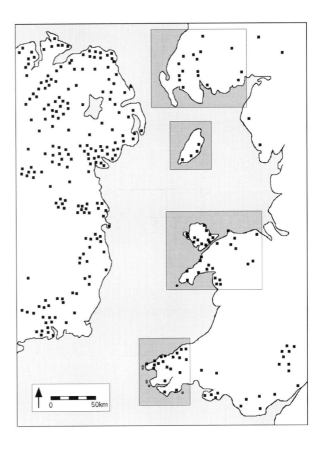

Figure 4.1. The distribution of monuments along the eastern Irish Sea zone. The study areas in this paper are highlighted by boxes: south-west Wales, north-west Wales, the Isle of Man and south-west Scotland

1954; Sheridan 2000). This has been reinforced by the study of the movement of material culture such as stone axes (Cooney 2000b, 204–28; Saville 1999; Sheridan 1986; Sheridan *et al.* 1992). However, the differences between monuments and the sheer diversity of monument styles has meant that it has been impossible to pinpoint precise interactions between communities along the Irish Sea coasts. Here I will suggest why specific areas along the Irish Sea had concentrations of monuments, emphasising the importance of their setting in the landscape.

Connections across the Irish Sea: mountains

The significance of the landscape in relation to Neolithic monuments has been explored in recent years (e.g. Bergh 1995; Cooney 2000b; Tilley 1994; Watson 2001). It seems that the landscape was an integral part of the configuration and experience of monuments in the Neolithic and that sites were carefully positioned in relation to a whole range of distinctive topographic features. All the monuments in the eastern Irish Sea zone are found around mountains, and although no sites were actually built in the mountains themselves, they have clear views towards them. For example, in south-west Wales many sites have views of the Preselis, especially sites in the Nevern Valley such as Llech y Dribedd and Pentre Ifan (Cummings 2001; Tilley 1994). The Bargrennan monuments of south-west Scotland have views of the Merrick Mountains (Cummings 2002b) and all bar one of the monuments on Anglesey in north Wales have views of Snowdonia (Cummings and Whittle 2004).

For the most part, however, discussion has focussed on what landscape features were visible *from* each site. Here I would like to emphasise the importance of what is visible from the mountains of the Irish Sea zone. The intervisibility of the mountains of the Irish Sea zone has been noted for many years (e.g. Bowen 1970, 24). For example, from the Preselis in south-west Wales it is possible to see the Wicklow Hills in Ireland and Snowdonia (Miles 2001). From the Merrick Mountains in south-west Scotland it is possible to see the Cumbrian Mountains, Snowdonia, the Isle of Man and the Mourne Mountains in northern Ireland (de Ferranti 1995a). It has also been noted that it is possible to see the five kingdoms of north Wales, southern Ireland, northern Ireland, south-west Scotland and Cumbria from the summit of Snaefell on the Isle of Man (Bowen 1970, 24 and Fig. 4.2). Therefore the monuments of the eastern Irish Sea have views of mountains which in turn have views out over the Irish Sea. Thus the landscapes of the Irish Sea zone are connected through the intervisibility of its mountains.

It is not just the mountains of the Irish Sea zone which have views of distant places. A number of monuments themselves have views of distant landscapes. From the monuments of Cairnholy I and II in south-west Scotland, for example, it is possible to see the Isle of Man on a clear day (Cummings 2002b). At Cashtal yn Ard on the Isle of Man the Cumbrian Mountains are visible on the horizon behind the forecourt. From Barclodiad y Gawres in north Wales, Ireland can be seen to the west (Powell and Daniel 1956, 2). And the small concentration of six monuments on the Ardudwy peninsula have views south to the Preselis in south-west Wales. It seems, then, that these monuments may have been carefully positioned so that there were views of distant places. Had they been sited lower down the slopes on which they stand, these

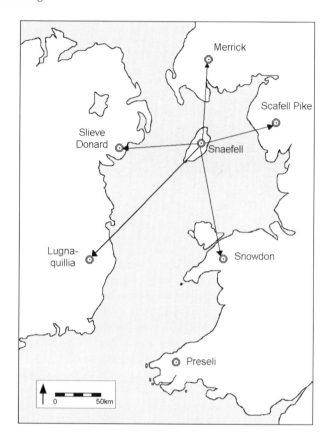

Figure 4.2. *The intervisibility of the Irish Sea zone. It is possible to see the five kingdoms from Snaefell on the Isle of Man: southern Ireland, northern Ireland, Scotland, England and Wales*

long distance views would not have been visible: at Barclodiad, had the site been located just 50m to the north or south, the view of Ireland would have disappeared (Cummings and Whittle 2004).

If mountains were important reference points in the landscape, where the intervisibility over the Irish Sea zone was particularly significant, should we therefore understand the Isle of Man as the very centre of a Neolithic world in the Irish Sea, as all five 'kingdoms' are visible from Snaefell? There is some evidence which suggests that this may have been the case. The Isle of Man has a number of different monument forms which are similar to those found elsewhere along the Irish Sea zone (Henshall 1978, 172). Cashtel yn Ard and King Orry's Graves can be paralleled with court cairns in Ireland and south-west Scotland (Megaw 1938, 226), while the first-phase box-like structure at King Orry's Grave SW is similar to those found on Anglesey, such as Trefignath, and Clyde monuments in south-west Scotland such as Mid Gleniron I. Axes are also found on the Isle of Man from Wales, Cumbria and Ireland (Coope and Garrad 1988; also see Cummings and Fowler this volume).

However, although the Isle of Man may *seem* to sit at the centre of the Irish Sea, I would like to suggest that in

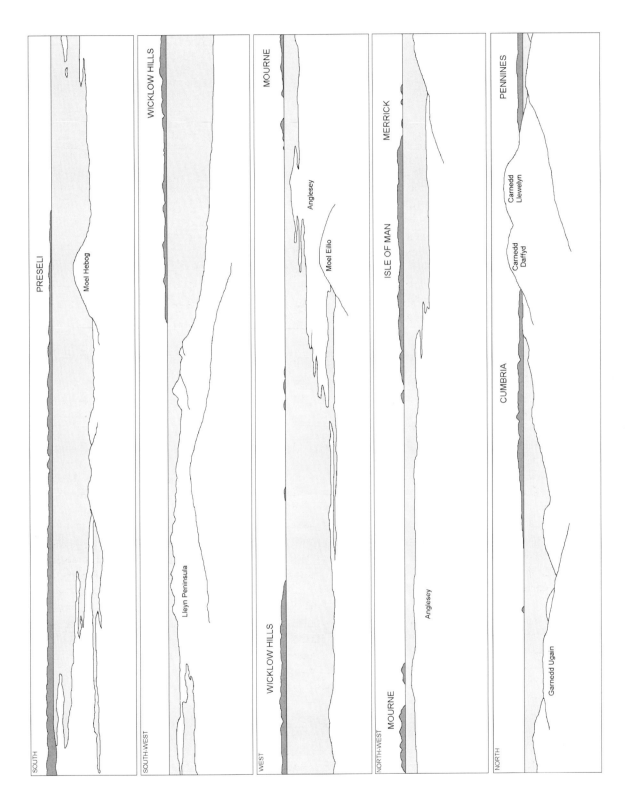

Figure 4.3. *The landscapes visible from the summit of Snowdon from the south to the north-east (after de Ferranti 1995).*

the Neolithic it was not understood in this way. Instead, I would like to suggest that it was north Wales, in particular Snowdonia and Anglesey, that were understood as being at the very heart of a Neolithic world which was centred and focussed around the Irish Sea. This is because from the summit of Snowdon it is possible to see the mountains of each of the areas along the Irish Sea (de Ferranti 1995b) all of which have densities of Neolithic monuments. From Snowdon it is possible to see the Preselis in south-west Wales, the Wicklow mountains in southern Ireland, the Mourne mountains in northern Ireland, the Isle of Man, mountains in south-west Scotland including the Merrick and the Cumbrian mountains (Fig. 4.3). People may well have recognised these distant landmasses, especially if we envisage people moving across the Irish Sea regularly (see below). Therefore, Snowdon literally sits at the very centre of the Irish Sea which is connected through the inter-visibility of mountains (Fig. 4.4). Snowdonia may have been significant as it not only has views of the entire Irish Sea area but there is also an axe factory at Graig Lwyd on its edge. Virtually all the monuments on the nearby island of Anglesey have views of Snowdonia, as do the monuments along the Lleyn peninsula (Cummings and Whittle 2004) and I would like to suggest that it was the presence of Snowdonia which explains the density of monuments on Anglesey. Anglesey has the densest concentration of monuments anywhere along the eastern Irish Sea with 17 definite sites and another 26 possible or destroyed sites on the island (Lynch 1969). It provides a landscape of low-lying fertile land with views of mountains, and also of the sea, which seems to have been the perfect combination of landscape elements that megalithic builders sought throughout the Irish Sea zone (for more detail see Cummings 2001; 2002b; Fowler and Cummings 2003). If Anglesey was conceived as being at the very heart of the Irish Sea it may also explain the sheer diversity of monument forms on the island. Anglesey has dolmens, multi-phase long cairns, sub-megalithic tombs and passage graves (Lynch 1991) and these are all forms of monument which are found in the surrounding Irish Sea areas.

Not all of the monuments in north-west Wales have views of Snowdonia, however. The small concentration of six monuments on the Ardudwy peninsula do not have views of Snowdon. Instead, all of these sites have views south to the Preselis in south-west Wales. Architecturally these monuments are more similar in form to the south-west Welsh monuments than those in north Wales. What is even more striking is they are set in remarkably similar landscape settings. The Ardudwy sites are located with views of a locally prominent hill, Moelfre, the Lleyn peninsula and the sea while the monuments around the Preselis are set with views of a locally prominent hill, Carn Ingli, Dinas Head and the sea (Cummings and Whittle 2004). At these sites it is the landscape which creates connections between the two areas, through intervisibility and also in the similarity of setting.

It seems, then, that monuments may have been located

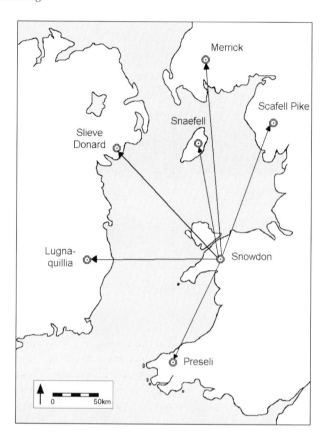

Figure 4.4. *The intervisibility of Snowdon. It is possible to see the mountains of all the other parts of the Irish Sea zone from the summit of Snowdon.*

in order to have views of distant places, or of mountains which had views of distant places from their summits (Fig. 4.5). However, the long distance views of landscape features would not have been visible all the time. Mountains are not always visible from the monuments. For much of the year mountains are shrouded in mist and cloud, or haze in the summer. Long distance visibility from the mountains themselves is even rarer. The person who first noted that south-west Scotland was visible from Snowdon saw the distant Merrick mountains only twice in 400 ascents (Jesty 1980). Therefore, the significance of mountains may have been only in part because of their views over the Irish Sea. The significance of mountains may also relate to their visual characteristics (see Bradley 2000; Watson this volume). For example, a number of monuments in south-west Wales have views of Carn Meini in the Preselis. This hillside has distinctive outcrops which erupt out of the earth, many of which appear to be built by people (Cummings 2002a). Richard Bradley (2000, 95) has suggested that the distinctive charac-teristics of Carn Meini may explain why it was used as a source for stone axes and also for the Stonehenge blue-stones. Mountains are also places where the land meets the sky, where you can stand in the clouds, or even

Figure 4.5. *The monument of Hen Drefor, Anglesey, with the Snowdonia mountains visible in the distance.*

overlook clouds when above the cloudline. Mountains are where water, earth, sky and stone meet, places perhaps where other worlds could be seen or entered. These otherwordly places would have been liminal, removed from everyday activities (Watson 1995) and they were likely to have been sacred places, perhaps connected with spirits and myths. In many ethnographic cases, mountains are often tied into creation myths (Martin 1999; Sundstrom 1996). We could therefore suggest that mountains had a special place in a Neolithic cosmology. Not only were mountains visible from monuments but they were also used as the source of stone axes. By quarrying stones from these mountains, people were able to move around parts of mountains and by building monuments at their bases these highly symbolic places could be referenced time and again.

The sea

Even though mountains seem to be a critical reference point in the landscape none of the monuments are actually built on top of the mountains themselves. Instead, monuments are always constructed on lower ground frequently with views of the sea (see Cummings and Whittle 2004; Fowler and Cummings 2003), and it is to the sea that we shall now turn. Over two thirds of monuments in the eastern Irish Sea area have views of the sea (Fig. 4.6) and many sites seem to be positioned so that the sea is visible as you approach the front of the monument. This relationship does not seem to be a coincidence and can be directly contrasted with the location of stone circles in the area, of which only 7% have views of the sea (Fowler and Cummings 2003). Just like mountains, a view of the sea may relate to connections with other parts of the Irish Sea zone. Instead of seeing the sea as a barrier, it seems likely that the sea would have been easier to traverse

than many of the heavily wooded inland areas of Britain. During the Neolithic period we know that material culture was moving across the Irish Sea, documented clearly by the movement of stone axes (from Ireland to Britain and *vice versa*), Arran pitchstone (Finlay 1997, 132; Williams Thorpe and Thorpe 1984) and Antrim flint (Saville 1999). Evidence dating back to the Mesolithic suggests that people would have been able sailors (such as evidence for deep-sea fishing: Coles 1971, 353; Mithen 1994, 106), and the first domesticated animals would have arrived by boat from the continent (Case 1969). Crossing the Irish Sea may well have been a regular occurrence. It is interesting, however, that people in the Neolithic do not seem to have used marine resources (see Schulting this volume). Instead, the sea may now have been understood as a connecting substance, linking together various parts of the Irish Sea zone. Therefore, a view of the sea may have been a reference to distant places, and a metaphor for journeying and travelling (Richards 1996).

Local features

Monuments were not just located in the landscape in relation to mountains and the sea. More localised features also seem to have been of significance in the creation of monumental places. In south-west Wales many sites have views of distinctive local outcrops (Cummings 2002a). These appear on the horizon as at Pentre Ifan (Tilley 1994, 105–6) while other sites were built right beneath these outcrops. Cairnholy II in south-west Scotland is also built on an outcrop. A number of sites are positioned in relation to rivers (Cummings and Whittle 2004; Fowler and Cummings 2003 and this volume) which may have been significant local features as well as connecting parts of the landscape. Many sites have views of smaller hills which may have been significant in local mythologies.

Figure 4.6. The monument of Bachwen, north-west Wales, which has a clear view of the sea.

Figure 4.7. Monuments are also positioned in relation to significant local features, such as Trefignath which has clear views of Holyhead Mountain.

Trefignath and other sites on Anglesey have views of Holyhead Mountain. This mountain seems to form an integral part of the structure at Trefignath. If one is standing in the forecourt looking towards the final-phase portal stones, Holyhead Mountain rises up in the centre of the portal (Fig. 4.7). Many sites are located next to streams and springs. King Orry's Graves on the Isle of Man are positioned next to a stream (see Fowler, and Cummings and Fowler this volume) while Gwal y Filiast in south-west Wales is close to rapids (Tilley 1994, 109). Sites may also have been built over locales that had previous activity. This is best documented in the Cotswold-Severn monuments but may also have occurred along the Irish Sea. Pre-cairn activity was found at Trefignath (Smith and Lynch 1987) and a microlith was found in Carreg Samson (Lynch 1975) hinting that these places may already have been significant before the construction of the monument. Megaliths may even have been built out of rocks that were already named and

significant places (see Richards and Whittle this volume). The distinctive capstone at Lligwy, for example, may have been an important landmark before it was used to construct a megalith. It is through reference to these more immediate landscape features that the builders of monuments were able to tie sites into a local understanding of the world, and we could even suggest that these local mythological understandings of the immediate topography may have had their origins in the Mesolithic (Cummings 2000; 2003).

Creating connections: discussion

It seems that monuments along the eastern Irish Sea worked at a number of different levels. At one level, they were tied into a local understanding of the landscape, while references to the sea and mountains created connections across the whole Irish Sea zone. And across all areas of the Irish Sea zone monuments were located in broadly similar locales, even though the architecture of the sites varied.

At this point it is relevant to address the issue of why there were not any monuments in the 'blank' areas along the Irish Sea coasts. I would like to suggest that the areas that do not have any monuments do not have the right 'combination' of landscape features which were appropriate for the construction of a chambered monument. For example, the stretch of coastline between Barmouth and Cardigan in mid Wales has no stone monuments, and we could argue that the absence of monuments in this area meant it was not possible to built a site with views of distinctive mountains, with long distance views, and also views of the sea. Further along the eastern Irish Sea coast, Cumbria does not have the density of stone-built monuments found elsewhere in the Irish Sea zone (although see paper in this volume by Evans). However,

I would argue that this area did play a critical role in the Irish Sea area because the mountains were incorporated into the Irish Sea zone through the extensive quarrying and exchange of stone axes from Langdale (Bradley and Edmonds 1993). Furthermore, these mountains **are** visible from some of the monuments in the Irish Sea area such as Cashtal yn Ard on the Isle of Man and Lligwy on Anglesey.

So how can we begin to interpret the significance of monuments placed to have views of mountains and the sea? It is possible to suggest that although monuments may have been built in relation to localised features which were part of an established, essentially Mesolithic understanding of the landscape, the creation of monumental places represented a new way of engaging with the world. I would like to suggest that the construction of monuments related to a new set of social relationships which were concerned with the creation of a broader community which spanned the Irish Sea area. In these areas, the Neolithic may have been about a new sense of social identity and community which was shared across the Irish Sea and manifested in monumental form as well as a common material culture. 'Being Neolithic' in these areas may have concerned a new set of social connections across the Irish Sea, reinforced through exchange networks. This involved the movement of material culture across the Irish Sea, and we could also envisage the movements of people and animals or even ancestral relics. However, a crucial part of this new sense of identity may have been linked to landscape and was expressed in the construction of monuments which had views of mountains and sea, the two substances which connected the Irish Sea, and also in the exchange of parts of the landscape in the form of axes.

I would also like to suggest that the location of monuments in relation to mountains and sea also had an impact on the ways these places were used. Perhaps the visibility of the mountains from the monuments, or the visibility of the broader Irish Sea zone from the mountains dictated what activities could take place or the types of material culture that could be deposited. Since the visibility of mountains and the long distance visibility of the Irish Sea zone from mountains would not have occurred all the time, this could have affected when and how each monument was used. Is it even possible that the Neolithic represented a new way of seeing the world where visuality became an increasingly significant way of engaging with the world (see also discussion in Cummings and Whittle 2004). The beginnings of the clearance of the landscape and the intervisibility of monuments could have been part of a process where the visual became increasingly important in people's lives, and the increasing importance of the visual could also have been part of what it was to 'be Neolithic' in these areas.

Conclusion

Although I have suggested that the Irish Sea zone was an area of interaction, where people may have felt part of a broader Neolithic community, this is not to suggest that this area existed in complete isolation. There were clearly links with other parts of the country. Stone axes from the Irish Sea zone are also found beyond the Irish Sea, for example, Group VI and VII axes are found throughout eastern Britain. Likewise, court tombs are found throughout northern Ireland. There were also visual connections with these areas. For example it is possible to see the Black Mountains and the Peak District from Snowdonia. Perhaps we should understand the monuments along the Irish Sea zone as variations on a common theme where permanent locales are created in the landscape which in turn referred to distant places. Sites were both connected to the local topography by referencing features of local significance, but also positioned in relation to the mountains and the sea. Mountains may have been sacred and a key component of a symbolic and inscribed landscape, and by having views of mountains, people building and using monuments could reference all the parts of the Irish Sea zone. The sea also seems to have been significant, as it was able to physically connect people across this area. It was these key landscape features, mountains and sea, which I have suggested were used to create connections across the Irish Sea zone, and a new Neolithic community within it.

Acknowledgements

I would like to thank the Board of Celtic Studies who funded the 'Megaliths in the Neolithic landscapes of Wales' project, and the School of History and Archaeology in Cardiff for their continued support. This paper has benefited enormously from discussions with Chris Fowler, Robert Johnston, Aaron Watson, Alasdair Whittle and Howard Williams. Many thanks to Jonathan de Ferranti for allowing me to reproduce one of his landscape panoramas.

References

Bergh, S. 1995. *Landscape of the monuments*. Stockholm: Riksantikvarieämbet Arkeologiska Undersöknigar.

Bowen, E.G. 1970. Britain and the British Seas. In D. Moore (ed.), *The Irish Sea province in archaeology and history*, 13–28. Cardiff: Cambrian Archaeological Association.

Bradley, R. 2000. *An archaeology of natural places*. London: Routledge.

Bradley, R. and Edmonds, M. 1993. *Interpreting the axe trade*. Cambridge: Cambridge University Press.

Burrow, S. 1997. *The Neolithic culture of the Isle of Man*. Oxford: British Archaeological Reports British Series 263.

Case, H. 1969a. Neolithic explanations. *Antiquity* 43, 176–86.

Coles, J. 1971. The early settlement of Scotland: excavations at Morton, Fife. *Proceedings of the Prehistoric Society* 37, 284–366.

Cooney, G. 2000a. Coping with death, changing the landscape: people, places and histories in the Irish Neolithic. In A. Ritchie (ed.), *Neolithic Orkney in its European context*, 247–58. Oxford: Oxbow.

Cooney, G. 2000b. *Landscapes of Neolithic Ireland*. London: Routledge.

Coope, G. and Garrad, L. 1988. The petrological identification of stone implements from the Isle of Man. In T. Clough and W. Cummins (eds), *Stone axe studies volume two*, 67–70. London: Council for British Archaeology.

Cummings, V. 2000. Myth, memory and metaphor: the significance of place, space and the landscape in Mesolithic Pembrokeshire. In R. Young (ed.), *Mesolithic lifeways: current research from Britain and Ireland*, 87–95. Leicester: Leicester University Monographs.

Cummings, V. 2001. *Landscapes in transition? Exploring the origins of monumentality in south-west Wales and south-west Scotland*. Unpublished PhD Thesis: Cardiff University.

Cummings, V. 2002a. All cultural things: actual and conceptual monuments in the Neolithic of Western Britain. In C. Scarre (ed.), *Monumentality and landscape in Atlantic Europe*, 107–21. London: Routledge.

Cummings, V. 2002b. Between mountains and sea: a reconsideration of the monuments of south-west Scotland. *Proceedings of the Prehistoric Society* 68, 125–46.

Cummings, V. 2003. Mesolithic world-views of the landscape in western Britain. In L. Larsson (ed.), *Proceedings of the Mesolithic 2000 conference*, 74–81. Oxford: Oxbow.

Cummings, V. and Whittle, A. 2004. *Places of special virtue: megaliths in the Neolithic landscapes of Wales*. Oxford: Oxbow.

Darvill, T. 2000. Neolithic Mann in context. In A. Ritchie (ed.), *Neolithic Orkney in its European context*, 371–85. Oxford: Oxbow.

de Valera, R. 1960. The court cairns of Ireland. *Proceedings of the Royal Irish Academy* 60, 9–140.

de Ferranti, J. 1995a. *Panoramic map of the view from Merrick, Galloway*. Newburgh, Fife: Viewfinder: viewfinder@taynet.co.uk.

de Ferranti, J. 1995b. *Panoramic map of the view from Snowdon*. Newburgh, Fife: Viewfinder: viewfinder@taynet.co.uk.

Finlay, N. 1997. Lithics from the Arran sites; summary and discussion. In J. Barber (ed.), *The archaeological investigation of a prehistoric landscape: excavations on Arran 1978–1981*, 131–6. Edinburgh: Scottish Trust for Archaeological Research.

Fowler, C. and Cummings, V. 2003. Places of transformation: building monuments from water and stone in the Neolithic of the Irish Sea. *Journal of the Royal Anthropological Institute* 9, 1–20.

Henshall, A. 1972. *The chambered tombs of Scotland, volume two*. Edinburgh: Edinburgh University Press.

Henshall, A. 1978. Manx megaliths again: an attempt at structural analysis. In P. Davey (ed.), *Man and environment in the Isle of Man*, 171–6. Oxford: British Archaeological Reports British Series 54.

Jesty, C. 1980. *A guide to the view from Snowdon*. Bridport: Jesty's Panoramas.

Lynch, F. 1969. The megalithic tombs of north Wales. In T.

Powell, J. Corcoran, F. Lynch, and J. Scott (eds), *Megalithic enquiries in the west of Britain*, 107–48. Liverpool: Liverpool University Press.

Lynch, F. 1972. Portal dolmens in the Nevern Valley, Pembrokeshire. In F. Lynch and C. Burgess (eds), *Prehistoric man in Wales and the west*, 67–84. Bath: Adams and Dart.

Lynch, F. 1975. Excavations at Carreg Samson megalithic tomb, Mathry, Pembrokeshire. *Archaeologia Cambrensis* 124, 15–35.

Lynch, F. 1989. Wales and Ireland: a fluctuating relationship. *Archaeologia Cambrensis* 138, 1–19.

Lynch, F. 1991. *Prehistoric Anglesey: second edition*. Llangefni: Anglesey Antiquarian Society.

Martin, J. 1999. *The land looks after us: a history of Native American religion*. Oxford: Oxford University Press.

Megaw, B. 1938. Manx megaliths and their ancestry. *Proceedings of the Isle of Man Natural History and Antiquarian Society* 4, 219–39.

Miles, D. 2001. The Presely Hills. *Rural Wales* 2001, 14–15.

Mithen, S. 1994. The Mesolithic age. In B. Cunliffe (ed.), *Prehistoric Europe: an illustrated history*, 79–135. Oxford: Oxford University Press.

Piggott, S. 1954. *The Neolithic cultures of the British Isles*. Cambridge: Cambridge University Press.

Powell, T.G.E. and Daniel, G.E. 1956. *Barclodiad y Gawres: the excavation of a megalithic chamber tomb in Anglesey 1952–1953*. Liverpool: Liverpool University Press.

Richards, C. 1996. Henges and water: towards an elemental understanding of monumentality and landscape in late Neolithic Britain. *Journal of Material Culture* 2, 313–36.

Saville, A. 1999. A cache of flint axeheads and other flint artefacts from Auchenhoan, near Campbeltown, Kintyre, Scotland. *Proceedings of the Prehistoric Society* 65, 83–123.

Sheridan, A. 1986. Porcellanite artefacts: a new survey. *Ulster Journal of Archaeology* 49, 19–32.

Sheridan, A. 2000. Achnacreebeag and its French connections: vive the 'Auld Alliance'. In J. Henderson (ed.), *The prehistory and early history of Atlantic Europe*, 1–15. Oxford: British Archaeological Reports International Series 861.

Sheridan, J., Cooney, G. and Grogan, E. 1992. Stone axe studies in Ireland. *Proceedings of the Prehistoric Society* 58, 389–416.

Smith, C. and Lynch. F. 1987. *Trefignath and Din Dryfol: the excavation of two megalithic tombs in Anglesey*. Bangor: Cambrian Archaeological Association.

Sundstrom, L. 1996. Mirror of heaven: cross-cultural transference of the sacred geography of the Black Hills. *World Archaeology* 28, 177–89.

Tilley, C. 1994. *A phenomenology of landscape*. Oxford: Berg.

Watson, A. 1995. Investigating the distribution of Group VI debitage in the central Lake District. *Proceedings of the Prehistoric Society* 61, 661–2.

Watson, A. 2001. Composing Avebury. *World Archaeology* 33, 296–314.

Williams Thorpe, O. and Thorpe, R. 1984. The distribution and sources of archaeological pitchstone in Britain. *Journal of Archaeological Science* 11, 1–34.

5 The searchers: the quest for causewayed enclosures in the Irish Sea area

Kenneth Brophy

The search

John Ford's 1956 movie, *The Searchers*, depicts the desperate and increasingly ambiguous search by Ethan Edwards (played by John Wayne) for his niece Debbie who has been kidnapped by the Comanche. During this snatch they also killed most of Edwards' brother's family. His search lasts for many years. As the search continues, it is increasingly unclear as to what the motives for the search are. Edwards' hatred of the indigenous Americans ('Red Indians') is based not just on the time-honoured Western movie tradition of revenge, but also his obsessive racism (Pye 1996). The act of searching is itself ambiguous: after years beyond the white frontier Debbie has become tainted and Edwards resolves not just to find her but to kill her. She has become disgraced and outwith 'decent' society to Wayne's character, and in searching for her he also changes her in his own mind. The searcher is an ambiguous character 'who is both monstrous *and* John Wayne' (Pye 1996, 229), and his motivations are driven by personal need and the norms of the society he belongs to (Maltby 1996).

Ford's epic western was set in the equally epic landscape of Monument Valley. This generic location was later subverted and parodied in Sergio Leone's *Once Upon a Time in the West* (Frayling 1998). But films such as Leone's retained the general Western movie theme of searching as an *obsession*. In Leone's westerns the search for 'revenge' rarely leads to closure for the hero. Even after killing an ancient enemy, his Men with No Names (Clint Eastwood; Charles Bronson; Terence Hill) move on, restless, unable to reach closure or peace, always searching (Frayling 2000). Through both American and European westerns, then, searching is seen as more important than the end result, and as a process where through looking for something we usually change it. The climax of the film may be the duel, or the partial resolution, but the narrative is all about the search. It is a cathartic process.

As archaeologists we are always searching, often beyond our known frontiers, sometimes in our own monumental valleys. What we are searching for in some cases is to extend those frontiers, which in our case are often graphically depicted as dotted lines or areas of shading on distribution maps (see Fig. 5.1 and also Brophy forthcoming a). In the case of this paper I am particularly interested in the (re)searchers looking for, and expanding the frontiers of, causewayed enclosures. Through looking at recent advances in this frontier northwards and westwards, I hope to show that the results are ambiguous and the search un-resolved; and also that the processes of data gathering and typology in archaeology may be altering and constraining the evidence before we actually find it.

A fistful of enclosures

This paper, then, is about a type of monument that is not readily associated with the Irish Sea zone. It would be fair to say, however, that in recent years strenuous efforts have been made to change the image of causewayed enclosures from being the archetypal earliest Neolithic enclosure type in southern England. Through (re)analysis of aerial photographs, excavation, and trawling through SMRs, a number of regional syntheses have been published. These include for Scotland (Barclay 2001a), northern England (Waddington 2001), Ireland (Sheridan 2001) and the Isle of Man and surrounding coastal fringes (Darvill 2001). There has also been the publication of a wider gazetteer and interpretive volume by English Heritage (Oswald *et al.* 2001) as well as several high profile conferences. All have argued persuasively for extending the known distribution of causewayed enclosures (or large sub-circular early Neolithic enclosures) into previously uncharted territory. Not all of these enclosures have been explicitly linked to the causewayed enclosure type, but implicitly they fall within that tradition.

Rather than go over the ground these contributions cover, I want to argue here that these attempts to extend the causewayed enclosure frontier are not merely based on the premise that these sites may be early Neolithic (causewayed) enclosures – but that these areas simply *must have had them*. This is reminiscent of the rapidly extending distribution of cursus monuments, another class of Neolithic enclosure, witnessed in the 1980s and 1990s

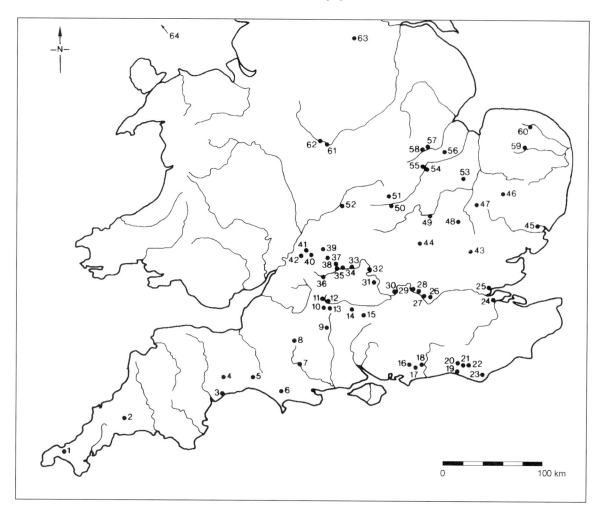

Figure 5.1. *Typical distribution map of causewayed enclosures, cutting off Scotland and depicting the only listed Irish site with an arrow pointing off the page (from Mercer 1990).*

across the British Isles. Similar regional syntheses were published (mostly in Barclay and Harding 1999) indicating that cursus monuments may have existed in some numbers in Scotland, Wales, Ireland and so on. By way of footnote, I find it a peculiar contradiction of the recent moves towards acknowledging regional variation in the Neolithic of the British Isles (see Barclay and Brophy forthcoming) that we are still trying to find pan-British Isles monument distributions.

In this paper, then, I will look firstly at the iconic status causewayed enclosures appear to have in Neolithic studies, and then address the tensions and contradictions inherent in attempts to look for these sites in northern Britain and the Irish Sea area. From this, I will suggest that our fresh knowledge about potential causewayed enclosure sites is at the same unreflective stage as cursus monument studies 5 or 6 years ago. Finally, I will suggest a few ways forward – and acknowledge, like John Wayne's character, that the search for us will never reach a truly satisfactory conclusion.

Causewayed enclosures – the Holy Grail?

Waddington has recently written, 'archaeologists looking for evidence of these enclosures outwith southern England have been encumbered by the pervading form of the causewayed enclosure' (2001, 1). Geographic and typological baggage, then, have inevitably shaped late 1990s causewayed enclosure studies. Worryingly, attempts to go beyond what Waddington calls the 'straitjacket of monument typology' have usually ended up in one breaking free from the straitjacket only to find oneself still trapped in a typological padded cell. This is because, like all monument classifications or types, 'causewayed enclosure' (the label, not the site) has transcended the useful archaeological shorthand it once was.

The term formerly known as causewayed camp has come to represent an idealised image (really a snapshot in time of one incarnation of a monument in the biography of a place); and is also encumbered with the baggage of a specific geographical distribution (Brophy forthcoming a; Waddington 2001). It is little wonder that attempts to locate this image or package wholesale elsewhere has had mixed results. Furthermore, causewayed enclosures have come to represent a particular type of Neolithic economy and social organisation (Oswald *et al.* 2001; Thomas 1999, chapter 3).

In the recent English Heritage volume, *The creation of monuments*, it is stressed almost immediately that the understanding of what causewayed enclosures were used for – what went on within their porous boundaries – is some kind of key for understanding how communities in the early Neolithic organised their subsistence strategies (Oswald *et al.* 2001, chapter 1). In recent years they have – as Barclay (2002) and Cooney (2001) have suggested – come to represent an important cog in the idea of a mobile pastoral economy in the early Neolithic. The discourse over whether this represents a new orthodoxy for the Neolithic of the British Isles has been well rehearsed (see Cooney 2001 and Thomas' response in the same volume) but clearly the implication that these monuments represent this type of subsistence strategy adds more significance to their apparent existence in the Irish Sea area.

So when we start to search for causewayed enclosures beyond the known frontiers, not just 'filling maps' but 'extending distributions' as Darvill and Thomas (2001a, 4) have characterised it, we are not merely looking for the familiar physical form of a cropmark or earthwork enclosure. Actually we are looking for a myth, an idea, an icon of the early Neolithic, all baggage included (Fig. 5.2). These indeed are created monuments, but much of the creation has happened in the present. This may seem a superficial, and unnecessarily obtuse argument – an idealistic and naïve position to take. But I feel that there are issues of fundamental importance here, a number of questions that archaeologists have not as yet fully theorised.

Firstly, this is clearly an area where regional Neolithic monumental traditions overlap larger scale (even universal?) processes such as the act of enclosure *per se*. How do we as archaeologists engage with such overlapping scales and ideas? Secondly, the order of discovery of sites by archaeologists has been allowed in some cases to become some kind of real chronology of the past. Yet there are several types of Neolithic monument including henges and cursus monuments that were first discovered in southern England but have been pre-dated by more recent discoveries in northern Britain. Finally, why should we expect to find similar site types everywhere, whole suites of monuments replicated up and down the country? There is no reason why there had to be causewayed enclosures in Scotland. Are we in danger of searching for something that did not ever exist, and in the process creating a marginalised and secondary group of eclectic non-conforming enclosures?

These thoughts will be developed through the course

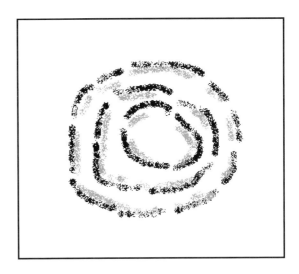

Figure 5.2. This is not a causewayed enclosure: the archetypal image of this kind of site

of this paper. But now, to make a start, I want to look at the work of the searchers so far, in particular assessing the effects and implications of extending the distribution and expanding the morphological form of the causewayed enclosure type.

For a few causewayed enclosures more

As mentioned already, a series of similar and significant papers have been published on possible causewayed enclosures in the Irish Sea area and northern Britain in general. Not all of these sites have been explicitly called causewayed enclosures, but all are implicitly connected to the early Neolithic tradition of causewayed ditch enclosures. Often these candidate sites are graded in terms of the likelihood that they do form part of that tradition, with adjectives like possible, probable, potential and classic being applied. These groups of sites have often been collected from painstaking trawls of SMR and NMRS records, and are heavily biased towards aerial photographic evidence, although there are also a number of candidates that are undated hilltop enclosures (Horne *et al.* 2002). Much of the (re)interpretation, then, is based on morphological grounds or a loose association with Neolithic material.

The searches themselves look for specific traits that separate the sites from the large number of amorphous enclosures that are spread across much of the British Isles. These traits are seen in themselves as diagnostic, rather like the shape of a pottery vessel or the form of lithic arrowhead, and include:

– The landscape location – (causewayed) enclosure sites seem to be associated with water and/or promontories, and other apparently liminal locations;

– The enclosure boundaries – these should be causewayed or segmented in construction;
– The interior – should contain hints of ritualistic structures or activity, like structured deposition. Obviously this depends on fine air photo evidence or excavation.

Interestingly, these traits seem more important than some elements we more usually associate with causewayed enclosures. The clearest example of this is that, as we shall see, the constructional techniques used to create the boundaries (segmented; causewayed) are more important than the materiality of the boundary. Barnatt *et al.* (2001) argue that the extended distribution of early Neolithic causewayed enclosures into Ireland, Wales, the Isle of Man, northern England and Scotland have resulted in an extended or stretched definition of the monument type traits. Crucially, I would argue, in the absence of 'classic' examples, sites that would be discounted in southern England as amorphous or later prehistoric enclosures are counted as potential early Neolithic enclosures elsewhere.

So, for instance, a wider variety of sizes of sites are included. This happened in the 1960s with henge monuments, when atypically small enclosures were included within the tradition by being dubbed hengiform (Wainright 1969). More important has been the downplaying of the materiality of the boundaries of these enclosures. The sites put forward as candidates for being early Neolithic enclosures have earthwork boundaries, palisades, timber posts, stone and pebble banks and so on. Again, we have seen this process at work with cursus monuments (Brophy 1999; 2000) with the inclusion in Scotland of timber post-defined rectilinear enclosures within the class. Unusual northern variants of henges also inevitably found themselves included in the henge class too – Mayburgh in Cumbria with its pebble bank and lack of ditch for instance. Finally, as Waddington (2001) has noted, few of these sites are characterised by multiple concentric ditches (*classic* causewayed enclosure form). Therefore many of the candidate sites like Leadketty, Perthshire, and Sprouston, Borders, have single causewayed ditches (Fig. 5.3 and Barclay 2001a). Single ditched enclosures are also characterised by less frequent causeways.

It is small wonder that many of these sites have been absent from early Neolithic discourse for so long. In general they have been (and still are to some extent) discussed in altogether different discourses and frameworks resulting in wildly differing interpretations. In particular it is interesting to note how frequently these sites are linked to later Neolithic enclosure forms in recent publications. In particular palisaded enclosures like Hindwell, Powys; Forteviot, Perthshire; and even Dunragit, Wigtownshire, have been discussed within these same papers (e.g. Barclay 2001a; Gibson 1998; Waddington 2001). This is partly of course because some of these discussions are about Neolithic enclosures in general, although for me it is at times left unclear whether at least implicitly there is a relationship between all non-henge sub-circular Neolithic enclosures. It also of course indicates the diversity involved in producing these places, and an ease of re-invention as well as mimicry and allusion.

Perhaps an even greater indication of the way that discourse and typological interpretation allows the archaeological record to be shaped and structured (and so structures the 'past') is the way that these enclosures were previously recorded. This is particularly true of the cropmark record. To take Scotland as an example, the enclosures discussed by Barclay (2001a) and included in the English Heritage gazetteer (Oswald *et al.* 2001, page 158) have, and have had, a variety of class groups attributed to them in the NMRS. West Lindsaylands and Sprouston have both been interpreted as a 'fort', a class not denoting defence *per se* but rather defencibility through boundary form and/or location, with an assumption of Iron Age or early Historic date. Both have recently been re-thought not merely because of the causewayed nature of their artificial boundary (both are on river-sides so the river itself forms a natural boundary on one side), but also because of the presence of possible early Neolithic timber monuments nearby. In the case of Sprouston, this is a so-called timber hall, dateable by analogy to around 4000–3500BC (Smith 1991; Barclay *et al.* 2002); and at West Lindsaylands, a possible post-defined cursus monument (RCAHMS 1997). Leadketty is another candidate, and again has strong Neolithic associations, including Neolithic material recovered by fieldwalking in the same field (e.g. King 1993) and a presumably later Neolithic palisaded enclosure nearby (Barclay 2001a, see also Fig. 5.3). Leadketty has been classified in the NMRS as 'enclosure'.

Similar interpretations – fort, settlement, ritual enclosure, hillfort, hilltop enclosure and enclosure – have hidden many amorphous enclosures for many decades, both cropmark and upstanding, and it is only the recent searches that have started to uncover these as potentially earlier in origin. These labels are of course at the root of the problem – they are not mistakes or mis-identifications, but rather a product of earlier beliefs that there were almost no causewayed enclosures outwith southern England and Wales (e.g. Mercer 1990). Now, the opposite applies. People expect to find them and find them they have. I do not wish to criticise this valuable work here, but rather I want to use this process of searching, and the connection between what we are looking for and what we find, to draw some more general conclusions about the way that we structure the past in the present, the ways that we create the past. Enclosures are the plasticene of our expectations, malleable into whatever shape we want, nothing without us. But does the search for *causewayed* enclosures in the Neolithic of the Irish Sea zone really tell us anything about the Neolithic?

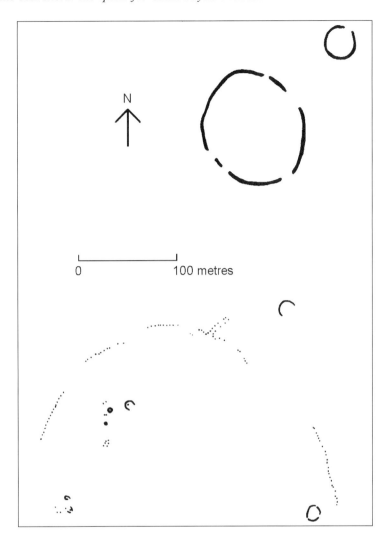

Figure 5.3. *One of Scotland's more probable causewayed enclosures, the single ditched Leadketty in Perthshire (from Barclay 2001a, after RCAHMS transcriptions).*

The good, the bad and Leadketty

What are the implications of such searches for types of monuments? Firstly, we must return again to the abiding image of causewayed enclosure distribution, part of the baggage of the label itself. The type of distribution map commonly used until recently (see Fig. 5.1) does not depict the distribution of absence. Rather, areas with no known causewayed enclosures by the 1980s were ignored. As Waddington (2001) suggests, this type of image is partly how we visualise the monument class itself. As has been discussed elsewhere, maps are powerful and persuasive tools for conveying just such information (Brophy forthcoming a). At face value, any attempt to re-write this map, to move the frontier (be it the edge of the illustration or a dotted line) is to be welcomed. And this is what the searchers have tried to do. But at what cost?

Sites beyond the frontier often re-enforce the frontier because these candidate sites appear peripheral to the southern English core. This is due to a combination of reasons, one of which must be simply that they were discovered later, once the type sites and characteristics had become engrained in archaeological discourse. However, perhaps more significantly, this feeling is based on the physical appearance of these Irish Sea sites. Possible early Neolithic enclosures in Scotland, northern England and Ireland in particular often appear as strange variations on causewayed enclosures, weird and atypical, even degenerate versions of the more familiar causewayed enclosures to the south. Implicitly at least they appear to be secondary regional variations on an established core tradition.

Yet logically this must be an illusion based on archaeological discourse and the nature of archaeological typology. It is archaeological discourse that has made sites like Windmill Hill and Maiden Castle 'typical' or 'classical' and of primary significance. These sites have been long known and had high profile excavations, and crop up even in basic textbooks on British prehistory. In

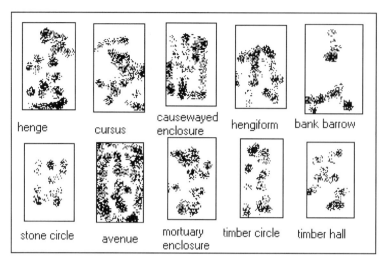

Figure 5.4. *Causewayed enclosures and pigeon-holes.*

short, they represent an orthodoxy based on familiarity, physical size and their location. Yet the overall distributional pattern of sites could just as well view southern England as atypical (Harding 1991), and even secondary. Billown, Isle of Man, has provided some dates that are very early in comparison to sites in southern England but has a 'classic' form (Darvill 2001).

Perhaps a more fundamental issue is the tension and uncertainty that the wide variety of possible early Neolithic enclosures being postulated brings. Even at a glance some sites in Scotland, Wales and Ireland indicate a wide array of architectural forms and designs. We are increasingly aware that the boundaries and final forms are an exploded diagram of various phases and acts focussed on each place. With this confusing array of sites, many of them difficult to classify, or forced uncomfortably into the causewayed enclosure pigeon-hole (Fig. 5.4), the safety net of typology is lost and it becomes increasingly difficult to reconcile local with wider scale concerns and influences. In short, is the only common Neolithic trait apparent from these sites that in the fourth millennium BC people built enclosures? If so, what are the implications for our understanding of wider social themes, regionality and identity?

Are we seeing in the fourth millennium BC – as Waddington (2001) and Barnatt *et al.* (2001) have suggested – local variants on general enclosure forms indicating group preferences in terms of ideological needs, raw material availability, and / or identity? Or are we seeing – as Barclay (2001a) seems to be suggesting – an indication of a more fundamental economic variation? The latter view suggests that the potential causewayed enclosure candidates in the Irish Sea area and beyond may indicate possible variations in settlement patterns across the British Isles; the former that it is futile to try to read socio-economic trends from the monuments that people leave behind. So here we have the possibility that types or forms of enclosure represent types of economy –

classic causewayed enclosures equal tethered/mobile pastoral economy; single ditch, stone bank or timber-defined enclosures associated with semi-mobile subsistence strategies such as transhumance.

These are the kinds of implications that these lists of sites bring with them. Firstly, that there are peripheral areas filled with weird, degenerate monuments. Secondly, that they potentially indicate different economic or subsistence strategies, and may indicate local or regional variations on a universal form. Left untheorised and unreflected, such ideas become orthodoxies or truths when they may or may not be. In the case of the extended distribution of cursus monuments in the mid to late 1990s, these issues had to be addressed, leading to a balanced approach to the apparently typical and atypical; and a mature suspicion of monument typology. I will now develop the parallel with 'cursus studies' in more depth.

The cursus experience

I was once a searcher, searching for cursus monuments in Scotland. Partly this was because previous research (e.g. Loveday 1985) had suggested that there must have been a number of cropmark cursus sites in Scotland, but also that there were lots of gaps in the distribution map that needed to be filled. In the mid 1990s various archaeologists started to look for cursus monuments where previously they had not been identified or had a very limited tradition – Ireland and Wales for instance. And wherever people looked for them, they found them, but they were a strange and eclectic group of monuments, some 'classic' types, but many others variations on the established form.

Sites with different boundaries – timber posts, even pits – were found in Scotland for instance in some numbers, and many sites displayed architectural variations such as kinks at the corners, and combinations of different boundary materials. At first in my research I made the mistake of regarding these as eccentric and secondary developments from the types of rectangular enclosures (such   as Springfield, Essex) found in southern England. But the mistake I made was this: I confused the sequence of discovery with the sequence of construction. The earliest known sites had become established in the archaeological literature as an iconic and typical form, and anything else would have to be atypical, or a copy. I used to call the sites tartan potatoes – Scottish and came in all shapes and sizes. Now, I realise that by searching for cursus monuments within a certain discourse and tradition, I was trying to reinforce the typological class – but may have ended up destroying it (Brophy forthcoming b).

Causewayed enclosure studies are now where cursus monument studies were around five years ago – the initial flush of excitement as the search bears fruit; the monument variations increasing; the number of known and suspected sites increasing; previously unclassifiable enclosures being classified; regional traditions identified; and of course the distribution expanding. Some of the more recent discoveries in Scotland and Ireland were the best-preserved examples of cursus monuments known. But there were also similar intellectual problems and concessions to make – the type group and definition was continually being compromised and stretched to include more and more sites; variation was seen as atypical; typology was reinforced; and ultimately difference was downplayed in the search for similarity.

However as more became known of the cursus sites in these peripheral areas (for instance through a series of high profile excavations in Scotland (e.g. Barclay and Maxwell 1998; Thomas 1998)) so re-evaluation of the monument class occurred and more localised and reflexive interpretations were applied to explain the architectural variations and wide distribution (see contributions in Barclay and Harding 1999). As importantly, the cursus monuments of England were reviewed afresh within this new context, and renewed searching there uncovered many potentially new monuments, often with strange variations on the cursus form such as post-defined cursus being identified (Alex Gibson *pers. comm.*). Within this new framework Scotland's sites could be viewed no longer as atypical but rather as part of more complex traditions of rectilinearity with no core or periphery. The 1990s excavations also suggested that the cursus monuments in Scotland had comparably early dates with their southern counterparts (see Barclay and Bayliss 1999).

The end of the search or just the beginning?

'At the end, he relents, rescuing Debbie instead of killing her, but he hasn't mellowed enough. In the last shot, he rides away from the community of friends and kin once more, destined, like the Comanche spirits, to wander forever' (Biskind 2001, 241)

'Every Western is a palimpsest, a manuscript written on the pages of an earlier, partially erased book, carrying traces of its previous inscriptions' (Maltby 1996, 40)

In this paper I have tried to make a number of points about the current stage of our knowledge about the distribution of causewayed enclosures (although is written in advance of the publication of an interpretive volume of papers on the topic (Varndell and Topping 2002)). This group of sites has been related at least implicitly to an increasing number of less complex single boundary early Neolithic enclosures. Excitingly, areas previously without traditions of early Neolithic enclosures, especially the Irish Sea fringes, have now been brought into this discourse. Sites recognisable as 'classic' causewayed enclosures have been excavated in the Isle of Man, Northern Ireland and Anglesey. I have compared the searching process by which we reached this stage with a similar process that went on for cursus monuments a few years ago.

This is an important horizon for our understanding of the earliest Neolithic monuments and built structures in the British Isles. A number of projects are starting to fill gaps in our knowledge, from revisited radiocarbon dating of passage graves in southern England (Alasdair Whittle *pers. comm.*), to the identification of a number of very early Neolithic timber buildings in lowland Scotland such as Claish Farm (Barclay *et al.* 2002). Ongoing debates about the nature of the subsistence economy and settlement patterns in the early Neolithic can only benefit from such projects as well as a re-evaluation of our knowledge about causewayed enclosures. This seems an ideal time to re-visit our assumptions of core and periphery (Barclay 2002); and how we view this important period of time.

To do this we must be aware of a number of inherent problems in the growth in knowledge we are experiencing regarding early Neolithic enclosures. The data as it stands – including a large number of unexcavated cropmark sites – rests on many assumptions on form and function, and sets up a few unhelpful patterns.

Firstly, these 'new' sites currently have the appearance of secondary, or atypical, causewayed enclosures, as if they slowly filtered northwards. This impression, as I have mentioned, made cursus monuments in Scotland seem like strange variations on English sites. But perhaps if we look back to the south again (as happened with cursus monuments) for potentially similar causewayed enclosure variants, we may well find them amidst the great number of un-interpreted and undated cropmark enclosures. Within the orthodox discourse of causewayed enclosures, these may never have been considered as having early Neolithic origins. We should let the imaginative interpretation of sites in northern and western British Isles re-inform our understanding of the early Neolithic of southern England.

Secondly, we have to investigate more of these enclosures to address issues of dating, meaning (rather than function) and development through time. Excavations at sites already suggest early dates (e.g. Darvill 2001), and unusual associations with settlement traces, natural features, lithic sources and so on. This is not to say that such investigation will not also uncover elements of what we would traditionally regard as being typical of causewayed enclosures, nor will it always provide early Neolithic dates (cf. Barclay 2001b; Mercer 1983).

Thirdly, as Waddington (2001) suggests, we have to move beyond our typological constructs. As more sites are identified, so we find our preconceptions continually being challenged, our labels becoming more and more inadequate, and ultimately our understanding altered. The very idea of looking for a causewayed enclosure is a tautology, an abstraction only made possible by being an archaeologist. As Thomas (2001) has successfully stressed, Neolithic enclosures in south-west Scotland and Anglesey were projects and processes – sites we choose to call causewayed enclosures, palisaded enclosures and henge monuments are simply 'enclosures', focal and special places. Ultimately these enclosures are the outcome of ritualised practice rather than (as we see them) the product of aerial reconnaissance or excavation strategy. They would have reflected and served localised concerns in some way rather than necessarily buying whole-heartedly into a universal Neolithic ideology.

This paper, then, has been a collection of observations and thoughts from somebody who a few years ago set out as an objective to find the first causewayed enclosure in Scotland. Partly this was a response to the orthodox position that there were none there to find. But I then realised that this was a meaningless and ridiculous objective. I was (and am) unsure what a causewayed enclosure was/is, so how would I know when I found one? Would it be enough to dig a site and conclude that, on the balance of probabilities, it was one? Or would I simply find yet another physical and monumental expression of people in the fourth millennium BC trying to make sense of the world for them in the only way they knew how? Causewayed enclosures are created monuments, created by our discourse and our needs, and in the end it does not matter what we call them. The endless search becomes all we have, because the goal in an illusion. Even when we apparently reach it, like a mirage or rainbow, it still remains frustratingly outwith our grasp because it does not really exist.

In Leone's film, *Once Upon a Time in the West*, Charles Bronson's character (the nameless hero) spends the entire file stalking his brother's killer, played by Henry Fonda. He has several opportunities to kill him, but does not take them. He wants and gets a stage-managed, delayed duel, a dance of death, extended to the 'point of dying'. As archaeologists we too are always searching, never truly succeeding, nor really wanting it to end. We always walk away from a project restless, searching again for gaps and maps to fill. Like the director, we are conscious of this process and how it works – but like the actors we are condemned to follow the script, to keep on searching.

Acknowledgements

I would like to thank the organisers of the session for inviting me to present a paper during the colloquium and for all of those who spoke to me about my paper. In particular, I must thank Gordon Barclay for his comments and conversation on our shared passion of Neolithic cropmark enclosures. Finally, I would like to stress to all of you searchers out there that to be a searcher is a good thing – it's what makes us archaeologists.

References

Barclay, A. and Bayliss, A. 1999. Cursus monuments and the radiocarbon problem. In A. Barclay and J. Harding, (eds) *Pathways and ceremonies: the cursus monuments of Britain and Ireland*, 11–29. Oxford: Oxbow.

Barclay, A and Harding, J. (eds), 1999. *Pathways and ceremonies: the cursus monuments of Britain and Ireland*. Oxford: Oxbow.

Barclay, G.J. 2001a. Neolithic enclosures in Scotland. In T. Darvill and J. Thomas (eds), *Neolithic enclosures in Atlantic Northwest Europe*, 144–54. Oxford: Oxbow.

Barclay, G.J. 2001b. The excavation of an early Medieval enclosure at Upper Gothens, Meikleour, Perthshire, *Tayside and Fife Archaeological Journal* 7, 34–44.

Barclay, G.J. 2002. 'Metropolitan' and 'parochial'/'core' and 'periphery': a historiography of the Neolithic of Scotland. *Proceedings of the Prehistoric Society* 67, 1–18.

Barclay, G.J. and Brophy K. (eds) forthcoming. *Regional diversity in the Neolithic of Britain and Ireland*. Oxford: Oxbow.

Barclay, G.J., Brophy, K. and MacGregor G. 2002. Claish, Stirling: a major Neolithic building in its context. *Proceedings of the Society of Antiquaries of Scotland* 132, 65–138.

Barclay, G.J. and Maxwell G.S. 1998. *The Cleaven Dyke and Littleour. Monuments in the Neolithic of Tayside*. Edinburgh: Society of the Antiquaries of Scotland.

Barnatt, J., Bevan, B. and Edmonds, M. 2001. A time and place for enclosure: Gardom's edge, Derbyshire. In T. Darvill and J. Thomas (eds), *Neolithic enclosures in Atlantic Northwest Europe*, 111–31. Oxford: Oxbow.

Biskind, P. 2001. *Seeing is believing or how Hollywood taught us to stop worrying and love the 50s*. London: Bloomsbury

Brophy, K. 1999. The cursus monuments of Scotland. In A. Barclay and J. Harding (eds), *Pathways and ceremonies: the cursus monuments of Britain and Ireland*, 119–29. Oxford: Oxbow.

Brophy, K. 2000. Excavations at a cropmark site at Milton of Rattray, Blairgowrie, with a discussion of the pit-defined cursus monuments of Tayside. *Tayside and Fife Archaeological Journal* 6, 8–17.

Brophy, K. forthcoming a. The map trap and the gap. Looking behind distribution maps. In G.J. Barclay and K. Brophy (eds), *Regional diversity in the Neolithic of Britain and Ireland*. Oxford: Oxbow.

Brophy, K. forthcoming b. *The cursus monuments of Scotland*. Edinburgh: RCAHMS.

Cameron, I. and Pye, D. (eds) 1996. *The movie book of the Western*. London: Studio Vista.

Cooney, G. 2001. Bringing contemporary baggage to Neolithic landscapes. In B. Bender and M. Winer (eds), *Contested landscapes: movement, exile and place*, 165–80. Oxford: Berg

Darvill, T. 2001 Neolithic enclosures in the Isle of Man. In T. Darvill and J. Thomas (eds), *Neolithic enclosures in Atlantic Northwest Europe*, 155–70. Oxford: Oxbow.

Darvill, T. and Thomas, J. 2001a. Neolithic enclosures in Atlantic Northwest Europe: some recent trends. In T. Darvill and J. Thomas (eds), *Neolithic enclosures in Atlantic Northwest Europe*, 1–23. Oxford: Oxbow.

Darvill, T. and Thomas, J. (eds) 2001b. *Neolithic enclosures in Atlantic Northwest Europe*. Oxford: Oxbow

Frayling, C. 1998. *Spaghetti westerns: cowboys and Europeans from Karl May to Sergio Leone*. London: IB Taurus.

Frayling, C. 2000. *Sergio Leone: something to do with death*. London: Faber and Faber.

Harding, J. 1991. Using the unique as typical: monuments and the ritual landscape. In P. Garwood, D. Jennings, R. Skeates and J. Toms (eds), *Sacred and Profane*, 141–51. Oxford: Oxbow.

Horne, P.D., MacLeod, D. and Oswald, A. 2002. The seventieth causewayed enclosure in the British Isles? In G. Varndell and P/ Topping (eds), *Enclosures in Neolithic Europe: essays on causewayed and non-causewayed sites*, 115–120. Oxford Oxbow.

Gibson, A.M. 1998. Hindwell and the Neolithic palisaded enclosures of Britain and Ireland. In A. M. Gibson and D. Simpson (eds), *Prehistoric ritual and religion. Essays in honour of Aubrey Burl*, 68–79. Stroud: Sutton Publishing.

King, M. D. 1993. Leadketty (Dunning parish): late Neolithic or EBA potsherd. *Discovery and Excavation, Scotland* 1993, 102.

Loveday, R. 1985. *Cursuses and related monuments of the British Neolithic*. Unpublished PhD Thesis: University of Leicester.

Maltby, R. 1996. A better sense of history. John Ford and the Indians. In I. Cameron and D. Pye (eds), *The movie book of the Western*, 24–49. London: Studio Vista.

Mercer, R.J. 1983. Spott Dod: crop-mark enclosure. *Discovery and Excavation in Scotland* 1983, 19.

Mercer, R.J. 1990. *Causewayed enclosures*. Princes Risborough: Shire.

Oswald, A., Dyer, C. and Barber, M. 2001. *The creation of monuments: Neolithic causewayed enclosures in the British Isles*. Swindon: English Heritage.

Pye, D. 1996. Double vision. Miscegenation and Point of View in *The Searchers*. In I. Cameron and D. Pye (eds), *The movie book of the Western*, 229–35. London: Studio Vista.

RCAHMS. 1997. *East Dumfries-shire: an archaeological landscape*. Edinburgh: Her Majesty's Stationary Office.

Sheridan, A. 2001. Donegore Hill and other Irish Neolithic enclosures: a view from the outside. In T. Darvill and J. Thomas (eds), *Neolithic enclosures in Atlantic Northwest Europe*, 171–89. Oxford: Oxbow.

Smith, I.M. 1991. Sprouston, Roxburghshire: an early Anglian centre of the eastern Tweed basin. *Proceedings of the Society of Antiquaries of Scotland* 121, 261–94

Thomas, J. 1998. Pict's Knowe, Holywood and Holm. Prehistoric sites in the Dumfries area. *Current Archaeology* 160, 149–60

Thomas, J. 1999. *Understanding the Neolithic*. London: Routledge

Thomas, J. 2001. Neolithic enclosures: reflections on excavation in Wales and Scotland. In T. Darvill and J. Thomas (eds), *Neolithic enclosures in Atlantic Northwest Europe*, 132–143. Oxford: Oxbow.

Varndell, G. and Topping, P. (eds) 2002. *Enclosures in Neolithic Europe: essays on causewayed and non-causewayed sites*. Oxford: Oxbow.

Waddington, C. 2001. Breaking out of the morphological straitjacket: early Neolithic enclosures in northern Britain. *Durham Archaeological Journal* 16, 1–14.

Wainright, G.J. 1969. A review of henge monuments in light of recent research. *Proceedings of the Prehistoric Society* 35, 112–33.

6 Tales of the land, tales of the sea: people and presence in the Neolithic of Man and beyond

Timothy Darvill

Introduction

Once it was all so easy. The sea was conceived either as a barrier to communication, or a superhighway that promoted and facilitated interaction between scattered communities. Cecil Fox indeed managed to have it both ways in his now classic work *The personality of Britain*, arguing that people who saw the sea as a barrier to be overcome tended to occupy eastern and southern Britain, while the early navigators occupied the Atlantic coasts (Fox 1933, 17). The Isle of Man, set in the middle of what Mackinder (1907, 20; and see Bowen 1970) fondly referred to as the British Mediterranean, lay firmly within the Atlantic province and was thus liable to influence not only from surrounding areas, but also those further afield to the north and south (Fig. 6.1). Davies (1945, 125) wrote of the seabourne nature of the 'megalithic cult' of southern and western Europe and suggested that megalith-using communities selected distinctive environments in which to settle.

With the emergence of a more explicitly cultural-historical approach through the middle decades of the twentieth century such a view came under scrutiny. Stuart Piggott saw the earlier Neolithic of Man as firmly within the primary colonization zone of his Clyde-Carlingford Culture (1954, 152), well represented by long barrows and chambered tombs, and the local tradition of Mull Hill style pottery. In Piggott's model these communities were replaced by the Ronaldsway Culture which he saw as a classic secondary Neolithic development with "notable insular individuality" (1954, 351). Superficially, this was a case of people colonizing an area and then cutting themselves off from surrounding communities. But the detail was rather different. When looking into the ancestry of the Ronaldsway Neolithic, Piggott cites *comparanda* suggesting links not just within the Irish Sea basin but as far afield as Iberia in the south and Norway to the north (1954, 351). Subconsciously perhaps, Piggott was perpetuating Fox's Atlantic seaways model, and while the seeds of an insular Neolithic had been sown, few took root.

Through the 1960s and 1970s descriptions and considerations of the Manx Neolithic tended to emphasize an eclectic mix of influences. Debates about the integrity of the Clyde-Carlingford Culture helped break down the coherence of that cultural province, and allowed A. E. P. Collins to exclude the Manx tombs from his separated Clyde and Carlingford Groups (1973, figure 1). He speculatively explained outliers to his core distributions as the work of adventurers who voyaged out from the homeland settlement areas. Michael Herity (1970, 30–3) emphasized the existence of provincial fashions in tomb building, while Audrey Henshall took a similarly eclectic approach to the inspirations behind what she considered to be a diverse group of megalithic monuments characterized by their individuality (Henshall 1978, 171). Peter Moffatt went further in his review of the Ronaldsway Culture by suggesting, perhaps rather blandly, that the term "Ronaldsway Culture" be abandoned and that the material culture of third millennium BC communities on the island should simply be seen as a local variation of those prevalent throughout the British Isles (Moffatt 1978, 215). By the time that Richard Bradley and Bob Chapman (1984; 1986) came to apply Colin Renfrew's Peer Polity Interaction model to western Britain, Man seems to be considered part of an indistinct but widespread cultural background, outside the hot-spots of passage grave building and Grooved Ware usage (Bradley 1984, figure 3.5). But to an extent such a view was based more on an absence of evidence than any real evidence of absence. Despite some important results from rescue excavations, occasional stray finds, and the picture gradually emerging from surface collections assembled by amateur enthusiasts, early farming communities on the island were not major research priorities during the later twentieth century and figure little in the archaeological literature of the period.

This began to change in 1995 with the establishment of the Billown Neolithic Landscape Project, based on the Southern Plain of the island (see Fig. 6.1), with the overall aim of developing an understanding of the changing landscapes of Billown area between about 5000 BC and 2000 BC (Darvill 1996, 9)[1]. Excavations at the Billown Quarry Site, extensive geophysical and geochemical surveys, and sample excavations in surrounding areas have provided new insights into the materiality of the fifth, fourth, and third millennia BC. Especially important

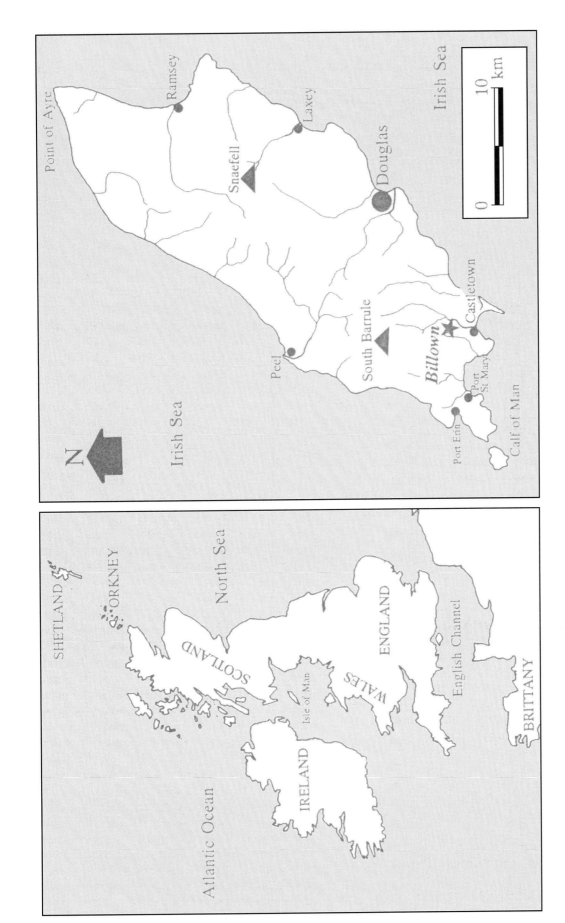

Figure 6.1. *Location of the Isle of Man in the Irish Sea area (left) and the position of Billown (right).*

was the discovery of kinds of archaeology previously unrecorded on the island: for example, enclosures, pit clusters, pit circles, timber settings, a mini-henge, and a possible cursus or long mound (see Darvill 2001 with earlier references). Along with the re-examination of previously recorded long barrows, passage graves, entrance graves, stone circles, standing stones, and domestic occupations, it is at last becoming possible to re-examine the archaeology of the island and relate it to that of adjacent lands around the Irish Sea, and indeed beyond to the Western Approaches, Celtic Sea, and English Channel coastlands.

Questions of interaction are far from simple. Notions of human agency and cultural practice take us far from the dualist, essentially deterministic, models of Fox's day, and the eclecticism of the 1970s, towards more socially constituted interpretations. Here I would like to argue for a nested scheme of cultural interaction around the Irish Sea and to regions beyond. On the one hand this involved the inward-looking production of local identity while, on the other hand, outward-looking region identities based around the manipulation and generation of common experiences. As illustrations, I would like briefly to consider three strands of material culture spanning different scales of action and engagement: pits; pottery and quartz pebbles; and the façade structures of long barrows.

Figure 6.2. Billown Quarry Site, Isle of Man. Two Neolithic pits part excavated. The scales each total 2m. [Photograph by Timothy Darvill].

Pits – form and process

Turning first to pits we encounter one of the most ubiquitous feature of fifth to second millennia BC archaeology. Julian Thomas memorably refers to the act of digging a pit as "part of the transformation of place" (1991, 76), but while it is tempting to see them all as somehow similar Christopher Houlder's analysis of the examples excavated at Hazard Hill, Devon (1963, 14–19) should warn against such a simplistic approach. His useful, if provisional, interpretive sequence included:

– Depressions
– Cooking-hole
– Quarry pit
– Food storage pit
– Water storage pit
– Pot stands

Similar variations can be seen in the evidence from other sites where pits are well-represented. With reference to the evidence from Hurst Fen, Suffolk, Clark (1960, 210–11) concluded that most of the 200 pits and hollows excavated at the site were the truncated remains of food storage pits, the larger examples being regarded as 'silos'. At Broome Heath, Norfolk, Wainwright (1972, 12) recognized three main types of pit amongst the 67 examples excavated: those with bowl-shaped profiles, those with a flat base, and those that appeared to have

been dug to contain square (presumably wooden) containers. Chronologically, the pits were distributed through a long period and suggested to the excavator that a community revisited the same site as part of a regular cycle (Wainwright 1972, 22). At Eaton Heath, Norfolk, the dozen or so Neolithic pits seem, from the published sections, to be similar to those from Broome Heath, but at Eaton there are also more than 20 deep pits or shafts with more or less vertical sides (Wainwright 1973, 12–23). These include shallow shafts (up to 2.8m deep), deep shafts (up to 8.0m deep), and double shafts. The quantity of finds from the pits and shafts was rather less than from similar features at Broome Heath and Hurst Fen. The character of the material was also different, especially the worked flint assemblage (Wainwright 1973, 9). Together, these three East Anglian sites illustrate the very considerable diversity that exists. The superficial simplicity of what is essentially a hole in the ground has perhaps clouded visions of the importance and potential of these features and serious research into their nature, content, and social context is urgently needed. Two points though are important here. First, is the longevity and wide distribution of the tradition of pit digging through the fourth and third millennia BC and the fact that the sequence and clustering of pits at many sites suggests periodic visits to a particular place, and the perpetuation of traditions based around delving into the ground (Pollard 2001). Second, is that while pits are rarely considered 'monumental' in the sense traditionally applied to far more spectacular Neolithic structures, they in fact embody many key elements of monumentality and sometimes form the earliest components of long constructional sequences that end in substantial and enduring structures such as tombs and enclosures. In this Thomas's (1991,76) recognition of the way that the digging of pits constitutes part of the process of creating the significance of place is perfectly right, but must be set against the need to isolate and archaeologically define the social context and intentionality of the acts represented.

At Billown pit digging began early, around the middle of the fifth millennium BC, with generally small, relatively shallow constructions that are perhaps better seen as sub-soil hollows than pits *per se*. Later examples included far larger and deeper structures (Fig. 6.2), some rather more in the form of shafts and others as distinct clusters. Most contain broken incomplete vessels and a few worked flints, but all contain either a hearth or spreads of charcoal-rich soil suggesting that a hearth had been situated adjacent to the pit and contributed material directly into the fills. Carbonized cereal grain, fruit stones, and hazelnut shells characterize the palaeobotanical assemblages; bone is not preserved on the site but may have been represented as another dimension to the character of the fills. What is clear from the excavation of these features and the preliminary analysis of the finds and environmental samples is that these are not directly connected with occupation, nor can they be considered repositories for carefully and deliberately placed deposits. It is suggested that the act of making a hole into the ground was the primary purpose, the material that became associated with the fills is the result of using that hole for a short period perhaps as the setting for a short vigil or 'watch', after which the hole was abandoned. Such pits may be referred to as *'fossa'*[2]. At Billown some were later re-cut by overlapping pits while others were presumably succeeded by new pits when the need to use one next arose. The distribution of these pits is also notable. All lie on the north side and perhaps just outside of a substantial Neolithic enclosure. Broadly similar groups of pits have been recorded outside Neolithic enclosures elsewhere in Britain. At Robin Hood's Ball, Wiltshire, the examination of a flint scatter recorded north-east of the main enclosure revealed five pits within an area 10m by 10m (Richards 1990, 61–5). At Windmill Hill, also in Wiltshire, the excavation of two areas to the south-east of the well-studied enclosure, within what was considered to be a depleted flint-scatter, revealed individual and clustered pits of early and late Neolithic date, some of which were interpreted as indicating a tradition of special visits to a special place (Whittle *et al.* 2000, 131). Attention to the areas around other sites would no doubt reveal more cases.

Elsewhere on the Isle of Man hollows, pits and pit groups have been noted at Phert, Ballavarry, Ballateare, and elsewhere (for a summary see Burrow 1997, 36–45), although they are not all directly comparable to the Billown cases. At Phert, for example, cliff erosion has

Figure 6.3. Billown Quarry Site. Excavation of a Ronaldsway earthfast jar within the small circular pit in which it had been buried. The alluminium foil around the top inside edge of the vessel was used to line the empty vessel before filling it with inert material prior to excavation. [Photograph by Timothy Darvill].

yielded large quantities of pottery and worked flint, a saddle quern, and a 'grain store' (Burrow 1997, 43). Pits are also found widely if sporadically around the Irish Sea and Atlantic fringe beyond, but again caution is needed as not all seem to be the same. One of the most well-known such group is at Goodland on a chalk ridge at the extreme northeast corner of Ireland. Excavated by Humphrey Case, there were about 170 identified pits within and outwith what appears to be a small ditched enclosure (Case 1973, figure 2). The presence of broken and incomplete pottery vessels and worked flint suggested to Case that the pits contained ritually deposited samples of settlement-soil brought to the site from elsewhere (1973, 188). Other interpretations have been offered however, Cooney (2000, 16) emphasizing the extraction and working of flint while Herity (1982, 265) includes the site in his list of habitations. The quantity and variety of finds from the Goodland pits stands in contrast to the evidence from Billown, as does the physical form of the pits themselves. Other pit groups are known at Linford, Co. Antrim, Ireland (Cooney 2000, 16); Luce Sands, Galloway (Cowie 1996) in south-west Scotland; and Llanilar adjacent to the Afon Ystwyth near Aberystwyth, Ceredigion, in west Wales (Briggs 2000). This last-

Figure 6.4. *Cashtal yn Ard long barrow, Isle of Man. View of the central façade and entrance to the chamber looking southeast. [Photograph by Timothy Darvill].*

mentioned site, known only as a result of salvage excavations carried out between 1980 and 1994, has more than a dozen scoops and pits, physically very similar to the smaller examples at Billown with burnt material incorporated in the fills as well as fragmentary pottery, worked flint, carbonized plant remains, and small amounts of cremated bone.

Changes through time are also important in looking at the nature of some kinds of pit and their use. Mainly on the basis of material from southern and eastern England, Josh Pollard has argued that a number of differences can be seen in the construction and use of ceremonial pits as between the earlier and later Neolithic, the later examples involving "a more explicit process of signification, and at the same time a greater degree of elaboration and invention in their enactment" (Pollard 2001, 325). Here attention is focused on content as much as structure, but similar traditions expressed in slightly different ways can perhaps be glimpsed in the Irish Sea area, and certainly there are important parallels on the Isle of Man which are best seen in the treatment of particular kinds of material culture.

The content of pits – pottery and quartz

Pottery and white quartz pebbles are amongst the most frequent finds from pits and ditches at Billown. Features of the fourth millennium BC tend to include pottery that is rather broken, the vessels represented fragmentary, and the sherds themselves well-scattered. This material is the classic Mull Hill style pottery first characterized by Stuart Piggott back in the 1930s on the basis of a large assemblage from the eponymous multiple passage grave overlooking Port Erin on the southern tip of the Island

(Piggott 1932). The Mull Hill tradition includes both plain and decorated round-bottomed shouldered vessels which share general appearances with other contemporary ceramics in Ireland and south-west Scotland, but as Stephen Burrow has pointed out "the specific design styles of these areas were adapted for use in the Isle of Man ... to create a unique interpretation of shouldered pottery" (1997, 16). Here then the Manx Neolithic communities are representing a distinct identity in the creation of their material culture, yet using it within more widely shared practices for the generation of experiences.

Rather different patterns emerge in the third millennium BC, when pottery in pits was more often deposited as whole vessels – the earthfast jars that represent such a distinctive feature of the Manx later Neolithic (Fig. 6.3). The process of deposition here involved: digging a neat circular pit; setting the pot into the pit with its top well below what would have been the contemporary ground surface; re-filling the pit at least to the top of the pot; and then placing a cover-slab over the mouth of the empty pot. Whether this structure was then fully covered with soil or remained accessible in the bottom of a hollow in the ground is not known, although most authorities prefer the latter. In such circumstances the pot may well be seen as a metaphor for what in earlier times, and in other contexts, was the ritual pit or shaft leading into the earth. The opportunity to re-open the pot may perhaps be a more 'inventive way', to use Josh Pollard's words cited above, of periodically re-digging a pit. Like the earlier pits, the earthfast jars seem to have been empty in the ground. This is how they are found when undamaged examples are excavated. Geochemical analysis of the Billown examples has yielded only negative results, although it is recognized that they could have held water or other liquids or substances that leave no distinctive

Figure 6.5. *Grey Mare and Her Colts long barrow, Dorset. View of the façade looking west. [Photograph by Timothy Darvill].*

geochemical fingerprint. Experiments are planned to examine the potential for these vessels to collect and hold natural rainwater and groundwater.

Closely associated with the pits, associated ditches, and earthfast jars at Billown and elsewhere are white quartz pebbles. These are beach pebbles brought to the site from at least 3–4km away and deliberately deposited at the site. I have argued elsewhere that the white colour is symbolically significant and that these stones may be seen as tokens of the human spirit (Darvill 2002). More than 600 were recovered from the site between 1995 and 1998, in some cases apparently carefully placed on the floors of ditches and pits. Again, white quartz is widely associated with fourth and third millennia BC sites around the Irish Sea, especially chambered tombs of various sorts. Examples in the Isle of Man include: around a standing stone in or under the cairn of Cashtal yn Ard (Fleure and Neely 1936, 388–9; Darvill and Chartrand 2000, 42) and in all of the chambers of the multiple passage grave on Mull Hill (Piggott 1932, 148). Further afield mention may be made of the quartz set around the revetment of Cairnholy I (Piggott and Powell 1949, 110) and amongst the façade blocking at Beacharra (Scott 1964, 150) in south-west Scotland (and see Henshall 1972, 97 and 150–1 for general comments). In Ireland, numerous court tombs, passage graves, and wedge tombs contain quartz (for details see Corcoran 1960, 107 and O'Brian 1999, 215–6), and it is also present in all three of the developed passage graves on Anglesey (Lynch 1969, 150). The acts associated with the use of white quartz pebbles, like the digging of *fossa*, must be seen as the materiality for a very broad and widely understood set of beliefs or understandings. It is most notable within the Atlantic coast area, perhaps because it is here that white quartz pebbles naturally occur very commonly on beaches and

in river valleys. The practice is perhaps represented in areas well-removed from good natural sources though, for example Nympsfield, Notgrove and Rodmarton, amongst the Cotswold Severn long barrows of Gloucestershire (Clifford 1950, 204). Here it is notable that another uniting element is the presence of long barrows that were constructed and used mainly in the fourth millennium BC.

Long barrow façades

The construction and architecture of chambered tombs has for decades provided one of the main strands in thinking about cultural interactions between regions of the British Isles and beyond. Indeed, Glyn Daniel recognized and discussed at some length the inter-related character of the Irish Sea groups in his analysis of the origins and dating of chambered tombs in England and Wales (Daniel 1950, 149–54). Perhaps not unexpectedly much of the discussion of these monuments has focused on their ground-plans and overall design, yet, as all visitors to extant examples know, these are very much three-dimensional structures in which architecture determines experience and engagement.

One of the most distinctive elements of the known long barrows on the Isle of Man, all of which seem to occur in the north-eastern part of the island (Darvill 2000, figure 32.2), is the use of large and distinctively shaped stones as components of the façades. At Cashtal yn Ard, a stone with tapering sides and a pointed top stands on the left as the observer looks towards the back of the forecourt in juxtaposition to a more parallel sided flat-topped stone to the right (Fig. 6.4. See Darvill and Chartrand 2000 for description of the site). The façade of the north-eastern chamber at King Orry's Grave has the flat-topped stone on the left and a more pointed one to the right; the same probably applies in the less well-preserved south-western chamber although only the right-hand (pointed) stone survives here (Gale *et al.* 1999). Around the Irish Sea a regular pattern emerges in the façades of long barrows. At Cairnholy I, for example, the eight stones of the façade are split into two groups one either side of the entrance. The southern half is laid out on a shallow but more or less regular curve and the stones are graded in height with the shortest on the outside and the tallest in the centre. They comprise two pairs of shaped stones with the pointed example to the left and the flat-topped example to the right. The northern half consists of an almost straight line of stones, not graded in height and with two flat-topped examples to the right and two pointed examples to the left (Piggott and Powell 1949, figure 5).

In Ireland, the pairing of flat-topped and pointed stones can be seen in court tombs, as for example at Ballymacdermot, Armagh (Collins and Wilson 1964) and Creevykeel, Sligo (Hencken 1939), and in wedge tombs as for example at Culleens, Sligo (Ó Nualláin 1989, 35 and plate 14). Crossing the Irish Sea, at Trefignath, Anglesey, the stones flanking the entrance to the chamber of the third-phase barrow appear from the front as a slender pointed stone to the left and a broader side-on stone to the right. The effect is achieved by the way the stones are positioned as much as their actual shape (Smith and Lynch 1987, figures 18 and 19).

To the south there are abundant further examples of what can be taken to be the same tradition. At Wayland's Smithy, Oxfordshire, the classic Cotswold-Severn long barrow (Barrow II) has a slightly lozenge-shaped stone to the left of the entrance into the chamber and a flat-topped example to the right (Whittle 1991). The Grey Mare and Her Colts near the Dorset coast of the English Channel, shows the same pattern in a monument that has many other similarities with long barrows in the Irish Sea province (Fig. 6.5. See Piggott 1945 for description of the site).

This same pairing of pointed-topped stones with flat-topped or rounded-topped pillars can be seen continuing into the third millennium BC and beyond with the pairing of stones in the stone circles and West Kennet Avenue at Avebury; the bluestones either side of the north-eastern axis of Stonehenge; and ultimately the widely occurring pairs of standing stones generally assigned a second millennium BC date (Burl 1993, 181–202).

Sexual symbolism has often been linked to this pairing of distinctively shaped stones. When discussing Cashtal yn Ard following its excavation in the early 1930s, Fleure and Neely suggested that the pointed (left-hand) stone was phallic in form and may thus be considered 'male', while the flat-topped (right-hand) stone should be considered 'female'. This possibility may be reinforced by the presence of a longitudinal groove in the top of the

'female' stone which, if not natural in origin, they suggested may represent a vulva (Fleure and Neely 1936, 394–5)[3]. Discussing the Avebury stones, Keiller and Piggott (1930, 420) note the two main forms: Type A generally tall and thin and Type B generally broad and lozenge shape, leaving Isobel Smith to postulate male and female symbolism (1965, 251). Estyn Evans (1966, 204) took the same view as Fleure and Neely when considering paired stones in Country Tyrone, and Burl (1993, 181) follows this through for paired stones generally. Interestingly, amongst standing stones it is the lozenge or flattish topped stones that tend to carry rock art in the form of cup-marks. The interpretation of this extremely common and widely used motif is fraught with difficulties, but in Scandinavian rock art at least their association with what appear to be depictions of females (the cup-mark is sometimes placed between the legs) suggests that they may be 'female' gendered and perhaps sexually charged symbols (see Coles 1990, 16 and 24–5; 2000, 31–47). Examples of cup-marked and cup- and ring-marked stone pairs in Britain include Crofthead, Perthshire (Burl 1993, 181), Barningham Moor, County Durham (Beckensall 1999, plate 4); and possibly the western stone in pair 25 of the West Kennet Avenue (cf. Keiller and Piggott 1936, figure 7; but cf. Smith 1965, 223). Indeed one may speculate that the cutting of cup-marks and hollows into a stone surface may not be so different from making pits in the ground in a way that perhaps begins to bind together some of the practices discussed in the foregoing sections.

Conclusions

This brief excursion into a few select aspects of the materialized Neolithic world of the Isle of Man and surrounding areas is in part an attempt to move away from the reconstruction of social and community relations through resort to distributions of broad monument classes and large undifferentiated categories of data. Such things may be useful in delineating general study areas, but in general relate to quite different scales of analysis to that which can be recovered through detailed fieldwork, survey, and the examination of human practice and social action in the archaeological record.

Taking the evidence from Billown and other Manx Neolithic sites I have proposed that there is a number of high-level similarities in material culture which are brought about by common patterns of social action and shared cultural conceptions that perhaps represent the visible materialized dimensions of more broadly-based and geographically widespread cosmologies. Pit digging, the use of quartz pebbles, and the incorporation of symbolically meaningful stones in the façades of long barrows are just examples of a much wider range of activities with strong material expression. In this sense it can be suggested that there was a fairly high degree of cultural interaction within the Irish Sea region – in human terms the 'Tales of the Sea' in my title. At a second level, and geographically much more restricted, the production and treatment of material culture suggests that local identities were produced and manipulated through the generation of distinctive experiences, for example the peculiarities of the local ceramic sequences and the idiosyncratic use of earthfast jars. These emphasize a quite different scale of thinking and may well have originated locally, prompted perhaps by 'Tales of the Land'. Thus rather than thinking in terms of simple oppositions as between communities that were highly interactive and those that were essentially insular, a more nested approach to social identity and materiality can be proposed in which practices in any particular area include multi-scaled translations of regionally derived and locally generated practice.

Notes

1   The Billown Neolithic Landscape Project is being undertaken by the School of Conservation Sciences at Bournemouth University in association with Manx National Heritage.
2   This follows the anatomical usage of the term to describe a hollow or depression in the surface of a bone or similar. Gerhard Bersu suggested the term *ustrinae* for comparable features uncovered at Ballateare, Isle of Man (1947, 167) but this terms implies a particular set of circumstances surrounding their formation which involved the cremation of human corpses over the holes. There is no evidence for this in the Manx examples.
3   A similar feature may be represented at the Grey Mare and Her Colts, Dorset. On the top of the right-hand flat-topped stone there is a slight ovoid indentation in more or less the same position as the one referred to here at Cashtal yn Ard.

Acknowledgements

I would like to thank Vanessa Constant, Louise Pearson, Damian Evans, Miles Russell, Kevin Andrews, and Roger Doonan for their help in working on the Billown material, and Peter Davey, Jenny Woodcock, Andrew Johnson, Andrew Foxon, Sinead McCartan, Robbie Farrar, Robbie Middleton, and Alan Skillan for comments and advice on the Manx material.

References

Beckensall, S. 1999. *British prehistoric rock art*. Stroud: Tempus.

Bersu, G. 1947. A cemetery of the Ronaldsway Culture at Ballateare, Jurby, Isle of Man. *Proceedings of the Prehistoric Society* 13, 161–69.

Bowen, E.G. 1970. Britain and the British Seas. In D. Moore (ed.), *The Irish Sea Province in archaeology and history*, 13–28. Cardiff: Cambrian Archaeological Association

Bradley, R. 1984. *The social foundations of prehistoric Britain*. London. Longman.

Bradley, R. and Chapman, R. 1984. Passage graves in the European Neolithic – a theory of converging evolution. In G. Burenhult (ed.), *The archaeology of Carrowmore*, 348–56. Stockholm: Institute of Archaeology at the University of Stockholm.

Bradley, R. and Chapman, R. 1986. The nature and development of long-distance relations in later Neolithic Britain and Ireland. In C. Renfrew and J. Cherry (eds), *Peer polity interaction and socio-political change*, 127–58. Cambridge: Cambridge University Press.

Briggs, S. (ed.), 2000. A Neolithic and early Bronze Age settlement and burial complex at Llanilar, Ceredigion. *Archaeologia Cambrensis* 146, 13–59.

Burl, A. 1993. *From Carnac to Callanish. The prehistoric stone rows and avenues of Britain, Ireland and Brittany*. London and New Haven: Yale University Press.

Burrow, S. 1997. *The Neolithic culture of the Isle of Man*. Oxford: British Archaeological Reports, British Series 263.

Case, H. 1973. A ritual site in north-east Ireland. In G. Daniel and P. Kjærum (eds), *Megalithic graves and ritual: papers presented at the III Atlantic Colloquium, Moesgård 1969*, 173–96. København: Jutland Archaeological Society.

Clark, J.G.D. 1960. Excavations at the Neolithic sire at Hurst Fen, Mildenhall, Suffolk, 1954, 1957 and 1958. *Proceedings of the Prehistoric Society* 26, 202–45.

Clifford, E.M. 1950. The Cotswold megalithic culture: the grave goods and their background. In C. Fox and B. Dickens (eds), *The early cultures of north-west Europe. H M Chadwick memorial studies*, 21–40. Cambridge: Cambridge University Press.

Coles, J. 1990. *Images of the past. A guide to the rock carving and other ancient monuments of Northern Bohuslän*. Uddevalla: Bohusläns Museum.

Coles, J. 2000. *Patterns in a rocky land: rock carvings in south-west Uppland, Sweden*. Uppsala: Department of Archaeology and Ancient History, Uppsala University.

Collins, A.E.P. 1973. A re-examination of the Clyde-Carlingford tombs. In G. Daniel and P. Kjærum (eds), *Megalithic graves and ritual: papers presented at the III Atlantic Colloquium, Moesgård*, 105–116. København: Jutland Archaeological Society.

Collins, A.E.P. and Wilson, B. 1964. The excavation of a court cairn at Ballymacdermot, Co Armagh. *Ulster Journal of Archaeology* 27, 3–22.

Cooney, G. 2000. *Landscapes of Neolithic Ireland*. London: Routledge.

Corcoran, J. X.W.P. 1960. The Carlingford Culture. *Proceedings of the Prehistoric Society* 26, 98–148.

Cowie, T. 1996. Torrs Warren, Luce Sands, Galloway. *Transactions of the Dummfriesshire and Galloway Natural History and Archaeological Society* 71, 11–105.

Daniel, G.E. 1950. *The prehistoric chamber tombs of England and Wales*. Cambridge: Cambridge University Press.

Darvill, T. 1996. *Billown Neolithic Landscape Project, Isle of Man, 1995*. Bournemouth and Douglas: Bournemouth University and Manx National Heritage.

Darvill, T. 2000. Neolithic Mann in context. In A. Ritchie (ed.), *Neolithic Orkney in its European context*, 371–85. Oxford: Oxbow.

Darvill, T. 2001. *Billown Neolithic landscape project, Isle of Man. Sixth report: 2000*. Bournemouth and Douglas: Bournemouth University and Manx National Heritage.

Darvill, T. 2002. White on blonde: quartz pebbles and the use of quartz at Neolithic monuments in the Isle of Man and beyond. In A. Jones and G. MacGregor (eds), *Colouring the past,* 73–91. Oxford: Berg.

Darvill, T. and Chartrand, J. 2000. A survey of the chambered long barrow at Cashtal yn Ard, Maughold. In T. Darvill, *Billown Neolithic Landscape Project, Isle of Man. Fifth report: 1999,* 34–44. Bournemouth and Douglas: Bournemouth University and Manx National Heritage.

Davies, M. 1945. Types of megalithic monuments of the Irish Sea and North Channel coastlands: a study in distributions. *Antiquaries Journal* 25, 125–44.

Davies, M. 1946. The diffusion and distribution pattern of the megalithic monuments of the Irish Sea and North Channel coastlands. *Antiquaries Journal* 26, 38–60.

Evans, E.E. 1966. *Prehistoric and early Christian Ireland: a guide.* London: Batsford.

Fleure, H.J. and Neely, G.J.H. 1936. Cashtal yn Ard, Isle of Man. *Antiquaries Journal* 16, 373–95.

Fox, C. 1933. *The personality of Britain: its influence on inhabitant and invader in prehistoric and early historic times.* Cardiff: National Museum of Wales.

Gale, J., Darvill, T., Chartrand, J. and Watson, C. 1999. A survey of the chambered long barrows at King Orry's Grave, Laxey. In T. Darvill, *Billown Neolithic landscape project, Isle of Man. Fourth report,* 54–63. Bournemouth and Douglas: Bournemouth University and Manx National Heritage.

Hencken, H.O'N. 1939. A long cairn at Creevykeel, Co Sligo. *Journal of the Royal Society of Antiquaries of Ireland* 69, 53–98.

Henshall, A.S. 1972. *The chambered tombs of Scotland. Volume 2.* Edinburgh: Edinburgh University Press.

Henshall, A.S. 1978. Manx megaliths again: an attempt at structural analysis. In P.J. Davey (ed.), *Man and environment in the Isle of Man,* 171–217. Oxford: British Archaeological Reports, British Series 54.

Herity, M. 1970. The early prehistoric period around the Irish Sea. In D. Moore (ed.), *The Irish Sea Province in archaeology and history,* 29–37. Cardiff: Cambrian Archaeological Association

Herity, M. 1982. Irish decorated Neolithic pottery. *Proceedings of the Royal Irish Academy* 82, 247–404.

Houlder, C. 1963. A Neolithic settlement on Hazard Hill, Totnes. *Transactions of the Devon Archaeological Exploration Society* 21, 2–30.

Keiller, A. and Piggott, S. 1936. Recent excavations at Avebury. *Antiquity* 10, 417–27.

Lynch, F. M. 1969. The contents of excavated tombs in North Wales. In T.G.E. Powell, J.X.W.P. Corcoran, F. Lynch and J.G. Scott, *Megalithic enquiries in the west of Britain,* 149–74. Liverpool: Liverpool University Press.

Mackinder, H.J. 1907. *Britain and the British seas.* Oxford: Clarendon Press.

Moffatt, P. 1978. The Ronaldsway culture: a review. In P.J. Davey (ed.), *Man and environment in the Isle of Man,* 177–217. Oxford: British Archaeological Reports, British Series 54.

O'Brian, W. 1999. *Sacred ground. Megalithic tombs in coastal southwest Ireland.* Galway: Department of Archaeology, National University of Ireland.

Ó Nualláin, S. 1989. *Survey of the megalithic tombs of Ireland. Volume V.* Dublin: Stationery Office.

Piggott, S. 1932. The Mull Hill Circle, Isle of Man, and its pottery. *Antiquaries Journal* 12, 146–57.

Piggott, S. 1945. The chambered cairn of 'The Grey Mare and Colts'. *Proceedings of the Dorset Natural History and Archaeological Society* 67, 30–34.

Piggott, S. 1954. *The Neolithic cultures of the British Isles.* Cambridge: Cambridge University Press.

Piggott, S. and Powell, T.G.E. 1949. The excavation of three Neolithic chambered tombs in Galloway, 1949. *Proceedings of the Society of Antiquaries of Scotland* 83, 103–61.

Pollard, J. 2001. The aesthetics of depositional practice. *World Archaeology* 33, 315–33.

Richards, J. 1990. *The Stonehenge environs project.* London: English Heritage.

Scott, J.G. 1964. The chambered cairn at Beacharra, Kintyre, Argyll. *Proceedings of the Prehistoric Society* 30, 134–58.

Smith, C.A. and Lynch, F.M. 1987. *Trefignath and Din Dryfol. The excavation of two megalithic tombs in Anglesey.* Cardiff: Cambrian Archaeological Association.

Smith, I.F. 1965. *Windmill Hill and Avebury. Excavations by Alexander Keiller 1925–1939.* Oxford: Clarendon Press.

Thomas, J. 1991. *Rethinking the Neolithic.* Cambridge: Cambridge University Press.

Wainwright, G.J. 1972. The excavation of a Neolithic settlement on Broome Heath, Ditchingham, Norfolk, England. *Proceedings of the Prehistoric Society* 38, 1–97.

Wainwright, G.J. 1973. Prehistoric and Romano-British settlements at Eaton Heath, Norwich. *Archaeological Journal* 130, 1–43

Whittle, A.W.R. 1991. Wayland's Smithy, Oxfordshire: excavations at the Neolithic tomb in 1962–63 by R.J.C. Atkinson and S. Piggott. *Proceedings of the Prehistoric Society* 57, 61–101.

Whittle, A., Davies, J.J., Dennis, I., Fairbairn, A.S., and Hamilton, M.A. 2000. Neolithic activity and occupation outside Windmill Hill causewayed enclosure, Wiltshire: survey and excavation 1992–93. *Wiltshire Archaeological and Natural History Magazine* 93, 131–180.

7   Fluid horizons

Aaron Watson

Introduction

This paper considers how perceptions of the Irish Sea are transformed along a journey that leads from Neolithic occupation sites near the shoreline of Cumbria, to major stone axe sources in the high mountains of the Lake District. We know that Neolithic perceptions of this walk are likely to have contrasted with our own, yet we rarely attempt to compensate for these differences. For instance, we use modern abstract knowledge to explain how distant islands are seen to appear over the curve of the earth, yet such understandings were unavailable to people over four thousand years ago. In this study, it is suggested that we try to disentangle our assumptions from the actual observations we make in the landscape, thereby revealing a world that is rather more fluid and dynamic than we might otherwise anticipate. The simplistic use of concepts such as 'intervisibility' is questioned, and a more reflexive and critical approach to landscape fieldwork suggested. While acknowledging that archaeologists may never be able to 'think Neolithic', it is proposed that we routinely challenge modern expectations in order to revitalise interpretation and expand our landscapes of the Neolithic.

Views over the sea

Figures 7.1 and 7.2 encapsulate two perceptions of the Irish Sea that are inextricably interlinked. Figure 7.1 is a map that has been drawn according to traditional conventions of cartographic representation. While the land is depicted with hills and place names, the sea itself is largely a featureless plane. This perspective was constructed from embodied perceptions that have been selectively integrated into an abstracted and objectified view (Thomas 1996, 85). The degree to which a reader will infer information from the diagram will depend to some extent upon their own knowledge and experience of the sea. In contrast, Figure 7.2 is an image of the Irish Sea that I photographed from the western coastline of Cumbria. Moving along this beach, I experienced the sea as a fluid topography of waves and reflections and heard the surf shifting sand and pebbles. I was immersed in a ever-changing multi-sensory encounter with the landscape, yet my perception and understanding of this experience was also being significantly informed and coloured by the knowledge that I had gathered from maps like that shown in Figure 7.1 (Bender 1993, 1–3). This paper will consider how this mixture of personal experience and preconceived knowledge impacts upon archaeological fieldwork. In the first half, I would like to consider these issues of landscape perception in relation to intervisibility and the Irish Sea. In the second half, I will consider some of the implications for our interpretation of the Neolithic.

Dwelling in the landscape

In recent years, there has been considerable discussion of landscape perception. Prehistoric spaces and places have been increasingly understood as multi-sensory experiences within a dynamic material and social world (e.g. Brück 1998; Cummings *et al.* 2002; Jones 1999; Tilley 1994; Whittle 1997; Watson 2001a; 2001b). Perceptions of the landscape need not be fixed, but may embody a multitude of meanings (Bender 1993; 1998; Hirsch and O'Hanlon 1995; Lowenthal 1961). Such an understanding is encapsulated by Ingold who describes landscape as 'the world as it is known to those who dwell therein, who inhabit its places and journey along the paths connecting them' (Ingold 2000, 193). This perspective acknowledges movement and temporality as central to revealing a landscape in which we are personally involved – we must dwell in order to see. For Ingold (2000, 189–90), the practice of archaeology is itself a form of dwelling, a perceptual engagement with the world that seeks 'the past in the landscape'.

Such approaches are being increasingly adopted across landscape archaeology. There has been considerable discussion of the implications of embodied perception in Geographical Information Systems (GIS) and other computer visualisation techniques such as virtual reality. The atheoretical stance once upheld by GIS is increasingly being challenged (Wheatley 1993; Witcher 1999), and questions have been raised as to whether such models

Figure 7.1. The Irish Sea region, showing places mentioned in the text. Ground over 200m is shown in dark grey.

Figure 7.2. Looking across the Irish Sea from a beach in west Cumbria.

represent surrogate realities or pure simulacra, and how they might be situated in relation to fieldwork observation (Earl and Wheatley 2002; Exon *et al.* 2000).

In search of intervisibility

An important component of landscape archaeology is the intervisibility between sites or places in the landscape.

One of the earliest accounts of intervisibility can be accredited to William Stukeley, who observed that round barrows on the hills near Avebury were carefully located so that they were visible from nearby valleys (cited in Fox 1942, 22). Similar observations have since been made elsewhere. For instance, many round barrows in the vicinity of Stonehenge seem to have been deliberately located upon ridges where they appear to surround the stone circle (Cleal *et al.* 1995; Watson 2001c). Intervisibility has also been noted at other prehistoric sites, ranging from megalithic tombs to the situation of rock art (e.g. Bergh 1995; Bradley 1997, 87–8; Phillips and Watson 2000; Phillips 2002), and in recent years GIS studies have increasingly enabled the simulation of these kinds of relationships (e.g. Exon *et al.* 2000; Lock and Harris 1996; Wheatley 1995). One aspect that has arisen from these approaches has been the definition of different kinds of intervisibility. For instance, 'viewshed' describes the region of a landscape that can be viewed from a given location, while 'false cresting' denotes the deliberate situation of a site upon a hill where it is seen against the sky.

I would now like to explore the assumptions under which intervisibility is observed by challenging the apparently straightforward notion that 'Point A is visible from Point B'. To consider this issue I will take a journey from the beach (Fig. 7.2) on the west coast of Cumbria to the top of the tallest mountain in the region. Ingold (2000, 208) has declared that archaeology is the study of 'the temporality of the landscape', and in describing my encounters with a landscape across several years I hope to convey a sense of its transient qualities. Rather than a telling of a spherical earth, we shall encounter islands that rise from the depths of the sea.

Lands beyond the horizon

Neolithic people inhabited the western lowlands of Cumbria (Fig. 7.3). Flint pebbles were collected from the shoreline and extensive scatters of artefacts have been found across the nearby coastal plain (Cherry and Cherry 1983; 1984; 1985; 1986; 1987). There were a number of stone circles in the vicinity (Waterhouse 1985), with the ring of Grey Croft being built within sight and sound of the sea.

Looking out to sea from a beach nearby, distant islands are visible on the horizon (Fig. 7.4). These views change continuously with the weather (Fig. 7.5), and over short periods of time the landforms can appear faint, translucent, or even fade away altogether. In the west of Britain, there are mythologies that describe phantom islands and mystical lands across the sea (Bord and Bord 1995, 68–86). Might such accounts reflect these transient characteristics?

Without the assistance of a map, it is extremely difficult to relate to the islands visible from the coast of Cumbria. There are isolated peaks to the north-west, several to the south-west and an extended island between. Most significantly, some of these 'islands' are actually illusions. Only the Isle of Man to the west is a true island (Fig. 7.4) whereas none of the others appear on any map. The islands to the south-west are, in reality, a distant view of the high peaks of north Wales, while the islands on the north-west horizon are the tops of prominent hills on the Scottish mainland (also see Cummings this volume).

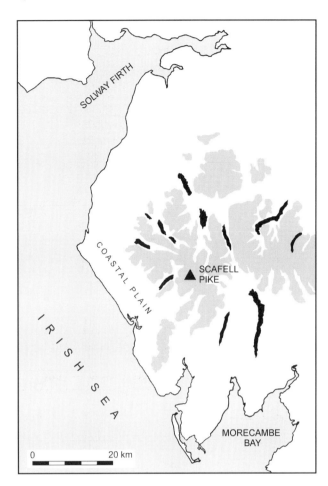

Figure 7.3. The topography of Cumbria. Ground over 300m is shown in dark grey.

The appearance of these real and illusionary islands can be transformed in relation to the location of the observer. By moving only a short distance onto the dunes above the beach, the view across the Irish Sea noticeably changes, with entirely new lands appearing to rise from the water. These first appear as mirage-like distortions on the horizon, appearing detached from the surface of the sea due to atmospheric refraction (Fig. 7.6). As the observer climbs higher above sea level, extensive areas of the Isle of Man emerge from beyond the horizon, along with headlands in south-west Scotland. Likewise, the mountains of Snowdonia gradually combine to create a unified land mass when observed from higher ground (Fig. 7.7). In the modern world we understand this effect as evidence for the curvature of the earth.

Where the land meets the sky

The Cumbrian coastline may have been a source of granite pebbles that were used as hammerstones in the Neolithic. These implements were carried from the lowlands into the mountainous interior of the Lake District where they

Figure 7.4. *A view of the Isle of Man from west Cumbria.*

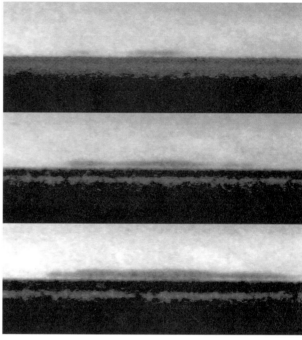

Figure 7.6. *The emergence of a distant landform across the Irish Sea.*

Figure 7.5. *Changing light over the Irish Sea.*

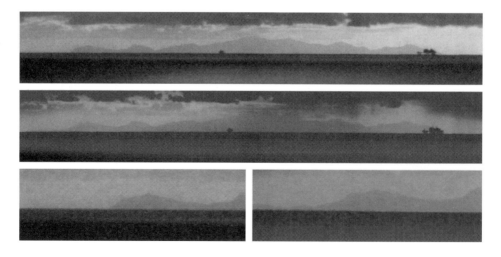

Figure 7.7. *An enhanced photographic montage showing how the appearance of Snowdonia changes as an observer climbs above the Cumbrian shoreline. The two lower images show details.*

Figure 7.8. Sunlight reflecting across the Irish Sea, seen from the Lake District mountains.

were used to work volcanic tuff into roughout stone axes (Bradley and Suthren 1990). If an observer traces possible routeways into the uplands, perceptions of the Irish Sea change entirely with increasing altitude. From the ridges and summits of the high mountains of the Lake District, the view of the sea contrasts entirely to that from the beach (Fig. 7.8). On a clear day, the Irish Sea now appears as a continuous arc of water from Morecambe Bay in the south to the Solway Firth in the north (see Fig. 7.3). Features that could only be viewed as discrete islands from the shoreline are now extensive landmasses. Snowdonia and Anglesey in north Wales are clearly visible, along with the entire southern coastline of south-west Scotland. The appearance of distant hills in Ireland is perhaps one of the most intriguing aspects (Jesty and Wainwright 1989), as this observation cannot be made from anywhere in Cumbria except the mountain tops. At the same time, a number of these extraordinary upland locations were among the most productive sources of ground stone axes in the British Isles. The spectacular views and dramatic situation of stone axe extraction sites might help to explain why stone axes from the Lake District possessed such high social value and were frequently carried to far-away regions (Bradley and Edmonds 1993). For example, stone axe sources near the summit of Scafell Pike (Claris and Quartermaine 1989) were located with views across the Irish Sea to Wales, Scotland and Ireland, some of the regions through which Lake District axes were widely circulated.

Fluid interpretations

This study of views over the Irish Sea suggests that there is no single defining experience of the phenomenon characterised as 'intervisibility'. While the term might superficially appear to reflect straightforward visual relationships, we have seen that visible phenomenon in the landscape can actually be rather more complex:

– To simply demonstrate that Point A is visible from Point B does not adequately characterise relations between two places, or possible movements between them. The views I encountered on my journey into the mountains changed in such subtle ways that they had to be described in some detail. The usefulness of terms such as 'false cresting' or 'viewshed' can also be questioned, as there is a danger that these might over-simplify or even classify experiences according to preconceived models from the literature. This does not encourage a reflexive and considered response to unique combinations of circumstances encountered in the field.

– Landscape studies often give primacy to demonstrating and illustrating intervisibility under optimal viewing conditions, denying the dynamic and transient nature of the environment within which the observer is situated.

Intervisibility is just one instance of how we tend to under-emphasise ambiguities inherent in the landscape. While acknowledging that the world was not a neutral backdrop against which Neolithic people lived their lives, we read and explain the landscapes of Cumbria in ways that are specific to our own time and place. As I have already described, we create relationships and connections between places based upon our understanding of maps, books, computer models and images of the earth from the air. Our understanding of topography is also bound within a history of landscape appreciation that ranges from the arts to the geographical sciences. For this reason, it is very difficult for us to isolate our abstract knowledge from the immediacy of our embodied experiences. For Neolithic people, however, the Irish Sea region was not a map or a computer model that could be 'examined, manipulated and visually devoured' (Gillings and Pollard 1999). It was a totally immersive and ever-changing world which was integral to the lives of the people who dwelt there. Today, we might only glimpse the fragmentary residue of the Neolithic cosmologies from which this world was constructed over four thousand years ago, but this need not prevent us from attempting to see beyond the boundaries of our twenty-first century lives.

- How might we perceive the transitory nature of views across the sea if we had no geological understanding of islands and mountains as permanent topographic features?
- What is the weather, if we have no knowledge of meteorology? Is it the land that changes, or the light? Are mountains a part of the ground, or the sky?
- Our knowledge of the earth as a globe is a concept that is rarely shared by non-Western societies (Ingold 2000, 209–18). How might the emergence of land over the horizon be understood otherwise?
- Why is it possible to see distant places from the top of mountains that are not visible from lower elevations?

In the next section, I will consider how we might begin to change our own perceptions of places if we try to disentangle modern abstractions from the subtleties of personal experience. While there will ultimately be many ways of telling, perhaps it is possible to formulate fresh interpretations that align rather more closely with perspectives such as Ingold's (2000) approach to dwelling in the landscape.

Transience and liminality

Neolithic people who inhabited the west coast of Cumbria were immersed within an extraordinary environment that we often take for granted in the modern world. To their east rose the mountains, where the land turned to rock. To their west was the sea, where the land turned to water. We might characterise these topographies in quite different ways because of their contrasting appearance and materiality, yet they arguably share many qualities. Just as the rocky and treeless uplands could have been perceived as a place apart from the inhabited lowlands (Fig. 7.9), the 'islands' across the sea might also have been liminal. While the hills merge with the sky and are often obscured by cloud, atmospherics across the sea can be equally enthralling, ambiguous, and unpredictable. In the modern world, it is stating the obvious to say that the most distant views are encountered from the most liminal spaces, because these are also the highest summits. But it is possible that this connection might have been understood quite differently by Neolithic people. Perhaps the character of the uplands provided a special, even supernatural, context within which extraordinary experiences could materialise. Across the world, upland landscapes are frequently understood to be inhabited by

mythical beings, sorcerers or spirits of the dead (Craig 1996; Malinowski 1922).

Mountains and monuments, time and space

In good visibility, travellers crossing the Irish Sea would have seen any land they approached emerge from behind the horizon in a manner that was not unlike their appearance when climbing a mountain. In this way, elements of the experience of climbing mountains to procure stone could have been reproduced in the act of transporting the finished axes. In this sense, perhaps the views to these far-away lands from the mountain summits might themselves have been envisaged as a kind of travel. In other words, the high ground facilitated a tangible connection between the observer and distant places that would not otherwise be encountered without undertaking a considerable expedition. At the same time, the uplands are generally a cooler environment than lower ground, causing the passage of the seasons to be progressively delayed or advanced with greater height. Indeed, whilst walking in the mountains it is common to encounter animals and plants at quite different stages in their annual cycle to those at sea level, and there can be snowfall on the high ridges at the times of the year that would be considered unseasonal at lower elevations (Pearsall and Pennington 1973). Taking these aspects together, it is possible to conceive of the extended views and changing climate in terms of a physical transformation of space and time.

If we accept that mountains were capable of profoundly transforming Neolithic peoples' sense of space and time, these 'natural' places then possess qualities which archaeologists often attribute to monumental buildings and ritual activities (Bradley 1993; 1998). To distinguish so rigidly between mountains and monuments might only perpetuate modernist distinctions between natural and artificial places (Bradley 1998; Ingold 2000). After all, topography can influence the movements of people in ways that are not dissimilar to formal architecture (Bradley 1997, 124, 132). There exists a tendency to explore a phenomenology of landscape (Tilley 1994) that actually gives primacy to *sites* and *monuments*. Therefore, it is important that archaeologists expand their experiences beyond monuments and into the wider world.

Movement and transformation

It seems that Neolithic landscapes were rather different to our own. When I walked from the Cumbrian beach onto Scafell Pike, I knew that I was seeing the distant mountains of Wales, Scotland and Ireland appear across the Irish Sea. My view was also informed by rigid geographical definitions that distinguish between a mountain that is surrounded by water (an island), and one that is part of a larger landmass. Logically, they cannot be both at the same time, and I could explain the transitory appearance

Figure 7.9. *A view of the Lake District mountains from Scafell Pike.*

of 'islands' as an illusion created by the curvature of the earth. Without such knowledge, however, Neolithic interpretations of the same phenomenon are likely to have been rather different. From their perspective, at what stage along the journey would the islands have become mountains? Could they have been both at the same time? Were geographical distinctions even relevant? Perhaps we should consider these metamorphosing islands not just in terms of a sequence of visible revelation, but one of *physical transformation*.

The critical element in transformation is movement. But the changing perspectives of a walk or a view are difficult to communicate in a written account. Indeed, the constraints of publication sometimes seem to influence fieldwork practice – it is quite acceptable to arrive at a view, take a photograph, and then depart. However, this denies the possibility that the appearances and meanings of places might substantially change in accordance with the ways in they are viewed as people move around them. Archaeologists identify monuments in relation to abstract and static conceptions of their architecture, yet this is entirely contrary to an embodied mobile perspective. As with the 'islands' across the Irish Sea we might ask 'when does a long barrow become a long barrow as we move towards it through the landscape'? At the point where the mound is only partially visible over the horizon, might Neolithic people have understood it to be something else entirely? Mayburgh in Cumbria provides an interesting example. The site is traditionally classified as a henge (Topping 1992), yet when viewed from outside its boundaries the monument takes on the appearance of an enormous circular mound that has affinities with Boyne Valley passage graves in Ireland (Watson and Bradley in press). In other words, an observer's comprehension of Mayburgh can vary entirely depending upon their viewpoint. While archaeologists are familiar with categorising monuments according to preconceived architectural schemes, we should consider the possibility that there may have been multiple readings in the Neolithic, each reflecting the individual viewpoint of an audience.

Discussion

While the importance of embodied perception is increasingly being acknowledged by archaeologists, this paper has discussed some of the ways in which modern knowledge informs our experiences of the world in ways that were unavailable to Neolithic people. While I am not suggesting that it will ever be possible for us to see the world through Neolithic eyes, it is important that we acknowledge and critically evaluate some of the assumptions inherent in our observations. The Cumbrian study I have outlined is the culmination of many years of my own experiences in the landscape, so my account will naturally be different to someone who is less familiar with these places. This is an important distinction which has potential implications for the results of archaeological fieldwork.

An archaeologist who has a cartographic knowledge of the Irish Sea will have a very different experience of the view from a beach in comparison to a visitor who does not. In other words, the archaeologist approaches the place with certain preconceived ways of 'reading' that landscape – they can identify distant landmasses and understand why the curvature of the earth partially conceals distant lands. Even if fog or rain obscures the view out to sea, the archaeologist can depart with the secure knowledge that intervisibility with Wales and Scotland would have been possible on a clear day. The essentially transitory nature of most experiences in the landscape is consciously rejected in order to cement a particular vision of reality. It seems that the 'true' view prioritised by the archaeologist is one that is not distorted by atmospherics, thereby denying the dynamic ever-changing experience of the observer who dwells in the world. Indeed, archaeologists seldom invest time or resources in order to engage with places in contrasting weathers, seasons, or different times of day or night, and it is equally rare for this diversity to be conveyed in published reports. There is a certain irony in this, since clear and settled weather can be uncommon across many regions of the British Isles, including the Irish Sea.

It appears that archaeologists neglect theories of

embodied perception at precisely the time when its concepts are most critical – their engagement with the landscape. Indeed, there seems to be a disconnection between the body of theory and acts of observation that underlie large areas of field archaeology. It seems that the theoretical implications of perception that receive so much discussion in the literature seem to fade quietly into the background during fieldwork, rather than being foregrounded at every moment as a continuous dialogue between theory and observation. We *know* that we understand apparently straightforward physical relationships on very different terms to Neolithic people, yet we persist in constraining our interpretations through the appliance of dogma that we know to be entirely our own creation. In this paper, I suggest that the integration of a rather more self-reflective experiential practice within research could begin to expand our interpretative capacity; not as a replacement for established methodologies, but a complementary approach that seeks to broaden the diversity of our experiences. Indeed, the advantages of encouraging more intense encounters with the landscape as part of traditional fieldwork strategies are already being acknowledged (Bradley 2000, 214–5). Overall, Ingold's (2000, 192) sentiment seems equally apt whether it is applied to the Neolithic dweller or a modern archaeologist: 'a place owes its character to the experiences it affords to those who spend time there'.

Concluding comments

I began this paper with two images. The first was an abstraction of the Irish Sea as a map, while the second represented my own encounter with the sea. From a modern perspective we encourage our knowledge of the first image to inform the second, yet in order to begin to interpret the Neolithic we have to try and *unlearn* these relations. Through an account of the illusionary islands and transient landscapes of Cumbria and the Irish Sea I hope to have communicated the multiple layers and readings inherent even in simple visual relationships. Such complex and subtle experiences are difficult to communicate to a wider audience in the context of a written paper, yet these properties seem utterly critical to our understanding and appraisal of Cumbrian topography. This is not about Neolithic perceptions, but our own. If uncritically applied, our approach to landscape can result in observations that are as bounded and predefined as plans of monuments or schemes of architectural classification. These issues should not prevent us from using a wide variety of techniques to investigate space and place, but it is absolutely critical that we remain constantly vigilant in how we make the fundamental observations upon which archaeological interpretations are ultimately founded.

There are many ways of telling the world. While we may never be able to think Neolithic, we can at least attempt to perceive the archaeological record in ways that challenge our preconceptions rather than moulding them to twenty-first century expectations. Our encounters with the world might at first appear to be static islands, but outside these boundaries lie rather more fluid horizons.

Acknowledgements

Many thanks to Vicki Cummings and Chris Fowler for inviting me to present the first version of this paper at the 'Neolithic of the Irish Sea' conference in Manchester, and for their constructive comments. I am also very grateful to Richard Bradley for reading and commenting upon the text, and Paddy Woodman for her advice. All images accompanying this paper were created by the author.

References

Bender, B. 1993. *Landscape: politics and perspectives.* Oxford: Berg.

Bender, B. 1998. *Stonehenge: making space.* Oxford: Berg.

Bergh, S. 1995. *Landscape of the monuments.* Stockholm: Riksantikvarieämbetet Arkeologiska undersökningar.

Bord, J. and Bord, C. 1995. *The enchanted land: myths and legends of Britain's landscape.* London: Thorsons, HarperCollins.

Bradley, R. 1993. *Altering the earth.* Edinburgh: Society of Antiquaries of Scotland.

Bradley, R. 1997. *Rock art and the prehistory of Atlantic Europe.* London: Routledge.

Bradley, R. 1998. Ruined buildings, ruined stones: enclosures, tombs and natural places in the Neolithic of south-west England. *World Archaeology* 30, 13–22.

Bradley, R. 2000. *The good stones: a new investigation of the Clava Cairns.* Edinburgh: Society of Antiquaries of Scotland Monograph 17.

Bradley, R. and Edmonds, M. 1993. *Interpreting the axe trade: production and exchange in Neolithic Britain.* Cambridge: Cambridge University Press.

Bradley, R. and Suthren, R. 1990. Petrographic analysis of hammerstones from the Neolithic quarries of Great Langdale. *Proceedings of the Prehistoric Society* 56, 117–22.

Brück, J. 1998. In the footsteps of the ancestors: a review of Christopher Tilley's A Phenomenology of Landscape: Places, Paths and Monuments. *Archaeological Review from Cambridge* 15, 23–36.

Cherry, J. and Cherry, P. 1983. Prehistoric habitation sites in west Cumbria. *Transactions of the Cumberland and Westmorland Antiquarian and Archaeological Society* 83, 1–14.

Cherry, J. and Cherry, P. 1984. Prehistoric habitation sites in west Cumbria: part two. *Transactions of the Cumberland and Westmorland Antiquarian and Archaeological Society* 83, 1–17.

Cherry, J. and Cherry, P. 1985. Prehistoric habitation sites in west Cumbria: part 3. *Transactions of the Cumberland and Westmorland Antiquarian and Archaeological Society* 85, 1–10.

Cherry, J. and Cherry, P. 1986. Prehistoric habitation sites in west Cumbria: part 4. *Transactions of the Cumberland and Westmorland Antiquarian and Archaeological Society* 86, 1–17.

Cherry, J. and Cherry, P. 1987. Prehistoric habitation sites in west Cumbria: part 5. *Transactions of the Cumberland and Westmorland Antiquarian and Archaeological Society* 87, 1–10.

Claris, P. and Quartermaine, J. 1989. The Neolithic quarries and axe factory sites of Great Langdale and Scafell Pike: a new field survey. *Proceedings of the Prehistoric Society* 55, 1–25.

Cleal, R., Walker, K. and Montague, R. 1995. *Stonehenge in its landscape: twentieth century excavations*. London: English Heritage.

Craig, D. 1996. *Landmarks: an exploration of great rocks*. London: Pimlico.

Cummings, V., Jones, A. and Watson, A. 2002. Divided places: phenomenology and asymmetry in the monuments of the Black Mountains, south-east Wales. *Cambridge Archaeological Journal* 12, 57–70.

Earl, G. and Wheatley, D. 2002. Visual reconstruction and the interpretative process: a case-study from Avebury. In D. Wheatley, G. Earl and S. Poppy (eds), *Contemporary themes in archaeological computing*, 5–15. Oxford: Oxbow/University of Southampton Department of Archaeology Monograph 3.

Exon, S., Gaffney, V., Woodward, A. and Yorston, R. 2000. *Stonehenge landscapes: journeys through real-and-imagined worlds*. Oxford: British Archaeological Reports.

Fox, C.F. 1942. A beaker barrow, enlarged in the Middle Bronze Age, at South Hill, Talbenny, Pembrokeshire. *The Archaeological Journal* 99, 1–32.

Gillings, M. and Pollard, J. 1999. Non-portable stone artefacts and contexts of meaning: the tale of the Grey Wether (www.museums.ncl.ac.uk/Avebury/stone4.htm). *World Archaeology* 31, 179–93.

Hirsch, E. and O'Hanlon, M. 1995. *The anthropology of landscape*. Oxford: Oxford University Press.

Ingold, T. 2000. *The perception of the environment*. London: Routledge.

Jesty, C. and Wainwright, A. 1989. *A guide to the view from Scafell Pike*. Bridport: Jesty's Panoramas.

Jones, A. 1999. Local colour: megalithic architecture and colour symbolism in Neolithic Arran. *Oxford Journal of Archaeology* 18, 339–50.

Lock, G. and Harris, T. 1996. Danebury revisited: an English Iron Age hillfort in a digital landscape. In M. Aldenderfer and H. Maschner (eds), *Anthropology, space, and geographic information systems*, 214–40. New York: Oxford University Press.

Lowenthal, D. 1961. Geography, experience, and imagination: towards a geographical epistemology. *Annals of the Associ-ation of American Geographers* 51, 241–60.

Malinowski, B. 1922. *Argonauts of the western Pacific*. London: Routledge and Kegan Paul.

Pearsall, W. and Pennington, W. 1973. *The Lake District*. London: Bloomsbury.

Phillips, T. 2002. *Landscapes of the living, landscapes of the dead: the location of chambered cairns in northern Scotland*. Oxford: British Archaeological Reports British Series 328.

Phillips, T. and Watson, A. 2000. The living and the dead in northern Scotland 3500–2000 BC. *Antiquity* 74, 786–92.

Thomas, J. 1996. *Time, culture and identity: an interpretive archaeology*. London: Routledge.

Tilley, C. 1994. *A phenomenology of landscape*. Oxford: Berg.

Topping, P. 1992. The Penrith henges: a survey by the Royal Commission on the Historical Monuments of England. *Proceedings of the Prehistoric Society* 58, 249–64.

Waterhouse, J. 1985. *The stone circles of Cumbria*. Chichester: Phillimore.

Watson, A. 2001a. Composing Avebury. *World Archaeology* 33, 296–314.

Watson, A. 2001b. The sounds of transformation: acoustics, monuments and ritual in the British Neolithic. In N. Price (ed.), *The archaeology of shamanism*, 178–92. London: Routledge.

Watson, A. 2001c. Round barrows in a circular world: monumentalising landscapes in Early Bronze Age Wessex. In J. Brück (ed.), *Bronze Age landscapes: tradition and transformation*, 207–16. Oxford: Oxbow.

Watson, A. and Bradley, R. in press. On the edge of England: Cumbria as a Neolithic region. In G. Barclay and K. Brophy (eds), *Regional diversity in the Neolithic of Britain and Ireland*. Oxford: Oxbow.

Wheatley, D. 1993. Going over old ground: GIS, archaeological theory and the act of perception. In J. Anderson, T. Madsen and I. Scollar (eds), *Computing the past: computer applications and quantitative methods in archaeology 1992*, 133–38. Aarhus: Aarhus University Press.

Wheatley, D. 1995. Cumulative viewshed analysis: a GIS-based method for investigating intervisibility, and its archaeological application. In G. Lock and Z. Stančič (eds), *Archaeology and geographical information systems: a European perspective*, 171–85. London: Taylor and Francis.

Whittle, A. 1997. Remembered and imagined belongings: Stonehenge in its traditions and structures of meaning. In B. Cunliffe and C. Renfrew (eds), *Science and Stonehenge*, 145–66. Oxford: Proceedings of the British Academy 92.

Witcher, R. 1999. GIS and landscapes of perception. In M. Gillings, D. Mattingly and J. Van Dalen (eds), *Geographical information systems and landscape archaeology*, 13–22. Oxford: Oxbow.

8   Falling off the edge of the Irish Sea: Clettraval and the two-faced Neolithic of the Outer Hebrides

Cole Henley

Introduction

The chambered cairn of Clettraval on North Uist (Fig. 8.1) is a confused monument. Situated near the top of the hill of Clettraval at around 100 metres above sea level, this considerable pile of stones, now grassed over, commands magnificent views across the loch-scattered western coast of North Uist below and outwards to the Atlantic Ocean. However, this site commands more than just these views, providing a near constant source of debate for archaeologists since its acknowledgement as a Neolithic monument by Erskine Beveridge at the turn of the twentieth century. In this paper, I want to look at Clettraval and use it as a means for examining the shifting history of archaeological attention towards the Neolithic of the Outer Hebrides over the past hundred or so years. In this history, we will see the interpretation of this monument change along with broader changes in British Neolithic studies and broader understandings for the role of the Outer Hebrides at this time. I ultimately hope to provide an interesting discussion that sets out the origins behind some underlying assumptions regarding the archipelago, and challenge its position in current British Neolithic studies, whether intended or not, as a peripheral and poorly understood region falling off the edge of the Irish Sea.

Figure 8.1. *Clettraval today.*

Describing Clettraval

Clettraval chambered cairn was excavated in 1934 by Walter Lindsay Scott (W. L. Scott 1935) having been identified as a Neolithic monument by Erskine Beveridge in his survey of North Uist (Beveridge 1911, 254). Despite considerable disturbance of the site, principally through the construction of an Iron Age house into the cairn itself, excavation revealed an elaborate range of architectural features and a detailed sequence of activity within the chamber.

Structures

W. L. Scott's excavations at Clettraval were focused on three main elements: the cairn interior, the façade, and the southern wall of the cairn (Fig. 8.2), in addition to the later, Iron Age structures. Excavation of the interior revealed a single, elongated chamber with no passage, divided along its length into five sections or compartments by low, vertical slabs set into the floor (sections I to V). An additional compartment defined the entranceway or portal to the interior (section VI). The chamber was slightly curved and widened with depth, the innermost compartment (section I) was the largest of the chamber. This compartment contained a small cist and provided the primary focus for deposits at the site.

The northern part of the cairn façade had been destroyed by the construction of the Iron Age house, but an elaborate convex façade survived to the south of the entrance to the chamber. This was constructed of large orthostats interspersed with dry-stone walling, fronted by a paved forecourt. Furthermore, set out from the narrow

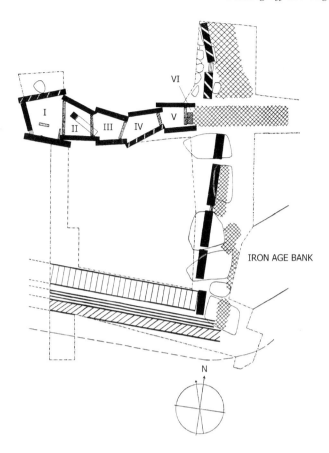

IRON AGE BANK

N

Figure 8.2. Extent of W. L. Scott's excavations at Clettraval.

chamber portal at the centre of the façade was a stone-built path running for over 5 metres, broadly aligned with the chamber axis (Fig. 8.3a). Excavation of the southern edge of the cairn revealed further elaborate structures. The cairn material was contained by a sophisticated tripartite peristalith (a wall framing or defining the cairn, from the Greek *peristellein*; to wrap around) made up of large upright stones set against the cairn material, abutted by horizontal slabs supported by a ramp of smaller slabs (Fig. 8.3b). W. L. Scott did not initially believe this peristalith design to be technological (W. L. Scott 1935, 492), although his later excavation of the nearby cairn of Unival, led him to re-interpret the Clettraval peristalith as structural (W. L. Scott 1948, 31).

Finds

Around 460 sherds of Neolithic pottery dominated the Neolithic finds from Clettraval (Squair 1998, 253), but also found were two granite balls, an irregular lump of pumice, charcoal, burnt human and animal bone, split pebbles of jasper and water-worn quartz pebbles (W. L. Scott 1935, 495). The finds were primarily derived from three distinct layers within the chamber: *stratum A*, an upper layer that post-dated the Neolithic use of the chamber; *stratum B*, an upper Neolithic layer; and *stratum C*, a lower Neolithic layer. All the bone from the site,

except for a single fragment, was found in the innermost compartment (section I) in stratum C. The animal bones were argued to be derived from sheep or goat (Jackson in W. L. Scott 1935, 499), whilst the human bone, restricted to a few examples due to the highly acidic local soils, showed evidence of burning from which it was suggested that they had been cremated (Tildesley in W. L. Scott 1935, 499).

The pottery assemblage contained over 45 Neolithic and Beaker vessels, almost half from stratum B of the innermost section (section I) of the chamber (Fig. 8.4). At least eighteen Neolithic vessels were found, from which a number of vessel forms and decorative elements were represented, the majority of which could be related to earlier Neolithic styles from western Scotland, notably 'Beacharra Ware' (Childe 1940, 53; Piggott 1954, 171–3; J. G. Scott 1969, 201–3; Sheridan 2000, 7–11), consisting of simple, lugged bag-shaped bowls and decorated carinated vessels. Also present were six Beaker vessels, restricted to the innermost compartments of stratum B (Table I), and twenty-one indeterminate vessels. The fragmentary condition of the assemblage led W. L. Scott to consider that some vessels may originally have been deposited incomplete; hinting at a ritual role for pottery at the site rather than just grave goods (W. L. Scott 1935, 496). In a reassessment of the Clettraval assemblage, Squair noted that some sherds may also have been selectively *removed* from the chamber (Squair 1998, 269).

Use

From the ceramic and mortuary evidence, W. L. Scott attempted to reconstruct the nature and sequence of practices that took place at Clettraval. The limited quantity and poor quality of human bone found suggested to W. L. Scott that rather than being the result of cremation, the burning of the bones represented secondary burning of the human remains shortly after being deposited in the cairn. He related this to the evidence from Mycenaean tombs in the Late Helladic and suggested this as a form of purification rite, possibly to drive out spirits or ghosts (W. L. Scott 1935, 530). The concentration of bone in section I led W. L. Scott to argue that this section was the focus for burial, each individual accompanied by one or more pots as grave goods. The presence of vessels outside of section I was argued to represent the clearing out of this section to facilitate new burials. W. L. Scott's ideas were confirmed in his excavation of the chambered cairn of Unival (W. L. Scott 1948). Here, a small polygonal chamber contained a cist within which was a large quantity of human bone, charcoal, as well as up to twenty-six ceramic vessels (Squair 1998, 271).

Although fragmentary and decayed, the bone from Unival was in considerably greater condition than that found at Clettraval, enabling W. L. Scott to attempt (with greater conviction) a reconstruction of the mortuary

Figure 8.3. a. Path and b. peristalith at Clettraval.

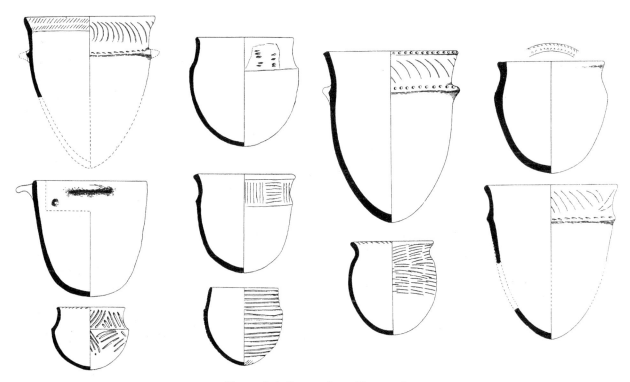

Figure 8.4. Pottery from Clettraval.

activity at this site. The majority of the bones were fragments of ribs, long bones, vertebrae and metacarpals, along with parts of a scapula. Of particular interest were several bones derived from a single, adult individual (Cave in W. L. Scott 1948, 37), plus rib fragments belonging to a younger individual (Jackson in W. L. Scott 1948, 37). The heavy calcinations of all the bones suggested that they had been burnt, a factor responsible for their preservation in the acidic soils, though the degree of calcinations was not consistent with cremation (Cave in W. L. Scott 1948, 38). This led W. L. Scott to conclude that 'though much distorted by fire these bones had not been cremated, and their condition must be due to the piling of burning charcoal on them as they lay in the cist' (W. L. Scott 1948, 13–4), supporting his earlier interpretation of Clettraval.

Clettraval in its Hebridean and broader context

Clettraval is one of over forty chambered tombs in the Outer Hebrides region, over twenty of these on the island of North Uist. I have already referred to Unival, again on North Uist, and further reference could be made to another of W. L. Scott's excavations at Rudh' an Dunain, on Skye. However, Clettraval is unique amongst these three sites; indeed it is arguably unique amongst all of the Neolithic chambered tombs in the region.

This poses intriguing questions for understanding the Hebridean Neolithic because the Neolithic period in this region is primarily understood through its chambered tombs. North Uist has provided evidence for settlement from this period at a number of sites, the islet sites of Eilean Domhnuill (Armit 1996) and Eilean an Tighe (W. L. Scott 1951) perhaps the most well known, but this handful of ephemeral sites – and those few known from the other islands of the region – are starkly contrasted by the abundant and substantial stone built megalithic tombs found throughout the region, North Uist in particular. The predominant form of the Hebridean tombs is the passage grave, defined by Childe as where 'the burial chamber is roughly circular or polygonal and is entered by a relatively long and narrow passage' (Childe 1933, 121). However, despite the predominance of the passage grave in the region, there exist a few examples of the Clyde cairn or gallery grave, where 'the chamber itself is long and narrow like a passage, and the entrance is reduced to a mere portal or shallow porch' (Childe 1933, 121). When Clettraval was excavated Scotland was considered in terms of a two-fold split between passage and gallery graves, each type representing a particular form of funerary architecture belonging to two distinct cultural populations (Childe 1933, 121; 1935, 24; Daniel 1941, 44; 1962, 72), with passage graves concentrated in the north of Scotland and gallery graves in the south-west. The Outer Hebrides presented a problem to this assumption though through the presence in the region of both monument forms. Yet this was further complicated by the merger of both forms in the construction of some individual sites. One such site was Clettraval.

In 1911, Erskine Beveridge had noted the similarity between Clettraval and similar 'long cists' or gallery graves on Arran (Beveridge 1911, 254), later confirmed by W. L. Scott's excavations. The shape of the cairn, the layout and construction of the chamber and the ceramic styles found, related Clettraval to a Clyde cairn tradition

of construction (Childe 1940, 53; Henshall 1972, 15; Piggott 1954, 152; J. G. Scott 1969). However, despite this classification, Clettraval did not conform to a 'typical' Clyde form and indeed elements of its architecture seemed to be directly influenced by a passage grave tradition of monument construction (Childe 1935, 40; Piggott 1954, 225; J. G. Scott 1969, 201; W. L. Scott 1935, 525). Childe commented that Clettraval could 'also be described as a chamber preceded by ante-chamber and segmented passage' (Childe 1935, 40–1), whilst Piggott noted 'the Clettraval chamber can only be interpreted as a structural hybrid between the passage-grave and the Clyde-Carlingford architectural traditions' (Piggott 1954, 225).

This did not fit into prevalent models for the Scottish Neolithic. According to Childe, passage graves and gallery graves were distinct phenomena employed by independent populations. The presence of both monument forms in the Outer Hebrides was confusing enough, a pattern that Childe struggled to explain, but that Clettraval represented an individual site employing both styles in its construction was hugely problematic for this dualistic interpretation. Childe's response was to propose that the presence of both styles in the region was a direct result of its peripheral location, the product of the isles' intermediate position between the two different cultural concentrations (Childe 1935, 40), an argument he had adopted for the monuments of Orkney which he believed to represent 'the outcome of long brooding in isolation' (Childe 1935, 50). Daniel, on the other hand was aware of the complications presented to Childe's model by the Hebrides and other parts of northern Scotland, where he observed that monument styles were 'so inextricably mixed that…there are no ordinary passage graves and gallery graves' (Daniel 1941, 44–5). However, Daniel ultimately offers the same explanation for this as Childe, reducing these regions to a series of sub-types situated on the periphery of the two main population concentrations.

W. L. Scott regarded this view of the Outer Hebrides as 'a confession of uncertainty' (W. L. Scott 1942a, 301) and highlighted the problems brought about by Childe and Daniel's emphasis on classification by monument architecture alone. Finds were frequently inconsequential to their findings, Childe noting 'though the traditions of funerary architecture seem to be radically different in the two principal areas, the culture of the people who built and used the tombs seems to have been the same' (Childe 1933, 136). W. L. Scott employed the evidence from his excavations at Clettraval, Unival and the settlement site of Eilean an Tighe, all on North Uist, in order to better understand the relationship between the Neolithic sites of the region and to construct a sequence for them, primarily based on the pottery from these excavations.

Contrary to Childe, Stuart Piggott had identified a broad diversity of pottery styles for the British Neolithic and noted the association of specific ceramic forms with particular monument types (Piggott 1931). W. L. Scott's work, however, demonstrated that despite architectural differences between Unival and Clettraval, the material culture and use revealed through excavation at these sites was remarkably similar. This suggested that rather than a homogenous Scottish Neolithic culture or cultural material specific to particular monument forms, a regional tradition of practice existed in the Hebridean Neolithic. Highlighting comparable developments in the ceramic and monument sequences of the western Mediterranean, the Outer Hebrides, and northern Scotland, W. L. Scott suggested that rather than a peripheral phenomenon ultimately influenced by continental developments, the Hebridean evidence represented continuous contacts and interaction between these regions through the Neolithic (W. L. Scott 1942, 302). This had significant implications for understanding and interpreting the place of the Outer Hebrides during the Neolithic, now centrally located within 'the main stream of sea traffic along the Atlantic route' (W. L. Scott 1942, 306), rather than a peripheral archipelago.

This view was supported by Piggott who noted the close relationship between the monuments and material culture from the Outer Hebrides, Orkney, and the Boyne in Ireland (Piggott 1954, 231–232). In this context, the merging of both traditions within the region, and individual monuments, could only be explained as the result of a head-on collision between two cultural strains rather than representing a mutation developed in isolation.

After Piggott, a refining of the chronology for the British and Scottish Neolithic, primarily through developments in radiocarbon dating, led to the realisation that this period involved significantly larger time-scales than had previously been appreciated. One result of this was a dramatic rethinking of the chronology and development of chambered cairns. With the spread of monuments being much slower than previously supposed, less radical causes for cultural change were considered and insular developments began to be favoured over colonization, migration, or diffusion through trade or religion. Most significantly, however, was the consideration that some, indeed many chambered cairns could not be considered just in their present form, but must be considered as composite, or multi-phase monuments. Initiated by the work of Jack Scott (J. G. Scott 1961; 1964; 1969; Selkirk 1972, 289–92) and John Corcoran (Corcoran 1966; 1969; Selkirk 1972, 281–87), this view was taken up by Audrey Henshall in her extensive cataloguing of Scottish chambered cairns (Henshall 1963; 1972; 1974).

The study of Scottish monuments was now the study of intricate developments in monument form, and rather than trace the movements of two broad strains of monumental architecture – as Childe and Daniel had done – archaeologists were now concerned with plotting local variability and sequence. Evolutionary models were applied to the main architectural forms, tracing sequences from simple to complex, championed by J. G. Scott in his search for the 'proto-megalith' (J. G. Scott 1969; Selkirk 1972, 289–92). Relating his sequence for the Clyde form to excavated remains, J. G. Scott was able to construct a ceramic sequence for the pottery styles associated with Clyde cairns. This had significant implications for the interpretation of Clettraval because although J. G. Scott thought Clettraval was essentially a passage-grave (J. G. Scott 1969, 201), the pottery deposited there was related to Clyde monuments in south-west Scotland. Specifically, bowls and jars found in the earlier levels from the site suggested direct contact between the two regions, but the fact that consequent styles were 'manifestly independent' (J. G. Scott 1969, 201) implied that contact between the Outer Hebrides and the Clyde region was brief and abrupt (J. G. Scott 1969. 201–3). The Outer Hebrides was now once more on the edge of the considered Neolithic world, a peripheral and insular region directly influenced from outside 'at a time when, and place where, both [passage-grave and Clyde traditions] were exerting a vigorous influence' (J. G. Scott 1969, 201).

Audrey Henshall made similar conclusions. Accepting the earlier two-fold division of Scottish Neolithic monuments, Henshall allotted the Outer Hebrides to a broader tradition referred to as the Orkney-Cromarty-Hebridean group of passage graves, essentially corresponding to the northernmost concentration of passage-graves considered by Childe and Daniel. In this context, the Outer Hebrides was on the westernmost fringe of a group of monuments whose core lay in the north-east of Scotland, concentrated in Caithness and Orkney. Henshall noted the presence of Clyde cairns in the Outer Hebrides but concluded that these were earlier outliers that represented shifting influences within the region from south-west to northern Scotland through time (Henshall 1972, 280), a view later supported by Müller (Müller 1988, 24). Some indigenous developments were noted, such as the overall larger scale of the cairns and the character of the peristalith at the Hebridean cairns, but these, once again, were regarded as insular peculiarities applied to an external template.

The influence of Henshall's survey has been considerable in Scottish Neolithic studies and our understanding of the period has benefited substantially from her work. However, our present understanding of the Neolithic of the Outer Hebrides has, I would argue, suffered from the peripheral view that has become associated with it. In order to more fully appreciate the nature of the Neolithic in the Outer Hebrides we must return to Clettraval and begin to examine in more detail the series of associations and also dis-associations that it reflects, within the Outer Hebrides, with the Irish Sea, and beyond.

The Clettraval connection?

Connections

Clettraval highlights a number of connections shared

between the Outer Hebrides, the Irish Sea zone, and other regions. Fundamentally, its architectural form is derived from a style of monument prolific in the Irish Sea zone, the Clyde form. Indeed, despite observations that Clettraval represents either a passage-grave/Clyde hybrid or simply an altered passage-grave, the continual reference to Clettraval as a Clyde cairn (e.g. Armit 1996; Henshall 1972; Kinnes 1985) constructs a connection between these two regions, in name if not exact parallel. Apart from Clettraval there are a further two examples of Clyde monuments in the Outer Hebrides, Geirisclett and Dun na Carnaich on North Uist, although the poor condition of Dun na Carnaich means that it can not definitely be labelled such. Geirisclett, however, has all the characteristics of an early Clyde monument (according to J. G. Scott's sequence) and as such may represent one of the earliest monuments in the region.

The pottery from Clettraval also displays a number of affinities with ceramics from the Irish Sea zone. The predominance in the Clettraval assemblage of partially decorated, collared round-based bowls and jars (Fig. 8.4) enabled J. G. Scott to confirm the connection between Clettraval and the Clyde monuments, similar to ceramics from Clyde cairns such as Achnacree, Beacharra and Glenvoidean, amongst others (Henshall 1972, 166–78, 302–9; Sheridan 2000, 10). Sherds from a developed 'carinated bowl' from Geirisclett (Henshall 1972, 310; Sheridan 2000, 10), a vessel form typical of the Clyde region, may further support this connection. Jasper pebbles were also found at Clettraval, a type of stone that could only have come from outside the region (Johnstone and Mykura 1989, 40), although the significance of jasper and the connotations surrounding its use may derive from even further afield (e.g. Cooney this volume). Other lithic materials found at Neolithic sites in the region can be provenanced to the Irish Sea zone, most notably Rhum bloodstone found at Rubh a' Charnain Mhor, North Uist (Finlayson in Downes and Badcock 1998), and several porcellanite axes from northern Ireland, the most impressive example being the hafted Shulishader axe from Lewis (Sheridan 1992, 198–201).

Disconnections

However, there are also elements of Clettraval that clearly do not relate to the Irish Sea zone. As noted, parts of its architecture share greater affinities with a passage-grave style of construction. There is an emphasis in both its architecture and use on the deepest part of the monument that is unusual in Clyde monuments and the chamber and portal to the site, as Childe noted (Childe 1935, 40), seems to be more indicative of a segmented chamber preceded by an ante-chamber than a Clyde form *per se*. Clettraval's location is also unusual, situated relatively highly on the slope of a prominent hill on North Uist. This is in contrast with the preference for these kinds of monuments to be situated on the coast, as is the case with

Geirisclett on North Uist, and comparable monuments in south-west Scotland (Childe 1934, 20; Cummings 2001).

Similar discontinuities can be observed in the ceramics from Clettraval. Although some of the Clettraval vessels were clearly paralleled by equivalent vessels from Clyde cairns, the later vessels from the site, although influenced in form and style by earlier Beacharra forms, were independent developments not featuring, for example, the corded decoration that was typical of later Beacharra vessels (J. G. Scott 1964, 151; 1969, 201).

Misconnections

At Clettraval then there are a series of connections and disconnections with the Irish Sea zone. The overall form of the monument, its trapezoidal cairn, its flat façade, and its chamber, divided into compartments and built of overlapping orthostats, arguably could only have been inspired by the monuments of south-west Scotland. Similarly, the ceramics from the site, despite local manufacture (W. L. Scott 1942b), can only have been influenced by comparable vessels from similar sites in south-west Scotland. However, the location and use of the site, and the later vessels deposited there, reflects local practices, probably influenced by passage-grave traditions from the north. Here we can see the playing out of two different worlds, a local interpretation of what a monument should be according to two different templates, the playing out of what Piggott referred to as 'the significance attached to specific forms of architecture' (Piggott 1954, 231). What is important at Clettraval is not the way that passage-grave architecture is incorporated into a Clyde-form, or *vice versa*, but how a Clyde-form is adapted to incorporate what it is that the passage-grave form embodies, namely a deep, closed focus for access and deposition. At passage-graves, it is the interior that is important where access is frequently restricted, prolonged, and ultimately distanced from the outside world. The cairn, peristalith, and entrance are frequently simple, in contrast to an impressive interior defined by large orthostats topped by a capstone and/or corbelling. The Clyde-form, in contrast, focuses attention on the exterior creating an open and accessible form with elaborate attention to the exterior and limited restriction to the interior.

Clettraval features elements of both of these forms but can perhaps best be understood as an attempt to embody the essence of a passage-grave within a Clyde-form. The innermost compartment of the chamber is the largest, contrasting with other Clyde monuments (J. G. Scott 1969, 201) and, like a passage grave, it is this that provided the focus for burial at the site. The location and orientation of the monument is also comparable to the passage-graves from the region, high up a substantial hill slope facing east. However, unlike a passage-grave, the exterior is elaborately defined with a complicated peristalith and a substantial flat façade and attention is drawn to the interior by a path leading directly towards the entrance.

Implications and conclusions

At this one site, we can see how during the Neolithic the Outer Hebrides experiences a series of connections with the Irish Sea and other regions, notably northern Scotland, yet also undergoes its own, insular developments. For me this example highlights a number of implications for studying and understanding the Neolithic of the Outer Hebrides of Scotland.

We must be more explicit about how we characterise the movement of particular social and cultural phenomena. When talking about the adoption of a Clyde form of monumental architecture at Clettraval are we talking about the movement of ideas, people, traditions, or materials? How and why did this specific form of monumental architectural arrive in the Outer Hebrides? Some may criticise such an argument for returning to the grand-narrative rhetoric of culture-history but we should not shy away from *explaining* the archaeology we are discussing. What was, as Piggott asked, the significance attached to specific architectural forms – the significance of specific traditions of practice – that led to the incorporation of both passage and gallery grave traditions in the construction and use of Clettraval? Why did the passage grave style come to dominate the region? Unless we are willing to start asking some of these questions, we will not be able to come to terms with the mixing of traditions represented at sites like Clettraval, and the Outer Hebrides as a whole.

To achieve this we must begin to address some of the chronological issues raised. The study of Clyde monuments, for example, has almost exclusively focused on their distribution through space. With the exception of J. G. Scott's work, there has been very limited effort to plot their movement through time. This leads to problems with interpreting sites like Clettraval because it simply does not fit into the typological sequences available. Relating particular monuments to the ceramic styles that are associated with them is not an adequate solution because without sufficiently well stratified sequences we are left with over-simplified typological schemes based on outdated assumptions concerning the evolution of particular monument forms. We have practically no basis for situating within any clear chronological framework the relationships within or between different regions, or between different characters of evidence. How does Clettraval relate to the settlement evidence from North Uist? Is the difference in ceramics between Clettraval and the settlement site of Eilean an Tighe functional or chronological? How can we answer these fundamental questions without a clear chronological framework? We can no longer use the absence of dates as an excuse. If there are no sequences then we must construct them. If there are no radiocarbon dates then we must get them.

Our priority must be the excavation of chambered tombs from the region. The nature of the architecture at Clettraval, and the character of the burial activities that took place there was conducive to the formation of a well-stratified sequence of deposits. It is plausible that a similar degree of preservation is present at other sites from the region. Although there has been moderate re-use of many of the chambered tombs from the region, particularly during the Iron Age (see Hingley 1996), the chambers and passages of most would seem to remain relatively undisturbed, sealed by collapsed cairn material. Most destruction is restricted to the cairn edges and to the capstones – an attractive source for large slabs of stone. In addition to the chamber and passage, a wealth of information may also be found underlying the sub-surface structures. The recent excavation of the kerb-cairn at Breasclete, near Callanish on Lewis, demonstrated the intriguing potential for evidence underlying early prehistoric monuments, with a series of ploughmarks and postholes predating the stone structures (Tim Neighbour *pers. comm.*).

Upon their excavation, it is likely that the contents of the tombs from the Outer Hebrides would reveal a broad range of evidence. In addition to pottery, the burial practices identified by W. L. Scott at Unival and Clettraval produced significant quantities of charcoal and where preservation permitted, both human and animal bone. It is unfortunate that these excavations were conducted prior to the availability of radiocarbon dating and that, where it has survived, the material from W. L. Scott's excavations is no longer suitable for dating. If further sites were to be excavated it is possible, if not probable, that such dateable material would be preserved and, with modern excavation techniques, that carbonised plant remains and ceramic residues suitable for dating and isotopic analysis may also be found. It should be noted that similar burial practices were revealed through excavations at Geirisclett, also on North Uist (Dunwell 1997), and had the site not been partially excavated by Beveridge (Beveridge 1911, 255–6; Dunwell 1997) and subjected to coastal erosion a great deal more material would probably have been found.

In our current situation, we cannot fully understand the Neolithic of this region because at present all we have are a series of places and practices isolated in time and space, tentatively connected by a handful of radiocarbon dates derived from an even smaller handful of sites. If we are to understand how these different places and practices inter-related through time or over space then a more thorough investigation of the sites from this region is required. The last time the evidence from this region was considered primarily on the basis of its surface remains, the result was its interpretation as an isolated place situated on the fringes of the Neolithic world. W. L. Scott's excavations demonstrated that there was much more to the Hebridean evidence than this and that the region had a great deal to offer British Neolithic studies.

Unless we are willing or able to excavate more sites and conduct a more thorough investigation of its monuments – dig deeper than the surface – then once more, we run the risk of restoring the Neolithic of this region to the peripheral and isolated region of Childe and Daniel's day. I believe that there is more to the Outer Hebrides than this and given the chance, this region has the potential to address some crucial questions that we must be asking of the Neolithic, questions that are not restricted to the Outer Hebrides and that should not just stop at the edge of the Irish Sea.

Acknowledgements

Thanks to Chris and Vicki for allowing a contribution from beyond the Irish Sea, for their unlimited patience in the production of this paper and for comments on earlier drafts. I am grateful to the Society of Antiquaries of Scotland for permission to use images from W. L. Scott's original excavation report from Clettraval, published in the Proceedings of the Society of Antiquaries of Scotland 1935.

References

Armit, I. 1996. *The archaeology of Skye and the Western Isles*. Edinburgh: Edinburgh University Press.

Beverige, B. 1911. *North Uist: its archaeology and topography*. Edinburgh: William Brown.

Childe, V. G. 1933. Scottish megalithic tombs and their affinities. *Transactions of the Glasgow Archaeological Society* 3, 120–37.

Childe, V. G. 1934. Neolithic settlement in the west of Scotland. *Scottish Geographical Magazine* 50, 18–25.

Childe, V. G. 1935. *The prehistory of Scotland*. London: Kegan Paul.

Childe, V. G. 1940. *Prehistoric communities of the British Isles*. London: Chambers.

Corcoran, J. X. W. P. 1966. Excavation of three chambered cairns at Loch Calder, Caithness. *Proceedings of the Society of Antiquaries of Scotland* 98, 1–75.

Corcoran, J. X. W. P. 1969. Multiperiod chambered cairns. *Scottish Archaeological Forum* 1, 9–17.

Cummings, V. M. 2001. *Landscapes in transition? Exploring the origins of monumentality in south-west Wales and south-west Scotland*. Unpublished Ph.D thesis: Cardiff University.

Daniel, G.E. 1941. The dual nature of the megalithic colonization of prehistoric Europe. *Proceedings of the Prehistoric Society* 7, 1–49.

Downes, J. and Badcock, A. 1998. *Berneray causeway: archaeological watching brief and excavations at the Screvan quarry site and Otternish, North Uist*. Sheffield: Archaeological Research and Consultancy at the University of Sheffield.

Dunwell, A. 1997. *Vallay strand project 1997: excavations at Geirisclett chambered tomb*. Edinburgh: Centre for Field Archaeology, University of Edinburgh.

Henshall, A. S. 1963. *The chambered tombs of Scotland, volume 1*. Edinburgh: Edinburgh University Press.

Henshall, A. S. 1972. The chambered tombs of Scotland, volume 2. Edinburgh: Edinburgh University Press.

Henshall, A. S. 1974. Scottish chambered tombs and long mounds. In C. Renfrew (ed.), *British prehistory: a new outline*, 137–164. London: Duckworth.

Hingley, R. 1996. Ancestors and identity in the later prehistory of Atlantic Scotland: the reuse and reinvention of Neolithic monuments and material culture. *World Archaeology* 28, 231–43.

Johnstone, G. S. and Mykura, W. 1989. *British Regional Geology: the Northern Highlands of Scotland*. London: Her Majesty's Stationery Office.

Kinnes, I. 1985. Circumstances not context: the Neolithic of Scotland as seen from outside. *Proceedings of the Society of Antiquaries of Scotland* 115, 15–57.

Müller, J. 1988. *The chambered cairns of the Northern and Western Isles*. Edinburgh: Edinburgh University Archaeology Department Occasional Paper 16.

Piggott, S. 1931. The Neolithic pottery of the British Isles. *Archaeological Journal* 88, 67–158.

Piggott, S. 1954. *The Neolithic cultures of the British Isles*. Cambridge: Cambridge University Press.

Scott, J. G. 1961. The excavation of the chambered tomb at Crarae, Loch Fyneside, Mid Argyll. *Proceedings of the Society of Antiquaries of Scotland* 94, 1–27.

Scott, J. G. 1964. The chambered cairn at Beacharra, Kintyre, Argyll, Scotland. *Proceedings of the Prehistoric Society* 30, 134–58.

Scott, J. G. 1969. The Clyde cairns of Scotland. In T. G. E. Powell, J. X. W. P. Corcoran, F. M. Lynch and J. G. Scott, *Megalithic enquiries in the west of Britain*, 175–222. Liverpool: Liverpool University Press.

Scott, W. L. 1935. The chambered cairn of Clettraval, North Uist. *Proceedings of the Society of Antiquaries of Scotland* 59, 480–536.

Scott, W. L. 1942a. Neolithic culture of the Outer Hebrides. *Antiquity* 16, 301–6.

Scott, W. L. 1942b. Local manufacture of Neolithic pottery. *Proceedings of the Society of Antiquaries of Scotland* 76, 130–2.

Scott, W. L. 1948. The chambered tomb of Unival, North Uist. *Proceedings of the Society of Antiquaries of Scotland* 82, 1–40.

Scott, W. L. 1951. Eilean an Tighe: a pottery workshop of second millennium BC. *Proceedings of the Society of Antiquaries of Scotland* 85, 1–37.

Selkirk, A. 1972. *Current Archaeology* 3 (11).

Sheridan, A. 1992. Scottish stone axeheads: some new work and recent discoveries. In N. Sharples and A. Sheridan (eds), *Vessels for the ancestors: essays on the Neolithic of Britain and Ireland*, 194–212. Edinburgh: Edinburgh University Press.

Sheridan, A. 2000. Achnacreebeag and its French connections: Vive the 'auld alliance'. In J. C. Henderson (ed.), *The prehistory and early history of Atlantic Europe*. Oxford: British Archaeological Reports International Series 861.

Squair, R. 1998. *The Neolithic of the Western Isles*. Unpublished Ph.D thesis: Glasgow University.

9   Labouring with monuments: constructing the dolmen at Carreg Samson, south-west Wales

Colin Richards

Introduction

This contribution focuses on dolmen, with its main object of study being the site of Carreg Samson, Pembrokeshire, south-west Wales. The theme however involves the social processes that lie behind the construction and constitution of monuments. Whilst wading through the large archaeological literature on prehistoric monuments in preparation for this paper, I came upon an interesting comment by Colin Renfrew (1997) in *Science and Stonehenge*. He said that 'I do not believe that we have yet learnt to think with sufficient coherence about the nature of monuments' (Renfrew 1997, 9). We must remember that Renfrew was saying this in the context of discussing a definition of monuments as edifices of commemoration, as mnemonic devices. However, given the huge volume of literature given over to investigating monuments is it reasonable to say that archaeological understandings of monuments are incoherent? More recently, this uncertainty about monuments has been expressed differently by Whittle (2002, 192) who questions whether "we can make any sort of sense, as outside observers, of the diversities visible at any time and through time, in any one place and from place to place?

I slowly came to realize that the problem may not be so much a lack of coherence as a possible misconception of the nature of certain monuments. This misconception may stem from our ideas of what constitutes a monument and the notion that it is built to provide a function only after completion. It is possibly this implicit assumption that lies behind numerous studies of the experience of architectural representation in monumental contexts (e.g. C. Richards 1993; Thomas 1992; Tilley 1994, and so on). That some monuments may have had an intended role or an identifiable purpose is beyond doubt, but such constructs are not immutable and besides should this be our sole focus of study? Whittle's question is pertinent to monuments such as dolmen that seem to maintain similar form over large areas of western Europe. However, we should be aware of the social practices that lie behind such forms. In particular, the acts of monumental construction where people in different places contributed in various ways to the building process and through their

Figure 9.1. Carreg Samson (photo: Vicki Cummings).

labour constructed both themselves and their relations with others. It is these ideas that I wish to draw out here.

The dolmen of Carreg Samson is a very impressive monument with its massive angled capstone which appears to 'float' in the air (Fig. 9.1). It is situated in an open position on gently rolling pasture overlooking the craggy inlet leading to Abercastle harbour. This early Neolithic monument is one of a group of dolmens, comprising various forms, that cluster around the Preseli mountains in south-west Wales. Cummings (2001; 2002) has pointed to the influence of the Preseli mountains and the ocean in the situation of these monuments. Carreg Samson is classified as belonging to a group of polygonal chambered megalithic tombs, taking its place within a meticulously researched typological sequence of Welsh megaliths (e.g. Lynch 1975, 25–34). Typological reasoning is grounded in distance, both physical and conceptual, and within a particular view of morphological order. Fortunately, such a framework tends to fall away with the physical encounter. When approaching this monument it is the striking visual appearance of a massive capstone of hewn rock held aloft by a group of smaller vertical pointed stones that eclipses notions of archaeological typology. With the sea and rugged coastline acting as a backdrop, this lone dolmen with its massive capstone is a spectacular sight. Such imagery cannot help but provoke questions of long passed intent and purpose. And, as so many have previously pondered, how did the builders create this amazing feat of construction, how was the quarrying and movement of this enormous stone achieved and how was it balanced so precariously in the air?

Archaeological analysis, particularly typological ordering, reflects our perspective on architecture so we tend to think about monuments, as we do other buildings, by privileging the built form. This is done with the knowledge that such form embodies socially constructed concepts of order, and its construction embraces the structuring of practice, the choreography of life. Consequently, we can speak of architecture as microcosm, but how applicable are such ideas to monuments such as Carreg Samson? In particular, to what degree should we privilege the final monumental form?

Figure 9.2. Natural rock formations near the passage grave of Barnenez, northern Brittany.

Reconstructing monuments

My point of departure is to suggest that in certain forms of Neolithic monumentality we may be witnessing a reversal of our own experiences of architecture. We are accustomed to construction being about creation; that something is built and only when completed can it fulfil its intended function. Alternatively, we should consider a situation where instead of seeing architecture as built to be used, its actual use lies in its *building*. Here, while there may well be an intended outcome, i.e. the dolmen, standing monolith, etc., the main social focus is the process of construction.

Most certainly, the builders of Carreg Samson had an architectural form in mind and a clear purpose of intent; to construct something outstanding that would provoke memories. Such memories would have been of people, perhaps named individuals, and memories of construction. In this respect the spectacular imagery of a dolmen is clearly related to remembrance. The architectural representation of dolmens has received much attention over recent years (e.g. Tilley 1994; 1996). Here the imagery of anomalous and spectacular rock formations as encountered, for instance, in Brittany (Fig. 9.2.), Cornwall and Wales may have been places imbued with cultural significance dating back hundreds if not thousands of years (Tilley 1994; 1996). Juxtaposition and imitation may feature strongly in this process and, in assuming a model of the sacred, monuments may be deployed and replicated elsewhere. Alternatively, Bradley (1998) has suggested a blurring of natural and cultural constructs with the implication that Neolithic people would have been unable to distinguish between the two (see also Cummings 2002). Whilst such interpretations have great merit in accounting for the architectural form of Neolithic dolmen attention remains focussed upon the finished form.

Regarding archaeological understandings of the large Wessex henges, Avebury and Durrington Walls, Barrett (1994, 13) criticises such attention when he suggests that the final plan did not reside in someone's head, 'but rather in the practice and in the project. It existed and it was known only through the moment of its execution. The project was guided by relatively simple principles of spatial order and it was upon these that it worked itself out' (Barrett 1994, 23). Although such a position with regard the final form is difficult to sustain in the example of Carreg Samson, Barrett does draw attention to 'practice and the project', namely labour and construction. If we reverse our idea of *building to create an entity that is then inhabited* and begin to consider the act of construction as the social focus *of inhabitation* then interpreting Neolithic monumentality takes on quite a different complexion (C. Richards *in prep*).

Methods of constructing monuments, in particular Stonehenge, are a well established archaeological topic. Numerous studies employ principles of engineering in experimental archaeology (e.g. J. Richards and Whitby 1997) in attempts to find out how monuments, were built. Even reconstruction models (Stone 1924, 104–12) have been employed in the search for possibilities. Unfortunately, this quest is beset with ethnocentric notions of technical ability and technological efficiency which has reached an extreme in the idea of architectural energetics (Abrams and Bolland 1999). Alongside these experiments are the calculations of labour requirements for monumental construction in which the amount of labour needed has consistently diminished (e.g. Atkinson 1956; Atkinson 1961; Bradley and Startin 1981; J. Richards and Whitby 1997 and so on.). What is so ironical about such calculations is that they completely misconceive monumental construction, namely, that it is an extravagant expression of social labour and effort and consequently by definition demands the presence and involvement of large numbers of people. It is not so much that monuments require a large labour force to be built but that large numbers of people are required for monumental construction. Any invocation of principles of least effort become redundant in such a social context because it is the number of people involved that constitutes the vehicle of prestige and occasion (*contra* J. Richards and Whitby 1997, 235). Equally, ideas concerning the employment of technological efficiency may also flounder when confronted with theories of tradition and traditionally accepted methods of practice and ritualised labour.

Again, by privileging the finished form there exists the tendency to compress construction into a unitary endeavour, a single event regardless of the temporality of practices embodied in the process of making. One implication of this view is that it supports discussions of monuments as, for example, territorial markers, because a unitary process has led to a single end product. Within this framework the scale of labour estimated to be involved in the building of a dolmen such as Carreg Samson – in the region of 10,000 – 15,000 worker-hours – is easily and unproblematically attributed to the work of a single kin group even if aided by others in return for a feast (Renfrew 1973, 547). Any real regard for a temporality of construction is unnecessary within this scheme because the finished monument represents the only goal, but as Edmonds (1999, 99) notes, it ignores the length of time taken for a monument to reach its final form. The point I am making here is that monumental construction is more than a means to an end. In the temporality of building lies practices that embody social transactions and the renegotiations of identities in the presencing and fusing of people together through their labour and the product of that labour. Here the monument may have many purposes but primarily it is a physical expression of peoples' labour.

So far I have suggested that the construction process of monuments may provide the social focus as opposed to the completed form (see Evans 1988). This now shifts the emphasis to human labour and on the accumulation of large numbers of people. It also highlights power and authority, obligation and debt, as ingredients of social exchange and construction of identity. The ability to mobilise a work force, as an index of political power, provided the basis of Renfrew's social typology of Neolithic monumentality (1973; 1979). Here the size of a monument created the calibration of a crude barometer of political organisation in Neolithic Wessex and Orkney. Problems of monumental scale and social evolution aside (Bradley 1984), there remains the assumption that a centralized political authority is necessary to initiate monumental architecture. Ethnographic evidence, quite simply, shows this to be a mistaken assumption (Hoskins 1986).

'And so we will raise this stone'

Returning to the chambered tombs of Wales, Daniel (1963) makes an insightful comment; 'when we are concerned with distributions and sequences of tomb plans and with objects of dateable type buried with the dead in these tombs, it is easy to forget the implications in human terms of these great monuments – the man hours of navvying and quarrying and dragging involved, and the ideas and ideals that prompted and inspired this hard work' (Daniel 1963, 22). While Daniel did forget these implications for the rest of the book, the point he makes is valid. How then could we think about such implications with regard the dolmen at Carreg Samson?

The motivation for its creation may have been the vocalized need for commemoration; to create a permanent material expression, perhaps relating to dead kin and acknowledge social obligation. Once such an undertaking was announced, much planning would be required because monumental construction begins not with a large labour force gathered together, but the creation of conditions under which such a labour force could act together. This matrix of production involves reaffirming a network of relationships between people who will not all necessarily directly participate in the physical movement of the stones. Importantly, these would have involved many different people in a range of different contexts all making preparations be they tools, materials, offerings and so on. In this sense they were producing things that were both pieces of themselves and yet were to be part of something greater (see Thomas 1996, chapter 5). Woven around the hearth in the evenings, many lengths of strong rope were required to drag the stone, levers, rollers and sledge required specific types of wood involving the felling of large numbers of trees in the forest. From a range of tools specially fashioned, to animals and food slowly accumulated, all these pursuits and more created a web of relationships that enmeshed many people in many different places. Therefore, these projects of the monument created their own rhythms and temporalities merging with the time cycles of production and daily life. In this way the activities surrounding the construction of a single monument brought a physicality and practicality to otherwise abstract social categories such as kin or community. Thus, although not yet physically built, Carreg Samson was already constructing and ordering social relationships and identities. The amount of preparation was likely to have been of great magnitude and in some cases these projects may have taken generations to realize.

As we all know, terminology goes a long way in shaping our expectations and understanding of archaeological evidence. The portal dolmens are a case in point where they fall within the category of chambered tomb. The expectation therefore is of their functioning as burial chambers and here lies additional weight to the idea that these monuments were built for a subsequent purpose – that of burial. However, while the remains from dolmens are very variable, on excavation they are consistently found to contain little in the way of human skeletal material. Indeed, if it was not for the historical legacy of understanding that defined dolmens as funerary monuments then such an interpretation would be difficult to

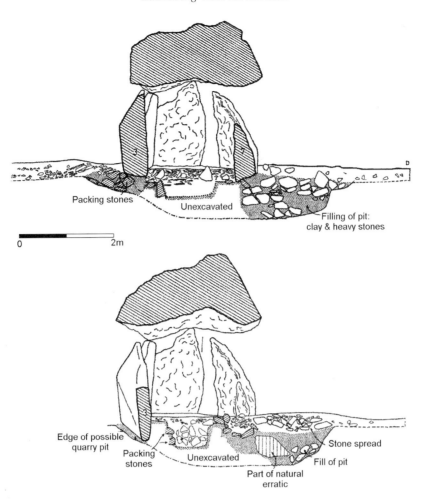

Packing stones

Unexcavated

Filling of pit:
clay & heavy stones

0   2m

Edge of possible
quarry pit

Packing
stones

Unexcavated

Stone spread

Fill of pit

Part of natural
erratic

Figure 9.3. Section drawing of Carreg Samson showing the possible quarry pit (after Lynch 1975).

arrive at on the evidence alone. This point is convincingly made by Leivers (2000, 126), in his examination of dolmens in north Wales, when he suggests that the western dolmen at Dyffryn Ardudwy contained nothing when it was sealed by the massive capstone. This contrasts with the eastern example which appears to be designed in order to facilitate repeated access and episodes of deposition (Leivers 2000, 130). This situation raises the possibility that some dolmens were erected as completed entities and not necessarily as containers. This would mean that once the capstone was elevated and positioned there was no expectation of any further use. In short, the monument had been completed once the capstone was set in place.

The dolmen effectively holds an enormous stone in the air. The capstone is difficult to visualize in all its detail as it towers above, indeed a large part of it cannot be seen by human eyes. In being the largest and heaviest stone it would have been the main focus of the preparation process as the majority of activities were tasks relating to its eventual movement. Given the great emphasis placed on the capstone, its choice would have clearly been of great importance. Shape, texture, substance, colour may

well have been of significance but was the stone renowned and acclaimed as something transcending these physical characteristics? Was it, for instance, gendered and did that alter with removal or elevation? To underline this significance, in some cases the selection of a suitable place for the monument appears determined by the *locale* of the stone. While recently Tilley (1994, 99) and Cummings (2001; 2002) have noted the significance of distant rock outcrops visible from Carreg Samson, there are also several large stone erratics of similar rock-type as the capstone in the same field.

On excavation the dolmen was found to be erected over a large pit; which was suggested to be quite possibly the source of the capstone (Fig. 9.3) (Lynch 1975, 16). In the fill of the pit were broken pieces of 'erratic' (Lynch 1975, figure 3), consistent with the pit being a product of quarrying. A similar large pit was found beneath the nearby site of Pentre Ifan and again there must remain a strong possibility that *in situ* stone was quarried and then raised up to form the capstone of the famous dolmen (also see Whittle this volume). At a number of other Pembrokeshire monuments, suggested to be of later date (Cummings 2002), such as Morfa Bycham D, Carn Wnda,

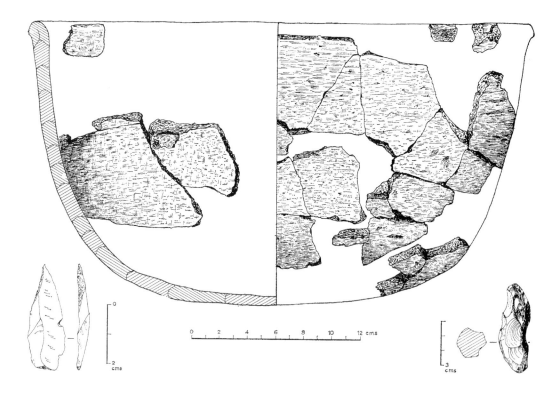

Figure 9.4. *A selection of artefacts recovered from Carreg Samson (after Lynch 1975).*

and Garn Gilfach, large natural stones are simply wedged up to form a capstone by inserting small blocks of stone beneath them (Barker 1992, 77). These occurrences are particularly illuminating. Here, I will extend Tilley's (1994, 76–109) and Cummings' (2002) arguments about the significance of natural features such as rock outcrops, whilst recalling Leivers (2000, 126) contention that some dolmen were built as monuments in themselves as opposed to containers of human remains, and suggest that the concept of a dolmen was not necessarily about creating a 'burial chamber' at all. Instead, the monument was more concerned with raising a mythical or sacred stone from the earth into the air (see Whittle, this volume). Under these circumstances the so-called contents of the 'chamber' could be better understood as offerings placed beneath the stone. At Carreg Samson such offerings were an interesting collection of materials and bone, 1.57 grammes of burnt bone, the partial remains of a round based bowl and 19 flints which included a microlith (Lynch 1975, 24–5). Clearly this deposit included disparate objects of different dates, most certainly the microlith would have represented something from, and representative of, the past (Fig. 9.4).

Capstone or tablestone, by whatever name the giant stone was called and however known, once it was chosen quarrying could begin. Traditional methods of quarrying may themselves have taken many years to complete the required cleavage of the stone from the earth. Its removal from its place would be the first act of construction requiring the coming together of a substantial labour force. The large stone supported at Carreg Samson weighs in the region of 25 ton. According to whichever calculation is accepted, dragging the stone free would have required at least 400 people for Atkinson's original estimates (1956, 10), 150 for Burl (1976, 74) and c. 75 for J. Richards and Whitby (1997, 240–56). These are estimated minimum numbers of individuals required, but imagine the visual spectacle and feelings of awe that the first attempts at moving the giant stone would arouse. Under these circumstance it is easy to conjure up a image of vast numbers of people gathering to witness such a momentous event.

From where did this number of people come and why did they join together in the labour of stone moving or dragging? Also, how do we conceive this act - as a pleasant and joyous occasion or one of toil, pain and injury? It is not necessary to invoke a centralized authority to account for the gathering of such a workforce. Networks of social relationships and exchange embracing communities and kin, are based on obligation and debt, achieved status and authority. It is through the playing out of practices that underlie such relationships that a large assembly of people could be realized. Here labour can be seen to be an element of exchange, which at one level is repaid through social debt and the provision of feasts, but at another builds an enduring monument embodying the many exchanges of labour. Finally, the people work together to cleave and drag the massive stone from the earth. In this act the many objects and materials specially prepared for the occasion fuse through the unity of social labour. As such, this moment serves to adhere the social relationships and personal identities embodied within the many practices and materials leading up to this special occasion. The stone is hauled free and a wave of excitement permeates through those assembled, from this point on stories will be told over generations about the time the earth gave up this great stone.

This act cannot be reduced to people simply coming together for a good feast, as Renfrew (1973, 547) suggests, nor some spontaneous display of social cohesion. For at such occasions different forms of social exchange occur and reconstructed identities are forged. Through the giving of goods and labour social debts may be re-paid and future obligations created. Feasts may be given and wealth sacrificed bestowing status on the hosts. At another level feasting is not merely a conspicuous display of wealth in the guise of payment for labour, but through subtleties such as the sequence of food serving, when and to whom, which cuts of meat are offered and what ceramic vessels are used, and so on, a kind of social mapping is effected; an arena where identities and relationships are re-negotiated.

Once the gathering has dispersed and the capstone had been quarried and laid to the side, the pit from which it had been excavated was refilled. At Carreg Samson several of the smaller supporting upright stones appear to come from different localities and sources. These are not massive stones but would still have required a large number of people dragging them across the land on wooden sledges. Through dense woodland and rough scrub, pathways would have been cut and cleared, tree trunk rollers laid, and slowly the land itself becomes scarred by acts of labour choreographed by the anatomy of the monument. Each stone may have referred to different groups and each act of stone dragging and erection constituted a different project possibly realized over several years. Here again, within the body of the monument, elements are brought together to create a new whole, a microcosm of an altered social and physical world.

The erection of a single standing stone may have been a primary and a significant act in the play of construction. Certainly in the eastern chamber at Dyffryn Ardudwy there is clear evidence of the back slab being the only orthostat set in a packed socket (Powell 1973); an assumption being that it was erected singly and stood isolated for some time before the rest of the chamber was built. Evidence from Carreg Samson for any similar sequence of orthostatic erection is unfortunately in-conclusive. Finally, after much preparation came the time for the capstone is to be born aloft at Carreg Samson. This was to be the great gathering of people to participate and witness the final act of construction.

Imagine the scene, hundreds of people working, some pushing with levers, the majority hauling on ropes, ritual

Figure 9.5. The massive capstone at Pentre Ifan.

specialists, the organizing social group, hundreds more watching. Within this mass, social choreography is at work ordering the labour force, for whom the organization of tasks is also a social microcosm, as the massive stone slowly moves into position (Fig. 9.5).

Cairns as mnemonics of construction

Just consider for a moment the focus of this final event; the practicalities of raising the capstone. Clearly, the building of a ramp or platform would have been necessary to lift and roll the giant stone onto the upright supporting orthostats. This ramp or platform would no doubt be composed of smaller stones heaped together in order to support such a great weight. Consequently, much stone would need to be gathered and built up at the site of the dolmen. At some dolmens there appears to be no special stone socket for the orthostats. Under these circumstances their main means of support is through compression by the great weight of the capstone. Given the delicate nature of balance and position, the orthostats would have to be carefully encased and supported in their correct place within the ramp or platform. In the final act, the massive stone would be rolled up the ramp or platform on wooded rollers into its correct position. Once the capstone had been correctly manoeuvred into place the stone platform would be carefully dismantled leaving the orthostats to support its weight.

Much debate and doubt has surrounded the provision of stone cairns at the portal dolmens (Kinnes 1975, 25). Inevitably, on excavation little remains of the cairn that is assumed to have originally encased the chamber (Daniel 1950, 38–9). At Carreg Samson a few stones were discovered around the dolmen but no form was apparent (Lynch 1975, 15–6). At Pentre Ifan a remodeled haphazard spread of stone was recognized as the remains of a cairn (Lynch 1972, 71–3). A similar small scatter of 'cairn' material was found at Carreg Coetan Arthur (Barker 1992, 19–20). At another example, further north,

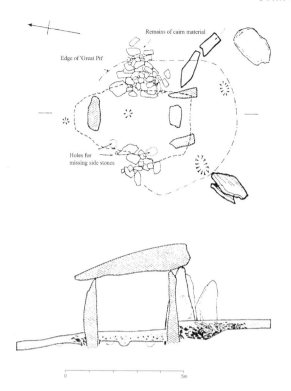

Remains of cairn material

Edge of 'Great Pit'

Holes for
missing side stones

0   5m

Figure 9.6. *Remains of stone cairn and 'Great Pit' from where the capstone may have been excavated at Pentre Ifan (after Grimes 1932).*

the 'cairn' surrounding Dyffryn Ardudwy (Powell 1973) was merely a low spread of rounded boulders. Accepting the likelihood of later stone-robbing, more often than not the putative 'cairn' is little more than a mass of stones strewn around the dolmen. That some examples do seem to show evidence of a certain formality in the definition of shape, for instance, at Pentre Ifan where the partial remains of a kerb is present (Lynch 1972, 73), should not be mistaken for evidence of an encasing mound of stones. On the contrary, I suspect that the notion of a cairn encasing the dolmen is slightly misconceived. This is because there seems to be an implicit expectation of such a presence at these sites. The evidence for such substantial encasing structures does not bear the weight of scrutiny and frequently amounts to little more than the noted spread of stones. Instead, the evidence interpreted as a cairn may simply be the remains of the dismantled ramp and platform, heaped around the dolmen, that was used to support the capstone. Yet, I would suggest this material is not symbolically neutral nor simply discarded material, but was highly potent in representing the physicality of construction and the deployment of peoples labour. Therefore, it is not accidental that it is either spread around the dolmen or is embanked against it (Fig. 9.6.).

Deliberately heaped around the dolmen, the physical remains of construction now adorn and fuse with the

monument. In this act we are not seeing the completion of a typical chambered tomb encased within a cairn, but a memorializing of the physical practices and social networks of construction. In visual constitution Carreg Samson could be seen to be made by people and symbolically composed of people through their labour and toil. When future generations came to confront and engage with this monument it was not simply the memories of a single person or social group that would be invoked. It also acted as a mnemonic for the social networks of labour and the great gathering of people that participated in its construction. They might not have asked, as we do, 'how was such an amazing feat achieved'? Instead through the architecture of Carreg Samson they were continually reminded of the process of construction and the drama of the great gathering long after the people had dispersed and died (Edmonds 1999, 103), and of the social relationships and identities that the monument was claimed to embody.

Garn Turne: a failure of construction

Finally, I want to consider an alternative scenario. When considering prehistoric constructions, particularly monuments, we tend to see completed forms and here ideas about 'ongoing projects' 'ideal types' and 'original meanings' become issues of debate (see Barrett 1994, 24). But what about monumental projects that failed, would they necessarily be recognized if we came across them? Sometimes plans can go wrong, as we all know, and implicitly it seems as if we expect the past to be composed of normative practices and clearly defined material forms and patterning.

Approximately 15 kilometres south-west of Carreg Samson is the collapsed dolmen Garne Turne (Barker 1992, 28–9). Cummings (2002, 111), has noted the views of the spectacular Great Trefgarne outcrops visible on the skyline from this site. However, the dolmen lies on slightly rising ground adjacent to a large rock outcrop, indeed, the monument is situated among a mass of natural stone. The interpretation of Garn Turne is contentious, for Grimes (1932, 92), it is a collapsed dolmen of 'Pentre Ifan type' while Barker disagrees with this possibility: 'the capstone is immense (c. 60 tons), and one must doubt whether it was ever entirely raised from the ground. It is possible that the tall uprights in front of the chamber were part of the facade, rather than supporters, and that the capstone was earthfast at the SW' (1992, 29). Given the elevation and size of the cap-stone, its scarred lower surface, the rear uprights clearly trapped beneath the stone, in conjunction with the large flakes removed from the inner side of the frontal uprights, I think that both Grimes (1932) and Barker (1992) are both partially correct in their interpretations. Garn Turne is a collapsed dolmen. However, as Barker (1992) notes, the capstone really is enormous and its estimated weight of 60 tons

Figure 9.7. *The collapsed dolmen of Garn Turne.*

significance between people and their physical world, and relationships between each other. But, as illustrated by the events at Garn Turne, failure is never far away.

Acknowledgements

I would particularly like to thank Vicki Cummings for generously spending time with me in Pembrokeshire and discussing her interpretations of these amazing monuments, many of the ideas expressed above were a product of our discussions at the different sites. Both Vicki Cummings and Chris Fowler kindly commented on this paper and I am grateful to both of them.

seems to be a cautious estimate (Fig. 9.7). A possible reinterpretation of this site is that it represents a failed attempt at building what would have been, had it met with success, a visually stunning and dramatic dolmen. Clearly, this would have been an inauspicious occasion, one remembered for the reverse of what was intended. The implications for the organizing social group, in terms of prestige and status, may have been devastating especially given the huge and lengthy preparations required for such an undertaking. Indeed, the scale of this act of construction may have been considered too ostentatious a display on the part of the sponsoring group and its failure a result of concealed social resistance (Hoskins 1986, 40–1). Perhaps exposure to failure and the element of social risk that such undertakings involve should be also taken into account when interpreting the sometimes extravagant and lavish displays of monumentality of the Neolithic period.

The possible collapse of Garn Turne during construction would have been a memorable event, probably more so than its successful erection. Here Thomas's (2000, 80) point about the destruction of material culture takes on dramatic dimensions because no-one would have forgotten the catastrophe at Garn Turne. Today, it lies as it was left several thousand years ago, a fallen and destroyed monument. Because, after such a technical and social disaster, there seems to have been no further attempt to re-erect the massive capstone.

Conclusion

To conclude, understandings of monuments have tended to focus on the completed form as opposed to the processes of construction. In some cases the social focus of a monument may have been solely in its building (C. Richards *in prep*). By examining the dolmens of Pembrokeshire I have hopefully drawn attention to the social practices that lie behind monumental construction and the way in which such practices forge webs of

References

Abrams, E.M. and Bolland, T.W. 1999. Architectural energetics, ancient monuments, and operations management. *Journal of Archaeological Method and Theory* 6, 263–91.

Atkinson, R.J.C. 1956. *Stonehenge*. London: Hamish Hamilton.

Atkinson, R.J.C. 1961. Neolithic engineering. *Antiquity* 35, 292–99.

Barker, C.T. 1992. *The chambered tombs of south-west Wales: a re-assessment of the Neolithic burial monuments of Carmarthenshire and Pembrokeshire*. Oxford: Oxbow.

Barrett, J.C. 1994. *Fragments from antiquity: an archaeology of social life in prehistoric Britain*. Oxford: Blackwell.

Bradley, R. 1984. Studying monuments. In R. Bradley and J. Gardiner (eds), *Neolithic studies*, 61–6. Oxford: British Archaeological Reports British Series 133.

Bradley, R. 1998. Ruined buildings, ruined stones: enclosures and natural places in the Neolithic of south-west England. *World Archaeology* 30, 13–22.

Burl, A. 1976. *The stone circles of the British Isles*. New Haven and London: Yale University Press.

Cummings, V. 2001. *Landscapes in transition? Exploring the origins of monumentality in south-west Wales and south-west Scotland*. Unpublished Ph.D. Thesis: Cardiff University.

Cummings, V. 2002. All cultural things: actual and conceptual monuments in the Neolithic of western Britain. In C. Scarre (ed.), *Monuments and landscape in Atlantic Europe: perception and society during the Neolithic and Early Bronze Age*, 107–21. London: Routledge.

Daniel, G.E. 1950. *The prehistoric chamber tombs of England and Wales*. Cambridge: Cambridge University Press.

Daniel, G.E. 1963. *The megalith builders of western Europe*. Harmondsworth: Pelican Books.

Edmonds, M. 1999. *Ancestral geographies of the Neolithic*. London: Routledge.

Evans, C. 1988. Acts of enclosure: a consideration of concentrically-organized causewayed enclosures. In J. C. Barrett and I. Kinnes (eds), *The archaeology of context: the Neolithic and Bronze Age*, 85–96. Sheffield: Collis Publications.

Grimes, W.F. 1932. Prehistoric archaeology in Wales since 1925. III The Neolithic period. *Proceedings of the Prehistoric Society of East Anglia* 7, 85–92.

Hoskins, J.A. 1986. So my name shall live: stone dragging and grave-building in Kodi, West Sumba. *Bijdragen tot de Taal-,Land-en Volkenkunde* 142, 31–51.

Kinnes, I.A. 1975. Monumental function in British Neolithic burial practice. *World Archaeology* 7, 16–29.

Leivers, M.A. 2000. *The architecture and context of mortuary practices in the Neolithic period in north Wales*. Unpublished Ph.D. thesis: University of Southampton.

Lynch, F.M. 1972. Portal Dolmens in the Nevern Valley, Pembrokeshire. In F.M. Lynch and C. Burgess (eds), *Prehistoric man in Wales and the West: essays in honour of Lily F. Chitty,* 67–84. Bath: Adams and Dart.

Lynch, F.M. 1975. Excavations at Carreg Samson megalithic tomb, Mathry, Pembrokeshire. *Archaeologia Cambrensis* 124, 15–35.

Powell, T.G.E. 1973. Excavation of the megalithic chambered tomb at Dyffryn Ardudwy, Merioneth, Wales. *Archaeologia* 104, 1–50.

Renfrew, C. 1973. Monuments, mobilisation and social organization in Neolithic Wessex. In C. Renfrew (ed.), *The explanation of culture change*, 539–58. London: Duckworth.

Renfrew, C. 1979. *Investigations in Orkney*. London: Thames and Hudson.

Renfrew, C. 1997. Setting the scene: Stonehenge in the round. In B. Cunliffe and C. Renfrew (eds), *Science and Stonehenge*, 3–14. Oxford: Oxford University Press.

Richards, C. 1993. Monumental choreography, architecture and spatial representation in later Neolithic Orkney. In C. Tilley (ed.), *Interpretative Archaeology*, 143–81. Oxford: Berg.

Richards, C. in prep. *Monuments in the making: constructing the great stone circles of northern and western Britain*.

Richards, J. and Whitby, M. 1997. The engineering of Stonehenge. In B. Cunliffe and C. Renfrew (eds), *Science and Stonehenge*, 231–56. Oxford: Oxford University Press.

Startin, B. and Bradley, R. 1981. Some notes on work organisation and society in prehistoric Wessex. In C. Ruggles and A. Whittle (eds), *Astronomy and society during the period 4000–1500BC*, 289–96. Oxford: British Archaeological Reports British series 88.

Stone, E.H. 1924. *The stones of Stonehenge*. London: Robert Scott.

Thomas, J. 1992. The politics of vision and the archaeologies of landscape. In. B. Bender (ed.), *Landscape, politics and perspectives*, 19–48. Oxford: Berg.

Thomas, J. 1996. *Time, culture and identity*. London: Routledge.

Thomas, J. 2000. The identity of place in Neolithic Britain: examples from southwest Scotland. In A. Ritchie (ed.), *Neolithic Orkney in its European context*, 79–90. Cambridge: McDonald Institute Monographs.

Tilley, C. 1994. *A phenomenology of landscap: places, paths and monuments*. Oxford: Berg.

Tilley, C. 1996. The power of rocks: topography and monument construction on Bodmin Moor. *World Archaeology* 28, 161–76.

Whittle, A. 2002. Conclusion: long conversations, concerning time, descent and place in the world. In C. Scarre (ed.), *Monuments and landscape in Atlantic Europe: perception and society during the Neolithic and Early Bronze Age*, 192–204. London: Routledge.

10   Stones that float to the sky: portal dolmens and their landscapes of memory and myth

Alasdair Whittle

Introduction

This paper considers the portal dolmens and related monuments of west Wales, with the assumption that they are early in the Neolithic sequences of the Irish Sea area. It stresses their difference from other kinds of monumental construction in the early Neolithic. It follows others in seeing fundamental links between these monuments and elements of their surrounding landscapes but suggests that portal dolmens can be further considered as statements or reworkings of indigenous myth concerned with creation and origin. From this perspective, it then briefly places this phenomenon into the broader context of the early Neolithic, and suggests an important contrast between western and central-southern Britain.

The paper has developed out of research with Vicki Cummings in 2001–2, and all the arguments touched on here will be dealt with in greater detail in a monograph (Cummings and Whittle 2004; and see Whittle 2003). It builds on recent suggestions by others about portal dolmens and landscapes (Bradley 1998a; 1998b; 2000; Cummings 2001; Tilley 1994; 1996; Tilley and Bennett 2001), and it uses the long established literature on Welsh monuments in general and portal dolmens and related constructions in particular (e.g. Barker 1992; Lynch 1972; 1975; 1976).

Achievements of special virtue

Portal dolmens and related monuments are widespread in the Irish Sea area, especially in eastern and northern parts of Ireland and in western parts of Wales and southwest England. They are characterised by substantial capstones of varied shapes. Some are thick and rounded, while others are thinner but often spectacularly tilted; all are supported by uprights forming a more or less rectangular, simple chamber. A number, but by no means all, are surrounded by the remains of stone cairns. Conventionally, these have been regarded as covering or enclosing cairns, but the evidence is both varied and ambiguous; in general, I prefer to see these cairns as more like surrounding platforms. I include in my dis-

cussion some variety of monuments, which others would prefer to break into separate categories (e.g. Lynch 1975; 1976). In my view this is problematic, since on the one hand it emphasises minor differences (such as very short 'passages') at the expense of the essence of these constructions and on the other rapidly reduces portal dolmens to a few claimed 'classic' examples and many exceptions or variants. I do, however, follow established opinion in seeing it as probable, on the basis of pottery associations and such few radiocarbon dates as exist, that many of these constructions were early in their regional sequences (Bradley 1998b; Cooney 2000; Lynch 1972; 1976; Tilley and Bennett 2001; see also Cummings and Whittle 2004). Though this is not the place for detailed discussion, they may have preceded perhaps the first court cairns or court tombs in Ireland and the earliest Cotswold-Severn outliers of south-east Wales. In some parts of south-west Wales, the portal dolmens are found in areas which had had numerous Mesolithic occupations (Cummings 2001; Cummings and Whittle 2004; Tilley 1994).

It is not hard to find the reasons for the comparative neglect of portal dolmens in discussions of Neolithic monumentality. They appear to be deceptively simple constructions. Their open character has made their original contents, if any, extremely vulnerable to disturbance and dispersal. They are hard to date, and were placed at first in the older literature at the end of the supposed developmental sequence. Crucially, and one may suggest correctly, Frances Lynch has advocated an early date, arguing from the associated pottery at monuments like Dyffryn Ardudwy (Lynch 1976, figure 1) and from the sequences of construction to be found at Dyffryn Ardudwy, Pentre Ifan, Carnedd Hengwm South, and elsewhere (Lynch 1976). Evidence from Ireland can also be seen in the same light (summarised in Cooney 2000), though the sequences on either side of the Irish Sea need not necessarily have run in parallel, and it is not entirely clear whether the early radiocarbon dates on human bone from Poulnabrone, Co. Clare, directly date the construction of the portal monument (Cooney 2000, 96). Finally, portal dolmens and related monuments have of course proved hard to classify. A notion of 'typical' and 'classic' has been dominant but probably unhelpful. Neat, rectangular chamber, twin portal stones with closing slab, and substantial if not massive capstone have all been seen as defining characteristics. These serve to separate other monuments with more polygonal chambers, a lack of defined portals, and possible short passages or at least additional stones outside the main stone construction; Carreg Samson is obviously a good case in point (Lynch 1975). But the notion of fixed types rapidly leads to difficulty. In discussing the monuments of the Nevern Valley, Lynch claimed Carreg Coetan as the 'most classic' example of a portal dolmen (1972, 69), but from this perspective Llech y Dribedd 'clearly belongs to the Portal Dolmen tradition but it is not an entirely classic example' (Lynch 1972, 77). Likewise, Powell saw the first, western construction at Dyffryn Ardudwy firmly as a portal dolmen, but the second, eastern one as something else, though he ends by conceding that it could be considered as 'a form of enlarged Portal Dolmen…adopting some new concepts of what an impressive funerary monument should be' (Powell 1973, 35). All such differences may have been significant, from the point of view of both sequence and development, and experience and meaning. But at this stage it may be much more profitable to think in terms of a western tradition of construction which produced and allowed a spectrum of forms. In that spirit, portal dolmens and related monuments can be discussed as early, distinctive constructions.

The older literature in general was inclined to see these monuments as tombs, and the Welsh literature in that tradition has been much concerned to track histories of migration and interaction. Most past models have tended to take the character of monuments for granted in discussions of this kind. In what we could call neutrally an older or pre-processual literature, the concerns were understandably for typology and sequence. Grimes's account of Pentre Ifan (1948) makes intriguingly suggestive remarks about the possible significance of the pit underlying the main stone construction and of the originally free-standing monolith stone IX, but otherwise restricts itself to detailed description, and discussion of sequence. The same concerns can be found in Powell's discussion of Dyffryn Ardudwy (e.g. Powell 1973, 31–3), and continue as a dominant theme in Frances Lynch's valuable papers (Lynch 1972; 1975; 1976). The general assumptions of the time are reflected in the reference to a 'widespread Neolithic desire to provide a lasting and monumental home for their dead' (Lynch 1975, 30). Commenting on the enormous capstone at Llech y Dribedd, Lynch strikingly reflected (1972, 77) that 'The lifting of such unnecessarily huge stones must have been an achievement of special virtue to the builders of Portal Dolmens…', but otherwise the discussions are almost wholly in terms of sequence, incoming populations and their landings and penetration inland, and subsequent relative dispersal and isolation. Nor was there much more consideration, in the first post-processual interpretations of these monuments, of the character of the constructions themselves. As Fleming has noted (1999, 119–20), Tilley's first account (1994) tended to downplay the structural diversity of monuments in south-west Wales, and while Tilley (1994) sought to examine the links between constructions and landscape forms, there was curiously little discussion of the monuments themselves.

More recently, other more integrated approaches have emerged. Bradley (1998a; 1998b; 2000) and Tilley and Bennett (2001) have discussed in more detail with reference to south-west England how these constructions appear to draw on and mimic features of the natural landscape such as tors and hilltops. Bradley (2000, 109–10) has drawn attention to how the building of monuments can add new meaning to already significant natural places. Tilley and Bennett have developed this point, to suggest that 'in elevating large stones, these people were emulating the work of a super-ancestral past' and 'the dolmens…were the tors dismantled and put back together again to resemble their original form' (2001, 345). Further:

> West Penwith is one of the few places in Britain from which the sun can be seen to have a watery death and birth at important points in the solar calendar…elemental cosmological themes of fire, water, stone, birth, death and the regeneration of life, may have had a particular resonance and symbolic power. (Tilley and Bennett 2001, 336)

Stones that float to the sky

In turn I want to suggest a further, specifically mythical dimension to these constructions. Whether dolmens resemble tors or *vice versa*, I believe there is more to the relationship than imitation or emulation. Construction involves transformation. Several features help to support this claim.

These were probably constructions rapidly made. A possible exception are the instances where the portal dolmen stands directly above a shallow pit, as at Carreg Samson or Pentre Ifan, though this may equally be an integral part of a single phase of construction. Nor do successive rebuildings, as at Dyffryn Ardudwy (Powell 1973) or Trefignath (Smith and Lynch 1987), invalidate the general claim. Though it has often been supposed otherwise, there is little evidence for the original presence of surrounding and concealing cairns, and there is good evidence in some cases for deliberately and carefully built platforms of smaller stones, from which the uprights appear to emerge.

Of the underlying pit at Pentre Ifan, Grimes (1948, 13) conceded that 'it may be that the pit was not dug for entirely structural reasons', such as to get a level floor for the stone construction. The deliberately refilled stone in the pit, much of it of igneous type rather than the immediately local shale, could suggest, together with the

Figure 10.1. Carreg Samson, south-west Wales (photos Vicki Cummings).

act of digging in the first place, an interest in the properties of the earth itself. A similar pit was also found under the main stone construction at Carreg Samson (in conventional formal terms, a chamber and passage monument rather than a portal dolmen), but without the same kind of stony backfill; following the suggestion of Hogg, the possibility was mooted that the pit represents where the capstone was dug out of the earth (Lynch 1975, 16). This is an attractive idea, and there are other stones still today partly buried, both close to Carreg Samson (Lynch 1975, 16) and Pentre Ifan. If this kind of explanation is preferred, it is still striking that builders chose to commemorate the act of extraction from the earth by placing the resulting stone construction directly above, in what might not from a purely practical point of view have been the easiest location.

The easy assumption has usually been made that a cairn was something which enclosed the whole, as is

undoubtedly the case in Irish as well as north Welsh passage graves, and probably in the great majority of Cotswold-Severn monuments; Hazleton North retained traces of a pitched axial ridge right along the top of its cairn (Saville 1990). Discussing Pentre Ifan, Grimes (1948, 10) noted the idea of the covering cairn as coming to prominence in the nineteenth century. The radical alternative for many portal dolmens and related constructions is that cairns were often never more than low platforms. It is unwise to be dogmatic when there is clearly such scope for later denudation, but it is striking how often very little survives of cairn material in contrast to the larger uprights and capstones. Had stone robbing been universally the main instrument of decay and destruction, we might well have expected many fewer major stone constructions (conventionally 'chambers') to have survived. The cairn at Pentre Ifan was already a minor feature at the start of the seventeenth century

(Grimes 1948), and putative robbing cannot be ascribed to intensifying land-use in more recent times. Frances Lynch (1972, figure 4) has suggested the presence of a small, squarish, first cairn at Pentre Ifan. At only about 11 by 15 m, with the main stone construction on the uphill side, and reaching a height at the top of the downhill end of the capstone or raised stone (i.e. its lowest part) of some 3 m, it is hard to see how such a cairn could have been a covering one at all. In other instances, there may have been little by way of surrounding material, as seems to have been the case at Carreg Samson (Lynch 1975). While some cairns may have had formal limits, as in the suggested second, more elongated phase at Pentre Ifan, or the rounded form of Carreg Coetan, others may have been much less well defined. At Pentre Ifan, there were signs of careful placing, diagonal stones alternating with smaller infill. To one side of the cairn at Twlc y Filiast (Savory 1956, 303), there were 'large glacial blocks apparently still in their natural positions but mixed with a certain amount of material derived from the cairn'; the distinction between placed and natural may have been blurred (cf. Tilley *et al.* 2000; Tilley and Bennett 2001). At Dyffryn Ardudwy, the thickest part of the cairn seems to have been due to a low bank connected to secondary blocking of the eastern stone construction (Powell 1973, 35–7).

From this base, whatever its nature, arise the substantial uprights which hold an often massive 'capstone' (Figures 10.1–10.5). But here the conventional terminology of megalithic archaeology lets us down (cf. Tilley 1998). Uprights are obviously integral to these constructions. Their arrangement in rectangles or other layouts may well have been significant, but this need not exhaust their significance. Uprights may have been important in their own right. The monolith stone IX at Pentre Ifan (Grimes 1948) might be seen as an earlier feature, following the model of Breton menhirs (Bradley 2002, and references). There are significant variations in colour and texture among uprights, including in the example of Carreg Samson, suggesting further that these stones were also themselves meaningful (Cummings 2001; 2002; Cummings and Whittle 2004). But there is a sense also in which their significance may have been misinterpreted, through the employment of a common language for all types of megalithic and monumental construction (Tilley 1998). In this regard the near-universal assumption in the relevant literature on portal dolmens and related monuments is that uprights serve to define and create 'chambers'; missing stones or inadequate provision of side stones are regarded as problematic, as in the main stone construction at Pentre Ifan (Grimes 1948; Lynch 1972). That a chamber-like space results in many instances is not in doubt, but the spectrum of construction also frequently allows much less formality, and it is legitimate therefore to consider whether the overriding role of the uprights was to act as supports for the larger stone raised above them. At the

least, these were not the same kind of chambers as in Cotswold-Severn monuments or in passage graves.

The top stones do indeed complete a box-like compartment, but there seems much more to them than this. They often overhang the uprights, and frequently are either pitched at a tilt or have an upper surface with a pronounced slope. The slope or tilt is formed either by the form of the upper sides or by the whole stone being literally tilted, sometimes dramatically. In several striking examples this arrangement mimics locally visible hilltops, such as the convincing link between Pentre Ifan and Carn Ingli in south-west Wales (Tilley 1994; Cummings 2001). In some cases, the link may be to a general resemblance to tors, as argued for Chun Quoit in West Penwith (Tilley and Bennett 2001, 346). In yet others, there may be no such reference, and it is possible therefore that the tilt has a significance of its own. This might be referred to some feature of daily life in forager or early farming existence, such as tents, but it may be equally plausible to think of what the raised stones actually stood for. Archaeological language and convention predispose us to call these stones 'capstones' or roofstones' but this is far too general, and misses what the architecture emphasises, that the stones have been carefully selected, dramatically raised, and placed in particular ways. These are surely stones which have been carefully selected for conspicuous presentation, after impressive amounts of concentrated labour to get them set up.

As often commented, the raised stones were often substantial. Lynch suggests weights of up to 50 tons (1972, 77). Many are thick, pregnant with their mass, but again there is a spectrum of variation, grading into the thinner examples at Dyffryn Ardudwy and Trefignath and elsewhere. Carreg Samson, formally a passage and chamber monument rather than a portal dolmen, shares the feature of a massive raised stone. Many are marked by a distinctive tilt on their upper surface. Sometimes this may just be the result of the shape of the stone dug out of the earth, but in others, as seems also often to be the case in Ireland, this feature is enhanced by subtle differential propping. It is even possible that some raised stones have been shaped rather than merely extracted from the earth. That at Pentre Ifan is one obvious candidate, and a wider study of this, though beyond the scope of the present study, would be very timely. Vicki Cummings has already drawn attention elsewhere to the visual effect of some of the raised stones, such as at Pentre Ifan, which seem to float in the air (Cummings 2001). Others, such as at Carreg Coetan, are rather different, giving the impression of either pressing down on the earth or a massive effort required to suspend them just above its surface.

Closely and directly linked to the use of the term 'chamber', the language employed on these stones has been universally that of 'capstones'. The easy assumption is made, often implicitly, that their principal structural purpose was to finish or close a chamber, rather in the manner of the beautifully engineered roofstones at

Figure 10.2. Pentre Ifan, south-west Wales (photos Vicki Cummings).

Knowth, which was in turn to be covered by a cairn or mound. Once again, it is hard to separate this question from that of cairns and mounds.

Relatively little of the contents of these constructions has survived. This paucity might also be a significant aspect of the character of these constructions, serving to emphasise what could be seen from the outside and roundabout, rather than what was deposited within, but this is hard to put into perspective. We know of depositions of both unaltered and cremated human bone. We know very little of the relative histories of construction and deposition. There may be a connection with human ancestry and descent, but it remains unclear whether this was a principal focus. Irish portal dolmens and court tombs may also largely share the same ambiguity.

While much variation can readily be envisaged, the separate strands of this discussion can be brought together. Surrounding cairns may often have had more the character of a low platform than a mounded and enclosing pile of stones, sometimes formally demarcated but on other occasions not rigidly separated from the natural stony surrounds. This is not unprecedented. Something of the kind may be seen in some at least of the Irish court tombs, and in late arrangements in some of the Orkney monuments. The emphasis is again on stone, generally much smaller than that used in the main vertical construction, with some evidence of gradations and deliberate placings. Out of this surface of stone rise uprights, to varying heights, and above these sit, hang or float a series of raised stones. It is as though there is a narrative connecting all these elements: pits dug into the earth and refilled with stone, a surface of stone from which uprights rise, and finally the great raised stones themselves. How different our normal

view of these raised stones might be if we could escape the confines of conventional terminology. Following ethnographic examples of the naming of places and features in the landscape (e.g. Basso 1984; Waterson 2000), we could at least make these constructions sound less familiar, for example on the following lines, with Welsh versions added for the sake of further unfamiliarity:

> stones-that-float-to-the-sky (*cerrig sy'n ymestyn i'r awyr*)
> places-where-the-creators-emerged (*y mannau lle yr ymddangosodd y creawdwyr*)
> mountain-raised-by-the-ancestors (*mynydd a godwyd gan yr hynafiaid*).

To repeat the claim made above, while there is clear evidence, already cited, of modifications over time to particular sites, it may well be that these monuments were not the result of prolonged construction. Whatever the social circumstances surrounding the selection of stones, the mobilisation of labour, or the choice of propitious times (see Colin Richards, this volume), the building process as such is likely to have been a fairly swift one. The Pentre Ifan monolith might serve to extend the sequence of use of this site, seen also in its possible secondary cairn and façade (Lynch 1972; 1976), but on the whole secondary modifications to these sites take the form of repetition, as at Dyffryn Ardudwy, rather than the wider process of transformation and eventual closure seen for example in southern English long barrows. The single act of creation may have added to the renown of builders, and may, as discussed further below, relate to other acts of creation and bringing the world into existence.

Figure 10.3. Carreg Coetan, south-west Wales (photos Vicki Cummings).

Landscapes of memory and myth

Even with portal stones and tilted raised stones, there is a sense in which these box-like, four-square constructions lack a single axis. In some cases, a prominent axis may indeed be proposed; Pentre Ifan, for example, seems quite simply to face uphill. But it also faces in other directions, and the 'gunsight' model of monument orientation does not seem to apply, in the way discussed for Cotswold-Severn monuments (Tilley 1994; Fleming 1999). In this way, portal dolmens appear from their careful placings in chosen settings (Cummings 2001; Cummings and Whittle 2004) to draw in a range of features of the surrounding landscape. Pentre Ifan affords views of outcrops, Carn Ingli, a partial view of the sea, and tracts of the Nevern valley. The prominent axis looks at the rising slope, with minor outcrops to one side, but other features are not excluded. Other discussions (Tilley 1996; Bradley 1998b; Tilley and Bennett 2001) have already usefully explored, in the context of south-west England, the resemblances between portal dolmens and natural landforms, especially tors, and the portal dolmens of Wales can certainly also be thought of in the same sort of terms. But it seems hard to confine their significance to this one relationship. They are built from materials rooted in particular places and localities, and yet refer to a series of wider features.

Among these wider features, outcrops, hills and mountains on the one hand, and the sea on the other, appear to be of recurrent significance. I concentrate here on elements of the earth and land (for discussion of the sea, see Cummings and Whittle 2004; cf. Scarre 2002a). If it can be suggested that portal dolmens and related monuments refer to or otherwise play on a connection with hills, mountains and rocky outcrops (Tilley 1994;

Cummings 2001), and if there is little evidence, though admittedly the circumstances for such survival are not favourable, for any pronounced interest in the deposition of human remains inside the compartments, it is important to think of the mythical agency of those natural features themselves. These constructions could better be seen as to do with creation myths, involving perhaps figures that emerged from the earth through mountains or rose from the earth to the sky via mountains, at the beginning of it all. This kind of belief can be found widely in other situations (e.g. Middleton 1960, 2; Waterson 2000, 184–5; Martin 2001, 116).

Mountains were a prominent feature of Lugbara mythology, for example, being a reference point or starting point in stories about creation and human origins (Middleton 1970, 36–9). In far western North America, mountains can be seen as male in relation to female locations with rock art (Whitley 1998). Tors and hills in the landscapes of the Irish Sea zone could be seen in this light as having a significance of their own, and there is thus a potential dialogue between natural places and built constructions, perhaps even an 'obviation' or alternation in Wagner's and Weiner's terms (Weiner 1988). The raised stones of portal dolmens might also, in conjunction with pits and platforms, have had a more general metaphorical or mythical significance. They could be seen as a version of creation, in which the earth was raised to the sky, or an account of how earth and sky were once joined. One Lugbara myth was about a time when people could move between the earth and the sky via a rope, a tree, and a tower; when these gave way, people were scattered over the earth into their present locations and social groupings in the world (Middleton 1970, 36).

Portal dolmens may therefore be seen, for all their

Figure 10.4. Llech y Dribedd, south-west Wales (photos Vicki Cummings).

apparent simplicity, to have complex associations and meanings. They are rooted in particular places by the choice of setting and materials. They may draw in a range of other landscape features. As with other monuments, some of this may have been less visible in summer, and more obvious in winter. It is not clear in the case of portal dolmens whether their primary emphasis was on the remains of the human dead, and by association on notions of human descent and ancestry. Other sets of ideas are suggested. Construction itself emphasises stone from the earth, and presents great raised stones for display and contemplation. The achievement of construction must surely have been a source of worldly renown, but it may also have played on a powerful mythical dimension, of stories of creation of the earth and of original creator figures that arose from the earth and waters. These might also have been associated with the outcrops, hills, mountains and sea visible from portal dolmens. A kind of reflexive relationship is possible. The monuments stand in sight of landscape features redolent of beginnings, and the monuments themselves recreate central features of that narrative. The presence or absence of human remains may be of secondary importance in this perspective. For all we know, the tilt of raised stones might have been far more significant than human remains, reflecting the first rising of the earth, or portraying the inversion of normality in that first time, like the beings who walked upside down in Lugbara myth (Middleton 1960).

Times and traditions of change: east and west

It seems to me more likely that, if this kind of interpretation is followed, this cosmology belonged to an indigenous population long familiar with the regional landscape (cf. Cummings 2001). There are no directly comparable constructions in possible source areas for colonists, such as north-west France (see Scarre 2002b; and discussed further in Cummings and Whittle 2004).

Long ago, Stuart Piggott (1955) posed the question of east or west, in relation to possible sources of the British Neolithic. The axes of identity and allegiance that he, and Childe before him, had indicated have remained the focus of research to this day. It is still legitimate to see major influences from the world of northern France, the Low Countries and the Rhineland and beyond on the formation of the Neolithic of the whole of eastern Britain. It is definitely beyond the scope of this paper to detail this relationship, but the character of the early Neolithic in southern England and eastern Britain as a whole is relevant to the nature of the early Neolithic in the west. Piggott left the relationship *between* east and west alone. Among other things, the presence in south-east Wales of long cairns of a very different tradition to the monuments of the west demands that this be examined. It is useful briefly to sketch some major differences, and then to reconsider relationships.

There are familiar difficulties in unravelling the competing claims for colonisation and acculturation in the eastern part of Britain. But there may be a case for seeing more colonisation there, by fissioning or filtering from the major established populations of the adjacent continent in the late fifth and earliest fourth millennium

Figure 10.5. The first-phase chamber at Dyffryn Ardudwy, north Wales (photo Vicki Cummings).

BC (cf. Schulting 2000). Diet change after the first two or three centuries may have been extensive, and there were few areas by this time without a Neolithic presence of some kind. East and west were certainly in contact, as seen in the movement of stone axes and in shared styles of pottery. The realm of ideas may have been rather different in the east. Memory of or reference to the old tradition of the LBK, in the form of the long mound and the ditched enclosure, was a dominant factor, absent in the west. On present chronology, however, this may not have come to the fore until two or three or even more centuries after the start of the Neolithic, a still unexplained delay in cultural memory (cf. Bradley 2002). Early monuments in the east were on the whole modest affairs, small constructions of wood, stone, earth and chalk, that were not monumentalised until the setting up of large long mounds and cairns, and the digging of ditched arenas. They might often be seen as an enhancement of the importance of place, and the landscape setting in itself may have been of less importance. Much early activity of this kind may have been concerned with the deposition of human remains, and specific genealogies as well as generalised notions of ancestry may have been to the fore. The foci were on the one hand distant memories and on the other recent persons. A rather different sort of belief system may have been at work.

By contrast, things may have been rather different in at least parts of western Britain. It could be conjectured generally that colonisation of coastal areas already occupied by well established indigenous communities is in fact unlikely, though that does not exclude colonisation of inland areas, as has been argued forcefully for Ireland

(Cooney 2000), leading to their gradual infilling. The case has also been made, on the basis of isotopic analysis and the pattern of radiocarbon dating, for rapid change in western Scotland, associated with at least some element of colonisation (Schulting and Richards 2002). It could be that the apparent turning away from use of the resources of the sea (Schulting 1998; Schulting and Richards 2002) belongs to this kind of context, and to a series of realignments in outlook and social practice. In other respects, however, and in parts or indeed the whole of western Britain, there may have been much continuity of belief systems. Many of the constructions under discussion (that is, those in western Wales) are placed close to rocky outcrops or with a view of them and prominent hills. In striking instances, the architecture of the monument seems to mimic the form of the hills, Carn Ingli being referenced by Pentre Ifan and Llech y Dribedd among others. Unlike the situation in central southern Britain, where what eventually became monumentalised began with a series of smaller constructions and interventions, there is relatively little sign of gradual development (though some sites do plausibly have sequences).

Why now? An answer must presumably lie in the changing situation over wide areas, even though contact between regions may have been fragmented and episodic. If there were a mixture of populations in western Britain and Ireland, the early monumental constructions could be seen as an assertion of indigenous identity, a statement that even if the sea was being slighted (Schulting 1998), the land endured. And interaction may have been played out at a wider scale too. If there were in fact more intrusive pioneer populations in southern and eastern Britain than in the Irish Sea zone, the early monumental constructions could be seen as an assertion of regional indigenous identity. There is little in western areas which directly evokes the longhouse world, though a general connection might be sought in the cairns of the court monuments. Orientation was to a different past, previously taken for granted perhaps but now open to contestation and the possibility of replacement.

It is then to this sort of context that the monuments of west Wales may belong in the early Neolithic. Many of these monuments, from portal dolmens and related constructions to earth-fast monuments (Cummings 2001), are distinctive. There are no compellingly similar antecedents in north-west France. If their meaning, as argued above, was to emphasise elements of a mythology involving the earth and creation or creators, it could be supposed that this refers best to indigenous belief systems, though of course the possibility of mutual influence and absorption (cf. Scarre 2002b, 55) cannot be discounted. The eastern part of the Irish Sea zone at the start of the Neolithic in the late fifth or early fourth millennium BC could have witnessed the reassertion and enhancement of indigenous beliefs in the face of and in reaction to the sets of changes in ideas and daily practices which had been affecting western Europe as a whole since the sixth millennium BC, and adjacent north-west France in particular since the mid-fifth millennium BC. This view might extend also to Ireland, *contra* prevailing Irish interpretations, and monuments and landscape could both have been part of a new sense of regional western community. On the other hand, the total distribution of Irish portal dolmens appears much wider than that of late Mesolithic populations on the island.

Bringing these two sets of possibilities together may further serve to underline the distinctive nature of what went on in the west in the early Neolithic. Communities in the Irish Sea area may have been reacting not only to ideas, events, contacts and new opportunities from over the sea, but also to changing populations and their ideologies to the east. The Gower and the Black Mountains may mark the westernmost extension of the eastern system, though there is no need, given the apparent variability in the Black Mountains situation, to suppose that every inhabitant there was of direct continental descent. Consideration of the Neolithic megaliths of Wales in their landscape settings can contribute significantly to wider histories of west and east.

Acknowledgements

Apart from the other sources noted in the text, I could not have written this paper without the help of Vicki Cummings. I also thank the Board of Celtic Studies of the University of Wales for funding our joint research.

References

Barker, C. 1992. *The chambered tombs of south-west Wales.* Oxford: Oxbow.

Basso, K.H. 1984. "Stalking with stories": names, places, and moral narratives among the Western Apache. In E.M.Bruner (ed.), *Text, play and the story: the reconstruction of self and society*, 19–55. Washington, DC: American Ethnological Society.

Bradley, R. 1998a. *The significance of monuments: on the shaping of human experience in Neolithic and Bronze Age Europe.* London: Routledge.

Bradley, R. 1998b. Ruined buildings, ruined stones: enclosures, tombs and natural places in the Neolithic of south-west England. *World Archaeology* 30, 13–22.

Bradley, R. 2000. *An archaeology of natural places.* London: Routledge.

Bradley, R. 2002. *The past in prehistoric societies.* London: Routledge.

Cooney, G. 2000. *Landscapes of Neolithic Ireland.* London: Routledge.

Cummings, V. 2001. *Landscapes in transition?: exploring the origins of monumentality in south-west Wales and south-west Scotland.* Unpublished PhD thesis, Cardiff University.

Cummings, V. 2002. Experiencing texture and touch in the British Neolithic. *Oxford Journal of Archaeology* 21:3, 249–61.

Cummings, V. and Whittle, A. 2004. *Places of special virtue: megaliths in the Neolithic landscapes of Wales.* Oxford: Oxbow.

Fleming, A. 1999. Phenomenology and the megaliths of Wales: a dreaming too far? *Oxford Journal of Archaeology* 18, 119–25.

Grimes, W. 1948. Pentre Ifan burial chamber, Pembrokeshire. *Archaeologia Cambrensis* 100, 3–23.

Lynch, F. 1972. Portal dolmens in the Nevern valley, Pembrokeshire. In F. Lynch and C. Burgess (eds), *Prehistoric man in Wales and the west*, 67–83. Bath: Adams and Dart.

Lynch, F. 1975. Excavations at Carreg Samson megalithic tomb, Mathry, Pembrokeshire. *Archaeologia Cambrensis* 124, 15–35.

Lynch, F. 1976. Towards a chronology of megalithic tombs in Wales. In G. Boon and J. Lewis (eds), *Welsh antiquity: essays mainly on prehistoric topics presented to H. Savory*, 63–79. Cardiff: National Museum of Wales.

Martin, J.W. 2001. *The land looks after us: a history of native American religion.* Oxford: Oxford University Press.

Middleton, J. 1960. *Lugbara religion: ritual and authority among an East African people.* London: Oxford University Press.

Middleton, J. 1970. *The study of the Lugbara: expectation and paradox in anthropological research.* New York: Holt, Rinehart and Winston.

Piggott, S. 1955. Windmill Hill – east or west? *Proceedings of the Prehistoric Society* 21, 96–101.

Powell, T. 1973. Excavations at the megalithic chambered cairn at Dyffryn Ardudwy, Merioneth, Wales. *Archaeologia* 104, 1–50.

Savory, H. 1956. The excavation of the Pipton long cairn Brecknockshire. *Archaeologia Cambrensis* 105, 7–48.

Saville, A. 1990. *Hazleton North: the excavation of a Neolithic long cairn of the Cotswold-Severn group*. London: English Heritage.

Scarre, C. 2002a. A pattern of islands: the Neolithic monuments of north-west Brittany. *European Journal of Archaeology* 5, 24–41.

Scarre, C. 2002b. Contexts of monumentalism: regional diversity at the Neolithic transition in north-west France. *Oxford Journal of Archaeology* 21, 23–61.

Schulting, R.J. 1998. Slighting the sea: stable isotope evidence for the transition to farming in northwestern Europe. *Documenta Praehistorica* 25, 203–18.

Schulting, R. 2000. New AMS dates from the Lambourn long barrow and the question of the earliest Neolithic in southern England: repacking the Neolithic package? *Oxford Journal of Archaeology* 19, 25–35.

Schulting, R.J. and Richards, M.P. 2002. The wet, the wild and the domesticated: the Mesolithic-Neolithic transition on the west coast of Scotland. *European Journal of Archaeology* 5, 147–89.

Smith, C. and Lynch, F. 1987. *Trefignath and Din Dryfol: the excavation of two megalithic tombs in Anglesey*. Bangor: Cambrian Archaeological Association.

Tilley, C. 1994. *A phenomenology of landscape: places, paths and monuments*. Oxford: Berg.

Tilley, C. 1996. The power of rocks: topography and monument construction on Bodmin Moor. *World Archaeology* 28, 161–76.

Tilley, C. 1998. Megaliths in texts. In M. Edmonds and C. Richards (eds), *Understanding the Neolithic of north-western Europe*, 141–60. Glasgow: Cruithne Press.

Tilley, C. and Bennett, W. 2001. An archaeology of supernatural places: the case of West Penwith. *Journal of the Royal Anthropological Institute* 7, 335–62.

Tilley C., Hamilton, S., Harrison, S. and Anderson, E. 2000. Nature, culture, clitter. Distinguishing between cultural and geomorphological landscapes; the case of hilltop tors in south-west England. *Journal of Material Culture* 5, 197–224.

Waterson, R. 2000. House, place and memory in Tana Toraja (Indonesia). In R.A. Joyce and S.D. Gillespie (eds), *Beyond kinship: social and material reproduction in house societies*, 177–88. Philadelphia: University of Pennsylvania Press.

Weiner, J.F. 1988. *The heart of the pearl shell: the mythological dimension of Foi sociality*. Berkeley: University of California Press.

Whitley, D.S. 1998. Finding rain in the desert: landscape, gender and far western North American rock-art. In C. Chippindale and P. Taçon (eds), *The archaeology of rock-art*, 11–29. Cambridge: Cambridge University Press.

Whittle, A. 2003. *An archaeology of people: dimensions of Neolithic life*. London: Routledge.

11   In touch with the past? Monuments, bodies and the sacred in the Manx Neolithic and beyond

Chris Fowler

Introduction

In this paper I focus on the constitution of material bodies – human, object and monument – in the Manx Neolithic. I argue that the principles which structured the organisation of one type of body were transferred over into others. I also suggest that contact between the living and the remains of the dead could be understood in the context of a broader contact with past and sacred things. In particular, old and fragmented things were revisited and revalued in negotiating spiritual connections with the past in a way that kept the dead, the past, and spiritual powers within the present community. The components of monumental and human bodies were given value as sacred substances. Manx Neolithic chambered cairns were repeatedly re-evaluated as sacred sites used to lodge, transform and provide regulated access to the remains of the dead. In the centuries following their construction chambered tombs were subject to alterations, visitations, acts of withdrawal and addition. Later Neolithic funerary practices and depositions of human remains moved away from chambered tombs, but, I suggest, continued to reflect on these past practices. The re-evaluation of past actions and remains therefore sometimes embellished existing structures, sometimes accessed old remains, and sometimes revisited older forms and practices in new geographical locales. As well as being reinterpretations of the past, I suggest that these activities commented on the flow of important substances through the community. The fragmented material culture of the past was given similar value to human remains, and both became vital sites for the re-negotiation of principles that structured social action. Repeated interaction with 'relic'[1] remains re-articulated relationships between those materials, their associated qualities and the living community. The earlier Neolithic focus on the movement of substances and potencies through the bodies of the living and the dead was maintained in the later Neolithic, even though this operated at different scales, through different tempos, and also through slightly different material media.

Fragmentation at Manx Neolithic monuments

From the ground up: pits, mounds and chambers

On the Isle of Man, the earliest Neolithic activity consisted of engagement with the earth. Shafts and pits were dug and filled with cultural debris at Billown Quarry, and in locations which are not seen as monumental, as at Phurt (Darvill 2001, 166). Burnt planks from one pit at Billown have been dated to 4938–4605 BC (5910±70 BP, Beta-110691) and several pits and shafts date to the earlier Neolithic (Chiverrell *et al.* 1999, 331; Darvill 1999). Mesolithic flint scatters were found around the area which later became one enclosure entranceway (Darvill 2001, 163). Plain bowls were placed in several of these pits – one of these was almost intact, others more fragmentary. We could think of these shafts into the ground as small earthen chambers where transformation and deposition took place, situated in arenas where large numbers of people could gather. Many display signs of burning – transforming wood, meat, bone or clay. The ditches contained a large number of sizeable quartz pebbles which Darvill (2001, 165) argues resembled human skulls placed in the base of ditches at southern English causewayed enclosures. Bone preservation from the area is poor, and while burnt bone fragments were found elsewhere on the site (e.g. from features within the later Neolithic 'mini-henge' Darvill 1997, 28–9), no bones survived from the earlier enclosure features. Whether or not the bones of the dead were placed here or the bodies of the dead laid out, Darvill's interpretation of the quartz pebbles as resembling skulls could indicate a system of equivalence between quartz and bone as a comparable material in this forum. The deposition of recently transformed materials in the earth was expanded through the growing scale of activity from pits to ditches at Billown.

Similar materials were deposited and transformed above ground at other earlier Neolithic sites. Ballafayle (Fig. 11.1) has been classified as a non-megalithic crematorium by Kinnes (1992), as a chambered long cairn by Darvill (2000), and as a court cairn by Mundin

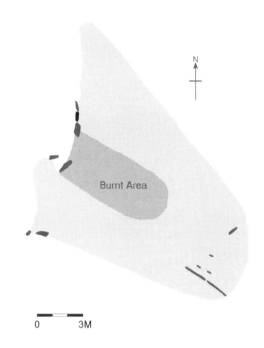

N

Burnt Area

0   3M

Figure 11.1. *Plan of Ballafayle trapezoid earthen mound with stone kerb and wooden chamber (after Kermode 1927).*

et al. (2000; see Davey this volume). The site consisted of a trapezoid cairn with orthostats along the façade and at the rear of the site (perhaps forming a screen or cist), and a low stone kerb. The chamber was probably made of wood, and was the scene of intense burning. Within this area charcoal, peat ash, and burnt and shattered stones were intermixed with layers of slate, cremated bones, ash, shattered flints and small white pebbles (probably quartz). Some of the cremated remains were in a relatively complete condition and one skeleton lay north-south across this area (Kermode 1927). The intermingling of human remains, burnt peat, wood, slate and quartz suggest that the human body was transformed alongside key substances from the surrounding landscape. Several megalithic monuments on the island also drew in different substances from the landscape so that the construction produced a place that gathered up diverse features of the physical world. Excavation of stone-holes for the façade at King Orry's Grave (NE) revealed that these were 'lined with water-worn pebbles' (Megaw n.d.). Each chamber at Mull Hill was paved and pottery, flint arrowheads, and cremated bone were found underneath and above the paving slabs. Chambers were later partially filled with quartz rubble, blocks, or pebbles. A burnt shale mound may be one of the earliest features at Cashtal yn Ard chambered cairn; here the portal stones to the entrance were marked by quartz nodules, and quartz pebbles were later strewn around the rear of the site (Fleure and Neely 1936). In these locales recently transformed materials are mounded above ground in a way that produced a lasting monument.

Both of these monumental strategies drew people together in acts that transformed the bodies of the living and the dead. They also produced bodies out of the materials of the landscape in a way that I will argue was analogous to the production of human bodies out of the community, and stood for the embodiment of the community itself.

The bodies of the living, the dead, and material things were transformed and fragmented at Ballaharra (Fig. 11.2) periodically throughout the Neolithic. Ballaharra is a complex site currently in publication, and most contextual information here comes from a detailed report prepared by David Higgins and Peter Davey (in press). This report (based on re-analysis of the archive following the excavator's death) makes the data from Ballaharra the most thoroughly researched from chambered tombs on the island.

A line of stake or postholes were found to the rear of the chamber which predate its construction, as well as two earlier Neolithic pits. The pits contained 50 flints (including a borer and scraper) and fragments from six undecorated bowls. Sherds from the same two bowls were found in both pits, indicating that fragments of these vessels were deposited in connected deposits. The chamber itself is likely to have been an enclosed box, but there is the possibility that further chambers were added to the front of the monument (Higgins and Davey in press). Some of the slabs were of Peel sandstone, some Manx Group rock, and one of the sandstone slabs was described as 'wave-washed', probably brought from coastal outcrops. The chamber deposits seem to have been disturbed during later Neolithic activity but some deposits were apparently undisturbed. The base of the chamber contained fragmentary unburnt bones and a skull. Stones and burnt material containing the sherds of earlier Neolithic shouldered bowls and cremated bones were lain over these remains. Flints from the chamber were mainly knapping debris. Much later on Bronze Age bones and pottery were inserted into the chamber. Quartz pebbles were found in and around the chamber, and in some deposits (the exact details were unspecified by the excavator). Ballaharra was composed of stones from different parts of the landscape, and became a locale where objects and bodies were fragmented and intermixed.

A series of other subsoil features were found around the chamber, including two troughs or channels and two further pits containing cremation deposits (Cregeen 1978, 146–9). Channel 1 contained fragmented objects and a piece of cremated bone; 5 sherds from an undecorated shouldered bowl were found along with debris from flint knapping, some burnt flint and two finished tools. Channel 2 contained 95 pieces of flint and 5 sherds from another plain bowl. Much of this flint debris has been identified as the product of earlier Mesolithic technology (Higgins and Davey in press). Fragments from old and new activity were intermixed from the earliest Neolithic activity at Ballaharra. Both human bodies and objects

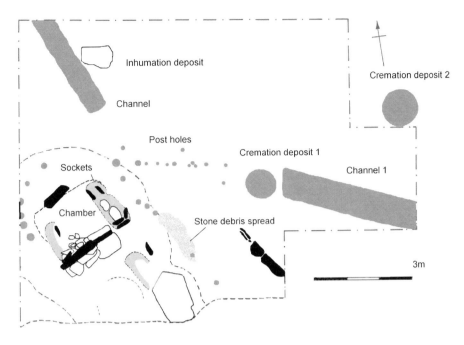

Figure 11.2. Plan of Ballaharra chambered tomb and surrounding features (after Higgins and Davey in press).

were fragmented. Human remains were intermixed with fragments of the histories or biographies of specific places and practices; pots (a new form of mineral body associated with display (Burrow 1997, 260) and consumption); flints both made in the recent past and also found as the remains of far older activity; and the extracted materials of the landscape itself (slate, sandstone and quartz). Cremation deposit 2, outside the chamber, contained a mixture of bones from three adults and two children and bones from at least two dogs and one other animal. This also intermixed the biographies and substances of many different bodies, creating a new corpus out of their components (Fowler 2001).

Chambers old and new: into the later Neolithic

Around 3000 BC the places where human bodies and their enduring remains were transformed and deposited on the island was changing. Timber-lined pits and large vessels acted as containers around which human remains were laid, in place of or alongside chambered tombs. Wooden-lined pits – perhaps kinds of chamber – were used in cremation rites at Killeaba around 3000 BC (Chiverrell *et al.* 1999, 330). Later, single jars were buried cut into the upper fills of these features (Cubbon 1978), emphasising the re-use of older locales where the dead had been transformed. Large intact earthfast jars, often covered with a slate, were placed in narrow pits across the island during the later Neolithic (Bersu 1947; Burrow 1997; Burrow and Darvill 1997; Piggott 1954, 346). At Ballateare cremated bones were found deposited in pits or around earthfast jars[2], and a number of burnt spreads

were found associated with postholes which may have supported a series of wooden screens (see figure 5; Bersu 1947; Burrow 1997; Burrow and Darvill 1997; Darvill 2000, 378; Moffatt 1978, 203–7). These screens could have emulated the form of a chambered tomb with a flat façade and with the main areas of burning either side of the 'entrance' through the façade (Fowler 1999; 2002). These fires and burnt areas could be compared to those either side of the entrance to the court cairn at King Orry's Grave NE. Radiocarbon dates taken from pot residues, 2920–2624 BC (OxA-5885, Chiverrell *et al.* 1999, 330) and 2614–2205 BC (OxA-5884, Chiverrell *et al.* 1999, 330), suggest a slightly later date than a fire-setting in the forecourt at King Orry's Grave NE, which is dated to 3368–2911 BC (4470+-80 BP, GU-2693 - Chiverrell *et al.* 1999, 330). These activities are, however, in chronological proximity to cremation deposit 1 outside the chamber at Ballaharra, and date to a period of interest in older remains at Ballaharra.

A large number of burnt pits, hollows, or spreads of burnt material, attest to repeated events of feasting and/ or cremation around Ballaharra chambered tomb continuing to the later Neolithic (phosphate evidence for bone in several of these features is cited by Higgins and Davey in press). Layers of burnt material were also found within the chamber fills. Two deposits including concentrations of cremated bone were found just outside the chamber. Charcoal from deposit 1 has been dated to 2922–2610 BC (4225±67 BP, BM-768) and 2920–2624 BC (4233±59 BP, BM-769) most likely locating these events at the beginning of the later Neolithic (Darvill 2000, 378; Chiverrell *et al.* 1999). This deposit contained the remains of bones from 33–40 humans, a sheep or goat, a dog and a 'pheasant-sized bird' as well as four kite-shaped arrowheads, other flints, slate, and potsherds (Cregeen 1978, 148). Unburnt largely intact bones probably from a single skeleton were found at the base of the deposit, indicating that older fully-decayed remains were mixed with the recently cremated bones (these remains may even have been brought out of the chamber: Higgins and Davey in press). That the bones within this deposit come from such a large number of different individuals suggests that it was the result of the intermixing and burning of a substantial number of older remains. The remains of the long dead were reconfigured at the locale. These remains, and the monument itself, again became a 'site' for the re-evaluation of relationships between past and present bodies.

It is clear that human bodies were fragmented in a variety of ways at Ballaharra, including *after* prior excarnation or interment, or following cremation. Some of these transformations were directly acted on the recently deceased, and some involved far older 'relic' remains. It seems likely that bodies were rendered partial during their time at the location through cremation or through decay, and these fragmentary remains were deposited alongside fragmented pottery and knapping waste. Activities at this locale repeatedly revised the status of past bodies of all kinds. In general these bodies were rendered partial and their parts were then recombined with one another, although this was not a monolithic process. One currently undated deposit contained the remains of three skeletons laid in a single feature as though they were one skeleton, and may reiterate the practices of recombination evident in the chamber and the cremation deposits. Activity at Ballaharra displays consistent re-engagement with a past place, the re-use of older remains, and repeated revisions in the forms of material things and associations between them. Some parallels could perhaps be drawn between the middle Neolithic fills over the earlier remains at West Kennet and the process of re-use at Ballaharra (cf. Thomas 1999, 203–6; Thomas and Whittle 1986). Both locations had been used to deposit decaying bodies and were later used to deposit fragmentary remains (including pots and/or other bodies, and organic waste perhaps from acts of feasting or other consumption), perhaps indicating an accentuation in the appropriate degree of fragmentation. Thomas (1999) argues that at West Kennet later uses mirror the decomposition of earlier remains with corpses now represented by pots. The later fragmentations at Ballaharra were perhaps more extreme and carried greater emphasis on burning than decay or fracturing. Yet both sites were revalued through repeated interest in the old remains of the dead.

While the change from chambered tombs to 'cemeteries' or cremation grounds around 3000 BC seems a major shift, the structuring principles through which engagements with past bodies were negotiated continued, albeit in slightly different ways and at a different scale. The way that space was delineated and used at Ballateare, and the way that token body parts were dispersed around containers, may suggest that similar practices were employed to those which took place at chambered tombs during the later parts of the earlier Neolithic, and the later Neolithic itself. This included contact with the remains of the dead and the decomposition of dead bodies, including through cremation. Cremation was perhaps not unknown in the earlier Neolithic – Mull Hill contained cremated remains which seem to have been in contexts with earlier Neolithic bowls (Kermode and Herdman 1914; Piggott 1935), though the re-mixing of past and present materials may call the security of this association into question. Through cremations soft, wet human bodies were rendered into hard and durable objects by the flames, just like pots during firing (see Tilley 1996, 115, 315–6). Pots, chambers and bodies were also potentially kinds of containers, as well as composites of different substances. The earthfast vessels were permeated with quartz inclusions as were the chambers and façades of the megalithic monuments, and they were durable containers which could be filled and emptied like chambers. Darvill (this volume) notes that the jars were often deposited empty, and with their mouths protruding from the ground. Many were covered with slates. These mini-chambers were accessible, and objects could have been left within them or removed from them, or the rainwater they accumulated utilised in ritual activity, perhaps at key points in a journey. We could also suggest a genealogy for the use of Ronaldsway jars as a kind of shaft (Darvill 2000). Earthfast jars drew on *multiple* factors in earlier traditions: pottery construction techniques and perhaps even the use of bowls as fixed objects in special locales; chamber-building and the repeated deposition and removal of objects from chambers; and pit or shaft excavation. Burial grounds were still places where physical contact with the transformed dead was possible, and where 'chambers' could be repeatedly accessed. While few deposits have been found in earthfast jars, this does not mean that deposits were not made and then recovered in prehistory. Furthermore, general cultural practices of fragmenting and combining different aspects of the physical world continued in a similar vein through to the later Neolithic, perhaps occurring at an accelerated rate. Past remains were still dragged back into the present, and sometimes reconfigured. While no further chambered tombs were built the process of bodily transformation was still heavily embedded in other activities which shared a similar field of *habitus* (dispositions towards practice, experience and understanding that are transposable from one social context to another; Bourdieu 1977, 72–3). At Ballvarry, for example, habitation debris included a fragment of an earlier Neolithic bowl and Grooved Ware sherds, as well as Ronaldsway pottery (Burrow 1997, 67, 193; Garrad 1984; 1987), merging the fragments of different pasts. This intermingling of fragmentary objects, can be contrasted with the dispersal of token cremation deposits at Killeaba and Ballateare, where cremated human bone had been carefully separated from any charcoal before deposition (Bersu 1947, 165; Cubbon 1978, 94–5; Fowler 1999, 177–9). Perhaps the bone was valued in one way, while charcoal was conceptually different. The original bodies and objects were rendered fully partial before deposition at both sets of sites, and the material deposited may even have been circulated for some time. Heavily fragmented remains were combined in ephemeral practices at later Neolithic campsites and gathering places as well as at cremation pyres and locales surrounding earthfast jars. These small-scale or ephemeral practices also had heritage in earlier Neolithic occupation sites, and the debris from habitation or feasting activity found in pits like those at Phurt and Billown.

From the earlier Neolithic ritualised activity had stressed interaction with past things and remains. In some cases these interactions were probably not continuations of past actions – the encounter with earlier Mesolithic remains at Ballaharra, for example. However, physical contact with and deposition of those remains alongside recently fragmented objects and bodies occurred repeatedly. This was also the case in the later Neolithic. There was also a clear continuation in the *value*, if not meaning, of particular materials over time. Quartz in particular continued to be a key symbolic substance clustered at a range of monuments. The distribution of such fractions of the world was a significant cultural practice which could be maintained *at a certain scale* even when material forms were changed.

In order to understand this manipulation of bodies at different scales, and provide a setting for understanding why objects could be seen as sacred alongside human remains, I turn to recent interpretations of bodies and substances.

Communities, bodies and substances

Recent studies by John Chapman (1996; 2000) have demonstrated that the circulation and deposition of fragmented things and bodies can form a deliberate strategy of employing material culture in interactions between people. I would like to suggest that we see in this fragmentation and relocation of parts in the Neolithic of the British Isles the interaction between a community *including* living people, the dead, things, and places; a community which mediated the flows of substance and energy between different features of the cosmos. To draw on an analogy, Howell (1989) describes how Indonesian Lio 'Houses' consist of people, gold valuables, the bones of the dead, and the House ancestors. A Lio House is an entity as well as a community that encapsulates people and things, and all Houses are encapsulated by the village and their collective ancestors. The enduring gold objects in particular, along with the dried bones of the dead, are

a connection with dead members of the House, and are key items in ritual ceremonies where spiritual entities nourish the living community. The dead still form part of the community, and their remains (including the gold objects associated with them) are a material filament of the House. The material world ties together past and present, and each entity (object, ancestor, person, House, village, etc) is simply one part of a larger entity in a fractal logic (Wagner 1991). A similar logic of permeable and interpenetrating social entities may be relevant to the Neolithic of the British Isles (Fowler 2001; 2003; Thomas 2002). Manx chambered cairns were durable traces of past action, the embodiment of the community containing the dead. These architectural forms acted upon people visiting them, shaping their bodies through inherited patterns of comportment. Performances conducted at megaliths were interactions with the dead whose agency pressed on them through the medium of the architecture and the propriety of ritualised action. Alterations to monuments and the remains within them indicate this was not a one-way process, and it seems likely that chambered cairns were an appropriate locale for negotiations between the living and the dead members of the community. These places acted as key interfaces between past and present, and between different scales of entity in the community. Actions at megaliths used the substances of the world to think about social relations, histories and genealogies.

The production of human bodies, places and things are often conceptualised as parallel to each other (e.g. Battaglia 1990; 1992; Berns 1988; Bloch 1982; 1995; Bourdieu 1970; Brück 2001; cf. Wagner 1991). Related human substances like fat, semen and bone may share qualities and affinities with worldly substances (e.g. Barraud *et al.* 1994; Bloch 1971). Perhaps the blocks and pebbles of quartz, the water-rounded stones brought from the beaches or waterways of the island, water itself and stone were parallel to human substances (see also Cummings and Fowler this volume; Fowler and Cummings 2003). Important generative energies may be controlled through the treatment and transmission of such materials (e.g. Strathern 1999; Strathern and Stewart 2000), which are often gendered events; the bodies produced may consist of multiple gendered substances and so may be multiply-gendered (e.g. Strathern 1988). The materials of the landscape and the human body may therefore have been analogous and also highly charged. Each material would have been the site for anchoring a host of polysemous meanings, and used to think about relations in the community, with the landscape, and through the body simultaneously. For example, analogies could be drawn between the cremation of bodies and the firing of finished vessels. Burrow (1997) points out that lumps of quartz in earlier Neolithic Manx pottery would have been visible to the potter and to whoever broke the vessel, but were kept beneath the smooth surface of the pot during its use-life (Burrow 1997, 259). This is rather like bones within the human body. Quartz crushed from granite or from quartz nodules was a key component of the temper for both earlier Neolithic bowls and later Neolithic jars. Perhaps the firing of vessels was analogous to cremation, or perhaps vessels were even fired in the pyres of the dead so that new incorruptible bodies were created when old 'soft' ones were transformed. Quartz pebbles and quartz rubble were intermixed with other materials including slate and peat or turf, and burnt along with human remains at Ballafayle. The construction of pots and monuments as analogous bodies may have involved similar processes. People were generated out of the relations between the community, including the bodies of their parents, and the substances that flowed from one generation to the next. Pots and monuments were built by extracting minerals from the landscape and combining those materials in the production of a new body.

The body is not the only metaphor that was employed in articulating social relations, and distinctive yet ambiguous materials like quartz may be significant precisely because they form a fulcrum around which many different metaphors revolved. Quartz could link features of human bodies with natural substance, mountains and coast, and even solid and liquid, for example (Fowler and Cummings 2003). Social relations and cultural understandings were structured through the movement and re-articulation of these substances in appropriate social contexts. Julian Thomas has elsewhere succinctly referred to an 'economy of substances' (Thomas 1998), in which the movement of human and non-human substances was crucial to multiple discourses of identity and social politics, and this seems an apposite description here. At times Manx Neolithic activity probably focussed on the substances moving between bodies, showing those bodies up as dividual (see LiPuma 1998; Strathern 1988), while at other times bodies, places and things were probably individuated from each other. In the rest of this paper I focus on the flows between these bodies which we could conceive of as permeable vessels. At times these acted as containers for essences and at other times the vessels were fragmented, their parts reduced to substances potentially contained by other vessels. Contacts between the bodies of the living and the fractions of other bodies in the Manx Neolithic may have been part of a carefully-monitored process of bodily transfers and exchanges between different entities, including the community and the person, and the ancestors and the living. These exchanges involved the remains of the past, to which I now turn.

Sacred bodies and the residue of their passing

Contact with human remains could be described as;

- funerary practice: the initial transformations of the dead
- ancestral rites (see Barrett 1988)
- the use of old remains to legitimate new narratives (e.g. supporting the status of a particular lineage, or the emergence of particular ideas about death, kinship, or what it means to be a person; see Fowler 2001; Lucas 1996; Richards 1988; Thomas 2000)
- cosmogenesis
- interaction with the sacred

Although none of these activities are mutually exclusive, here I would particularly like to consider the role of human remains as relics - sacred things containing potent and even supernatural energies. Cosmogenesis, the re-creation of the cosmos, may be implicit in Neolithic monument-building and also in mortuary practices, but I will not follow that up here. I have discussed both the production of changing narratives in the manipulation of human remains, and trends in Manx Neolithic funerary practice elsewhere (Fowler 1999; 2001; 2002). Ancestral rites have been discussed extensively in Neolithic studies as those activities which celebrate the place of the dead in the world of the living. Barrett (1988; 2001, 153) describes how chambered tombs act as conduits for transforming the remains of the dead and for securing ongoing relations between the living and the dead, as human bodies taken to the site are transformed into 'ancestral presence' drawn from the monument by the community. I am interested in the role of physical contact between human bodies and sacred materials as one mechanism of this process. I am also interested in the politics through which these remains were mobilised. I focus here on the re-use of remains through analogy with contemporary bodily interactions with sacred places.

Material culture is often valued based on the connections it retains with the past. Anthropologist Maurice Godelier (1999, 111, 161–7) defines three classes of things; commodities, valuables, and sacred things. *Commodities* are alienated from the context of their production – for example, through factory labour. Concrete or a polystyrene cup would normally be a commodity. The producer has no intimate relation with the thing produced, and the biography of the thing is unimportant. Commodities can be bought and sold for money. *Valuables* or precious things retain a connection with their producer, the place they were produced, and the materials they were produced from; they also become embedded in certain communities and places so that they are inalienable from those to some degree. While they are inalienable from the context of their production or the community that keeps them, they are also sufficiently alienable from that context to be given away. Gifts can often be described as valuable things, where the recipient holds but does not 'own' the valuable. Stone axes are a good contender for Neolithic gifts and precious objects (see Bradley and Edmonds 1993; Ray this volume). *Sacred* things are utterly inalienable from the context of their production, which is mythologised so that any human origin of the thing is subsumed within a sacred origin (Godelier 1999, 169–71). These things and places are retained by the community and cannot be given away, but their sacred properties can be passed on through contact with them. Their control and manipulation is a key arena in the legitimisation of social and cultural relations; authority is deferred to the past, and to things with sacred origins (Weiner 1992, 4).

I would also suggest that Godelier's scheme only makes sense in terms of negotiated arenas of value. Things may become more or less inalienable from people, places, or sacred origins, as they move through different social contexts. Human, animal, artefact and monument bodies may be valued differently through subsequent practices, and could be valued as sacred, as valuable, or as commodities. Furthermore, the status of any thing could be contested within such arenas of value. Sacredness is entirely contextual, so that human bones may be valued as sacred, making places where they are kept sacred – or alternatively, the transformation of bodies within locales that were either themselves sacred or made from sacred materials might have marked the remains produced there as sacred. Contexts where things are transformed, such as performances at chambered cairns, may be significant interstices where such changes in value are negotiated. I would argue that Neolithic pits, enclosures, and chambers like those on the Isle of Man were both liminal places for transformative acts and also key locales in these arenas of value. Deposition of early Neolithic material in these contexts may have marked that material as valuable or sacred due to its embeddedness in those locales, or transformed its value as it moved away from the community of the living. Whether or not this describes the value of these things at the time of initial construction and deposition, it may well describe their value to successive generations.

A recent study of holy wells in western Ireland (Casella 2002) illustrates that interaction with sacred sites places great emphasis on embodiment. Casella describes how objects intimate to the body are left by pilgrims visiting the wells; rags from clothes or used to wipe ailing bodies, eyeglasses and crutches. Objects relating to bodily consumption (cigarette packs, bottles of alcohol, confectionery wrappers) were left as symbols for fasts or personal sacrifice. The wells are used to wash the bodies of the afflicted, and the origin stories of the wells relate to the body parts of sacred characters; the footprints of saints' horses, or the marks made by kneeling saints. The features of the landscape were, in this sense, the relic remains of past sacred activity. At Kilbarry (Roscommon) a monk's skull was built into a wall, and visitors would touch the

skull before touching their own teeth (the relic was said to have special properties pertaining to diseases of the mouth and teeth). In each case bodily contact with the remains of the ancient and sacred dead were encouraged, and energies were transferred from these remains to the living through that contact. Finally, pilgrims also left two other types of objects at sacred sites; objects which were evidence of a distant journey like bottled holy water from foreign religious sites (i.e. evidence that they had undertaken pilgrimage); and stones. Casella (*pers. comm.*) considers that these stones were left as an enduring trace of bodily visitation at the site.

While this is a very specific Christian use of relics and holy places, the wider realm of sacred things are arguably important in connecting the bodies of the living with powerful spiritual forces. It is not just human remains that may be relics or spiritually charged, but also sacred objects and seemingly inanimate things like stones (e.g. see Bird-David 1993; 1999; Godelier 1999; Kahn 1990; Morris 1994, 8–10). Christian relics include objects which have been in touch with sacred bodies, like pieces of the True Cross or the Turin Shroud. The remains of past activity at Neolithic monuments could have acquired similar status, given their contact with human ancestors. In other traditions objects may themselves be sacred beings or possessed by sacred entities. These conduits of spiritual power are of high social and political value in the negotiation of identity, and have dramatic effects on the bodies of those who come into contact with them. Landscape features are often attributed to the actions of supernatural bodies, like those of saints, devils, giants, or ancestral entities, and their presence may have left certain places highly charged. The very material of the landscape may act as the point of contact between living bodies and these sacred entities. Building monuments assembled materials from such highly-charged places, and acts of construction articulated a spiritually significant place out of the diversely-charged components of the cosmos. In the increasing number of cases where archaeologists recognise that Neolithic monuments emulated landscape features, it seems that they may be skeuomorphs which redirected their origins from the human to the sacred (e.g. Cooney 1994; Cummings 2002, 119; Tilley 1994).

It often seemed to be important that contact between people and sacred places leave some trace, from wear-marks on stones to acts of deposition or construction. If Neolithic monuments – both natural and constructed – were sacred places, then perhaps the additions of material culture to these sites could be seen as traces of physical presence across the landscape. For example, the quartz pebbles deposited in abundance around the rear of Cashtal yn Ard and in the ditches at the Billown Quarry enclosures may have been the physical traces of a journey from the beach inland to the monuments, or even of a far longer journey. They articulated the relationship between the beach and the monument through bodily movement (see

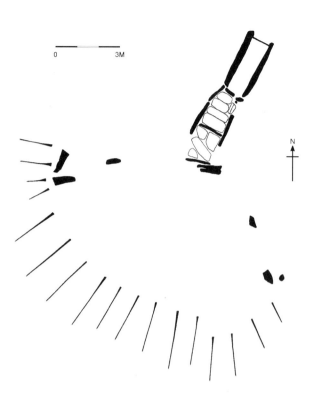

Figure 11.3. *Plan of King Orry's Grave SW (after Megaw, n.d.).*

Figure 11.4. *Photograph of King Orry's Grave (SW). View from the rear of the chamber, illustrating the small arch outside the rear chamber.*

also Cummings and Fowler this volume). Darvill (2002, 83) also attests to the historical deposition of quartz pebbles at holy wells around the Irish Sea, suggesting a sacred context for this activity. Likewise, arrows shot into the ditches at Billown may have been intimate objects projected from the person and embedded in the place. Bones, the core of the body and the person, may have become sacred through exposure to sacred places, while other features of the human body carried different qualities returned to the cosmos and community. While megalithic sites may have been used to transform the bodies of the dead, they were perhaps of more significance in transforming the *living* through their contacts and interactions with the remains of the dead, and other fractured remains of the past. Interactions with spiritual energies through the substances of human and monument bodies would have dramatic effect on a person and their well-being. The relationships that were negotiated changed the position of people in the human community, but may also have altered their relations with the non-human community, including spiritual beings. Such contact effected a connection between the living and the supernatural in an important arena of social power.

The unexcavated chambered cairn of King Orry's Grave SW (Fig. 11.3) was one place where the bodies of the living could come into contact with the remains of the past. It was probably initially built as an open box

chamber. Its slate side panels were over 2m long, and their heavy horizontal grains give the appearance of a split tree trunk. Two very small portal stones stand at the southerly 'entrance' to this chamber, and another two chambers and a concave façade were placed in front. The entrance-way would have been partly accessible, but a small curved slab which may have had a pair stands at one side of the entrance (Fig. 11.4). A deep gully with a fast-flowing stream runs parallel to the chambers less than 10 metres from the east horn of the façade, and the land slopes away steeply in front of the site. Less than 100m downhill the stream runs over a high waterfall, and the sound of 'white' water is clearly audible at the site. This natural feature may have been significant in the choice of location and the axis of the monument (Cummings and Fowler this volume; Fowler and Cummings 2003; cf. Brophy 2000; Richards 1996). Washing the living or dead body is a common symbolic action, cleansing or otherwise altering the person. It would appear that a small open box chamber was initially built

THE PREHISTORIC SOCIETY
Visit to the
Excavations at West Kennet Avenue: Booking Form

Led by Dr Josh Pollard (University of Southampton)

2pm, Sunday 3rd August 2013

Details:
The excavation focusses on a middle-late Neolithic settlement first encountered during Alexander Keiller's restoration and excavation of the West Kennet Avenue in 1934. The first season of this new phase of work during 2013 revealed an in situ scatter of worked flint and prehistoric ceramics (mostly Peterborough Ware) extending over an area of at least 100 x 50m - remarkable in this heavily cultivated landscape. This is associated with features including pits and at least one possible contemporary structure. It offers a rare glimpse into the character and structure of a well preserved settlement of this period. The excavations on the West Kennet site are part of a larger project (under the title of the Between the Monuments Project), which is investigating histories of settlement, routine activity and human-environment relations, and their ties to monument construction, during the 4th-early 2nd millennia BC within the Avebury landscape. The work is a collaboration between several institutions and individuals, including the Universities of Southampton and Leicester, Allen Environmental Archaeology and the National Trust.

Directions:
Please park at the main Avebury National Trust car park and then walk down through the henge and avenue. The site is c.600m south-east of the southern entrance of the Avebury henge, and is very visible.

The tour is free of charge, but so that we can assess how many people will attend the site visit please fill in the form below and return to: Tessa Machling, Prehistoric Society, Institute of Archaeology, 31-34 Gordon Square, London, WC1 0PY, by **1**$^{\underline{st}}$ **June 2014** or email to: prehistoric@ucl.ac.uk (electronic version available on our website: www.prehsitoricsociety.org)

Name.......................

Number of tickets:........................

Email (preferred method of contact) ....

Daytime Tel. ....

Mobile ....

by the side of the watercourse and this could have been used to store fragmentary or complete sets of human remains, as at Ballaharra. Unlike at King Orry's Grave NE the chambers are separated only by low sills, not upright slabs which would completely enclose the chambers. However, it is not possible to enter this rear chamber through the aperture provided by the two small portal stones, and it was probably equally difficult to access the outer chamber once that was built. A *degree* of repeated accessibility was ensured at King Orry's Grave SW. The construction of a low arch between two orthostats meant the rear chamber could be viewed and reached into but not entered (Fowler 2002). The architecture of the site suggests that it was possible to touch and see the remains, but not get amongst them. At other locales, particularly Cashtal yn ard and King Orry's Grave NE we could argue that the chambers were relatively difficult to access. Internal space was divided up into zones, with very high sill slabs separating the first and second chambers in particular. However, this creation of plural boundaries could be seen as one strategy in negotiating the value of those remains, another being deliberate access to the chamber contents, at least at Ballaharra. This may indicate that human remains became of higher value throughout the earlier Neolithic, and both more sought after and more heavily protected. By 3000 BC the remains of the dead were frequently transformed more rapidly after death, often through cremation, and evidence suggests these bones were cleaned of ash or charcoal if not further curated. Perhaps the bodies of some could be transformed to sacred remains more rapidly, or perhaps recent remains did not usually acquire such potency unless associated with older remains, older places, and older practices. The reconfiguration of remains at Ballaharra may have transformed the living persons involved in that event and created new ties with the long-dead, effecting the 'cosmological authentication' of present conditions by appeal to that particular subset of the community (Weiner 1992, 4).

The negotiation of the sacred at other Neolithic monuments

Sacred places and remains were constantly revalued throughout the Neolithic. There is no single pattern which can group together and explain the ongoing practices at Manx Neolithic monuments as a whole, let alone the Neolithic across the British Isles. Distinct regional differences can be observed in the sequences of chambered cairns from the Cotswold-Severn area, south-west Wales, north Wales, Anglesey, and south-west Scotland, for example. Some episodes in each sequence accentuate the exterior monumentality of the site, closing off access or hiding entrances and chambers, while others operate to choreograph experience of inner space and the remains of the dead, as with complex passage graves or complex terminally chambered monuments. Different experiences of past remains, of inner space, of the relationship with cosmos and landscape, and of the monumentality of the site were produced through the changing designs and embellishments of cairns. Manx chambers were not hidden, false entrances were not employed, and internal access was afforded yet also controlled. In the earlier phases of King Orry's Grave SW access would have been simple. In later phases external monumentality of sites like Cashtal yn Ard and King Orry's Graves was accentuated, and forecourts provided a focal point for activity. Archways provided access to antechambers potentially used in rites of passage. This spatial patterning allowed for the negotiation of complex relationships between the bodies of the living and the dead.

Thomas (1988; 1999, 145–151) suggests that Cotswold-Severn cairns were increasing designed to permit access to chambers and emphasize forecourt areas from after 3700 BC. Ditches along the sides of transepted cairns had previously cut off access to the dead, but terminally chambered cairns afforded that access. Discrepancies in the proportions of bones present suggest addition and removal at both types of site, though with different emphases (Thomas 1988, 552). Later interactions with the bones in some chambers articulated new skeletons from the jumbled remains of old ones. Interaction with the remains of the dead were of increasing importance in discourses on the identity of both living people and the dead themselves. These acts were statements about social relations expressed through the body (cf. Cummings *et al.* 2002), which may have used past remains to address current concerns and legitimate a revision in some of those relations (cf. Fowler 2001; Richards 1988). Furthermore some cairns (e.g. Gwernvale) were built to look far older than they were, creating the impression of extreme age. These cairns therefore also accentuated the age and perhaps value of the remains they contained (Thomas 1988, 555).

Re-orientations, the closing in of older chambers and the construction of 'false' entrances and forecourts were also common throughout many periods of the Neolithic in different regions. A number of chambered tombs were altered to partially close in and partially leave accessible or visible the remains of the dead. Portholes or small gaps between orthostats allowing visitors to touch remains, view remains, or insert partial remains into tombs, have been found at Bryn yr Hen Bobl, Anglesey, Luckington chamber B, Wiltshire, and Avening Court and Rodmarton, Gloucestershire (Powell *et al.* 1969, 94–5). At Pant y Saer on Anglesey the earlier chamber, filled with mainly articulated remains, was closed off (Lindsay-Scott 1933). Later human and animal bones were found outside the new 'false' entrance. Given the emerging observation that the choice of stones during megalithic projects could have been a significant form of engagement with the natural and spiritual world (e.g. Bradley 2000; Cummings 2002; Richards this volume; Whittle this volume), alterations could be seen as embellishments *accentuating* the value of the place. As access was restricted, so value was raised and attention drawn to the new conditions. Blocking stones in front of West Kennet were not *only* obstructions between the living and the ancestral dead, cutting their remains off from the community at large. Indeed, the spiritual value of these stones may have been claimed by some groups to justify the distraction of activity away from bones and small objects, and the bodies of the recent dead may have been processed in ways more openly visible to the community. Furthermore, in many cases, the stones of a monument mediated contact with the sacred, and spaces were created that afforded an experience of personal contact with these stones. At Cairnholy I, south-west Scotland, and at Cashtal yn Ard and King Orry's Grave SW, arches or ante-chambers provided access to at least the first chamber or antechamber, and allowed intimate contact with the chamber wall or the contents of the first chamber. Such spaces could be used in rites of passage or other changes to the living person, the dead, and the community. In other areas false portals focussed attention on stones which could form the focus or backdrop for activity without hiding older remains, as at Belas Knap. In these cases the stones themselves might act as symbolic portals for contact and communication.

Across the British Isles, different strategies were employed in relating to the dead, dependant on perceptions of their bodies both at death and during successive reuses of each site. Although we should not imagine that any strategy was directly linked to a single specific discourse, the variety of these strategies attest to a variety of discourses on the body, personhood and sacred potency. Interaction at chambered cairns involved political negotiations among the living, but also contact with the traces left by past bodies. Political interaction drew on and operated through access to the remains of past bodies – whether recently deceased or long dead, whether human or object. The political, personal and cosmological were closely intertwined through Neolithic encounters at each monument.

Conclusion

Neolithic trends in cosmological engineering (Thomas 1999, 46) did not only apply to monuments and landscapes but also extended to, and operated through, material culture and the human body. This cosmological engineering was not achieved in a singular event, but was an ongoing process of interaction with the world, involving the continual re-evaluation of past remains and inherited practices. Past accounts of the world could to a certain extent be revised through repeated engineering, including the mobilisation of human remains and material things with sacred associations. These discourses operated through regulating contact between the bodies of the living and the materials that composed them, including bone.

Human substances that flowed through the community were paralleled with other materials that composed the cosmos. The use, manipulation and later alteration of natural places (particularly outcrops of stone, bodies of water, the tops of hills or mountains, islands, and beaches) and materials should also be included in these analyses. All of these places and materials could form conduits for sacred energies, which nourished the bodies of human beings, the human community, places and things. The principles structuring the transformation of bodies changed throughout the Neolithic, and were also variable at any one time. As with other regions, while some Manx Neolithic practices involved monuments that bridged the smaller and grander scales many others carried out the cosmological engineering of the world through subtle alterations of natural places (Bradley 2000; Evans *et al* 1999; Mullins this volume) and through small-scale activities (see also Pollard 2001; Peterson this volume). Through each of these activities Neolithic people negotiated their place in the contemporary world, and revised the nature of that world, yet also kept firmly in touch with the past.

Acknowledgements

I would like to thank Peter Davey for making available a copy of the site report for Ballaharra ahead of its publication, for providing me with a copy of Megaw's unpublished draft report for King Orry's Grave (NE), and for comments on a draft of this chapter. I would also like to thank Vicki Cummings, Tim Insoll and Julian Thomas for their comments, Sarah Henson for preparing the illustrations, and Eleanor Casella for discussions on medieval relics and holy wells. I would also like to acknowledge the support of the Leverhulme Trust for funding my current Fellowship at the University of Manchester.

Notes

1 I use 'relic' here to denote objects recovered from past actions. I elected not to use the term relic throughout to refer to sacred things due to its very specific meaning in the Christian world. Both relics and other sacred objects can convey spiritual power in the way discussed here, but the specific relationship between Saints and Christians may not be an appropriate analogy for the relations between Neolithic people and their spiritual entities, human ancestors, and other cosmological features.

2 Only one jar contained any cremated bone, despite the amount of cremated bone deposits. It appears that, just as cremations took place outside Ballaharra, and dumps of cremated remains were strewn around the chamber, so cremated bones were placed near to or strewn around the mouths of jars. These were not funerary urns, unless their contents were emptied some time after deposition.

References

Barraud, C., de Coppet, D., Iteanu, A. and Jamous, R. 1994. *Of relations and the dead: four societies viewed from the angle of their exchanges*. Oxford: Berg.

Barrett, J. 1988. The living, the dead and the ancestors: Neolithic and early Bronze Age mortuary practices. In J. Barrett, and I. Kinnes (eds), *The archaeology of context in the Neolithic and Bronze Age*, 30–41. Sheffield: Department of Archaeology and Prehistory.

Barrett, J. 2001. Agency, the duality of structure, and the problem of the archaeological record. In I. Hodder (ed.), *Archaeological theory today*, 141–64. Cambridge: Polity Press.

Battaglia, D. 1990. *On the bones of the serpent: person, memory and mortality in Sabarl society*. Chicago: Chicago University Press.

Battaglia, D. 1992. The body in the gift: memory and forgetting in Sabarl mortuary exchange. *American Ethnologist* 19, 3–18.

Berns, M.C. 1988. Ga'anda Scarification: a model for art and identity. In A.Rubin (ed.), *Marks of civilization*, 57–76. Los Angeles Museum of Cultural History, UCLA: Los Angeles.

Bersu, G. 1947. A cemetery of the Ronaldsway Culture at Ballateare, Jurby, Isle of Man. *Proceedings of the Prehistoric Society* 13, 161–9.

Bird-David, N. 1993. Tribal metaphorization of human-nature relatedness. In K. Milton (ed.), *Environmentalism. The view from anthropology*, 112–25. London: Routledge.

Bird-David, N. 1999. 'Animism' revisited: personhood, environment, and relational epistemology. *Current Anthropology* 40, 67–92.

Bloch, M. 1971. *Placing the dead*. London: Seminar Press.

Bloch, M. 1982. Death, women and power. In M. Bloch and J. Parry (eds), *Death and the regeneration of life*, 211–30. Cambridge: Cambridge University Press

Bloch, M. 1995. Questions not to ask of Malagasy carvings. In I. Hodder, M. Shanks, A. Alexandri, V. Buchli, J. Carman, J. Last, and G. Lucas (eds), *Interpreting archaeology: finding meaning in the past*, 212–15. London: Routledge.

Bourdieu, P. 1970. The Berber house or the world reversed. *Social Science Information* 9: 783–802.

Bourdieu, P. 1977. *Outline of a theory of practice*. Cambridge: Cambridge University Press.

Bradley, R. 2000. *The archaeology of natural places*. London: Routledge.

Brophy, K. 2000. Water coincidence? Cursus monuments and rivers. In A. Ritchie (ed.), *Neolithic Orkney in its European context*, 59–70. Oxford: Oxbow.

Brück, J. 2001. Body metaphors and technologies of transformation in the English Middle and Late Bronze Age. In J. Brück (ed.), *Bronze Age landscapes: tradition and transformation*, 149–60. Oxford: Oxbow.

Burrow, S. 1997. *The Neolithic pottery of the Isle of Man and its relationship to that of surrounding areas: a study in production, decoration and use*. Unpublished PhD Thesis: Bournemouth University.

Burrow, S. and Darvill, T. 1997. AMS dating of the Manx Ronaldsway Neolithic. *Antiquity* 71, 412–19.

Casella, E. 2002. Tobar: an archaeology of the holy wells of Ireland. Paper delivered at *Archaeology and Religion* conference, Manchester, September 2002.

Chapman, J. 1996. Enchainment, commodification, and gender in the Balkan Copper Age. *Journal of European Archaeology* 4, 203–242.

Chapman, J. 2000. *Fragmentation in archaeology: people, places and broken objects in the prehistory of south-eastern Europe*. London: Routledge.

Childe, V.G. 1940. *Prehistoric communities of the British Isles*. Edinburgh: Edinburgh University Press.

Chiverrell, R., Davey, P., Gowlet, J. and Woodcock, J. 1999. Radiocarbon dates for the Isle of Man. In P. Davey (ed.), *Recent archaeological research on the Isle of Man*, 321–68. Oxford: British Archaeological Reports British Series 278.

Cooney, G. 1994. Sacred and secular Neolithic landscapes in Ireland. In D. Carmichael, J. Hubert, B. Reeves, and A Schanche (eds), *Sacred sites, sacred places*, 32–43. London: Routledge.

Cregeen, S. 1978. Ballaharra excavations 1971: a summary of work and results. In P. Davey (ed.) *Man and environment in the Isle of Man*, 141–51. Oxford: British Archaeological Reports British Series 54.

Cubbon, A. 1978. Excavation at Killeaba, Ramsey, Isle of Man. *Proceedings of the Prehistoric Society* 44, 69–95.

Cummings, V. 2002. All cultural things: actual and conceptual monuments in the Neolithic of western Britain. In C. Scarre (ed.), *Monuments and landscape in Atlantic Europe: perception and society during the Neolithic and early Bronze Age*, 107–21. London: Routledge.

Cummings, V., Jones, A. and Watson, A. 2002. Divided places: phenomenology and assymmetry in the monuments of the Black Mountains, southeast Wales. *Cambridge Archaeological Journal* 12, 57–70.

Darvill, T. 1996. *Billown Neolithic landscape project, Isle of Man, 1995*. Bournemouth and Douglas: Bournemouth University School of Conservation Sciences and Manx National Heritage, Research Report 1.

Darvill, T. 1997. *Billown Neolithic landscape project, Isle of Man, 1996*. Bournemouth and Douglas: Bournemouth University School of Conservation Sciences and Manx National Heritage, Research Report 3.

Darvill, T. 1998. *Billown Neolithic landscape project, Isle of Man, 1997*. Bournemouth and Douglas: Bournemouth University School of Conservation Sciences and Manx National Heritage.

Darvill, T. 1999. Billown Neolithic landscape project 1995–1997. In P. Davey (ed.), *Recent archaeological research on the Isle of Man*, 13–26. Oxford: British Archaeological Reports British Series 278.

Darvill, T. 2000. Neolithic Mann in context. In A. Ritchie (ed.), *Neolithic Orkney in its European context*, 371–85. Oxford: Oxbow.

Darvill, T. 2001. Neolithic enclosures in the Isle of Man. In T. Darvill and J. Thomas (eds), *Neolithic enclosures in northwest Europe*, 77–111. Oxford: Oxbow.

Darvill, T. 2002. White on blonde: quartz pebbles and the use of quartz at Neolithic monuments in the Isle of Man and beyond. In A. Jones and G. MacGregor (eds) *Colouring the past*, 73–91. Oxford: Berg.

Evans, C., Pollard, J. and Knight, M. 1999. Life in woods:

tree-throws, 'settlement' and forest cognition. *Oxford Journal of Archaeology*, 18, 241–45.

Fleure, H. and Neely, G. 1936. Cashtal yn Ard, Isle of Man. *The Antiquities Journal* 16, 373–95.

Fowler, C. 2001. Personhood and social relations in the British Neolithic with a study from the Isle of Man. *Journal of Material Culture* 6, 137–63.

Fowler, C. 2002. Body parts: Personhood and materiality in the Manx Neolithic. In Y. Hamilakis, M. Pluciennik and S. Tarlow (eds), *Thinking through the body: archaeologies of corporeality*, 47–69. London: Kluwer Academic Press.

Fowler, C. 2003. Rates of (ex)change: decay and growth, memory and the transformation of the dead in early Neolithic southern Britain. In H. Williams (ed.), *Archaeologies of remembrance - death and memory in past societies*, 45–64. London: Kluwer Academic Press.

Fowler, C. and Cummings, V. 2003. Places of transformation: building monuments from water and stone in the Neolithic of the Irish Sea. *Journal of the Royal Anthropological Institute* 9, 1–20.

Garrad, L. 1984. Rescue excavations 1980–82: Ballavarry, *Proceedings of the Isle of Man Natural History and Antiquarians Society* 9, 163–8.

Garrad, L. 1987. A Ronaldsway Neolithic site on West Kimmeragh, Isle of Man. *Proceedings of the Isle of Man Natural History and Antiquarians Society* 9, 420–26.

Godelier, M. 1999. *The enigma of the gift.* Chicago: University of Chicago Press.

Henshall, A. 1978. Chambered tombs of the Isle of Man: an attempt at a structural analysis. In P. Davey, (ed.), *Man and environment in the Isle of Man*, 171–6. Oxford: British Archaeological Reports British Series 54.

Higgins, D. and Davey, P. In press. Excavations by Sheila Cregeen at Ballaharra, German, 1969–1975. In F. Lynch (ed.), *Manx megaliths*. Liverpool: Liverpool University Press.

Howell, S. 1989. Of persons and things: exchange and valuables among the Lio of eastern Indonesia. *Man* 24, 419–438.

Kahn, M. 1990. Stone-faced ancestors: the spatial anchoring of myth in Wamira, Papua New Guinea. *Ethnology* 29, 51–66.

Kermode, P.M.C. 1927. Long barrow in the Isle of Man. *Antiquaries Journal* 7, 191–92.

Kermode, P.M.C. and Herdman, W.A. 1914. *Manks antiquities* Liverpool: Liverpool University Press.

Kinnes, I. 1992. *Non-megalithic long barrows and allied structures in the British Neolithic.* London: British Museum.

LiPuma, E. 1998. Modernity and forms of personhood in Melanesia. In M. Lambek and A. Strathern (eds) *Bodies and persons: comparative views from Africa and Melanesia*, 53–79. Cambridge: Cambridge University Press.

Lucas, G. 1996. Of death and debt. A history of the body in Neolithic and early Bronze Age Yorkshire. *Journal of European Archaeology* 4, 99–118.

Megaw, B. n.d. The Excavation of 'King Orry's Grave' (northeast). Unpublished manuscript held by the Centre for Manx Studies, consulted July 1998.

Moffatt, P. 1978. The Ronaldsway culture: a review. In P. Davey (ed.), *Man and environment in the Isle of Man, Volume 1*, 177–217. Oxford: British Archaeological Reports British Series 54.

Morris, B. 1994. *The anthropology of the self: the individual in cultural perspective.* London: Pluto Press.

Mundin, A., Chartrand, J. and Darvill, T. 2000. A survey of the long barrow at Ballafayle, Maughold. In T. Darvill (ed.), *Billown Neolithic landscape project, Isle of Man, 2000*, 31–39. Bournemouth and Douglas: Bournemouth University School of Conservation Sciences Research Report 9.

O'Sullivan, M. 2002. Earth, sea and sky: iconography in Irish passage tombs. Paper presented at the Neolithic of the Irish Sea: materiality and traditions of practice conference, Manchester, April 2002.

Piggott, S. 1954. *The Neolithic cultures of the British Isles.* Cambridge: Cambridge University Press.

Piggott, S. 1932. The Mull Hill Circle, Isle of Man, and its pottery. *Antiquaries Journal* 12, 146–57.

Pollard, J. 2001. The aesthetics of depositional practice. *World Archaeology*, 33, 315–33.

Powell, T., Corcoran J., Lynch, F. and Scott, J. 1969. *Megalithic enquiries in the west of Britain.* Liverpool: Liverpool University Press.

Richards, C. 1988. Altered images: A re-examination of Neolithic mortuary practices. In J. Barrett and I. Kinnes (eds), *The archaeology of context in the Neolithic and Bronze Age: recent trends*, 42–56. Sheffield: University of Sheffield.

Richards, C. 1996. Henges and water: towards an elemental understanding of monuments and landscape in Late Neolithic Britain. *Journal of Material Culture* 1, 313–36.

Strathern, M. 1999. The aesthetics of substance. In M. Strathern (ed.), *Property, substance and effect. Anthropological essays on persons and things*, 45–63. London: Athlone Press.

Strathern, M. 1988. *The gender of the gift: problems with women and problems with society in Melanesia.* London: University of California Press.

Strathern, A. and Stewart, P. 2000. Dangerous woods and perilous pearl shells –the fabricated politics of a longhouse in Pangia, Papua New Guinea. *Journal of Material Culture* 5, 69–89

Thomas, J. 1996. *Time, culture and identity.* London: Routledge.

Thomas, J. 1998. An economy of substances in earlier Neolithic Britain. In J. Robb (ed.) *Material symbols: culture and economy in prehistory*, 70–89. Carbondale: Southern Illinois University Press.

Thomas, J. 1999. *Understanding the Neolithic.* London: Routledge.

Thomas, J. 2000. Death, identity and the body in Neolithic Britain. *Journal of the Royal Anthropological Institute* 6, 653–68.

Thomas. J. and Whittle, A. 1986. Anatomy of a tomb: West Kennet revisited. *Oxford Journal of Archaeology* 5, 129–56.

Tilley, C. 1996. *The ethnography of the Neolithic: early prehistoric societies in southern Scandanavia.* Cambridge: Cambridge University Press.

Wagner, R. 1991. The fractal person. In M. Godelier and M. Strathern (eds), *Big men and great men: personifications of power in Melanesia*, 159–73. Cambridge: Cambridge University Press.

12   Rock art, identity and death in the early Bronze Age of Ireland and Britain

Edward Evans and Thomas A. Dowson

Introduction

When so-called 'cup and ring motifs' were found on early Bronze Age[1] cist slabs, it was generally accepted that all cup and ring art[2] found in the landscape could be dated to the early Bronze Age. More recently, however, a number of writers (Burgess 1990; Johnston 1993; Morris 1989, 49; Simpson and Thawley 1972) have observed that the taphonomic features of engraved cist slabs are such that the images on them could not have been executed specifically to 'decorate' the slabs. Not only are the images on the slabs definitely weathered, they are also truncated; the images could not have been made after the rock was quarried. Clearly, the builders of these monuments were quarrying rock on which cup and ring motifs had already been carved. And so a Neolithic date for the landscape art seemed the only alternative. Also, there are strong suggestions (Bradley 1997, 141) that in some areas at least the making of cup and ring motifs in the landscape continued into the Bronze Age.

Although the re-use of Neolithic rock art in the early Bronze Age is thought to be an intentional act, the imagery itself, its meaning and purpose, is widely thought to be part of a (Neolithic) belief system that was in decline and eventually abandoned. For instance, Beckensall suggests that 'whatever the meaning of these abstract designs, they eventually went out of use; and it may be their Neolithic symbolism was irrelevant to, and perhaps incompatible with, the basic cosmology of the Bronze Age' (Beckensall 1998, 8; see also Beckensall and Frodsham 1998, 55; Burgess 1990, 159). The physical interment of these decorated cist slabs in funerary contexts was equated with the death of cup and ring art; the tradition was literally 'laid to rest'. Bradley (1992; 1997, 136–50), however, went beyond merely assessing the chronological significance of the re-use of Neolithic art in the early Bronze Age, and discussed the purpose of these decorated stones in terms of mortuary practice. The already engraved stones, he argued, 'brought the landscape, and the past itself, into direct relationship with the dead' (1992, 175; cf. Jones 2001).

In this paper we show that during the early Bronze Age the re-use of rock art imagery was not irrelevant.

The re-use of Neolithic imagery in the early Bronze Age was not random. Rather, there are specific patterns in the re-use of cup and ring art; patterns that can be regionally defined. This regionally consistent pattern suggests that re-use of rock art was not only intentional, but it had a particular significance. Exploring this significance, we develop and expand upon the relationship described by Bradley. Far from being laid to rest, the art remained as active in early Bronze Age communities as it had been in the Neolithic, and its study can contribute to current thinking on the changing social relations of this time.

Theorising Neolithic rock art

Although we only discuss the re-use of Neolithic rock art in Bronze Age mortuary monuments, it is necessary to comment on the character of Neolithic rock art (for a more detailed discussion see Evans 2003). Rock art of the Irish and British Isles was initially deployed in the open, on what has been termed 'living' rock, during the Neolithic. This imagery is commonly referred to as 'cup and ring' art. Use of this term implies a single artistic tradition composed of very simple motifs: small cupules, which are often surrounded by one or more concentric circles. But the term, although apparently neutral and innocuous, does in fact discourage deeper interpretative analysis. While researchers are beginning to look beyond a stereotypical notion of 'cup and ring' and identify regionally specific traditions, it is difficult to go beyond descriptive accounts of this truly enigmatic imagery, and be more interpretative. As we ourselves have found, when all else fails, there is always description. There have been numerous classifications of motif types, but these typologies have not produced or enabled any greater understanding of the tradition. This is largely because they have focussed entirely on formal and temporal aspects of the images without any understanding or interpretation of how and why these qualities might come together. Like Yates (1993, 35) we believe 'the way forward for rock art analysis is not to address issues of chronology but to theorize the art – a theorization which must extend

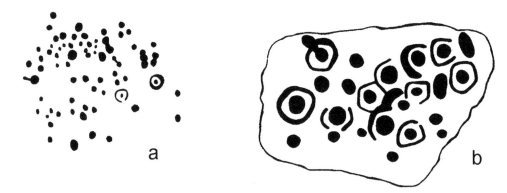

Figure 12.1. *Standard imagery a) from Glen Lochay, central Scotland, and, b) on cist slab from Glen Corse Church, central Scotland (after Morris 1981).*

beyond the stale discussions of terminology – and study its appearance and meaning in local and regional terms'.

By analysing the appearance of the art, and offering a more interpretative account, we identify three fundamental features of this art. Panels of images can appear as if simple or what we prefer to call *standard*, having a basic range of variability. These panels are either comprised of groups of cupules (cup marks) which are often surrounded by a single concentric ring, or they are made up entirely of cup marks (Fig. 12.1a). Panels can also appear more *elaborate*, where there is a greater diversity of motif type and combination (Fig. 12.2a). These include cupules, rings around cupules and curvilinear grooves. Two or more, in some cases even eight, concentric rings surround cupules. Curvilinear grooves either make up a motif alone or they join a series of cup and rings together. The way in which these types of motif are brought together varies considerably.

Although there is great diversity in the way in which these motifs are combined, there are obviously limits to this diversity. Elaborate panels differ from each other only slightly. The third, and final, feature we draw attention to is the *idiosyncratic* character of some rock art panels. In localised groups of rock art sites, one can always find a panel that includes an image that is distinctive and unique to that particular area. For instance, in the rock art sites found in the Kilmartin valley, south-west Scotland, a number of sites each have an idio-syncratic motif: the rosette at Ormaig and the so-called 'horned spiral' at Achnabreck (Fig. 12.3). These images do not represent a general range of diversity, instead they are markedly different and clearly unique to that cluster of sites.

The characterisation of rock art panels we outline here is not only necessary, it does, we believe, go beyond a simple classification of the art in terms of formal qualities, and the temporal relationships between them. Our characterisation of 'cup and ring' rock art is not a means to an end in itself. Theorising the appearance of the art enables a more sensitive approach to discern its

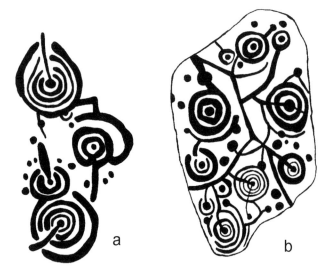

Figure 12.2. *Elaborate imagery a) from site 5 at Weetwood Moor, north-east England (after Beckensall 1983), and, b) on a cist slab from Gainford, north-east England (after Beckensall 1999).*

meaning and social role, which in turn allows us to use the art as an informing context, and so understand the way in which art actively negotiates social interaction (see Dowson 1998).

Bronze Age re-use of rock art – a local and regional view

Neolithic rock art was then re-used in Bronze Age mortuary monuments including cist interments, barrow architecture, wedge tombs, standing stones and stone circles. In some cases the re-used rock art is standard (Fig. 12.1b), and on others it is elaborate (Fig. 12.2b). To demonstrate that this re-use of art was meaningful and intentional, we consider the specific way in which rock art imagery was re-used in seven regions of the Irish and British Isles. We are therefore examining its appearance in local and regional terms.

South-west Ireland

Although rock art is found in the east, it is more heavily concentrated in western Ireland (Harding 2000, 341; Johnston 1989, 42; Lacy 1983, 98; Shee 1968, 144; Van Hoek 1985, 123; 1987, 23–5; 1997, 12) and mostly in the Cork-Kerry region (Johnston 1989, 19). In this area there is a significant concentration of so-called wedge tombs, funnel shaped stone monuments that contain the remains of the dead and date to the final Neolithic and early Bronze Age (Johnston 1989, 295; O'Brien 1993; 1994; 1999; Walsh 1995). The rock art of south-west Ireland is particularly elaborate, exhibiting strong regional characteristics. In contrast, the imagery re-used in wedge tombs is much more standard in character. The monument at Ballyvoge Beg (Kerry), for example, contains only cup-marks whilst that at Ballyhoneen, also in Kerry, consists of 12 cup-marks, one of which exhibits a single broken ring (Johnston 1989, 119; O'Brien 1999, 209). The same standard imagery is also evident on the stone circles found in the south and west (see Burgess 1990, 166; Burl 1979, 147; Johnston 1989, 226; O'Brien 1999, 218–23).

Western Scotland

Along the western Scottish coast there is limited evidence for the re-use of imagery in Ayrshire (Morris 1981), but more noticeable evidence in the Kilmartin valley of Argyll. The Kilmartin valley has a substantial concentration of rock art and a large number of early Bronze Age cist burial cemeteries. Seven cairns are located along the centre of the valley floor, two of which (Nether Largie North and Nether Largie Mid) have evidence for the re-use of imagery. Leaving aside the locally recurrent axe motif, which was later carved on quarried outcrops prior to inclusion (Bradley 1998a; Beckensall 1999, 111; Butler 1999, 56–3; Oram 1997, 139–40), the imagery re-used in these cists is standardised, very different to the elaborate rock carving encountered on living rock throughout the valley. This same pattern is also evident at other sites in the valley, such as the clusters of standing stones at Ballymeanoch, Nether Largie and Torbhlaran (see Beckensall 1999, 123; Burgess 1990, 166). Jones (2001) has also noted the marked difference between the rock art in the landscape and the imagery on cist slabs.

The Temple Wood stone circle, also in the Kilmartin valley, has a complex and unique history (see Bradley 1998a, 136; Burl 1979, 148), and requires specific consideration here. The first, Neolithic phase of the more substantial stone circle is comprised of a ring of stone uprights, two of which are decorated; one with a double

Figure 12.3. The double spiral from Achnabreck, Kilmartin valley, Scotland.

spiral spread over two faces and the other a pair of concentric circles (Beckensall 1999, 120), as is the case in the landscape. Significantly, for the purposes of our discussion, the phase of construction that dates to the early Bronze Age saw the construction of a stone kerb between the uprights (Bradley 1998a, 136). On this kerb Beckensall (1999, 121) has identified a slab decorated with two cup-marks – the same patterning of re-use observed at other local early Bronze Age sites.

In the Kilmartin valley there are a few sites at which the imagery that is re-used is not standard. But, as with the rest of the valley, the cist imagery from these sites, for example Badden and Carn Ban, demonstrate a concern to avoid the re-use elaborate imagery, using instead motifs that are more characteristic of passage tomb art (see Beckensall 1999, 122; RCAHMS 1988). We believe the passage tomb art to be something different, and we address this elsewhere (see Evans 2003).

Eastern Scotland

In the far north-east some 50 stone built passage graves, ring cairns and circles, known collectively as the Clava cairns, are clustered around the Moray Forth. These early Bronze Age structures combine features normally associated with passage graves and stone circles in a new expression of monumentality with a pronounced regional similarity (Bradley 2000). The rock art re-used in these monuments is standard in character (Bradley 1998b, 111; 2000, 206), as is the rock art in the landscape. A similar pattern is also evident amongst the nearby recumbent stone circles, with which the Clava cairns share many architectural features and an association with the dead (see Bradley 2000, 3–7; Burl 1969–70, 18). This pattern of re-use, in which the re-used imagery is similar in character to that in the local landscape, continues down the eastern side of Scotland. In Fife, early Bronze Age cist burials have slabs on which standard imagery occurs, as is the case for rock art in the landscape there. Around Edinburgh and in the Borders area it is a more elaborate imagery that is found in both the landscape and re-used in mortuary monuments.

Central Scotland

Little in the way of cist imagery is found in the inland areas of Scotland between the Forths of Clyde and Firth. The only concentration of note can be found around Glasgow. Here, the cist imagery is as elaborate as the imagery of the landscape. In areas where there are no decorated cists, around Loch Tay in Perthshire for example, rock with standardised imagery is used in the stone circle monuments generally accepted to be dated to the early Bronze Age (Morris 1981), emulating the standard character of art in the landscape. Despite a degree of variation in the character of rock art re-used in Bronze Age monuments, the pattern is locally consistent: rock art re-used in mortuary monuments is the same in character as the rock art in the landscape.

North-east England

In the north-east of England rock art in the landscape is predominantly elaborate in character. The art on the cist slabs is also elaborate. Often there was a more intimate connection between rock art sites in the landscape and the Bronze Age mortuary monuments. At Weetwood Moor, for example, a number of early Bronze Age cairns were built on top of previously carved outcrops (Beckensall 1999, 144–9). These monuments were constructed, however, in a manner that allowed the majority of imagery to remain visible. The idea of a connection between mortuary monuments and the landscape as suggested by rock art was being made much more explicitly.

North-west England

In the two major valley systems of the Lake District are a small number of open air rock art sites (Beckensall 2002). Although this imagery occasionally includes standard images of cup-and-rings it is the concentric circles, curvilinear grooves and meandering linear motifs of the recently discovered Chapel Stile site that characterise the rock art of this region. The elaborate character of the open air rock art sites is re-used at a number of Neolithic stone circle monuments. Perhaps the most well known example of this is found at the circle complex of Long Meg. The single, decorated outlying stone has spirals, concentric circles and meandering lines on it. This massive block is thought to have once stood in the red sandstone cliffs of the river Eden (Frodsham 1989, 111–13) where they occupied the same vertical plane as the Chapel Stile motifs. The circle at Long Meg shares many architectural characteristics with the monuments at Kemp Howe, Grey Yauds and Castlerigg (Barnatt 1989a, 344; 1989b, 183). The imagery at Castlerigg is comparable with the elaborate imagery at Long Meg, as well as the stones recovered from the Neolithic burial monument at Old Parks.

Significantly, Burl (1976, 60) places Long Meg and Castlerigg amongst the earliest of British stone circles, locating them in the Neolithic, the same chronological horizon as the decorated burial structure at Old Parks (Beckensall 1999). Because of comparable imagery, Burl (1994, 7) argues that Little Meg is also Neolithic in age, while extending Burl's argument suggests the decorated cairn at Glassonby is the same age. Neolithic re-use of rock art in Cumbria is such that it is similar in character to the rock art in the landscape. Considering the three decorated stones at Little Meg, however, suggests an alternative interpretation of the age of this site. Two of these stones belong to the standardised cup-and-ring range whilst the so-called Maughanby stone has elaborate imagery, as in the landscape. Significantly, the two unnamed stones were associated with a cist-like structure, whilst the Maughanby stone retained the striking physical appearance it once had in the landscape (Frodsham 1996). Almost certainly the cist is a later structure. Evidence to support this suggestion comes from the Shap Avenue, a monument that according to Burl's scheme has a construction life that straddles the boundary of the Neolithic and the Bronze Age. Two of the few remaining stones of this monument, Aspers Field and Goggleby, have standard cup-and-ring imagery, as is the case in the cist structure of Little Meg. This emphasis on standard imagery continues into monuments that are unequivocally dated to the early Bronze Age (including the ring cairn of Moor Divock, the double ring cairn of Hardendale, and cist covers at Redhills and Maryport). The carved rocks of Stag Stone Farm, Honey Pots, Dean and Penrith museum can also be added to this list (data from Beckensall 1999; Frodsham 1989). Although these rocks are not accurately provenanced, the material form and the truncation of motifs are reminiscent of early Bronze Age cist slabs encountered elsewhere.

During the change from the Neolithic to the early Bronze Age in Cumbria, the re-use of imagery changed from resembling the imagery seen in the landscape to imagery that was very different to that on living rock. The contrasting characteristics of landscape imagery and early Bronze Age redeployments evident in Cumbria is more pronounced in the Peak District. The landscape imagery of Derbyshire is highly elaborate, containing little of the standard imagery (see Barnatt and Firth 1983; Barnatt and Reader 1981). In contrast, the imagery found in monumental contexts rarely includes anything other than cup marks.

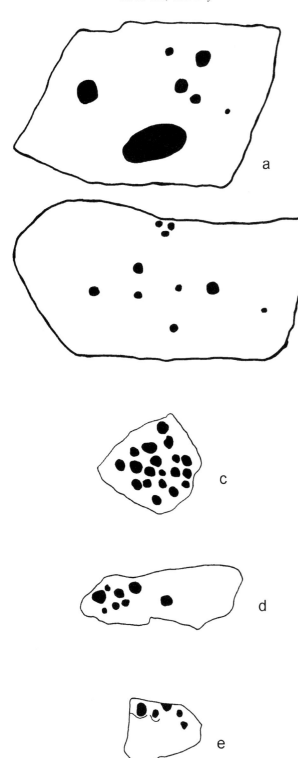

Figure 12.4. *Examples of carved rocks from Starapark (a, b) and Stithians (c, d, e), Cornwall (after Trudgian 1976; Hartgroves 1987 respectively).*

South-west England

The rock art in south-west England presents a particularly interesting challenge. At one site, 12 cup-marked stones were found below the high-water line at the Stithians reservoir (Fig. 12.4). The archaeological context of these decorated stones has been interpreted in significantly different ways. On the one hand, Hartgroves (1987) sees these as an incidence of landscape rock art. On the other, Christie (1985) argues that the stones come from a denuded barrow. In a similar vein, Beckensall (1999, 83–7) believes there to be no engraved outcrops of living rock in Cornwall. But he does detail 14 sites in which cup-marked rocks were interred in the central structures or mound fill of barrows dating to the early Bronze Age (see also Bradley 1997, 148; Christie 1985 for chronological evidence). It appears then that in the south west of England, carved cist slabs are not the result of the re-use of landscape imagery. Rather, it appears slabs of rock were being specifically carved with standard imagery for inclusion in barrow cists (see Fig. 12.4).

Re-use as a strategy of re-production

From the foregoing discussion of seven rock art regions in the Irish and British Isles it is clear the re-use of carved, living rock in the early Bronze Age mortuary monuments was not random. If this were the case we should not expect to find such consistent local patterning.

In three of the regions discussed above, eastern Scotland (see Fig. 12.5a), central Scotland and north-east England (Fig. 12.5b), carved rock that was quarried for inclusion into monuments had imagery that is similar in character to that in the landscape. For instance, in north-east England, where the rock art panels in the landscape are predominantly elaborate, the rock art on stone incorporated into monuments is also elaborate. In three of the other areas discussed, north-west England (Fig. 12.5c, d), western Scotland (Fig. 12.5e) and south-west Ireland, builders of those monuments chose to quarry rock on which a more standard character of imagery had once been carved; specifically ignoring the elaborate panels in the landscape. Builders were selecting rock art to be incorporated into monuments such that the imagery on the cist slab was made to appear as if it was strikingly different in character to the overall character of rock art found in the landscape. The final region discussed, south-west England, is quite different to all the other regions in that here there is no rock art in the landscape. The character of imagery carved onto rocks used in barrows in this region is standard.

This apparently sudden appearance of rock art in the Bronze Age of Cornwall can be explained by exploring connections with south-west Ireland. Here too, as discussed above, redeployed imagery is standard in character. The wedge tombs of south-west Ireland were constructed

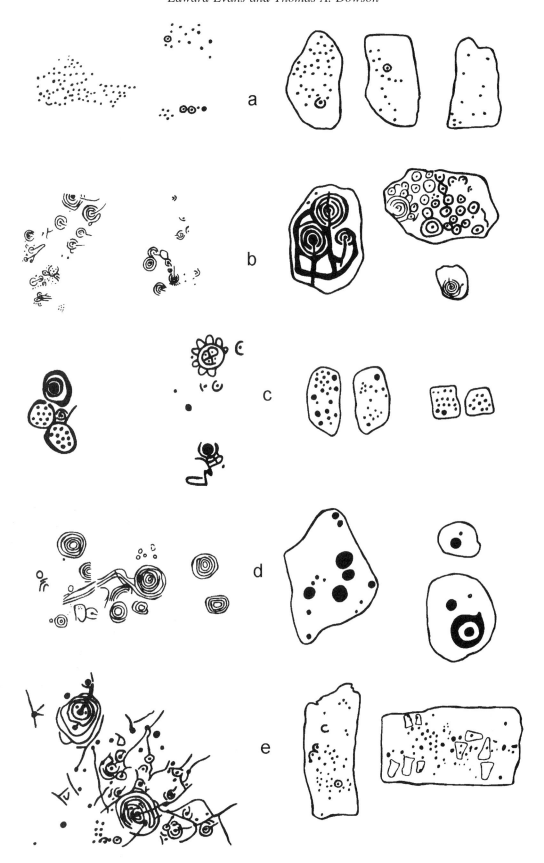

Figure 12.5. *Landscape art (left hand column) and cist-slab art (right hand column): a – eastern Scotland (after Beckensall 1999; Bradley 2000), b – north-east England (after Beckensall 1999; Simpson and Thawley 1972), c – Peak District (after Barnatt and Reeder 1982), d – Cumbria (Beckensall 1999; 2002), e – Kilmartin (after Morris 1981; Beckensall 1999).*

on the metalliferous peninsulas of Cork and Kerry at about the same time as there was a rapid expansion of metal production. Although copper was common to this area a lack of tin provided a significant incentive for exchange with other metal producing communities. It is generally accepted that the rich alluvial deposits of south-west England were the most likely source of tin for the Irish metal workers (Harding 2000, 200; O'Brien 1994, 241–9; O'Sullivan and Sheehan 1996, 74–7). In fact there is considerable archaeological evidence for exchange between these two regions. We propose that the cup-marked cist slabs that were placed in Cornish barrows were a way of mimicking the re-use of rock art in south-west Ireland.

Two scholars have already noted an inter-regional patterning in the re-use of rock art in the early Bronze Age. Haddingham (quoted in Beckensall and Frodsham 1998, 52), writing as far back as 1974, suggested that 'the distribution of carved cists may confirm the assumption that complex cup-and-ring carving had died out in some western districts by Bronze Age times, but that in eastern areas its influence persisted'. This explanation does not suitably explain why it was that in the west people should only re-use standard imagery despite the abundance of complex, or elaborate, art in the landscape. More recently, and in contrast to Haddingham, Bradley (1997) has argued for a north-west divide: a western tradition in Wales and the south-west of England, and a northern tradition taking in the well documented areas of rock carving in Scotland and the north of England. Grouping the various regions of Scotland and the north of England together hides regional variations that are not only stark, but also, we believe, significant. Extending the scope of investigation to include south-west Ireland, as well as mortuary monuments other than only cist burials suggests that it is more profitable to speak of an east-west divide; a divide that appears to run down the centre of mainland Britain.

Such is the manner in which rock art is re-used throughout the Irish and British Isles that we argue this 're-use' of imagery represented a new series of strategies of production, or rather re-production. The art was initially deployed in the open landscape on living rock. Towards the end of the Neolithic and during the early Bronze Age, rock art was redeployed in new contexts, with new purposes, meanings and social roles. The change of archaeological context is easily observable: rock art being made on exposed rock outcrops in the landscape to those same images being quarried and buried in the making of mortuary monuments. But, it is understanding the change of purpose that proves to be more difficult to construct. Not only are there locally consistent patterns, i.e. redeployed rock art either resembles that in the landscape or it does not, there is also inter-regional patterning. In the Irish and British Isles there is an east-west divide of these locally consistent patterns of redeployment. It is in the east where redeployed art

resembles imagery seen in the landscape, whereas in the west redeployed art is not the same in character as the art in the landscape. In attempting to make sense of these local and regional patterns and unravel the new purpose rock art had for the community in which it was reproduced and consumed, we are reminded of a comment Yates (1994, 70) makes, that archaeological data are not limited but the minds that think about them are. This comment applies as equally here for our discussion of Irish and British rock art as it does the interpretation of Swedish rock art for Yates.

Redeployment of rock art and the construction of identity

The redeployment of rock art into mortuary monuments coincides with an introduction of single burial graves and the regional decline of communal tombs towards the end of the Neolithic. Understanding the purpose in redeploying rock art alongside the interment of individuals is possible if we can theorise a relationship between the two contexts for action: redeployment of art and interment of individuals. During the 1990s there was a considerable mind-shift in thinking about the change from communal tombs to single grave burial. This change in thinking was led principally by Barrett (see, for example, 1988; 1990; 1994), who concentrated on the architectural setting of mortuary practice, and further developed by Thomas (1996; 2000), who explored the part played by the human body in mortuary practices. For these scholars mortuary practices are not some passive reflection of ethnic affiliation, nor do they represent the relative prestige of the interred. On the contrary, mortuary practices – the architectural setting, material goods and the deceased bodies – are a means by which social relations are continually created, transformed and reinforced, not only between the dead and the living, but, as importantly, amongst the living in the present (cf. Fowler 2001; Lucas 1996). These social relations included people's duties, obligations between individuals, positions of authority, as well as the affiliations individuals construct.

Barrett (1988) makes a distinction between the mortuary practices of the Neolithic and those of the early Bronze Age. The earlier Neolithic is characterised by communal burials and ancestor rituals where bodies are deposited and continuously redeposited, in the belief that the ancestors are continually evoked to structure and sanction social relations amongst the living. Towards the end of the Neolithic and in the early Bronze Age funerary rites became focussed on the death of a particular individual. The single burial grave located the social death of an individual in the landscape. By adding further burials to the grave mound, or digging new grave mounds nearby – an individual's death was fixed in both space and time. Funerary practices then ensured the physical remains of the dead were inaccessible to the living or, as Thomas (2000, 663) suggests, distanced the dead from the living. Not only did the ritual locate individuals' death, but also the burial placed them in the past, within a recognisable line of descent (Thomas 2000, 665). Thomas (1996) argues that the increased cultural diversity archaeologists observe during the late Neolithic resulted from a series of overlapping social networks and contexts for action that began to emerge then. These would have generated a diverse range of experiences and forms of authority. Consequently, individuals, with differing access to specific combinations of artefacts, spaces and contexts for action began to develop different life histories. It was these individual life histories, which were socially and historically situated within identifiable lines of descent, that increasingly negotiated personal identities of the living. This may have been the case as people ceased to see themselves as being part of a bounded community with widely held beliefs and shared experiences.

The social production (and re-production) and consumption of art was an integral part of these social processes. The act of carving images on rocks, as well as the images themselves, were but one element of daily life through which the social was continually brought into being. Originally produced in the open, on living rock, for all to see, rock art negotiated shared communal experiences. The redeployment of art in single grave burials, on the other hand, represented peoples' life experiences.

It is safe to assume that not all individuals would have identified intimately with the experiences associated with the production and consumption of art. But certainly some did. For these people the quarried rocks in their graves were a testament to that life history. Also, the act of quarrying carved rock, by the deceased's descendants was, as importantly, a part of reinscribing on the living those duties associated with the rock art once held by the deceased. In so doing, they were re-affirming their affiliation to a particular line of descent with specific character of ancestry. The art was not being laid to rest, it continued to negotiate social relations amongst the living.

The contrasting strategies for redeployment observed in the west and in the east allow us to make more specific comments. In the west the redeployed imagery in early Bronze Age mortuary monuments is strikingly different in character to that in the landscape. Making the body inaccessible in single grave burials was just one means by which descendants distanced the dead. The particular strategy of redeploying art observed in the west was specifically used as a further way of distancing the dead from the living. The memory of the deceased was 'fixed' in the present (cf. Jones 2001). In Cumbria the strategy of redeploying imagery changes from the Neolithic to the early Bronze Age. In the Neolithic the redeployed art resembles the elaborate landscape imagery, whereas in the early Bronze Age redeployed art is standard. This is evidence, perhaps, of the shift in attitudes about the dead; increasingly distancing them from the present, placing them in the past.

On the other hand, in the east imagery redeployed in mortuary monuments is similar in character to that in the landscape. On some of these easterly regions, notably north-east England, the burial cairns, which often include carved cist slabs, was placed directly on top of outcrops of rock that were previously carved. Placing the dead in the landscape, with cist-slab imagery that resembled the art in the landscape, drew attention to the relationship that that particular individual had with the land as constructed by rock art. Going one step further and placing the dead directly on top of existing carved rock made that relationship between rock art and the dead more explicitly direct and immediately observable. This strategy of linking the dead to specific locales was a means of identifying the deceased with a fixed point in the landscape and ritual activities that may have taken place there. But also, and perhaps more significantly, the implicit or explicit strategies of redeployment were a way of acknowledging and re-inscribing a continued relationship between the living, by virtue of their descent from the deceased, to that landscape and the associated rock art activities that took place there. Further, it is not inconceivable that making blatantly explicit links to rock art, not only through the use of redeployed art but also by placing the dead directly on top of the rock art, was a means by which contested land claims, whether real or potential, were challenged or pre-empted.

This interpretation of the redeployment of rock art is obviously a general one. In this paper we present an initial and tentative attempt at understanding this enigmatic artistic tradition. The understanding we offer is one in which the active role of the art can be conceptualised, which allows the re-production and consumption of redeployed art to be considered alongside other lived experiences of this time. This interpretative framework will be significantly enhanced and developed at specific sites when considering the specific archaeology of those places.

Acknowledgements

We have benefited greatly from discussions on the ideas presented here with Julian Thomas and Colin Richards. Chris Fowler kindly commented on a draft of this paper, making invaluable suggestions.

Notes

1   Although we refer throughout this paper to 'early Bronze Age' cists there is no evidence to suggest all of these cists are early Bronze Age in date. Some are said to be 'Final Neolithic/early Bronze Age', while others are thought to be late Neolithic. This apparent uncertainty strikes at the once cherished Neolithic/Bronze Age divide. The significance of this more fluid situation will become clearer later in the paper.

2   We recognise that the use of the term 'art' is highly problematic (for a recent, considered discussion see

Tomásková 1997). Like Wolff (1981) we find the generally accepted definition of 'art', the one most archaeologists attempt to move away from, to be as restrictive and misleading for contemporary art as it is for prehistoric art. We do, however, believe the term can be rehabilitated.

References

Barrett, J.C. 1988. The living, the dead, and the ancestors: Neolithic and early Bronze Age mortuary practices. In J.C. Barrett and I.A. Kinnes (eds), *The archaeology of context in the Neolithic and Bronze Age*, 30–41. Sheffield: Department of Archaeology and Prehistory.

Barrett, J.C. 1990. The monumentality of death: the character of early Bronze Age mortuary mounds in southern Britain. *World Archaeology* 22, 179–89.

Barrett, J.C. 1994. *Fragments from antiquity*. Oxford: Blackwell.

Barnatt, J. 1989a. *The stone circles of Great Britain*. Oxford: British Archaeological Reports British Series 215(i).

Barnatt, J. 1989b. *The stone circles of Great Britain*. Oxford: British Archaeological Reports British Series 215(ii).

Barnatt, J and Firth, P. 1983. A newly discovered 'cup and ring' carving in Ecclesall Wood, Sheffield. *Derbyshire Archaeological Journal* 103, 41–2.

Barnatt, J and Reeder, P. 1982. Prehistoric rock art in the Peak District. *Derbyshire Archaeological Journal* 102, 33–44.

Beckensall, S. 1983. *Northumberland's prehistoric rock carvings*. Rothbury: Pendulum Press.

Beckensall, S. 1998. An ideology that faded into a new age. *British Archaeology* 1988, 8–9.

Beckensall, S. 1999. *British prehistoric rock art*. Stroud: Tempus.

Beckensall, S. 2002. British prehistoric rock art in the landscape. In G. Nash and C. Chippendale (eds), *European landscapes of rock art*, 39–70. London: Routledge.

Beckensall, S and Frodsham, P. 1998. Questions of chronology: the case for Bronze Age rock art in northern Britain. *Northern Archaeology* 15/16, 51–69.

Bradley, R. 1992. Turning the world – rock carving and the archaeology of death. In N. Sharples and A. Sheridan (eds), *Vessels for the ancestors*, 168–76. Edinburgh: Edinburgh University Press.

Bradley, R. 1997. *Rock art and the prehistory of Atlantic Europe*. London: Routledge.

Bradley, R. 1998a. *The significance of monuments: on the shaping of human experience in Neolithic and Bronze Age Europe*. London: Routledge.

Bradley, R. 1998b. A new investigation into the Clava cairns. *Proceedings of the Society of Antiquaries of Scotland* 128, 1125–6.

Bradley, R. 2000. *The good stones: a new investigation of the Clava Cairns*. Edinburgh: Society of Antiquarians of Scotland Monograph 17.

Burgess, C. 1990. The chronology of cup-and cup-and-ring marks in Atlantic Europe. *Rev. archéol. Quest, Supplément* 2, 157–71.

Burl, A. 1969–70. The recumbent stone circles of Scotland. *Proceedings of the Society of Antiquaries of Scotland* 102, 56–81.

Burl, A. 1976. *Stone circles of the British Isles*. New Haven: Yale University Press.

Burl, A. 1979. *Rings of Stone*. London: Frances Lincon.

Burl, A. 1994. The stone circle of Long Meg and her daughters, Little Salkeld. *Transactions of the Cumberland and Westmoreland Antiquarian and Archaeological Society* 94, 1–11.

Butler, R. 1999. *Kilmartin*. Kilmartin: Kilmartin House Trust.

Christie, P. 1985. Barrows on the north Cornish coast: wartime excavations by C.K. Croft Andrew 1939–1944. *Cornish Archaeology* 24, 23–121.

Dowson, T. A. 1998. Rock art: handmaiden to studies of cognitive evolution. In C. Renfrew and C. Scarre (eds), *Cognition and material culture: the archaeology of symbolic storage*, 67–76. Cambridge: MacDonald Institute for Archaeological Research.

Evans, E. 2003. *Focus, effect and meaning: Writing history from art in the Neolithic of Ireland and the British Isles*. Unpublished PhD Thesis: University of Manchester.

Fowler, C. 2001. Personhood and social relations in the British Neolithic with a study from the Isle of Man. *Journal of Material Culture* 6, 37–163.

Frodsham, P. 1989. Two newly discovered cup-and-ring stones from Penrith and Hallbankgate, with a gazetteer of all known megalithic carvings in Cumbria. *Transactions of the Cumberland and Westmoreland Antiquarian and Archaeological Society* 89, 1–18.

Frodsham, P. 1996. Spirals in time: Morwick Hill and the spiral motif in the British Neolithic. *Northern Archaeology* 13/14, 101–38.

Harding, A. 2000. *European societies in the Bronze Age*. Cambridge: Cambridge University Press.

Hartgroves, S. 1987. The cup-marked stones of Stithians reservoir. *Cornish Archaeology* 26, 69–84.

Johnston, S. 1989. *Prehistoric Irish petroglyphs: their analysis and interpretation*. Ann Arbour: University Microfilms.

Jones, A. 2001. Enduring images? Image production and memory in earlier Bronze Age Scotland. In J. Brück (ed.), *Bronze Age landscapes: tradition and transformation*, 217–28. Oxford: Oxbow Books.

Johnston, S. 1993. The relationship between prehistoric Irish rock art and Irish passage tomb art. *Oxford Journal of Archaeology* 12, 257–79.

Lacy, B. 1983. *An archaeological survey of county Donegal*. Lifford: Donegal County Council.

Lucas, G.M. 1996. Of death and debt. A history of the body in Neolithic and early Bronze Age Yorkshire. *Journal of European Archaeology* 4, 99–118.

Morris, R. 1981. *The prehistoric rock art of southern Scotland*. Oxford: British Archaeological Reports.

Morris, R. 1989. The prehistoric rock art of Great Britain: a survey of all sites bearing motifs more complex than simple cup marks. *Proceedings of the Prehistoric Society* 55, 45–88.

O'Brien, W. 1993. Aspects of wedge tomb chronology. In E. Shee-Twohig and M. Ronayne (eds), *Past perceptions*, 63–74. Cork: Cork University Press.

O'Brien, W. 1994. *Mount Gabriel: Bronze Age mining in Ireland*. Galway: Galway University Press.

O'Brien, W. 1999. *Sacred ground. Megalithic tombs in coastal south-west Ireland*. Galway: National University of Ireland.

Oram, R. 1997. *Scottish Prehistory*. Edinburgh: Binlinn.

O'Sullivan, A. and Sheehan, J. 1996. *The Inveragh peninsula; an archaeological survey of south Kerry.* Cork: Cork University Press.

RCAHMS. 1988. *Argyll: an inventory of the monuments, volume 6.* Edinburgh: Her Majesty's Stationary Office.

Shee, E. 1968. Some examples of rock art from Co. Cork. *Journal of the Cork Historical and Archaeological Society* 63, 144–52.

Simpson, D. and Thawley, J. 1972. Single grave art in Britain. *Scottish Archaeological Forum* 4, 81–104.

Thomas, J. 1996. *Time, culture and identity: an interpretative archaeology.* London: Routledge.

Thomas, J. 2000. Death, identity and the body in Neolithic Britain. *Journal of the Royal Anthropological Institute* 6, 653–68.

Tomásková, S. 1997. Places of art: art and archaeology in context. In M. Conkey, O. Soffer, D. Stratmann and N.G. Jablonski (eds), *Beyond art: Pleistocene image and symbol,* 265–87. San Francisco: California Academy of Sciences.

Trudgian, P. 1976. Cup-marked stones from a barrow at Starapark, near Camelford. *Cornish Archaeology* 15, 49.

Van Hoek, M. 1985. A new group of cup and ring marked rocks at Inisnown, Co. Donegal. *Ulster Journal of Archaeology* 48, 123–27.

Van Hoek, M. 1987. The prehistoric rock art of Co. Donegal (PtII). *Ulster Journal of Archaeology* 51, 21–97.

Van Hoek, M. 1997. The distribution of cup-and-ring motifs along the Atlantic seaboard of Europe. *Rock Art Research* 14, 3–16.

Walsh, P. 1995. Structure and deposition in Irish wedge tombs: an open and shut case? In J. Waddell and E. Shee-Twohig (eds), *Ireland in the Bronze Age,* 113–27. Dublin: Office of Public Works.

Wolff, J. 1981. *The social production of art.* London: Macmillan.

Yates, T. 1993. Frameworks for an archaeology of the body. In C. Tilley (ed.), *Interpretative Archaeology,* 31–72. Oxford: Berg.

13   The setting and form of Manx chambered cairns: cultural comparisons and social interpretations

Vicki Cummings and Chris Fowler

Introduction

The Isle of Man is found at the heart of the Irish Sea and is roughly 40 kilometres long and 20 kilometres wide at its broadest point. Topographically, the island is quite diverse, incorporating high mountains and low coastal plains. The north of the island consists of a low plain which, while rich in occupational debris (particularly from the later Neolithic), contains no known megalithic monuments (Darvill 2000). The centre of the island is a highland area which shelves down the to sea on the east and west through rolling foothills and steep glens. The north-west coast is exposed, and devoid of sheltered beaches. The south-west and eastern coasts are a mixture of rocky cliffs and sheltered bays, with rocky and pebble beaches. Hills extend along the west coast to the tip of the island, but the south-east part of the island is a lowland region of gently rolling hills. The southern-most tip of the island contains rocky outcrops and a few high hills. There are 10 known chambered cairns on the island (Fig. 13.1), found primarily to the east of the island in the foothills or lowlands between the mountains and the coast.

The Neolithic monuments of the Isle of Man were constructed and embellished in the earlier Neolithic[1] (Darvill 2000; Fowler this volume; Lynch in press). Three sites (Ballaharra, Clay Head and Port St. Mary's) have been destroyed, and their landscape locations are not discussed here. As a group, the monuments are diverse in form: writing in 1978, Henshall said 'the most striking feature of the Manx sites are their diversity and individuality' (Henshall 1978, 171). Cashtal yn Ard and King Orry's Grave NE and SW are court cairns with the closest parallels in eastern Ireland. Ballafayle seems to be the remains of a long barrow, or possibly a court cairn with a wooden chamber similar to that found within the cairn at Ballymacaldrack (Evans 1938; Mundin *et al.* 2000). The Cloven Stones, Ballakelly and Kew remain unclassified, although it has been suggested that the small box-chamber at Ballakelly could be similar to the first phase at Mid Gleniron (Henshall 1978, 172) and Kew the remains of a passage grave (Darvill 2000, figure 32.5c). Finally, the circular six-chambered monument at Mull Hill (Fig. 13.2) remains unparalleled in Britain, although connections have been suggested with south-west Scotland (Davey this volume; Henshall 1978) and south-west Wales (Lynch 1972).

Monuments and landscape

The past 15 years has seen a growing interest in the landscape setting of Neolithic monuments (e.g. Bergh 1995; Tilley 1994). Over the last few years the landscape setting of the monuments along the eastern Irish Sea have been considered in some detail (see Cummings 2001; 2002b; this volume; forthcoming; Cummings and Whittle forthcoming; Fowler and Cummings 2003). As part of an wider interpretation of the Manx megaliths it was decided to examine the landscape settings of the monuments against the broader Irish Sea background. Were trends in the landscape location of particular forms of chambered cairns that were taken up in other regions also employed on the Isle of Man? In this contribution we examine the surviving monuments on the Isle of Man in particular focussing on the connections between monument location, monument form and the local topography. This work is provisional, and an abundance of tumuli and other remains which have not been fully investigated on the island may contain the remains of further megalithic monuments. Recent fieldwork (e.g. Davey and Woodcock forthcoming) may suggest not only that far more earlier Neolithic sites exist but also that there were a far greater *range* of sites, and locations used to build them. The chambered cairn at Ballaharra was buried under 2m of overburden, and other finds of stone monuments cited by P.M.C. Kermode (1930), and Pitts (1999) could be borne in mind as potential chambered cairns or contemporary monuments. Our discussion is therefore limited only to the extant standing chambered cairns known on the island at present.

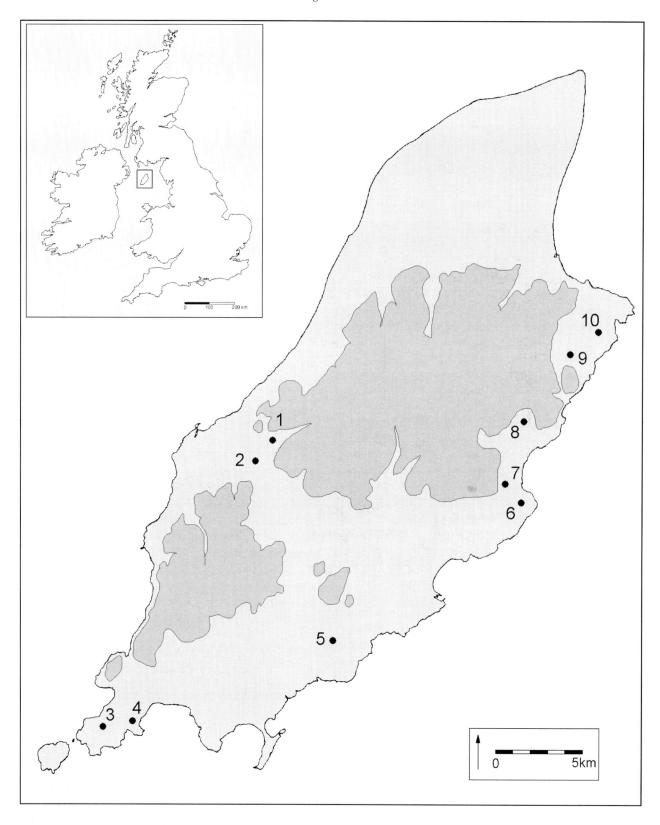

Figure 13.1*. Location map of the Isle of Man. Darker shading on the island is land over 150m. 1. The Kew. 2. Ballaharra. 3. Mull Hill. 4. Port St. Mary. 5. Ballakelly. 6. Clay Head. 7. The Cloven Stones. 8. King Orry's Graves. 9. Cashtal yn Ard. 10. Ballafayle.*

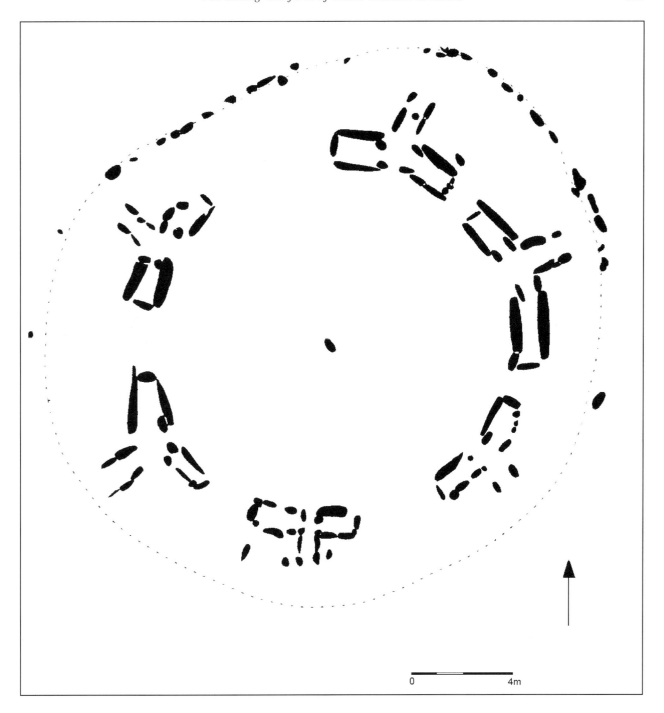

Figure 13.2. The monument of Mull Hill (after Burrow 1997).

Mountains

Recent work on the settings of monuments around the Irish Sea has demonstrated that mountains were key reference points in the landscape. Many monuments in north Wales, for example, are located with clear views of Snowdonia (Cummings and Whittle forthcoming). Like-wise, the Bargrennan monuments of south-west Scotland cluster around the Merrick Mountains (Cummings 2002b). Mountains are often shrouded in cloud and mist, hidden from the everyday world of the living, and blurring the land and the sky. They are often wet as well as rocky places, with rapidly-changing weather conditions different from those in the lowlands. From a distance, mountains are important features in navigating around the landscape and across the Irish Sea. Some of these mountains were also used for quarrying stone axes (Clough and Cummins 1988). It has been suggested that mountains would have been key places in the Neolithic, connected with spirits, other-worldly beings or even ancestral beings (see Cummings this volume; Watson this volume; Whittle this volume; and Cooney this volume on islands and mountains). Mountains, then, seem to have been highly potent places in the Neolithic around the Irish Sea.

Snaefell is the highest mountain on the Isle of Man, and it has long been noted that from its summit it is possible to see Snowdonia, Cumbria, the Merrick mountains, the Mourne mountains and the Wicklow mountains (also see Cummings this volume). However, Snaefell itself is not visible from much of the island, lying in the northern highlands and obscured from the lowlands by lesser peaks. It is not visible from any of the extant monuments on the island. Instead, monuments have views of distinctive local peaks. North Barrule is visible from Cashtal yn Ard, while South Barrule is visible from Mull Hill, as are the Calf of Man, and Bradda Head (see Davey, this volume for the full range of landscape features visible from Mull Hill). South Barrule is also referenced in the design of Billown Quarry enclosure, with the entrance between the south and the north enclosed areas framing the mountain along the path of a hollow way (see Darvill 1996; 1997; 1998; 2000; 2001). South Barrule is obscured from view at Ballakelly, but had the monument been located only 100m to the west of its present location, South Barrule would have been visible. At a point some 100m inland from the monument, the land reaches a broad knoll, and from this spot it is possible to view both South Barrule and Ballakelly. Unmarked locations like this may have been significant in the use of megalithic monuments, though excavations rarely extend so far from the stone features of monuments. Alternatively the location of the monument may be designed to obscure the peak. This suggests that while a view of a mountain may have been desirable at some sites, not all monuments were positioned so that there was a direct mountain view.

Water: streams and the sea

All of the monuments on the island seem to be located in relation to streams. There is a general connection between the monuments and the watercourses which run from the foothills of the central mountains and the southern hills through nearby glens to the sea. However, in many cases it would be hard to position a monument without it being relatively close to a stream, so it is difficult to assess the significance of streams at all of the monuments. Yet there are still a few cases where cairns seem to have been very carefully positioned in relation to watercourses. Cashtal yn Ard is surrounded by streams in most directions so that it is essentially encircled by water: it is necessary to cross water to reach the site. King Orry's Graves are located above a stream and waterfall, and running water is audible from King Orry's Grave SW.

At this site the lie of the hill, the stream, and its gully are part of the architecture of the monument and affect how it could be approached. The stream runs only 10m from the forecourt at King Orry's Grave SW, and the ground directly outside the forecourt slopes away dramatically to the south-east, meaning that very few people would actually have been able to stand in the immediate forecourt area or witness acts in the entranceway. The forecourt at King Orry's Grave NE does not share this restriction, and lies uphill of the chambers and the stream. Here the wide forecourt leads into a hillside from which many people could observe activities at the monument.

The sea is visible from all of the sites on the island. Ballakelly overlooks the coastal strip with much of the horizon to the east occupied by sea. Likewise, at both Ballafayle and Cashtal yn Ard there are wide views of the sea to the east of each monument. Mull Hill, Cashtal yn Ard, Ballaharra, Port St Mary's, King Orry's Graves, and Ballakelly were all positioned in lofty vantage points giving extensive views of the sea and the horizon. Many of the monuments found along the eastern Irish Sea have similar views of the sea (see below, and Cummings 2001; 2002b; Fowler and Cummings 2003).

Bays and harbours

It has often been suggested that Neolithic monuments are found close to bays and harbours that would have been suitable landing places for small Neolithic craft (for example in relation to Barclodiad y Gawres in north Wales – Powell and Daniel 1956). On the Isle of Man a number of sites are positioned close to bays and harbours, most often at the heads of glens. This is of particular interest given that there is clear evidence of seafaring throughout the Neolithic from the presence of imported axes from both Ireland and Britain (and see Cooney this volume for further evidence). The Cloven Stones at Baldrine lie on a sloping path between the hills and the coast, less than 1km from the sheltered beach at Garwick and 1km from Laxey Bay. King Orry's Graves are 1km from Laxey Bay, a sheltered bay that is still used as a harbour today. At this site we could envisage people arriving at the bay by boat and following the stream up to the monuments. Elsewhere on the island, Cashtal yn Ard is approximately 1.5km from the sheltered beach at Port Cornaa and at the south of the island Mull Hill is located close to Port Erin Bay.

Outcrops and sources of stone

Elsewhere it has been noted that monuments are frequently located in relation to distinctive natural features (e.g. Bradley 1996; Cummings 2002a; Tilley 1996). In some cases the stones used to build monuments are very local, in other cases they have been brought from more distant landscape features. A similar mixture of the local and distant can be observed across Manx sites. Mull Hill is located in an area with a number of outcrops, some of which were used to construct the monument itself. Mull Hill is constructed from slate, but at the very centre of the circle is a large lump of quartz. Quartz veins run through the local slate, and are visible in the slabs of several chambers. While the majority of stones employed in building Manx megaliths were of local origin, at least one of the orthostats at the now destroyed site of Ballaharra was constructed from a wave-washed sandstone slab, and stones were also brought from at least two other locales (Higgins and Davey in press; cf. Fowler this volume for the admixing of different local materials in monument construction and use on the island). Furthermore, it could be suggested that stones with specific qualities were located at important points in a monument. At Cashtal yn Ard quartz veins and inclusions in the orthostats are concentrated around the forecourt façade. Similarly, at King Orry's Grave SW the sill stones contain thin strands of quartz, and quartz inclusions can be seen in the portal stones at both King Orry's Grave NE and Cashtal yn Ard.

Restricted view

One of the characteristics of monuments found along the eastern Irish Sea is their location on the side of a hill, with a restricted (or 'closed') view in one direction (Cummings 2001; Cummings and Whittle forthcoming). This has also been noted in relation to monuments elsewhere where it has been described as 'false-cresting' (e.g. Phillips 2002). This effectively means that a monument appears skylined when approached from the ground beneath it, although it does not actually sit on the summit of the hill. Many of the Manx monuments have a restricted view in one direction and are false-crested. Mull Hill is located on the side of hill which means that almost half the view of the surrounding landscape is restricted from view. Approaching Mull Hill from below also means that the site appears silhouetted on the skyline. King Orry's Graves, Ballakelly, Ballafayle and the Cloven Stones are also located on the side of hills which means that there is a restricted view in one direction - inland, in each case. Kew, interpreted elsewhere as a passage grave, is similarly positioned on the side of hill, yet passage graves found on both sides of the Irish Sea are typically positioned on the summit of a hill with wide views in all directions (e.g. Loughcrew: Cooney 2000). Even those in lower settings have wide views (e.g. Bryn Celli Ddu). It is also notable that Cashtal yn Ard does not have a restricted view in any direction.

Discussion

Morphology and landscape

What can the landscape settings of these sites tell us about the classification of the known monuments? The location of Kew in a landscape setting very similar to the other monuments on the island, and very unlike the setting of passage graves from Anglesey and Ireland, may suggest it is not a passage grave. The other monuments seem to be located in the landscape in ways that match wider patterns along the Irish Sea. The two court cairns, for example, are in comparable locations with their Irish counterparts (Cooney 2000, 139–40). However, there is one exception: Mull Hill. The setting of this monument is unusual for a number of reasons. It is set in a more rocky upland setting than the other monuments. It is now located in very marginal land, although it may be that present conditions do not reflect prehistoric ones. Other sites have a direct view down towards the sea, yet this site overlooks the sea while being divided from it directly by a rise in the landscape at Shenvalley. The mountains of the west coast are also only visible as distant peaks. Its setting is more reminiscent of the Bargrennan group of monuments (Cummings 2002b) than other Manx megaliths. The monument itself is also morphologically unique in the Irish Sea area. Its six tripartite chambers arranged in a circle are not found elsewhere (Fig. 13.2) although Henshall (1978, 174) has suggested it may be a variation of a Bargrennan monument. Whatever its affinities with monuments elsewhere, and despite its rather unusual landscape setting, it references the wider landscape in a parallel way to the other monuments on the island. One of the passages is aligned with the Calf of Man, another directly out to sea, and another into the outcrop and summit behind the monument. It would seem, therefore, to link the mountains and the sea, and to draw these into the sphere of the monument (Fowler 2001; 2002).

Local landscapes as arenas for performance

Monuments not only relate to the wider world but also to their immediate topography. The chambered long cairn at Cashtal yn Ard provides a good example of the placing of monuments in relation to local landscape features (Fig. 13.3). Cashtal yn Ard is set on the flat, broad summit of a domed hill with wide views in most directions. A large flat area along the top of the hill lies immediately outside the forecourt providing a significant space for gatherings. To the west of the site is a wide view inland towards the two distinctive hills of Slieau Ouyr and North Barrule, and the Corrany Pass between these two hills (Fig. 13.4). To the north and south of the monument are views of other smaller hills; all of these hills form a natural semi-circle. Therefore, the view from the forecourt is framed by a natural horse-shoe inverse to that provided by the

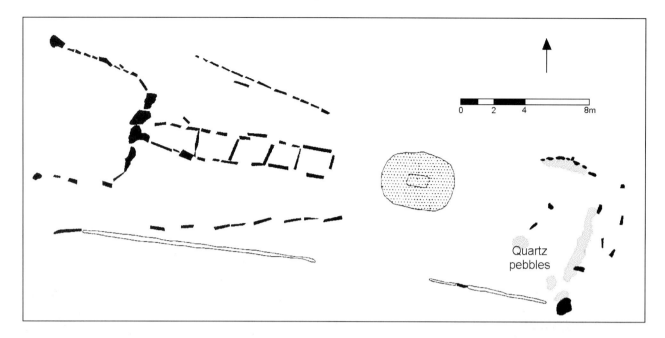

Figure 13.3. Plan of Cashtal yn Ard (after Fleure and Neely 1936 and Burrow 1997).

monument façade. We have already noted that the site is surrounded by streams on three sides so a visitor would have to cross water in order to the reach the site, unless approaching over the hills from Snaefell, via Clagh Ouyr or Sileau Ouyr. One of these streams, the Corrany, runs around the site from north-west to south-east, where it flows into the sea at Cornaa. This beach contains a very high proportion of quartz pebbles very similar to those found during excavations at Cashtal yn Ard. Looking directly into the forecourt the monument is framed against the sea along the skyline providing a striking setting. Distant mountains may also have played a part in the choice of this location as the Cumbrian mountains are visible in clear conditions on the horizon directly behind the monument. The cairn is aligned east-west, and the sun rises from the sea in the direction of Cumbria, and sets over the central highlands of the Isle of Man. Therefore, Cashtal yn Ard is located on a natural rise enclosed by water and set within a wider bowl of hills, and exhibits connections to both the mountains and the sea beyond that bowl. This provides a very distinctive position in the local landscape, and the monument marks out what may already have been an important gathering place. In effect then, Cashtal yn Ard creates a cosmological arena, drawing in the local and wider landscape into the very fabric of the monument. Movement towards the monument through the local landscape, and from the coast, involves prescribed interaction with landscape features like streams and hills, and this control of movement may be referenced in the patterns of quartz pebbles deposited around the rear of the site. These routes of movement may have been in use for some time, and memorialised in additions to the tail of the site after the

earlier Neolithic. The forecourt itself raises stones to enclose the visitor in rocks and hills. From the forecourt the two passages through these rocks are the Corrany pass inland, and the entrance to the monument itself. Movement at the monument choreographs an interaction with the wider cosmos: the landscape is a critical part of the construction and orientation of the site, and of the human experience of it. The design and use of the monument provide a juncture for interpretation of the broader landscape.

Monuments, landscape and regions

The landscape settings of the monuments on the Isle of Man are, for the most part, very similar to the location of monuments elsewhere along the Irish Sea coast. Elsewhere it has been suggested that one of the defining features of monuments found along the eastern Irish Sea is their setting between the mountains and the sea (Cummings 2001; 2002b; Cummings and Whittle forthcoming; Fowler and Cummings 2003). This is in direct contrast to monuments found elsewhere in Britain such as the Cotswold-Severn group. Furthermore, the majority of monuments on the Isle of Man have a restricted view in one direction, and, like monuments elsewhere along the eastern Irish Sea, are not positioned on the tops of hills or directly on the coast but have clear views of both. This suggests that the builders of the Manx monuments were drawing on a set of common themes for the location of sites in the landscape.

We can therefore interpret these monuments as the result of repeated patterns of engagement with local landscapes, histories and mythologies. There was perhaps

Figure 13.4. View looking west along the chamber and forecourt at Cashtal yn Ard.

a *habitus* (Bourdieu 1977) involved in the way that monuments were built and used, a set of ways of doing things that were partly conscious and partly unconscious. The general language of these patterns of engagement were shared across a large area, but were manifested in different ways partly due to differences in local topography, myth and history. Chambered cairns are predominantly located on the side of hills with views over a range of local topographic features such as streams, the sea and mountains. However, the location of monuments probably guided specific encounters with the landscape as a whole, encounters that were made sense of through the *habitus* of engagement appropriate in visiting chambered cairns.

Elsewhere we have suggested that quartz was a crucial media in the relationship between mountains and sea, and that the use of quartz cited connections to both zones (Fowler and Cummings 2003). Quartz was an anchor for a host of metaphorical connections that drew on its physical properties. The colour, translucence, texture and reflectivity of quartz meant that it could connote properties of the human body, the landscape and perhaps the wider cosmos. Quartz was therefore a key symbol in Neolithic cosmology, an ambiguous symbol that could be interpreted in many ways. It was predominantly used to mark out places of transformation, connection and liminality. Quartz pebbles and rubble have also been found at sites on the Isle of

Man. Large numbers of quartz pebbles were found around the rear of Cashtal yn Ard (Fleure and Neely 1936), for example. Quartz veins are frequently found in the fabric of the monument, located at significant points, particularly portals. We suggest that the use of quartz at monuments connected different parts of the landscape. Veins in quartz rocks had a biographical connection with rock outcrops and the mountains, while water-rolled quartz pebbles came from the coast and the sea. Furthermore, the deposition of quartz pebbles at these monuments (e.g. as traces of journeys; see Fowler this volume) and their broader setting close to significant bays or harbours may hint at the ways these monuments were used. Perhaps people arrived by sea, or travelled down to the coast, where they collected quartz pebbles. From the beach, they could have followed streams inland through the foothills to the monuments. This pattern could also be imagined for the earlier Neolithic enclosure at Billown Quarry. Here quartz pebbles were also deposited in the enclosure ditches (Darvill 2000; 2001; this volume). Both the cairns and the enclosure could be seen as interstitial points of entry and exit to the island, places often used in gatherings and ceremonial transitions. Causewayed enclosures often form island-like spaces, and the setting of Cashtal yn Ard on a hilltop surrounded by flowing water may indicate it was also a conceptual island. Gabriel Cooney (this volume) has noted that the small coastal islands around the east coast of

Ireland were used in similar ways to causewayed enclosures, as points of transition from one region to another, from Ireland were used in similar ways to causewayed enclosures as points of transition from one region to another, from one landscape to another (e.g. from Cumbria, south-west Scotland or northern Wales to eastern Ireland). The Isle of Man is a large island with several landing places. Each may have formed staging points in routes along which monuments were placed. Taking these paths lead to places where personal and group identities might be altered, material culture was fragmented and/or deposited, and the remains of the past could be encountered. Monuments were therefore located in liminal places, much like other Neolithic monuments in the British Isles. While some of these spatialised liminality like Manx monuments (i.e. by lying between the mountains and the sea), others achieved this effect through different uses of the topography (cf. Cummings *et al.* 2002; Edmonds 1993).

By positioning sites with views of mountains and sea, the builders of Manx chambered cairns may also have been making references to more distant parts of the Irish Sea zone (see Cummings this volume for more detail). In fact, one site makes explicit reference to a distant place: the view of Cumbria from Cashtal yn Ard. There are also material connections between the Isle of Man and the rest of the Irish Sea zone, most notably in the distribution of stone axes. Axes from both Cumbria and Ireland have been found on the island, suggesting connections with both of these areas. Cumbrian axes are found almost exclusively along the west coast, again the opposite side of the island from their expected source. Manx axes (Group XXV) are found around Peel to the south-west of the island with two examples from Ronaldsway. Irish axes have also been found, although their origin and location need verification (Coope and Garrad 1988). The distribution of both cairns and axes, then, suggest a complex set of relations between things, their distant origins and their Manx contexts.

The Isle of Man in its regional context: a social view

The Isle of Man might have been an important cross-roads within the wider Irish Sea Neolithic, and the mixture of monuments may reflect a role of translator and interstitial place (cf. Cooney this volume). The three court cairns are found on the eastern side of the Ireland, whereas one might expect to find them on the western side of the island which is closer to Ireland. The two sites that have been paralleled with monuments in south-west Scotland are the two monuments to the south of the island, Ballakelly and Mull Hill. The location of monuments and material culture perhaps translates the relationship between things (cairns, axes) and their origins or affiliations. The landscape location of Manx court cairns near glens, in hills near the sea or overlooking bodies of water, may relate to the wider location of court cairns in

Ireland. The variety of Manx monuments could be seen as a claim to encapsulate and translate between experiences of many of the lands surrounding it.

This leads to an important realisation about discourse on Manx Neolithic identity. As we have outlined in the introduction to this volume, patterns in practice do not equal patterns in ethnic identity. Earlier Neolithic monuments on the island draw on a broad field of practices which can be seen across parts of Ireland, Scotland, Wales and England. The diversity of sites on the island is not unique, and other regions include chambered cairns of more than one type. However, a more eclectic mixture of monument forms and locales was drawn on here than in many other areas of equivalent size. This eclecticism may not relate to different ethnic groups, and makes a nonsense of approaches that delineate cultural groups by the presence or absence of monument types (*qua* Davey this volume). On the other hand, it is possible that local identities were created in an active *bricolage* of neighbouring material symbols. Alternatively, these patterns may relate to the island's place as a mediator between slightly discordant social practices and cultural phenomena that were prevalent in a range of different neighbouring communities. Perhaps the eclecticism of Manx chambered tombs provided a special opportunity for the combination of different kinds of experience, subtly revealing a set of connections between them. It is even possible that the production of such a collection of monuments might make the Isle of Man seem to successive generations of visitors like a place of origin for those living with chambered cairns in Ireland, Scotland, England and Wales. Manx monuments may have later been mobilised in such a discourse on origins in conflict with other discourses, such as one which employed the connections between mountains across the Irish Sea presented by Cummings (this volume) which locates Snowdonia as a central focus point.

Conclusion

The Isle of Man sits at the very heart of the Irish Sea and as such has attracted the attention of scholars for many years. However, the island does not offer easy answers to the broader study of interaction and cultural identity in the Neolithic. The number of cairns is relatively small, making it difficult to assess whether the differences and similarities between them relate to issues of preservation and contemporary recognition rather than Neolithic practices. In this short piece we have examined one element of the monumental record on the island, the landscape setting of the surviving chambered cairns. It seems that the diversity of monument form is matched by the diversity of landscape settings employed. However, as with other areas of the Irish Sea, monuments were located in relation to a range of specific topographic features, most notably the sea, streams and mountains as well as other local features. History and mythology would have been important in locating the monuments; it seems likely that a locale like the hilltop at Cashtal yn Ard would have been an important gathering place before the monument was constructed. The 'empty' places referred to by the setting of cairns (such as the rise separating Ballkelly from a view of South Barrule, or the Calf of Man referenced by Mull Hill), or by the presence of stones from specific locales in the cairn fabric, may have referenced significant places of human gathering, or affinities with spiritual entities and sacred properties, or both. We would also suggest that the proximity of cairns with, and experiential and material connections to, streams, waterfalls and beaches underlies an affinity with those natural places imbued with connotations of fluidity and transformation (Fowler 1999; 2002; Fowler and Cummings 2003). The construction of a monument cemented the choreography of movement around the meaningful landscape. This choreography may have been incorporated into rites of passage. These rites were concerned the transformation of the bodies of the living as well as the dead, and perhaps drew on contact with the remains of the dead (Fowler this volume). Much as they did elsewhere around the Irish Sea, practices which moved people through one state to another therefore took place in locales which were between two zones of the landscape; the highland regions and the rocky coasts. Whether earlier Neolithic communities lived the majority of their lives on the lowland strip, or whether they frequently moved between highland, lowland and coast (and overseas), monuments gathered together the entire local world in a single cosmological arena. In these local arenas people were able to come together and translate the wider world in which they lived, making connections with the other parts of the Irish Sea world. Over time these connections may have been re-evaluated, and the designs and locations of chambered cairns used in supporting claims about the relationship between the island, its inhabitants, and other lands and people.

Acknowledgements

We would like to thank Peter Davey for his kind assistance with our visits to the island, and for providing information on the site at Ballaharra in advance of publication. We would also like to thank Siân Jones for discussions about Kermode's list. Vicki would like to thank the Board of Celtic Studies for funding a visit to the island. Chris would like to thank the Leverhulme Trust, for providing funding both for his Fellowship, and for a visit to the Isle of Man.

Notes

1 We use the division earlier/later, hinging around 3000BC. Earlier here covers the ascription of Manx chambered cairns to the middle Neolithic by Darvill (e.g. 2000) and Davey (e.g this volume).

References

Bergh, S. 1995. *Landscape of the monuments*. Stockholm: Riksantikvarieämbet Arkeologiska Undersöknigar.

Bourdieu, P. 1977. *Outline of a theory of practice*. Cambridge: Cambridge University Press.

Clough, T. and Cummins, W. 1988. *Stone axe studies volume two*. London: Council for British Archaeology.

Cooney, G. 2000. *Landscapes of Neolithic Ireland*. London: Routledge.

Coope, G. and Garrad, L. 1988. The petrological identification of stone implements from the Isle of Man. In T. Clough and W. Cummins (eds), *Stone axe studies volume two*, 67–70. London: Council for British Archaeology.

Cummings, V. 2001. *Landscapes in transition? Exploring the origins of monumentality in south-west Wales and south-west Scotland*. Unpublished PhD Thesis: Cardiff University.

Cummings, V. 2002a. All cultural things: actual and conceptual monuments in the Neolithic of Western Britain. In C. Scarre (ed.), *Monumentality and landscape in Atlantic Europe*, 107–21. London: Routledge.

Cummings, V. 2002b. Between mountains and sea: a reconsideration of the monuments of south-west Scotland. *Proceedings of the Prehistoric Society* 68, 125–46.

Cummings, V. and Whittle, A. forthcoming. *Places of special virtue: megaliths in the Neolithic landscapes of Wales*. Oxford: Oxbow.

Darvill, T. 1996. *Billown Neolithic Landscape Project, Isle of Man, 1995*. Bournemouth and Douglas: Bournemouth University School of Conservation Sciences and Manx National Heritage, Research Report 1.

Darvill, T. 1997. *Billown Neolithic Landscape Project, Isle of Man, 1996*. Bournemouth and Douglas: Bournemouth University School of Conservation Sciences and Manx National Heritage, Research Report 3.

Darvill, T. 1998. *Billown Neolithic landscape project, Isle of Man, 1997*. Bournemouth and Douglas: Bournemouth University School of Conservation Sciences and Manx National Heritage.

Darvill, T. 2000. Neolithic Mann in context. In A. Ritchie (ed.), *Neolithic Orkney in its European context*, 371–85. Oxford: Oxbow.

Davey, P. J. and Woodcock, J. J. forthcoming. Rheast Buigh, Patrick: middle Neolithic exploitation of the Manx uplands? In I. Armit, E. Murphy, E. Nelis and D. Simpson (eds), *Neolithic settlement in Ireland and western Britain*. Oxford: Oxbow Books.

Evans, E.E. 1938. Doey's cairn, Dunloy, Co. Antrim. *Ulster Journal of Archaeology* 1, 49–78.

Fleure, H. and Neely, G. 1936. Cashtal-Yn-Ard, Isle of Man. *The Antiquities Journal* 16, 373–95.

Fowler, C. 1999. *On discourse and materiality: personhood in the Manx Neolithic*. Unpublished PhD thesis: University of Southampton.

Fowler, C. 2001. Personhood and social relations in the British Neolithic with a study from the Isle of Man. *Journal of Material Culture* 6, 137–63.

Fowler, C. 2002. Body parts: personhood and materiality in the Manx Neolithic. In Y. Hamilakis, M. Pluciennik and S. Tarlow (eds), *Thinking through the body: archaeologies of corporeality*, 47–69. London: Kluwer Academic Press.

Fowler, C. and Cummings, V. 2003. Places of transformation: building monuments from water and stone in the Neolithic of the Irish Sea. *Journal of the Royal Anthropological Institute* 9, 1–20.

Henshall, A. 1978. Manx megaliths again: an attempt at structural analysis. In P. Davey (ed.), *Man and environment in the Isle of Man*, 171–6. Oxford: British Archaeological Reports British Series 54.

Higgins, D. and Davey, P. in press. Excavations by Sheila Cregeen at Ballaharra, German, 1969–1975. In F. Lynch (ed.), *Manx megaliths*. Liverpool: Liverpool University Press.

Kermode, P.M.C. 1930. List of Manx Antiquities. Available on-line: http://www.ee.surrey.ac.uk/Contrib/manx/fulltext/lma1930/index.htm#contents

Lynch, F. (ed.) in press. Manx Megaliths. Liverpool University Press.

Lynch, F. 1972. Portal dolmens in the Nevern Valley, Pembrokeshire. In F. Lynch and C. Burgess (eds), *Prehistoric man in Wales and the west*, 67–84. Bath: Adams and Dart.

Mundin, A., Chartrand, J. and Darvill, T. 2000. A survey of the long barrow at Ballafayle, Maughold. In T. Darvill (ed.), *Billown Neolithic landscape project, Isle of Man, 2000*, 31–39. Bournemouth and Douglas: Bournemouth University School of Conservation Sciences Research Report 9.

Phillips, T. 2002. *Landscapes of the living, landscapes of the dead. The location of chambered cairns of northern Scotland*. Oxford: British Archaeological Reports British Series 328.

Tilley, C. 1994. *A phenomenology of landscape*. Oxford: Berg.

Tilley, C. 1996. The powers of rocks: topography and monument construction on Bodmin Moor. *World Archaeology* 28, 161–76.

14   Where is the Cumbrian Neolithic?

Helen Evans

Introduction

Archaeological interpretations of Cumbrian prehistory have traditionally been influenced by the geographical situation of the region, defined by the Pennine ridge to the east and the Irish Sea coast to the west. Within Cumbria, discussion has been split between the east and west of the Cumbrian Massif, in particular between the Eden Valley and the south-western coast and fells. While aspects of the prehistoric record in western Cumbria suggest shared traditions with the Irish seaboard regions, the character of monuments situated in the Eden Valley has meant that links have often been drawn with east Yorkshire. As a result, discussions have traditionally concentrated on charting the similarities between Cumbria and its neighbours, rather than focusing on the variety of localised sequences and traditions which define the region's prehistoric record.

Stone circles and 'the axe trade'

Since the 1930s, grand narrative approaches to the Cumbrian Neolithic have been based exclusively on two interlinked categories of evidence; the 'great' stone circles, and the production and exchange of the ubiquitous group VI axe (Bradley and Edmonds 1993; Collingwood 1933; Fell 1964; Manby 1965). The work of Burl (1976) in particular has been instrumental in understandings of the regional and national context of the Cumbrian stone circles and the so-called axe trade. Although Burl's rather speculative narrative drew heavily on culture historical themes, his study of the morphological characteristics of the stone circles has been taken on verbatim by subsequent authors. This has impeded further interpretation of the dating and significance of many of the Cumbrian circles. Burl's 'grand narrative' approach, alongside more recent interpretations of architectural similarities between the Cumbrian monuments and those of Ireland and Scotland, has maintained the link between diffusionist ideas and the trade of Langdale axes (e.g. Bradley and Watson in press). The siting of the large Neolithic stone circles close to major rivers and mountain passes has consistently

been interpreted as relating to passages of movement used by 'axe-traders' as they passed through Cumbria between areas with more strongly defined Neolithic traditions. This has further encouraged an inter-regional focus to interpretations of the Cumbrian Neolithic:

> 'The importance of Cumbria....is shown through its use by Neolithic groups passing through the Stainmore Gap in the Pennines on their way from Yorkshire to Northern Ireland or to the north along the Tyne Gap towards south-west Scotland' (Burl 1976, 55).

Interpretative scale

Interpreted inter-regional and national chronologies have consistently relied on a 'bridge-building' scale of analysis, focusing on the broad similarities between regions rather than the closer investigation of localised sequences. The existence of distinctive regional traditions has been confronted at a number of different levels since it was first discussed during the first half of the twentieth century (Bradley 1984; Childe 1940; Piggott 1954; Thomas 1998). Recent interpretative shifts towards a more contextual archaeology have stressed the diffusion and exchange of ideas and practices rather than the migration of people (e.g. Bradley 1993; Thomas 1991). However these themes have been confronted almost exclusively at a theoretical level and discussions of regional diversity remain based on the same patterning of stylistic similarities identified by the proponents of culture history.

Recent theoretical accounts (e.g. Thomas 1998) have argued that the shared distribution of particular styles of monument and material culture is not solely indicative of long distance contacts. If so, the use of particular elements of material culture and architectural style to identify links across very different areas is detrimental to the closer understanding of particular regional sequences. Prehistoric communities may have taken on particular aspects of these traditions in very different contexts. Therefore shared styles need not represent shared practices or commonly held understandings of the same material traditions.

Closer scales of reference have been used in site-specific studies. Focussed on aspects of particular monuments or 'ritual landscapes', often those situated in the better studied areas of southern Britain, these approaches frequently draw on specific architectural features and the ways in which these could be experienced (e.g. Barrett 1994; Thomas 1993). Insights into aspects of sensory experience at particular monuments are important themes to address, however we prioritise those often to the detriment of understanding the significance of these structures in their own local context.

The problem with these varying scales of analysis is that monuments in particular have either been studied at too small or too large a scale (Bradley 1998). Whilst particular sites have seen the investigation and interpretation of the minutiae of architectural practice, more generalised syntheses and classificatory schema have stressed broad stylistic similarities over wide areas. Sitting uncomfortably in the middle ground between these approaches is the characterisation of prehistoric sequences at a local landscape level. Only by considering monuments in terms of their place in the seasonal routines of the communities that built and used them, can we begin to understand them both in their local context and at wider regional and inter-regional levels.

There are various reasons for the lack of emphasis on the close characterisation of the prehistoric landscapes of Cumbria. Partly due to problems of secure dating and the integration of evidence at a landscape scale, the varied traditions of the Cumbrian Neolithic have never seen consistent or detailed analysis at a close regional level. Practical issues concerned with landuse and fieldwork bias have traditionally dogged archaeological visibility, and the lack of modern investigation in the region has further inhibited detailed interpretation and discussion.

Neolithic monuments in Cumbria

The monumental record of Neolithic Cumbria boasts a variety of features including long mounds, cairns, barrows, stone circles and a small number of henge monuments. These features have seen relatively little investigation since the nineteenth and early twentieth centuries. Early explorations revealed a wide variety of architectural, funerary and mortuary traditions. However, records are generally poor, with interpretation of the excavated evidence set within culture historical frames of reference whereby emphasis was placed on the identification of particular styles of material culture to the detriment of understanding burial and stratigraphic sequences.

Largely due to the lack of sustained excavation, most monuments in Cumbria have been characterised according to their external morphology and their association with other features. This is problematic on a number of levels primarily as it has been presumed that features in close physical association are of a contemporary date. As external

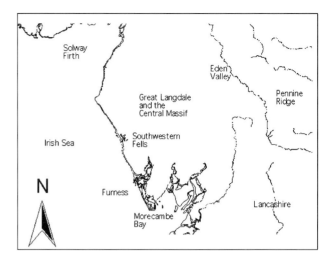

Figure 14.1. *Cumbria and the main areas mentioned in the text.* © *Crown Copyright Ordnance Survey. An EDINA Digimap/JISC supplied service.*

appearance relates only to the final form of the structure, this method of classification has had a detrimental impact on the number of Neolithic monuments identified. Excavated monuments often illustrate several phases of use, and considerable alteration. The issue of time depth is of crucial importance not only in relation to particular classes of monument, but also in that the evidence suggests communities returned to particular places in the landscape over long periods of time.

Alongside examples in other regions of northern Britain (Oswald *et al.* 2001), Neolithic enclosures previously thought to be Iron age in date are beginning to be recognised in Cumbria. A hillfort on Aughertree Fell, northern Cumbria, has recently been re-interpreted as being of Neolithic date (Horne 2000). The feature overlooks the Solway Plain and encloses a long mound which, although possibly of natural origin, may have influenced the location and significance of the enclosure (Horne 2000). On the Furness Peninsula of southern Cumbria, the hilltop enclosure at Skelmore Heads may also date to the Neolithic. Commanding views of the south-western fells and the Cumbrian Massif, Skelmore Heads is situated towards the centre of a dense concentration of prehistoric activity including a long barrow of the same name located one hundred and fifty metres north of the enclosure entrance. Skelmore Heads has traditionally been interpreted as an Iron Age hillfort. However although excavation revealed several phases in the construction of the monument, no dating evidence was recovered (Powell 1963). A cache of four roughout stone axes was found in the limestone grykes which partly define the enclosure, and one of six socketed bronze axes was discovered close by (Powell 1963). These instances of deliberate deposition and the presence of a long barrow are strongly suggestive that this location held some importance from the Neolithic onwards into later prehistory.

Although Cumbria has been understood to lack a long cairn tradition, over twenty possible examples have been identified (Masters 1984; Cumbria County SMR). The external morphology of a number of long cairns on the west coast does suggest some shared characteristics with chambered examples from south-west Scotland whilst examples in the south and east have been linked to the east Yorkshire long barrow tradition (Masters 1984). However very few have seen excavation and as such there are a number of questions relating to their antiquity, as well as the possibility that some are natural features. Many of these long cairns are situated in the high uplands, and on the west coast in particular they lie in or close to extensive cairnfields. As such a number of these features have been regarded with suspicion as it is possible that they are the result of linear clearance during the Bronze Age.

Round barrows in Cumbria have generally been considered to be Bronze Age in date. As with a proportion of the long cairns in the region, this presumption has been based on classification through external morphology as well as the common association with cairnfields. Although it may be erroneous to draw direct analogies with other regions, a similar situation has existed until relatively recently in other upland areas of northern England. Recent excavations in the Peak District have identified Neolithic barrows associated with Bronze and Iron Age cairnfields and field systems (Barnatt 1996). There are a large number of prominent oval and round barrows in Cumbria, however in many upland contexts problems with characterisation and the association with cairnfields has meant they have seen limited excavation. The existence of Neolithic burials in round or oval cairns is well attested in many areas of northern England and the Irish seaboard, and includes further examples in Cumbria, for example Greenwell's Crosby Garrett CLXXIV and CLXXIII (1877). The probability of a Neolithic round barrow tradition in Cumbria may be further suggested by the morphology of the two excavated 'long' cairns; Raiset Pike was formed by a pair of adjoined round cairns (Clare 1979), and Skelmore Heads is more oval than it is long (Powell 1972). Evidence from these long barrows has led numerous authors to link them with similar examples in east Yorkshire (Bradley and Edmonds 1993; Manby 1970; Masters 1984; Powell 1972) where the existence of a Neolithic round barrow tradition is perhaps more strongly established.

There are a number of excavated barrows in Cumbria where Bronze Age burials appear to involve the re-use of existing features, or where burial traditions suggest a Neolithic date. Evidence illustrates an emphasis on communal or individual disarticulated inhumation, a tradition commonly associated with Neolithic burial (Kinnes 1979). However disarticulation alone cannot be used to ascribe a Neolithic date as both communal and disarticulated burials are well attested through the Bronze Age (Peterson 1972). Although some of these barrows contain finds and grave goods that could be ascribed, typologically, to the later part of the Neolithic, early Bronze Age material has been found associated with a number of burials. There are 'formal' burial traditions in Cumbria during the final Neolithic and early Bronze Age, evidenced by beaker inhumations and urned and unurned cremations occurring in a variety of contexts. However some communities, or perhaps particular groups within these communities, made no clear cut distinction between the burial and depositional practice that we, as archaeologists, would usually ascribe to the either the Neolithic or the early Bronze Age.

With the exception of the large stone circles, there are few known Neolithic ceremonial monuments in Cumbria, the henges at Mayburgh and King Arthur's Round Table in the Eden Valley being the exceptions. Whilst these features have seen some attention we still know relatively little about them as discussion has almost exclusively been based on identifying links with other regions, largely through the perceived associations with the 'axe trade' (Bradley and Edmonds 1993; Bradley and Watson 2001; Burl 1976). Although there are no more extant examples, the characterisation of aerial photographs is beginning to identify further putatively Neolithic monuments in the region. For example, hengiform features with evidence of internal timber circles (John Hodgson *pers. comm.*), have recently been identified on the southwest coast, adjacent to the site of a destroyed concentric stone circle (Cumbria County SMR 1478). A large and again 'putatively' Neolithic enclosure at Long Meg has also been identified from aerial photographic evidence (Soffe and Clare 1988). Taken with the Neolithic timber circle sealed by a Bronze Age ring cairn excavated at Oddendale (Turnbull and Walsh 1997), these features suggest of a degree of time depth and complexity not previously identified in the region's prehistoric record.

While it is possible to characterise a degree of broad patterning in burial traditions and the monumental record, what is lacking at present is a closer understanding of how these monuments operated at a landscape level. In other words, how did they fit into the seasonal patterns and routines of everyday life? Little is known about the Neolithic occupation of Cumbria, largely as a result of interpretative focus on culture historical themes and the lack of modern excavation in the area. However through the integration of evidence at a landscape scale, it is possible to fill in some of the blank spaces of the 'middle ground' between monument specific studies and the broader issues of exchange and interaction which have characterised previous approaches to the Cumbrian Neolithic.

Neolithic occupation

The environmental record from Cumbria is particularly strong, covering a wide variety of topographical zones from the upland tarns and peats to lowland mosses and estuarine contexts (e.g. Oldfield 1963; Pennington 1975). Despite the uncertainties surrounding the archaeological interpretation of palynological data there is with some distinct patterning in the location, nature and extent of forest disturbance over the later Mesolithic and Neolithic. The environmental evidence suggests that during the fifth, fourth and third millennia, communities were actively involved in the creation and maintenance of forest clearings in a variety of landscape settings. Both upland and lowland areas were exploited, evidence suggesting occasional small scale cultivation on the coastal plain and the eastern limestone plateau. Upland clearances appear mainly to be associated with the maintenance of open or grassland areas at the edge of the treeline, occasionally through the use of fire (Pennington 1975; Skinner 2000).

The pollen record is strongly suggestive of seasonal movement between the uplands and lowlands into and throughout the Neolithic. With the exception of axe production sites in the central Lakes there is very little material evidence for these occupation strategies at a landscape scale. However evidence of coastal occupation in the region is considerable. Environmental evidence has illustrated the occurrence of several marine transgressions over the course of the later Mesolithic and the Neolithic (Bonsall *et al.* 1994). The rise and fall of sea-levels in the region meant that the coastline underwent a number of changes over this period, attested by lithic evidence from a number of raised beach and sand dune contexts (Bonsall *et al.* 1994).

Erosion of the southern and western coastline has revealed a large number of lithic scatters and a variety of occupation features. Assemblages from the west coast alone contain over 80,000 pieces (Cherry and Cherry 1996), where the density of microlithic assemblages has been taken to suggest year round occupation of the coastal plain during the Mesolithic (Bonsall *et al.* 1994). Recognition of these sites is due largely to long term surveys being undertaken by local archaeologists between the 1930s and 1980s. Smaller scale surveys have also been undertaken in the eastern uplands (Cherry & Cherry 1987; Skinner 2000). However, in general, the lithic resource suffers from problems of unequal distribution across all topographical zones, and as such it is difficult to integrate this data at a landscape scale. Alongside these problems however, the history of research, along with the character of the lithic raw materials, has meant that there are more basic problems concerning the attribution and definition of a Neolithic technology in the region. The vast proportion of the scatters identified from the region have occurred as a result of erosion although a small number of assemblages have been identified as wider surface scatters in plough-zone contexts. However, although a number of small-scale excavations have been carried out on the west coast, there are no assemblages from stratigraphically sealed contexts. As such the identification of single period assemblages is problematic.

Alongside more widely recognised technological changes there is a distinction between blade and flake based lithic technologies in Cumbria. Flake based assemblages are often associated with later Neolithic and early Bronze Age typological forms, but blade based scatters have largely been ascribed to the later Mesolithic on the basis of the occurrence of large numbers of microliths. Blade based typological forms usually taken to be indicative of an early Neolithic date are always associated with these microlithic scatters. As such the presence of leaf shaped arrowheads, extremely rare in the region, has been taken to be the sole flint form indicative of an early Neolithic date (Cherry and Cherry 1996). Scatters associated with Group VI axes, either complete or re-worked, have also been used to indicate early Neolithic occupation. However these forms are consistently associated with assemblages containing either later typological forms, or scatters of microlithic material (Cherry and Cherry 1996). At a very basic level, the use of this package to indicate an early Neolithic date remains questionable. Axe production in the region took place into the later Neolithic, and we do not have an exact date for its onset. Additionally, leaf-shaped arrowheads, although commonly found in earlier Neolithic contexts, are also known to occur into the early Bronze Age. Mixed scatters such as these are relatively common in northern contexts and have thrown up similar sets of interpretative problems (e.g. Waddington 2000; Young 1987). The presence of both Group VI axes and leaf-shaped arrowheads in apparently later Mesolithic contexts may indicate that a largely microlithic technology persisted in Cumbria throughout the Neolithic. However if so the distinction between scatters of later Mesolithic and early Neolithic date is problematic as microlithic scatters not containing typologically later forms are still routinely ascribed to the later Mesolithic.

The identification of the first lithic scatters along the Cumbrian coastline has had a considerable effect on subsequent interpretations of lithic material from the area. During the 1930's assemblages from Walney Island were described by Clark (in Cross 1939) as being indicative of a 'poverty industry', with similarities to sandhill and raised beach sites in Northern Ireland and the west coast of Scotland. Affinities to Irish and Scottish assemblages were defined on the basis of shared tool forms such as hollow scrapers, occasional finds of Bann River points as well as the diminutive size and poor quality of the naturally occurring lithic resource (Cross 1939). Characterising a regional technology on the basis of its affinities with other areas has illustrated a degree of contact between these communities. However to some extent, ill-defined affinities to the traditions of the Irish Seaboard have led to interpretative efforts based on charting these similarities rather than looking at the character and distribution of local technological traditions in their own right. The legacy of culture historical approaches to the so-called 'poverty industries' has meant that little effort has been made to fully characterise the Cumbrian material. More recent approaches to understanding the lithic record in the area have been based on wider typological chronologies based on assemblages from the southern English downlands (e.g. Pitts and Jacobi 1979) where the character and availability of raw materials is very different. As a result, although the presence of particular lithic forms has been taken as indicative of long distance contacts, an early Neolithic flint technology cannot be ascribed with any confidence in its own regional context.

Conclusion

So what was the nature of the Neolithic in Cumbria? The archaeological record suggests a number of distinctive regional traditions within the area, illustrative of dispersed valley based communities with a network of contacts stretching throughout and beyond the region. Although the evidence is difficult to interpret at a landscape scale it does suggest seasonal movement between the uplands and lowlands where axe production in the central Cumbrian Massif probably took place in conjunction with leading or following domesticated or wild animals. On the high ground, these seasonal routines may be reflected by the landscape setting of monuments, many of which are situated on natural routeways between the uplands and more low-lying areas, along the major river valleys. Evidence from the coastal and lowland areas illustrates woodland exploitation and occasional cultivation, and mixed scatters of occupation debris occasionally associated with evidence for the final grinding and polishing of stone axes. This narrative is, however, rather ambiguous and insubstantial, not dissimilar in character to those forwarded in previous accounts that have dealt with the Cumbrian Neolithic at a grand scale (e.g. Bradley and Edmonds 1993). With the exception of evidence for the production of stone axes, the broad patterning described here could be taken as illustrative of many Neolithic regions. As such it is detrimental to the understanding of the localised and diverse nature of traditions within Cumbria itself. This situation serves to further highlight the need for detailed scrutiny and integration of the region's prehistoric record at a local landscape level.

Some aspects of technology, occupation and monumental practice in Cumbria illustrate broad similarities with Neolithic traditions identified in other regions. However the evidence also suggests a degree of insularity of practice, the long-term maintenance of a variety of material traditions, and the continued use of particular places over the later Mesolithic, the Neolithic and into the Bronze Age. Given the existence and importance of regional diversity over the course of later prehistory, it is perhaps the relationship between these aspects of continuity and change that should be of concern if we are to do justice to the variety of archaeological evidence from the diverse landscapes of Cumbria. Additionally, with the themes and problems set out over the course of this discussion in mind, we have to ask to what extent our period definitions and concomitant models of social change really work, especially in areas to the north and west of the southern British chalklands.

Cumbria has seen the investigation of many aspects of the prehistoric record, however this work has largely focused on charting the distribution of particular monuments and elements of material culture in relation to regions with more strongly defined Neolithic traditions. Whilst detrimental to understandings of time depth, occupation strategies and associations between monuments and their local landscape, these approaches have helped to elucidate aspects of the regional chronology.

However problems interpreting the monumental and lithic record have rendered the Neolithic almost invisible in Cumbria, as such little attempt has been made to identify and integrate the disparate aspects of this period and discuss them at the varying scales of their local, regional and inter-regional contexts. This sort of multi-scale analysis is essential if we are to create a regional chronology within which we can discuss the statics and dynamics of prehistoric landscape occupation in the area. Only then can we look more confidently at the wider issues concerning the relationship between Cumbria and its neighbouring regions, and towards the wider trajectories of British prehistory.

Acknowledgements

Many thanks are due to Mark Edmonds, Tim Allen and Bean for their advice and comments on earlier drafts of this text.

References

Barnatt, J. 1996. Barrows in the Peak district: a corpus. In J. Barnatt and J. Collis (eds), *Barrows in the Peak District: recent research*. Sheffield: Collins.

Barrett, J. 1994. *Fragments from antiquity*. Oxford: Blackwell.

Bradley, R. 1984. *The social foundations of prehistoric Britain*. Harlow: Longman.

Bradley, R. 1993. *Altering the earth*. Edinburgh: Society of Antiquaries of Scotland.

Bradley, R. 1998. *The significance of monuments*. London: Routledge.

Bradley, R. and Edmonds, M. 1993. *Interpreting the axe trade: production and exchange in Neolithic Britain*. Cambridge: Cambridge University Press.

Bradley, R. and Watson, A. In press. On the edge of England: Cumbria as a Neolithic region. In G. Barclay and K. Brophy (eds), *Regional diversity in the Neolithic of Britain and Ireland*. Oxford: Oxbow.

Bonsall, C., Sutherland, D. and Payton, R. 1994. The Eskmeals coastal foreland: archaeology and shoreline development. In J. Boardman and J. Walden (eds), *Cumbria field guide*, 90–103. Oxford: Quaternary Research Association.

Burl, A. 1976. *The stone circles of the British Isles.* New Haven: Yale University Press.

Cherry, J. and Cherry P. 1996. Coastline and upland in the Cumbrian Neolithic. *Northern Archaeology* 13/14, 63–6.

Cherry, J. and Cherry P. 1987. *Prehistoric habitation sites on the limestone uplands of eastern Cumbria.* Kendal: Cumberland and Westmorland Archaeological and Antiquarian Society.

Childe, G. 1940. *Prehistoric communities of the British Isles.* London: Chambers.

Clare, T. 1979. Rayset Pike long cairn in the Matchell MSS. *Transactions of the Cumberland and Westmorland Antiquarian and Archaeological Society* 79, 144–6.

Collingwood, R. 1933. An introduction to the prehistory of Cumberland, Westmorland and Lancashire-North-of-the-Sands. *Transactions of the Cumberland and Westmorland Antiquarian and Archaeological Society* 33, 163–200.

Cross, M. 1939. A prehistoric settlement on Walney Island, Part II. *Transactions of the Cumberland and Westmorland Antiquarian and Archaeological Society* 39, 262–83.

Fell, C. 1964. The Cumbrian type of polished stone axe and its distribution in Britain. *Proceedings of the Prehistoric Society* 30, 39–55.

Greenwell, W. 1877. *British barrows.* Oxford: Clarendon Press.

Horne, P. 2000. A Neolithic causewayed enclosure in Cumbria. *Archaeology North* 17, 13.

Kinnes, I. 1979. *Round barrows and ring ditches in the British Neolithic.* London: British Museum.

Manby, T. 1965. The distribution of rough-out 'Cumbrian' and related axes of Lake District origin in Northern England. *Transactions of the Cumberland and Westmorland Antiquarian and Archaeological Society* 65, 1–37.

Manby, T. 1970. Long barrows of northern England: structural and dating evidence. *Scottish Archaeological Forum* 2, 1–27.

Masters, L. 1984. The Neolithic long cairns of Cumbria and Northumberland. In R. Miket and C. Burgess (eds), *Between and beyond the walls*, 52–73. Edinburgh: John Donald.

Oswald, A., Dyer, C. and Barber, M. 2001. *The creation of monuments: Neolithic causewayed enclosures in the British Isles.* Swindon: English Heritage.

Oldfield, F. 1963. Pollen analysis and man's role in the ecological history of the south-east Lake District. *Geografiska Annaler* 45, 23–40.

Pennington, W. 1975. The effect of Neolithic man on the environments of north-west England: the use of absolute pollen diagrams. In J. Evans, S. Limbrey & H. Cleere (eds), *The effect of man on the landscape: the highland zone*, 74–86. London: Council for British Archaeology.

Peterson, F. 1972. Traditions of multiple burial in later Neolithic and early Bronze Age Britain. *Archaeological Journal* 129, 22–55.

Piggott, S. 1954. *The Neolithic cultures of the British Isles.* Cambridge: Cambridge University Press.

Pitts, M. and Jacobi, R. 1979. Some aspects of change in flaked stone industries of the Mesolithic and Neolithic in southern Britain. *Journal of Archaeological Science* 6, 163–7.

Powell, T.G.E. 1963. Excavations at Skelmore Heads near Ulverston, 1957 and 1959. *Transactions of the Cumberland and Westmorland Antiquarian and Archaeological Society*, 63, 1–30.

Powell, T.G.E. 1972. The tumulus at Skelmore Heads near Ulverston. *Transactions of the Cumberland and Westmorland Antiquarian and Archaeological Society* 72, 53–6.

Soffe, G. and Clare, T. 1988. New evidence of ritual monuments at Long Meg and Her Daughters, Cumbria. *Antiquity* 62, 552–7.

Skinner, C. 2000. *Recognising and reconstructing prehistoric landscapes: a new case study from eastern Cumbria.* Unpublished PhD Thesis, University of Leicester.

Thomas, J. 1991. *Rethinking the Neolithic.* Cambridge: Cambridge University Press.

Thomas, J. 1993. The politics of vision and the archaeologies of landscape. In B Bender (ed.), *Landscape: politics and perspectives*, 19–48. Oxford: Berg.

Thomas, J. 1998. Towards a regional geography of the Neolithic. In M. Edmonds and C. Richards, (eds),*Understanding the Neolithic of north-western Europe*, 37–60. Glasgow: Cruithne Press.

Turnbull, P. and Walsh, D. 1997. A prehistoric ritual sequence at Oddendale, near Shap. *Transactions of the Cumberland and Westmorland Antiquarian and Archaeological Society* 97, 11–44.

Waddington, C. 2000. The Neolithic that never happened? In J. Harding and R. Johnston (eds), *Northern pasts: interpretations of the later prehistory of northern England and southern Scotland*, 33–44. Oxford: British Archaeological Report British Series 302.

Young, R. 1987. *Lithics and subsistence in north-eastern England.* Oxford: British Archaeological Report British Series 161.

15   The Isle of Man: central or marginal in the Neolithic of the northern Irish Sea?

Peter Davey

Introduction

The Isle of Man, located in the northern Irish Sea within sight, on a clear day, of the mountains of Mourne, the Antrim plateau, the Dumfries granite domes, the Lake District, Anglesey and Snowdonia, retains some ten megalithic tombs (Fig. 15.1).

The subject of this paper is the place that these monuments occupy both in the intellectual constructs of archaeologists over the last century or so and in the folk consciousness of the Manx people. In particular, the changing position of the Manx tombs within the typologies and geographical development of archaeological thinking will be set against a range of native knowledge and understandings of the sites. The main objective of the paper is to suggest not only that the insular history and tradition surrounding the megaliths should be given full weight, but also that the central role of the Isle of Man in Neolithic regional consciousness should be better recognized.

Background

Documented archaeological investigation of Manx megaliths begins in the mid nineteenth century with the accounts by Jeffcott (1866) and Barnwell (1868) of the Meayll Circle[1], followed in 1893 by the excavations of Kermode and Herdman (1894; 1914). More recently five further excavations have been carried out on megalithic sites: Ballafayle in 1926 (Kermode 1926; 1927), Cashtal yn Ard in 1935 (Fleure and Neely 1936), King Orry's Grave (North-East) in 1953 (Megaw forthcoming), Ballaharra between 1969 and 1975 (Cregeen 1978; Higgins and Davey forthcoming) and a small exploratory excavation on the revetment of the Meayll Circle in 1971 (Henshall forthcoming). Henshall (in Cubbon 1971) reviewed all of the sites on the occasion of a visit of the Prehistoric Society to Man and again for the 1977 Douglas Conference (Henshall 1978). In 1971 she also agreed to begin work for the Manx Museum on a monograph on the Manx sites to parallel her Scottish series. After a delay caused by lack of data from the 1953 King Orry's

Grave excavations and absence of a full account of Ballaharra, this project is now well advanced under the editorship of Frances Lynch (forthcoming), both missing reports now being complete.

More recently, Fowler has assessed the sites and their funerary practise in light of contemporary ethnographic debates about personal identity and the body (Fowler 1999; 2001; 2002; this volume), and Darvill has prepared new descriptive and interpretative accounts, including geophysical survey of a number of the sites: Meayll Circle (Gale et al. 1997), Ballakelly (Gale and Darvill 1998), King Orry's Grave (Gale et al.1999), Cashtal yn Ard (Darvill and Chartrand 2000) and Ballafayle (Mundin et al. 2001). Despite this welcome increase in research activity the definition of discrete phases of activity and their absolute dating at a majority of the sites is still in its infancy.

The aim of this paper is twofold. Firstly, the place of the Manx megaliths in contemporary discussions of the geography and sociology of the Northern Irish Sea area will be considered. Secondly, a number of lines of evidence will be used to propose an explanation for the location and role of the Meayll Circle.

Problems of distribution and classification

The map of the expansion of the Celts into both eastern and western Europe published by Megaw and Megaw (1989, 11; Fig. 15.2) may, at first site appear to be politically neutral and not relevant to the period discussed at the Manchester conference. Two apparently minor points suggest a mind-set that is steeped in the contemporary mythologies of national origins. The arrow showing the movement of the Celts into Ireland very specifically links Brittany to Ireland. There is no arrow from continental Europe to Britain and none from Britain to Ireland. The effect, whether overt or subconscious, is to reinforce the purity of the Irish claim to Celtic origins, unsullied by contact with the Anglo-Saxon world that eventually produced the British Empire.

Manx Megaliths

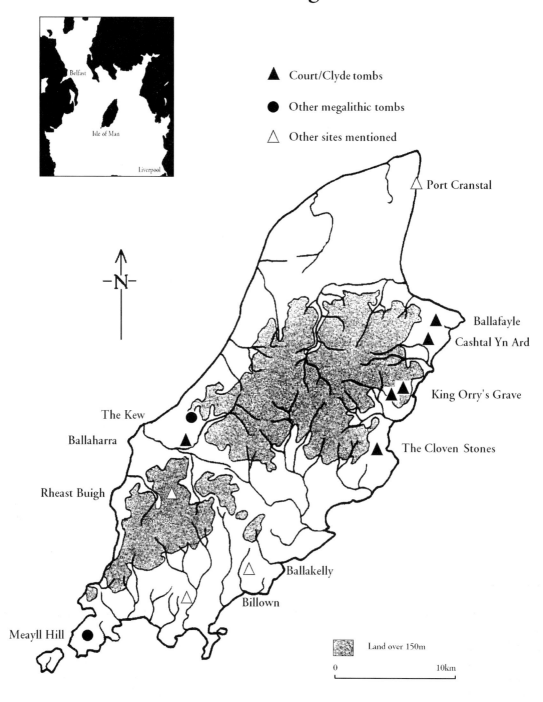

Figure 15.1. *The Isle of Man showing the main sites referred to in the text. Inset: the island and its visible neighbours.*

A second feature of the map is the absence of the Isle of Man – a phenomenon dubbed by a regular column in the Manx press as the 'Miss Isle of Man Syndrome' – along with Anglesey and the Isle of Wight. It is not simply a question of the scale of a map that shows most

of Europe and parts of North Africa, as many other islands of similar size or smaller are shown (e.g. Harris, Skye, Islay, Ibiza, Minorca, Kithira, Naxos, Karpáthos and so on). Whilst Anglesey and the Isle of Wight are very close to the mainland of Britain, Man is centrally placed in the

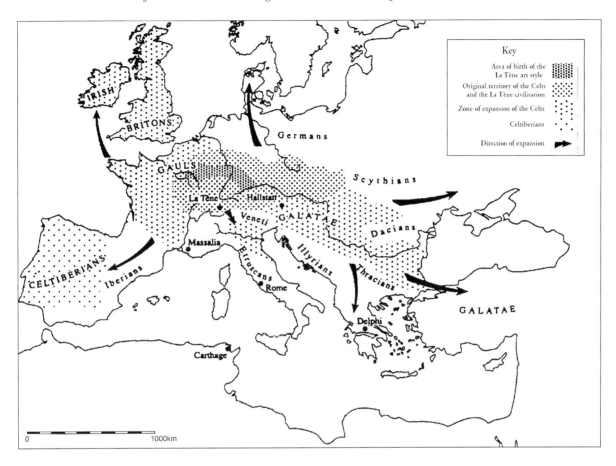

Figure 15.2. Map showing the postulated expansion of the Celts in later prehistory (after Megaw and Megaw 1989).

northern Irish Sea. In the minds of the Megaws the central feature of the British Isles is the antithesis between Ireland and Britain, reflecting the ongoing tension between the UK and Irish Republic about the future of Northern Ireland. The political entity represented by the Isle of Man has no significance. However anachronistic these attitudes might be, it is the contention of this paper that such considerations play a role in much prehistoric interpretation, including that of the Manx megalithic tombs in many synthetic approaches to site morphology across the British Isles.

A further problem encountered in the study of the British and Irish megalithic tombs is that of classification and the weight given by archaeologists to matters of morphology. Frances Lynch's recent book on *Megalithic tombs and long barrows in Britain* (1997) provides an excellent example of the difficulties and especially how these have affected understanding of the Manx evidence. In her composite map of the regional groupings *of* megalithic tombs (Fig. 15.3) the lines dividing the different types often wobble eccentrically in order to include examples in the Island. The boundary of the non-megalithic mound distribution that otherwise runs from south to north separating eastern from western Britain lurches violently to the west in order to incorporate

Man, including as it does part of Strangford Loch and the Ards peninsular (Lynch 1997, figure 21, No 5). It does this to include the site at Ballafayle described by Henshall most recently as 'long cairn to stone chamber' lying 'at the limit of the distribution of the type of monument to which it belongs' (Henshall 1978, 172–3). Having accepted Kermode's interpretation of the site as having a curved façade and projecting horns (Cubbon 1971, 28), the implication that the three surviving orthostats at the west end would have formed part of a megalithic chamber is not considered. A new survey and interpretation by (Mundin *et al.* 2000) has concluded that the site is probably a badly damaged court cairn/ Clyde tomb, similar in form and possible sequence to its neighbour at Cashtal yn Ard. Thus, 'it can be proposed that Ballafayle is re-united with the main group of Manx long barrows' (Mundin *et al.* 2000, 39). This persuasive solution will remove the wobble from the non-megalithic mound divide and free the inhabitants of the Ards and Man from a peripheral position. The significance that had to be placed on the apparent morphology of a single very damaged site in order to produce an inclusive distribution map is a matter of concern.

The same issue also applies to the line encompassing the portal dolmens, though to a much less marked degree.

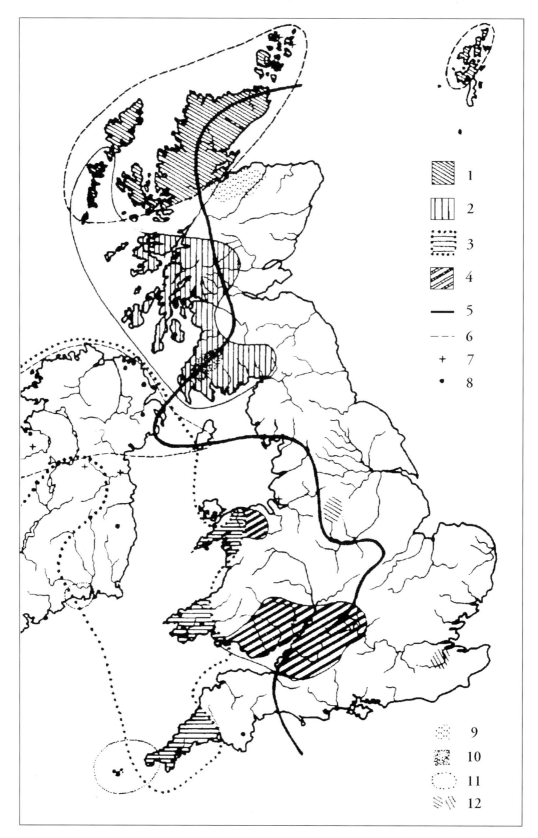

Figure 15.3. *The distribution of regional groups of megalithic tombs (after Lynch 1997, 36, figure 21). 1. Scottish passage graves; 2. Clyde tombs; 3. portal dolmens (Britain and Ireland); 4. Cotswold-Severn cairns; 5. Boundary of non-megalithic mopund distribution; 6. Court tombs (Ireland); 7. Isolated short-passage Passage graves; 8. Cruciform passage graves; 9. Clava cairns; 10. Bargrennan tombs; 11. Entrance graves (Britain and Ireland) 12. Stone chambers in Derbyshire and Kent.*

A single damaged and partly reconstructed site at Ballakelly is included. Whilst this monument has normally been considered as a megalithic tomb (e.g. Cubbon 1971, 10; Gale and Darvill 1998; Henshall 1978, 172), the discussion has centred on its Neolithic affinities. Given its extremely small size – the internal length of the 'chamber' is less than two metres – the lack of period specific artefactual evidence and the presence of cup marks on the outside of one of the orthostats there must be a possibility that the site is Bronze Age, rather than early Neolithic in date. A nineteenth century plan in the Manx Museum, apparently predating the Barnwell (1866) survey, shows a central cist surrounded by a complete circle of stones. In form this arrangement would appear close in size and style to the nearby Arragon Mooar monument, normally interpreted as a Bronze Age burial set within a circle of standing stones and incorporated into a cairn. If Ballakelly is Bronze Age the portal dolmens are confined to Cornwall, west Wales and Ireland.

More significant to the present discussion is the ambiguous affiliation of the bulk of the Manx tombs amongst contemporary archaeologists. If Ballafayle, Ballaharra (Cregeen 1978; Davey and Higgins forthcoming) and the two sites at King Orry's Grave (Gale *et al.* 1999; Henshall 1978) are included, the island has six trapezoidal chambered tombs with horned forecourts (Fig. 15.4). How these are placed in relation to the surrounding islands is crucial to the present argument. In Lynch (1997) the sites are defined as 'court tombs (Ireland)' and so included in her distribution map (Lynch 1997, figure 21, No 6). In contrast, Waddell's maps of Clyde and court tombs, in his *'Irish Sea in prehistory'* (Waddell 1991, figure 2; and Fig. 15.5), places the Manx sites (only 2 are shown) firmly within the Clyde group (Waddell 1991, figure 2). The map of Clyde tombs contained in Ashmore's *Neolithic and Bronze Age Scotland* (Ashmore 1996, 57, figure 32; Fig. 15.6) gives no indication that any similar tombs exist beyond the boundaries of modern Scotland. His discussion of the monuments is contained within a chapter entitled 'Regional diversity increases: 3500 to 3000 BC'. Throughout, there is an anachronistic presupposition that the regionality he describes is contained within the present pseudo-state. Waddell's later discussion of court tombs in The Prehistoric Archaeology of Ireland (1998, 78–82) also restricts discussion to that island. It is clear from his discussion of over 390 court tombs that the regional variation in Ireland *within this tomb type alone* is greater than that between either the Clyde tombs or the Manx chambered tombs and their Irish equivalents. No serious evidence has been adduced by either author for their apparent nationalisation of a sub-group of these monuments.

It would seem that archaeologists are in the grip of a post-colonial need to assert regional and national identities through their classification and presentation of prehistoric monuments. They are viewing the past through

the agency of contemporary political structures such as Historic Scotland and book markets whose readers will relate most easily to nationalist agendas. Imagine the sales potential of a book entitled *The megalithic tombs of northern Ireland, south-west Scotland and the Isle of Man*? Lynch is clearly aware of the difficulty for the classification of the Manx tombs as she comments: 'The Isle of Man contains several very impressive megalithic tombs...which share features with the Clyde cairns and court tombs of northern Ireland' (Lynch 1997, 39–40).

It is hard to resist the temptation to return to Piggott's classification of the monuments as key elements within his 'Clyde-Carlingford Culture' (Piggott 1954, figure 7) in which he combines the distribution of a specific pottery type (Lyles Hill Ware) with the distinctive trapezoidal chambered tombs with horned forecourts to produce a regional 'culture'. His map is substantially out of date. The Isle of Man, for example, now has one major new site at Ballaharra (Burrow 1997, 67–72; Cregeen 1978) with the local form of Lyles Hill, and another at King Orry's Grave (Burrow 1997, 105–6; Gelling and Megaw forthcoming). Two important settlement sites have been located; one at Port Cranstal, Bride (Burrow 1997, Gonzales *et al.* 2000, 355–8) in the process of eroding from a cliff section, the other is now under excavation at Billown, Malew (Darvill 1999, 16–20). A further site of the period has recently been identified in the Manx hills at Rheast Buigh, Patrick (Davey and Woodcock 2003; Pitts 1999, figure 4). His terminology and its underlying presuppositions has also been the subject of much revision. For example Sheridan (1995) questions not only the application and use of the term Lyles Hill Ware, but also its place in Piggott's view of European ceramic families (Sheridan 1995, 17–18). But Piggott, like Lynch, does not attempt to deconstruct a British Neolithic imperial geography and to replace it with regional culture groupings that reflect the contemporary mythologies or aspirations of the post-colonial inhabitants of these islands.

Although there is a reasonable number and concentration of tombs in the Isle of Man, the sheer numbers present in neighbouring areas of Scotland and Ireland, combined with the present relative insignificance of the Manx state, has meant that, whatever regional combinations are proposed, the island is seen as either peripheral or problematic, or both. There is some reason to question this assumption. If Piggott's 'Clyde-Carlingford Culture' does reflect to some degree the prehistoric human geography of the northern Irish Sea area, with whatever contemporary qualification and amendment is necessary, is the Isle of Man a marginal or focal component of it? Whilst it is not possible to provide a definitive answer to this question, a number of factors, both prehistoric and more recent may suggest that the island was seen as the physical and psychological focal point of the region (cf. Cummings this volume).

The dominance of a small island over a much larger

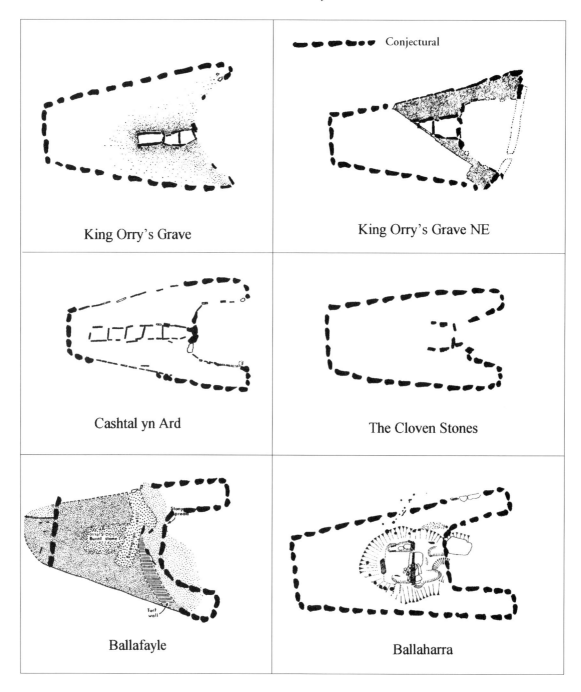

Figure 15.4. *Megalithic tombs and related monuments in the Isle of Man.*

area is not as inherently unlikely as may be imagined. Quite apart from historic examples such as Venice or the British Empire itself, the political and economic geography of the medieval Kingdom of the Isles saw the Isle of Man as the political, religious and economic capital of a scattered empire significantly more far flung than the court/Clyde tombs (Fig. 15.7).

The importance of local tradition

Theoretical archaeologists – post-processual and others – have reacted against what they see as an arid, typological discourse, such as has been the subject of the first part of this paper, and have adopted a range of philosophical and practical models to aid discussion and interpretation of prehistoric societies. In particular the work of social anthropologists has provided a basis for new approaches to the archaeological evidence and the place of the individual in society. As far as the Manx Neolithic is

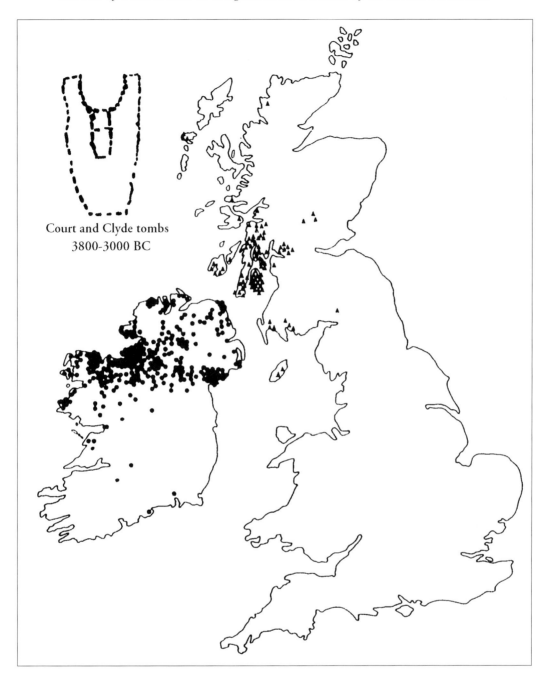

Court and Clyde tombs
3800-3000 BC

Figure 15.5. *Waddell's map of Clyde and Court tombs (after Waddell 1991, figure 2).*

concerned, Chris Fowler has made a series of suggestions about the interpretation of the sites and their physical location and the detailed significance of the excavated burial and related assemblages, in his PhD thesis (1999) and a number of subsequent papers (Fowler 1999; 2001; 2002; Fowler and Cummings 2003). Cummings and Fowler (this volume) discuss the landscape settings of the Manx megaliths in some detail and provide a number of novel suggestions.

The thesis of the second part of this paper is that, whilst this approach has provided many novel and useful

insights into the possible cultural attitudes of the tomb-builders, is it is inherently more likely that an examination of the place of the sites in their present and recent historical and cultural context will provide a firmer foundation for their interpretation. This is especially so given the substantial continuity of population and lack of evidence for large-scale folk movements in the Isle of Man since the Neolithic period. To some degree the megalithic tombs are the burial places of the ancestors of contemporary Manx society. Three strands of evidence will be considered – literary and place-name, geographical

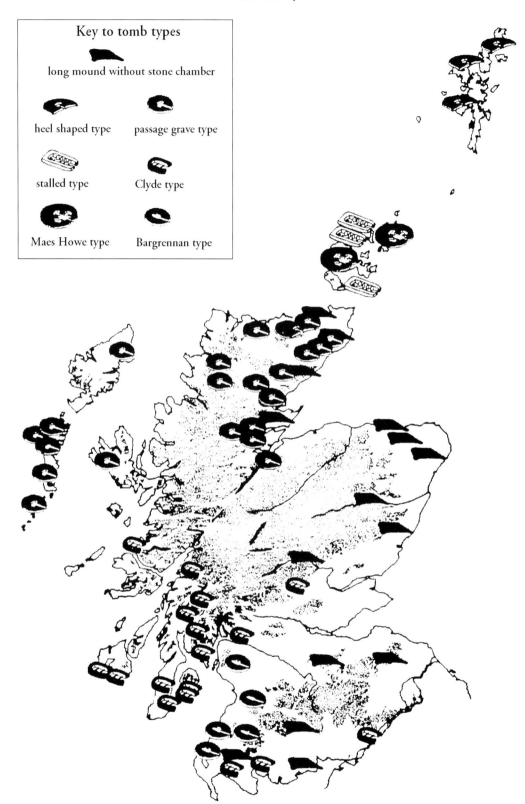

Figure 15.6. *Map of regional types of chambered tomb in Scotland (after Ashmore 1996, 57, figure 32).*

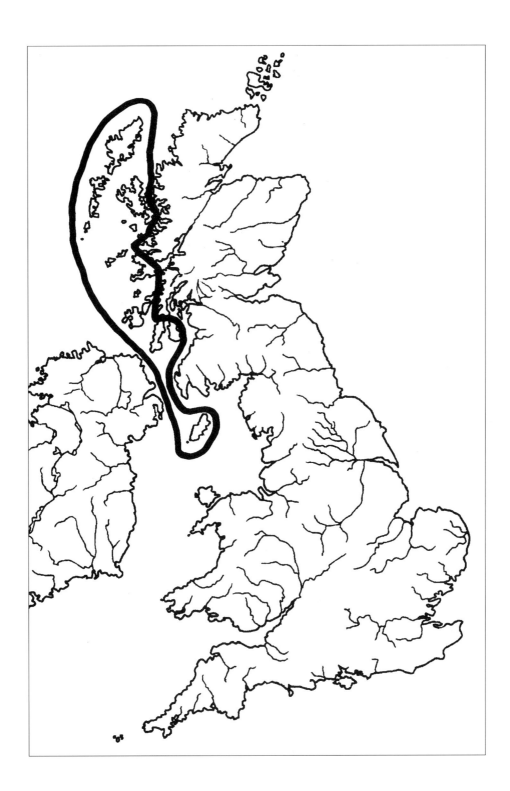

Figure 15.7. Norse Kingdom of the Isles.

and contemporary folklore, the latter with special reference to the Meayll Circle.

Man and Mannanán

The name of the Isle of Man and its mythological progenitor Mannanán can be traced back around 1,500 years in Old Irish literature (Muhr 2002, 38–40). The tradition as then received, and subsequent versions of it, is multi-layered, complex and sometimes internally contradictory. Many of the texts exist only in much later medieval copies, so that it is often difficult to separate out myth from 'historical' statement, or a pagan from a Christianized world-view. In spite of these difficulties a number of core ideas can be isolated that almost certainly represent a view of the island in the minds of the later prehistoric peoples of the northern Irish Sea.

In the case of Man itself the Island appears to have been highly valued both for its fertility and as a physical manifestation of the otherworld. The former doubtless due to its demonstrable economic advantages of soils, climate, minerals, marine produce and strategic location, the latter probably because of its mysterious way of appearing and disappearing on the horizon – depending on visibility and cloud cover – as seen from the neighbouring lands (see Watson this volume). The combination of these two attributes produced in the minds of the early Ulster writers a local Eden or Elysium.

A mysterious woman from an unknown land appears to Bran son of Febal and invites him to follow her:

Crób dind abaill a hEmain	'A branch of the apple tree from Emain
Do-fet samail do gnáthaib	I bring like those well-known'
(Muhr 2002, 38–40).	

This land of promise is clearly echoed in the twelfth century Gaelic praise-poem to King Raghnall of Man in which the island is likened to Tara, the legendary seat of the high-kings of Ireland:

Emain na n-aball cumra	'Eamhain of the fragrant apple-trees
Teamair Mhanann cin mhebhla	[is the?] Tara of Man without deceit,
As siat cuaine saer Sadha	the noble progeny of Sadhbh are
Abhla craebh n-uaine nEamhna	the green-branched apple-trees of Eamhain
(Ó Cuív 1957, 289).	

The traditions relating to Mannanán are much more complex (MacQuarrie 1997). In the same story of *Immran Bran* (the voyage of Bran) he is seen sometimes as a sun god 'stirring the sea until it is blood', sometimes as a sea-god 'riding atop the waves' (MacQuarrie 1997, 22–4). He is a creator figure, emanating from the east (from an Ulster perspective) and producing earth from water chaos.

'First he reveals the other world which is all around Bran and identified the sea as the land of Mannanán mac Lir; secondly, he tells of the nature of the world and relates the way it has come to its present state, in contrast to the Otherworld which has remained pristine since the time of creation; and finally he reveals knowledge of the future regarding the coming of a champion/saviour who will perform conquests in battle as well as reveal knowledge of the world' (MacQuarrie 1997, 37).

Although the evidence from Manx Gaelic literature is much more modern it contains some of the same essential elements. In the opening of the *Traditionary Ballad*, which is a potted history of the human settlement of the Island written down in the late fifteenth or early sixteenth century, the connection between island and god is fundamental:

Mananan beg va Mac y Leirr	(Young Mannanán who was son of Ler [ie the Sea]
shen yn chied er ec row rieau ee	was the first who ever owned her).

In another anonymous poem of similar date entitled *Mannanan beg, mac y Leirr* this picture is expanded somewhat:

Dy neaishtagh shin agh rish my skeayll	If you would listen to my story
As dy ving lhieu ayns my chant;	I will pronounce my chant as best I can;
Myr share dy voddyms lesh my veeal	I will with my Mouth
Yinnin diu geill dán ellan sheeant.	Give you notice of the enchanted Island.
Manannan beg va mac y Leirr,	Little Manannan was son of Leirr,
Shen yn chied er ec row rieau ee;	He was the first that ever had it;
Agh myr share oddym's cur-my-ner,	But as I can conceive,
Cea row eh hene agh an-chreestee.	He himself was a heathen.
Cha nee lesh e Chliwe ren eh ee reayll	It was not with his sword he kept it,
Cha nee lesh e Hideyn, ny lesh e vhow	Neither with arrows or bow;
Agh tra aikagh eh lhuingys troailt	But when he would see ships sailing,
Oallagh eh my geayrt lesh kay.	He would cover it round with fog.
Yinnagh eh doinney ny hassoo er brooghe,	He would set a man standing on a hill,
Er-lhieu shen hene dy beagh ayn keead;	Appear as if he were a hundred;
As shen myr dreill Mannanan keole,	And thus did wild Mannanan protect
Yn Ellan shoh' n-ayn leash coisney bwoid	That island with all its booty
(Harrison 1873, 26–29, stanzas 1, 3–5).	

Figure 15.8. Quartz pebbles in Early Christian grave marker post-packing at Peel Castle.

The tradition of Mannanán cloaking the island in mist to protect it from unwanted visitors, including the present Lord of Man (Queen Elizabeth II), persists to this day.

Although it is impossible to be sure that the Island and its supernatural protector held the same or equivalent place in the minds of the middle Neolithic inhabitants of the northern Irish sea area, given the lack of substantial population change and demonstrable continuity in many aspects of cultural life, it would seem at least as likely as that regional prehistoric societies should have followed norms observed in much more recent populations in Oceania, the Arctic or West Africa. A strong argument for the antiquity of Man and its supernatural role is that in the thematic 'cycles' that form the basis of early Irish literature Mannanán is the only significant figure to appear in all of them (Macquarrie 1997, 10) implying not only his psychological importance but also his prior existence within the tradition out of which the cycles were formed.

Meayll Circle

The distribution and typology of Clyde cairns and court tombs and their Manx equivalents has been discussed above. In terms of its material culture the Meayll Circle (also known as Mull Hill in the literature) is clearly contemporary with burial sites such as Cashtal yn Ard, King Orry's Grave and Ballaharra, open settlements such as Port Cranstal (Phurt) and Billown (Burrow 1997, 67–121) and with the newly discovered quartz mounds (Davey and Woodcock 2003; Pitts 1999). Despite attempts to relate its unique plan of six chambers arranged in a circle within a cairn to sites in Derbyshire and Galloway

(Henshall 1978, 174) the Meayll circle has no credible parallels. The best that can be said is that the doubling of chambers in some sites of the Bargrennan group in Galloway 'is a step towards the orderly arrangement of the six chambers at Meayll Hill' (Henshall 1978, 174). Lynch has suggested a comparison with Cerrig y Gof in Pembrokeshire where five chambers are somewhat randomly placed in the side of a small cairn (Lynch 1972, 80, Fig. 15.8). The Welsh site is barely one quarter of the area of the Meayll Circle (110sq^m as against 410 sq^m), the chambers are square of sub-rectangular in form and are laid out in rather irregular spacing and orientation. The contrast with the passage and twin chamber complexes at Meayll Hill and its size and symmetry is very marked. It is surely a huge stride to move from two to six chambers or from simple box graves to micro passage tombs. Whilst 'the components of the site and indeed its totality, fit comfortably within the earlier Neolithic monument building traditions found along the western seaways' with a range of analogies being noted in a number of sites in northern France (Gale *et al.* 1997, 57), no other site has the same form of chamber in an equivalent symmetry. It is the suggestion of the present writer that this uniqueness is directly related both to the central place held by the Isle of Man in the geography and cosmology of the region, as described above, together with topographical and mythological elements that are tied to the location of the site itself.

The present form of the name and usage in the designation of the site (pronounced 'mule') must be of relatively recent origin. Whilst the Manx *meayl* denotes a bare hill, the upper part of the peninsular has only become denuded of soil in the last few centuries, lying within late medieval quarterland, (cf. Woods 1867; for

Rushen, Davies 1956, 102–3) and the word order is English. The Manx Gaelic name for the site has been the subject of some confusion. According to Kermode and Herdman it was called *Rhullick y Lag Sliggagh* meaning 'graveyard of broken slates', whilst the nearby hut circles are called *Lag-ny-Boirey* or 'hollow of trouble, strife, lamentation or botheration' (Kermode and Herdman 1914, 37–40). Charles Roeder, however, collecting Manx names in 1898 is quite clear: *Lhiaght ny Borragh* 'is the proper name of the Druidical circle on the Mull as ascertained by me from many Cregneish people', a finding that agrees with this use of the name by Manx fishermen using the circle as a leading mark to find one of the fishing grounds off the Calf. It seems that the antiquarians transposed the names of the two sites. Kneen (1925–28, 44), on the basis of contemporary pronunciation derives the meaning from *Lhiack ny Virragh* and the Irish *leac*, a stone, and the genitive plural of *forrach*, a meeting or assembly place. On the basis of the spelling *Lack-ne-Moiragh* in an 1811 deed Broderick, on the other hand, derives the Gaelic name of the Meayll Circle from *leacht + biorach*, meaning 'grave of the pointed (stones)' (Broderick 2002, 455). Thus in the Manx tradition the name of the site both described its physical position and nature and also implies that it may have functioned as a focus for the regular experience or re-experience of communal strife or lamentation.

Both the landscape setting of the site and its specific structure and funerary deposits deserve comment. Fowler, in his PhD, in a series of recent papers, and in this volume, has discussed a range of issues to do with 'place, path and event' in a 'living social landscape' (Fowler 1999, 104–111) personhood and social relations (Fowler 2001, 153–5), the orientation of the passages and the contents of the chambers (Fowler 2002). In addition, Fowler and Cummings (2003) have also reviewed the use of beach pebbles and quartz in the Meayll Circle and elsewhere in the earlier Neolithic of the Irish Sea. In the final section of this paper, a number of additional suggestions derived mainly from more recent communal understandings of the site will be made, in an attempt to provide further possible insights into its functions within Neolithic society.

The site as a whole, which is located on a terrace near the summit of the peninsular, faces mainly north, west, south-west and north-east. Fowler noted that lines of site through the passages in Chambers II and IV are directed into the hill itself, whilst the other four passages provide more distant views of the Calf of Man (V), sky and sea (V1), Bradda (I) and Billown (II) (Fowler 2001, 153, figure 3). Whilst this latter suggestion may be somewhat anachronistic, as no early Neolithic upstanding structure has as yet been identified at Billown, the passage of Chamber II certainly points to the Plain of Malew, the most fertile area in the Isle of Man (Harris *et al.* 2001, 18 and Fig 15.4), and probably the immediate homeland of the builders of the site. Given the number of suitable landscape features that might have been used it is notable that the alignment of the chambers does not appear to be related to them. Neither distant features such as the Mountains of Mourne, the Mull of Galloway or Black Coombe nor local landmarks such as Bradda Head, Peel Hill, Cronk ny Errey Laa, South Barrule, Archallagen, Douglas Head or the summit of the Calf of Man appear to have been used. The relationships are as follows (magnetic bearings in clockwise order):

020	Corrins Tower
023	Chamber I
029	Cronk ny Aree Laa
043	South Barrule
064	Archallagan
070	Douglas Head
070	Chamber II
084	Black Coombe (Lake District, England)
128	Chamber III
160	Axis of monument
189	Chamber IV
245	Chamber V
249	Summit of the Calf of Man
298	Mountains of Morne (Co Down, Ireland)
304	Chamber VI
340	Axis of monument
346	Bradda Head (west end profile)
350	Bradda Head (summit)
358	Mull of Galloway (Scotland)[2]

If the chamber alignments were not determined by local or distant topographical features, some other locational factor must be sought. For example, the Meayll Circle is situated on the only area in the south of the Isle of Man, apart from Maughold Head, from which the northern half of the Island is visible. Peel Hill and Dalby Mountain can be seen through the Fleshwick gap. If the site was significant in the context of the whole island, rather than a sub-region within it, this would have been important. From the earliest historic times the Island was divided both legally and culturally into a Northside and a Southside, delineated by the central line of hill ridges running from north-east to south-west (Davey 2002, 91–99). Peel Hill and Dalby, both visible from the Meayll, are in the north. It is even possible that the six chambers reflect an early manifestation of the six sheading medieval divisions.[3]

More significantly for the argument of this paper the site provides a platform from which it is possible to see, on a clear day, the Mull of Galloway and the Mountains of Mourne. The Circle is focused on north-east Ireland and south-west Scotland, the same area that boasts the major concentration of distinctive middle Neolithic sites and finds designated by Piggott as the 'Clyde-Carlingford Culture'. Is it so located so that the builders and users of the site could connect with their own homelands when on Man?

The importance of quartz, both in pebble and veinous

Figure 15.9. *Quartz topped pillars marking the entrance to Staward Farm Cottages, Sulby.*

form to contemporary understandings of the site and its rituals has been discussed by Fowler and Cummings (2003), Fowler (1999; 2002), and Darvill (2002; this volume). The ritual use of quartz beach pebbles continued on the Isle of Man and elsewhere in the Irish Sea area until recently (Crowe 1982), being especially prominent in Early Christian burials (e.g. Freke 2002, 66; Fig. 15.8). In a Christian context each pebble represented a link with the other world in the form of a prayer (Garrad 1989–91, 88). Quite apart from the finds of quartz pebbles at Cashtal yn Ard and the quartz vein that features prominently in one of the standing stones that forms its entrance (Darvill and Chartrand 2000, 42–4), the island can boast a group of quartz boulder Bronze Age sites that appear to be unique in the Irish Sea area (Woodcock 2001, 176–215, 345). A form of pebbledash called spardash, and quarried until recently on Meayll Hill, is still in favour as a weatherproof cladding for domestic houses. Modern gatehouse pillars are normally topped with quartz boulders - a contemporary recognition, albeit usually subconscious, of the power of the metaphysical over the human (Fig. 15.9).

Although the site contains a prominent quartz block at its centre and Meayll Hill itself is traversed by numerous quartz veins, some passing close to the circle, this feature could not have been the primary reason for the location of the monument. Mineralized veins occur frequently for the whole length of the central uplands of the Island. Equally the Mountains of Mourne and the hills of Galloway can be seen from many upland locations throughout Man. A more specific, local reason that links well with the place-name evidence can be suggested.

The Circle provides a panoramic view of the north side of Port Erin Bay from Bradda Head to Spaldrick. This section of cliff-line is still actively described and discussed by local people in a variety of ways; as the grave of a Buggane – a sort of Manx super troll (Moore 1891, 55) – who was killed by Mannanán during his conquest of the island, or as representing Finn Mac Cooil in one or more versions of the legend in Irish folklore (Morrison 1929, 15–19), or as the final resting place of Mannanán himself following his defeat by St Patrick (Morrison 1929, 20–24). Bradda Head is seen as his forehead, the vertical line of the copper mines his eye socket, Ghaw Roole as his mouth and Gawe ny Pharick as the underneath of his chin. All of these features have been bisected by the shore line along the long axis of the figure which is lying recumbent, horizontally in the sea (Fig. 15.10). The eye socket, which has been greatly exaggerated by recent mining activity, would have appeared in prehistory as the biggest visible quartz vein in view from the Hill – the most tangible link to the otherworld. The site of the Meayll Circle is the first and only level location on Meayll Hill from which both the distant lands of Scotland and Ireland and the recumbent giant can be seen.

Whilst the research of Fowler and others has illuminated the complex of social and cultural phenomena involved in the burial rituals found in the chambers at the Circle, it seems likely that these events provided a foundation consecration of the site, whose main function was not for burial, for which many conventional tombs were in use in the Isle of Man and elsewhere, but for the enactment of ritual. At midsummer sunset, on the axis of

Figure 15.10. Meayll Circle – view to Bradda Head (detail inset).

the Meayll Circle, Mannanán, the creator, would stir the sea until it became the blood out of which life was born. The cult may have been initially related to a military or political leader in the same area, but by the time the tradition was first recorded it is as a supernatural entity that the progenitor of the Isle of Man was known. The Meayll Circle provided a focus for the social expression of this knowledge, combining as it does a visual link by air to southwest Scotland and northeast Ireland and a physical contact, through the quartz within and beneath the site, to the metaphysical realms beyond.

Thus the Isle of Man, despite its apparent contemporary political marginality, may have occupied an unique central place within the Northern Irish Sea cultural zone at which a creation ritual connected with Mannanán or his ancestor was re-enacted by the peoples of the region.

Notes

1   Throughout this paper Manx place-names will be used. Meayll Circle is also known by its English name, Mull Hill Stone Circle, or simply as Mull Hill.
2   Bearings taken, 3rd november 2002, with a *Plastimo* nautical handbearing prismatic compass.
3   I am grateful to Andrew Johnson of Manx National Heritage for this suggestion.

References

Ashmore, P. J. 1996. *Neolithic and Bronze Age Scotland*. London: Batsford.
Barnwell, E. L. 1866. Notes on the stone monuments in the Isle of Man. *Archaeologia Cambrensis* 45, 46–60.
Broderick, G. 2002. *Placenames of the Isle of Man, Volume 6; Sheading of Rushen*. Tübingen: Max Niemeyer Verlag.
Burrow, S. 1997. *The Neolithic culture of the Isle of Man*. Oxford: British Archaeological Reports British Series 263.
Cregeen, S. 1978. Ballaharra excavations 1971: a summary of work and results. In P.J. Davey (ed.), *Man and environment in the Isle of Man*, 141–51. Oxford: British Archaeological Reports British Series 54.
Crowe, C.J. 1982. A note on white quartz pebbles found in Early Christian contexts on the Isle of Man. *Proceedings of the Isle of Man Natural History and Antiquarian Society*, 8, 413–5.
Cubbon, A.M. (ed.) 1971. *Prehistoric sites in the Isle of Man*. Douglas: Manx Museum and National Trust.
Darvill, T. 1999. Billown Neolithic Landscape Project 1995–1997. In P.J. Davey (ed.), *Recent archaeological research on the Isle of Man*, 13–26. Oxford: British Archaeological Reports British Series 278.
Darvill, T. 2002. White on blonde: quartz pebbles and the use of quartz at Neolithic monuments in the Isle of Man and beyond. In A. Jones and G MacGregor (eds), *Colouring the past*, 73–91. Oxford: Berg.
Darvill, T. and Chartrand, J. 2000. A survey of the chambered

long barrow at Cashtal yn Ard, Maughold. In T. Darvill (ed.), *Billown Neolithic landscape project, Isle of Man, 1999*, 34–44. Bournemouth and Douglas: Bournemouth University School of Conservation Sciences Research Report 7.

Davey, P.J. 2002. At the crossroads of power and cultural influence: Manx archaeology in the high Middle Ages. In P.J. Davey and D.M. Finlayson (eds), *Mannin revisited: twelve essay on Manx culture and environment*, 81–102. Edinburgh: Scottish Society for Northern Studies.

Davey, P.J. and Woodcock, J.J. 2003. Rheast Buigh, Patrick: middle Neolithic exploitation of the Manx uplands? In I. Armit, E. Murphy, E. Nelis and D. Simpson (eds), *Neolithic settlement in Ireland and western Britain*, 128–135. Oxford: Oxbow Books.

Davies. E. 1956. Treens and quarterlands: a study of the land system of the Isle of Man. *Transactions and Papers of the Institute of British Geographers* 22, 97–116.

Fleure, H.J. and Neely, G.J.H. 1936. Cashtal yn Ard, Isle of Man. *Antiquaries Journal* 16, 373–95.

Fowler, C. 1999. *On discourse and materiality: personhood in the Neolithic of the Isle of Man*. Unpublished Ph.D. Thesis: University of Southampton.

Fowler, C. 2001. Personhood and social relations in the British Neolithic with a study from the Isle of Man. *Journal of Material Culture* 6, 137–63.

Fowler, C. 2002. Body parts: personhood and materiality in the Manx Neolithic. In Y. Hamilakis, M. Pluciennik and S. Tarlow, (eds.), *Thinking through the body - archaeologies of corporeality*, 47–69. London: Kluwer/Academic Press.

Fowler, C. and Cummings, V. 2003. Places of transformation: building monuments from water and stone in the Neolithic of the Irish Sea. *Journal of the Royal Anthropological Institute* 9, 1–20.

Freke, D. 2002. *Excavations on St Patrick's Isle, Peel, Isle of Man 1982–88*. Liverpool: Liverpool University Press.

Gale, J., Chartrand, J., Fulton, A., Laughlin, B. and Darvill, T. 1997. The Mull Hill tomb. In T. Darvill (ed.), *Billown Neolithic landscape project, Isle of Man, 1996*, 52–60. Bournemouth and Douglas: Bournemouth University School of Conservation Sciences Research Report 3.

Gale, J. and Darvill, T. 1998. A survey of the Ballakelly chambered tomb, Santan. In T. Darvill (ed.), *Billown Neolithic landscape project, Isle of Man, 1997*, 38–42. Bournemouth and Douglas: Bournemouth University School of Conservation Sciences Research Report 4.

Gale, J., Darvill, T., Chartrand, and Watson, C. 1999. A survey of the chambered long barrows at King Orry's Grave, Laxey. In T. Darvill (ed.), *Billown Neolithic landscape project, Isle of Man, 1998*, 54–63. Bournemouth and Douglas: Bournemouth University School of Conservation Sciences Research Report 5.

Garrad, L.S. 1989–91. The archaeology and tradition of some prehistoric and early Christian religious practices in the Isle of Man. *Proceedings of the Isle of Man Natural History and Antiquarian Society* 10, 413–5.

Gelling, P. and Megaw, B.R.S. forthcoming. The excavation of King Orry's Grave (North East). In F. Lynch (ed.), *Manx megaliths*. Liverpool: Liverpool University Press.

Gonzales, S., Innes, J., Huddart, D., Davey, P. and Plater, A. 2000. Holocene coastal change in the north of the Isle of Man: stratigraphy, palaeoenvironment and archaeological evidence. In K. Pye and J.R.L. Allen (eds), *Coastal and estuarine environments; sedimentology, geomorphology and geoarchaeology*, 343–63. London: the Geological Society, Special Publication No.175.

Harris, J., Fullen, M.A. and Hallett, M.D. 2001. *Agricultural soils of the Isle of Man*. Douglas: Centre for Manx Studies Research Report 9.

Harrison, W. 1873. *Mona miscellany: a selection of proverbs, sayings, ballads, customs, superstitions, and legends, peculiar to the Isle of Man*. Douglas: Manx Society, Volume 21.

Henshall, A.S. 1978. Manx megaliths again; an attempt at structural analysis. In P.J. Davey (ed.), *Man and environment in the Isle of Man*, 171–6. Oxford: British Archaeological Reports British Series 54.

Henshall, A.S. forthcoming. The 1972 excavations at Meayll Hill. In F. Lynch (ed.), *Manx megaliths*. Liverpool: Liverpool University Press.

Higgins, D.A. and Davey, P.J. forthcoming. Excavations at Ballaharra, German, 1969–1983, by Sheila Cregeen. In F. Lynch (ed.), *Manx megaliths*. Liverpool: Liverpool University Press.

Jeffcott, J.M. 1866. Circle on the "Mule", Isle of Man. *Archaeologia Cambrensis* 47, 306–9.

Kermode, P.M.C. 1926. The cairn at Ballafayle. *Proceedings of the Isle of Man Natural History and Antiquarian Society*, 3, 151–4.

Kermode, P.M.C. 1927. Long barrow in the Isle of Man. *Antiquaries Journal* 7, 191–2.

Kermode, P.M.C. and Herdman, W.A. 1914. *Manks antiquities*. Liverpool: Liverpool University Press.

Kermode, P.M.C. and Herdman, W. A. 1894. The excavation of the Neolithic stone circle near Port Erin, Isle of Man. *Proceedings and Transactions of the Liverpool Biological Society* 8, 159–72.

Kneen, J.J. 1925–1928. *The place-names of the Isle of Man*. Douglas: Yn Çheshaght Ghailckagh.

Lynch, F. 1972. Portal dolmens in the Nevern Valley, Pembrokeshire. In F. Lynch and C. Burgess (eds), *Prehistoric man in Wales and the West*, 67–84. Bath: Adams and Dart.

Lynch, F. 1997. *Megalithic tombs and long barrows in Britain*. Princes Risborough: Shire.

Lynch, F. (ed.) forthcoming. *Manx megaliths*. Liverpool: Liverpool University Press.

Macquarrie, C.M. 1997. *The waves of Mannanán: a study of the literary representations of Mannanán mac Lir from Immram Brain (c700) to Finnegans Wake (1939)*. Unpublished PhD Thesis: University of Washington.

Megaw, M.R. and Megaw, J.V.S. 1989. *Celtic art from its beginnings to the Book of Kells*. London: Thames and Hudson.

Moore, A.W. 1891. *The folk-lore of the Isle of Man*. (Reprinted 1994). Felinfach: Llanerch Publishers.

Morrison, S. 1929. *Manx fairy tales*. Douglas: The Manx Experience. (Second Edition 1992).

Muhr, K. 2002. 'Manx place-names: an Ulster view'. In P.J. Davey and D.M. Finlayson (eds), *Mannin revisited: twelve essay on Manx culture and environment*, 37–52. Edinburgh: Scottish Society for Northern Studies.

Mundin, A., Chartrand, J. and Darvill, T. 2000. A survey of the long barrow at Ballafayle, Maughold. In T. Darvill (ed.),

Billown Neolithic landscape project, Isle of Man, 2000, 31–39. Bournemouth and Douglas: Bournemouth University School of Conservation Sciences Research Report 9.

Ó Cuív, B.O. (ed.) 1957. 'A poem in praise of Raghnall king of Man *Baile Suthach Sídh nEamhna*. In *Éigse* 8, 283–301.

Piggott, S. 1954. *Neolithic cultures of the British Isles.* Cambridge: Cambridge University Press.

Pitts, M.B. 1999. Quartz mounds: a preliminary assessment. In P.J. Davey (ed) *Recent archaeological research on the Isle of Man*, 63–73. Oxford: British Archaeological Reports British Series 278.

Sheridan, A. 1995. Irish Neolithic pottery: the story in 1995.

In I. Kinnes and G. Varnell (eds), *'Unbaked urns of rudely shape': essays on British and Irish pottery for Ian Longworth*, 3–21. Oxford: Oxbow.

Waddell, J. 1991. The Irish Sea in prehistory. *Journal of Irish Archaeology*, 6, 29–40.

Waddell, J. 1998. *The prehistoric archaeology of Ireland.* Galway: Galway University Press.

Woodcock, J.J. 2001. *In search of a cultural identity: a study of the Manx Bronze Age in its Irish Sea context.* Unpublished Ph.D. Thesis: University of Liverpool.

Woods, J. 1867. *A new atlas and gazetteer of the Isle of Man.* London: Day and Son.

16   Neolithic worlds; islands in the Irish Sea

Gabriel Cooney

Introduction

In thinking about the Irish Sea, we often seem to concentrate on it as a space between the two large islands of Ireland and Britain, or more specifically the lands bordering the Irish Sea Basin (e.g. Bowen 1970). More rarely do we consider it, including the North Channel and St George's Channel, as a maritime setting for islands, ranging in size and location. While it is recognised that the western coast of Scotland to the north of the Irish Sea and the North Channel, and the western and southern coasts of Ireland, are characterised by irregular coastlines and a large number of islands, by contrast the Irish Sea tends to be perceived as an expanse of open water. However, I want to draw attention to and discuss islands, particularly the smaller islands, in our understanding of the Neolithic of the Irish Sea. The importance of large islands – Anglesey, Mann, Arran and the Hebrides to the north – has been recognised, but the number and significance of smaller islands along the Irish Sea littoral has been not been the subject of the same degree of interest. When these small islands in the Irish Sea have been considered, they have been discussed in isolation and in an immediate, local context. In Broodbank's (2000) work on the archaeology of the Cyclades he suggests that we need to rethink some of the basic assumptions we make about islands to open the way to a more culturally informed island archaeology. This includes a need to move away from the concept of individual islands as the best units for analysing island societies. We should focus instead on connections and linkages between islands and mainlands, forming what might be termed *islandscapes*. Broodbank's work can be seen as part of a broader re-assessment of island archaeology (e.g. Gosden and Pavlides 1994; Robb 2001). Central to these new ways of thinking about islands is the recognition that the material culture used on islands plays a very active part in island life and identity and also offers us the opportunity to explore inter-island and island-mainland relationships.

By way of background I should explain that I have been involved in survey and excavation on an Irish Sea island, Lambay, off the Dublin coast, for several years

(Cooney 1998; 2000; 2002). This has led to a increasing awareness on my part that this island cannot be seen in isolation but should be considered in the context of the adjacent mainland of Ireland and of the other islands off the coast of Dublin (Cooney forthcoming a). With the experience of recognising the significance of the group of islands off the Dublin coast, I was struck by the occurrence of other small islands and island groups along the western Irish Sea coast, such as the Saltee and the Copeland Islands. Similarly on the eastern side, especially in the St. George's Channel area, there are islands such as Lundy, Caldey, Skomer, Ramsey and Bardsey (Fig. 16.1). My contention would be that these and other islands, while relatively few in number, should be seen as a significant feature of the Irish Sea zone. Of course we have to bear in mind the reality of changes in relative sea-level before, during and since the Neolithic. For example, looking at the pattern of sea-level change around the Irish coastline (Carter 1991; Taylor *et al.* 1986), along the southern Irish Sea coastline there has been a rising relative sea-level trend during the post-glacial period. An initial rapid rise has been followed by a decelerated rise over the last three thousand years. There has been a more complex pattern in the north Irish Sea because of the isostatic factor. Here rapidly rising sea-level in the early post-glacial was followed by a fall from the maximum post-glacial level dating to before 4000 BC, then a rise again to the present day. This raises the question as to when islands actually became islands and also their former extent. Because of the pattern of sea-level change in the northern part of the area places that were islands in prehistory may now part of mainlands, as in the case of the Howth peninsula north of Dublin.

Seeing and moving between Neolithic islands

In a paper considering the islands off the coast of Dublin (Cooney forthcoming a), which should be read as a complement to the present one, I discussed the general significance and attraction of islands in the Neolithic.

Gabriel Cooney

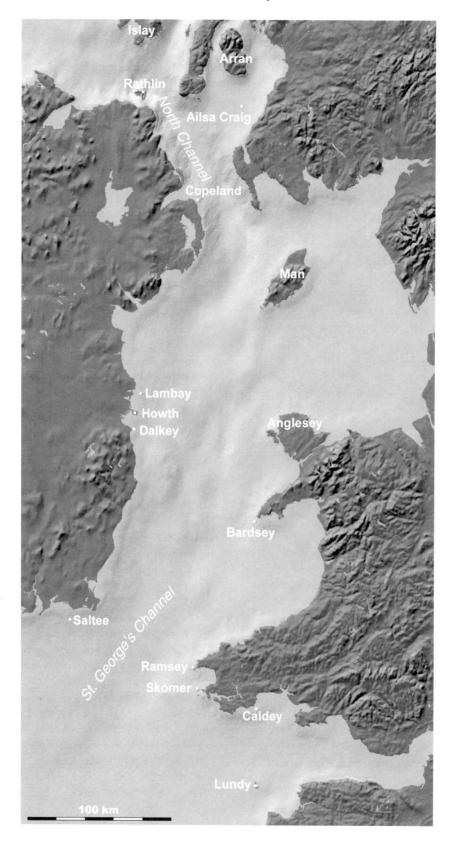

Figure 16.1. *Islands in the Irish Sea.*

More specifically in examining the role of islands in the Irish Sea it becomes important to try to understand why in Bowen's phrase (1970, 28) the waves were easier to negotiate than the land. The first step is to think of people at home on the water. In coastal areas movement by sea would have been part of everyday life. People were aware of the power of the sea and guided by its daily and seasonal rhythms. Indeed in making this shift in perspective, from the land to the sea and its shores, the enduring attraction of islands becomes more understandable. Islands then become places, seamarks and landmarks, where the land begins rather than ends and where the rest of the world is held at bay by the sea (Nicholson 2001, 61). As well as the generally forested nature of the landscape of Neolithic Ireland and Britain the other factor that would have made movement by water attractive is that travel by boat was significantly quicker than walking (e.g. Woodman and Johnson 1996). It is often argued that throughout prehistory and into historic times, because communication was easier and quicker by sea than by land, the Irish Sea was a centre of influence and activity (Bowen 1970, 28; Waddell 1991/2). During the Neolithic movement across and along the Irish Sea was a key articulating agent in the establishment and maintenance of cultural contacts. The material evidence for these contacts can be seen, for example, in the distribution pattern of objects such as stone axes from specific sources that had to have been transported across the Irish Sea (Cooney 2000).

There have been valuable discussions of the nature of water transport in the Neolithic (e.g. Bowen 1972, 39–42; Case 1969; Cunliffe 2001, 65–8; McGrail 1998). It is widely agreed that of the three widespread traditions of boat building in north-west Europe; log boats, hide boats and plank boats, the first two were in use at this time. The earliest known log boats from Ireland are late Mesolithic in date and there are a number of Neolithic examples, including the one from Lurgan, Addergoole, County Galway, the longest surviving log boat from Ireland or Britain (Fry 2000, 9; Lanting and Brindley 1996; McGrail 1998, 83; see also Gregory 1997; McGrail 1978; Mowat 1996). The log boat is best suited to movement on relatively sheltered inland and estuarine waters, the low freeboard would have made its use in turbulent coastal waters or the open sea more problematic. However, two log boats dating to 3700–3400 BC were recently located in Larne Lough, a sea lough in County Antrim (Fry 2000, 24). Cunliffe (2001, 65) points out that with additional stabilizing features log boats could have been used sailed in more open waters. Fry (1995; 2000, 25) has argued that even in the absence of evidence for such features there is no reason why log boats could not have sailed successfully offshore in reasonably calm conditions.

While direct evidence of hide boats has not been found in Neolithic contexts the long tradition of the use of such craft, as in the Irish *currach*, their documentation by

classical and later writers and the presence of potential later prehistoric models such as the gold decorated shale boat from Caergwrle, Flintshire, Wales (Green 1985) and the gold boat forming part of the hoard from Broighter, County Derry, Ireland (Raftery 1983, 268–70) argue very strongly that such craft were in use during the Neolithic. McGrail (1998, 185–7) has shown that the technology to built such craft was certainly current in the Neolithic. Indeed consideration of issues such as the introduction of domesticated livestock to islands, large or small, makes it clear that craft such as keeled currachs, with a crew of several people, using oars and sail would have been needed (see Case 1969). At the smaller end of the scale one-person hide craft were probably also in use on rivers, such as the Boyne coracle (Stout 2002, 91–2). The presence of plank boats of later prehistoric date from the Welsh side of the Severn Estuary (see discussion in Davies and Lynch 2000, 177–8; McGrail 1998) raises the question of when this third boat-building tradition began in the Irish Sea area.

In an important paper considering the diffusion and distribution of megalithic monuments around the Irish Sea and North Channel Margaret Davies (1946) discussed the conditions that a sea traveller would have faced using the kind of craft outlined above, given that the modern pattern of tidal circulation can be assumed to broadly resemble conditions in the Neolithic (McGrail 1998, 259; Fig. 16.2). The pattern of tidal currents would clearly have encouraged movement along coastlines. It also makes it easier to appreciate why the Isle of Man is such a crucial island link for movement across and along the Irish Sea, meriting Norman Davies's (1999, 9) description of it as 'Midway Island'. Interestingly the tidal streams flowing into the Irish Sea basin from the north and south meet to the south-west of Mann. In turn we can now perhaps appreciate more fully why there are such a variety of cultural components, drawn from different areas in the Irish Sea, in the material culture of the Manx Neolithic (e.g. Darvill 2000). Of course people would have known by tradition and passed-on experience to wait for favourable stages of the tide and to use the tidal currents to best benefit. As Nicolson (2001, 128) remarks 'pick your moment and the sea will do what it can for you, however small the boat and however unpractised the helm'. But it would be misleading to underestimate the dangers involved in sea travel. Constant dangers in the Irish Sea would have been the tidal eddies, whirlpools and strong tidal races. Many of these are located in very significant locations when considering maritime travel close to coasts as they occur off major promontories, headlands and islands (Fig. 16.3). For example there are difficult passages due to tidal race funnelling effects around Anglesey and in the North Channel. Allied to the ever-present possibility of changing weather conditions, particularly in winter (McGrail 1998, 259–60), we can appreciate how the Irish Sea provided both an invitation and a threat to travel.

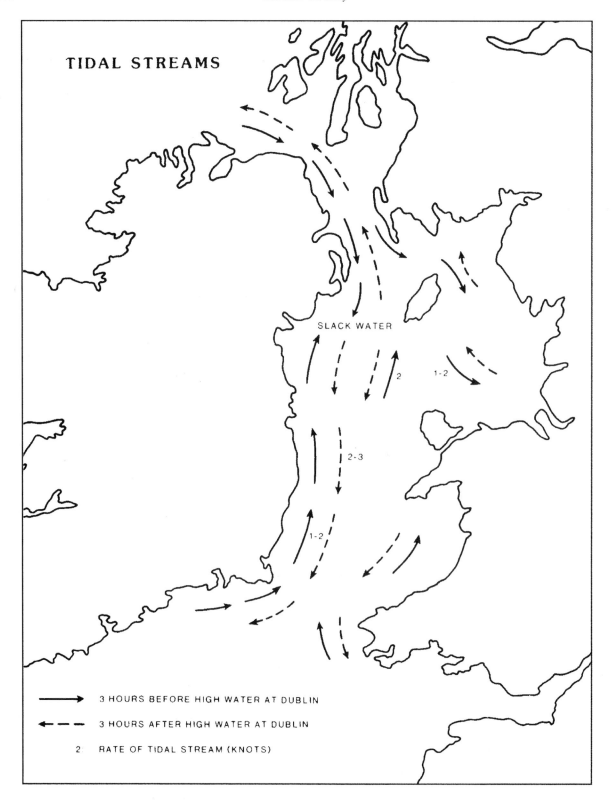

Figure 16.2. *Tidal regime in the Irish Sea (after Reed's Nautical Almanac and Tide Tables for 1977).*

One reason why the hazards of travel on the open sea may have been lessened for Neolithic as for later seafarers on the Irish Sea is that they would have rarely been out of sight of land. Raban (1986, 52) has described the archipelago effect created by the land visible from a boat in the mid-Irish Sea. Interestingly the best long-distance visibility often follows rainstorms as cold, clear air from the north replaces the damp, foggy weather coming in

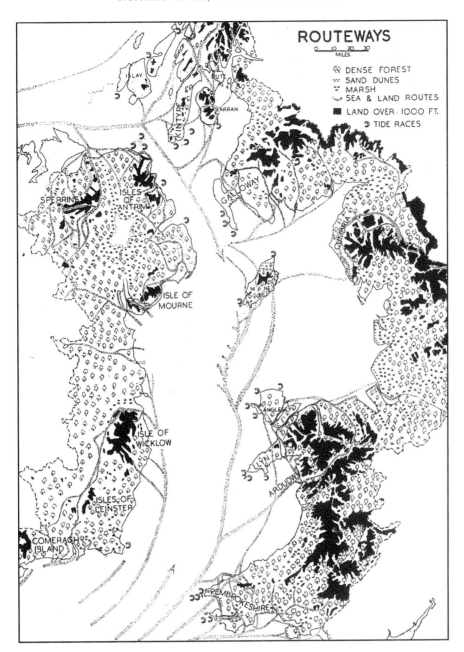

Figure 16.3. *Irish Sea routeways, mountain 'islands' and tidal races (after Davies 1946).*

from the west (Bowen 1972, 40). In these circumstances one can imagine the relief of the wet, wave-tossed sailor on sighting familiar landmarks. A critical observation made by Margaret Davies (1946, 42–4) was that from the sea these landmarks would have appeared as 'islands', or mountains rising from the sea (Fig. 16.3). The basin of the Irish Sea is ringed with such islands: the Wicklow Mountains, the Mourne (including the Cooley) Mountains, the mountain core of the Isle of Man, the Lake District Fells and Snowdonia. Over the long duration of the Neolithic people would have become familiar with all the Irish Sea coastlands and their varying character, but we can appreciate why these 'islands' would have continued

to guide and facilitate movement, making the journey across open water seem shorter and in that sense less hazardous (Woodman 1981, 96). Helms (1988, 25) has argued that islands have a particular character as sacred, special places because they are where the land, the sea and the sky meet. This creates two liminal zones setting islands apart; at the junction of the land and sea and the island and the sky (see also discussion in Scarre 2002). This may also help us understand the particular attractions of mountains that appear to rise from the sea as islands' and the blurred perceptual lines between actual, water-surrounded islands and places perceived to be islands (see Watson this volume).

As the conditions of tide and current in the Irish Sea would have favoured north-south movement this re-inforces the importance and attraction of 'actual' islands close to the coast such as Lundy, Lambay or Rathlin that rise sharply out of the sea and hence would have been visible as markers on the horizon for considerable distances along coastlines. The strategic position of such islands in terms of travel around the Irish Sea should not be downplayed. Also in the light of the offshore location of these islands, the question arises as to their potential role as contact points in networks of linkage and exchange between the larger islands of Britain and Ireland. Al-though discussing the problem in the context of maritime trade rather than exchange McGrail (1983, 311–13) usefully set out the different requirements that participants in such exchanges may have had. The interesting point for the present discussion is that he identified small islands as one of the ideal locations for such activity. Locally such islands could also be useful places from which to monitor and if necessary control the movement of boats along coastlines. On the other hand it is also worth bearing in mind that the tidal conditions around some islands, such as Rathlin (see Fig. 16.3), would have made them difficult places to access and leave. Hence islands could have been viewed both as gateways to a wider world, but also as dangerous, liminal places, set apart from the rest of the world.

The use of islands during the Neolithic

This examination of communication and the relationship of land and sea in the Irish Sea forms a background for a discussion of the role of small islands during the Neolithic. Here I want to tack between the Dublin group (Cooney forthcoming a) and other islands in the Irish Sea. Islands clearly could have a role as a source of food (marine, bird and in the case of larger islands terrestrial) and related resources. Indeed this is the role that is seen as the dominant one when their utilisation during the Mesolithic is discussed (e.g. Finlayson and Edwards 1997; McCartan 2000). Clearly subsistence requirements would have continued to have an influence on the way islands were used in the Neolithic. Wild resources, such as birds, fish and cetaceans may have been a reason for seasonal visits to islands. If such visits were of any duration or indeed where sustained occupancy of an island occurred then people would have needed to live off island-based resources. To take a couple of examples, while the impressive range of field boundaries and field enclosures on the island of Skomer off the coast of Dyfed in south-west Wales (Evans 1990; Grimes 1950) are now regarded as most likely being of late prehistoric date (Davies and Lynch 2000, 169), their presence indicates that where the soil cover had agricultural potential, small islands could have been cultivated in prehistory. Other indications of this kind of extended island usage may by indicated by Schofield's

(1994) field-walking and test-pit survey on Lundy, 20km off the north Devon coast in the approaches to the Bristol Channel (Fig. 16.4). The evidence was interpreted as suggesting intermittent visits during the Mesolithic prior to a more permanent occupation (but perhaps still short-lived) in the Bronze Age (Schofield 1994, 430). On Lambay the abundant quantity and widespread distribution of struck flint turning up in rabbit-burrow disturbance systematically recorded over several years suggests at the very least repeated and extensive use of the island (Fig. 16.5). The use of bi-polar technology makes much of this material difficult to date but it does appear to span the later Mesolithic, Neolithic and early Bronze Age.

Alongside this pattern of island usage it is important to raise again the issue of the defined, bounded character of islands. It has been pointed out above that small islands may also have been regarded as special places (see relevant discussion in Scarre 2002). In this regard they can be linked to other places such as caves, mountains, springs, and rivers. In small-scale, traditional societies such special places are widely held to have a religious or cosmological significance because of their spatial location or form. They provide dangerous but critical linkages between the lived-in world and the other world of spirits, ancestors and gods . A useful framework for examining the significance of natural places has been posited by Bradley (2000, 36). He suggests that the deliberate deposition of material, the embellishment of striking features of the landscape with monuments and the deployment of objects made at and from these places provide us with opportunities to identify such special places. All of these patterns of human behaviour can be seen on small islands in the Irish Sea during the Neolithic.

Two islands where there is good evidence for the deliberate deposition of material are Dalkey and Caldey. Dalkey is a small island which forms the southernmost of the Dublin group of islands. Lying about 400m offshore, it is separated from the mainland by a deep sound where the currents can be dangerous. It is only about seven hectares in extent, and certainly justifies the title of a small island. Dalkey is probably known best known for the Mesolithic evidence recovered during the excavation of midden material at the northern end of the island (Liversage 1968). Dating of mammal bone (Woodman et al. 1997; Woodman 2000) indicates that the island was used over the course of the later Mesolithic period. Activity also went on through much of the Neolithic. The site has been interpreted in economic terms (Liversage 1968; McCartan 2000) but recent re-ex-amination of the stone axes and associated material from the site by Leon (2001) suggests that it is open to a different interpretation. There are a series of features post-dating and in some cases dug into the middens which the excavator (Liversage 1968) interpreted as domestic but which contain deliberate deposits and in some cases appear to mark or be marked by boulders. There is at least one definite Neolithic human burial. The location

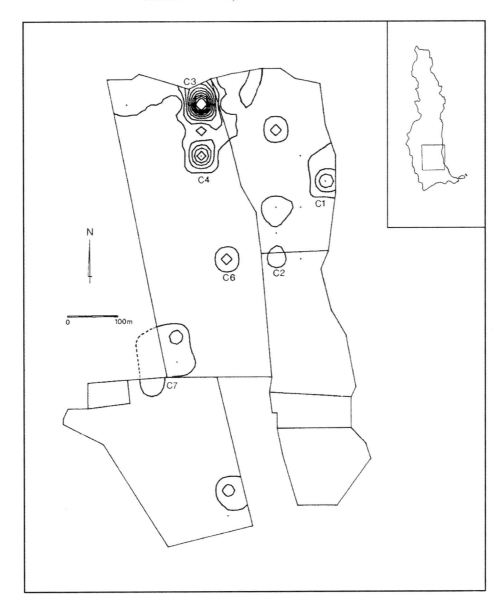

Figure 16.4. *Overall distribution and concentrations of lithics from the extensive survey at the southern end of Lundy (after Schofield 1994).*

of the site on the island is also relevant. It is at the base of a low cliff, facing and overlooking the sound and the mainland. The pattern of material being brought here and being deposited on the island appears to have started in the Mesolithic and continued during the Neolithic.

On Caldey island in Carmarthen Bay there is evidence that it shared with Dalkey a role as a special place during the Neolithic (and perhaps in the Mesolithic). Caldey island (Fig. 16.6) is 2.4 kilometres by 1.2 kilometres in extent and has a long history of settlement (Lacaille and Grimes 1955; 1961), beginning in the Palaeolithic when it was part of the mainland. It has close links with and is within sight of the mainland to the north-west across Caldey Sound. A notable feature are the limestone caves and fissures along the northern and eastern coastline. A

number of the caves have produced archaeological deposits, including the Daylight Rock fissure at the east end of the island (Fig. 16.7). In their programme of stable isotope analysis combined with AMS radiocarbon dating Schulting and Richards (2000) have shown that there was deposition of human bone in caves on Caldey from before 7500 BC down to the Neolithic and later. There is no direct association between the scattered human remains and the important material assemblages of Mesolithic (David 1989) and Neolithic date. Interestingly the human remains from the Daylight Rock fissure and other cave sites on Caldey dated to the Neolithic illustrate the wider trend in Britain of a lack of significant use of marine resources and a great degree of reliance on terrestrial foods, in contrast to those individuals dating to the Mesolithic (Schulting and

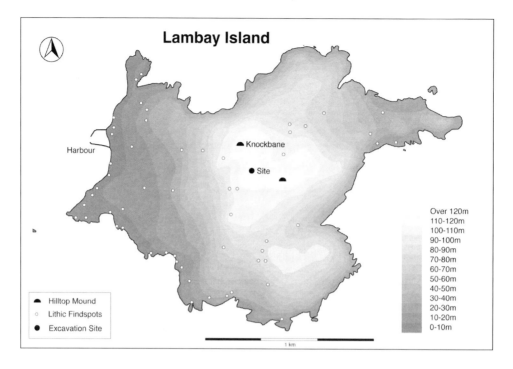

Figure 16.5. *General distribution of lithics recovered from areas of disturbed ground on Lambay.*

Richards 2000, 62; see discussion in Richards and Hedges 1999; Schulting and Richards 2002). In this context the placement of human bone in island caves, suggests that these were places of special significance, a significance that continued despite the major alteration in dietary regime at the beginning of the Neolithic (Lynch 2000, 75–7). It is tempting to suggest that the combination of caves and an island setting would have been imbued Caldey with a special meaning, particularly as the origin of the island would have taken place during the course of the Mesolithic as a consequence of sea level rise (David 1989, 243). This change literally set Caldey apart from the world, and is very likely to have been an integral part of the oral memory of communities with a long history of occupation of this area.

Lacaille and Grimes (1961, 32) observed that the two highest points on Caldey were marked by round mounds (see Fig. 16.6). The monumentalisation of the landscapes of the larger islands in the Irish Sea, such as Arran, Mann and Anglesey, is well-known but it also occurs not just on Caldey but on other smaller islands. Today Howth forms a peninsula on the north side of Dublin Bay, protecting the bay from northerly winds, but in the Neolithic it was an island, about a kilometre off the coast, and roughly 700 hectares in extent, an island which had also been utilised during the later Mesolithic (Mitchell 1956; 1972; Woodman 2000). A portal tomb was built approximately at the centre of the island, facing south-east into a cliff face which probably was the source for the structural stones. On the uplands to the south of the tomb there are three small cairns. What is interesting is

that we are seeing in microcosm on this island the pattern that occurs on the Dublin mainland south of the river Liffey where the portal tombs are placed in low-lying locations, some in dramatic local settings, while passage tombs and other cairns are placed on the hilltops in the south Dublin/Wicklow uplands (Cooney 2000, 143–5). We could also see the portal tomb on Howth as a local representation of an Irish Sea monument tradition as portal tombs are found widely around the Irish Sea Basin.

Writing about the concentration of monuments on Arran, Hughes (1988, 52) suggested that part of the attraction of the island as a place for monuments was its visual dominance and its geographical position in the Firth of Clyde. The island mountains gave a sense of permanence and a link with the world of the past and the ancestors. Thinking of monuments on islands and the power of place, it is interesting to pose the question of whether a small island itself could have been regarded as a monument. As one example one might suggest Ailsa Craig at the mouth of the Firth of Clyde (Fig. 16.8). This island rises to a height of 340m and is about 100 hectares in extent. Of volcanic origin as an igneous intrusion the microgranite of the island has a dramatic dome shape, making it a distinctive landmark rising up out of the sea. The dome impression is created by the sheer cliffs on three sides, with the eastern side being less precipitous. The name of the island comes from the Gaelic for 'fairy rock' and this may reflect the way in which the island was viewed in prehistory, as somewhere powerful, with connections to the other world. That it resembles a monument is captured in Craig's (1996, 284)

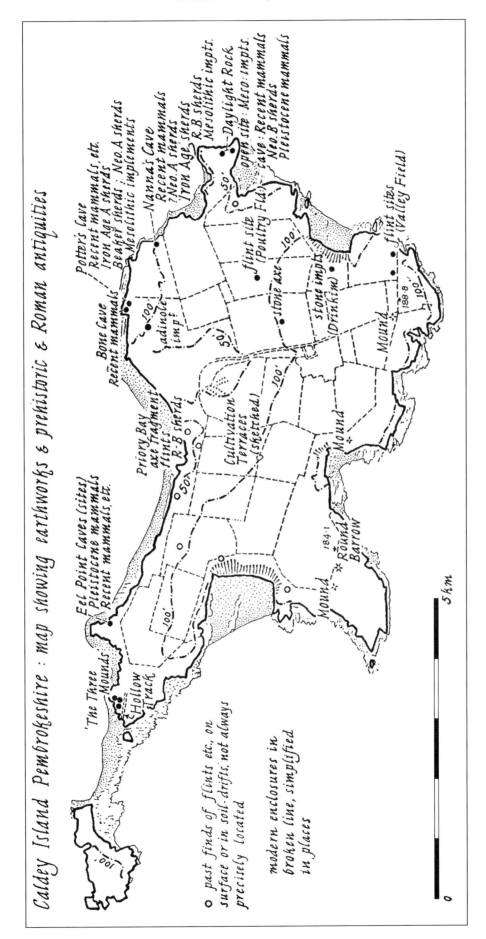

Figure 16.6. Caldey Island (after Lacaille and Grimes 1961).

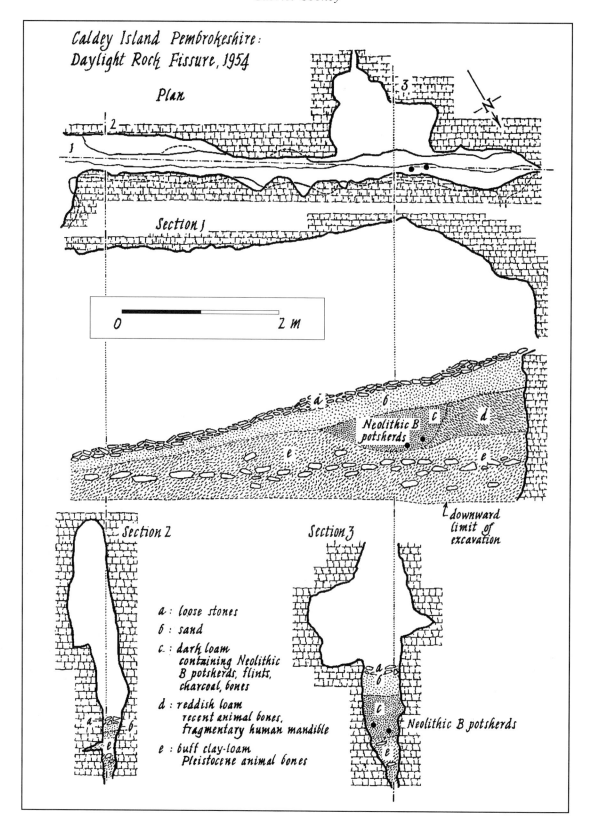

Figure 16.7. Daylight Rock, Caldey (after Lacaille and Grimes 1961).

***Figure 16.8.** Ailsa Craig (photograph by Ann Bowker).*

observation that Ailsa Craig (and a number of other rocks in Scotland) looks like the remains of a monument-building culture whose humans and artefacts have long gone.

Ailsa Craig then is clearly named from the perspective of the seafarer, it is also referred to as 'Paddy's Milestone', being located roughly half-way on the voyage between Glasgow and Belfast. Another intriguing insight into the possibility that the particular character of places as *islands* was crucial to their meaning is provided by the Irish name for Lambay and Rathlin. This is *Reachrú* in both cases. The similarity of this name has provided an interesting historical problem in that the historical sources referring to the earliest Viking raids in Ireland in AD 795 refer to Reachrú. This has given rise to continuing debate as to which is being referred to, Lambay or Rathlin (e.g. O Muraíle 1997, 203). Linguistically the term seems to be a very old one and to signify something like rugged or indented cliffs or island (McKay 1999; O hogáin *pers. comm.*). Given the nature of the coast of the two islands it is an apt name that describes the predominant character of both when viewed from the sea.

Ailsa Craig also provides a curious modern example of the link between the working of island sources for the production of artifacts which could then become a micro-cosm of the power of that place when taken away from the island. From the early nineteenth century until the 1970s the microgranite was quarried to provide setts for streets and the roughouts for curling stones (e.g. Craig 1996, 289). Traditionally Ailsa Craig microgranite was seen as the best source for curling stones and these stones ended up all over Scotland and in other countries, such as Canada, where the game was played. There are a number of examples where lithic sources on islands were regarded as being of significance during the Neolithic, as indicated by their exploitation and the movement of products off-island. The best known example are the porcellanite axeheads from Brockley, Rathlin Island. This

is one of two sources of porcellanite, the other being Tievebulliagh on the mainland to the south. While the importance of Brockley has been underplayed it appears to have been at least as significant as Tievebulliagh in terms of scale of production and there are extraction galleries there (Cooney 2000; Mandal *et al.* 1997; Sheridan 1986). The use and distribution of pitchstone from Arran (Simpson 1995; Simpson and Meighan 1999) is another example of an island source being highly valued. One important and literally obvious point is that in both of these cases the sources are visually distinctive. Porcellanite is an interesting problem in that the products from the island (Brockley) and mainland (Tievebulliagh) source, while distinguishable in geochemistry, are visually identical. Bearing this in mind it does seem likely that part of the narrative history around such objects would have been built on attributes, such as distinctive colour and appearance, which could be read as indicating where they came from. As mentioned above tide and current conditions make Rathlin difficult to approach. In the Neolithic as at present it is probable that the main landing place would have been Church Bay (located on the southern coast where the island bends to the south). Approaching the bay from the south on a clear day there is a dramatic view of the cliffs stretching to the west; white flint overlain by dark coloured basalt. Just as with monuments these different colours and forms of stone may have structured the way in which Rathlin was experienced and provided a very special local context for the movement of axes from the island (see relevant discussion in Jones 1999).

Lambay – an island in an Irish Sea world

I wanted to end by coming back to the island I started from, Lambay off the Dublin coast (Fig. 16.5). In a number of papers (Cooney 1998; Cooney 2002, forthcoming a;

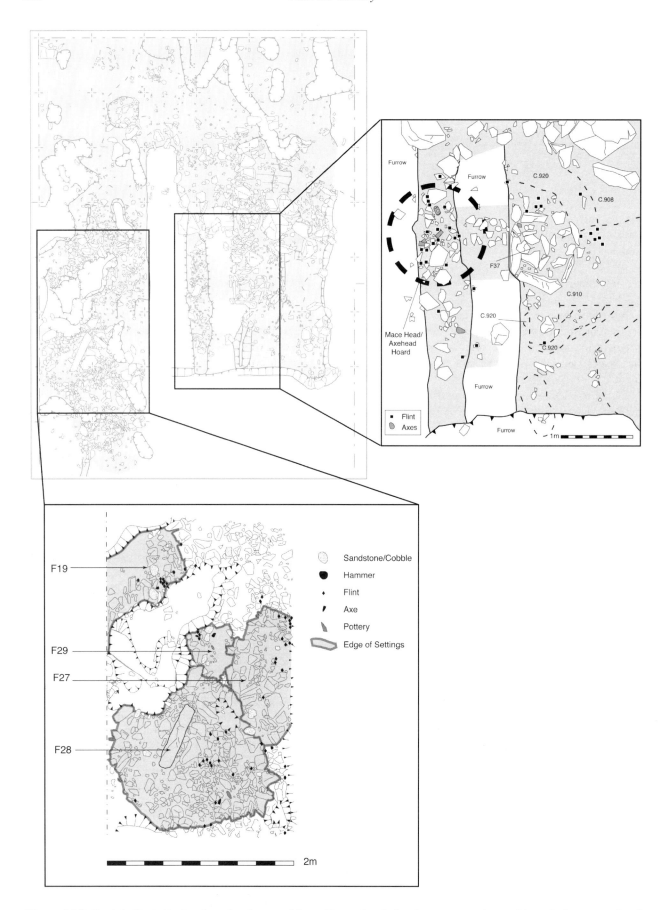

Figure 16.9. *Eagle's Nest site, Lambay, focal area of deposition at level showing stone setting and hoard of stone axeheads and macehead.*

forthcoming b) I have explored the results of the excavation of a Neolithic 'quarry' site and ongoing survey on the island. What we have are components of material culture and human events that evoke both the particular character of Lambay as an island and that link it to the wider world. Our central focus on Lambay has been the excavation of a production site (the Eagle's Nest) where a visually distinctive medium-grained volcanic rock, porphyry or porphyritic andesite was exploited for the production of axeheads. There is evidence of quarrying in the middle/ late Neolithic, but also of deposition, both in the quarry areas and on the floor of a small valley between two worked outcrops. Here a sequence of activity appears to begin with pits, which are frequently recut. Then there is a switch to the placement of features and material (Fig. 16.9). For example, one event involved the deposition of a hoard including a pestle type macehead and a porphyry roughout and a finished axehead. Some of the contemporary features are reminiscent of the settings outside passage tombs. One of the notable features of the material culture is the deposition of jasper pendants and beads and evidence that jasper was worked, at the site or elsewhere on the island.

At the moment it is attractive to think of the Eagle's Nest as a place where rock (porphyry) is being worked, while other material is being brought and left there, enabling connections and linkages to be actively created through material culture. Away from the site it is worth noting that there are pieces of quarried porphyry in the makeup of the hilltop mound at Knockbane, the most notable prehistoric landmark on the island. Knockbane also takes us out to the wider world, it is placed to be seen. It seems to mirror the shape of the most striking of the peaks in the Wicklow mountains on the mainland, namely the Sugarloaf (Cooney forthcoming a). From Knockbane not only are the Dublin/Wicklow mountains visible to the south, but there is also the view north to the Cooley mountains, Slieve Gullion and the Mournes. On a very clear day looking to the north-east you can see the peak of Snaefell on Isle of Man. Given these links the activities on Lambay cannot be seen in isolation. Matching this visual world to be seen from the island are the links in the material between activities on a specific island and a wider cultural setting. The wider cultural tradition certainly appears to be strongly linked to the construction and use of monuments such as passage tombs. The stone settings at the Eagle's Nest and the broader pattern of deposition echoes that seen outside large passage tombs, as at the Knowth complex (Eogan 1986; Eogan and Roche 1997). Jasper pendants and beads like those from the site usually occur with cremated human bone deposits in Irish passage tombs (Eogan 1986). The pestle macehead at the Eagle's Nest is an important contexted addition to those found in Ireland and in Orkney in settlement and tomb contexts (Simpson and Ransom 1992, 227). The dominance of Carrowkeel and Goodland bowls in the ceramic assemblage again is consistent with wider links to the passage tomb tradition (Sheridan 1995). Material appears to be have been brought to the island from the Irish Sea world as a number of axeheads found with other material close the main landing place on the west coast of Lambay in the 1920s are consistent with a linkage with sources in Preseli in south-west Wales (Cooney and Mandal 1995). On the other hand the way this material is being actively used on the island is clearly to do with a local frame of reference. At the Eagle's Nest site deposition was happening as a complement to the quarrying of a local rock source rather than in a standard monumental context. While Knockbane clearly looks out to the wider world, to the south-east on the only other point on the island over 120m there is an unusual cairn which is really only visible on the island itself. It is of local prominence and significance, particularly in those areas to the south of Knockbane where that hilltop monument goes out of view due to the local topography. On this island world people carried on their lives in a distinctive way, within the physical, perceptual and material framework of a wider Irish Sea seascape.

This echoes the emphasis placed by other authors in this volume (e.g. Cummings; Darvill) on the active interplay between material culture being worked and re-worked in local contexts, creating a local sense of identity and colour, but articulating with a more broadly based and geographically widespread cosmology (Robb 2001). What is particularly important about islands is they help us understand how these two frames of reference could be brought together.

Acknowledgements

My thanks firstly to Barbara Leon for all her work on the illustrations. Stephen Harrison, Barbara Leon and Aidan O'Sullivan kindly read earlier drafts of the text and the paper has been benefited greatly from their comments. My thanks also to the editors for their patience!

References

Bowen, E.G. 1970. Britain and the British Seas. In D. Moore (ed.), *The Irish Sea province in archaeology and history*, 13–28. Cardiff: Cambrian Archaeological Association.

Bowen, E.G. 1972. *Britain and the western seaways*. London: Thames and Hudson.

Bradley, R. 2000. *An archaeology of natural places*. London: Routledge.

Broodbank, C. 2000. *An island archaeology of the early Cyclades*. Cambridge: Cambridge University Press.

Carter, R.W.G. 1991. *The impact on Ireland of changes in mean sea-level*. Dublin: Department of the Environment and Local Government.

Case, H.J. 1969. Neolithic explanations. *Antiquity* 43, 176–86.

Cooney, G. 1998. Breaking stones, making places. In A. Gibson and D.D.A. Simpson (eds), *Prehistoric ritual and religion*, 108–18. Stroud: Sutton Publishing.

Cooney, G. 2000. *Landscapes of Neolithic Ireland*. London: Routledge.

Cooney, G. 2002. So many shades of rock: colour symbolism in Irish stone axeheads. In A. Jones and G. MacGregor (eds), *Colouring the past*, 93–107. Oxford: Berg.

Cooney, G. forthcoming a. The role of islands in defining identity and regionality during the Neolithic: The Dublin coastal group. In G.J. Barclay and K. Brophy (eds), *Regional Diversity in the Neolithic of Britain and Ireland*. Oxford: Oxbow

Cooney, G. forthcoming b. Stereo porphyry: quarrying and deposition on Lambay Island, Ireland. In P. Topping and M. Lynott (eds), *Prehistoric extraction*. Oxford: Oxbow.

Cooney, G. and Mandal, S. 1995. Getting to the core of the problem: Petrological results from the Irish Stone Axe Project. *Antiquity* 69, 969–80.

Craig, D. 1996. *Landmarks: an exploration of great rocks*. London: Pimlico.

Cunliffe, B. 2001. *Facing the ocean: the Atlantic and its peoples*. Oxford: Oxford University Press.

Darvill, T. 2000. Neolithic Mann in context. In A. Ritchie (ed.), *Neolithic Orkney in its European Context*, 371–85. Oxford: Oxbow.

David, A. 1989. Some aspects of the human presence in west Wales during the Mesolithic. In C. Bonsall (ed.), *The Mesolithic in Europe*, 241–53. Edinburgh: John Donald.

Davies, J.L. and Lynch, F. 2000. The late Bronze Age and the Iron Age. In F. Lynch, S. Aldhouse-Green and J.L. Davies (eds), *Prehistoric Wales*, 139–219. Stroud: Sutton.

Davies, M. 1946. The diffusion and distribution pattern of the megalithic monuments of the Irish Sea and the North Channel coastlands. *Antiquaries Journal* 26, 38–60.

Davies, N. 1999. *The isles: a history*. Oxford: Oxford University Press.

Eogan, G. 1986. *Knowth and the passage tombs of Ireland*. London: Thames and Hudson.

Eogan, G. and Roche, H. 1997. *Excavations at Knowth 2*. Dublin: Royal Irish Academy.

Evans, J.G. 1990. An archaeological survey of Skomer, Dyfed. *Proceedings of the Prehistoric Society* 56, 247–67.

Finlayson, B. and Edwards, K.J. 1997. The Mesolithic. In K.J. Edwards and I.B.M. Ralston (eds), *Scotland: environment and archaeology, 8000 BC-AD 1000*, 109–25. Wiley: Chichester.

Fry, M.F. 1995. Communicating by logboat: past necessity and present opportunity in the north of Ireland. *Irish Studies Review* 12, 11–6.

Fry, M.F. 2000. *Coití: logboats from Northern Ireland*. Belfast: Environment and Heritage Service Department of the Environment.

Gosden, C. and Pavlides, C. 1994. Are islands insular? Landscape vs. seascape in the case of the Arawe islands, Papua New Guinea. *Archaeology in Oceania* 29, 162–71.

Gregory, N.T.N. 1997. *A comparative study of Irish and Scottish logboats*. Unpublished PhD thesis: University of Edinburgh.

Green, H.S. 1985. The Caergwrle Bowl, not oak but shale. *Antiquity* 59, 116–7.

Grimes, W.F. 1950. The archaeology of Skomer Island. *Archaeologia Cambrensis* 101, 1–20.

Helms, M.W. 1988. *Ulysses' sail: an ethnographic odyssey of power, knowledge and geographical distance*. Princeton: Princeton University Press.

Hughes, I. 1988. Megaliths: space, time and the landscape - a view from the Clyde. *Scottish Archaeological Review* 5, 41–58.

Jones, A. 1999. Local colour: megalithic architecture and colour symbolism in Neolithic Arran. *Oxford Journal of Archaeology* 18, 339–50.

Lacaille, A.D. and Grimes, W.F. 1955. The prehistory of Caldey. *Archaeologia Cambrensis* 104, 85–165.

Lacaille, A.D. and Grimes, W.F. 1961. The prehistory of Caldey: part II. *Archaeologia Cambrensis* 110, 30–70.

Lanting, J.N. and Brindley, A.L. 1996. Irish logboats and their European context. *Journal of Irish Archaeology* 7, 85–95.

Leon, B. 2001. *A reassessment of stone axeheads from Dalkey island, Co. Dublin*. Unpublished MA thesis: University College Dublin.

Liversage, G.D. 1968. Excavations at Dalkey island, Co. Dublin, 1956–1959. *Proceedings of the Royal Irish Academy* 66C, 53–233.

Lynch, F. 2000. The earlier Neolithic. In F. Lynch, S. Aldhouse-Green and J.L. Davies (eds), *Prehistoric Wales*, 42–78. Stroud: Sutton.

McCartan, S. 2000. The utilisation of island environments in the Irish Mesolithic: agendas for Rathlin island. In A. Desmond, G. Johnson, M. McCarthy, J. Sheehan and E. Shee Twohig (eds), *New agendas in Irish prehistory*, 15–30. Bray: Wordwell.

McGrail, S. 1978. *Logboats of England and Wales with comparative material from European and other countries*. Oxford: British Archaeological Reports British Series 51.

McGrail, S. 1983. Cross-channel seamanship and navigation in the late 1st millennium BC. *Oxford Journal of Archaeology* 2, 299–337.

McKay, P. 1999. *A dictionary of Ulster place-names*. Belfast: Institute of Irish Studies.

McGrail, S. 1998. *Ancient boats in north-west Europe: the archaeology of water transport to AD 1500*. London: Longman.

Mandal, S., Cooney, G., Meighan, I. and Jamison, D.D. 1997. Using geochemistry to interpret porcellanite axe production in Ireland. *Journal of Archaeological Science* 24, 757–63.

Mitchell, G.F. 1956. An early kitchen-midden at Sutton, Co. Dublin. *Journal of the Royal Society of Antiquaries of Ireland* 86, 1–26.

Mitchell, G.F. 1972. Further investigations of the early kitchen-midden at Sutton, Co. Dublin. *Journal of the Royal Society of Antiquaries of Ireland* 102, 151–9.

Mowat, R.J.C. 1996. *The logboats of Scotland*. Oxford: Oxbow.

Nicolson, A. 2001. *Sea room: an island life*. Harper Collins: London.

O Muraíle, N. 1997. The Columban onomastic legacy. In C. Bourke (ed.), *Studies in the cult of Saint Columba*, 193–246. Dublin: Four Courts Press.

Raban, J. 1986. *Coasting*. London: Picador.

Raftery, B. 1983. *A catalogue of Irish Iron Age antiquities*. Marburg: Veröffentlichung des Vorgeschichtlichen Seminars Marburg, Sonderband 1.

Richards, M.P. and Hedges, R.E.M. 1999. A Neolithic revolution? New evidence of diet in the British Neolithic. *Antiquity* 73, 891–7.

Robb, J. 2001. Island identities: ritual, travel and the creation of difference in Neolithic Malta. *European Journal of Archaeology* 4, 175–202.

Scarre, C. 2002. A pattern of islands: the Neolithic monuments of north-west Brittany. *European Journal of Archaeology* 5, 24–41.

Schofield, A.J. 1994. Lithic artefacts from test-pit excavations on Lundy: evidence for Mesolithic and Bronze Age occupation. *Proceedings of the Prehistoric Society* 60, 423–31.

Schulting, R.J. and Richards, M.P. 2000. The use of stable isotopes in studies of subsistence and seasonality in the British Mesolithic. In R. Young (ed.), *Mesolithic lifeways: current research from Britain and Ireland*, 55–65. Leicester: Leicester University Press.

Schulting, R.J. and Richards, M.P. 2002. The wet, the wild and the domesticated: the Mesolithic-Neolithic transition on the west coast of Scotland. *European Journal of Archaeology* 5, 147–89.

Sheridan, J.A. 1986. Porcellanite artifacts: a new survey. *Ulster Journal of Archaeology* 49, 19–32.

Sheridan, J. A. 1995. Irish Neolithic pottery: the story in 1995. In I.A. Kinnes and G. Varndell (eds), *Unbaked urns of rudely shape': essays on British and Irish pottery for Ian Longworth*, 3–21. Oxford: Oxbow Books.

Simpson, D.D.A. 1995. The Neolithic settlement at Ballygalley, Co. Antrim. In E. Grogan and C. Mount (eds), *Annus Archaeologiae*, 37–44. Dublin: Office of Public Works and OIA.

Simpson, D.D.A. and Rasom, R. 1992. Maceheads and the Orcadian Neolithic. In N. Sharples and A. Sheridan (eds), *Vessels for the ancestors,* 221–43. Edinburgh: Edinburgh University Press.

Simpson, D.D.A. and Meighan, I. 1999. Pitchstone - a new trading material in Neolithic Ireland. *Archaeology Ireland* 48, 26–30.

Stout, G. 2002. *Newgrange and the bend of the Boyne.* Cork: Cork University Press.

Taylor, R.B., Carter, R.W.G., Forbes, D.L. and Orford, J.D. 1986. Beach sedimentation in Ireland: contrasts and similarities with Atlantic Canada. *Current Research, Canadian Geological Survey* 1986A, 55–64.

Waddell, J. 1991/2. The Irish Sea in prehistory. *Journal of Irish Archaeology* 6, 29–40.

Woodman, P.C. 1981. The post-glacial colonisation of Ireland: The human factors. In D. O Corráin (ed.), *Irish antiquity: essays and studies presented to Professor M.J. O'Kelly*, 93–100. Cork: Tower Books.

Woodman, P.C. 2000. Getting back to basics: transitions to farming in Ireland and Britain. In T. D. Price (ed.), *Europe's first farmers*, 219–59. Cambridge: Cambridge University Press.

Woodman, P.C. and Johnson, G. 1996. Excavations at Bay Farm 1, Carnlough, Co. Antrim and the study of Larnian technology. *Proceedings of the Royal Irish Academy* 96C, 137–235.

Woodman, P.C., McCarthy, M. and Monaghan, N. 1997. The Irish quaternary research project. *Quaternary Science Reviews* 16, 120–59.

17   Axes, kula, and things that were 'good to think' in the Neolithic of the Irish Sea regions

Keith Ray

Introduction

The aim of this paper is to open up discussion about the materiality of key items that were mobile within Neolithic societies. It seeks to explore one instance of the way in which the active maintenance of social relations over long distances – and potentially also long periods of time – is implicated in such mobility. The regions bordering the Irish Sea provide a useful context for examination of these links, due to both the proximity and diversity of regions otherwise united by the quasi-landlocked sea.

For some time, contacts mediated at least in part through the transfer of stone axes have been discussed in Neolithic studies. Recent studies of source locations and more precise analyses of source materials are beginning to open up new standpoints from which the question of inter-group relations across time can be examined. Moreover, ethnographic research into networks such as the *kula* of the Massim peoples of Melanesia has provided insights into how long distance exchange practices could become formalised and sustained over centuries, while accommodating changes in content and emphasis.

This paper explores these new possibilities in reference to an aspect of stone axe studies that has so far received less attention. This is consideration of the role that the materiality of axes had in promoting and sustaining their movement. While economic and political dimensions of exchange were no doubt important, the degree to which the properties of the exchanged items themselves sustained exchange practices needs also to be taken into account. The suitability of axes as exchange media is considered in reference to the key location of source areas around the Irish Sea. Moreover, the evidence for an exchange system is seen to be present in the non-coincidental occurrence of axes from one source area found in another. That this extends to highly specialised forms of axe is taken as a further indicator of a system of 'controlled' movement of axes, perhaps along with other items.

Background

In Neolithic studies in Britain and beyond, stone and flint axes (equally referenced as 'axe-heads' or 'axe-blades') have become inextricably linked with the idea that inter-community exchange was a feature of life in the fourth and third millennia BC. The existence of sites attributable to the Neolithic period containing evidence for apparent large-scale production of stone axes, and the presence of axes from such source locations ('quarries' or 'axe factories') at some distance away, has been known from at least the early twentieth century (Clark 1940, 60–1). For a long period in Neolithic studies, a postulated 'axe trade' has been seen by many prehistorians as a means of supplying a key commodity used for the opening up of the post-Glacial climax forests to energetic first farmers (cf. Fowler 1983, 165; Houlder 1976). This is not to suggest that alternative explanations for the movement of axes have not been proposed. An example, based in ethnography, was the idea that the distribution of axes was symptomatic of the operation specifically of gift exchange (Clark 1965).

More recently, axe movements have become a taken for granted aspect of the Neolithic social world in Britain. Sourcing and spatial studies have sought to map the direction of flow of items and to deduce distribution patterns that may have distinctive explanations (Chappell 1987; Clough and Cummins 1979; 1983; Hodder and Lane 1982). The often simplistic nature of such reasoning has led to some extreme scepticism about the degree to which exchange movement of axes existed at all (Berridge 1994; Briggs 1976). In the last ten years or so, more structured investigative approaches have emerged. These have involved source-critical and inter-disciplinary work (for example Cooney and Mandal, 1998), and the investigation of source locations in depth (Bradley and Edmonds 1993). Ways now need to be found to extend these integrative approaches to consider the materiality of axes in its own right.

This paper, therefore, looks at the question of Neolithic axe exchange from a perspective that focuses primarily on the materiality of the items concerned. Firstly, the material properties of axes are considered, in relation to a series of defined dimensions. The relevance of ethnographically documented exchange mechanisms to the consideration of exchange in prehistory is then considered. The *kula* exchange ring of Melanesia is explored as a metaphor for structured social interconnection mediated by key items of material culture. Some key attributes of axes, axe finds-contexts and distributions in Neolithic Britain are reprised. There is then a consideration of the way in which Irish Sea distributions can be understood. Finally, a return is made to the question of what sustains or disrupts exchange practices. While power games and inter-group rivalry on the one hand, and the circulation of commodities on the other, necessarily play a part, it is proposed that some items are also manipulated because they are 'good to think'.

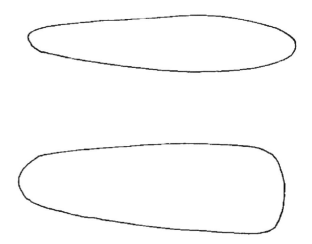

Figure 17.1. *Neolithic stone axe: an archetype. Profile (above) and laid flat (below).*

The materiality of stone axes

The functionality of stone axes has been explored in a variety of ways, perhaps most graphically in numerous 'experimental archaeology' studies (Coles 1973). This was perhaps initially due to perceived difficulties in chopping down trees using such axes. It has been deduced through experiments that individual trees can easily be felled using stone axes. However, to achieve the scale of clearance that can now be attributed to Neolithic activity (cf. Gearey and Charman 1996), trees would need to be felled that had been subject to prior ring-barking or fire-setting (Rackham 1986, 71). Meanwhile, a different understanding has been achieved through the study of woodworking debris. As a result axes are seen more as evidence for woodworking than simply for felling trees, and various forms have been taken to imply use as adzes, chisels and so on. This has been substantiated in reference to the form of facets and spalls among the debris (cf. Taylor 1998, 147–8). One current explanation for variation in size and form that is evident among stone axes is therefore linked to different kinds of axe/adze/wood-working requirements. Such discussion has drawn attention away from subtleties of variation in form, and the evident fine finishing and presentation of many of these objects. This is an aspect that, presumably because aesthetic judgements might be brought to bear, has been almost entirely neglected in the study of Neolithic axes (although some discussion has taken place about how polishing gives axes a distinctive appearance: see Bradley 1998, 44).

It should perhaps have been evident all along that the seed-like form of the axes, with tapering or splayed straight sides, often a clear 'belly' evident in profile, a blade-like distal end and a butt-like proximal end, represents an archetype (Fig. 17.1). There was an idea and an aesthetic of 'axe-ness' at work here, that evoked a variety of associations, and that rendered a variety of forms around this central theme appropriate. That the axe itself was a pervasive motif within Neolithic Britain is demonstrated also, by the existence of miniature examples (for instance from Irish tomb contexts) and by the production of skeuomorphs (for instance in chalk from Woodhenge near Amesbury in Wiltshire). Such formal representations stand alongside axes that are exotic and special in other ways. Slender and finely polished jadeite and flint specimens occur as comparative rarities, but are widely distributed, for instance. All these forms conveyed the idea and evoked the presence of axes and axe-ness all the more powerfully for not actually being 'usable'.

Yet this is not a 'style versus function' debate. The conceptual centrality of stone axes arose precisely because they had both a definite purpose and use, and because this functional importance lent them a symbolic significance that could be distilled through abstractions of their form into fine non-functionality. The materiality of axes, then (as of most items of material culture), was in part physical and in part conceptual. It also resided in, and accrued from, properties arising from the raw materials chosen, attributes produced in production or modification, uses to which the items were put, associations which were implied or evoked, and histories of actions involving axes that were connoted or implicated. The workings of a purposive aesthetic were also made manifest through the choice of materials that would for instance provide weight and density, or could be ground and/or polished to produce particular effects of shininess or reflection of light.

Why should these items have been made attractive in these ways? In the days when a 'trade' in stone axes was seen to have followed the principles of the market, the answer would have been self-evident: to attract purchasers by being distinctive. Here, acquisition alone is seen as the purpose and as an act of closure. In contrast, in the context of 'situated exchange' no item is entirely alienable (see below), and so exchange is socially engendered: there is no 'consumption' in the sense of classical

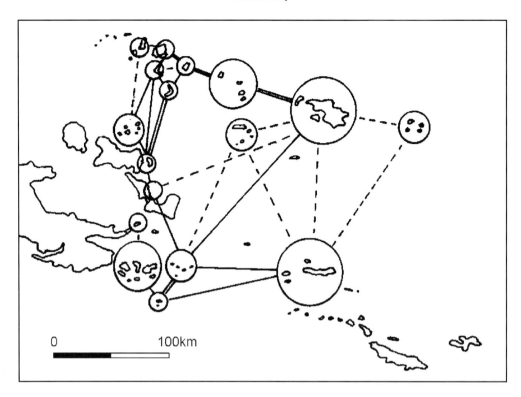

Figure 17.2. *The Kula ring in 1922. Double lines represent close exchange links, solid lines less frequent contacts and dotted lines occasional contacts (simplified from Irwin 1983, 55).*

economics. Rather, it is the capacity that the items possess to attract attention and appreciation, to convey meanings and messages, and to evoke less tangible associations, that stimulates the 'demand' for (albeit often temporary) acquisition.

Archaeologically, of course, we do often 'locate' axes and other such exchanged items at points of 'consumption', usually where they have entered the ground. And yet most of the deposits they are found in are now recognised as somehow 'special', in the care taken to produce physical associations and conceptual links with other materials in the structured manner of deposition itself. Axes, again, are the quintessential deposited item, in the British Neolithic context either placed or thrown whole into watery contexts, or buried whole or in pieces with myriad items that include other artefacts and pieces of dead people and animals (Bradley 1998; Thomas 1999). Arguably, such consumption is therefore simply an attenuated form of exchange: a removal of the 'dialogue' of contact and association into another sphere.

In this light it can justifiably be claimed that it was the quality of axes as metaphor (that is, it was their allusive potential and habitual reference) that both moved them and on occasion deposited them within exchange networks. This metaphoric power elicited a shared concern to acquire and use them among peoples often far removed from one another's immediate physical orbit. In the process, they became media for the co-transfer of

other goods and services, by establishing the threads that connect communities and individuals. The way that this can occur has been well illustrated in ethnography through studies of the *kula*, a complex institution of Melanesia. It is perhaps worth exploring the case of the *kula*, not because it provides a direct parallel for the Neolithic case, but because its complexity and persistence throws light on sea-going exchange practices more generally.

The lessons of the *kula*

The *kula* is primarily a practice of the Massim speaking peoples in the islands at the eastern end of Papua New Guinea. When Malinowski published his study of their ceremonial exchange system in 1922, he was concerned to lay some myths about 'primitive trade'. He phrased his canoe voyagers as 'Argonauts of the Western Pacific' because he viewed their ocean-bound exploits as quests – for fame and connectedness – and not as commercial enterprises (Malinowski 1922). He characterised the essence of the *kula* as involving the circulation of shell necklace and arm-shell valuables around a 'ring' of exchange locations and individuals on different islands (Fig. 17.2).

Each necklace ornament could only be exchanged for an arm-shell ornament of equivalent value, and the progress of exchanges produced a continual clockwise movement of the former that balanced the counter-clockwise movement of the latter. In this network, some individual ornaments acquired names through famous transactions, and associations with legendary 'players'. Individual people (mostly but not exclusively men) thereby became famous through association with the (compounded and attenuated) 'ownership' of the most celebrated of the ornaments. The network provided a 'map' of social contacts, therefore, even though no one person could have drawn its extent.

Some named ornaments clearly had a super-ordinate value (Fig. 17.3), and no item within the *kula* was ever entirely alienable. For both these reasons, unlike currency-based or otherwise formalised exchange systems there was no systematic system of equivalents. Instead, there was a deliberate ambiguity whereby relative value was highly negotiable, and was determined by the outcome of particular enactments of exchange. These occasions were when, almost like prize cockerels in early nineteenth century rural England, two renowned items 'met' each other in the ring and the relative skills of the keepers determined what happened.

These overtly symbolic exchanges co-existed with an extensive flow between these islands, of yams, coconuts, various woods, feathers, betelnut, and stone axe-blades. Some of these exchanges of goods coincided with the twice-yearly *kula* sea-going canoe expeditions, but the latter were not simply a vehicle for the former. Rather, to kula was to participate in a wide forum of contact mediated according to complex exchange rules, accompanied by elaborate rituals and ceremonies (Leach 1983).

While many institutions within traditional societies recorded in the early years of the twentieth century have disappeared, the *kula* has persisted, despite some profound changes in Massim life. As a result, through a series of researches in the 1970s it has been possible to qualify some aspects of the Malinowskian portrayal (Leach and Leach 1983). In particular, two key concepts not considered at length in the earlier studies have been explored (Leach 1983, 24–5). The first concept is that of the *kitom*. This is a term applied to an ornament that for a variety of reasons is not moving around or under some obligation within the *kula* ring. Appreciation of the reasons why *kitom* stand outside the *kula*, yet are implicated in its operation, has enabled a fuller understanding of the process whereby a person can expand their place in the system. The second now better understood concept is that of a *kula* 'path', or *keda* (Campbell 1983a). These paths are viewed simultaneously as linear or circular chains of trusted (but calculating) partners, as routes along which ornaments move, as linkages between *kula* communities, as channels of resource transfer and reserve food supply, and as avenues for the making of *kula* reputations. This helps us to understand exactly how the 'value' of both objects and traders is defined reciprocally within the *kula* (the one continually in reference to the other) through the specific pattern of achieved exchanges (Campbell 1983b).

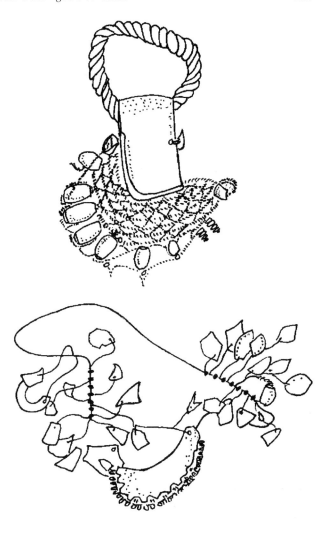

Figure 17.3. Mwari armshell (upper) famed already in 1922 when identified to Malinowski as Nanoula. It was still in circulation in the 1970s and was photographed by Shirley Campbell at Vakuta. Shell necklace (lower) also recorded at Vakuta.

What has also been re-emphasised from the recent studies (although it was understood well enough by Malinowski) was the ritualisation of the journeying itself, and the way in which the building, launching and elaboration of the canoes was integral to the *kula* process. What is particularly interesting in this context is the way in which the canoes are decorated. The prows are highly elaborate and upon approaching the 'destination' of the expedition, they are festooned with *kula* items. This is said to be so that the host community is overwhelmed by the negotiatory power of the incoming exchange voyagers (Munn 1983). It is interesting also to note that the connection between Gawan canoes and *kula* shells is carried over into prominent representations of canoes on the shell-adorned prows (Fig. 17.4). At the same time the canoe itself has been transformed through its use within the *kula* from a solid material form into something less confined: a 'field of influence'. Members of the

Figure 17.4. Prow of a canoe from Gawa, beached on northern Kiriwina in the Trobinand Islands in 1973 (after J. Leach). The figurehead has no fewer than three superimposed stylised representations of a canoe.

matriline concerned are 'attached' to each exchanged ornament brought to the group by the canoe 'transaction'. A link has thereby been created simultaneously, between those individuals, and the movement of the canoe itself. On the island of Gawa, for instance, both the canoe that a matrilineal grouping has exchanged for the purchase of shell ornament valuables, and the valuables themselves, become transformed by this action (Munn 1983). The ornaments become *kitom*, since they have temporarily at least ceased their movement within the *kula*. The presence of the *kitom* on Gawa is therefore seen to magnetically draw other ornaments back to the island.

Malinowski's research was based primarily on a single island, Kiriwina, and the more recent studies have extended the close documentation of the system over the whole Massim area. Recent research has also included archaeological investigations that have suggested that shell valuables were being produced up to 2,000 years ago, and that pottery was once widely exchanged (Irwin 1983). This information of course involves recognising a paradox. On the one hand, it substantiates the idea that contact and exchange within a system has great longevity in island Melanesia. On the other hand it does not and

cannot be taken to imply that the *kula*, as an institution, necessarily therefore has such a long history.

A number of conclusions with relevance to British prehistory can be drawn from the suite of exchange systems that we can now envisage as linked by the Melanesian *kula* network. The first of these concerns the relation of exchange and value. Cultural practices such as *kula*-type networked exchanges provide both mechanisms and metaphors for the fulfilment of social relations between individuals and between groups of people, both close at hand and separated by extensive distances. The movement of ambiguously utilitarian items (such as fine polished axes) can operate as a central articulation of such a system, just as much as more obviously non-utilitarian shell ornaments. Moreover, artefacts engaged within such systems accrue associations with the historical pattern of exchanges itself. They also serve to evoke the paraphernalia of myths and rituals that articulate and perpetuate both the rationale for and the traditions of exchange. The 'good' arising from the relations mediated through this kind of exchange is not the 'satisfied want' of classical economics. Rather, it is a tangible expression of social connectedness and personal worth. This resides in, is felt through, and is sometimes manifestly expressed by, the specific materiality of the objects transferred between exchangers. This means that their value is measured at least in part in terms of their role in making and sustaining ties. As such, as I have implied in the title of this paper, the objects concerned effect a non-material exchange between the medium and the social message. As well as being 'good to consume', in the process of association they become 'good to think' (Tambiah 1969).

Another conclusion concerns the inter-linked value of persons and the objects with which they are regularly or distinctively associated. Identified and identifiable exchange items may be seen not so much as indicating trade routes, as following 'pathways' that have established and have served to maintain links between communities and individuals. In turn, the existence of such links implies the likelihood of social and material exchanges of other kinds, and the possibility that specific spatially and temporally referenced 'biographies' were developed for both items and people. Moreover, at any one time the physical disposition of items within the exchange system is not entirely arbitrary. Rather, it is contingent upon the 'state of play' of both socio-political relations within a linked network, and upon an accumulated history of exchanges. While we should clearly not therefore expect that a complexity of relations and histories can simply be 'read off' against any particular identified pattern of eventual deposition, the pattern itself should be understood as embracing such potential complexity.

New contextualisations of Neolithic axes in Britain

Recent studies of axes in Neolithic Britain have developed a focus upon their context. This has been in terms of their provenance and distribution on the one hand, and upon the circumstances of their manufacture on the other. Most progress has occurred through studies that have sought to link these two kinds of contextualisation.

Although this is nowhere quantified, my impression is that most of the complete or near-complete examples of axes that are discovered (or at least reported) today are chance finds. There is clearly a recovery bias here, to a considerable but unknowable extent. The assumption in the past has often been that these casual finds represent chance losses – either during forest clearance, or along trade routes. Recent experience of the associations of finds of prehistoric bronze objects (also thought previously to be chance or unassociated losses) suggest that such random processes are unlikely to account for the majority of finds (R. Bradley *pers. comm.*). Rather, most chance finds of axes will have been from locations close to centres of activity of various kinds – marked in the Neolithic context by pit-groups, ring-ditches and other ephemeral traces. In contrast, the specific location of axes within certain kinds of site such as causewayed enclosures has been noted ever since Keiller's excavation of Windmill Hill. There has been some suggestion that within such enclosures, whether Staines, Etton or Hambledon Hill, for instance, axes occur mostly as broken fragments, and in some locations rather than others (Edmonds 1993; Pryor 1998). The assumption here in recent years has been that the deposition of axes and fragments of axes in particular deposits represents series of acts of 'consumption', while their presence in these sites at all represents the operation of forms of exchange or re-distribution (Oswald *et al.* 2001, 123–4).

Another phenomenon that has received some attention has been the degree to which some axes were reworked during their lifetime. Some of these observations have been substantiated quantitatively. For instance, it has been claimed that size variation among axes from different sources suggests a down-the-line pattern of exchange, whereby some axes exhibit a greater degree of reworking, the further away from their source they are found (Hodder and Lane 1982).

These and other studies that considered aspects of distribution (for instance Darvill 1989) led to a situation by the late 1980s where it was felt necessary to provide a new perspective on axe production and exchange by looking again at the axe 'factories'. This new phase of work began with a study of the Cumbrian axe sources, and in particular those to the north and west of Great Langdale (Bradley and Edmonds 1993). This work produced many insights into rock extraction procedures, primary flaking and working, and finishing, of the Cumbrian axes. What this research, particularly on the Cumbrian axes, has done, is

to provide a benchmark for future work looking at both source locations and distribution. While some of these studies will, like the Irish Stone Axe Project, provide a series of comparative data, and expand knowledge of the workings of exchange systems involving axes among other items (see below), there are other avenues of research that are worth pursuing.

For example, little sustained and co-ordinated research work has been done so far on the specific co-variation of material, form and context among the axes themselves, despite the generalised observations on the context of deposition noted above. If one thing has become clear from work on 'structured deposition' in Neolithic Britain, it is that there was a continual process of deliberate selection of items for co-burial (Thomas 1999, 62–88). One of the more specialised kinds of depositional context is that of 'hoards', which despite being noted early on in Neolithic studies remains a little-explored phenomenon (Sheridan *et al.* 1992, 395; see below).

In this context, it is perhaps worth also reconsidering what new work on both distributions and the source-provenancing of stone axes might have to tell us. One prospect held out by recent studies of the macroscopic, microscopic and chemical properties of the stone used for axes is some discrimination between those sourced further from and nearer to their finds location. For example, a study of twelve axes from the Weaver Hills in north Staffordshire compared the results of 'total petrography' with x-ray flourescence geochemistry (Ixer *et al.* forthcoming). It was found that four and five axes respectively in the sampled group produced a workable match with rocks from in the Great Langdale and Graig Lwyd series. However, two other axes were made from two different porphyritic andesites, and the twelfth axe was made from a coarse-grained andesitic tuff. It was concluded that these rocks were so far most closely matched with Lake District sources, but were not the same as the known Langdale series. While the twelfth axe may come from a so far unstudied central Lake District quarry source, it was noted that the geological memoir for the central Staffordshire area lists altered porphyritic andesites from Borrowdale as being found in boulder clay locally. In this case, it was considered likely that the axes were produced locally from erratics.

Although the quantities of axes from the major quarrying areas are massive, when these are taken out of the equation, there can be some surprising results. For instance, in the recent macroscopic identification study of Irish axes, of a total of 13,569 objects studied, 7294 were of porcellanite. Of the remaining 6275, it might have been expected that igneous rocks (including gabbro, dolerite and basalt) or metamorphic rocks (including schist) might have accounted for the majority. However, it was sedimentary rocks that provided 4334 of this total. Of these, there were only 452 flint axes, while mudstone and shale accounted for 1296 and 1847 artefacts, respectively (Cooney and Mandal 1998, 55).

It can perhaps be assumed that these latter axes were less likely to be traded further afield, given the widespread distribution of sedimentary rocks of these kinds. In this case, the occurrence of otherwise exotic items of similar forms and the presence of large quantities of axes from major quarrying areas potentially represent 'independent' phenomena. This is not to say that a single cause can be adduced for the distributions, but rather that different series of mechanisms could have been responsible for distributing different kinds of carefully discriminated forms of axe. Again, stylistic variability and context become more rather than less crucial, in trying to establish the grain of the pattern of distribution.

The relation between morphology and material has been explored in yet another approach, which has considered the place of flint axes and flintworking as much more central than previously acknowledged, especially in previous provenancing studies (Pitts 1996). This work has provided some important insights, via multivariant morphological analysis, into the clustering of axe forms into seven taxa (Pitts 1996, 334). It has moreover correctly stressed the typicality of the local in sourcing and use (Pitts 1996, 326–8).

However, the whole undertaking is interpretively flawed by unwarranted, and in some cases palpably misguided, assertions. One is that, in effect, all meaningful variability (particularly between the seven taxa) is determined by the source material used (Pitts 1996, 338–9). Another is that encapsulated within the view that 'found at the consumption or discard site, a stone axe can have limited value to the archaeologist' (Pitts 1996, 339). This is apparently due to the possibility that such axes (or, worse still, fragments) had already been in circulation for a long time, somehow rendering associations of contextual location meaningless.

Neolithic axes and the Irish Sea

One of the most striking insights concerning the source and primary processing locations of quarried material, concerns the westerly distribution of such places (Fig. 17.5). Within this general distribution, a striking correlation is the presence of quarrying areas among mountains directly bordering the northern part of the Irish Sea, and recent work at Lambay island in the Dublin Bay area has served to emphasise this (Cooney 1996; this volume). I want to suggest here that this is the most 'robust' clue we have at present to the way in which the Irish Sea may have had a pivotal role in facilitating both contact and exchange not only in the areas around its shores, but also further afield.

In this section, I shall identify three separate phenomena as indicative of the nature of contact between and beyond these areas. The first is simply new evidence for the range of contacts and movement, as revealed in the results of the Irish Stone Axe Project. One aspect that is highlighted here is the previously noted phenomenon of axes from one source being present in another source area. The second is the question of 'hoards'. The location as well as the nature of such groups may be significant, with the occurrence of pairs or groups of axes within source areas, and at key locations between them. The third is the presence and movement of end-perforated stone axes, the significance of which may also have been understated.

Axe distributions and forms

One of the key aspects of the Irish Stone Axe Project (ISAP) has been the use of both transmitted and reflective light microscopy in the petrographic study of the sampled axes (Mandal 1997). This has enabled, for instance, the discrimination of axes from the two known Antrim porcellanite sources of Brockley (Rathlin Island) and Tievebulliagh (Mandal and Cooney 1997). Besides showing that the former may have been the more prolific source, this has also demonstrated that axes from either source are present in areas immediately adjacent to the other. Given the relative closeness of the source locations, this may not be entirely surprising. However, it does *also* indicate some possibility that the products were exchanged. Meanwhile, products from these sources are known from across Ireland, and in a scatter across England and Scotland (where they have become known as Group IX, and number over 180 so far identified: Cooney *et al.* 1998, 146), but with a marked trend into north-east Scotland.

The results of the study of axes in materials not apparently local within Ireland in ISAP have been more dramatic still. For example, it has been shown that at least 32, and probably over 100 Cumbrian (specifically, Group VI) axes are known in Ireland. The distribution includes a scatter primarily from north-east to south-west, with a concentration in the Antrim area. Perhaps significantly, most finds have come from rivers or bogs (Cooney *et al.* 1998, 144–5). However, the strength of the ISAP studies analytically, lies also in the detailed work on morphology that has been done. This has enabled some conventional wisdom about the Cumbrian axes to be challenged. For instance, it has been questioned whether it really was the larger sized axes that were traded further afield, since smaller sized items are found just as widely dispersed. Moreover, the assumption that the smaller axes were largely reworked appears also to lack justification when the axe forms across a range of items are more closely studied (Cooney and Mandal, 1998, 136–7). It is perhaps also significant to their potential use in wider patterns of less utilitarian exchange, that both the Cumbrian and the gabbro axes in Ireland are predominantly finely ground and polished, as are the porcellanite axes (Mandal 1997, 304).

The gabbro axes were also the subject of special study within ISAP, and the conclusions were instructive. Two distinct gabbroic rocks were defined from 33 of the 45

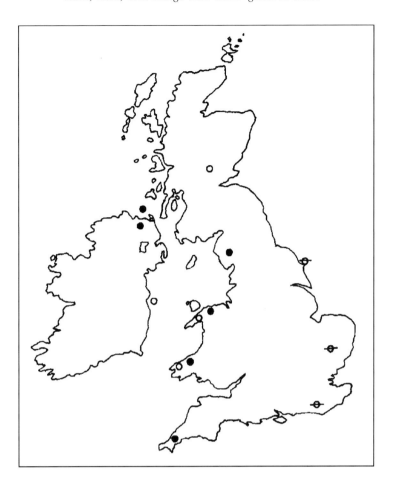

Figure 17.5. *Source locations especially relevant to Irish Sea Neolithic axe distributions. Solid circles represent prolific sources, barred circles flint sources.*

cored axes that were subject to thin-section examination (Mandal 1997, 298). Further geochemical study was carried out on 23 of the 45 cored axes. This confirmed the coherence of the two main gabbro types, and indicated that they are sufficiently distinct from those from local Irish sources as to suggest that most if not all of the 383 hand-examined gabbro axes were imports to Ireland. Moreover, the gabbro type with the strongest geographical focus, in north-east Ireland, was indicated as being very close in character to the previously-defined Group I axe source area in west Cornwall. The full implications of this study cannot be understood until comparable work is done on the Cornish series of axes and sources, and the previously defined groupings of 'Cornish' axes elsewhere in Britain. However, the likelihood remains that again, the phenomenon of axe-producing areas also being recipients of axes from other producing areas is in operation here. That the ISAP studies suggest this also obtains for Pembrokeshire axes adds further strength to the case. Petrological and petrographic study of three spotted dolerite axes from Lambay (a source location for porphyritic andesite) indicated a likelihood of a doleritic source close to the Preseli mountains, although no exact

match was found with the Group XIII source reference material (Cooney and Mandal 1995, 973).

Axe 'hoards'

One of the most dramatic images published in recent years has been of the group of porcellanite axes from 'Danesfort', Malone Road, Belfast (Sheridan *et al.* 1992, Plate 20a; Bradley and Edmonds 1993, 47, Plate 3.1). This is due to the large number of axes present (19 found at various times between 1869 and 1918) and perhaps their generally large size and high degree of polish. However, in light of discussion about the forms of Cumbrian axes above, perhaps at least as significant is the inclusion of numbers of examples of specifically different morphological classes. This, and the presence of 'non-axe' stone items and materials, is a recurrent feature of the large groupings of axes referred to in the literature as 'hoards'.

The discovery of stone axes in hoards occurs across north-west Europe. For instance, they are found in small groups in Brittany (Bradley 1998, 51), and in similar locations to later finds of copper axes in Scandinavia

(Bradley 1998, 64). Explanations for the deposition of axes in groups goes back at least to Armstrong's survey of associated finds of axes (1918; quoted in Sheridan *et al.* 1992). These explanations include caches, manufacturer's hoards, and votive deposits, and most frequently of course, trader's stock (Cummins 1979). From the limited evidence of multiple stone axe finds in Ireland, it was concluded that it is difficult to distinguish caches from votive deposits (Sheridan *et al.* 1992, 395). However, several deliberate deposits were noted, including the 'Danesfort' finds, a group of finely polished axes from a bog near Oughterard, County Galway, and a flint group from the socket of a forecourt orthostat of a court tomb at Ballyalton, County Down. Among manufacturer's hoards, groups of roughouts have been noted at various locations, but a celebrated example from Ireland was the find of a group of axes at Culbane, County Derry, in apparent close association with a grinding stone.

There exist a variety of practical, economic, votive and otherwise intentional reasons for placing artefacts of particular kinds in multiples together in the ground and sometimes with other items, at different junctures in prehistory (Bradley 1998, 23–41). It is perhaps instructive that in his review of the Scandinavian and Breton evidence for finds contexts of axes, however, Bradley adduced no single mechanism for hoarding. Moreover, having constructed an elaborate narrative for the changing contexts of deposition of exchanged axes in the British Isles, Bradley appeared deliberately to avoid specific interpretation of the phenomenon (Bradley 1998, 64–75).

Part of the problem here is perhaps a failure so far to attempt to characterise the hoards themselves as deliberate assemblages of items. In reference to hoards of Bronze Age metalwork in Scandinavia, it has been suggested that contrasts were being made between exotic and locally produced items, between unique and standard items, and between material associated with men and with women (Sørensen 1987). In the case of groups of axes and other material, distinctions exist between deliberately contrasting forms and numbers of axes of similar form. To take the 'Danesfort' example, among the 19 items, only one is routinely distinguished for its narrow form, as a 'chisel'. However, far from formal variation being continuous among the remaining 18, there is a group with broader, flatter blades (and other co-variant attributes), a group with markedly shorter, narrower blades, and a group roughly between these two featuring similar attributes to the first group, but being smaller in size. Regardless of the context of deposition, it seems likely that these represent a series that embodied specific exchange values and were the subject of deliberate transport as a group.

This extends to the discovery of groups of flint axes along with other flint objects, as at Auchenhoan, near Campbeltown in Argyll (Saville 1999; Sheridan 1992). Here, five elaborately worked flint axes were found only 500m from the present shoreline. Most significantly, they were found along with two bifacial preforms and 171 flint flakes (Saville 1999, 85). Much of the focus regarding the Auchenhoan case has been on the nature of the apparently unused flakes, and the suggestion that the group therefore represents goods for practical use, in transit (Saville 1999, 108–10). This accords well with the view that buried flintwork found in groups represents a deliberate storage of valued goods in a safe repository below ground (Pitts 1996, 340). This may well be, but it does not mean that these 'caches' are necessarily therefore the stock of a flintworking (or for that matter, stoneworking) trader.

One attribute of the Auchenhoan axes that has not been remarked upon is the size-grading, which interestingly in some degree mirrors that of the 'Danesfort' group. So, among these flint axes deposited in Kintyre, the largest axe and the smallest share some shape characteristics and not others: and in this respect they are like the Malone Road, Belfast, porcellanite ones. Meanwhile, the other three have a more elongated and largely parallel-sided shape (as do the majority of the 'Danesfort' ones). Such similarities may be coincidental, but this observation does raise the possibility that systematic type selection was a regular feature of the *exchange* of groups of axes.

As to why 'hoards' were buried in such coastal locations (cases are known from Cumbria and Wales as well as Scotland and Ireland), other possibilities should be entertained. Some reasons can be adduced that relate to the operation of exchange networks that moved items in groups, perhaps as part of specific exchange voyages. For instance, the 'caching' of objects could represent the temporary removal of items from exchange networks. Or indeed the intent may have been the safe-keeping of items and groups in preparation for the 'next' round of exchanges that, by definition, did not then occur.

Perforated axe-heads

The form and distribution of perforated axe-heads has attracted notice in the past, especially concerning the two kinds of perforation – near the butt and in the centre of the axes in question – and the potential significance of their contrasting distribution (Bradley 1990). In both cases, it is interesting how the perforations have been interpreted. Firstly, it has been assumed that their similarity to maceheads renders them a late Neolithic phenomenon. Secondly, it has been inferred that the perforations were a secondary phenomenon, and moreover that they represent modifications of axes after they had reached the area that they had travelled to from their source locations (Bradley and Edmonds 1993, 189).

It is of interest to note that, of the four butt-perforated axes identified, the two jadeite examples were found in south Dorset, perhaps near the point where they entered Britain, and the two Langdale examples were found in Perthshire and Norfolk, respectively (Fig. 17.6). In the case of the jadeite axes, therefore, presumably long-

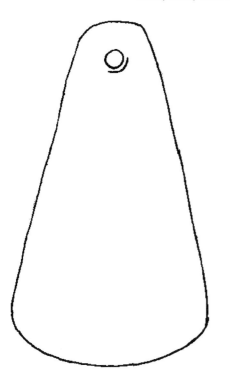

Figure 17.6. *Cumbrian perforated axe found at Cargill, Perthshire. NMS af 408.*

distance (and at least in part, sea-borne) exchange is implicated. Meanwhile, it is perhaps significant in light of the above discussion about axes from one source area 'attracted' to another, that both Perthshire and Norfolk were axe-producing areas.

This is yet more pronounced in the case of the axes with perforations at or near the centre of their blades. The seven examples of perforated Cumbrian axes are found in eastern England, spreading down into Norfolk again. Meanwhile almost all the other examples are Cornish gabbroic axes. The latter comprise one example from Devon, and the rest in a north-east trending pattern with again a concentration in eastern England. The assumption about the date of these centre-perforated axes and the secondary nature of the hole-drilling has led in turn to a further inference. This is that, because 'some of these well-travelled artefacts were converted into locally appropriate forms', the status of non-flint axes was being called into question in this late period (Bradley and Edmonds 1993, 189). The 'locally appropriate forms' were thought to be personal ornaments in the case of the butt-perforated examples, and maceheads in the case of the centre-perforated ones.

Our Melanesian cases, however, should perhaps lead us to question these assumptions. Most particularly, no-one has yet actually established (other than by analogy with maceheads), what the perforations are telling us. It is certainly true that, once the axe-blades had centre perforations, they were rendered useless as woodworking tools. But it has to be borne in mind, that, quite probably, many of these objects never were intended as such anyway. What if the perforations were intended solely to enable the axes to be used as key components of otherwise *composite* exchange items? Realisation of such a possibility potentially transforms our understanding of how these objects were used within local systems, but there remains a problem. This is the apparent absence of perforated axes from the source areas around the Irish Sea. However, at least five examples of perforated axes are known from Ireland (Sheridan *et al.* 1992, 398). The one from Portrush, Antrim, intriguingly has a perforation near its cutting edge. This is clearly very close indeed to the porcellanite sources and has a coastal location. Moreover, the location of the perforation rules out use both as a macehead, and quite probably also, as an ornament.

Some implications

Together with the coastal location of many groups of axes around the Irish Sea, we have noted that there is scope to consider ways in which axes singly, in groups, and associated with other items, could have existed within a network of deliberate movement. While the details of the pattern of exchanges implicated in such co-presences of axes cannot be reconstructed closely, I think that we are here in similar social territory as the *kula*. Here is an extended network of contact that moves material between key locales, and renders the 'source' areas not simply centres of supply, but as nodal points within an exchange system.

What we do not have so far very clearly is an indication of the kinds of materials that could have journeyed along with axes. There is no shortage of candidates, however. For smaller items whose numerical presence could have been substantial, we have noted that there are worked flint items. In some areas, pitchstone implements, with source locations on the west coast of the Isle of Arran, and that appear on many sites around the littoral, can also have moved in this way (Derek Simpson *pers. comm.*). For food items, there is the grain that appears to have been bulked at key locations, in Scotland at least in the 'lodges' now attested both at Balbrinie on Deeside and at Claish Farm, Perthshire (Barclay *et al.* 2002). These are of course very much on the north-east 'trail' of the north-eastwards distribution of porcellanite axes from Ireland.

The materiality of the *kula* and the shape of axes: further insights

There are two further aspects of the materiality of the *kula* shell valuables that were not explored in any depth until recently. The first was the variability that exists in the forms of the key exchanged shell ornaments. For example, the shape of many of the individual elements, and their position within the composite item, evokes and records both their history and their individual identity. It is precisely this individuation that enables them to be recognised and which also reinforces the sense of their possession of a biography. Like people, this biography 'contains' the memory of associations with other people. So for the shell valuables, this memory is referenced both to people and to the history of exchange with other valuables.

In this light it is surprising that in studies of the movement of axes across Neolithic Britain so little attention has been paid to the optimal characteristics of axes as exchange items. Their capacity for fulfilling both functional and aesthetic requirements is a good starting-point, but the 'satisfactory' and connotative nature of their form was perhaps equally central. However, perhaps the most useful characteristic they shared was the scope they had for almost infinite but yet subtle variability. It was precisely this characteristic that appears to have secured supremacy for the shell valuables within the *kula* system. That stone axes had great metaphorical and allusive resonances in Neolithic Britain can hardly be doubted. One of the particular references that they carried may have involved their generalised seed-like shape. Perhaps both this shape, and the sometimes prodigious quantities of axes that were produced, evoked the qualities of seed in generating and regenerating life. There was certainly an attachment to the generalised form across many generations, and to the traditions of variation based upon alternative ways of working the same material, and persistent ways of producing key attributes (witness the side-facets of the Cumbrian axes).

The rich ethnography of the Massim of Melanesia nonetheless provides another twist here, concerning how axes themselves are conceptualised in at least one place. On Sabarl island, axes are constituted as a rich field for metaphorical expression and action (Battaglia 1983; 1990). Their form and hafting are expressive of individual social being, and of social relations and obligations. They evoke conditions, including productivity, reproductivity, and death. They allude to the movement of wealth within and between social entities. And they are central to rituals associated with both exchange and mortuary rituals. These manipulations of axes express the articulation of the kinship links and the agency of both living and newly deceased individuals. In turn the axes are themselves individuated as agents and as metaphoric persons.

In the context of understanding the dynamic field for symbolism contained within axes as composite items and individuated forms, the recent formal studies undertaken within ISAP take on a greater importance than simply for their linkages to source analyses. They can be seen to open up further possibilities for discrimination among the properties of individual axes (witness the morph-ological 'syntax' revealed in the study of fine attributes:

Cooney and Mandal 1998, 14–25, 44–51). In turn, this conjures the prospect of our eventually being able to reveal the faint outlines of a rich geography of social ties that bound the peoples of the Irish Sea area, and beyond, into a living cultural world.

Such ties would have been dissolved as well as created. This is perhaps where a more sophisticated understanding of some of the circumstances of deposition can be reached. For instance, it represents something of a paradox that, while some axes are found individually or in groups, only fragments of other axes are found, apparently deliberately broken and deposited. Such deposits are especially well documented so far in southern Britain, in causewayed enclosures (Oswald et al. 2001). The studies of the *kula* might be used to suggest that, while some items are in some terms inalienable, some aspects of linkage can be dissolved, perhaps to maintain a particular direction of contact within the wider exchange system. What better way to effect such a dissolution could be found, than through the fragmentation and burial (and thereby perhaps symbolic 're-seeding') of the 'person' of the axe in an exchange location?

The gift of axes and the nature of what was 'good to think'

It would of course be possible to return simply to Clark's (1965) ethnographic insights about Neolithic axes, and to suggest that they constituted bride-wealth payments or some such particular exchange medium. Or it might be possible to construct a more elaborate model, and to attempt to explain the current Irish Sea patterns of distribution in terms of Britain's own early *kula*. This is not however an issue of the appropriateness or otherwise of the use of ethnographic analogy. What I have instead tried to do here is to sketch out the need for an approach to the study of axes that sees the variability of key items as a matter of deliberate significance in the world of Neolithic Britain. Most prehistorians today agree that axes were an important item in the Neolithic, and that they were bound up in patterns of exchange. Yet the axes themselves have tended to be regarded simply as the 'dye in the water' that makes those patterns visible. Attention needs rather to be directed to the pattern of individuation of items, and the way that each of their associations has lent further discrimination to their 'context'. This context includes reference to the people behind the objects. Anthropologists have eventually understood the significance of the representation of the 'distributed person' (Strathern 1988). This is maintained and developed in part through the projection of the essence of certain individuals via the proxy of objects evoking their being, but at a distance. I have termed this practice 'presencing', and have related it to archaeological contexts through the use of material items to convey complex allusions evoking not only persons but even whole mythic histories and associations. Moreover, it is the relatively powerless as well as the powerful people in society who can manipulate presence and association through material culture and choreographies in this way (Ray 1987).

In the case of axes in Neolithic Britain, if a series of exchange practices are implicated in the apparent mobility of these and other items, the question of the longevity of such practices, and changes occurring across hundreds of years must be considered. Throughout this paper I have discussed axes and their finds contexts as if they were to all intents contemporary. The longevity of the different forms was no doubt variable, and we now know that the quarried sources became fewer and yet more abundant (Bradley and Edmonds 1993). The detailed field research of the late 1980s in Great Langdale in Cumbria indicated also the likelihood that the extraction process became more highly ritualised, dangerous and restricted in scope through time.

What sustains or disrupts exchange practices in such circumstances? The engine and motive for the sustenance of the Melanesian *kula* and inter-group exchange appears to have been varied. It included the 'biographical' incentive to aggrandisement and competition among individuals (Leach 1983). There appears also to have been long-term inter-group rivalry based upon access to resources, and the motivation of specialised producers to acquire goods through the manufacture and exchange of pots (Irwin 1983). However, I think that it has to be accepted that once a series of practices as intricate as these emerge, and myths form that 'explain' their existence, they can become deeply embedded. The role assumed by key items can become symbolically pivotal, as the case of the Sabarl axe noted above illustrates.

I have proposed therefore that some items are manipulated within such exchange systems because they have become 'good to think'. But there is clearly an extent to which 'good to think' is a time-dependent thing. It may be that the instability of the Neolithic 'axe trade' in Britain arose precisely because a generalised pattern of exchange was replaced by a more 'brittle' focus on only a few sources and the prestige accumulation of only certain types of object.

Important though such chronological resolution is, it is the mobility of axes in the British Isles and specifically Irish Sea Neolithic context that is such an outstanding phenomenon. Axes travelled. And, as in the seas of western Melanesia, it is most likely that a significant element of such travel was undertaken by canoe – or, in this setting, we should say, curragh. By comparison with the western Pacific Ocean case, the sea journeys involved were quite possibly short, although the presence of coastal caches in the Western Isles (Saville 1999) should warn us against assuming that a 'shortest crossing' principle determined the extent of voyaging.

The idea of an 'Irish Sea Zone' in the Neolithic is probably no more sustainable than the idea of a similar unified sphere in the Iron Age (Thomas 1972). The regions such a 'zone' encompasses clearly present as many contrasts as parallels. Nonetheless, it is the only large area of sea in Britain that it is possible to comprehend as a bounded entity visually (that is, not just from a map), and to experience specifically as being land-girt. So not only famously from Man, from the mountains of Cumbria or of Mourne, but also from Galloway, from Snowdonia and from the Preselis, it is possible to see the glassy surface of the sea rimmed with land (see Cummings this volume). As such, this land-fringed sea provided the would-be 'Argonauts' of the Neolithic with much the same kinds of opportunities as those grasped by the Trobriand Islanders of the Pacific. Not only were there opportunities to engage in long-distance exchange as such, but they could also develop a supra-regional network of social relations. Perhaps it was a growing awareness of the scope for aggrandisement of key individuals within and beyond this Irish Sea area (and taking in also at least north-east Scotland, north-east Yorkshire and Norfolk) that helped to stimulate the increased volume of specialised production of axes in the later Neolithic. Yet it was in this sense of a shared world of sea-based contact that the connections may have made themselves felt most directly to these Neolithic communities. In this context, we can envisage the possibility that it would not only have been the axes, but also the Irish Sea itself that became, for these people, 'good to think'.

Acknowledgements

I would like to thank the organisers of the meeting, and the editors of the present volume, Vicki Cummings and Chris Fowler, for their patience and their continuing interest in my work. A number of the contributors have generously shared perceptions and provided information. I thank in particular, Gabriel Cooney, Gordon Barclay and Derek Simpson. I also wish to thank Rob Ixer for information about recent provenancing research in England.

References

Barclay, G.J., Brophy, K., and MacGregor, G. 2002. A Neolithic building at Claish Farm, near Callander, Stirling Council, Scotland, UK. *Antiquity* 76, 23–4.

Battaglia, D. 1983. Projecting personhood in Melanesia: the dialectics of artefact symbolism on Sabarl island. *Man* 18, 289–304.

Battaglia, D. 1990. *On the bones of the serpent: person, memory and mortality in Sabarl Island society*. Chicago: University of Chicago Press.

Briggs, S. 1976. Notes on the distribution of some raw materials in later prehistoric Britain. In C. Burgess and R. Miket (eds), *Settlement and economy in the third and second millennia BC*, 267–82. Oxford: British Archaeological Reports British Series 33.

Berridge, P. 1994. Cornish axe factories: fact or fiction? In N. Ashton and A. David (eds), *Stories in stone*, 45–56. London: Lithic Studies Society Occasional Paper No. 4.

Bradley, R. 1990. Perforated stone axe-heads in the British Neolithic: their distribution and significance. *Oxford Journal of Archaeology* 9, 299–304.

Bradley, R. 1998. *The passage of arms: an archaeological analysis of prehistoric hoard and votive deposits.* Oxford: Oxbow Books.

Bradley, R. and Edmonds, M. 1993. *Interpreting the axe trade: production and exchange in Neolithic Britain.* Cambridge: Cambridge University Press.

Campbell, S.F. 1983a. Kula in Vakuta: the mechanics of keda. In J.W. Leach and E. Leach (eds), *The Kula: new perspectives on Massim exchange,* 201–27. Cambridge: Cambridge University Press.

Campbell, S.F. 1983b. Attaining rank: a classification of *kula* shell valuables. In J.W. Leach and E. Leach (eds), *The Kula: new perspectives on Massim exchange,* 229–48. Cambridge: Cambridge University Press.

Chappell, S. 1987. *Stone axe morphology and distribution in Neolithic Britain.* Oxford: British Archaeological Reports British Series 177.

Clark, J.D.G. 1940. *Prehistoric England.* London: Batsford.

Clark, J.D.G. 1965. Traffic in stone axes and axe blades. *Economic History Review* 18, 1–28

Clough T.H. and Cummins, W. A. (eds) 1979. *Stone axe studies.* London: Council for British Archaeology.

Clough T.H. and Cummins, W. A. (eds) 1983. *Stone axe studies, volume 2.* London: Council for British Archaeology.

Coles, J. 1973. *Archaeology by experiment.* London: Hutchinson

Cooney, G. 1996. Lambay Island. In I. Bennett (ed.), *Excavations 1995,* 25–6. Dublin: Wordwell.

Cooney, G., Byrnes, E. and Mandal, S. 1998. Case study: Group VI axes in Ireland. In G. Cooney and S. Mandal, *The Irish stone axe project, monograph I,* 111–73. Dublin: Wordwell.

Cooney, G. and Mandal, S. 1995. Getting to the core of the problem: petrological results from the Irish stone axe project. *Antiquity* 69, 969–80.

Cooney G. and Mandal, S. 1998. *The Irish stone axe project, monograph I.* Dublin: Wordwell.

Darvill, T. 1989. The circulation of Neolithic stone and flint axes: a case study from Wales and the mid-west of England. *Proceedings of the Prehistoric Society* 55, 27–43.

Edmonds, M. R. 1993 Interpreting causewayed enclosures in the past and the present. In C. Tilley (ed.), *Interpretative archaeology,* 99–142. Oxford: Berg.

Fowler, P. J. 1983. *The farming of prehistoric Britain.* Cambridge: Cambridge University Press.

Gearey, B. and Charman, D. 1996. Rough Tor, Bodmin Moor: testing some archaeological hypotheses with landscape scale palynology. In D. Charman, R. Newnham and D. Croot (eds), *The quaternary of Devon and east Cornwall: field guide,* 101–19. London. Quaternary Studies Association.

Hodder, I. R. and Lane, P. 1982. A contextual examination of Neolithic axe distribution in England. In J. Ericson and T. Earle (eds), *Contexts for prehistoric exchange,* 213–35. London: Academic Press.

Houlder, C. 1976. Stone axes and henge monuments. In G. Boon and J. Lewis (eds), *Welsh antiquity,* 55–62. Cardiff: National Museum of Wales.

Irwin, G. J. 1983. Chieftainship, kula and trade in Massim prehistory. In J.W. Leach and E. Leach (eds), *The Kula: new perspectives on Massim exchange,* 29–72. Cambridge: Cambridge University Press.

Ixer, R.A., Williams-Thorpe, O., Bevins, R.E. and Chambers, A.D. Forthcoming. A comparison between 'total petrography' and geochemistry using portable X-ray flourescence as provenancing tools for some Midlands axe-heads. In E. Walker, F.F. Wenban-Smith, and F. Healey (eds), *Lithics in action: papers from the lithics studies in the year 2000 conference.* London: Lithics Study Society.

Leach, J.W. 1983. Introduction. In J.W. Leach and E. Leach (eds), *The Kula: new perspectives on Massim exchange,* 1–26. Cambridge: Cambridge University Press.

Leach, J.W., and Leach, E. (eds) 1983. *The Kula: new perspectives on Massim exchange.* Cambridge: Cambridge University Press.

Malinowski, B. 1922. *Argonauts of the Western Pacific: an account of native enterprise and adventure in the archipelagoes of Melanesian New Guinea.* London: Routledge and Kegan Paul.

Mandal, S. 1997. Striking the balance: the roles of petrography and geochemistry in stone axe studies in Ireland. *Archaeometry* 39, 289–308.

Mandal, S., Cooney, G., Meighan, I.G. and Jamieson, D.D. 1997. Using geochemistry to interpret porcellanite stone axe production in Ireland. *Journal of Archaeological Science* 24, 757–63.

Munn, N.D. 1983. Gawan kula: spatiotemporal control and the symbolism of influence. In J.W. Leach and E. Leach (eds), *The Kula: new perspectives on Massim exchange,* 277–308. Cambridge: Cambridge University Press.

Oswald, A., Dyer C. and Barber, M. 2001. *The creation of monuments: Neolithic causewayed enclosures in the British Isles.* London: English Heritage.

Pitts, M. 1996. The stone axe in Neolithic Britain. *Proceedings of the Prehistoric Society* 62, 311–71.

Pryor, F. 1998. *Etton: excavations at a Neolithic causewayed enclosure near Maxey, Cambridgeshire, 1982–7.* London: English Heritage.

Rackham, O. 1986. *The history of the countryside.* London: Dent.

Ray, K. 1987. Material metaphor, social interaction and historical reconstructions: exploring patterns of association and symbolism in the Igbo-Ukwu corpus. In I. Hodder (ed.), *The archaeology of contextual meanings,* 66–77. Cambridge: Cambridge University Press.

Saville, A. 1994. Exploitation of lithic resources for stone tools in earlier prehistoric Scotland. In N. Ashton and A. David (eds), *Stories in stone,* 57–70. London: Lithic Studies Society.

Saville, A. 1999 A cache of flint axeheads and other flint artefacts from Auchenhoan, near Campbeltown, Kintyre, Scotland *Proceedings of the Prehistoric Society* 65, 83–123.

Sheridan, A. 1992. Scottish stone axeheads: some new work and recent discoveries. In N. Sharples and A. Sheridan (eds), *Vessels for the ancestors: essays on the Neolithic of Britain and Ireland,* 194–212. Edinburgh: Edinburgh University Press.

Sheridan, A., Cooney, G. and Grogan, E. 1992 Stone axe studies in Ireland. *Proceedings of the Prehistoric Society* 58, 389–416.

Sorensen, M.L.S. 1987. Material order and cultural classification: the role of bronze objects in the transition from the Bronze Age to the Iron Age in Scandinavia. In I. Hodder (ed.), *The archaeology of contextual meanings*, 90–101. Cambridge: Cambridge University Press.

Tambiah, S. 1969 'Animals are good to think and good to prohibit'. *Ethnology* 8, 424–59.

Taylor, M. 1998. Wood and bark from the enclosure ditch. In F. Pryor, *Etton: excavations at a Neolithic causewayed enclosure near Maxey, Cambridgeshire, 1982–7*, 115–59. London: English Heritage.

Thomas, C. (ed.) 1972. *The Iron Age in the Irish Sea province*. London: Council for British Archaeology.

Thomas, J. 1999. *Understanding the Neolithic*. London: Routledge.

18   Materiality and traditions of practice in Neolithic south-west Scotland

Julian Thomas

Introduction: from domination to implication

Over the past two decades, archaeologists' conceptions of the stone and earth monuments of the European Neolithic have changed in important ways. However, some of these changes have been gradual and incremental, and not always easy to identify. This is perhaps because the debate on monumentality has not been characterised by polarised schools of thought, or by the radical critique of one community of scholars by another. Instead, new ideas and new evidence have slowly been assimilated, and particular authors have repeatedly revised their own arguments. One consequence of this process of revision and reformulation is that it is important to periodically stand back and question whether all of the concepts and language that we employ in discussing prehistoric monuments are still adequate. In this contribution I want to critically evaluate the notion of 'monumental tradition'. We still routinely talk about 'traditions of monument-building', but it may be that by now this locution is poorly matched with our broader understanding of Neolithic monumental architecture.

The initial recognition of monumentality as a significant phenomenon worthy of study in its own right can be attributed to a number of papers published in the 1970s which sought to generalise about the social role of monument-building (Cherry 1978; Renfrew 1973). However, in these arguments monuments were presented as the correlates or symptoms of particular social processes, whether political centralisation or the status-building activities of social elites. It was not until the early 1980s that the materiality of prehistoric monuments was directly addressed, in terms that explicitly evoked the contemporary reconceptualisation of material culture (Bradley 1984; Shennan 1983). Rather than representing the material manifestation of a certain form of social organisation, monuments were presented as being in some senses 'active', capable of causing effects in the human world. In particular, it was pointed out that structures like megalithic tombs and cursus monuments were at once massively large and supremely durable (Bradley 1984, 61). Consequentially, they might be expected to

continue to exert an influence over the ways in which landscapes were inhabited and understood for generations after their construction.

This conception of monuments as dominant presences in the landscape was a fruitful new departure, and opened the way for a consideration of the experience of architecture and landscape by embodied human subjects (e.g. Barrett 1994; Tilley 1994). But at the same time the implied message that monuments represent a form of material culture suggested that they were simply objects, 'non-portable artefacts', imposed upon and opposed to the landscape. This reading of monumentality is one that construes architecture as 'culture', quite distinct from the 'nature' that surrounds it. In other words, human labour takes a series of raw materials from the world (earth, stone, timber, clay) and transforms them into something utterly different, which stands in opposition to the natural realm. This is broadly what Tim Ingold refers to as 'the building perspective', a modernist western outlook which presumes that meaning is introduced into the world by human action (Ingold 1993). As long as prehistoric monuments could still be seen as isolated and bounded entities that stood apart from the landscapes onto which they had been imposed it remained possible to discuss them as abstract forms. That is, they could be considered in isolation from their physical or topographic context, and arranged into typological systems or developmental sequences, just as readily as if they had been palstaves or pots. In this sense, the prehistoric archaeology of the 1980s had still not definitively broken with Grimes' 'devolutional' sequence of Cotsword-Severn tombs or the Piggotts' and Atkinson's division of henge monuments into a series of 'classes' (Atkinson 1951; Grimes 1960, 90–101; Piggott and Piggott 1939).

The element that needed to be relinquished before a more radical view of Neolithic monuments could be achieved was the productionist metaphysics that drew an absolute distinction between things that had been 'made' and the natural world. This is all the more difficult to do in relation to monuments because one of their most distinctive characteristics is the vast quantity of labour that has been invested in them. They appear pre-eminently to be the products of human creative agency. Yet this view is implicitly challenged by Chris Tilley's study of the prehistoric landscape of Bodmin Moor, which focuses on funerary monuments and stone circles but also addresses the stone tors of the moor. Tilley concludes that these natural features would have been significant to Neolithic communities, representing 'non-domesticated megaliths' (Tilley 1996, 165). Perhaps they were understood as having been created by spirits, deities, giants or ancestors, and indeed the kind of cosmology that lays much stress on origin myths begins to erode any distinction between landscape features that were built by humans and the 'natural' topography. Furthermore, it is conceivable that some Neolithic monuments were themselves eventually attributed to supernatural agencies.

Tilley's argument rests on the proposition that the rocks from which megalithic chambers and stone circles were constructed would have been understood as possessing an inherent power, which was merely appropriated or redirected through the act of building. This suggests that archaeologists might need to pay more attention to the substances and materials from which monuments were made. In a similar way, Colin Richards (1996, 331) drew attention to the architecture of henges, suggesting that their ditches and banks embodied the relationship between water and hills, thereby representing a microcosm of their surrounding landscapes. Just as portable artefacts in the Neolithic were not so much alienated commodities as things that were embedded in flows of substance that linked persons, places and abstract ideas (Thomas 1999a), so monuments were combinations of significant materials which brought together meanings that were well established before any event of construction. As Kenny Brophy points out in the case of cursus monuments, a monumental structure can enclose space, but it also does a great deal more through the way that it re-orders a set of materials into a specific relationship with hills, streams, rivers and woodland (Brophy 2000, 68). This suggests that our efforts to typologise Neolithic architecture obscure as much as they enlighten, neglecting both the materiality of built structures and the contextual topographic relationships which contributed so much to their meaning.

Recently, Aaron Watson has discussed the monumental complex of Avebury in north Wiltshire in very much these terms (Watson 2001, 304). Watson draws attention to some very particular aspects of the way that the Avebury henge fits into the immediate topography: how three of the entrances are lower than the central area of the enclosure, and the way in which the surrounding hills 'substitute' for the bank at certain places in the interior, for instance. This indicates that the builders must have had a detailed and intimate knowledge of the landscape, rather than simply imposing a complex geometric design onto a more-or-less flat space in an arbitrary way. Watson also argues that the stones that make up the great circles at Avebury might themselves have possessed histories of their own, just as some of the orthostats of the West Kennet long barrow had demonstrably been used as axe-

grinders before they were incorporated into the tomb. Suggesting that the choice of constructional elements and location might have been governed by imperatives that were broadly aesthetic, Watson uses the term 'composition' to cover the processes of selection and building. We might equally describe monument-building as a kind of *collage* or *montage* in which materials, substances, people, animals, plants and places, and their meanings, were brought together and new relationships between them were forged. Neolithic monuments made use of materials that would have been familiar, including undressed stones, tree-trunks and masses of subsoil, but combined them together in configurations that were unfamiliar. As Victor Turner (1969, 39) once argued, the essence of ritual practice lies in bringing a range of materials which represent the world together in a single place so that they can be manipulated and re-ordered. We might say, then, that the building of monuments in the Neolithic was itself a form of ritual, which involved a kind of 'cosmological engineering' (Thomas 1999b, 46). In building their enclosures and tombs, Neolithic people were re-constructing the world itself.

Traditions of practice

Clearly, we have come a long way in the past twenty years, from built objects that dominate their surroundings to an architectural practice that is implicated in the relationships that make up a landscape and partakes of the materiality of place. Indeed, the very notion of an 'archaeology of natural places' (Bradley 2000) is one that would scarcely have been conceivable until recently. But as I have already suggested, these changes require us to reconsider other aspects of the way in which we conventionally address the Neolithic. In particular, the concept of *tradition* is one that now requires some re-evaluation. Very often, when the word is used in archaeology today it is employed as a placeholder for more obviously contentious terms like 'culture' or 'culture group'. It is interesting that while processual archaeology has had only the most limited influence on the study of the British Neolithic, largely restricted to matters of methodology, quantification and sampling (as opposed to explanation), culture-history continues to exercise a potent and malign force. So when we talk about 'the Peterborough tradition', or 'the Cotswold-Severn tradition', we implicitly smuggle much of the baggage of culture-history back into our archaeology. That is to say, we relax into the comforting belief that the outward morphology of structures and artefacts can be used as the basis for ordering them according to typology, because similarities of form can ultimately be attributed to cognitive templates or shared cultural norms. These norms generate material culture variation, so that each material thing is understood as the more or less perfect manifestation of a kind of Platonic ideal that precedes its instantiation. I would like to suggest that we could more profitably think about tradition in terms of *what people do*: ways in which human beings engage with the material world. The traditions that human communities hand down from generation to generation are sets of practices, rather than abstract forms.

These issues have proved to be of critical importance to a field project that the author has conducted in the south-west of Scotland over the past eight years, investigating a number of Neolithic ceremonial monuments. These have included the henge at the Pict's Knowe, Dumfries (Thomas 1999c; 2001), the cursus monuments at Holywood (Thomas *et al.* 1999), and the post alignments at Holm Farm (Thomas 2000). The results of this work have been clarified and brought into focus by the findings of the most recent phase of the project, which has been concerned with the excavation of a complex of monumental structures at Dunragit, south of Stranraer in western Galloway. At Dunragit there is the unusual combination of a post-defined cursus of early Neolithic date, and a later Neolithic palisaded enclosure (Figs 18.1 and 18.2). The enclosure is itself a multi-phase structure, composed of a free-standing timber circle, which was renewed on at least one occasion, surrounded by two rings of palisade composed of large posts interspersed with smaller uprights, the larger ring being around 300 metres in diameter. These two palisade rings may not be contemporary, for they have entrance structures that do not respect each other. The massive entrance passageway connected with the middle palisade ring aligns on a very large earthen mound at Droughduil, 400 metres to the south. While the mound has been recorded as a medieval motte, it is arguable that it is more comparable with prehistoric mounds like Silbury Hill and the Conquer Barrow, both of which are associated with later Neolithic enclosures.

The Dunragit complex, and other Neolithic monuments in the south-west of Scotland, demonstrate the virtue of turning away from a morphological classification of sites in favour of a focus on their materiality, and the ways in which they were built, used and destroyed. This can be achieved by comparing three sets of structures that were materially different from each other, and which as a consequence had different *temporal* structures. In this respect, Dumfries and Galloway is a particularly interesting area: it contains megalithic chambered tombs, timber monuments that have been deliberately burned down, and timber monuments that have been allowed to decay. My suggestion is that each of these ways of building and using monumental structures implies a different kind of relationship between the human community and its past. In this respect my argument draws on Paul Connerton's insight that social memory can be sustained both through recollection and through bodily performance, especially ceremonial performances that commemorate past events or persons (Connerton 1989, 72). Monuments, as mnemonic objects and as the stages or

settings for embodied ritual action, are potentially instrumental in both of these kinds of remembering.

Monumental materialities in SW Scotland

Megalithic tombs, for instance, had a very particular temporal character in which episodes of construction were followed by long periods of relative changelessness, and this is demonstrably the case amongst the long cairns of Dumfries and Galloway. Structures like the Mid Gleniron cairns (Fig. 18.3) were multi-phase, with initial, smaller monuments encapsulated in subsequent larger mounds (Corcoran 1969, 35). Yet the consequence of this constructional accretion was that the monument became a physical reminder of the past, which existed in the present. The chambers of the first phase tombs were rendered inaccessible, but they and their contents remained a permanent material presence that would have to be accommodated by subsequent activities. Indeed, this kind of presence has the effect of both locating and orientating performative actions, at the same time rendering them significant. Both the Mid Gleniron and the Cairnholy tombs had forecourt spaces, so that performances on the part of the living, involving the lighting of fires and elaborate acts of deposition, could be conducted in relation to the remains of the dead. At Cairnholy, both tombs had chambers that were essentially closed cists (Piggott and Powell 1949, 116), so there was a strong sense of a relationship between a fixed and unchanging past, and fleeting or transitory actions in the present. The acts of the living were given their form and location by an architecture that related to the past, and the dead generations. Moreover, in its changelessness this architecture seems to demand repetition: the same acts, in the same sequence, in the same location. At the very least it facilitates the citation and reiteration of past acts (see Jones 2001, 343 on the significance of cultural citation in social reproduction). When these tombs and their forecourts were blocked, this would have amounted to a further episode of construction, which changed the conditions of performance and established a greater distance between the living and the dead. However, these clearly continued to be places of great significance, for at both Mid Gleniron and Cairnholy there was intrusive late Neolithic and Early Bronze Age pottery in the tomb chambers (Corcoran 1969, 60; Piggott and Powell 1949, 117). Megalithic tombs, then, were landmarks and places to come back to, irrespective of whether they were still in use for the deposition or processing of the remains of the dead.

These are all fairly unremarkable points, but they start to take on a greater importance when we compare them with another tradition of monument building and use. Throughout much of Scotland and northern England in the earlier Neolithic it appears to have been commonplace to build rectilinear timber structures and then to burn

***Figure 18.1.** Dunragit: structures visible on aerial photographs, showing the areas excavated 1999–2001.*

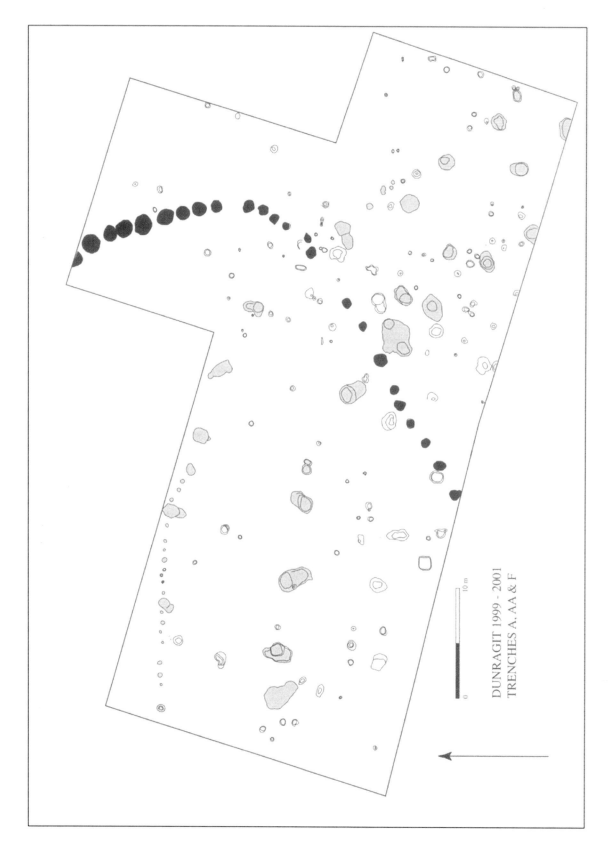

Figure 18.2. *Dunragit 1999–2001, Trenches A, AA and F, showing the post-defined cursus (in black) and the inner and middle rings of the late Neolithic enclosure (shaded).*

DUNRAGIT 1999 - 2001
TRENCHES A. AA & F

10 m

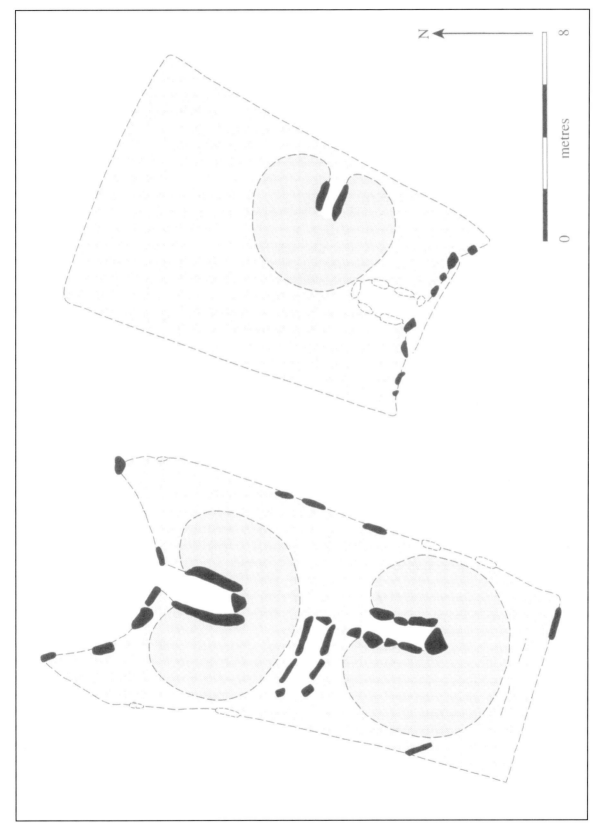

Figure 18.3. *The chambered cairns at Mid Gleniron Farm, to scale but not in their relative locations (after Corcoran 1969).*

them down. This practice applied to post-defined cursus monuments (Kendrik 1995), rectangular mortuary enclosures (Barclay and Maxwell 1991), and timber buildings (Barclay *et al.* 2002). In some cases the firing of the monument demonstrably took place soon after its construction. At the Holywood North cursus, for instance, the ditch surrounding the burnt timber structure was deliberately back-filled after no more than a single winter. This structure itself replaced and cut through the post-hole of a massive, isolated timber upright, which had also been deliberately burnt and collapsed (Thomas 2000, 81).

At Holm Farm, within a mile of Holywood, a structure composed of an avenue of posts running parallel with the River Nith and terminating in a circular enclosure of some kind (a ring-ditch or a timber circle in different phases of construction) had been burned down and rebuilt on as many as eight occasions. Some of the individual post-holes contained the burnt stumps of as many as three successive posts (Thomas 2000, 86). It appears that this structure has been created to facilitate a particular pattern of bodily movement: a procession along the course of the river, beginning or terminating in a small enclosed space. It is arguable that on each occasion that this procession took place the monument was re-constructed and then set on fire. The resulting traces of the structure on the ground amounted to a dense and initially confusing scatter of post-holes. Finally, at Dunragit the burning of the uprights of the cursus had been sufficiently intense to scorch the gravel surface around the post-holes and redden the packing-stones. Clearly, firing such a structure would involve an enormous amount of effort, as brushwood would have to be piled up around the free-standing uprights in order to make them burn at all. Indeed, in the case of thick oak posts it is possible that more than one episode of burning would have been required to char the timbers through to the core. Yet even after this it seems that the location of the Dunragit cursus was recalled after its destruction, for lines of features were later cut, continuing the alignment of the southern side of the enclosure. These included two very deep post-holes flanking a cremation deposit.

I have suggested elsewhere that it was the spectacular character of the destruction of these monuments that rendered them memorable (Thomas 2000). We might argue that given the short elapse of time between the construction and burning of each timber structure the whole process of building, use and destruction can be seen as a single continuous performance. Moreover, at each site there was an element of reiteration. The Holywood cursus was built on a site that had held a previous burnt timber structure. The Holm alignments established and then decommissioned the architecture that framed a particular pattern of human movement, over and over again. And at Dunragit the later post lines re-established the orientation of the cursus. If the megalithic tombs provided a changeless setting within which repeated bodily performances could be enacted, these

burnt timber structures, their construction and destruction, were themselves *part of* the performance, and their building and rebuilding was itself a citational or re-iterative practice that re-presented the past in the present.

Dunragit: death, decay, dilapidation and deposition

However, the later Neolithic enclosure at Dunragit, while also composed of timber uprights, had a material history that was quite different from these burnt structures. The entire edifice was constructed and then allowed to rot away without repair on two separate occasions, presumably over a period of some decades. So this was a monument that was neither stable like the megaliths, nor part of a performative episode, like the cursus. Recently, Chris Fowler (2003) has discussed the significance of decay in Neolithic societies. The rotting and corruption of human and animal bodies and foodstuffs has a tempo that meshes with the temporality of social life, embedding social rhythms in the processes of the natural world. We might go so far as to say that social relationships were naturalised through this association. If we imagine that ceremonial monuments like the Dunragit enclosure were not continuously occupied, but were returned to at intervals, then on each occasion the structure would be subtly different, as it slowly fell into dilapidation. Over time, the declining condition of the monument would serve as a reminder of its age, and encourage the re-collection of its construction and past events of use. Rot and decay come to stand as the evidence of the structure's authenticity.

Moreover, decay and dilapidation make up a continuous process that links the present with the past. This gradual decline forms a background against which other acts and events can be set. In the case of the Dunragit enclosure, the free-standing posts of the timber circle had been treated in an entirely different way from the uprights of the surrounding palisade rings. Not only had the post-holes for the post-ring been dug much larger than was strictly necessary (Fig. 18.4), representing a kind of conspicuous expenditure of effort, but in both phases of the circle some of the posts had been deliberately removed. The rocking back and forth that this had necessitated had resulted in very disrupted profiles in the post-holes. But in every case where a post had been withdrawn, some kind of deliberate deposit of cultural material had been placed in the resulting crater.

Each one of these deposits was unique and distinctive. In one case, a deposit of Beaker pottery was placed in the post-removal, while a small pit containing more Beaker sherds and a hammer-stone was dug beside the post-hole. In another, sherds of Grooved Ware and fine flint objects including an oblique arrowhead were incorporated into a mass of burnt organic material that filled the post-crater. In a third, the cremated remains of a woman and

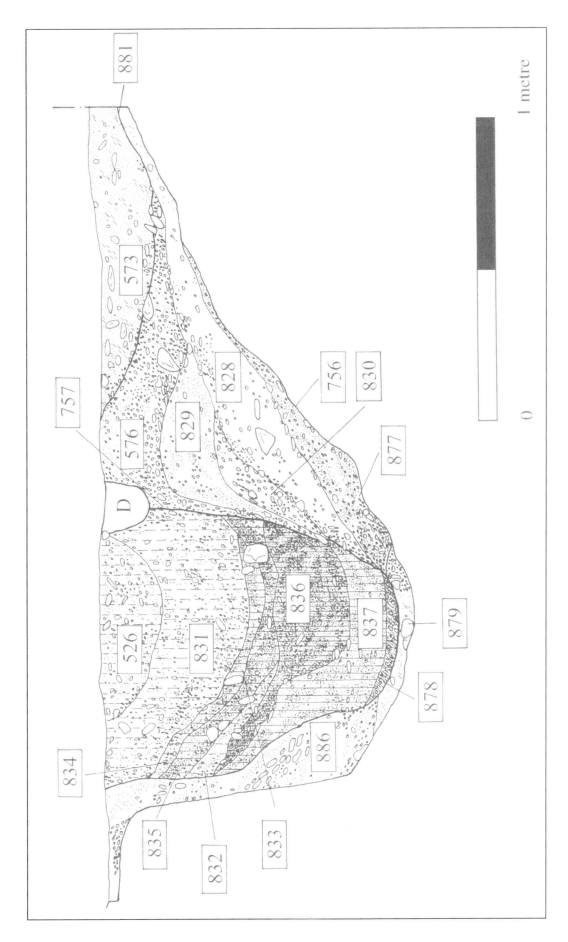

Figure 18.4. *Dunragit, Feature 879, a large post-hole of the inner post-ring, showing two distinct phases of use. 878 is the cut of the second phase of the post-hole, the fill of which is notably darker than that of the first.*

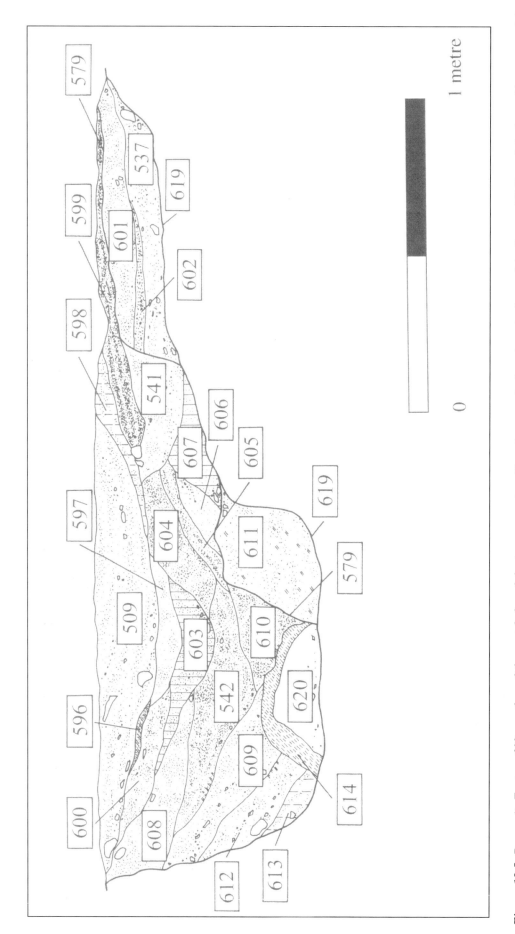

Figure 18.5. *Dunragit, Feature 619, another of the post-holes of the inner post-ring. Note the mound of sand on the base of the feature (620), and the lens of burnt material immediately above (614).*

a sheep were placed flat on the bottom of the post-removal, and the remainder of the void back-filled. Finally, one post-hole was completely cleaned out, and a small mound of clean sand placed on its base. A single sherd of early Neolithic pottery was placed on top of this, and then a mass of oak charcoal containing fragments of burnt animal bones was dumped over the top, before the whole was backfilled (Fig. 18.5).

Now, the significance of these events is that the removal of the posts formed part of the decline or decommissioning of the enclosure. They took place while the other posts were still in place but rotting away. Because only a minority of the posts were actually removed, the place where they had been would have been conspicuous as a gap in the otherwise regular arrangement of uprights in the post-ring. One paradox of the practice that we have come to describe as 'structured deposition' is that while placing an assemblage of symbolically-charged objects in the ground is a powerful means of fixing meaning in space, it leaves no physical trace. At Dunragit, the deposits that replaced the withdrawn posts were *visible in their invisibility*, for the absence of the post would serve as a reminder that some significant set of items and materials had been deposited in precisely that location. This kind of deposition, of course, is only possible in the case of a monument that has a particular temporal signature, and which falls gradually into disrepair over a period of time. It is a monument that does its work by wasting away.

Conclusion

I have argued that when we talk about 'traditions' of monumentality we should focus a little less on the forms of structures, and more on the ways in which people negotiate the material world, in building and occupying constructed spaces. I have described three different ways in which the Neolithic communities of south-west Scotland established relationships between the past and the present through monumental architecture. Stone monuments like megalithic tombs are not really timeless, but they fall into disrepair over a very long period of time, so that they still remain in the landscape today. Both for ourselves and for Neolithic people they represent the physical trace of a distant past that is nonetheless here with us in the present. Timber monuments, however, decay at a rate that is comprehensible on a human time-scale. Their decline would have been appreciated by people who visited them at intervals, and would have invited a recollection of their own past experiences. This suggests a past that is demonstrably receding from the present. In contrast, when those timber structures were not allowed to decay, but were deliberately burned, they were consigned to memory as spectacular events whose remembering at a later date would require an active 'hauling-back'. In effect, these different strategies of monumentality imply different kinds of memory-work, through which the past was inserted into the present in different ways.

References

Atkinson, R.J.C. 1951. The henge monuments of Great Britain. In R.J.C. Atkinson, C.M. Piggott and N.K. Sandars, *Excavations at Dorchester, Oxon.*, 81–107. Oxford: Ashmolean Museum.

Barclay, G.J., Brophy, K. and MacGregor, G. 2002. A Neolithic building at Claish Farm. Near Callander, Stirling Council, Scotland, UK. *Antiquity* 76, 23–4.

Barclay, G.J. and Maxwell, G.S. 1991. The excavation of a Neolithic long mortuary enclosure at Inchtuthill, Perthshire. *Proceedings of the Society of Antiquaries of Scotland* 121, 27–44.

Barrett, J.C. 1994. *Fragments from antiquity.* Oxford: Blackwell.

Bradley, R.J. 1984. Studying monuments. In R.J. Bradley and J. Gardiner (eds), *Neolithic studies: a review of some current research*, 61–6. Oxford: British Archaeological Reports 133.

Brophy, K. 2000. Water coincidence? Cursus monuments and rivers. In A. Ritchie (ed.), *Neolithic Orkney in its European context*, 59–70. Oxford: Oxbow.

Cherry, J. 1978. Generalisation and the archaeology of the state. In D. Green, C. Haselgrove and M. Spriggs (eds), *Social organisation and settlement*, 411–37. Oxford: British Archaeological Reports S47.

Connerton, P. 1989. *How societies remember.* Cambridge: Cambridge University Press.

Corcoran, J.W.X.P. 1969. Excavation of two chambered tombs at Mid Gleniron Farm, Glenluce. *Transactions of the Dumfries and Galloway Natural History and Antiquarian Society* 46, 29–90.

Fowler, C. 2003. Rates of (ex)change: decay and growth, memory and the transformation of the dead in early Neolithic southern Britain. In Williams, H. (ed.), *Archaeologies of remembrance - death and memory in past societies*, 45–63. Kluwer Academic/ Plenum Press.

Grimes, W.F. 1960. *Excavations on defence sites, vol.1 mainly Neolithic-Bronze Age.* London: Her Majesty's Stationary Office.

Ingold, T. 1993. The temporality of the landscape. *World Archaeology* 25, 152–74.

Jones, A. 2001. Drawn from memory: the archaeology of aesthetics and the aesthetics of archaeology in earlier Bronze Age Britain and the present. *World Archaeology* 33, 334–56.

Kendrik, J. 1995. Excavation of a Neolithic enclosure and an Iron Age settlement at Douglasmuir, Angus. *Proceedings of the Society of Antiquaries of Scotland* 125, 29–67.

Piggott, S. and Piggott, C.M.1939. Stone and earth circles in Dorset. *Antiquity* 13, 138–58.

Piggott, S. and Powell, T.G.E. 1949. The excavation of three Neolithic chambered tombs in Galloway, 1949. *Proceedings of the Society of Antiquaries of Scotland* 83, 103–61.

Renfrew, A.C. 1973. Monuments, mobilisation and social organisation in Neolithic Wessex. In A.C. Renfrew (ed.), *The explanation of culture change*, 539–58. London: Duckworth.

Shennan, S.J. 1983. Monuments: an example of archaeologists' approach to the massively material. *Royal Anthropological Institute Newsletter* 59, 9–11.

Richards, C.C. 1996. Henges and water: towards an elemental understanding of monumentality and landscape in late Neolithic Britain. *Journal of Material Culture* 1, 313–36.

Thomas, J.S. 1999a. An economy of substances in earlier Neolithic Britain. In J. Robb (ed.), *Material symbols: culture and economy in prehistory*, 70–89. Carbondale: Southern Illinois University Press.

Thomas, J.S. 1999b. *Understanding the Neolithic*. London: Routledge.

Thomas, J.S. 1999c. The Pict's Knowe: Neolithic to late Iron Age archaeology. In R.M. Tipping (ed.), *The quaternary of Dumfries and Galloway*, 57–61. London: Quaternary Research Association.

Thomas, J.S. 2000. The identity of place in Neolithic Britain: examples from south-west Scotland. In A. Ritchie (ed.), *Neolithic Orkney in its European context*, 79–90. Oxford: Oxbow.

Thomas, J.S. 2001. Neolithic enclosures: some reflections on excavations in Wales and Scotland. In T. Darvill and J. Thomas (eds), *Neolithic enclosures of north-west Europe*, 132–43. Oxford: Oxbow.

Thomas, J.S., Brophy, K., Fowler, C., Leivers, M., Ronayne, M. and Wood, L. 1999. The Holywood cursus complex, Dumfries: an interim account 1997. In A. Barclay and J. Harding (eds), *Pathways and ceremonies: the cursus monuments of Neolithic Britain and Ireland*, 107–18. Oxford: Oxbow.

Tilley, C.Y. 1994. *A phenomenology of landscape: places, paths and monuments*. Oxford: Berg.

Tilley, C.Y. 1996. The powers of rocks: topography and monument construction on Bodmin Moor. *World Archaeology* 28, 161–76.

Turner, V. 1969. *The ritual process*. Harmondsworth: Penguin.

Watson, A. 2001. Composing Avebury. *World Archaeology* 33, 296–314.

19   Evidence of absence? The Neolithic of the Cheshire Basin

David Mullin

Introduction

A glance at any textbook distribution map of Neolithic burial monuments will show not only a concentration of monuments in areas such as Wessex and Yorkshire, but also, by implication, large gaps in the distribution in Devon, Norfolk/Suffolk, Mid Wales and the entire English Midlands. This is a distribution largely echoed by that of causewayed enclosures, which are generally located to the south of the River Trent. Archaeologists have been attracted to large highly visible monumental complexes and the analysis of 'monument rich' areas has, as a result, dominated narratives for the Neolithic of Britain as a whole. It is the intention of this paper to explore the Neolithic archaeology of one 'empty' area in an attempt to redress the balance and suggest some possibilities for alternative ways for looking at the Neolithic utilisation of such regions.

Models for the early Neolithic in the Cheshire Basin

In contrast to much of the Irish Sea zone, the Cheshire Basin is largely lacking in Neolithic monuments, despite being located between north Wales and Derbyshire, both areas rich in sites from this period. This absence has led to the construction of explanatory models which have generally been argued in terms of environment, based on the work of Sir Cyril Fox (1932). Such models have actively discouraged research in the region, as it has been assumed 'empty' and lacking a Neolithic presence. Fox suggested that soil types could be classified into two dominant groups: light, sandy soils and heavy, clay soils. The areas with sandy soils would support open woodland and were therefore easier to clear, easier to till, and more fertile. Heavy clay soils, on the other hand, would have supported dense, damp oak woodland and would have been unattractive for settlement and farming. Further work in Wales supported this pattern (Crampton and Webley 1960) and it became accepted that Neolithic 'colonisers' from the Continent sought out light soils on which to practice agriculture. These ideas were per-petuated by Childe and Piggott and have dominated narratives of the Neolithic until relatively recently (see Barclay 2001, 9–13).

In the Cheshire Basin, the lack of prehistoric find sites from the heavy glacial tills of the low lying Cheshire Plain and their concentration on the sands and gravels above fifty feet was noted by Varley (1932). This followed Fox in stating that the Plain would have been heavily wooded or swampy and therefore unattractive to settle-ment. This was reiterated in Varley and Jackson's 'Prehistoric Cheshire' (1940): it was assumed from the lack of monuments that the Plain was ignored during the Neolithic and that people settled on the more attractive, higher limestone of the Peak District and North Wales. The concept of the prehistoric population as 'pioneer settlers' choosing the best soils on which to grow crops followed the dominant explanatory frameworks of the day, but have become established even in recent histories of the county. Higham (1993), whilst pointing out the difficulties of identification of Neolithic and Bronze Age sites, still maintains that only a very low-level use was made of the Plain with settlement occurring only on the higher land or on islands of sands and gravels amongst the heavier soils.

Such environmentally deterministic ideas were questioned by Mary Alexander in the pages of the Cheshire Archaeological Bulletin (Alexander 1977). Informed by a reading of Evans' *Environment of early man in the British Isles* (Evans 1976), Alexander posited the idea that thin soils overlying the boulder clays of the Plain could have been utilised in prehistory and, as a result, destroyed. The relative absence of Neolithic sites was suggested as being due to the result of a more mobile lifestyle than previously appreciated and the lack of evidence for woodland clearance accounted for through a dependence on pigs and cattle, which are happy in a wooded environment. These ideas seem to have been precursors to the popular 'mobility model' offered by Thomas *inter alia* (Cooney 1997, 24–6; Edmonds 1999; Thomas 1991; 1999).

The present day environment of the Cheshire Basin certainly poses some problems to the discovery, recovery and interpretation of archaeological sites and monuments.

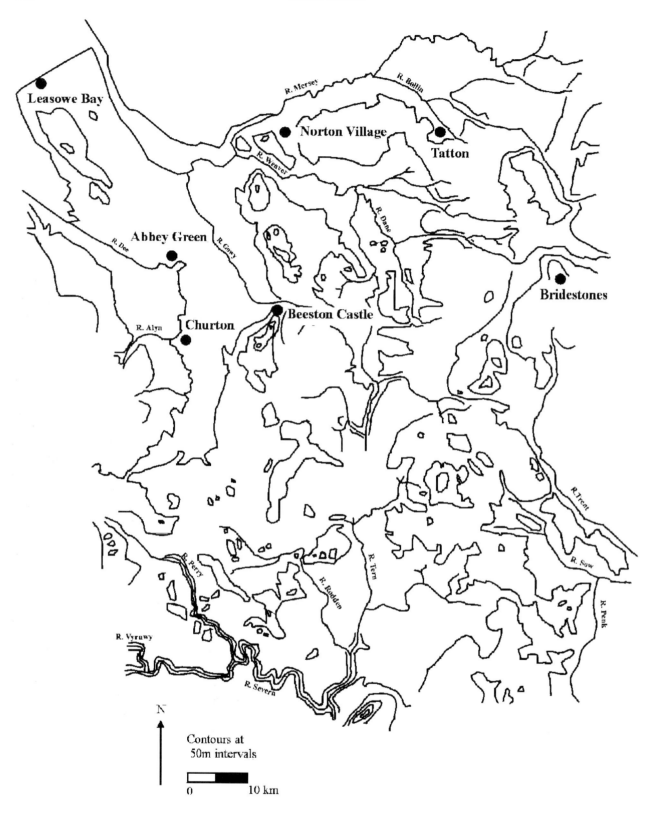

Figure 19.1. *Sites mentioned in the text.*

The nature of the soils makes geophysical survey difficult and surface collection is hampered in the region, due to the high incidence of pasture. Recovery rates from surface scatters also tend to be low due to the poor visibility of material in the soil and the special conditions presented by these soils means that pottery and other material is often rapidly destroyed after deposition (Carver 1991, 6; Limbrey 1987). Much of the prehistoric record has also been destroyed by medieval and later agriculture, with many sites existing only as crop marks, which do not form well on the regions soils. The present soil conditions in the region may, however, bear no relation to those of prehistory. Limbrey (1978, 23) has pointed out the changes which soils undergo as a result of forest clearance and these involve erosion, a loss of nutrients and in-creasing wetness due to a rise in the water table. Soils under primary forest are thought to have been high in nutrients, with the forest canopy sheltering the soils from rain water and therefore lessening erosion and leeching. Indeed, wetness, heaviness and the potential for erosion only develop on these soils *after some utilisation* (Limbrey 1978, 22). Thus, the soils which are now the distinctive heavy glacial tills in the Cheshire Basin would have had radically different characteristics under the primary woodland of the Neolithic. Recent work by Clare (1995) suggests that prehistoric forest cover would have been a mosaic of heavy and light woodland, with some species more common than others in certain areas. This is contrary to the traditional model offered by Fox (1932) of impenetrable, dense undergrowth in a closed, damp forest on poor soils and light, open forest on light soils. Indeed, Limbrey (1978, 22) suggests that these conditions are not found in undisturbed forest, nor in the botanical and ecological sources on which Fox drew.

The presence of heavy glacial soils cannot then be used as an explanation for the absence of a Neolithic population from a region. This may indeed indicate that the Cheshire Basin was in fact an *attractive* area for mobile Neolithic populations dependent to an extent on wild resources (Edmonds 1999; Moffett *et al.* 1989; Thomas 1991; 1999) as it may have been rich in wild resources and of high potential for settlement.

Evidence of absence?

Recent research is beginning to show that the Cheshire Basin was indeed utilised during the Neolithic. During excavations at the medieval Beeston Castle, Cheshire, a series of terraces and hollows were excavated close to the Outer Gateway (Ellis 1993). Three postholes and a pit were excavated here, and the area of the terraces was found to be covered in 'occupation debris' associated with early Neolithic pottery and charcoal (Ellis 1993, 19). The pottery consisted of two sherds of Grimston Ware (Ellis 1993, 66–9) and four leaf-shaped arrowheads with two Neolithic axe fragments also being recovered. The

Grimston Ware was locally made (Ellis 1993, 65–7), but the flint was from a non-local source, possibly Yorkshire (Ellis 1993, 59). Early Neolithic radiocarbon dates of 4340–4003 cal BC and 4036–3816 cal BC (HAR 6461 and HAR 6462) were obtained from this debris and from a nearby ditch. A low bank was associated with the terracing and this was interpreted as possibly being an enclosure, although this feature was not dated. A further posthole and a deep pit containing a single sherd of early Neolithic pottery were excavated c.10m to the west of the terracing.

Grimston Ware was also recovered during excavations at the medieval village of Norton, Cheshire. Here two pits containing a distinctive sandy fill were excavated. One pit contained charcoal, ten sherds of Neolithic pottery and nine flint flakes whilst the other contained a single sherd of similar pottery (Greene and Hough 1977, 80, Mullin 2002). Further finds of Grimston Ware have been made within the city of Chester where, during excavations at the Roman fortress on Abbey Green (McPeake *et al.* 1980), several sherds of prehistoric pottery were discovered in a secondary context, as were a number of flints. The pottery was originally interpreted as being Iron Age, but has been re-interpreted as Grimston Ware (for a more complete discussion of these sites see Mullin 2002).

Early Neolithic occupation evidence was encountered during the excavation of a deserted medieval village at Tatton, Cheshire (Higham and Canc 1999). Three features were assigned a Neolithic date: two post-built structures and a pit. The first post-built structure (hereafter Structure 1) was described as 'ill defined' (Higham and Cane 1999, 31) and consisted of a series of four postholes, one of which contained a flint flake and another a core. Material from one of these postholes was radiocarbon dated to 3500–2945 cal BC (HAR 4495). The second post-built structure (hereafter Structure 2) was excavated c.35m to the NNW of the first and was formed of an arc of six postholes, the fill of one of which was radiocarbon dated to 2195–1680 cal BC (HAR 5716). This was interpreted by the excavators as an 'end date' for the structure, the use of which was thought to be probably contemporary with Structure 1. A pit (TV82.81) was also excavated at the site and contained a sandy fill above a layer of burnt material. This material contained 40 grains of hulled 6–row barley, 12 seeds of sun spurge, 1 fruit of black bindweed and 6 nutlets of dock, common weeds found on cultivated land. Material from this pit was radiocarbon dated to 3370– 2925 cal BC (HAR 5146). Pollen evidence was also analysed from the pit and from Structure 2. There was a similar pollen balance and composition from these samples, which were dominated by grasses with cereals with grassland weeds also present. Tree pollen was low from the samples, with only elm and juniper represented, probably indicating an open landscape in the immediate area (Higham and Cane 1999).

Although the evidence from Tatton may suggest a level of agricultural exploitation in the later Neolithic, wild resources were also being utilised during this period as can be seen from the material from a midden at Leasowe Bay, North Wirral. Here an auroch's skull, red deer antlers, dog and horse skulls and several vertebrae was excavated from a layer of blue silt in the 1960s (Huddart *et al.* 1999, 569). A sample from these deposits was radiocarbon dated to 2700–2200 cal BC (Birm 1013) by Kenna (1986, 5) and appears to relate to the exploitation of a now submerged forest off the north and west Wirral coast. During this period, the sea level was rising, with alder and fen carr and *Sphagnum* bog the dominant vegetation in the immediate area.

Environmental evidence for the exploitation of wetland locations during the Neolithic was recovered by the North West Wetland Survey and is summarised in Leah *et al.* (1997) and Leah *et al.* (1998). The region is also relatively rich in finds of Neolithic axeheads, with a total of 81, dominated by flint and Groups VI and VII, recovered from Cheshire (information compiled from the Cheshire SMR).

Places and monuments: places as monuments

Although the evidence outlined above demonstrates a Neolithic presence in the Cheshire Basin, this is a record dominated by 'occupation' sites and single chance finds. There is but a single example of a chambered tomb on the very edge of the Cheshire Basin: the Bridestones near Congleton (Dunlop 1938; Longley 1987, 43–6). The only other potential monument from this period is a rectangular ditched enclosure close to the River Dee south west of the village of Churton, Cheshire (Cheshire SMR 1807), interpreted as a Neolithic mortuary enclosure (Longley 1987, 46). The enclosure is orientated north/south and measures c.33m x 18m and has bowed sides and rounded corners with a 10m gap in the southern side. The site has not been excavated and a magnetometer survey carried out in 1988 by John Gater (Cheshire SMR) failed to locate the ditches seen from the air. Fieldwalking on the site has produced only a single abraded medieval potsherd (Longley 1987, 46) and its status should be regarded as questionable.

The preceding raises some interesting questions about the relationships between people and monuments. Traditionally, the Cheshire Basin has been seen as a no mans land of dense impenetrable woodland, best avoided. The arguments outlined above, however, illustrate not only the dangers of reading off past environments from modern data, but also that people were indeed present in the area during the Neolithic, interfering with the environment; building post-built structures; using and discarding stone tools and digging pits. The absence of monuments cannot therefore be seen simply as due to a lack of population. The construction of monuments has been seen as central to the definition of 'being Neolithic' and part of the 'package' of material culture and subsistence

strategies introduced during this period. Recent work is beginning to suggest, however, that a range of natural phenomena may have been exploited in a 'monument-like' fashion with ritual significance being attached to events such as tree throws and lightening strikes.

The wind throw of trees is a common phenomena in woodland and is increasingly being identified in archaeological contexts (for example see Bell 1983; Bradley and Ellison 1975; Evans *et al.* 1999; Hey 1997, 107). Although modern storms cannot be used as direct analogy for those in the past, wind throw can clear large areas of woodland, as evidenced during the 'Great Storm' of 1987. A storm of even one tenth of this size in the past would have affected c.2,500 km² (Brown 1997, 141), but it is thought that large storms are exceptional, with clearings of less than 2ha a more usual occurrence (Brown 1997). Archaeological evidence for the exploitation of the areas created by wind throw has been found at several sites, including Hinxton and Barleycroft Farm in Cambridgeshire, where Neolithic flintwork and pottery were found in association with the root hollows of wind thrown trees (Evans *et al.* 1999). In the Nene Valley, root bowls exposed by wind throw were burnt and Neolithic flint and pottery found in the hollows (Brown 1997) and at Farnham, Surrey, tree throw hollows were modified and possibly used as dwellings (Evans *et al.* 1999, 249).

Strikes by lightening against dead wood may have also held significance during the Neolithic, and offer an alternative mechanism for the clearance of woodland areas. Pine is the only native species that is naturally pyrophytic in that it increases its susceptibility to fire as part of its adaptive strategy (Brown 1997, 135). Broad leafed woodland is not naturally combustible, even during dry seasons, as the RAF discovered during World War II when incendiary devices dropped on such woodlands found that they 'refused to burn at any time' (quoted in Brown 1997, 136). This has obvious implications for models of the Neolithic, where charcoal found in deposits is often accounted for by episodes of forest clearance. It seems unlikely that large areas could have been cleared by fire, although selective clearance of the underbrush, especially gorse and bracken, would have been possible. It may be the case that many fires were natural in origin, resulting from lightening strikes on dead timber or on pine, resulting in small scale clearance and the opening up of the forest canopy.

Natural events such as lightening strikes and tree throws would have left a mark on the landscape which may have needed to be explained on a cosmological level. These explanations may have formed part of the mesh of stories, myth and metaphor that articulated life in the woods. One possible outcome of the natural clearance of an area may have been the construction of a monument in the space created as a way of cementing and making visible the associations between people, the environment in which they dwelt and the meanings that this may have held. However, construction of a monument may have only been one of a range of possible outcomes in response to natural clearances. Indeed, just as a monument illustrates the transformative power of people over a space, an event such as a forest fire as a result of a lightening strike may have illustrated the transformative powers of nature itself. Such clearances may not have needed to have monuments constructed within them and may have been used as the location for structured deposition in pits, or may have been used in ways which leave no archaeological trace such as for gatherings and meetings.

If naturally cleared spaces acted as a focus for attention, they may have formed part of a spectrum of practice which included the use of artificial, monumentalised and natural spaces for ritual activity. Indeed, the boundaries between these categories of space may have been, perhaps intentionally, blurred. Moreover, these divisions are a product of post-enlightenment thinking and are not necessarily useful categories when thinking about prehistory. Tilley (1994) and Bradley (2000) have explored the ways in which natural landforms such as hills, rivers, caves and rocks form a focus for ritual attention and the ways in which natural landforms were perhaps intentionally mis-identified as monuments during prehistory has been examined by Mullin (2001). These concepts are part of a broader movement to look beyond monuments and examine the way in which natural phenomena may have been incorporated into ritual practice and how they may have provided an alternative or parallel practice to formal monument construction. Natural phenomena have usually been seen as the inspiration for monuments, with monumentality a cultural response to natural forms or events (for example see Evans *et al.* 1999). The line of the Springfield cursus, for example, deviates to include two tree throw hollows (Buckley *et al.* 2001, 152–3) and tree throws are known at the cursuses at Drayton, Oxfordshire and Barford, Warwickshire. The construction of monuments and the ritual exploitation of natural phenomena temporally overlap, however, and should perhaps be seen as two aspects of the same behaviour: just as acts of formal deposition and monument building may have referenced occupation and/or settlement (Pollard 1999, 88) such events may also have referenced natural episodes such as tree throws or lightening strikes.

Conclusion

It may be the case, then, that the non-construction of Neolithic monuments is a regional trait, perhaps reflecting a degree of continuity with Mesolithic practices. A lack of certain categories of Neolithic monuments has been noted from areas such as Kent (Barber 1997) and more attention should perhaps be paid to regional differences, rather than viewing the Neolithic as a homogenous, coherent phenomenon across Britain as a whole (Thomas 1993). Regional responses may have included conscious rejection of otherwise widespread practice, perhaps with

repeated small scale, discreet ritual acts such as the deposition of selected elements of material culture in rapidly backfilled pits (Thomas 1999, 64–74), contrasting to the large scale, long lived monuments constructed elsewhere. The act of clearance of vegetation cover to create open space may also have been an aspect of ritual activity, which did not *necessarily* require the construction of a monument. The detection of such small scale acts, may, however, be at the limits of archaeological resolution. This should not mean that they are seen as less important than the construction of monuments but rather that we need to look in detail at the spaces between major monument distributions in an attempt not only to 'fill in the gaps', which may in fact never be filled, but to draw a more complete picture of the range and diversity of Neolithic ritual practice. Indeed, regional studies in these 'blank' areas may throw further light on the way in which people during the Neolithic behaved as active agents, transforming the land in ways which they saw fit, utilising the possibilities it offered and choosing the way in which they expressed their identities. Apparently empty areas, such as the Cheshire Basin, should not be ignored when considering the Neolithic of the Irish Sea zone, but rather need to be drawn from the sidelines and incorporated into our narratives.

References

Alexander, M. 1977. Notes on the prehistory of Cheshire. *Cheshire Archaeological Bulletin* 5, 7–9.

Barber, M. 1997. Landscape, the Neolithic and Kent. In P. Topping (ed.), *Neolithic landscapes*, 77–86. Oxford: Oxbow.

Barclay, G. 2001. 'Metropolitan' and 'parochial/core' and 'periphery': a historiography of the Neolithic of Scotland. *Proceedings of the Prehistoric Society* 67, 1–18.

Bell, M. 1983. Valley sediments as evidence of prehistoric land-use on the South Downs. *Proceedings of the Prehistoric Society* 49, 119–50.

Bradley, R. 2000. *An archaeology of natural places.* London: Routledge.

Bradley, R. and Ellison, A. 1975. *Rams Hill.* Oxford: British Archaeological Reports Number 19.

Brown, T. 1997. Clearances and clearings: deforestation in Mesolithic/Neolithic Britain. *Oxford Journal of Archaeology* 16, 133–46.

Buckley, D., Hedges, J. and Brown, N. 2001. Excavations at a Neolithic cursus, Springfield, Essex, 1979–85. *Proceedings of the Prehistoric Society* 67, 101–62.

Carver, M. 1991. A strategy for lowland Shropshire. *Transactions of the Shropshire Archaeology and History Society* 67, 1–8.

Clare, T. 1995. Before the first woodland clearings. *British Archaeology* 8, 6.

Cooney, G. 1997. Images of settlement and the landscape in the Neolithic. In P. Topping (ed.), *Neolithic landscapes*, 23–32. Oxford: Oxbow.

Crampton, C. and Webley, D. 1960. The correlation of prehistoric settlement and soils in the Vale of Glamorgan. *The Bulletin of the Board of Celtic Studies* 18, 387–96.

Dunlop, M. 1938. A preliminary survey of the Bridestones, Congleton, and related monuments. *Transactions of the Lancashire and Cheshire Antiquarian Society* 53, 14–31.

Edmonds, M. 1999. *Ancestral geographies of the Neolithic.* London: Routledge.

Ellis, P. 1993. *Beeston Castle, Cheshire.* London: English Heritage Archaeological Report No.23.

Evans, C., Pollard, J. and Knight, M. 1999. Life in woods: tree throws, 'settlement' and forest cognition. *Oxford Journal of Archaeology* 18, 241–54.

Evans, J. 1976. *Environment of early man in the British Isles.* London: Book Club.

Fox, C. 1925. *The personality of Britain.* Cardiff: National Museum of Wales.

Greene, J. and Hough, P. 1977. Excavations in the Medieval village of Norton 1974–1976. *Journal of the Chester Archaeological Society* 60, 61–93.

Hey, G. 1997. Neolithic settlement at Yarnton, Oxfordshire. In P. Topping (ed.), *Neolithic landscapes*, 99–112. Oxford: Oxbow.

Higham, N. 1993. *The origins of Cheshire.* Manchester: Manchester University Press.

Higham, N. and Cane, T. 1999. The Tatton Park Project, part I: prehistoric to sub-Roman. *Journal of the Chester Archaeological Society* 74, 1–62.

Huddart, D., Gonzalez, S. and Roberts, G. 1999. The archaeological record and mid Holocene marginal coastal Palaeoenvironments around Liverpool Bay. *Quaternary Proceedings* 7, 563–74.

Kenna, R. 1986. The Flandrian sequence of North Wirral. *Geological Journal* 21, 1–28.

Leah, M., Wells, C., Appleby, C. and Huckerby, E. 1997. *The wetlands of Cheshire.* Lancaster: Lancaster Imprints.

Leah, M., Wells, C., Stamper, P., Huckerby, E. and Welch, C. 1998. *The wetlands of Shropshire and Staffordshire.* Lancaster: Lancaster Imprints.

Limbrey, S. 1978. Changes in quality and distribution of the soils of lowland Britain. In S. Limbrey and J. Evans (eds), *The effect of man on the landscape: the lowland zone*, 21–27. CBA Research Report 21. London: Council for British Archaeology.

Longley, D. 1987. Prehistory. In B. Harris (ed.), *A history of the county of Chester. Volume*, 1 36–92. Oxford: Oxford University Press

McPeake, J. and Bulmer, M. 1980. Excavations in the garden of No.1 Abbey Green, Chester 1975–77. *Journal of the Chester Archaeology Society* 63, 14–37.

Moffett, L., Robinson M., and Straker, V. 1989. Cereals, fruit and nuts: charred plant remains from Neolithic sites in England and Wales and the Neolithic economy. In D. Miles, A. Williams and N. Gardner (eds), *The beginnings of agriculture*, 243–61. Oxford: British Archaeological Reports International Series 496.

Mullin, D. 2001. Remembering, forgetting and the invention of tradition: burial and natural places in the English early Bronze Age. *Antiquity* 75, 533–7.

Mullin, D. 2002. Early Neolithic pottery from Cheshire. *Journal of the Chester Archaeological Society* 77, 1–7

Pollard, J. 1999. 'These places have their moments': thoughts on settlement practices in the British Neolithic. In J. Bruck and M. Goodman (eds), *Making places in the prehistoric world*, 76–93. London: UCL Press.

Thomas, J. 1991. *Rethinking the Neolithic.* Cambridge: Cambridge University Press.

Thomas, J. 1993. Discourse, totalisation and 'the Neolithic'. In C. Tilley (ed.), *Interpretative archaeology*, 357–94. Oxford: Berg.

Thomas, J. 1999. *Understanding the Neolithic.* London: Routledge.

Tilley, C. 1994. *A phenomenology of landscape.* Oxford: Berg.

Varley, W. 1932. Early man in the Cheshire Plain. *Transactions of Chester and North Wales Architectural, Archaeological and Historic Society* 29, 50–65.

Varley, W. and Jackson, J. 1940. *Prehistoric Cheshire.* Chester: Cheshire Rural Community Council.

20 Away from the numbers: diversity and invisibility in late Neolithic Wales

Rick Peterson

Introduction

This paper will describe what I believe to have been distinctive about later Neolithic society in the area that is now Wales. I also want to consider why the character of these societies has been obscured within a more generalised account of the second part of the Neolithic period and what strategies we might adopt to recover more detail.

I want to begin by considering the evidence from Wales for the later Neolithic, in this case the period between 3000 and 2400 BC. Given the nature of this evidence, it will be necessary to treat the resulting synthesis with some degree of caution. I am trying to make a narrative, an understanding, of the later Neolithic in Wales, which will give us a framework to work in and to react against. In places, I may have been more detailed and more specific than is strictly justified by the evidence. I want to look at what is distinctive about the late Neolithic in Wales and why some of this detail might have escaped us in the past.

So, what happened in Wales in the third millennium BC? I will begin by looking first at those sites which have produced radiocarbon dates of the relevant age. There is now a large literature on the limitations and possibilities radiocarbon dating (Buck *et al.* 1996, 200–52; Herne 1988; Kinnes 1988 for example). I examined this evidence as part of my PhD research (Peterson 1999), in that case looking at dated sites from Wales for the whole of the Neolithic. I began by gathering together all of the radiocarbon dates which pre-dated 3500 bp. Only those dates which appeared to be reliably associated with human activity and did not appear problematic for other reasons were used (see Peterson 1999, appendix A for a site by site discussion of all of this evidence). The dating evidence has been summarised as a series of maps, one for each hundred years throughout the period, to try and give some indication of changing patterns of occupation and activity.

Later Neolithic evidence from Wales

Looking at the maps from the beginning of the third millennium BC onwards we can see certain patterns. The symbols for Gwernvale (Britnell and Savory 1984, 138–9), Graig Lwyd (Williams and Davidson 1998, 19–20), Pontnewydd (Richards and Hedges 1999, 859), Parc le Breos Cwm (Whittle and Wysocki 1998) and Carreg Coetan (Barker 1992, 20–1) relate to the extreme tail of distributions for earlier Neolithic dates. The dates from Moel-y-Gerddi come from a series of hearths (Dresser 1985, 373), sealed by Iron Age contexts, while the single date from Ogmore came from a Peterborough ware associated hearth within a wind-blown sand deposit (Hamilton and Aldhouse-Green 1999). A ring ditch at Four Crosses (Warrilow *et al.* 1986, 64) probably also continued in use until around 3000 BC. The first phase of activity at Upper Ninepence, Walton (Gibson 1999, 43) consisted of a scatter of small pits associated with Peterborough Ware. Evidence of slightly more substantial structures was provided at Sarn-y-bryn-caled 2 with dates from the phase 2 silts of a small pennanular ring ditch (Gibson 1994, 159–61). A single large pit or small ditch segment (number 27) provided the dates from Hendre, Rhydymwyn (Brassil and Gibson 1999, 96). The distribution pattern seems to be predominantly lowland and possibly linked to major communication routes, particularly river valleys and the sea. Although Moel-y-Gerddi appears to be an exception at *c* 500m OD, it would still have overlooked Tremadog Bay, continuing the link to major communication routes.

If we move away from the radiocarbon evidence, and in contrast to the small scale sites noted so far, there was a tradition in North Wales of large complex passage graves, for which later Neolithic dates have been suggested (Lynch 1976, 77). The two classic sites are Barclodiad y Gawres (Powell and Daniel 1956) and Bryn Celli Ddu (Hemp 1931), both of which are on Anglesey. There are also two destroyed sites, Tregarnedd near Llangefni and the Calderstones in Liverpool, which have been claimed as belonging to this group (Lynch 1969, 111; 1976, 77). I would see these monuments as part of a wider tradition of large chambered cairns with round

Rick Peterson

Figure 20.1a. *3000BC*

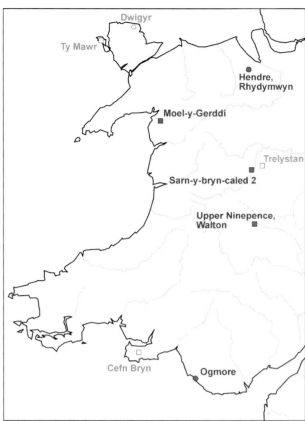

Figure 20.1b. *2900BC*

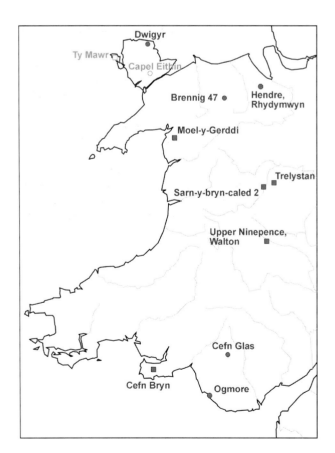

Figure 20.1c. *2800BC*

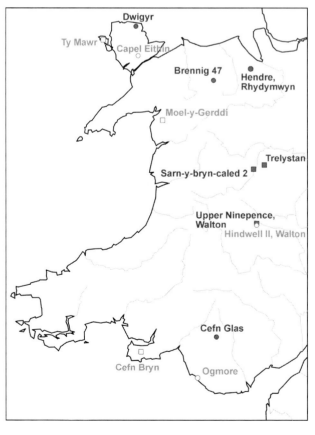

Figure 20.1d. *2700BC*

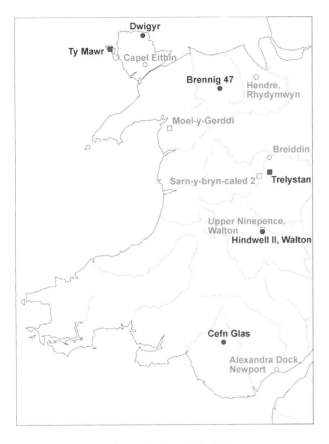

Figure 20.1e. 2600 BC

Figure 20.1f. 2500 BC

Figure 20.1g. 2400 BC

Figure 20.1. Radiocarbon activity between 3000 and 2400 BC (data from Peterson 1999, Appendix A). Two kinds of symbols have been used on these maps. Boxes indicate sites where multiple radiocarbon dates were combined with a phased stratigraphy, to allow an estimation of both when and for how long the site was in use. Solid boxes show the shortest probable range of occupation, and the open boxes indicate the maximum possible limits of the range of occupation. The sites which are represented by circles are those where only a single event has been radiocarbon dated. Solid circles show the range of that date at one standard deviation, open circles at two standard deviations. Consequently, the circles do not give any indication of how long a site was in use.

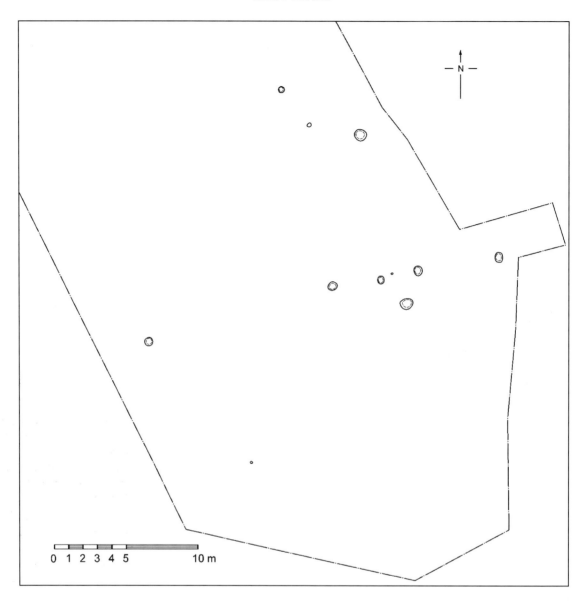

Figure 20.2. *Peterborough Ware associated structures beneath Upper Ninepence barrow (after Gibson 1999, fig 33).*

mounds. Possible examples include Gop, near Prestatyn (Lynch 1990, 6) and Bryn yr Hen Bobl, on Anglesey (Hemp 1936), which may have had a circular ditch around the mound (Driver *et al.* 2000), similar to the one associated with Bryn Celli Ddu.

My feeling about this whole group of sites is that they should be regarded as middle Neolithic rather than late Neolithic in date. That is to say I do not believe they continued in use much after 3000 BC. They are certainly distinct from the vast majority of other chambered cairns in Wales, which seem to have been in use between 3800 and 3500 BC. Precise dating evidence is lacking from any of the excavated sites, although re-analysis of the archive from Bryn yr Hen Bobl has shown that at least part of that site was built after 3500 BC (Leivers *et al.* 2001). Barclodiad y Gawres has its closest parallels

amongst the large cruciform cairns in the Boyne valley in Ireland. Its relatively small size might suggest a date early in Sheridan's (1986) developmental sequence for Irish passage graves. Brindley (1999, 134–5) dates the Irish passage grave tradition as a whole to the middle Neolithic, between 3400 and 3100 BC. Bryn Celli Ddu could also be considered as early on typological grounds, although Lynch (1976, 77), building on O'Kelly's (1969) interpretation of the features beneath the cairn as a henge, suggested a very late date for the site. However, subsequent debate about the character of the pre-cairn features (Bradley 1998, 8–10; Eogan 1983; Lynch 1991, 91–8) may have cast doubt on this identification.

Returning to the radiocarbon evidence and moving towards the middle of the third millennium BC, the most striking pattern seems to be an apparent drift of

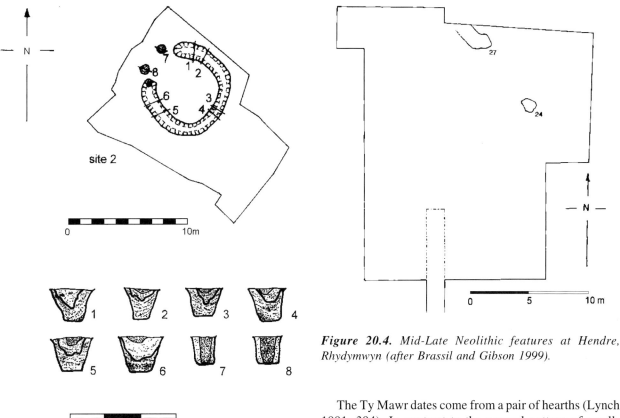

Figure 20.3. Sarn-y-bryn-caled ring ditch (after Gibson 1994).

Figure 20.4. Mid-Late Neolithic features at Hendre, Rhydymwyn (after Brassil and Gibson 1999).

occupation northwards. By 2500 BC there is no dated occupation of south-west Wales at all. While it is probable that some of this pattern is an effect of the relatively small sample of dates from Wales as a whole, it possibly reflects a general trend away from the south. At the very least it should be regarded as evidence of a much lower density of occupation in the south and west. Together with this move into the north came, for the first time, a significant amount of activity in the upland areas of Wales. Despite this general trend there *were* two new sites in the south dated to this period. A collection of pits, postholes and hearths at Cefn Bryn (Ward 1987) and a 'hut floor' associated with a late Neolithic flint scatter at Cefn Glas (Clayton and Savory 1991, 15).

Further north, new sites were also largely ephemeral in nature: a single pit on a later site at Dwigyr (Lynch 1991, 395); part of a surface sealed beneath a later cairn at Brenig (Lynch 1993, 206). Two very similar groups of stake built structures at Trelystan (Britnell 1982) and Upper Ninepence (Gibson 1999, 29–34) were associated with hearths, pits and substantial quantities of Grooved Ware, and appear to form a distinct class of site at this period.

The Ty Mawr dates come from a pair of hearths (Lynch 1991, 394). In contrast to the general pattern of small-scale sites, the dates from Hindwell II (Gibson 1999, 15–19) are from the timbers of the massive palisade enclosure. This is the only example so far discovered in Wales of the tradition of large scale Late Neolithic monument construction seen in many other parts of the British Isles. The evidence of the date from Capel Eithin (White and Smith 1999, 34) relates to a setting of five timber posts, once again associated with Grooved Ware. A human skull fragment recovered from a former river channel in Alexandra Dock, Newport (Bell *et al.* 2000, 69) provided the date from that site. The second date from Hendre came from an arc of small pits containing Grooved Ware sherds, lithics and charcoal (Brassil and Gibson 1999, 96), while the date from the Breiddin (Burleigh *et al.* 1976, 34) came from a single pit. There is also Grooved Ware pottery from Llanilar, near Aberystwyth (Briggs 2000, 24) which is undated and appears to be residual in a series of later pits. Similarly unstratified sherds from Stackpole Warren on the south Pembrokeshire coast may also include some Grooved Ware vessels (Benson *et al.* 1990, 210–1). The presence of these sherds does indicate that there was a late Neolithic presence in West Wales not visible in the radiocarbon evidence.

However, the general pattern revealed for the late Neolithic in these maps is one of small scale and temporary occupations concentrated in the north, with a significant number of upland locations in use for the first time.

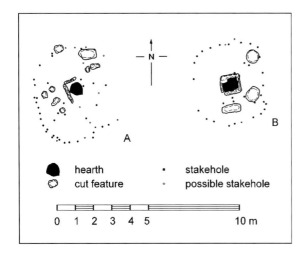

hearth   · stakehole
cut feature   ∘ possible stakehole

0 1 2 3 4 5   10 m

Figure 20.5. *Structures A and B at Trelystan (after Britnell 1982).*

The character of the later Neolithic in Wales

If the postulated middle Neolithic date for the complex passage graves is accepted, what we seem to have is a situation where there is very little evidence for any activity after 3000 BC other than transient occupations. Late Neolithic sites in Wales seem to have been dominated by small stake shelters such as Trelystan and Upper Ninepence, and by small groups of pits or hearths such as those at Hendre or Cefn Bryn. The striking exception to this statement is the Hindwell palisade enclosure. Although only a very small portion of Hindwell has been excavated (Gibson 1999, 15–19) it is noticeable that there appears to be no tradition of repeated formal deposition at the site, in contrast to the similarly vast late Neolithic monuments in central southern England and Scotland: the West Kennet enclosures (Whittle 1997), Durrington Walls (Richards and Thomas 1984) and Dunragit (Thomas 2001, 138–40), for example. This is not an effect caused by any regional poverty in the material culture. The enormous contemporary assemblage of Grooved Ware from Upper Ninepence was discovered only a kilometre from Hindwell.

Late Neolithic society in Wales seems to have been mobile rather than sedentary. We might gather this purely from the nature of the occupation evidence but other hints can be added to build a fuller picture. Thin section analysis of later Neolithic pottery from Trelystan, Sarn-y-bryn-caled, the Breiddin and Four Crosses (Darvill *in* Britnell 1982; Gibson 1994; Musson 1991; and Warrilow *et al.* 1986) seems to indicate long-range exchange contacts. Pottery from all of these sites appears to have been produced at a variety of distant locations. Moving pottery does not necessarily imply a mobile population, but it is easier to imagine the long distance exchange of

fragile pottery within a mobile society. A pastoral economy has been suggested for Neolithic Wales in several studies (Moore-Colyer 1999; Webley 1976 for example). Specifically late Neolithic evidence to support this is rather rare and it may be that a more varied range of subsistence strategies needs to be considered, although stable isotope evidence from Ifton (Rick Schulting *pers. comm.*) and Alexandra Dock (Bell *et al.* 2000, 69) does show a meat-dominated diet.

The limited environmental data that is available tends to support the idea that society was mostly pastoral. Pollen evidence from the Severn estuary levels (Bell *et al.* 2000, 208–44); the Black Mountains (Crampton and Webley 1964; 1966) and the Walton Basin (Caseldine *in* Gibson 1999, 141–50) seems to show that there was some forest regeneration around 3000 BC, following widespread woodland clearance early in the Neolithic. Charred plant remains at Upper Ninepence are dominated by wild species, particularly hazelnut (Caseldine *in* Gibson 1999, 141–50), similar results from Trelystan (Britnell 1982) also indicate a mixed woodland environment and the exploitation of hazelnuts. Important work on the material from beneath the Upper Ninepence round barrow offers a glimpse of the ways in which later Neolithic subsistence may have changed on a localised and episodic basis. The pits at this site can be divided into two later Neolithic phases: one associated with Peterborough Ware and the other with Grooved Ware. Microwear studies on the use of stone tools (Donahue *in* Gibson 1999, 100–12) shows that a wide range of tasks was being carried out in the earlier period. The much larger assemblage of Grooved Ware associated flint was dominated by hide processing tools, with a few used for cutting meat and working wood. A similar shift in the use of the pottery is revealed by lipid analysis (Dudd and Evershed *in* Gibson 1999, 112–20). Peterborough Ware appears to have been used almost exclusively for cooking pork and Grooved Ware for cooking beef, with neither pottery style showing much evidence for cooking plant foods.

To summarise, during the late Neolithic (*c* 3000–2400 BC) society seems to have been centred on the uplands and the north and east. The population appear to have become almost entirely mobile, but unlike early mobile populations in Wales or contemporary societies in other parts of Britain, they did not use any kind of monument as a fixed point in their seasonal round. It is certainly striking that where there is evidence of later chambered cairn re-use in Wales it can be dated to the early Bronze Age rather than the late Neolithic. Examples include Food Vessel associated cremation burials at Trefignath (Smith and Lynch 1987, 79, subsequently re-assessed by Alex Gibson, *pers. comm.*) and a late burial at Parc le Breos Cwm (Whittle and Wysocki 1998, 175). Dates from stone and timber circles in Wales also seem to be exclusively Early Bronze Age: Moel Goedog 1 (Callow *et al.* 1963, 35) and Sarn-y-bryn-caled 1 (Gibson 1994, 150–9), for example.

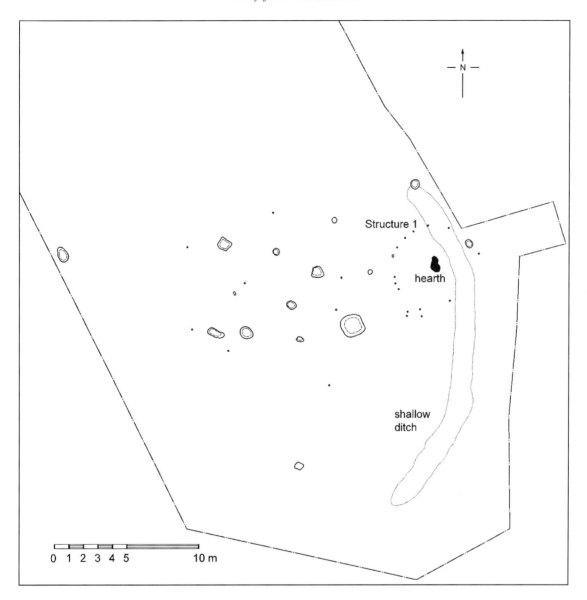

Figure 20.6. *Grooved Ware associated structures beneath Upper Ninepence barrow (after Gibson 1999, fig 33).*

Past studies of the late Neolithic in Wales have not really explicitly addressed these distinctive elements. There has been a concentration on the earlier part of the Neolithic, with an assumption that the later part of the period might be interesting if and when more evidence was forthcoming (Olding 2000, 27 for example, or the more extreme case of Children and Nash 2001, in which the later Neolithic is not considered at all). I would regard this assumption as wrong. I think that we already have evidence for the late Neolithic from Wales but, as it does not fit the usual picture in many respects, it has been ignored.

Studying later Neolithic society

What is troubling about these assumptions is the possibility that we are missing similar evidence of diversity in other areas, perhaps even in areas which have more traditionally 'late Neolithic' archaeology. I think this is because of the ways in which we have approached the archaeology of the period. The late Neolithic, perhaps even more than the earlier Neolithic, has been defined by the study of monuments and monument complexes. These monuments have become the stages on which late Neolithic social relations were acted out, negotiated in the manipulation of earth, timber and stone, of Grooved Ware and pig bone. Away from the monuments, off the stage, the social relations recede and the actors are put back in their box.

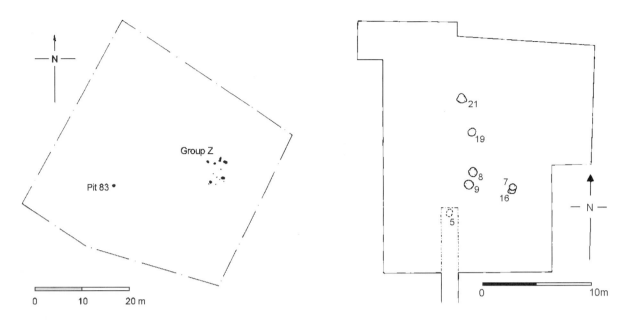

Figure 20.7. *The timber post setting (group Z) at Capel Eithin (after White and Smith 1999).*

Figure 20.8. *Grooved Ware associated features at Hendre, Rhydymwyn (after Brassil and Gibson 1999).*

This is not to argue that people in the late Neolithic did not use monuments and the deposition of material culture at those monuments as part of their network of social relationships. However, I would argue that our understanding of the late Neolithic in mainland Britain has been fabricated from a particular sub-set of the available evidence. From Renfrew (1973) onwards monuments have been important in social theory. Is it the case in Neolithic studies that a society without monuments is a society without complexity? Richard Bradley (1984, 11) once pointed out an invidious distinction in the older literature between Neolithic populations imagined as having 'social relations with one another' and Mesolithic populations imagined as having 'ecological relations with hazelnuts'. Did this split arise solely because of the lack of monumental architecture in the Mesolithic? In attempting to understand social relations in the period we seem to have focussed particularly on two very productive strategies.

We have studied the active use of material culture, particularly the structured deposition of large assemblages of pottery, animal bone and lithics from monument complexes. It is true that meaningful acts of deposition have been identified from smaller sites such as groupings of pits, but it remains the case that the classic examples, those which are held to characterise late Neolithic society, are studies of the archaeology of large monumental complexes. The sort of study I am thinking about includes work like Richards and Thomas (1984) on Durrington Walls, Joshua Pollard on the Sanctuary (1992) and Woodhenge (1995), Colin Richards (1993) on Balfarg, and Julian Thomas on Mount Pleasant (1996, 183–233). In these studies social relations are revealed through the statistical study of artefact variability. Away from these

numbers society becomes invisible once again. We have also studied the way in which these monument complexes themselves were situated within and manipulated the landscape to achieve certain ends. Obviously this tradition of research is even more restricted to those areas with substantial architectural remains. I am thinking of work like Aaron Watson's (2001) study of Avebury, Christopher Tilley's (1994) work on the relationship between chambered cairns and the landscape in the early Neolithic in Wales, or Colin Richards' (1996) on Orcadian monumentality. In these cases some of the nature of society is revealed by a close study of the architectural practice of making monuments. Meaningful actions and order can be established as long as we are around monuments but as we move away this detail is lost. These research agendas have served us well in areas rich in monumental archaeology, but in regions like Wales they fail us. The problem we have is that if we look for society using these criteria there is simply no evidence from late Neolithic Wales to study. The whole country shows up as blank. So a possible distinction between north and east Wales where there may have been a largely non-monumental late Neolithic, and an area like south-west Wales, where there may not have been any significant late Neolithic activity at all, escapes us.

So what we have in Wales is a situation where we know we have a late Neolithic population, at least in the north and the east, but if we want to talk about society in that period we seem to be reduced to importing our explanations wholesale from areas with monumental archaeology. This is fine as long as we assume that late Neolithic society was more or less uniform throughout Britain and Ireland. However, if that was the case, why did this uniform society leave such different remains in different places? There are two possible answers to this question. It might be the case that there were substantial numbers of late Neolithic monument complexes in Wales but that they have yet to be discovered. Alternatively we may not have recognised the dates of those monuments we have discovered. However, the other possible answer is that there never were substantial numbers of monuments in Wales, that no matter how much fieldwork we do we are never going to be able to discover social complexity by digging up monuments. What if we were to assume this was the case and try and study social complexity in the archaeology we do have, to look at this pattern of shifting occupation on its own terms. Late Neolithic society in what is now Wales had neither regressed from some complex fourth millennium BC monumental state nor was it peripheral to a series of late Neolithic 'core areas'; it was merely organised differently, meaning that we need to investigate its remains differently.

It seems clear to me why understandings of late Neolithic society in what is now Wales are vague, or second-hand, or both. The nature of the archaeology means that assemblages are not associated with monumental structures open to analysis. Contextual information is often 'good' (most diagnostically late Neolithic material comes from recent fieldwork). However, a lot of this material comes from pit scatters, generally of small pits with single fills. Many assemblages are small and bone rarely survives in Welsh soils. We understand social relations in the late Neolithic by looking at the interplay between large numbers of artefacts and complex monumental structures. There is no surviving evidence we can use for this sort of study, what different kinds of approach might we try?

Pottery and society in later Neolithic Wales

I looked at the histories of manufacture and use of Neolithic pottery from Wales as part of my Ph.D. thesis. Forced by the nature of the evidence away from the monumental late Neolithic, I have found other pointers to understanding how society changed in the third millennium BC.

Looking at the processing and gathering of raw materials used in pottery, a few very simple and widespread techniques seem to have been in use (Peterson 1999, 185–6). This is a marked contrast to earlier Neolithic pottery over the same area, which was made according to large numbers of different, very complex recipes. I have suggested that this change is in part the result of the very mobile nature of late Neolithic society, as borne out by the number of vessels which appear to have been made a substantial distance from where they were deposited. Grooved Ware was the most mundane of all the Neolithic pottery styles, at least in terms of the processing and gathering of the raw materials used to make it.

The order and shape of vessel construction tell a slightly different story. Late Neolithic pottery is made in a wider range of shapes and styles than earlier vessels, and these styles are more fragmented and localised (Peterson 1999, 188). This may be telling us something about the kinds of strong and very small-scale senses of identity which existed alongside the mobility and long-range contact referred to earlier. Once again it may also be telling us something about the changing status of pottery. Early pottery was made in a number of relatively restricted shapes throughout Wales, implying a concern with uniformity and the importance of distant ideal forms. The breakdown of this uniformity may be as much to do with the changing status of the pottery as any absence of long distance contacts.

The wide-ranging nature of social contacts in the late Neolithic is perhaps indicated most clearly by the widespread adoption of the range of decorative styles and motifs associated with Grooved Ware (Peterson 1999, 192). Here is a piece of evidence which can be used to tie the problematic late Neolithic of Wales to the ordered monumental period of the 'core areas'. However it is by no means necessarily the case that uniformity of decorative style implies uniformity of meaning. There is no doubt that the late Neolithic population of what is now Wales knew about the monumental societies to the east and west of them. The fact that they appear not to have imported their distinctive monuments along with their pottery decoration may imply that they believed different things or that their society was ordered differently.

Interestingly it is only in the late Neolithic that there appear to have been a number of vessels in circulation which were never used for cooking (Peterson 1999, 201). It is always tempting to label vessels like these as 'non-utilitarian' and from that point to drift into thinking about these vessels as special 'ritual' vessels. I have tried to resist this line of thinking for a number of reasons. In studying the early Neolithic material it became clear that practically all of the pottery had been used for cooking. The high status ascribed to fine carinated bowls (Herne 1988, 26), such as the carefully deposited vessels from Dyffryn Ardudwy (Powell 1973, 8–15), seems to have been bound up with their use as cooking vessels. During the early Neolithic there we cannot see distinct classes of ritual and mundane pottery, all pottery seems to have had special meaning and all pottery seems to have been used for cooking. Moving into the later Neolithic, when there do appear to have been vessels which were never used for cooking, there is little evidence that this 'non-utilitarian' pottery was being treated differently. What I would suggest is that all later Neolithic pottery had meanings which we might categorise as ritualistic, and which were connected with the idea of food preparation and consumption. What was distinctive about the late Neolithic is that, for the first time, these meanings were applied to pottery which was not actively used for cooking.

Conclusion

In this short paper there is only space to present a few, broad brush, statements about the late Neolithic arising from my work. A lack of monumental architecture does not equate either to a lack of social complexity or to an inability to discuss society. Other studies on other aspects of the archaeology of areas like Wales could fill in much more detail. Returning to my outline of the history of the area between 3000 and 2400 BC: what we appear to have in the north and east of Wales is a highly successful group of very small-scale societies who carried on a distinct way of life for around six hundred years. They were highly mobile and used the contacts that mobility brought them to preserve a number of common traditions. They also selectively borrowed or appropriated aspects of the material culture of neighbouring groups in what is now southern England and eastern Ireland. They appear to have been the first societies in the area to move into the uplands in relatively large numbers. Distinctively they did not build monuments. It may be that societies like these were more common in the late Neolithic than we have assumed, and that rather than being at the margins of a world dominated by the Boyne, Orkney and Wessex, non-monumental societies formed the bulk of the late Neolithic population of Britain and Ireland.

Acknowledgements

My thanks are due to Vicki Cummings and Chris Fowler for the invitation to contribute a version of this paper to the colloquium at Manchester and to everyone who contributed to the stimulating discussions over the two days of the event. Thanks also to Julia Roberts and Joshua Pollard for reading and commenting on earlier drafts of the paper and to Chris and Vicki for editorial comments.

References

Barker, C. T. 1992. *The chambered tombs of south-west Wales. A re-assessment of the Neolithic burial monuments of Carmarthenshire and Pembrokeshire*. Oxford: Oxbow.

Bell, M., Caseldine, A. and Neumann, H. 2000. *Prehistoric intertidal archaeology of the Welsh Severn estuary*. York: Council for British Archaeology.

Benson, D.G., Evans, J.G., Williams, G.H., Darvill, T. and David, A.1990. Excavations at Stackpole Warren, Dyfed. *Proceedings of the Prehistoric Society* 56, 179–245.

Bradley, R. 1984. *The social foundations of prehistoric Britain, themes and variations in the archaeology of power*. London and New York: Longman.

Bradley, R. 1998. Stone circles and passage graves – a contested relationship. In A. Gibson and D. Simpson (eds), *Prehistoric ritual and religion*, 2–13. Stroud: Sutton.

Brassil, K. and Gibson, A. 1999. A Grooved Ware pit group and Bronze Age multiple inhumation at Hendre, Rhydymwyn, Flintshire. In R. Cleal and A. MacSween (eds), *Grooved Ware in Britain and Ireland*, 89–97. Oxford: Oxbow.

Briggs, C.S. (ed.) 2000. A Neolithic and early Bronze Age settlement and burial complex at Llanilar, Ceredigion. *Archaeologia Cambrensis* 146, 13–59.

Brindley, A. 1999. Sequence and dating in the Grooved Ware tradition. In R. Cleal and A. MacSween (eds), *Grooved Ware in Britain and Ireland*, 133–44. Oxford: Oxbow.

Britnell, W. 1982 The excavation of two round barrows at Trelystan, Powys. *Proceedings of the Prehistoric Society* 48, 133–201.

Britnell, W.J. and Savory, H.N. 1984. *Gwernvale and Penywyrlod: two Neolithic long cairns in the Black Mountains of Brecknock*. Cardiff: Cambrian Archaeological Association.

Buck, C.E., Cavanagh, W.G. and Litton, C.D. 1996. *The Bayesian approach to interpreting archaeological data*. Chichester: Wiley.

Burleigh, R., Hewson, A. and Meeks, N. 1976. British Museum natural radiocarbon measurements VIII. *Radiocarbon* 18/1, 16–43.

Callow, W., Baker, M. and Pritchard, D. 1963. National Physical Laboratory radiocarbon measurements I. *Radiocarbon* 5, 34–9.

Children, G. and Nash, G. 2001. *The prehistoric sites of Breconshire: ideology, power and monument symbolism*. Woonton Almeley: Logaston.

Clayton, D. and Savory, H.N. 1991. The excavation of a Neolithic hut floor on Cefn Glas, Rhondda, 1971–4. *Archaeologia Cambrensis* 139, 12–20.

Crampton, C.B. and Webley, D. 1964. Preliminary studies of the historical succession of plants and soils on selected sites in South Wales. *Bulletin of the Board of Celtic Studies*, 20, 440–9.

Crampton, C.B. and Webley, D. 1966. A section through the Mynydd Troed long barrow, Brecknock. *Bulletin of the Board of Celtic Studies*, 22, 71–7.

Dresser, Q. 1985. University College Cardiff radiocarbon dates I. *Radiocarbon* 27/2b, 338–86.

Driver, T., Hamilton, M., Leivers, M., Roberts, J. and Peterson, R. 2000. New evidence from Bryn yr Hen Bobl, Llanedwen, Anglesey. *Antiquity* 74, 761–2.

Eogan, G. 1983. Bryn Celli Ddu. *Antiquity* 57, 135–6.

Gibson, A. 1994. Excavations at the Sarn-y-bryn-caled cursus complex, Welshpool, Powys, and the timber circles of Great Britain and Ireland. *Proceedings of the Prehistoric Society* 60, 143–223.

Gibson, A. 1999. *The Walton basin project: excavation and survey in a prehistoric landscape 1993–7*. York: Council for British Archaeology.

Hamilton, M.A. and Aldhouse-Green, S.H.R. 1998. Ogmore-by-Sea. *Archaeology in Wales* 38, 113–5.

Hemp, W.J. 1931. The chambered cairn of Bryn Celli Ddu. *Archaeologia* 80, 179–214.

Hemp, W.J. 1936. The chambered cairn known as Bryn yr Hen Bobl near Plas Newydd, Anglesey. *Archaeologia* 85, 253–92.

Herne, A. 1988. A time and a place for the Grimston bowl. In J.C. Barrett and I.A. Kinnes (eds), *The archaeology of context in the Neolithic and the Bronze Age: recent trends*, 9–29. Sheffield: University of Sheffield.

Kinnes, I.A. 1988. The cattleship Potemkin: reflections on the first Neolithic in Britain. In J.C. Barrett and I.A. Kinnes (eds), *The archaeology of context in the Neolithic and the*

Bronze Age: recent trends, 2–8. Sheffield: University of Sheffield.

Leivers, M., Roberts, J. and Peterson, R. 2001. Bryn yr Hen Bobl, Anglesey: recent fieldwork and a reassessment of excavations in 1935. *Archaeology in Wales* 41, 3–9.

Lynch, F.M. 1969. The megalithic tombs of North Wales. In T.G.E. Powell, J.X.P.W. Corcoran, F.M. Lynch and J.G. Scott, *Megalithic enquiries in the west of Britain*, 107–74. Liverpool: University of Liverpool Press.

Lynch, F.M. 1976. Towards a chronology of megalithic tombs in Wales. In G.C. Boon and J.M. Lewis (eds), *Welsh antiquity*, 63–79. Cardiff: National Museum of Wales.

Lynch, F.M. 1990. Wales and Ireland in prehistory: a fluctuating relationship. *Archaeologia Cambrensis* 138, 1–19.

Lynch, F.M. 1991. *Prehistoric Anglesey, the archaeology of the island to the Roman conquest*. Llangefni: Anglesey Antiquarian Society.

Lynch, F.M. 1993. *Excavations in the Brenig valley: a Mesolithic and Bronze Age landscape in North Wales*. Cardiff: Cambrian Archaeological Association and Cadw.

Moore-Colyer, R.J. 1999. Agriculture in Wales before and during the Second Millennium BC. *Archaeologia Cambrensis* 145, 15–33.

Musson, C.R. 1991. *The Breiddin hillfort: a later prehistoric settlement in the Welsh Marches*. London: Council for British Archaeology.

O'Kelly, C. 1969. Bryn Celli Ddu: a reinterpretation. *Archaeologia Cambrensis* 118, 17–38.

Olding, F. 2000. *The prehistoric landscapes of the eastern Black Mountains*. Oxford: British Archaeological Reports British Series 297.

Peterson, R. 1999. *The construction and use of categories of Neolithic pottery from Wales*. University of Southampton: Unpublished PhD Thesis.

Pollard, J. 1992. The Sanctuary, Overton Hill, Wiltshire: a re-examination. *Proceedings of the Prehistoric Society* 58, 213–26.

Pollard, J. 1995. Inscribing space: formal deposition at the later Neolithic monument of Woodhenge, Wiltshire. *Proceedings of the Prehistoric Society* 61, 137–56.

Powell, T.G.E. 1973. Excavation of the megalithic chambered cairn at Dyffryn Ardudwy, Merioneth, Wales. *Archaeologia* 104, 1–49.

Powell, T.G.E. and Daniel, G.E. 1956. *Barclodiad y Gawres*. Liverpool: University of Liverpool Press.

Renfrew, C. 1973. Monuments, mobilisation and social organisation in Neolithic Wessex. In C. Renfrew (ed.), *The explanation of culture change*, 539–58. London: Duckworth.

Richards, C. and Thomas, J. 1984. Ritual activity and structured deposition in later Neolithic Wessex. In R. Bradley and J. Gardiner (eds), *Neolithic studies: a review of some current research*, 189–218. Oxford: British Archaeological Reports British Series 133.

Richards, C. 1993. Contextual analysis of Grooved Ware at Balfarg. In G.J. Barclay and C.J. Russell-White (eds), Excavations in the ceremonial complex of the fourth to second millennium BC at Balfarg/Balbirnie, Glenrothes, Fife. *Proceedings of the Society of Antiquaries of Scotland*. 123, 185–92.

Richards, C. 1996. Henges and water: towards an elemental understanding of monumentality and landscape in late Neolithic Britain. *Journal of Material Culture* 1, 313–36.

Richards, M.P. and Hedges, R.E.M. 1999. A Neolithic revolution? New evidence of diet in the British Neolithic. *Antiquity* 73, 891–7.

Sheridan, A. 1986. Megaliths and megalomania: an account, and interpretation, of the development of passage tombs in Ireland. *Journal of Irish Archaeology* 3, 17–30.

Smith, C.A. and Lynch, F.M. 1987. *Trefignath and Din Dryfol: the excavation of two megalithic tombs on Anglesey*. Bangor: Cambrian Archaeological Association.

Thomas, J. 1996. *Time, culture and identity*. London: Routledge.

Thomas, J. 2001. Neolithic enclosures: reflections on excavations in Wales and Scotland. In T. Darvill and J. Thomas (eds), *Neolithic enclosures in Atlantic northwest Europe*, 132–43. Oxford: Oxbow.

Tilley, C. 1994. *A phenomenology of landscape: places, paths and monuments*. Oxford: Berg.

Ward, A.H. 1987. Cefn Bryn, Gower. *Archaeology in Wales* 27, 39–40.

Warrilow, W., Owen, G. and Britnell, W. 1986. Eight ring ditches at Four Crosses, Powys. *Proceedings of the Prehistoric Society* 52, 53–87.

Watson, A. 2001. Composing Avebury. *World Archaeology* 33, 296–314.

Webley, D.P. 1976. How the west was won: prehistoric land use in the southern marches. In G.C. Boon and J.M. Lewis (eds), *Welsh antiquity*, 19–35. Cardiff: National Museum of Wales.

White, S.I. and Smith, G. 1999. A funerary and ceremonial centre at Capel Eithin, Gaerwen, Anglesey. *Transactions of the Anglesey Antiquarian Society*.

Whittle, A. 1997. *Sacred mound, holy rings. Silbury Hill and the West Kennet palisade enclosures: a later Neolithic complex in north Wiltshire*. Oxford: Oxbow.

Whittle, A. and Wysocki, M. 1998. Parc le Breos Cwm transepted long cairn, Gower, West Glamorgan: date, contents, and context. *Proceedings of the Prehistoric Society* 64, 139–82.

Williams, J.L and Davidson, A. 1998. Survey and excavation at the Graig Lwyd Neolithic axe-factory, Penmaenmawr. *Archaeology in Wales* 38, 3–21.

21   By way of illustration: art, memory and materiality in the Irish Sea and beyond

Andrew Jones

Introduction

Since the rediscovery of Newgrange at the end of the seventeenth century the great passage tombs of the Boyne Valley, Ireland, have exercised a power on the imagination of both antiquarian and archaeologist. Two aspects of these monuments continue to have a singularly powerful effect on the imagination today. Foremost is the spectacular nature of the art associated with these monuments which lead to questions relating to meaning and significance. Related to this, with the recognition of related monumental and artistic traditions around the Irish Sea region and further afield, queries arise about the possible origin of these monuments. In this paper I want to reassess both of these questions by reviewing the intellectual and practical conditions within which we study passage tomb art. By doing so I wish to question the desire to continue to search for a unity to the 'passage tomb phenomenon' within the Irish Sea region.

By way of illustration

I want to begin this reassessment by taking a look at a decorated stone from the western tomb at Knowth. My example is orthostat 45. This stone is decorated with angular incised motifs followed by angular picked motifs, dispersed picking, picked ribbons and close area picking (Fig. 21.1). The stone is covered with a total of five overlays of motifs. How are we to understand this phenomenon? I argue that traditional accounts tend to emphasise each set of motifs as distinct chronological styles (Eogan 1986; 1997), and thereby overlook the cultural specificity of this practice.

Many of our problems with passage tomb art arise because, when examining these images, we tend to privilege form over process. One consequence of the subordination of process to form is the tendency to dislocate either panels or motifs from their contexts. For example in the classic corpus of megalithic art Shee Twohig (1981, 107, 137, see also corpus catalogue) presents both motifs and panels in isolation. In part, this is a precondition of academic discourse; motifs and panels

are transferred to the medium of paper so that we can compare and analyse them (Jones 2001a). Nevertheless, a consequence of this is that images then appear to us as spatially and temporally static. For this reason we often overlook the context of motifs and feel compelled to compare motifs that are spatially and temporally disparate (see Kinnes 1995). It is this strategy that lies at the heart of schemes of cultural interaction (Bradley and Chapman 1986, 132; O'Sullivan 1993, 10–11; Shee Twohig 1981, 137) and chronologically based narratives of art styles (e.g. Eogan 1986; 1997; O'Sullivan 1986). Interestingly, while endogenous interpretations of passage tomb art (Bradley 1989a; Dronfield, 1995a; 1995b; 1996; Lewis-Williams and Dowson 1993) provide an understanding of how motifs and panels may have functioned in terms of the human nervous system, these schemes are similarly reliant on a notion of temporal stasis. This is particularly true of Dronfield's statistical analyses, which depend upon the incorporation of all panels into a single atemporal scheme (Dronfield 1996). As Cooney (1996, 60) notes in the comments to this article such analyses depend upon the visibility of panels which were not easily accessible during the use of the monument. Cooney's point underlines the fact that this methodology, and the mode of representation to which it is allied, is synoptical and tends not to take account of the position of the viewing subject.[1] Effectively, as archaeologists, we are beguiled by formal similarity at the expense of a deeper investigation of the context of production of images. The aim of this paper is to explore what the study of passage tomb art might look like if we focus on process rather than form. I will argue that by focusing on process we can circumnavigate some of the problems arising from the discussion of origins and interaction.

If we are to focus on process rather than form, then it is critical that we consider the relationship between images and memory. While the relationship between the two is not immediately apparent, it is important since, in focusing on *making* images, we are simultaneously examining the effect both the images and the act of production have on cognition.

Like other forms of inscription, such as writing (Connerton 1989; Fentress and Wickham 1992; Moreland

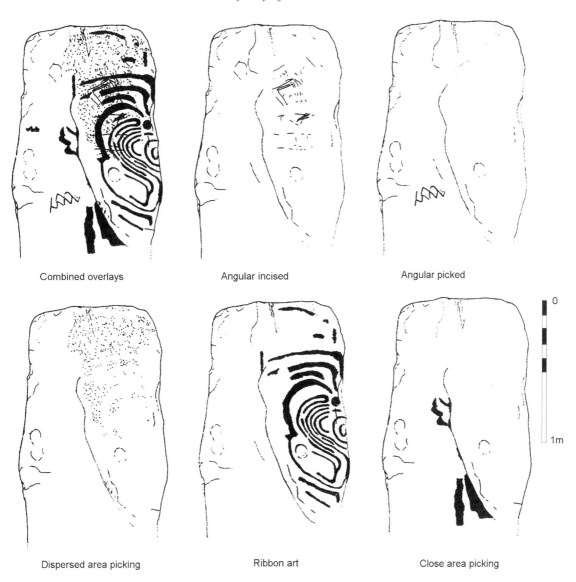

Combined overlays Angular incised Angular picked

Dispersed area picking Ribbon art Close area picking

0

1m

Figure 21.1. Orthostat 45, western tomb, Knowth, illustrating the succession of decorative techniques beginning with angular incised motifs followed by angular picked motifs, dispersed picking, picked ribbons and close area picking (after Eogan 1997).

2001), we traditionally treat images as the products, or traces of, prior mnemonic functions. The production of images is treated then as an expression of memory. This is obviously a passive model of *images* in which visual images simply reflect memory, or act as surrogates for memory (Melion and Küchler 1991). Such a view presupposes a static model of *memory* in which memories are hermetically retained or stored. I argue that this model of images and memory is implicit to the stadial notion of art styles.

I suggest that we take an alternative view of the relationship between visual images and memory. Instead of speaking in terms of discrete stored memories, we need to consider memory as a continuous and interactive process of engagement between person and world. The

relationship between image production and remembrance should then be viewed as a dynamic process, in which the production of visual images shapes the form of remembrance (see also Jones 2001b). Remembrance is performed and, as an active component of this process, images do not so much represent memories as help to create them (Melion and Küchler 1991, 3–4). The act of producing images is therefore responsible for projecting memory, while the visual traces of image are mnemonics for the act of production. Images therefore have a dual function in terms of their relationship to memory. If we are to consider images as active participants in the production of memory we need to consider how it is that images function. This is particularly important if we are to understand how the material qualities of images visually affect the viewer. Of special note here are the works of David Freedberg (1989) and Alfred Gell (1998) who both stress the point that we need to consider art as a form of technology which acts to captivate or enchant the viewer. In addition, if we are to consider the role of image production and reception in the process of remembrance, it is worth also considering the multiple ways in which the production of images may be embodied through a range of sensory mediums. With Serematakis (1994), I argue that the senses evoke memory and that we should think of embodied memory as a form of metasense (see also Hamilakis 2002). As we shall see it is important to consider a number of sensory registers, particularly the aural and haptic senses, when considering the production and reception of passage tomb art.

Making passage tomb art

With these considerations in mind, I will now turn to passage tomb art. Instead of examining distinct art styles, or abstracted motifs, in the passage tomb art repertoire my intention is to examine the *practice* of motif production and reception. This approach shifts us away from a chronologically driven comparative perspective, to instead examine the process of art production. I am not interested in defining the meaning of art motifs, rather in examining how art functions in certain architectural and social settings (see also Bradley 1989a; 1989b; Thomas 1991; 1992). In doing this I wish to provide an interpretative framework for understanding the observations and insights of Muiris O'Sullivan (1986) and George Eogan (1997). This account is indebted to their prior observations.

I will begin with an examination of the well-documented passage tombs from the Boyne Valley. Finally as a counterpoint to the Irish evidence I will compare Irish passage tombs with other monuments further afield, especially the passage graves of Orkney.

I will examine three aspects of image production:

1. The location of superimposed images versus non-superimposed images, and the technique used in their production.
2. The location and technique employed on re-used panels in the construction of monuments.
3. The significance of the material qualities of the stones on which art is executed.

Superimposition, location and technique

Let us start by looking at the nature and location of superimposition in the exterior and interior of passage tombs. The best evidence comes from Knowth site 1 and the main Newgrange mound, while some evidence for superimposition can also be gleaned from Dowth. At the outset we will distinguish between incision and picking as distinctive techniques (see Eogan 1997; O'Sullivan 1986).

We will begin with an investigation of Knowth. Faintly incised angular motifs are rare on the exterior kerbstones at Knowth. They are found on only six stones, or 7% of the total (Eogan 1986, 150). These motifs are always superimposed by other picked designs, usually of a curvilinear form. O'Sullivan (1986, 77) identifies a further stage of superimposition of picked ornamentation on 15, or 16%, of the kerbstones. It would appear that two, occasionally three, episodes of superimposition occurred on the kerbstones at Knowth. In some cases superimposed designs cross-cut previous designs, such as K52 where a picked spiral was cut by picked ribbons. In most cases, however, subsequent picked designs seem to enhance previous designs.

When we come to examine the interior of Knowth the first thing that is so striking is the intense degree of superimposition. Faintly incised angular motifs are more common in the interior of the monument, and are on a total of 30 stones in the chamber and passage of the eastern tomb and 11 stones in the chamber and passage of the western tomb. Like the kerbstones, incised stones also seem to have superimposed picking on their surfaces. This picking takes a number of forms: angular; formless loose area picking; formless close area picking and broad picked lines in ribbon/serpentiforms (Eogan 1997, 221). If we include the incised motifs, five episodes of superimposition can be identified in the interior of the passage tombs at Knowth. These episodes appear to follow in temporal succession and they both relate to and cross-cut previous motifs. On some occasions the primary angular incised designs are used as guidelines for subsequent angular picking, as in corbel 37/38 (Eogan 1997, 225). On other occasions as in orthostat 41, incised and picked angular motifs are cross-cut (Eogan 1997, 226).

Other forms of picking often appear to cross-cut subsequent designs, this is especially true of the loose area picking and ribbon designs. Close area picking seems to often be used to sculpt areas of decorated stones not otherwise covered by previous designs.

This distinction in the number and intensity of episodes of activity is also a feature of Newgrange. Incised angular motifs are absent from the visible surfaces of exterior kerbstones at Newgrange (C. O'Kelly 1982). Most stones have picked angular and curvilinear designs, and there is less absolute evidence for secondary picking, although O'Sullivan (1986, 79) suggests that K1, K52 and K67 – the most elaborate of the kerbstones – may have been enhanced with secondary picking.

The interior of Newgrange is quite different. Here we see a small number of stones with incised angular motifs (six in total), but more importantly a great many stones have evidence of superimposition, with at least four episodes of superimposition, in particular of picked angular motifs and loose and close area picking. In some cases this reworking is extensive. Indeed, O'Sullivan (1986, 79) notes that loose area picking is found on nearly all the stones of the passage. Close area picking at

Newgrange is particularly spectacular since it is used to sculpt the form of the stone – clearly seen in stones R21 and R22 – flanking the transition between passage and chamber.

At Dowth (O'Kelly and O'Kelly 1983), the evidence is more partial, particularly on the exterior where the original number of kerbstones is unknown. All kerbstones with evidence for art have picked curvilinear designs. There is some possible evidence for loose area picking on K16 (O'Kelly and O'Kelly 1983, 163). However in general there appears to be only a single episode of working on the exterior of the monument.

This contrasts with the tombs in the interior. There is evidence for incised angular motifs on orthostats C2, C7 and C8, north tomb (O'Kelly and O'Kelly 1983, 169– 71), and on recess orthostat C12, south tomb (O'Kelly and O'Kelly 1983, 177). Curvilinear picked motifs are present on many of the structural stones of the interior, and there is evidence for the reworking of picked motifs, especially on orthostat C19, north tomb where a picked radial design cross-cuts an earlier picked curvilinear design (O'Kelly and O'Kelly 1983, 172). Loose and close area picking are also evident. Loose area picking is evident on C1, C7, C19, north tomb and R1, the lintel of the recess, south tomb. Evidence for close area picking is most apparent on the recess orthostat C12, south tomb where it is used to both obliterate earlier picked designs and accentuate incised designs (O'Kelly and O'Kelly 1983, 177).

At each monument we appear to observe numerous episodes of reworking in relation to artistic production, with distinctions in the amount of reworking in monument interiors and exteriors (Fig. 21.2). Eogan has noted that there are distinctions in the design of motifs at Knowth, with curvilinear art predominating on the exterior kerb and angular motifs in the interior (Eogan 1986, 188–9, 194–5). At Dowth the exterior of the monument consists of curvilinear designs whereas the interior has a propensity of angular designs. A similar pattern can be observed at Newgrange where the exterior of the monument has both curvilinear and angular pecked motifs (Eogan 1986, 193). Again these are more often executed as a single episode, as distinct from the multiple episodes of reworking identified in the interior (Fig. 21.2).

If we combine this observation with the observed distinctions in the practice of reworking, it follows that the exterior curvilinear art is largely the result of a single episode of *in situ* execution and is executed as a holistic design, often covering the entirety of the stones' surface. This is in contradistinction to the interior panels where motifs are executed over a lengthier period of time, and where the execution of motifs follows an ordered sequence from faintly incised motifs to boldly realised pecked motifs. While there is a sequence we cannot relate this sequence to specific chronological stages. For example in the case of the later picked motifs both the position and execution of motifs on stones is more haphazard,

and often only covers certain sections of the stone. In both cases, the mode by which the motifs on the exterior and in the interior operate visually is quite distinct, and this relates to the manner of their execution.

We also have to consider the role of other senses in the production of the later picked images. The later picked images at Newgrange are continuous across the interior of the monument and were produced when the monument was complete. Given that their execution leaves little visible trace and what we know of the acoustic properties of these monuments (Watson 2001) it is likely that the production of this later picked art would have been as much acoustic as visual in its impact (see also Ouzman 2001).

The incorporation of art

The practice of artistic reworking is related to the incorporation of art within the body of monuments. At Knowth, a series of panels with art are hidden within the fabric of the monument. These include orthostats 17, 18, 74 and 81 in the western tomb. A number of panels of art are also difficult of access, especially those used in the corbelling of the central chamber (Eogan 1986). At Newgrange the corpus of hidden art includes the back of kerbstones K13 and K18 (Fig. 21.3), the roof-stone of the east recess, art placed on the back of the roof of the passage RS3 and RS7 as well as stones X, Y and Z. Furthermore, panels of art are also a feature of three of the structural stones of the roof-box (C. O'Kelly 1982). Finally, buried in the cairn make-up at Newgrange were three boulders bearing pecked curvilinear and angular designs (M. O'Kelly 1982, 190–2). At Dowth, hidden art is found on the back of Kerbstone K51 (O'Kelly and O'Kelly 1983, 164–6).

Interestingly, this hidden art appears to consist of both incised and picked techniques; this is especially evident in the panels hidden on the back of kerbstones K13 and K18 at Newgrange. On K51 at Dowth there is a distinction in the manner of execution on either side of the panel with the hidden motifs being haphazard in their overall effect, in contrast to the more ordered designs on the front of the stone. Picked angular motifs are also a feature of the corbelling of Knowth and the art on the roof-box at Newgrange. Obviously some of these panels have been incorporated from elsewhere bearing preexisting art motifs (especially the stone used in the eastern recess and the kerbstones K13 and K18 at Newgrange). In other cases, as with the art found on the Knowth corbels and Newgrange lightbox, this is more likely to have been executed *in situ*. Eogan (1998) suggests that much of the hidden art from both Knowth and Newgrange may have been derived from a now dismantled monument standing in the position of the present Knowth 1.

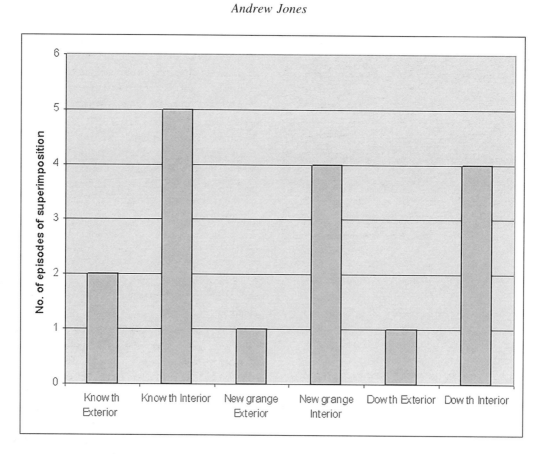

Figure 21.2. *Episodes of superimposition in the major Boyne Valley passage tombs.*

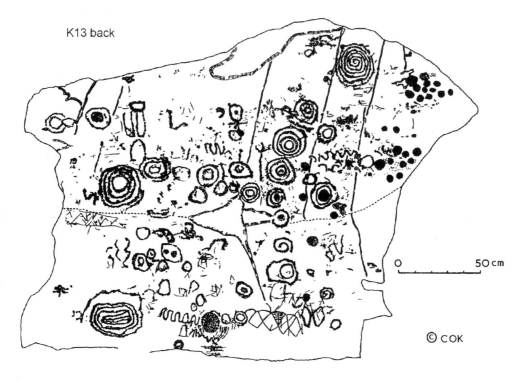

Figure 21.3. *An example of the 'hidden art' from the back of kerbstone K13 at Newgrange. Note the haphazard nature of the design (after C. O'Kelly 1982).*

Figure 21.4. *K52 at Newgrange. Note the series of natural cup marks which inform the from and execution of the overall design.*

The qualities of stone

The recognition of the importance of the material qualities of stone in influencing the production of images has long been a feature of the analysis of Palaeolithic cave art (Clottes and Lewis-Williams 1996; Lorblanchet 1989). It has also now been recognised as a feature of open air rock art sites (Bradley *et al.* forthcoming; Helskog 1999; Nash and Chippindale 2001, 3–4). For this reason I believe it is important to consider how the material qualities of stone influence the execution of passage tomb art. Notably, some stones have pre-existing hollows or cupmarks which are embellished by picking. Examples of this include Newgrange K52, K67, K82 and R21. In other cases, the form of the stone itself affects the layout of the motifs. This is most spectacularly observed on Newgrange K52 (Fig. 21.4). Dowth also has plentiful evidence for the embellishment of natural hollows, on the back of kerbstone K51 and on orthostat C7, north tomb. Large natural hollows are also a feature of kerbstone K1 outside the south tomb at Dowth.

The material qualities of the stone are particularly important when we examine the layout of close and loose area picking in both monuments. Curiously, rather than preparing the stone for subsequent decoration the picking instead appears to have been employed to accentuate the undulating character of the stone at a later stage in its life (O'Sullivan 1986).

Passage tomb art, performance and place

How are we to understand these processes of reworking? They are difficult to comprehend if we subordinate form to process since we simply assume that art was simply made to be viewed because of the spectacular visual nature of passage tomb art. If we are to re-evaluate this aspect of passage tomb art, we need to contextualise these processes of reworking alongside other contemporary activities at passage tombs.

We know that the two major passage tombs at Knowth and Newgrange were constructed of materials from several widespread sources (Mitchell 1992). At Knowth and Newgrange, quartz from County Wicklow and granodiorite, granite and siltstone from Dundalk Bay were used in the construction of the façade. The greywacke, sandstone and limestone used in the construction of both Newgrange and Knowth was probably quarried some kilometres from the site. As Cooney (2000, 135–8) cogently argues, the use of both local and non-local stone is significant since each material embodies a sense of place which is then re-articulated in the form of the passage tomb. Moreover, places of significance are embedded in monuments, as Knowth incorporates both an earlier settlement and a later passage tomb (passage tomb 16).

In a sense these individual components are *material citations* of the significance of place and identity. Nowhere is this more apparent than in the construction of the curious stone settings outside the entrances of Knowth and Newgrange (Figure 21.5). The Newgrange setting was a stone pavement bounded by low uprights of schist, the setting contained two pieces of flint and an unusual piece of polished sandstone and was subsequently covered by a mound composed of fragments of quarried quartz, water-rolled quartz and grey granite pebbles (O'Kelly 1982, 75–6). At Knowth stone settings were abundant outside both the eastern and western tombs (Eogan 1986, 46–8, 65). The largest of these, outside the eastern tomb, was edged with glacial erratics and ironstone and the internal paving was covered by two successive layers of quartz chips. Like the use of materials in the passage tombs themselves, these stone settings reiterated and re-articulated the significance of place through the deposition of materials of differing origins. Similar features occur on the top of passage tomb 16 at Knowth (Eogan 1984) and further afield beneath the passage tomb at Townleyhall II (Eogan 1963).

The connection between these circular features and the curvilinear images in contemporary art has been highlighted by Bradley (1998, 104–9). However, I believe that these circular features and the curvilinear designs of passage tomb art are related by more than just their formal similarities: they are also connected by their association with a specific form of cultural practice. To begin with, the circular stone settings give us a critical insight into an understanding of the qualities of stone. Stone is a material that embodies the significance of place. Its use, through its incorporation within, around and beneath monuments is a citation of this significance. What is more, as we see with the stone settings, the significance of the relationship between stone and place is reiterated or replenished through repeated episodes of deposition. More importantly, the process of reiteration that characterises the use of stone in both the monuments and

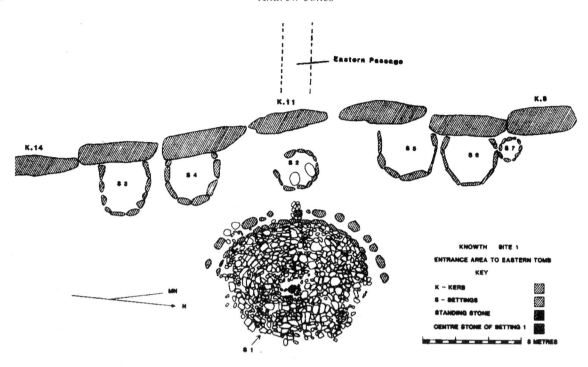

Figure 21.5. *Stone settings outside Knowth (after Eogan 1986).*

the stone settings also occurs in relation to passage tomb art. In some instances panels of art are incorporated into the body of the monument, possibly from earlier monuments, just as stones from differing sources are incorporated in the mound construction. Likewise, in the interior of the monument, the connection between the significance of place and identity is reiterated by the episodic replenishment of images on stones. Here the process of superimposition is of the utmost importance since the execution and repetition of images is a visible citation of events of prior significance, as fainter images are pecked over, or drawn attention to by subsequent pecking. Moreover, images are executed in sympathy with the material qualities of stone. Rather than thinking of images being carved onto stone, then, perhaps we need to consider images to be drawn *out of* stone. This is of particular significance when we think of the sculptural qualities of later pecking. Once we consider this, alongside the observation that the execution of images within the passage tomb produces an acoustic effect, it becomes clear that it is the *work* of image creation that is critical to the reception and meaning of passage tomb art.

In some ways we can think of the art as activating and reactivating the material and conceptual link between stone, place and identity. That images are indeed active is evinced by the location of images on the structural stones of the Newgrange roof-box – itself a conduit for the episodic source of celestial energy – and on the external surfaces of the great basin stones at Knowth and Newgrange, which may have been used to contain the remains of the dead (Sheridan 1986).

Furthermore, images are active in a number of different ways, depending upon the nature of their composition and their overall visual effect in relation to the viewing subject. On the exterior of the monument images are easily available for visual inspection and are composed as a whole. The images on the exterior kerbstones are executed *in situ*, probably during the monument's construction. As such these images are architectural –they are an integral part of the monument – and as a whole they act to visually define the perimeter of the monument. One consequence of their composition as a continuous whole is that the images are visually complex, and the involutions of spiral and concentric curvilinear designs serve to cognitively captivate the viewer, drawing them into the design. This is especially interesting since many of the most complex compositions are on the kerbstones at the entrance to the passages of Knowth and Newgrange and K52 and K67 at Newgrange (Bradley 1989a; Thomas 1991). Might this art be so placed on the perimeter kerbstones to provide a visual barrier, drawing the viewer's attention to the art rather than the activities occurring inside the monuments? Interestingly O'Kelly (1982, 72) notes that complex panels of art such as K52 at Newgrange, placed diametrically opposite K1 at the entrance, may have created a visual axis for the monument. Indeed, the concept of art as a visual cue defining points of transition in and around monuments has been discussed in the context of the contemporary settlement of Skara Brae, Orkney (Richards 1991) and the passage tombs at Louchcrew, County Meath (Thomas 1992).

The art in the interior of the tombs works quite

differently. In the interior of the monument images are encountered in semi-darkness as the subject moves down the passage and into the chambers (see also Bradley 1989b). Notably the art in the passage at Newgrange is heavily picked, while picked ribbons dominate the Knowth passage, making the encounter of the art a partially textural experience. Images in the chambers and recesses are often placed in inaccessible places making their visual appreciation difficult; this is especially true of the incised images. At the outset these images did not visually captivate the viewer. Rather the presence of images actively shaped the production of successive images, each made with (either negative or positive) reference to the primary image. Over time, as earlier images were embellished, the art became more visually arresting. Like the exterior motifs, it is so placed in the recesses of the chambers to draw in the viewer. Through repeated performance images are visually drawn out of the rock.

So, I have argued that we need to consider the passage tomb art of the Boyne Valley monuments as a form of technology executed to instantiate the relationship between place and identity. Importantly the images on the exterior and interior of the monument operate in quite different ways. Since the images on the exterior of the monument are architecturally integral, are executed as a whole, and are designed to captivate the viewer they are not the context for subsequent reworking. In the interior of the monuments images are less visually arresting, however images provide a visual trace for subsequent reworking. On both the exterior and interior art acts as a 'technology of remembrance' since it is executed to memorialise the significance of place and identity. In both cases images act as visual cues for remembrance. Due to their spectacular manner of execution images on the exterior simply elicit remembrance visually; in the interior, images also act as cues for remembrance, as remembrance is materially expressed through the repetitive action of image making.

Art, technology and memory in the Boyne Valley and beyond

Traditionally differences in the manner of execution and the form of art motifs are assumed to be chronological, however this presupposes a stadial scheme of stylistic reproduction in which one style simply replaces another. If we assume that the production and reproduction of images was part of a process of visualising remembrance, then the differences in the processes of production and the number of episodes of reworking relate to distinct mnemonic practices. The framework I have proposed here allows us to consider the production of art as one means of materially expressing remembrance; it is a strategy of remembrance that will be expressed in different ways in different cultural contexts.

If we compare the practice identified at Knowth and Newgrange with other passage tombs (Fig. 21.6), such as the smaller tombs at Knowth, it is notable that while incised motifs are found at the smaller tombs there are only two phases of reworking (Eogan 1997). Similar practices of reworking are found in other areas of Ireland. At Fourknocks I, County Meath angular incised motifs are found on stones R2, R5 and L4 (Shee Twohig 1981, figures 246–7). In the case of R5 and L4 these motifs influence the execution of pecked angular motifs. The motifs on L4 infill the area delineated by the angular designs, while the motifs on R5 seem to refer to prior motifs in their overall design. Most of the art at Fourknocks, however, consists of pecked angular motifs probably executed as a single event and is located at specific transitional points in the tomb interior. At Fourknocks I we observe two episodes of reworking.

At the passage grave cemetery at Loughcrew, County Meath again we see the overlaying of sparse incised motifs with a single phase of picked motifs (Shee Twohig 1981, figures 213–44). A number of tombs suggest evidence for angular incised motifs, such as Cairn F, R4, Cairn L, C16, Co1/16 and C19, Cairn T, cell 3 roof-stone and Cairn W, C2. Most motifs on the Loughcrew monuments are picked, however there is also evidence for dispersed picking as on Cairn L, R4. The material qualities of stones appear to be critical to the execution of motifs, since a number of natural hollows are embellished by working as on Cairn F, L4 and C1, Cairn H, L2 and C18, Cairn I, C1 and cell 3, Cairn L, L1, L3, R4, C1 and C17, Cairn S, L3, C2 and C6, Cairn T, L5, R5, C2, C3 and C15, Cairn U, C3 and Cairn V, C4. Probably the most notable feature of the art at Loughcrew is its haphazard nature. Like the art in the interior of the Boyne Valley passage tombs it does not appear to have been composed in a single episode, although there is less evidence for the overlaying of motifs, with a likelihood of at least two episodes of reworking.

Many of the features identified in the major Boyne Valley monuments appear to be found in other monuments in eastern Ireland. While the practice of reworking appears to be a feature of the production of art in this region, it would appear that this practice was of special significance in the major Boyne Valley monuments. In fact it is precisely due to this specific 'technology of remembrance' that the art of the major Boyne valley passage tombs is so spectacular, as the significance of place and identity is continually reiterated through artistic production.

Practices appear to differ in monuments around the Irish Sea and further afield. The images on the Anglesey monuments, Barclodiad y Gawres and Bryn Celli Ddu, appear to have been executed in a single episode of pecking, there is little apparent evidence for super-imposition of images in either case. The qualities of the stone appear to have been critical to the execution of images on some of the stones at Barclodiad y Gawres,

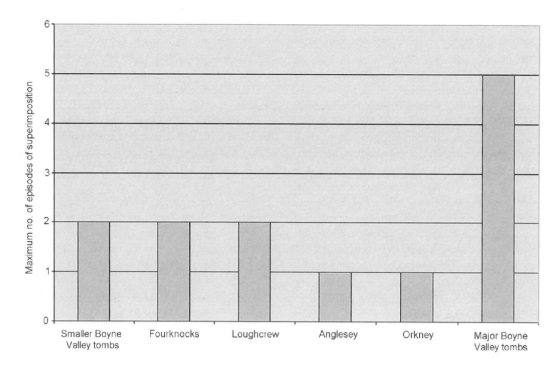

Figure 21.6. *A comparison of episodes of superimposition in passage tombs in Ireland, Anglesey and Orkney.*

such as C1 where the images are fitted between natural undulations in the rock and C3 where images cluster around and work within a natural crack in the surface (see Shee Twohig 1981, figures 266–7). Nevertheless it is worth noting that the reiteration of the significance of place is certainly a feature of Bryn Celli Ddu where the position of the passage tomb incorporates an earlier henge (O'Kelly 1969).

As a final point I want to examine the practice of remembrance in a related group of monuments in Orkney. On the face of it there are a number of similarities with Ireland and Wales; in each case monuments incorporate earlier structures, such as the houses beneath the passage graves at Howe of Howe (Smith 1994) and Maes Howe (Richards 1993). They are also built from materials from significant places in the landscape (Jones forthcoming). Again, in Orkney, curvilinear compositions, where they are found, are often on the exterior of monuments, such as at Pierowall Quarry, Westray (Sharples 1984). More common are faint angular incised motifs (Bradley *et al.* 2001). Again these motifs are difficult to see in the interior of the monument, as evinced by their relatively recent discovery. As I have argued in relation to Ireland, the execution of these designs are a citation of the relationship between stone, place and identity, as motifs represent visible features of the Orcadian landscape (Jones forthcoming) and are also cited at contemporary settlements. In Orkney this art represents *ephemeral* acts of repetition in different parts of the tomb, unlike Ireland where the repetition of images is *cumulative*. The designs are

executed on monuments to activate the relationship between place and identity, but a reiteration of this relationship is not a feature of Orcadian passage grave art. Remembrance was instead enacted through the reworking of the bones of the dead and the deposition of material culture.

Art, process and passage tombs in the Irish Sea region and beyond

As a technology, passage tomb art was a powerful medium for defining the relationship between substance, place and identity. However, we need to be aware that while the medium appears formally similar, in practice the art is implicated in quite different 'strategies of remembrance' in differing regions. Certain elements of the mnemonic practices outlined for Ireland occur in other regions, such as the reuse of decorated stones in the construction of monuments in France and Spain (Bueno Ramirez and de Balbín Behrmann 1998; Le Roux 1984). But the intensity and nature of the reworking of designs in the interior of Irish passage tombs appears to constitute a specific cultural practice.

Given this realisation we need to reconsider the role that formal analysis plays in the discussion of the origins of passage tombs around the Irish Sea region and further afield to the Orkney Isles, Brittany and Iberia (Bradley and Chapman 1986; Eogan 1999). I believe that an analysis which foregrounds the process of image production problematises the conclusions we draw regarding origins and interaction based on purely formal analysis. As noted in the introduction, one of the consequences of the emphasis on form is the desire to dislocate images from their context. Elsewhere I have argued that this rhetorical strategy is partly a precondition of an academic discourse which seeks to construct a comparative taxonomy of artefacts and monuments (Jones 2001a). An apt example of this rhetorical strategy for the Irish Sea region is Sheridan's (1986; 1995; this volume) analysis of the relationship between art motifs on bipartite pottery and the morphology of passage tomb architecture. In these analyses the comparison of the formal appearance of art motifs and the formal layout of monuments is used to draw connections between pottery and passage graves from north-east Ireland, south-west Scotland and north-west France, thereby advancing an argument for the origin of both monuments and artefacts in France. While connections between these areas cannot be entirely discounted[2] we need to remember that it is only possible to draw these connections together through the medium of the printed page; it is unlikely that such a synoptic perspective would have been available to communities around the Irish Sea in prehistory. Of course, this approach to the formal similarities of art motifs, artefacts and monuments has a deep intellectual history and is the legacy of a number of such approaches to the Neolithic of the Irish Sea region (Collins 1973; Davies and Evans 1933; 1962; de Valera 1960; Eogan 1986; 1999; Waddell 1992).

Needless to say, there is plentiful evidence of interaction around the Irish Sea region during the Neolithic (Bradley and Chapman 1986; Cooney 2000, 212–32; Waddell 1992) as well as between this region and areas further afield. It goes without saying that interaction certainly occurred between those areas in which we find passage tombs or passage graves. Nevertheless, with Tilley (1999, 82–101), I suggest that we should also be aware of the intellectual constraints that the construction of typological categories such as 'passage tombs' or 'passage tomb art' place on the way in which we both describe and ask questions of the data (for a related argument see Brophy this volume). We need to be aware that the specific rhetorical devices we use to discuss phenomena will tend to shape our research questions.[3]

I am not arguing that we need to abandon formal analysis or discussions of cultural interaction. Rather I am suggesting that we need to frame questions with a prior awareness of the intellectual legacies and constraints of such approaches. Instead, borrowing from the recent literature on the cultural interaction engendered by colonial encounter (e.g. Thomas 1991), we need to consider the role that material culture plays in the performance of cultural reproduction. By focusing on passage tomb art as a form of mnemonic practice I hope to have re-framed the way in which we think of this art

operating in relation to the passage tomb. Images therefore relate to distinct modes of cultural reproduction; art is implicated in differing strategies of remembrance in different regions around the Irish Sea as well as further afield. I will recapitulate this point by returning to the comparison of Ireland and Orkney. In Ireland and Orkney remembrance is performed in different ways. In Orkney, remembrance is enacted by the continuous deposition of material culture and the reworking of the bones of the dead. The production of art in Orkney is a component of the performance of remembrance that leaves an ephemeral visual trace. In Ireland, by contrast, it is critical that remembrance is visualised through the medium of art, as memories are imaged by being literally drawn out of stone.

Acknowledgements

I would particularly like to thank Yannis Hamilakis and Hannah Sackett for their helpful comments on this paper.

Notes

1 I am aware that superimposition, aurality and attention to the quality and topography of stone are characteristics that have been discussed under the rubric of shamanism or shamanic practice (e.g Lewis-Williams and Dowson 1988, Clottes and Lewis-Williams 1996, Ouzman 2001). While my analysis does not preclude a shamanic interpretation, I believe that this does not adequately encompass all aspects of image production in relation to passage tomb art. Instead, by focusing on the relationship between memory systems and images a series of other interpretative possibilities can be drawn out, including a discussion of the relationship between image production and place.

2 Of course, accounts of this sort have a deep history within the discipline. However it is notable that these accounts are characterised by a set of convoluted connections between geographically disparate regions; they have less to say about the mechanics of contact and the consequences these have for our understanding of the reproduction of social practices. To borrow from AEP Collins (1973), there is a 'deficiency in economy of hypothesis'

3 Tilley's argument relates to the way in which our descriptive language creates a series of intellectual traps or snares which come to have their own veracity and then require explanation. For example, as soon as we create the descriptive category 'megalith', the category serves as a linguistic bridge between phenomena related only by their construction using large stones. These phenomena are then grouped as a whole and demand explanation. In a similar way, I suggest that the formal representations we deploy to depict phenomena channel or shape discourse in certain directions and come to have a degree of veracity.

References

Bradley, R. 1989a. Death and entrances: a contextual analysis of megalithic art. *Current Anthropology* 30, 68–75.
Bradley, R. 1989b. Darkness and light in the design of

megalithic tombs. *Oxford Journal of Archaeology* 8, 251–9.

Bradley, R. 1998. *The significance of monuments: on the shaping of human experience in Neolithic and Bronze Age Europe.* London: Routledge.

Bradley, R. and Chapman, R. 1986. The nature and development of long-distance relations in Later Neolithic Britain and Ireland. In C. Renfrew and J.F. Cherry (eds), *Peer polity interaction and socio-political change,* 127–36. Cambridge: Cambridge University Press.

Bradley, R., Phillips, T., Richards, C. and Webb, M. 2001. Decorating the houses of the dead: incised and pecked motifs in Orkney chambered tombs. *Cambridge Archaeological Journal* 11, 45–67.

Bradley, R., Jones, A., Nordenborg-Myhre, L. and Sackett, H. forthcoming. Sailing through stone: carved ships and the rock face at Revheim, south-west Norway, *Norwegian Archaeological Review.*

Bueno Ramirez, P. and de Balbín Behrmann, R. 1998. The origin of the megalithic decorative system: graphics versus architecture. *Journal of Iberian Archaeology* 0, 53–67.

Clottes, J. and Lewis-Williams, D. 1996. *The shamans of prehistory: trance and magic in the painted caves.* New York: Abrams.

Collins, A.E.P. 1973. A re-examination of the Clyde-Carlingford tombs. In G. Daniel and P. Kjaerum (eds), *Megalithic graves and ritual,* 93–103. Copenhagen: Jutland Archaeological Society Publications.

Connerton, P. 1989. *How societies remember.* Cambridge: Cambridge University Press.

Cooney, G. 1996. Comments on Dronfield. *Cambridge Archaeological Journal* 6, 59–60.

Cooney, G. 2000 *Landscapes of Neolithic Ireland.* London: Routledge.

Davies, O. and Evans, E.E. 1933. Excavations at Goward, near Hilltown, Co. Down. *Proceedings of the Belfast Natural History and Philosophical Society* 1932–3, 90–105.

Davies, O. and Evans, E.E. 1962. Irish court cairns. *Ulster Journal of Archaeology* 24–5, 2–7.

de Valera, R. 1960. The court cairns of Ireland. *Proceedings of the Royal Irish Academy* 60C, 9–140.

Dronfield, J. 1995a. Subjective vision and the source of Irish megalithic art. *Antiquity* 69, 539–49.

Dronfield, J. 1995b. Migraine, light and hallucinogens: the neurocognitive basis of Irish megalithic art. *Oxford Journal of Archaeology* 14, 261–75.

Dronfield, J. 1996. Entering alternative realities: cognition, art and architecture in Irish passage tombs. *Cambridge Archaeological Journal* 6, 37–72.

Eogan, G. 1963. A Neolithic habitation site and megalithic tomb in Townleyhall townland, Co. Louth. *Journal of the Royal Society of Antiquaries of Ireland* 93, 37–81.

Eogan, G. 1984. *Excavations at Knowth 1.* Dublin: Royal Irish Academy.

Eogan, G. 1986. *Knowth and the passage-tombs of Ireland.* London: Thames and Hudson.

Eogan, G. 1997. Overlays and underlays: aspects of megalithic art succession at Brugh Na Boinne, Ireland. *Brigantium* 10, 217–34.

Eogan, G. 1998. Knowth before Knowth. *Antiquity* 72, 162–72.

Eogan, G. 1999 Megalithic art and society. *Proceedings of the Prehistoric Society* 65, 415–46.

Fentress, J. and Wickham, C. 1992. *Social memory.* Oxford: Blackwell.

Freedberg, D. 1989 *The power of images: studies in the history and theory of response.* Chicago: Chicago University Press.

Gell, A. 1998. *Art and agency: an anthropological theory.* Oxford: Clarendon.

Hamilakis, Y. 2002. The past as oral history: towards an archaeology of the senses. In Y. Hamilakis, M. Pluciennik and S. Tarlow (eds), *Thinking through the body: archaeologies of corporeality,* 121–36. New York: Kluwer Academic/Plenum.

Helskog, K. 1999. The shore connection. Cognitive landscape and communication with rock carvings in Northernmost Europe. *Norwegian Archaeological Review* 32, 73–94.

Jones, A. 2001a. Drawn from memory: the archaeology of aesthetics and the aesthetics of archaeology in earlier Bronze Age Britain and the present. *World Archaeology* 33, 335–57.

Jones, A. 2001b. Enduring images?: Image production and memory in earlier Bronze Age Scotland. In J. Brück (ed.), *Bronze Age landscapes: tradition and transformation,* 217–31. Oxford: Oxbow.

Jones, A. forthcoming. Natural histories and social identities in Neolithic Orkney. In E. Casella and C. Fowler (eds), *The archaeology of plural and changing identities: beyond identification.* Kluwer Academic/Plenum Press.

Kinnes, I. 1995. An innovation backed by great prestige: the instance of the spiral and twenty centuries of stony sleep. In I. Kinnes and G. Varndell (eds), *'Unbaked urns of rudely shape': essays on British and Irish pottery,* 49–53. Oxford: Oxbow.

Le Roux, C.T. 1984. A propos des fouilles de Gavrinis (Morbihan): nouvelles données sur l'art mégalithique Armoricain. *Bulletin de la Société Préhistorique Française* 81, 240–5.

Lewis-Williams, J.D. and Dowson, T.A. 1993. On vision and power in the Neolithic: evidence from the decorated monuments. *Current Anthropology* 34, 55–65.

Lorblanchet, M. 1989. From man to animal and sign in Palaeolithic art. In H. Morphy (ed.), *Animals into art,* 109–43. London: Unwin Hyman.

Melion, W. and Küchler, S. 1991. Introduction: memory, cognition, and image production. In W. Melion and S. Kuchler (eds), *Images of memory: on remembering and representation,* 1–47. Washington: Smithsonian Institute Press.

Moreland, J. 2001. *Archaeology and text.* London: Duckworth.

Nash, G. and Chippindale, C. 2001. Images of enculturing landscapes: a European perspective. In G. Nash and C. Chippindale (eds), *European landscapes of rock art,* 1–19. London: Routledge.

O'Kelly, C. 1969. Bryn Celli Ddu, Anglesey: a reinterpretation. *Archaeologia Cambrensis* 17, 17–49.

O'Kelly, C. 1982. Corpus of Newgrange art. In M. O'Kelly (ed.), *Newgrange: archaeology, art and legend,* 146–85. London: Thames and Hudson.

O'Kelly, M. 1982. *Newgrange: archaeology, art and legend.* London: Thames and Hudson.

O'Kelly, M. and O'Kelly, C. 1983. The tumulus of Dowth,

County Meath. *Proceedings of the Royal Irish Academy* 83C, 135–90.

O'Sullivan, M. 1986. Approaches to passage tomb art. *Journal Royal Society of Antiquaries of Ireland* 116, 68–83.

O'Sullivan, M. 1993. *Megalithic art in Ireland*. Dublin: Country House.

Ouzman, S. 2001. Seeing is deceiving: rock art and the non-visual. *World Archaeology* 33, 237–56.

Richards, C. 1991. Skara Brae: revisiting a Neolithic village in Orkney. In W. Hanson and E. Slater (eds), *Scottish archaeology: new perceptions*, 24–43. Aberdeen: Aberdeen University Press.

Richards, C. 1993. *An archaeological study of Neolithic Orkney: architecture, order and social classification*. Unpublished PhD thesis: Glasgow University.

Serematakis, N. 1993. *The senses still: perception and memory as material culture in modernity*. Chicago: University of Chicago Press.

Sharples, N. 1984. Excavations at Pierowall Quarry, Westray, Orkney. *Proceedings of the Society of Antiquaries of Scotland* 114, 75–125.

Shee Twohig, E.S. 1981. *The megalithic art of western Europe*. Oxford: Clarendon.

Sheridan, A. 1986. Megaliths and megalomania: an account, and interpretation, of the development of passage tombs in Ireland. *Journal of Irish Archaeology* 3, 17–30.

Sheridan, A. 1995. Irish Neolithic pottery: the story in 1995. In I. Kinnes and G. Varndell (eds), *'Unbaked urns of rudely shape': essays on British and Irish pottery*, 3–21. Oxford: Oxbow.

Smith, B.B.1994. *Howe: four millennia of Orkney prehistory*. Edinburgh: Society of Antiquaries Monograph Series 9.

Thomas, J. 1991. Monuments from the inside: the case of the Irish megalithic tombs. *World Archaeology* 22, 168–78.

Thomas, J. 1992. Monuments, movement and the context of megalithic art. In N. Sharples and A. Sheridan (eds), *Vessels for the ancestors: essays on the Neolithic of Britain and Ireland*, 141–55. Edinburgh: Edinburgh University Press.

Thomas, N. 1991. *Entangled objects*. Cambridge, Mass: Harvard University Press.

Tilley, C. 1999. *Metaphor and material culture*. Oxford: Blackwell.

Waddell, J. 1992. The Irish Sea in Prehistory. *Journal of Irish Archaeology* 6, 29–40.

Watson, A. 2001. The sounds of transformation: acoustics, monuments and ritual in the British Neolithic. In N. Price (ed.), *The archaeology of shamanism*, 178–92. London: Routledge.

22   The early Bronze Age on the Isle of Man: back into the mainstream?

Jenny Woodcock

Introduction

From the early Mesolithic period (*c* 7000 cal BC) through to the end of the Bronze Age, (*c* 750 cal BC) archaeological evidence clearly indicates that some form of regular contact, possibly varying in constancy through time, was established and maintained between any groups of people living on the Isle of Man at that time and their near neighbours around the northern Irish Sea. For a period during the late Neolithic, however, there is evidence of what appears to be a significant break in continuity of contact.

Around the beginning of the third millennium BC, life on the Isle of Man became dominated by a clearly-defined, apparently insular society – the Ronaldsway Neolithic Culture group. The earlier regular interaction demonstrable from both artefactual and structural evidence appears to have been interrupted during this time. Communication between the Manx groups and their contemporaries around the Irish Sea was ostensibly restricted, either, it is suggested, voluntarily by the early Manx themselves or, less likely, as the result of some organised policy of exclusion by their neighbours. Yet at some stage during the 'metal using Neolithic' (*c* 2500–2050 cal BC) to early Bronze Age (*c* 2050–1500 cal BC) (Needham 1996), the artefactual evidence from the island suggests that, once again, the Manx had become comparatively rapidly reintegrated into the mainstream of social and cultural activity evident amongst their neighbours. Decorative and stylistic evidence, combined with a limited number of archaeological radiocarbon dates, suggests that the initial contact was from Ireland and that the process was relatively rapid.

This paper will discuss the archaeological evidence which supports the suggestion of a renewal of contact between the Manx and contiguous communities around the northern Irish Sea at this time of innovation and change. It will also consider the possible reasons why, during this period, the Manx should have chosen or have been encouraged to renew the relationships formerly apparent between this island people and their near neighbours to the west.

The late Neolithic Ronaldsway period

The distinctive late Neolithic Ronaldsway Culture of the Isle of Man was first defined by Bruce, Megaw and Megaw (1947, 139–160) following the discovery and wartime excavation of the rectangular domestic structure, Ronaldsway House – the type-site – which lay within the confines of the Fleet Air Arm base at Ronaldsway in the southern parish of Malew. The following year at Ballateare, Jurby in the north of the island, the fortuitous discovery beneath a Viking mound of a cemetery of this early period provided further evidence of this distinctive culture (Bersu 1947, 161–9). Piggott (1954, 346–51) summarised the Ronaldsway Culture describing it as 'well defined in all its major aspects' and falling within the 'secondary Neolithic complex'. In 1978 Peter Moffatt, in the light of current knowledge, undertook a comprehensive review of the known sites and the cultural evidence (Moffatt, 1978, 177–217). Subsequently, Burrow (1997, 19–27; 1999, 31–4) endeavoured to define more closely the duration of the Ronaldsway influence and establish possible relationships between the Manx groups and their contemporaries around the Irish Sea.

Evidence for this manifestly insular Manx culture appears abruptly at around 3000 BC and Burrow and Darvill (1997, 412–419) have been able to establish, through a systematic programme of AMS dating of the characteristic substantial Ronaldsway jars from a variety of sites, that this period of cultural isolation seems to have lasted for anything between about 600 to 900 years (Fig. 22.1). Whilst Burrow (1999, 31–4) never claims that the Manx of the late Neolithic Ronaldsway Culture were totally isolated from their neighbours, he proposes that they had succeeded in establishing a certain degree of social/cultural independence at this time. He suggests that the adoption of essentially distinctive forms of pottery and lithics might imply that they had succeeded in 'establishing their own cultural norm, distinct from that of their neighbours, stepping out of the spiral of competitive emulation, possibly to off-set the possibility of being judged by the increasingly high standards this required'.

Despite the significant artefactual evidence of cultural

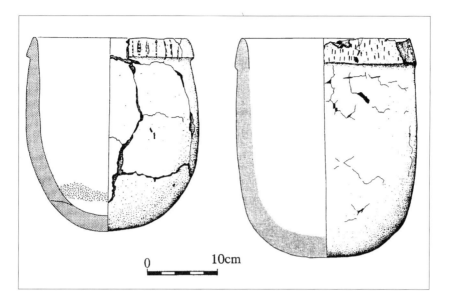

Figure 22.1. Characteristic round-based jars of Ronaldsway type from Billown Quarry (after Burrow 1997, 86–87).

isolation, however, the trade/exchange in stone axes (Langdale – Group VI; Graig Lwyd – Group VII and Tievebulliagh – Group IX) appears to continue throughout the Ronaldsway period, with four examples of Group VI and seven locally produced axes of the distinctive roughened and truncated butt form (RTB) (Group XXV) coming from secure contexts at Ronaldsway house alone (Burrow 1997, 22). The presence of polished axes of 'foreign' origin, together with the reported presence of Grooved Ware pottery from Ronaldsway sites such as Glencrutchery, Ballacottier and at Ronaldsway House itself (Burrow 1999, 34), and the evident utilisation of some decorative elements of Grooved Ware culture on the remarkable group of slate plaques from Ronaldsway House and Ballavarry (Burrow 1997, figure 6.3, 30) certainly substantiate observations that, whilst some apparently formal attempt at segregation had been attempted, a total break in contact never occurred. The limited evidence of polished stone axes of RTB type from Ireland (Rynne 1992, 97–9), albeit limited, would further support this continuation of contact.

Complete isolation would seem unlikely amongst the maritime peoples of the northern Irish Sea (Fig. 22.2) with their inherited tradition of contact and communication throughout the area. Quite apart from routine expeditions with trading/exchange in mind, informal meetings between fishing groups from different areas are likely, then as now, to have continued, and communities living in the west and north of the island probably regularly met up with or acted as hosts to groups or individuals taking refuge in bad weather.

The 'interface' period between the late Neolithic Ronaldsway and the early Bronze Age periods

Traditional terms such as Neolithic and Bronze Age do not truly represent tangible phases of time and cannot be defined by linear temporal boundaries. They represent no more than various stages in the development of material usage and achievements which followed one upon the other. Throughout much of the British Isles there is considerable evidence of continuity across the interface between the late Neolithic and the early Bronze Age (Parker Pearson 1993, 11). On the Isle of Man, however, the arbitrary separation between Neolithic and Bronze Age is confusingly both clearer, and in some cases, more clouded than elsewhere. Single-period sites of Ronaldsway Neolithic and Bronze Age date can be easily discriminated on the basis of material culture. The typical Ronaldsway-style pottery sherds from both funerary and settlement sites have largely proved to be distinctly chronologically early and should be seen as evidence of a fairly long-lived late Neolithic phenomenon (Burrow and Darvill 1997, 412–18).

Although the clearly discernible cultural change evident from the archaeological record suggests it might be possible to identify a distinct period by which time the term 'Bronze Age' becomes relevant to the island, there are some sites, both domestic and funerary, which appear to span the interface between late Neolithic and early Bronze Age (Fig. 22.3). Evidence from these sites suggests that there was some continuity and overlap between these two, ostensibly very different, 'cultures'.

A mingling of domestic evidence, incorporating Neolithic and Bronze Age pottery and flint, may be found

Figure 22.2. *The Isle of Man in its Irish Sea setting.*

at Glencrutchery in Onchan and at Ballachrink, Jurby, where late Neolithic and possible Beaker material occur closely associated with flint of Neolithic and Bronze Age type (Johnson and Woodcock *in prep.*; McCartan and Johnson 1992, 110). A combination of domestic and industrial debris has been found at Billown in Malew (Darvill 1995–2000) and marine erosion at Port Cranstal (Phurt) in Bride continues to produce evidence to suggest middle and late Neolithic (Ronaldsway) and some Bronze Age exploitation of the area inland of the present coastline (Gonzales *et al.* 2000, 355–8). Along the north-west coast of Ballaugh and Kirk Michael small hearths and pits together with finds of Neolithic and Bronze Age date have been exposed in the eroding Crawyn, Ballakoig/ Ballaugh and Orrisdale Brooghs for many centuries. In addition, years of meticulous observation and field-walking, particularly in the northern parishes of Bride, Andreas and Jurby has resulted in the accumulation of a vast amount of evidence of multi-period exploitation over widespread and ill-defined areas. Whilst there is much distinctive Mesolithic and Neolithic material amongst the assemblages, including much of Ronaldsway type, there is also some Bronze Age flint.

Funerary evidence includes a site, Kerrowmooar Farm at Ballig Bridge, where a modern road has artificially divided two areas of unmarked urn burials. Here ploughing exposed three Ronaldsway Neolithic urns in the plot north of the road (Burrow 1997, 38 and 48) and two Cordoned Urns in the plot to the south (Woodcock 1999a and b). A mound on Black Mountain has not been adequately investigated but has some marked affinities to the cemetery mound of Killeaba in Ramsey, where excavation (Cubbon 1978, 69–95) shows that the Bronze Age graves clearly respected those of Ronaldsway type. Whilst the funerary evidence, particularly that at Killeaba, clearly suggests a continuity of use through this 'interface' period, Brodie (1994, 24–6) proposes caution suggesting that, where settlement assemblages include material from different traditions, the evidence could indicate 'several, discrete, episodes of occupation'.

The problems of understanding the boundary between the two ostensibly very different Manx groups – the people of the Ronaldsway culture and those represented by the traditional trappings of the early Bronze Age –cannot easily be resolved. This subject has recently been broached by Peter Davey who suggests that one should perhaps be

Figure 22.3. *Distribution of 'interface' sites with both Ronaldsway Neolithic and Bronze Age evidence.*

looking for a slightly different framework and local terminology when addressing an insular situation (Davey 2002).

The early Bronze Age period

Abruptly, towards the end of the third millennium BC, the archaeological evidence suggests a comparatively swift cessation of the customs and practices of the Ronaldsway Culture and an adoption of the trappings of the early Bronze Age which is apparent in neighbouring areas,

particularly those to the west. It remains unclear whether the abrupt change was instigated by the Manx themselves or by the adjacent communities.

The early copper and bronze metallurgical evidence

Little is known of the early history of metalworking on the Isle of Man but methodical fieldwork, such as that currently being undertaken by the School of Conservation Sciences, Bournemouth University (Doonan and Eley 2000, 45–53), is beginning to define the questions

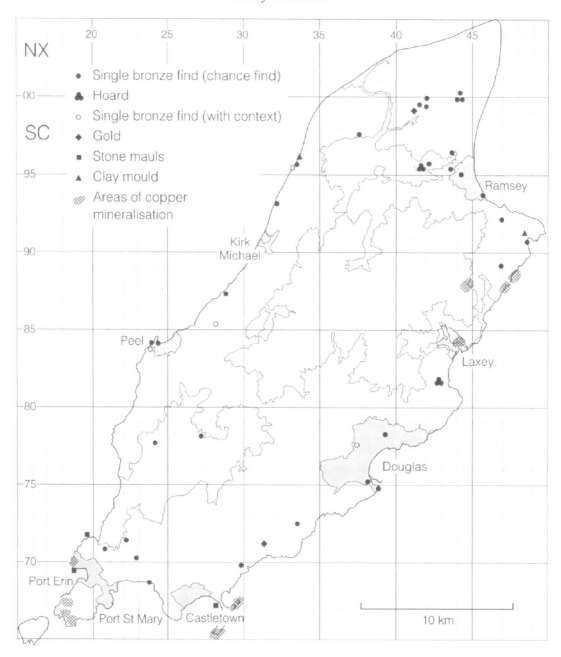

Figure 22.4. *Distribution of copper mineralisation and metalworking evidence.*

involved. There are no sources of tin on the island, but both copper and lead ore deposits are present and have been successfully mined in historic times (Fig. 22.4). Copper staining is likely to have been clearly visible to prehistoric peoples at coastal localities such as Bradda Head in the Parish of Rushen, but as Northover points out (Davey *et al.* 1999, 59) 'the availability of a natural resource does not necessarily mean that it was exploited'. The discovery of a number of possible hammerstones or mauls from around the southern sites has led to the suspicion that copper may have been mined during the Bronze Age, particularly at Bradda Head. The evidence

to date, however, is purely circumstantial as none of the finds can be clearly associated with irrefutable mining contexts. Bearing in mind that tools of this type are known to have continued in use into the medieval period and the Manx 'mauls' are all chance finds, there is, no un-ambiguous evidence to indicate exploitation of copper during the Bronze Age and only equivocal evidence for local metal working.

It is of note that Northover's recent analyses of bronze and copper objects from the Isle of Man have not succeeded in identifying a local metal type and O'Connor points out that there is no evidence of a recognisable

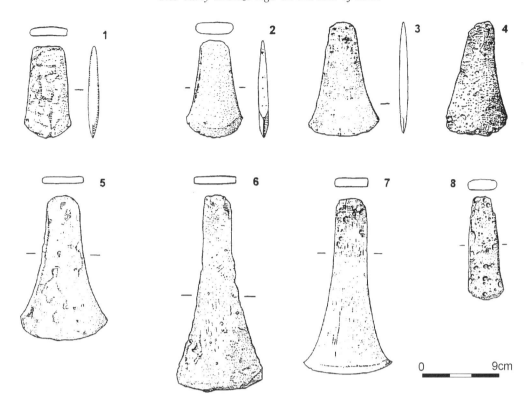

Figure 22.5. *Copper and bronze axes of metal using Neolithic and early Bronze Age date (after Davey* et al. *1999, 47).*

indigenous Manx metalwork type (Davey *et al.* 1999, 55–60). O'Connor indicates that knowledge of local Manx metalworking is currently limited to some later evidence which suggests a degree of probable local skill in repairing or re-working; a broken, but re-worked sword from Foxdale; fragments of bronze vessel with a rivetted patch from Strandhall and a portion of copper ingot together with an incompletely cast sword from a small hoard from Ballagawne. There is, in addition, the unstratified tip of a baked-clay sword mould from the Crawyn Brooghs on the north-west coast of the island.

Whilst there is no contextual evidence for any of the early copper and bronze flat axes from the Isle of Man – all being chance finds – Needham's work on the application of radiocarbon and dendrochronological dating to establish dates and a chronology of metalworking phases. Needham (1996, 121–40) has demonstrated that the five earliest copper axes found on the island belong to his 'Metal Using Neolithic' periods 1 (2500–2300 cal BC) and 2 (2300–2050 cal BC). A further three flat axes can be dated to the early Bronze Age – Needham's period 3 (2050–1700 cal BC) – (Fig. 22.5). The former group clearly encroach upon the 'interface' period between the influence of the late Neolithic Ronaldsway Culture and the beginning of the early Bronze Age. Typologically, or on the basis of metal analysis, Brendan O'Connor (Davey *et al.* 1999, 43–55) has been able to suggest reasonably secure origins for these axes. All except one (of apparent Welsh origin) appear likely to be Irish in type. This contact with Ireland,

apparent through the bronze metallurgy, appears to have continued and remained prevalent up to the middle Bronze Age at which time the Irish influence, through the medium of metalwork at least, appears, for some reason, to have declined.

The early pottery evidence

Additional evidence in support of the renewal of Manx-Irish contact at the beginning of the Bronze Age may be implied from two sets of peripherally related ceramic evidence – from Beakers and from vessels of the Bowl tradition.

Whilst in England, Scotland and Wales, Beakers are consistently associated with crouched skeletons in graves, on the Isle of the Man there is only a single Beaker – Group N3, of late northern type (Clarke 1970, 484, No 374) – from a cist found at Baroose in Lonan (Quine 1925, 270–72). A limited number of possible Beaker fragments have been found, either poorly stratified in the vicinity of later funerary mounds or from probable domestic contexts, but in general the Beaker influence on the Isle of Man seems to have been very limited. In view of the apparent insularity of the preceding period, it is perhaps surprising that this generally ubiquitous vessel is found on the island at all. The paucity of Beakers in Manx cists is similar to the scenario observed by Waddell in Ireland (Waddell 1998, 119). On the Isle of Man, as in Ireland, it would appear that it is the makers of pottery of

Bishopcourt Farm (IOMMM 7368 [smaller] and IOMMM 7371 [larger])

Bishop's Demesne (IOMMM 995)

Figure 22.6. Vessels of bowl form from Bishopscourt Farm and Bishop's Demesne, Ballaugh, Isle of Man.

the Bowl and Vase tradition of the late third millennium who seem to be adopting the funerary practice of crouched inhumation with an accompanying pot in classic Beaker fashion.

A total of fourteen vessels of Bowl form and three of Vase type are known from the island. Of these, ten Bowls (six from cists) and one Vase from a cist, come from clear funerary contexts. Only two of the Bowls have been radiocarbon dated (Chiverrell *et al.* 1999, 47–8, 321–36) (Fig. 22.6). At Bishopscourt Farm in Ballaugh, in the north-west of the island, one mound concealed two cists, the larger of which held an inhumation and the smaller a cremation. Both burials were accompanied by markedly similar Bowls of typically Irish form and decoration - perhaps coincidentally, the larger bowl was associated with the larger cist (Woodcock 1999c, 99–110).

If the radiocarbon date achieved from the Bishopscourt Farm inhumation (2122–1688 cal BC) and that from human bone (1974–1696 cal BC) from a neighbouring cist with inhumation and a small vessel of Bowl type – Bishop's Demesne – are compared with a series of dates from Irish Bowls (Fig. 22.7) it appears that this vessel type is appearing on the Isle of Man slightly later than in Ireland. This may provide tentative evidence of a movement from west to east. The current absence of radiocarbon dates on Bowl burials from Dumfries and Galloway in south-west Scotland remains an impediment to extending this line of thought to include the area of Scotland closest to the Isle of Man. The radiocarbon dates collected for Bowl and Vase burials from Ardnave, Kilellan and from Kentraw on Islay (Stewart and Barclay 1997, 39) – currently amongst the earliest from Scotland – compare very favourably with those from the Isle of Man. The Islay evidence might, therefore, equally support the suggestion of a similarly timed movement to the north and east out of Ireland to Scotland at the start of the early Bronze Age (Woodcock 2001, 326–8). A further group of marginally later dates associated with Bowl and Vase forms from central and eastern Scotland - from Angus, Perthshire and Tayside – (Stewart and Barclay 1997, 39; Taylor *et al.* 1998, 65; Woodcock 2001 326–8) could also be said to reinforce this proposed west to east movement.

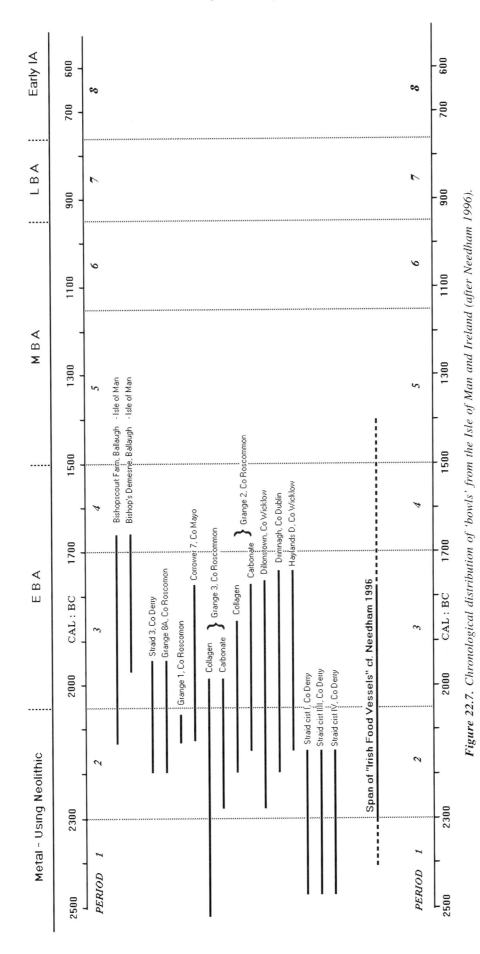

Figure 22.7. *Chronological distribution of 'bowls' from the Isle of Man and Ireland (after Needham 1996).*

Conclusions – the 'resumption of contact'

What could account for the changes evident from the archaeological record which took place at around 2,000 BC? What precipitated the disappearance of the Ronaldsway culture which faded at this time, almost as suddenly as it had emerged some 1,000 or so years earlier?

The type of interaction and motivation which is likely to have existed between the essentially self-sufficient prehistoric fishing and farming groups of the northern Irish Sea province is difficult to evaluate. It is hard to determine what the early Bronze Age communities could not have acquired for themselves without the obvious perils involved in crossing the Irish Sea. It can only have been the promise of mineral wealth which precipitated the Manx re-entry into the mainstream of interaction between the communities around the Irish Sea. It is highly probable that the early Manx inhabitants were totally unaware of the potential of their own mineral resources and had no knowledge of the mechanisms of prospecting or exploiting metalliferous deposits. Certainly, as Davey *et al.* (1999) indicate, the evidence of the sword mould, the copper ingot and reworked or repaired bronze sword of Ewart Park type suggests that the knowledge of working copper and bronze arrived on the island some time after the pioneering phase was complete. It seems reasonably safe, therefore, to presume that prospecting and metal-working technology must have initially been introduced from beyond the Isle of Man (Davey *et al.* 1999, 55). As the presence of the early flat axes and the introduction of Bowl and Vase forms suggests, it is likely that the drive, in the initial stages, came from Ireland.

On the assumption that the decision for Manx 'isolation' was purely elective, and presupposing that social contact was never totally abandoned but maintained informally throughout the regime of the Ronaldsway Neolithic culture, it can be suggested that once the knowledge of procuring and working copper was established in Ireland, the awareness of the new metallurgy and its advantages circulated rapidly amongst all the communities of the Irish Sea province, including the inhabitants of the Isle of Man. Following the spread of information, it is perhaps reasonable to suggest that with an awareness of the early metal technology, the aspirations of the Manx may have outstripped their desire to remain 'different'. The more influential members of Manx society are likely to have coveted both the knowledge of metallurgy and ore procurement and the practicality and status afforded by the objects of copper themselves. Such ambitions may have been strong enough to prompt the resumption of both economic and cultural contacts with their neighbours to the east. Alternatively, and possibly more likely, once mineral claims in Ireland had been established, pioneering metallurgists and prospectors from that country, seeking to extend their wealth and influence by identifying and laying claim to new sources of copper and tin, had of necessity to explore beyond their own shores. Viewed from the north-east coast of Ireland, the Isle of Man and indeed south-west Scotland will have appeared both extensive and full of potential.

At the end of the Neolithic and beginning of the Bronze Age, therefore, the ancient, familiar social and cultural contacts which had previously existed between the peoples of the Irish Sea province were once again extended to include the inhabitants of the Isle of Man. What the incentive was and from which direction the impetus lay is conjectural. Whether contact was purely commercial, or if this small island was ever sufficiently highly regarded to be included in an overarching social, political and economic federation of north-west groups cannot be determined from the archaeological record alone.

Acknowledgements

This paper derives from research undertaken for a Ph.D. at the University of Liverpool between 1994 and 2001. The writer would like to thank Anna Brindley and Jan Lanting of the Groningen radiocarbon laboratory for access to a number of the Irish radiocarbon dates included in Figure 22.7 in advance of their formal publication.

References

Bersu, G. 1947. A cemetery of the Ronaldsway culture at Ballateare, Jurby, Isle of Man. *Proceedings of the Prehistoric Society* 12, 161–9.

Brodie, N. 1994. *The Neolithic – Bronze Age transition in Britain*. Oxford: British Archaeological Reports British Series 238.

Bruce, J.J., Megaw, E.M. and Megaw B.R.S. 1947. A Neolithic site at Ronaldsway, Isle of Man. *Proceedings of the Prehistoric Society* 13, 139–60.

Burrow, S. 1997. *The Neolithic culture of the Isle of Man*. Oxford: British Archaeological Reports British Series 263.

Burrow, S. 1999. Neither east nor west: a social history of the Manx Neolithic. In P.J. Davey (ed.), *Recent archaeological research on the Isle of Man*, 27–38. Oxford: British Archaeological Reports British Series 278.

Burrow, S. and Darvill, T. 1997. AMS dating of the Manx Ronaldsway Neolithic. *Antiquity* 71, 412–19.

Chiverrell, R.C., Davey, P.J., Gowlett, J.A.J. and Woodcock, J.J. 1999. Radiocarbon dates for the Isle of Man. In P.J. Davey (ed.), *Recent archaeological research on the Isle of Man*, 321–36. Oxford: British Archaeological Reports British Series 278.

Clarke, D.L. 1970. *Beaker pottery of Great Britain and Ireland, 1 and 2*. Cambridge: Cambridge University Press.

Cubbon, A.M. 1978. Excavation at Killeaba, Ramsey, Isle of Man. *Proceedings of the Prehistoric Society* 44, 69–95.

Darvill, T. 1995–2000. *Billown Neolithic landscape project, Isle of Man 1995–2000*. Bournemouth and Douglas: Bournemouth University School of Conservation Sciences Research Reports 1,3,4,5,7 and 9.

Davey, P.J., Northover, P., O'Connor, B. and Woodcock, J.J. 1999. Bronze Age metallurgy on the Isle of Man: a symposium. In P.J. Davey (ed.), *Recent archaeological research on the Isle of Man,* 39–62. Oxford: British Archaeological Reports British Series 278.

Davey, P.J. 2002. Innovation, continuity and insular development in the Isle of Man. In W. Waldren (ed.) *Islands in prehistory.* Oxford: British Archaeological Reports International Series 1095.

Doonan, R.C.P. and Eley, T. 2000. The Langness ancient mining survey. In T. Darvill (ed.), *Billown Neolithic landscape project, Isle of Man,* 45–53. Bournemouth and Douglas: Bournemouth University School of Conservation Sciences Research Report 7.

Gonzales, S., Innes, J., Huddart, D., Davey, P. and Plater, A. 2000. Holocene coastal change in the north of the Isle of Man: stratigraphy, palaeoenvironment and archaeological evidence. In K. Pye and J.R.L. Allen (eds),*Coastal and estuarine environments; sedimentology, geomorphology and geoarchaeology,* 343–63. London: The Geological Society, Special Publication No. 175.

Johnson, A. and Woodcock, J. in prep. Excavations at Ballachrink, Jurby 2000. In P. Davey (ed.), *Recent archaeological research on the Isle of Man 1998–2000.*

McCartan, S. and Johnson, A. 1992. A rescue excavation at Ballachrink, Jurby. *Proceedings of the Isle of Man Natural History and Antiquarian Society* 10, 105–22.

Moffatt, P.J. 1978. The Ronaldsway culture: a review. In P.J. Davey (ed.), *Man and environment in the Isle of Man,* 177–217. Oxford: British Archaeological Reports British Series 54.

Needham, S. 1996. Chronology and periodisation in the British Bronze Age. In K. Randsborg (ed.), *Absolute chronology: archaeological Europe 2500–500 BC,* 121–140. Copenhagen: Munksgaard.

Parker Pearson, M. 1993. *Bronze Age Britain.* London: Batsford.

Piggott, S. 1954. *The Neolithic cultures of the British Isles.* Cambridge: Cambridge University Press.

Quine, J. 1925. Note re discovery of cist with urn at Baroose, Lonan. January, 1919. *Proceedings of the Isle of Man Natural History and Antiquarian Society* 2, 270–2.

Rynne, E. 1992. Miscellanea: Adare, Athenry and the Isle of Man – coincidence or a late Neolithic connection? *North Munster Antiquarian Journal* 34, 97–99.

Stewart, M.E.C. and Barclay, G.J. 1997. Excavations in burial and ceremonial sites of the Bronze Age in Tayside. *Tayside and Fife Archaeological Journal* 3, 22–54.

Taylor, D.B., Rideout, J.S., Russell-White, C.J. and Cowie, T.G. 1998. Prehistoric burials from Angus; some finds old and new. *Tayside and Fife Archaeological Journal* 4, 31–66.

Waddell, J. 1998. *The prehistoric archaeology of Ireland.* Galway : Galway University Press.

Woodcock, J.J. 1999a. *Report on the excavation of the contents of a Bronze Age urn from Kerrowmooar Farm, Andreas – Loan No 22149/1.* Unpublished report submitted to Manx National Heritage, December 1999, 5. (Library mss no: 10434/1).

Woodcock, J.J. 1999b. *Report on the excavation of the contents of a second Bronze Age urn from Kerrowmooar Farm, Andreas - Loan No 22149/2.* Unpublished report submitted to Manx National Heritage, January 2000, 3. (Library mss no: 10434/2).

Woodcock, J.J. 1999c. Bronze Age burials from Cottier's Field, Bishopscourt Farm, Ballaugh. In P.J. Davey (ed.), *Recent archaeological research on the Isle of Man,* 99–110. Oxford: British Archaeological Reports British Series 278.

Woodcock, J.J. 2001. *In search of a cultural identity: a study of the Manx Bronze Age in its Irish Sea context.* Unpublished PhD thesis: University of Liverpool.

23 Layers of life and death: aspects of monumentality in the early Bronze Age of Wales

Marcus Brittain

Introduction

The Neolithic chambered tombs of the Welsh coastline, particularly the peninsular from Fishguard to Strumble Head, have been afforded a recent resurgence of discussion (Cummings 2001; this volume; Fleming 1999; Tilley 1994). This, set within the focus of the symbolic nature of mythical and memorable landscapes and viewscapes, has provided a range of possibilities for creative interpretation. The relationships between these monuments and the natural features nearby has opened an ambiguity between the artificial (cultural) and the found (natural) (Bradley 2000; Cummings 2002, 115). The following paper explores a similar relationship from the perspective of the early Bronze Age in Wales. Using examples from the Welsh coastline (Fig. 23.1), particularly from north Pembrokeshire, I take the position that typologically distinct monuments are in fact part of a wider monumental landscape. Rather than being constructed through a preconceived form, I suggest that these are a part of the land, and that the natural environment was an intrinsic element of social knowledge in which monuments were conceived through the metaphor of growth.

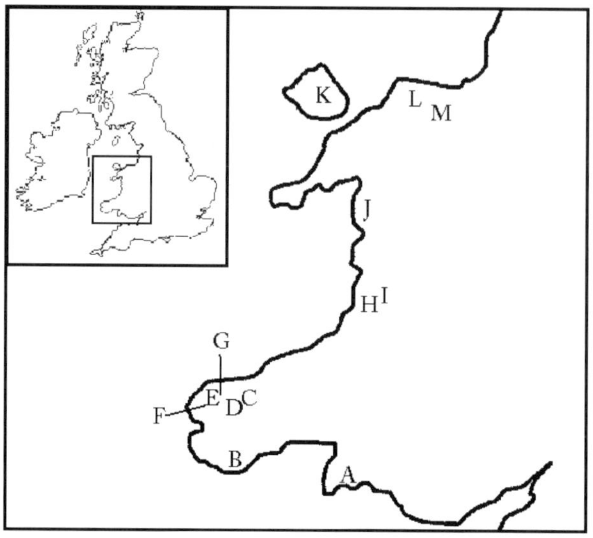

(A) Great Carn Ring I, Cefn Bryn. (B) Stackpole Warren. (C) Croes-mihangel. (D) Letterston. (E) Rhos-y-Clegyrn. (F) Ffyst Samson (G) Ffynnon Druidion. (H) Aber Camddwr. (I) Hystrad-Hynod, Llanidloes. (J) Moel Goedog ring cairn I. (K) Bedd Branwen. (L) Druid's Circle, Penmaenmawr. (M) Brenig.

Figure 23.1. *Sites mentioned in the text.*

Background

Arguments for the social function of Bronze Age monuments in Wales have generally debated their use as territorial and boundary markers (Roese 1980), graves or 'political memorials' (Lynch 2000, 127). Lynch (1980, 237; 2000, 121) has acknowledged that many of these monuments were constructed and elaborated through a number of compositional stages over a prolonged time-span. Others have problematised the relationship between the past and the present through tracing their construction above the remnants of structures or residues of activity that may have been left to rest for hundreds of years (Lane 1986). For further arguments of social function to be explored, there needs to be an analysis of the material that constitutes these monuments, questioning how these materials are important to those that used them, and why they were used in such a way. Such work has been taking

place for Bronze Age archaeology elsewhere in the British Isles (Brück 2001; Owoc 2000; Parker Pearson and Ramilisonina 1998; Tipping 1994). Furthermore, the relationship of these monuments to the dead needs to be addressed. While cremation is the primary treatment of the dead in early Bronze Age Wales, the deposition of partial cremation remains or no human remains at all makes the relationship between these monuments and mortuary rituals difficult to define. Very few monuments in Wales house any evidence of a pyre in the near vicinity, thus suggesting that any inclusion of human remains came late in the mortuary rite (McKinley 1997). Most of the monuments explored in this paper are associated in some way with human remains, cremated or otherwise, at some point in their biography.

The perception of a built form has been explored

through the relationship of monuments to their natural surroundings (Bradley 2000), suggesting that they may be imitations of symbolic natural forms (Tilley 1996; Tilley and Bennett 2001), or that natural forms were recognized as ancient monuments prior to the advent of geology around 300 years ago (Barnatt and Edmonds 2002; Bradley 1998; Mullin 2001). Taking a different approach, this paper explores the relationship between monumental construction and natural processes, rather than monument and landscape form. This does not presume any particular relationship between natural features and monuments, but looks instead for the way that knowledge is created and recreated by bringing together particular materials from the environment into a monumental location. I am therefore trying to interpret a series of underlying grammars that were manipulated over time, resulting in the 'final' form of the monuments that we can see today. I will consider past actions as the materialization of memory, and analyze a process where various materials that embodied particular meanings were layered in a dialogue where growth and decay temporalise social practice (cf. Fowler 2003; Thomas this volume), linking various locations conceptually and physically in a monumental landscape.

Forms of growth, growing forms

Modern western thinking induces an innate difficulty for archaeological interpretation when the relationship between making and producing, form and substance is considered as an unproblematic given. There are other ways of looking at monuments. For example, Williams (1988, 33) has suggested that standing stones were not considered to be the most important focal aspects of the monument to which they belonged. If this was also the case for mounds, cairns, or the even 'primary' deposits, then this may be a first step beyond what Merleau-Ponty (1962, 243) has called the 'world of static represent-ations', in which space is merely an arrangement of things, rather than the *means* of the possibility for the arrangement *of* those things. Here the focus of the monument is not necessarily the focus of meaning. This allows for a contextual archaeology in which the nature of material deposits *makes* the site, as opposed to a preconception of the site's form preceding the material itself (Brittain forthcoming). How then, is it possible to discern between the form of a site and the layers of practice and substance that make that form?

In a recent paper, Ingold (2000a) uses the analogy of weaving a basket to situate the manufacturing of a surface as a building-up of layers as opposed to a simple trans-formation of form. He argues that, 'Form is said to be applied from without, rather than unveiled from within [... T]he world of substance – of brute matter – must present itself to the maker of artefacts as a surface to be transformed' (Ingold 2000a, 339). Here Ingold proposes

a process that is similar to organic growth, with a series of external and internal forces allowing the form of the artefact to unfold itself in relation to the building up of other 'cells', rather than being determined by a genetic blueprint or preconceived idea (Ingold 2000a, 345). This is in direct contrast to metaphysical boundedness that sees a construction of form as a living 'natural' substance being transformed into dead 'cultural' matter, making things the passive products of social performance.

Ingold's metaphor of growth is an area that holds a number of potentials for the Welsh Bronze Age material. It may be regarded as an environmental process that, along with decay, could be imprinted upon the image of social transformation and temporality. For example, all practical knowledge of the world for the Huaorani of Amazonia is understood through the cycle of organic growth. It is ritualized, symbolized and performed, thus defining the conceptual apparatus for political symbolism through material, garden produce and exchange (Rival 1993). It may also be that in certain contexts the degrees of these processes are elaborated in order to facilitate a transformation of some kind, maybe invoking a product of reproduction and regeneration (Weiner 1980, 72). This may apply to the human body where organic growth is a metaphor for bodily reproduction (Giambelli 1998; Munn 1992, 296), or where substances are brought together to form beings (Busby 1997; Pool 1984), or where objects may be understood as or of bodies or persons (Thomas 2002, 41). Different substances may be analogous to different beings of similar rates of growth; Ingold (2000b), for example, outlines various ethnographic contexts where organic plant species with a fast rate of growth may serve as metonymic devises for the growth of children, both requiring a particular form of nurturance, whereas the slow rate of growth of trees facilitates a different relationship that may be analogous to the changes in being of adults. But the substances that are brought together to form these objects (or persons) may have also gone through various processes of transformation before they are fused together. Each stage of this transformation may be imbued with specific meaning, and the substances are invariably organic or mineral at their outset.

Layering the past

'The earth god formed him of wood or clay, the god of heaven gave life'.

Exert from a Madagascan myth, in Abrahamsson (1977, 115).

In early Bronze Age Wales, the layering of various materials to form a mound or a platform associated with standing stones, embanked stone circles and the numerous cairn types, utilized an array of different substances. These generally included stones, clays, soil and turf, each with other additional inclusions such as cremated bone, pottery or charcoal of varying types of organic species. Owoc (2002) has noted the important role of minerals in the cosmological and technological constructions of barrows in south-west England, with the various materials being brought from specific locations in the wider landscape, the deposition of which may be understood in terms of colour, texture, location, depth and consistency. The transformation of these substances through the natural weathering process may also provide a means for monitoring temporal and social change (Owoc 2002, 133). A similar Welsh example may be the central space of Great Carn Ring I on Cefn Bryn, which was comprised of soils that were grey, white and yellow-brown in colour with flecks of charcoal inclusions (Ward 1988). Similarly, the Croesmihangel barrow in north Pembrokeshire displays a process of 'raising the ground' to form a platform surface. The platform, covering four urns, was raised from the soil and clay of an encircling ditch before a number of posts or stakes were inserted into it to form a circular enclosure, then removed allowing the holes to fill with clay. After a short period of time, a mound was erected over the platform consisting of layers of non-local dark earth and stones, followed by a small kerb of quartz blocks (Nye *et al.* 1983).

In addition to this, various ethnographic cases show how a great number of other organic materials are used in the construction of special places. Differing combinations of materials in specific contexts may then have been interpreted in different ways by different people (e.g. Strathern and Stewart 2000). In North Wales, oak was imported from up to 16km to the Brenig cemetery for the majority of structural construction (Keepax 1993), but at the Brenig 44 ring-cairn it would appear that pits filled solely with charcoal were of birch, alder and hazel species, compared to the oak charcoal associated with cremated remains (Lynch 1993, 136). The same relationship is found at Aber Camddwr ring-cairn (see below). The functional explanation is that oak burns longer than other species and is therefore more efficient for a pyre, but within an upturned urn at Moel Goedog ring cairn I, Harlech, a layer of earth and oak charcoal was associated with a separate layer of the complete remains of a cremated adult, whereas the charcoal pits contained a much more varied mixture of species. Furthermore, it also appears that different species were being burnt in different locations before being brought together in deposition (Lynch 1984, 22–3, 27), suggesting a particular categorization, knowledge and social meaning of tree species (Seeland 1997). These carbonised remains, still identifiable by the fossilised grain structure, may have embodied a different meaning to the tree category having been set through the process of fire and heat transformation. The majority of cremated remains in Wales were deposited inside either an upturned or an upright urn, and the often partial cremated remains are generally accompanied by some form of organic deposit other than charcoal. At Bedd Branwen on Anglesey, at least seven

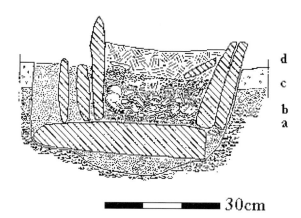

Figure 23.2. Cist with a layered fill at Hystrad-Hynod, Llanidloes (after ApSimon 1973).

of the vessels recovered contained layers of a black, red or brown soil with a burnt deposit of charcoal and/or bone (with a preference for ear bones) (Lynch 1971, 22–4). This selection of dark soil and burnt material is also found at Moel Goedog ring cairn I in both pits and urns, where many of the cremated bone deposits associated with these organics had a soil adhered to them that was foreign in origin, and had therefore been imported to the site. Similar patterns are found at solitary cists. At Hystrad-Hynod, Llandiloes, a small stone cist beneath a soil, clay and stone-layered cairn and standing stone contained four different organic layers:

a. black silt with charcoal and small stones
b. cremated bone set in brown clay
c. dark brown earth with burnt bones and some charcoal with a bronze awl
d. dark brown earth with charcoal and small stones (ApSimon 1973; Fig. 23.2).

The Druid's Circle, an embanked stone circle near Penmaenmawr, North Wales, also contained a central cist, but filled with wet white clay and small fragments of stone. Within the clay was an Enlarged Food Vessel containing cremated bones and a fill of unburnt earth. A later secondary urn was inverted into the soil near the primary cist, and was 'plugged' with thick clay, cremated bone and a bronze knife (Griffiths 1960, 315–6). A language of composition is evident for these deposits.

Significantly, these materials are not just imported pyre debris, but soils and clays of a sort that are clean of burning, and often foreign to the respective sites in which they were deposited, suggesting the resonance of other places and performances embedded within the materials. Owoc has convincingly argued that 'soil as material culture' could be manipulated for special occasions of transformative power in the lifecycle of an individual or community, and that it played an important part in ritual practice in the Bronze Age (Owoc forthcoming b). Furthermore, 'subterranean landscapes' played a key role in the knowledge and cosmology of the community, and were integral for the positioning of monuments in the landscape (Field 1998, 323; Owoc 2000, 129). Owoc's example is the Crig-a-Mennis early Bronze Age barrow on Bodmin Moor in Cornwall, that was constructed above a 'geological break' where the soft pink sandstone meets the harder green slate (Owoc forthcoming a). In Pembrokeshire, an interesting comparison is found at Letterston where a barrow was constructed in a location where two different clays of yellow and blue met beneath the thin sandy subsoil (Savory 1949, 69), suggesting that similar importance was given to soil categories in Wales.

Containers for life

The possibility for a complex understanding of soil and mineral categories is supported by a number of ethnographic examples (e.g. Boivin 2000; Descola 1996; Ollier *et al.* 1971; Wilshusen and Stone 1990). It may be useful here to turn again to an ethnographic analogy without taking it as a direct example for Bronze Age practice. I would like to consider these monuments and the deposits within them as containers that are both active and acted upon. This is not in the sense that the monument is just a container of things, like human remains, but the locale for a fusion of substances that can bring forth a process of transformation and change. A monument, then, would act as a container like pots and bodies, which have been understood in the same light by a number of societies either through association (David *et al.* 1988; Kan 1989, 49–64), form (Berns 1990), or through the process of coming into being (Herbert 1993, 210–5).

In the Kongo, the term *nkisi* represents an ancestral spirit that resides within a container (also *nkisi* (singular), or *minkisi* (plural)) that is a pot or idol imbued with magic, the power of which depends on the substances that are incorporated into the fabric of the container, or those that are contained inside it (MacGaffey 1991, 4–5; Fig. 23.3). The invisible and formless *nkisi* can only be contacted and given form through the earth, so *minkisi* are made of clays, stones and soil from the graves of the dead, so to incorporate disembodied spirits through the metaphor of the land (MacGaffey 1988). Each substance is a medicine that embodies its own power and meaning, and the most common substance used to fill the container with power is a white clay that represents the ancestor's bones (Hottot 1956, 29). This is found in underwater streambeds – the land of the dead (MacGaffey 1988, 191). Red and yellow clays are also frequently used as well as various other substances ranging from bark, thorns and charcoal, to snail shells, claws and feathers (Van Wing 1941). Different substances are chosen depending on the spirit that is being captured by the ritual specialist (*nganga*) who owns the *nkisi*, and significance is captured in the symbolic properties of these substances as opposed to their pharmacological properties. Their containment

Figure 23.3. *Varying forms of Bakongo* nkisi *(after VanWing 1951, by permission of the Royal Anthropological Institute).*

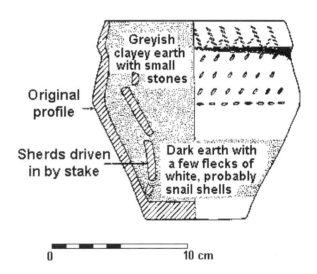

Figure 23.4. *Urn from Aber Camddrw (after Hogg 1977).*

in *minkisi* is necessary 'as though the forces they represented were under constraint' (MacGafey 1993, 63).

This may be comparable to the way that a variety of materials were used in the Welsh Bronze Age. For example, a ring-cairn at Aber Camddwr, Cardiganshire, was comprised by a less clear process of layering, but covered a central cluster of postholes, the cremated burial of a headless child, and a series of pits. One pit to the south-east of the burial, was filled with the charcoal of birch and alder, and housed a Collared Urn which, placed upright, contained a clean soil humus with white snail shells at the base, and layers of greyish clayey earth with small stones at the neck (Fig. 23.4). The urn had then been capped by a 'bun-shaped lump of white quartzite',

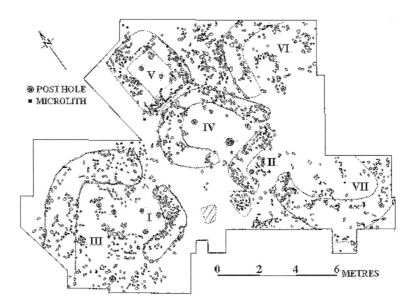

Figure 23.5. Early Bronze Age huts at Rhos-Y-Clegyrn (after Lewis 1974, with modifications).

covering its contents before it was later broken by a stake inserted into the monument (Hogg 1977, 28–34). Clearly the separate materials have been selected, sorted, and combined in a particular way before being sealed and contained as a single entity. But the relationship of this to the other deposits further combines fragmented objects, substances and beings to form a space that is new and intelligible. Here the mound builds upon previous notions of growth and layering, imprinting a permanent image of social reproduction on the landscape.

Time and practice

These examples all display a process of highly structured deposition (Richards and Thomas 1984), from the pre-mound or platform deposits to the platforms or mounds that were then constructed above, possibly several generations or hundreds of years later. By superimposing successive layers upon these already established places of significance, time and space is transformed in the present (Lane 1986).

There are, however, certain contexts where this process appears to be much more frequent or even seasonal in occurrence. This can be seen at Rhos-y-Clegyrn in Pembrokeshire, where eight sub-rectangular structures were found beneath a standing stone and stone setting within a stretch of enclosed marshland (Lewis 1965; 1974; Fig. 23.5). Only three of these structures (1, 3 and 5) displayed a repeated cycle of occupation after brief periods of abandonment, the others being used only once (Brittain forthcoming). Nowakowski (2001) describes the process of abandonment as a highly structured sequence of clearing and back-filling of hearths, postholes and other features, which at times was then followed by the spreading of a

layer of debris that may have accumulated away from the dwelling. In contrast to the early Bronze Age roundhouse at Stackpole Warren, Pembrokeshire, which was burnt either during or before being demolished, (Benson *et al.* 1990), those at Rhos-y-Clegyrn were dismantled, the post-holes and hearths filled with layers of clay and small stones, and then left to the elements before being re-surfaced with grey or yellow clay, with the post-holes re-cut for use. Rather than a closure of past practice it appears that the past is being built upon and incorporated into the present as a continuity of the life cycle and growth. This process may be analogous to a ritualised burial (Nowakowski 2001, 141), followed by a period of re-generation and then reproduction, with different floor materials being used for particular times of occupation and periods of transformation (Boivin 2000).

After a period of less than 200 or so years, five or six partial cremation remains were placed within the buried imprint of the interior of structure 5, and a series of stone deposits, urn fragments and pits formed a concentric order of deposition towards the central cremations (Fig. 23.6). These pits contained layers of highly varied organic deposits, including clays and soils of differing colour and texture. A wooden post (PH 1) remaining from the period of the hut structures acted as the marker for a series of alignments running between newly erected wood and stone uprights, and a pair of standing stones (Brittain 2002). Two of these were directed towards two Neolithic chambered tombs at Ffynnon Druidion and Ffyst Samson, and the other was directed towards the three Letterston barrows (Savory 1949; 1963) three kilometres to the south-east, with which there appears to be a number of similarities in the structural biography (see Brittain forthcoming). The alignments crossed directly upon two small stone uprights (pit D) associated with the cremations, thus

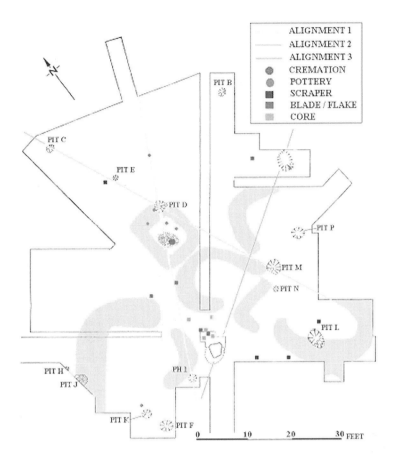

Figure 23.6. Outline of underlying Early Bronze Age hut structures beneath later phases of activity (modified from Lewis 1974).

drawing the landscape into the centre of the monument, the meanings and performances associated with the tombs, and an ancestral authority (Brittain forthcoming). Other sites with house-like structures appear to contain similar deposits or alignments, such as the roundhouse at Stackpole Warren, in which a hollow contained a deposit of multi-coloured clay (Benson *et al.* 1990, 186). This lay beneath a later alignment of upright stones leading towards a large standing stone and stone setting with a number of substances and a later cremated deposit.

These hut structures may have been part of a wider cycle of growth, regeneration and reproduction by means of layering places, culminating with the deposition of specific substances and partial human remains, and drawing on the efficacy of ancient monuments in the landscape. This legitimised the introduction of deposited substances through the appropriation of the ancestral past, reaffirming and recreating social relations by spatialising performance upon established notions of continuity. At Rhos-y-Clegyrn the alignments and deposits were eventually covered and sealed by a stone setting, hardening and drying the once soft and wet nature of the monument, like a prolonged act of finishing within mortuary exchanges or obligations beyond death (e.g.

Battaglia 1992). This does not necessarily require a human body but may be constructed through the growth of a conceptual body, container or place, in which the worldly elements or substances of being are brought together to comprise an orienting image for the (re-) production of practice.

Conclusion: materiality, knowledge and action

There are similarities in the material and structure of deposits across classes of early Bronze Age sites along the Welsh coast. What differ are the various combinations of substances that are brought together in a meaningful dialogue. These substances combine a series of local and non-local sources, and appear to have been specifically selected and differentiated for deposition, even after burning. These objects and materials may have been in circulation for some time before they were brought together (Thomas 1996, 141). The partial nature of the cremation remains and urns suggests that these were brought to the site from at least one other location, and this may be significant in light of the growing number of disturbed graves which had been either removed or added to (Owoc 2001, 194–5). The movement of these substances from place to place established particular connections between locations, weaving the landscape together by ties of meaning.

The actions producing these signatures did not move towards a preconceived idea or form, but resulted from a way of knowledge that is both fluid and transient. This knowledge is based on the concept of growth. The monument becomes the image of this process, being grown from the inside-out, but through materials that are external to the monument's location, and the substances being brought together to make this image also become metaphors for this process, transgressing many other social arenas. The transformative process need only require a 'token' of each substance from their respective origins within the landscape. This is particularly true for the cremated remains and associated urns. In many ways, this partiality displays the 'temporal rhythms of life' that are embedded within their eventual form (Ingold 2000, 345). Pot fragments display their structural layers along the broken edge – a structure that would otherwise have been invisible when the pot was intact. These may even be a sign of continuity, displaying their temper elements and trans-formed minerals, thus opening interpretation of their origin and allowing a reading of their embedded meaning and skeletal layering (Smith 1989). Similarly, by digging through the layers of the monument, the structure of growth is revealed, affirming yet at the same time transforming practice in the present. In summary, monument form in early Bronze Age Wales may be secondary to processes of monument growth. Furthermore, substance comes prior to form in the unfolding of a monument. By questioning the idea of a preconceived form, a closer understanding of materiality is achieved through which temporal processes of the built monument may be appreciated through the construction of knowledge, and the relations and under-standing that the builders had with the materials and the substances themselves.

The conception of growth and decay in the early Bronze Age may offer a new way of interpreting the emergence of a formalised landscape in Wales as differing relations with the land begin to take place (Evans 1990; Kissock 1993; Moore-Colyer 1996; Murphy 2001; Ward 1989a; 1989b). Elsewhere in the British Isles, plough-marks beneath barrows may be interpreted in a similar way as a particular form of relation with the environment (Tarlow 1993). The metaphor of growth, however, is neither universal nor fixed, and may be understood in different ways both regionally and through time. This may also be the case for monumental forms in the Welsh Neolithic (Cummings 2002) where landscape features neither represent nor inspire the construction of monuments, but where both landscape features and monumental forms are a part of the same process of the transformation of the world, neither natural nor cultural, but imbricated in a unified cosmology.

Acknowledgements

I must convey my thanks to Chris Fowler and Vicki Cummings for their invitation to contribute to this volume, and for their comments on earlier drafts of this paper. I am most grateful to Mary Anne Owoc for providing me with various forthcoming and unpublished papers, and Julian Thomas whose advice on aspects of this paper has been greatly appreciated. Thank you also to Mark Lodwick at the National Museum and Gallery, Cardiff, for his help with the archive material of Rhos-y-Clegyrn, and for providing me with various slides and digital images. The content of the piece is my own responsibility.

References

Abrahamsson, H. 1977. *The origins of death: studies in African mythology*. New York: Arno Press.

ApSimon, A. 1973. The excavation of a Bronze Age barrow and a Menhir at Ystrad-Hynod, Llanidloes (Mont.), 1965–66. *Archaeologia Cambrensis* 122, 35–54.

Barnatt, J. and Edmonds, M. 2002. Places apart? Caves and monuments in Neolithic and earlier Bronze Age Britain. *Cambridge Archaeological Journal* 12, 113–29.

Battaglia, D. 1992. The body in the gift: memory and forgetting in Sabarl mortuary exchange. *American Ethnologist* 19, 3–18.

Benson, D., Evans, J., Williams, G., Darvill, T. and David, A. 1990. Excavations at Stackpole Warren, Dyfed. *Proceedings of the Prehistoric Society* 56, 179–245.

Berns, M. 1990. Pots as people: Yungur ancestral portraits. *African Arts* 23, 50–60.

Bradley, R. 1998. Ruined buildings, ruined stones: enclosures, tombs and natural places in the Neolithic of south-west England. *World Archaeology* 30, 13–22.

Bradley, R. 2000. *An archaeology of natural places*. London: Routledge.

Brück, J. 2001. Body metaphors and technologies of trans-formation in the English Middle and Late Bronze Age. In J. Brück (ed.), *Bronze Age landscapes: tradition and trans-formation*, 149–60. Oxford: Oxbow.

Boivin, N. 2000. Life rhythms and floor sequences: excavating time in rural Rajasthan and Neolithic Çatalhöyük. *World Archaeology* 31, 376–88.

Brittain, M. forthcoming. Traditions of Substance: form v's formation in the monumentality of early Bronze Age Wales. In A. Lopez Royo (ed.), *Archaeology and Performance*. Los Angeles: Cotsen Institute of Archaeology.

Busby, C. 1997. Permeable and partial persons: a comparative analysis of gender and the body in south India and Melanesia. *Journal of the Royal Anthropological Institute* 3, 261–78.

Cummings, V. 2001. *Landscapes in transition? Exploring the origins of monumentality in south-west Wales and south-west Scotland*. Unpublished Ph.D. Thesis: Cardiff University.

Cummings, V. 2002. All cultural things: actual and conceptual monuments in the Neolithic of western Britain. In C. Scarre (ed.), *Monumentality and landscape in Atlantic Europe*, 107–21. London: Routledge.

David, N., Sterner, J. and Gavua, K. 1988. Why pots are decorated. *Current Anthropology* 29, 365–89.

Descola, P. 1996. *In the society of nature. A native ecology in Amazonia.* Cambridge: Cambridge University Press.

Evans, J. 1990. An archaeological survey of Skomer, Dyfed. *Proceedings of the Prehistoric Society* 56, 247–67.

Field, D. 1998. Round barrows and the harmonious landscape: placing early Bronze Age burial monuments in south-east England. *Oxford Journal of Archaeology* 17, 309–26.

Fleming, A. 1999. Phenomenology and the megaliths of Wales: a dreaming too far? *Oxford Journal of Archaeology* 18, 119–25.

Fowler, C. 2003. Rates of (ex)change: decay and growth, memory and the transformation of the dead in early Neolithic southern Britain. In H. Williams (ed.), *Archaeologies of remembrance - death and memory in past societies*, 45–63. London: Kluwer Academic Press.

Giambelli, R. 1998. The coconut, the body and the human being. Metaphors of life and growth in Nusa Penida and Bali. In L. Rival (ed.), *The social life of trees: anthropological perspectives on tree symbolism*, 133–57. Oxford: Berg.

Griffiths, W. 1960. The excavation of stone circles near Penmaenmawr, North Wales. *Proceedings of the Prehistoric Society* 36, 303–39.

Herbert, E. 1993. *Iron, gender, and power: rituals of transformation in African societies.* Bloomington and Indianapolis: Indiana University Press.

Hogg, A. 1977. Two cairns at Aber Camddwr, near Ponterwyd, Cardiganshire. *Archaeologia Cambrensis* 126, 24–37.

Hottot, R. 1956. Teke fetishes. *Journal of the Royal Anthropological Institute of Great Britain and Ireland* 86, 25–36.

Ingold, T. 2000a. On weaving a basket. In T. Ingold, *The perception of the environment: essays in livelihood, dwelling and skill*, 339–48. London: Routledge.

Ingold, T. 2000b. Making things, growing plants, raising animals and bringing up children. In T. Ingold, *The perception of the environment: essays in livelihood, dwelling and skill*, 77–88. London: Routledge.

Kan, S. 1989. *Symbolic immortality: the Tlingit potlatch of the nineteenth century.* Washington and London: The Smithsonian Institute.

Keepax, C. 1993. Analysis of the Brenig wood: identification results. In F. Lynch, *Excavations in the Brenig Valley. A Mesolithic and Bronze Age landscape in North Wales*, 199–201. Bangor: Cambrian Archaeological Monographs No. 5.

Kissock, J. 1993. Some examples of co-axial field systems in Pembrokeshire. *Bulletin of the Board of Celtic Studies* 40, 190–7.

Lane, P. 1986. Past practices in the ritual present: examples from the Welsh Bronze Age. *Archaeological Review from Cambridge* 5, 181–92.

Lewis, J.M. 1965. The excavation of four standing-stones in south Wales. *Bulletin of the Board of Celtic Studies* 21, 249–64.

Lewis, J.M. 1974. Excavations at Rhos-y-Clegyrn prehistoric site, St Nicholas, Pembs. *Archaeologia Cambrensis* 123, 13–42.

Lynch, F. 1971. Report on the re-excavation of two Bronze Age cairns in Anglesey: Bedd Branwen and Treiorwerth. *Archaeologia Cambrensis* 120, 11–83.

Lynch, F. 1980. Bronze Age monuments in Wales. In J. Taylor (ed.), *Culture and environment in prehistoric Wales*, 233–41. Oxford: British Archaeological Reports British Series 76.

Lynch, F. 1984. Moel Goedog Circle I: a complex ring cairn near Harlech. *Archaeologia Cambensis* 133, 8–50.

Lynch, F, 1993. *Excavations in the Brenig Valley. A Mesolithic and Bronze Age landscape in North Wales.* Bangor: Cambrian Archaeological Monographs No. 5.

Lynch, F. 2000. The later Neolithic and earlier Bronze Age. In F. Lynch, S. Aldhouse-Green and J. Davies (eds), *Prehistoric Wales*, 79–138. Stroud: Sutton.

MacGaffey, W. 1988. Complexity, astonishment and power: the visual vocabulary of Kongo Minkisi. *Journal of Southern African Studies* 14, 188–203.

MacGaffey, W. 1991. *Art and healing of the Bakongo commented by themselves: Minkisi from the Laman collection.* Stockholm: Kolkens museum-etnografiska.

MacGaffey, W. 1993. The eyes of understanding: Kongo Minkisi. In W. MacGaffey and M. Harris (eds), *Astonishment and power*, 21–103. Washington: National Museum of African Art.

McKinley, J. 1997. Bronze Age 'barrows' and funerary rites and rituals of cremation. *Proceedings of the Prehistoric Society* 63, 129–45.

Merleau-Ponty, M. 1962. *Phenomenology of perception.* London: Routledge.

Moore-Colyer, R. 1996. Agriculture in Wales before and during the second millennium BC. *Archaeologia Cambrensis* 145, 15–33.

Mullin, D. 2001. Remembering, forgetting and the invention of tradition: burial and natural places in the English early Bronze Age. *Antiquity* 75, 533–7.

Munn, N. 1992. *The fame of Gawa.* Cambridge: Cambridge University Press.

Murphy, K. 2001. A prehistoric field system and related monuments on St David's Head and Carn Llidi, Pembrokeshire. *Proceedings of the Prehistoric Society* 67, 85–99.

Nowakowski, J. 2001. Leaving home in the Cornish Bronze Age: insights into planned abandonment processes. In J. Brück (ed.), *Bronze Age landscapes: tradition and transformation*, 139–48. Oxford: Oxbow.

Nye, A., Harrison, W. and Savory, H. 1983. Excavations at the Croesmihangel Barrow, Pembrokeshire, 1958–59. *Archaeologia Cambrensis* 132, 19–29.

Ollier, C., Drover, D. and Godelier, M. 1971. Soil knowledge amongst the Baruya of Wonenara, New Guinea. *Oceania* 42, 33–41.

Owoc, M. 2000. *Aspects of ceremonial burial in the Bronze Age of south-west Britain.* Unpublished Ph.D. thesis: University of Sheffield.

Owoc, M. 2001. The times, they are a changin': experiencing continuity and development in the early Bronze Age funerary rituals of southwestern Britain. In J. Brück (ed.), *Bronze Age landscapes: tradition and transformation*, 193–206. Oxford: Oxbow.

Owoc, M. 2002. Munselling the mound: the use of soil colour as metaphor in British Bronze Age funerary ritual. In A. Jones and G. MacGregor (eds), *Colouring the past*, 127–140. Oxford: Berg.

Owoc, M. forthcoming a. Beyond geoarchaeology: pragmatist explorations of alternative viewscapes in the British Bronze

Age and Beyond. In *The Odyssey of Space*. Calgary: University of Calgary Press.

Owoc, M. forthcoming b. A phenomenology of the buried landscape: soil as material culture in the Bronze Age of south-west Britain. In M. Owoc and N. Boivin (eds), *Soil, stones and symbols: cultural perceptions of the mineral world*.

Parker Pearson, M. and Ramilisonina. 1998. Stonehenge for the ancestors: the stones pass on the message. *Antiquity* 72, 308–26.

Pool, F. 1984. Symbols of substance: Bimin-Kuskusmin models of procreation, death, and personhood. *Mankind* 14, 191–216.

Richards, C. and Thomas, J. 1984. Ritual activity and structured deposition in later Neolithic Wessex. In R. Bradley and J. Gardiner (eds), *Neolithic studies*, 189–218. Oxford: British Archaeological Reports British Series 133.

Rival, L. 1993. The growth of family trees: understanding Huaorani perceptions of the forest. *Man* 28, 635–52.

Roese, H. 1980. Some aspects of topographical locations of Neolithic and Bronze Age monuments in Wales. *Bulletin of the Board of Celtic Studies* 28, 645–55.

Savory, H. 1949. Two middle Bronze Age palisade barrows at Letterston, Pembrokeshire. *Archaeologia Cambrensis* 88, 67–86.

Savory, H. 1963. Excavations at a third round barrow at Pen-Dre, Letterston (Pemb.), 1961. *Bulletin of the Board of Celtic Studies* 20, 309–25.

Seeland, K. 1997. Indigenous knowledge of trees and forests in non-European societies. In K. Seeland (ed.), *Nature is culture: indigenous knowledge and socio-cultural aspects of trees and forests in non-European cultures*, 101–12. London: Intermediate Technology Publications.

Smith, F. 1989. Earth, vessels, and harmony among the Gurensi. *African Arts* 22, 60–5.

Strathern, A. and Stewart, P. 2001. Dangerous woods and perilous pearl shells. *Journal of Material Culture* 5, 69–89.

Tarlow, S. 1993. Scraping the bottom of the barrow: an agricultural metaphor in Neolithic/ Bronze Age burial practice. *Journal of Theoretical Archaeology* 3/4, 123–44.

Thomas, J. 1996. *Time, culture and identity: an interpretive archaeology*. London: Routledge.

Thomas, J. 2002. Archaeology's humanism and the materiality of the body. In Y. Hamilakis, M. Pluciennik and S. Tarlow (eds), *Thinking through the body: archaeologies of corporeality*, 29–46. New York: Kluwer Academic/Plenum Press.

Tilley, C. and Bennett, W. 2001. An archaeology of supernatural places: the case of West Penwith. *Journal of the Royal Anthropological Institute* 7, 335–62.

Tilley, C. 1994. *A phenomenology of landscape: places, paths and monuments*. Oxford: Berg.

Tilley, C. 1996. The powers of rocks: topography and monument construction on Bodmin Moor. *World Archaeology* 28, 161–76.

Tipping, R. 1994. "Ritual" floral tributes in the Scottish Bronze Age – palynological evidence. *Journal of Archaeological Science* 21, 133–39.

Van Wing, J. 1941. Bakongo magic. *Journal of the Royal Anthropological Institute of Great Britain and Ireland* 71, 85–97.

Ward, A. 1988. Survey and excavation of ring cairns in south Wales and on Gower, West Glamorgan. *Proceedings of the Prehistoric Society* 54, 153–72.

Ward, A. 1989a. Land allotment of possible prehistoric date on Mynydd Llangyndeyrn, south-east Dyfed. *Archaeologia Cambrensis* 138, 46–58.

Ward, A. 1989b. Cairns and 'cairn fields'; evidence of early agriculture on Cefn Bryn, Gower, West Glamorgan. *Landscape History* 11, 5–17.

Weiner, A. 1980. Reproduction: a replacement for reciprocity. *American Ethnologist* 7, 71–85.

Williams, G. 1988. *The standing stones of Wales and south-west England*. Oxford: British Archaeological Reports, British Series 197.

Wilshusen, R. and Stone, G. 1990. An ethnoarchaeological perspective on soils. *World Archaeology* 22(1), 104–114.

24 Memory, tradition and materiality: the Isles of Scilly in context

Trevor Kirk

Introduction

If future archaeological research in the Isles of Scilly (Fig. 24.1) is to enhance our understanding of memory, materiality and traditions of practice in prehistory, we must first take stock of current thinking on these issues. The last major synthetic works on the prehistory of Scilly were published in 1974 (Paul Ashbee's *Ancient Scilly*) and 1985 (Charles Thomas's *Exploration of a Drowned Landscape*). Their scope is remarkable, ranging from earliest prehistory to the first millennium AD, and from ecology and marine transgression to monumentality, settlement, economy and place-name evidence. These two books are also important because they explicitly model networks of cultural interaction linking Scilly to Cornwall, Ireland, Wessex and Brittany. Ashbee and Thomas skilfully marshal environmental, artefactual, ethnographic and historical evidence to identify the first prehistoric settlers, probably arriving on virgin islands from their Cornish base during the early second millennium BC. Thomas confidently identifies five 'founder settlements' and five associated 'founder cairns' (Fig. 24.2) established, in Thomas's own words, 'within Year One, certainly inside Decade One [of colonisation]' (1985, 103). Following Renfrew (1976), Thomas (1985, 107–9) models a segmentary society for Scilly on the basis of prehistoric settlement patterns and forms of monumentality. Thomas and Ashbee also highlight the early settlers' struggle to replicate their parent culture in a new setting that rapidly succumbs to soil degradation. Most notably Ashbee (1976, 11) views 'chambered cairns on Scilly… as repositories for occupation earth…which reflect a non-material approach to the problems of soil fertility'.

It might therefore be argued that traditions of practice – the motif of the Manchester colloquium – are for Thomas and Ashbee driven by folk movement and defined by the quest to replicate socio-economic systems in new territories through pragmatic and symbolic behaviour. This paper considers how future work in Scilly might develop different approaches to memory, tradition and materiality; approaches which highlight agency and the forging of identity through social practice. The paper is concerned with the historical and material conditions of human life; with the processes whereby identities and social relations are created through immersion in specific material, cultural and political worlds. I view traditions of practice as dynamic networks of memories and dispositions through which the world is encountered and interpreted. Tradition is not simply adopted but is constantly 'modified in accordance with changed historical circumstances' (Warnke 1987, 92). Andy Jones (2001) has recently adopted Judith Butler's (1993) metaphor of citation to explain this process. He argues that 'the performance of a citation both encapsulates previous ideas or things while also rearticulating them afresh in order to create or define novel categories' (Jones 2001, 340). I intend to carry forward the theme of citation, and not least its focus on performance and action – the 'inscribing practices' of Connerton (1989, 72–9) – as the medium for reworking tradition. In short, this paper asks how traditions were 'passed down' and transformed through lived experience in later prehistoric Scilly.

Establishing tradition: the fifth to third millennia in Scilly

Scillonian prehistory is unusual because it appears to start so late. Mesolithic communities are only dimly glimpsed when they impact on the native tree cover. A pollen core from Higher Moors, St Mary's shows mixed oak forest, including birch and hazel, in the late sixth millennium BC (5520–5035 BC – HAR-3695) (Scaife 1983). The presence of birch scrub in this context may indicate woodland regeneration following small-scale clearance by hunter-gatherers (Scaife 1983). Mesolithic artefacts are rare in Scilly, the only securely identified pieces being two obliquely blunted microliths (one unprovenanced, the other from Halangy Down, St Mary's), an axe sharpening flake found near The Town on Bryher, two unprovenanced pieces in the Alec Gray collection in Truro (a curved-backed point and a microlith), a pecked pebble hammer from Porth Cressa, St Mary's, and small surface collections of *débitage* such as that from the cliff face at Old Quay, St Martin's (Ashbee 1986, 195;

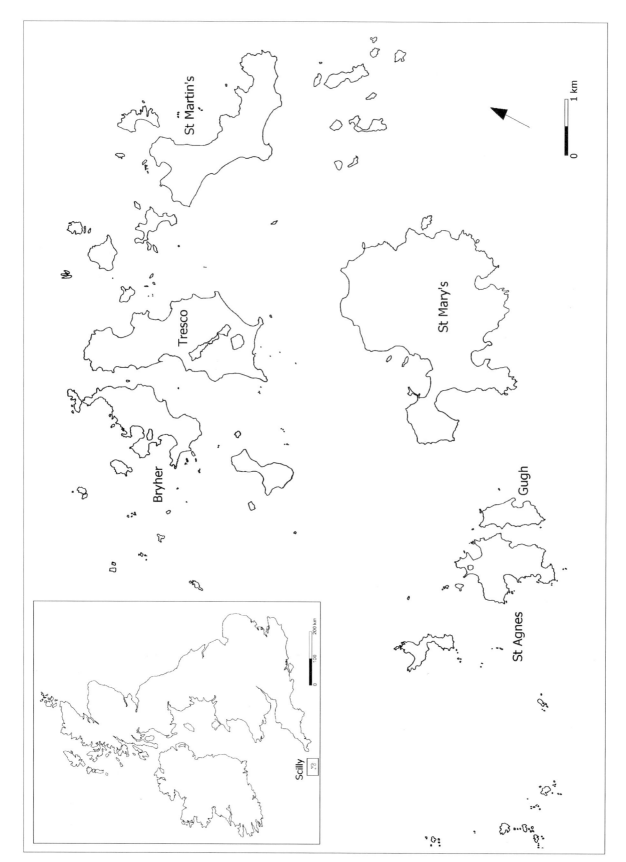

Figure 24.1. *The Isles of Scilly (after Ratcliffe 1989).*

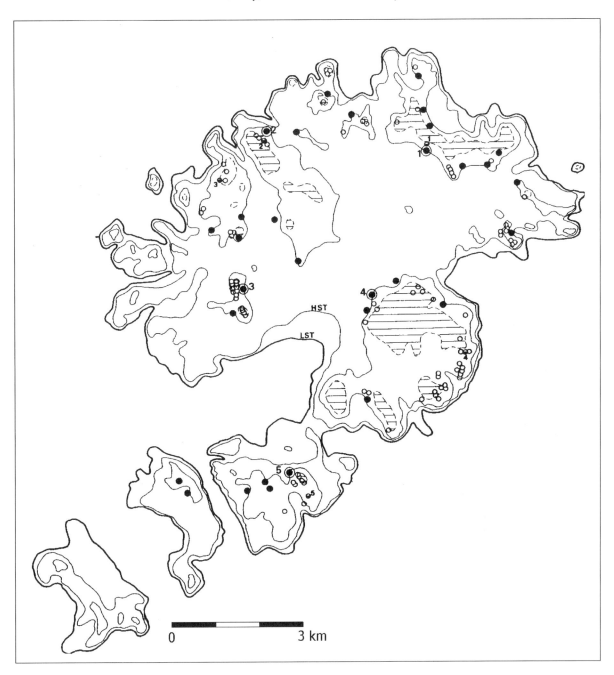

Figure 24.2. *Scilly in the second millennium BC (after Thomas 1985, 104, figure 43). Key: Black symbols – settlements (circled symbols, 'founder settlements'); Open symbols – cairns (circled symbols, 'founder cairns'); LST – low spring tide; HST – high spring tide.*

Berridge and Roberts 1986, 30; Ratcliffe 1989, 33). Large trimmed Larnian-style blades and flakes are relatively common in surface collections (Ashbee 1986, 195).

Despite the paucity of Mesolithic evidence, it is hard to imagine that Scilly was not part of the known Mesolithic world along the Irish seaboard, particularly in light of the evidence for thriving Mesolithic communities in Brittany, south-east Ireland, south-west England and Wales (Bonsall 1989). Granted, rising sea-levels (Fig. 24.2) have drowned much of the coast-line and central

plain that would have attracted Mesolithic fishing, gathering and hunting communities. Also, the late Flandrian islands may never have been large enough to support a permanent hunter-gatherer-fisher community (Mercer 1986, 61). Rather, Scilly may have been 'a seasonal station for the exploitation of specific aspects of the marine resource' (Mercer 1986). Nonetheless, it is notable that the majority of Scilly's flint collections have not been analysed in detail: not least with an eye to identifying Mesolithic material. Analysis of these assem-

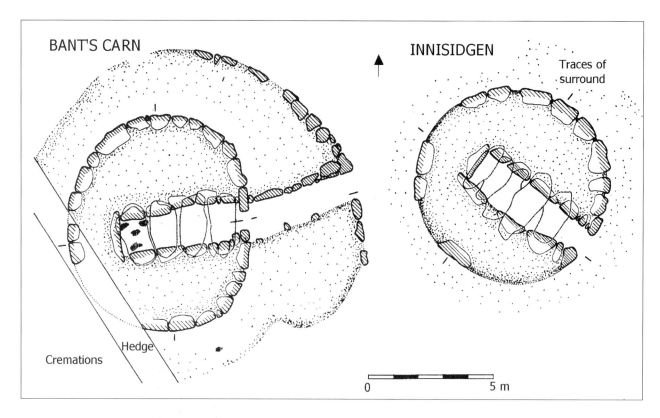

Figure 24.3. Bant's Carn and Innisidgen entrance graves (after Ashbee 1974, 81, figure 10).

blages, together with systematic surface survey and further environmental sampling, may well enhance our understanding of the place of Scilly in the Mesolithic world. Whether periodically visited or more extensively inhabited, it seems likely that traditions of practice (for example, seasonal rounds of movement through the landscape, fishing, the collection of flint and other material resources) were established in Scilly from, perhaps, the sixth millennium. With the high concentration of later prehistoric monuments in Scilly in mind, Roger Mercer has asked if 'such specialist seasonal occupation could have taken on other special connotations in the eyes of descendant populations' (1986, 61). In short, we would do well to consider the extent to which later communities referred back to the earliest occupation and traditions of practice in Scilly. Indeed, it is with this thought in mind that I now turn to the second millennium BC, the period for which we have evidence for the earliest long-term occupation in Scilly.

Practice and tradition in second millennium BC Scilly

At the moment it is difficult to gain any meaningful insight into the process of Neolithic transition in Scilly. Indeed, the Scillonian Neolithic is itself incredibly elusive: so much so, that it hardly exists at all. Pottery is limited

to a handful of middle Neolithic sherds from Bant's Carn, St Mary's and from pits at East Porth, Samson (Ratcliffe 1989, 34). Diagnostic stone tools are also rare, and often date to the late Neolithic/early Bronze Age. Axes are notably rare, despite the fact that glacial tills on St Martin's, Bryher and Tresco yield large flint nodules suitable for axe production (Ashbee 1974, 231). Axes and associated heavy tools include a pointed-butt greenstone axe from Gugh (Ashbee 1974, 236), an edged-cushion macehead from Bryher (Ashbee 1974) and an adze from the old ground surface beneath Knackyboy cairn, St Martin's (O'Neil 1952, 22). Diagnostic arrowheads are mainly barbed and tanged (Ratcliffe 1989, 34) but also include a petit-tranchet derivative form at Samson Hill, Bryher, and lozenge and triangular-based forms at Normandy Farm, St Mary's (Ashbee 1974, 233 and 235). Blade and flake based industries, often featuring scrapers, are known, but lithic assemblages have rarely been studied in detail. Local flint and hardstone sources were predominantly used (Ashbee 1974, 231; Evens *et al.* 1972), the only imported items being a tourmaline granite battle-axe found at Normandy Farm, St Mary's and a Group I greenstone ball from Nornour (Ashbee 1974, 237).

It is true that entrance grave architecture (Figs. 24.3 and 24.4) appears to recall Neolithic traditions of monument building, with a central chamber that may have been periodically accessed. However, with the exception of sherds of middle Neolithic pottery from Bant's Carn, St

Figure 24.4. Innisidgen entrance grave (after Ashbee 1974, 85, plate 5a).

Figure 24.5. Urns from Knackyboy Cairn, St. Martin's and Obadiah's Barrow, Gugh (after Ashbee 1974, 157, plate 13).

Mary's the material from entrance graves is almost entirely Bronze Age (Ashbee 1976, 14; Thomas 1985, 102). Cremation burials in biconical urns (Fig. 24.5) suggest a second millennium BC date for the main phases of monument use. Sadly, and surprisingly, there are no published C-14 dates for any of the Scillonian entrance graves, though the primary use of Tregiffian in Cornwall dates from the early second millennium (1995–1680 BC – BM-935) (Thomas 1985, 94). Sherds of biconical urn sealed beneath the chamber paving at Knackyboy cairn, St Martin's strongly suggest that, here at least, the entrance grave was built during the second millennium (O'Neil 1952, 30). Also, entrance graves such as Bant's Carn overlie field boundaries which are taken to be Bronze Age at earliest (Ashbee 1976). Entrance graves elsewhere in the Irish sea zone were, to judge from their cremation

deposits and Beaker-derived pottery, also used (and perhaps built) in the second millennium BC. This is certainly the case in Cornwall (at Greenburrow, Pennance and Brane), in south-east Ireland (Tramore, Co. Waterford) and in south-west Scotland (White Cairn at Bargrennan) (Thomas 1985, 96 and 119–20).

It therefore appears that several of the entrance graves were indeed late constructions. Only at Obadiah's Barrow, Gugh is there evidence for an early 'pre-cremation' phase represented by a 'hard blackish soil' underlying the urn burials (Ashbee 1974, 110–11; Hencken 1933, 22). It was in this layer that the disarticulated remains of one or more individuals were deposited in a fashion reminiscent of practices at Neolithic chambered tombs and long barrows in southern England. Indeed, back in 1960 Grimes noted that 'while some chambered tombs in the

Scilly Isles are Neolithic in date as well as in ancestry...
at least one [Knackyboy] seems to have been built at a
more advanced date in the Bronze Age' (Grimes 1960,
177). While I accept the notion of a Neolithic ancestry
for the entrance graves, their construction and use
probably occurs more frequently in the second millennium
BC than Grimes would have it. Also, the clearance of
primary chamber deposits during the Bronze Age is not
demonstrable at any of the excavated entrance graves.
The entrance graves do not appear, in the current state of
knowledge, to be Neolithic monuments that were cleared
and re-used in the Bronze Age, though further excavation
is required to clarify this important issue.

Of course many prehistoric monuments do have long
life-histories. They are used and re-used, their functions
and meanings reworked through the generations. In this
respect I am not claiming anything special for any
Scillonian entrance graves that may have been built in
the third millennium BC. However, many entrance graves
appear to have been built late. Just as post-modern
architecture draws on past styles and designs, so early
Bronze Age Scillonians may have recalled traditions from
a different time and from a different place, traditions
which were reworked to produce effects relevant for their
new context. The point is perhaps best illustrated by
examining building practices, monument biographies and
patterns of material deposition at entrance graves
(especially deposits of occupation debris, pottery and
human remains).

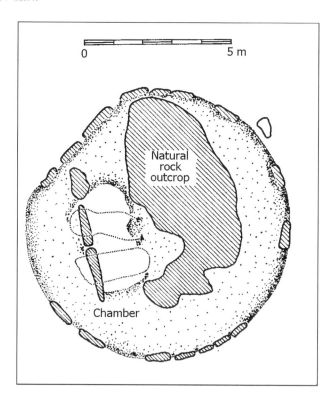

Figure 24.6. *Outcrop incorporated into entrance grave at*
Porth Hellick, St. Mary's (after Ashbee 1974, figure 12).

Building practices and monument biographies

People are aware of the historical context in which they
live. They are aware that the material world is replete
with meanings, associations and connotations that are
the result of other people's thoughts and actions. The act
of monument building is, like all human action, shot
through with tradition. That is to say, the resources with
which people labour – such as a place in the landscape,
stone, earth and timber – carry forward meanings from
other times and, in the case of portable materials, from
other places. Cultural meanings are not fixed, much less
are they single. Matrices of meaning emerge through
discursive practices (ranging from formalised story-telling
to day-to-day conversation) and through lived-experience,
that domain of habitual practice which produces meaning
and effect that is not readily rendered in language. The
cultural traditions that people inherit are resources with
which to work in the daily routines of life and in formal
contexts of ritual.

Monuments are rarely built on virgin territory; the
landscape has been known and lived in. Take, for
example, the granite outcrops incorporated into entrance
graves as elements of chamber walls (at Knackyboy,
Cruthers Hill, Porth Hellick and Obadiah's Barrow), as
part of cairn kerbing (Salakee Down) or embedded in the
fabric of the cairn (Porth Hellick) (Fig. 24.6). This

recurrent architectural feature may simply represent
pragmatic utilisation of available resources. Also, the
outcrops are small; they do not dominate the landscape
in the way that Tilley (1994; 1996a) views the meaning-
laden outcrops associated with Neolithic monuments in
Pembrokeshire and on Bodmin Moor. However, people
inscribe meanings around the smallest objects. Janet
Hoskins (1998) charts the complex biographies of betel
bags and spindles in Eastern Indonesia, objects around
which elaborate meanings are woven. Identity, belonging
and self-worth emerge through people's engagement with
such objects. The capacity of relatively small objects to
support cultural biographies is therefore well-known.
However, why might we feel that some small granite
outcrops were significant in prehistoric Scilly? We know
that granite was used to build entrance graves in Scilly.
One might argue that with trees and earth in short supply
granite was the only available resource. However, this
assumes that the idea of monument building (presumably
introduced to Scilly?) is primary, and that only later do
people work out how to produce the desired effect with
locally available resources. This is perhaps to overstate
the power of mental templates. Or, more importantly, we
risk overlooking the fact that monuments are built, that
their material forms and associated cultural meanings
emerge in the flow of human practice. It may well be that
alternative building materials were in short supply, but

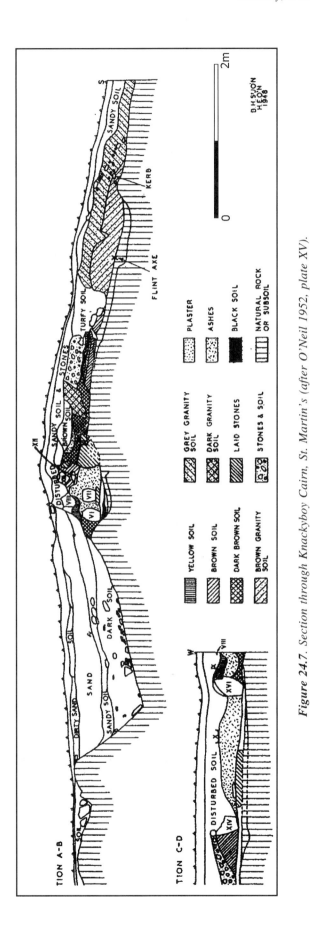

Figure 24.7. Section through Knackyboy Cairn, St. Martin's (after O'Neil 1952, plate XV).

that does not lessen the potential of that which does exist to attract and sustain cultural meaning. If anything, in a world of limited resources, one might actually go about distinguishing between superficially similar materials. Archaeology's brush with post-structural theory teaches us that meaning emerges through structured networks of difference. In a small bounded landscape, one might start to categorise the world in quite subtle ways, distinguishing between different outcrops, places and spaces on a micro-scale.

Until we know more about early prehistory in Scilly it is difficult to assess how and why specific places and natural features may have developed cultural biographies. Future research might usefully reflect on routes, pathways and places associated with hunting, gathering, fishing and early farming. Relational analogies and 'analogies of materiality' (Parker Pearson and Ramilisonina 1998, 309–11) might also allow us to envisage rocks as enduring landscape features that may have acted as metaphors or actual embodiments of spirits, ancestors and the other world (Gillings and Pollard 1999). A 'natural pit in the rock' beneath the Salakee Down entrance grave, St. Mary's (Grimes 1960, 173) may represent a further referencing of natural features. While the origins of the natural hollow are not clear, I am reminded of recent work on relationships between Neolithic sites and monuments and relatively ephemeral natural features such as tree throws (Buckley *et al.* 2001; Evans *et al.* 1999). Questions about the tempo, rhythms and cycles of monument building, use and abandonment might therefore be useful avenues of future research in Scilly (Thomas this volume). Temporalities of durable stone may run parallel with more rapid tempos of organic growth and decay associated with, say, trees and, of course, the people buried in entrance graves. Metaphors linking organic decay to issues of human mortality and cultural identity (Fowler this volume, 2003) are fertile areas for further research. Indeed, it is to this area that I now turn, with particular interest in the deposition of occupation debris and pottery in entrance graves.

Earth, pots and people

Entrance graves primarily contain midden debris – dark organic earth, ash, charcoal and abraded sherds (Ashbee 1976) (Fig. 24.7). These deposits are reminiscent of the occupation debris deposited at southern English long barrows and causewayed enclosures and of the 'black earth' in some Scottish chambered tombs (Ashbee 1976, 21). These symbols of life (rich organic soil), of trans-formation (ash and charcoal) and of decay (broken pottery) have the potential to convey a variety of contextual meanings, perhaps relating to the fluidity and mutability of social identities, perhaps framing relationships between the living and the dead (see also Brück's (1995) discussion of fertility, human remains and 'refuse' in Bronze Age Britain). However, in Scilly the meaning of these deposits may also relate to a specific problem – soil degradation.

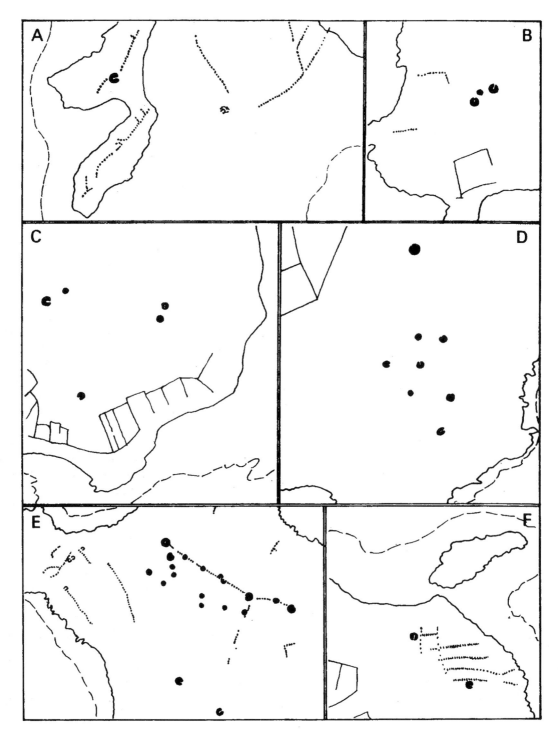

Figure 24.8. Entrance graves, cairns and enclosure walls (after Thomas 1985, 137, figure 59) Key: A – Tean, Old Man and West Porth; B – Bryher, Gweal Hill; C – Bryher, Samson Hill; D – St. Mary's, Porth Hellick Down; E – Gugh, Kittern Hill; F – St. Mary's, Innisidgen.

Pollen cores (notably from Higher Moors, St Mary's) show extensive woodland clearance by the second millennium BC (Scaife 1983; Thomas 1985, 116–7), while field enclosure (Fig. 24.8) may herald shifting attitudes towards land tenure and the introduction of a short-fallow system of agriculture (Barrett 1994). Manuring may also have been practised in an attempt to maintain the fertility of Scilly's shallow acidic soils. Worked flint associated with boundary walls on the flats (especially on Samson) may be the only durable residue of household waste spread on fields, while sea-shells and beach pebbles associated with early field boundaries may indicate the use of seaweed as manure (Thomas 1985, 121–2). Ashbee (1976, 11) has indeed argued that entrance graves were ostensibly 'repositories of occupation earth, sometimes leavened with human remains, which reflect a non-material approach to the problems of soil fertility'. In short, symbols of fertility (organic deposits) – symbols with an ancestry spanning several centuries – were used to address a major concern amongst the living in second millennium Scilly: deteriorating soil quality.

Some entrance graves were also stages for complex rites during which ancestral remains were manipulated over a substantial period of time. At Knackyboy cairn, St Martin's the deposition of seven cremation urns (Fig. 24.9) is followed by one or more episodes of 'tidying up' or 'rededication' (O'Neil 1952, 24). This involved the emptying of cremation urns (or the introduction of cremated material, perhaps following temporary storage elsewhere?) to form a thick ashy deposit into which further urned cremations were placed. A similar sequence is also seen at Obadiah's Barrow, Gugh (Hencken 1933) (Fig. 24.10). It is tempting to see here an echo of the Neolithic practice of circulating ancestral remains within or between monuments (Ashbee 1974, 117). This practice may have served to ground the social identities of people living in small-scale lineage societies within genealogies stretching back into the past. Indeed, the absence of major public monuments (henges, stone circles, stone rows) suggests that a small-scale segmentary society with minimal social hierarchy was maintained in Scilly, long after the decline of such systems in many parts of the Irish Sea zone.

As only occasional Neolithic artefacts are found in Scilly, we might envisage occasional seasonal sorties to the islands by Neolithic groups, perhaps from Cornwall. The islands appear not to have been permanently settled until the late Neolithic/early Bronze Age. When settlement does occur, Thomas (1985, 102) models the 'communal movement' of a 'mature and non-experimental system'. He further argues that '...we could and should expect that after the move these pioneers would reproduce within a familiar, if scaled-down, setting, all the house-types, farming practices and burial customs long dictated by social habit and stubborn empiricism' (Thomas 1985, 102). To my mind there is a lack of dynamic in this account. Inherited experience is important, but it is a resource with which to work rather than a template that determines outcome. We have already seen how ideas with a Neolithic ancestry (chambered monuments, the symbolism of occupation debris, manipulation of ancestral remains) may have been reworked in novel ways in the second millennium BC in Scilly. Tradition is not static. Neither is it a restrictive structure which prohibits and says 'no'. Rather, tradition is a dynamic and shifting network of knowledge, memories and dispositions through which the world is experienced and interpreted. Tradition may also paradoxically support the opposing world-views of individuals or interest-groups. It is a dynamic resource

on which to draw rather than a prescribed list of normative behaviour.

Earlier I suggested that a lack of major public monuments may mean that social structure in Scilly was less hierarchical than that in many other parts of the Irish Sea zone during the late-third and second millennia BC. This suggestion may appear to be at odds with the presence of field systems in Scilly, perhaps relating to new definitions of land tenure comparable to those in southern England during the second millennium (Barrett 1994). However, many of the major field systems (Shipman Head Down, Bryher; Castle Down, Tresco and Chapel Down, St Martin's) are in areas that were probably always too marginal to have ever supported agriculture (Thomas 1985, 129–123). Rather, Thomas suggests that 'boulder-walls running from cairn to cairn may be closer to the concept of a power-line cable than to that of an estate boundary' (Thomas 1985, 140). Charged with symbols of life (occupation debris) and, on occasion, with ancestral remains, the entrance graves were stages on which people worked to maintain or restore the fertility of soils, animals, plants and people. In this light 'we can look again at the walls linking cairns, walls that can be extended into side-enclosures that seem to symbolise, rather than actually to constitute, the fields and plots of everyday life' (Thomas 1985, 142). Agriculture was undoubtedly practised in Scilly, but it's expansion into a system of permanent land tenure may have been, at best, short-lived. If this is the case, then some of the so-called 'field systems' may be symbolic references to the problem of soil degradation (real or threatened?) rather than agricultural enclosures. Once again, memory and structural forms may have been reworked to produce new effects and meanings.

Entrance graves were also charged with symbols of transformation and decay (ash, charcoal, broken pottery, cremated human bodies). These monuments may therefore have been public stages on which people addressed the fluidity and ambiguity of social identities. This may have involved rites of passage which formally marked major transitions in the life-cycle of individuals, interest groups or entire communities. However, I also have in mind the minute-on-minute, day-to-day fluidity of human person-hood; the way in which we dismantle, reformulate and change our place in society through the flow of everyday life (Fowler 2001). Dispersal of the self, something along the lines of Marilyn Strathern's (1988) *dividual*, is a concept that may have been grappled with in prehistoric Scilly.

The common association of the dead with pottery may also be significant here. Cremated bodies are buried in urns or cremation ashes scattered in thick layers inter-leaved with broken pottery. Bodies are reduced to ash by the heat of fire, the same technology that is used to produce pottery. Bodies are transformed from flesh and blood to dry ashes, just as moist clay is fired to produce hard dry ceramics. Parallel transformations from moist/

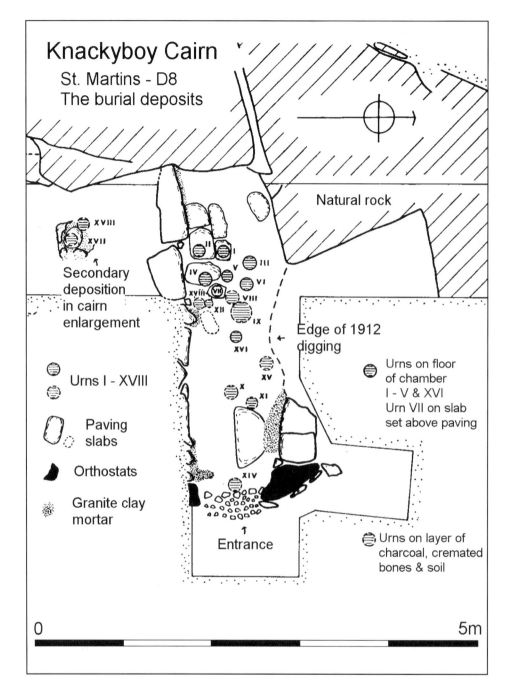

Figure 24.9. Chamber deposits at Knackyboy Cairn, St. Martin's (after Ashbee 1974, 114, figure 18).

wet to dry may have been played out in the biographies of people and pottery (see Tilley (1996b) for a discussion of comparable metaphorical links in the Neolithic of Scandinavia). It is also notable that high concentrations of surface mica give some of the vessels from Bant's Carn an 'almost iridescent quality, which would have made many vessels conspicuous when newly made' (Ashbee 1976, 17). The individual identities of some pots may, in some contexts, have contrasted the anonymity of the dead whose remains were scattered on the floors of entrance graves. However, the wealth of broken pottery,

for example at the sealed entrance to Obadiah's Barrow (Ashbee 1974, 112) suggests that the integrity of pots was also compromised on some occasions. Human actions and performances were clearly diverse and strategic rather than rote implementations of cultural norms.

The ambiguity and mobility of human identity may also be metaphorically represented by granite clay mortar plastered on the chamber walls at Knackyboy cairn, St. Mary's (O'Neil 1952, 23) and Innisidgen, St. Mary's (Ashbee 1974, 100). Durable granite, a material referenced in the architecture of the entrance graves, is

OBADIAH'S BARROW
GUGH DI:H5
THE BURIAL DEPOSITS
AFTER G. BONSOR

A : LARGE FRAGMENT OF POTTERY

B : URN FRAGMENTS

C : INVERTED URN BASE OVER CREMATION

D : UNURNED CREMATION

E : CORD-ORNAMENTED URN FRAGMENT

F : CRUSHED CORD-ORNAMENTED INVERTED URN

G : PELVIS & FEMUR HEAD

H : INVERTED INURNED CREMATION

I : FEMUR PART BELOW POTSHERD

J : ARTICULATED FOOT-BONES

K : SEVERAL BROKEN URNS

L : URN BASE OVER CREMATION

M : URN FRAGMENT OVER CREMATION,
JAW-BONE BENEATH

N : BRONZE AWL

O : INTACT URN INVERTED OVER CREMATION

P : LARGE FRAGMENTS OF BROKEN URN

Q : CREMATION & SHERDS, FINGER-BONES
BENEATH

R : FOREARM & KNEE-CAP

S : HAMMER-STONE

T : SEVEN ARTICULATED VERTEBRAE

U : RIB BENEATH CREMATION & SHERDS

FLAT
STONE

AREA
OF CREMATIONS
& BROKEN
URNS

DISTURBED
AREA

ENTRANCE
CLOSING STONE

POTTERY

0   5m

Figure 24.10. *Chamber deposits at Obadiah's Barrow, Gugh (after Ashbee 1974, 109, figure 17).*

transformed (albeit through a combination of natural and human agencies) from a dry inflexible form through a moist pliable state to a further state of dry durability and permanence. Interwoven biographies of people and materiality (cf. Marshall and Gosden 1999) (notably pottery and building materials such as granite and clay mortar) may prove to be fruitful avenues for future research into traditions of practice in prehistoric Scilly.

Conclusion

I feel that we now need to work towards a better understanding of the historically-contingent meanings inscribed in Scilly around monumentality, material culture, agriculture and the human body, themes and concerns that are common throughout the Irish Sea zone and beyond. The role of cultural memory and the reworking of the same through embodied performance lies at the heart of this project. More specifically, the passing down of tradition is a process of citation (Butler 1993; Jones 2001), of reformulating existing cultural ideas to produce meanings relevant for changing times. However, theoretical and interpretive questions remain, not least the precise meaning of agency in our accounts of prehistory. Ian Hodder (2000) recently re-iterated his view that 'constructivist' approaches often fail to take adequate account of intentionality (of creative forward-thinking) and of indeterminacy (the view that events are not determined by social structure). In his view, many approaches to agency ironically focus on agentless power relations and on cultural traditions for controlling material and symbolic resources: 'agency is seen in terms of resources: what is available to allow action to take place, rather than in terms of individual forward-looking intentionality and creativity' (Hodder 2000, 23). For Hodder the result is a failure to grapple fully with the dialectics of structure and agency; 'Rather, the focus is on the social construction of subjectivities as part of the unfurling of long-term processes' (Hodder 2000, 24). Hodder offers a timely reminder of the danger of privileging long-term processes over people's real lives and lived-experiences. Perhaps citation of tradition through lived-experience is one way of envisaging the mutuality of agency, material resources and long-term processes of social reproduction and change.

References

Ashbee, P. 1974. *Ancient Scilly. From the first farmers to the early Christians.* Newton Abbot: David and Charles.

Ashbee, P. 1976. Bant's Carn, St Mary's, Isles of Scilly: an entrance grave restored and reconsidered. *Cornish Archaeology* 15, 11–26.

Ashbee, P. 1986. Ancient Scilly: retrospect, aspect and prospect. *Cornish Archaeology* 25, 186–219.

Barrett, J. 1994. *Fragments from antiquity. An archaeology of social life in Britain, 2900–1200 B.C.* Oxford: Blackwell.

Berridge, P. and Roberts, A. 1986. The Mesolithic period in Cornwall. *Cornish Archaeology* 25, 7–34.

Bonsall, C. (ed.) 1989. *The Mesolithic in Europe.* Edinburgh: John Donald.

Brück, J. 1995. A place for the dead: the role of human remains in the Late Bronze Age. *Proceedings of the Prehistoric Society* 61, 245–77.

Buckley, D., Hedges, J. and Brown, N. 2001. Excavations at a Neolithic cursus, Springfield, Essex, 1979–85. *Proceedings of the Prehistoric Society* 67, 101–62.

Butler, J. 1993. *Bodies that matter. On the discursive limits of 'sex'.* London: Routledge.

Connerton, P. 1989. *How societies remember.* Cambridge: Cambridge University Press.

Evans, C., Pollard, J. and Knight, M. 1999. Life in woods: tree-throws, 'settlement' and forest cognition. *Oxford Journal of Archaeology* 18, 241–54.

Evens, E., Smith, I. and Wallis, F. 1972. The petrological identification of stone implements from south-western England. *Proceedings of the Prehistoric Society* 38, 235–75.

Fowler, C. 2001. Personhood and social relations in the British Neolithic with a case study from the Isle of Man. *Journal of Material Culture* 6, 137–63.

Fowler, C. 2003. Rates of (ex)change: Decay and growth, memory and the transformation of the dead in early Neolithic southern Britain. In Williams, H. (ed.) *Archaeologies of remembrance - death and memory in past societies,* 55–74. Kluwer Academic/ Plenum Press, New York.

Gillings, M. and Pollard, J. 1999. Non-portable stone artefacts and contexts of meaning: the tale of Grey Wether (www.museum.ncl.ac.uk/Avebury/stone4.htm). *World Archaeology* 31, 179–93.

Grimes, W. 1960. Salakee Down chambered cairn, St Mary's, Scilly. In W. Grimes (ed.), *Excavations on defence sites, 1939–1945. I: mainly Neolithic and Bronze Age,* 170–80. London: Her Majesty's Stationery Office.

Hencken, H.O'N. 1933. Notes on the megalithic monuments in the Isles of Scilly. *Antiquaries Journal* 13, 13–29.

Hodder, I. 2000. Agency and individuals in long-term processes. In M. A. Dobres and J. Robb (eds), *Agency in archaeology,* 21–33. London: Routledge.

Hoskins, J. 1998. *Biographical objects. How things tell the stories of people's lives.* London: Routledge.

Jones, A. 2001. Drawn from memory: the archaeology of aesthetics and the aesthetics of archaeology in earlier Bronze Age Britain and the present. *World Archaeology* 33, 334–56.

Marshall, Y. and Gosden, C. (eds) 1999. *The cultural biography of objects (World Archaeology* 31). London: Routledge.

Mercer, R. 1986. The Neolithic in Cornwall. *Cornish Archaeology* 25, 35–80.

O'Neil, B.H.St.J. 1952. The excavation of Knackyboy cairn, St Martin's, Isles of Scilly, 1948. *Antiquaries Journal* 32, 21–34.

Parker Pearson, M. and Ramilisonina, 1998. Stonehenge for the ancestors: the stones pass on the message. *Antiquity* 72, 308–26.

Ratcliffe, J. 1989. *The archaeology of Scilly. An assessment of the resource and recommendations for the future.* Truro: Cornwall Archaeological Unit.

Renfrew, C. 1976. Megaliths, territories and populations. In S. De Laet (ed.), *Acculturation and continuity in Atlantic Europe,* 198–220. Bruges: De Tempel.

Scaife, R. 1983. A history of Flandrian vegetation in the Isles of Scilly: palynological investigations of Higher Moors and Lower Moors peat mires, St Mary's. *Cornish Studies* 11, 33–47.

Strathern, M. 1988. *The gender of the gift. Problems with women and problems with society in Melanesia.* Berkeley: University of California Press.

Thomas, C. 1985. *Exploration of a drowned landscape. Archaeology and history of the Isles of Scilly.* London: Batsford.

Tilley, C. 1994. *A phenomenology of landscape.* Oxford: Berg.

Tilley, C. 1996a. The power of rocks: topography and monument construction on Bodmin Moor. *World Archaeology* 28, 161–76.

Tilley, 1996b. *An ethnography of the Neolithic. Early prehistoric societies in Southern Scandinavia.* Cambridge University Press.

Warnke, G. 1987. *Gadamer: hermeneutics, tradition and reason.* Oxford: Polity Press.